Introduction to Microprocessors:
Software, Hardware, Programming

Introduction to Microprocessors: Software, Hardware, Programming

Lance A. Leventhal

Engineering and Technology Department
Grossmont College

PRENTICE-HALL, INC., Englewood Cliffs, New Jersey   07632

Library of Congress Cataloging in Publication Data

LEVENTHAL, LANCE A (date)
  Introduction to microprocessors.

  Includes bibliographies.
  1. Microprocessors.   I. Title.
QA76.5.L486   001.6'4'04   78-7800
ISBN   0-13-487868-X

Printed in the United States of America

10 9 8 7 6

PRENTICE-HALL INTERNATIONAL, INC., *London*
PRENTICE-HALL OF AUSTRALIA PTY. LIMITED, *Sydney*
PRENTICE-HALL OF CANADA, LTD., *Toronto*
PRENTICE-HALL OF INDIA PRIVATE LIMITED, *New Delhi*
PRENTICE-HALL OF JAPAN, INC., *Tokyo*
PRENTICE-HALL OF SOUTHEAST ASIA PTE. LTD., *Singapore*
WHITEHALL BOOKS LIMITED, *Wellington, New Zealand*

To Dr. Gerald Pournelle,
in appreciation of his guidance and friendship.

Contents

3 MICROPROCESSOR INSTRUCTION SETS *72*

4 MICROPROCESSOR ASSEMBLERS *127*

5 ASSEMBLY LANGUAGE PROGRAMMING *166*

6 SOFTWARE DEVELOPMENT FOR MICROPROCESSORS *238*

7   MICROCOMPUTER MEMORY SECTIONS   *284*

8   MICROPROCESSOR INPUT/OUTPUT   *337*

9   MICROPROCESSOR INTERRUPT SYSTEMS   *433*

APPENDICES

Preface

Microprocessors have already had far-reaching effects in almost every industry. New processors, new hardware and software intended for use with processors, and new products that incorporate microprocessors seem to appear daily. As usual, textbooks and other educational materials have lagged far behind the spread of the technology itself. The manuals written for specific microprocessors are intended as references for users rather than as textbooks; articles in the trade press or technical journals discuss limited subjects or particular applications. This book is a general introduction to microprocessors for advanced undergraduate students; the students are assumed to have had introductory courses in programming and digital circuits. This textbook should prove useful and interesting to undergraduate and graduate students in electrical engineering, other engineering disciplines, the physical and natural sciences, mathematics, computer science, and the health sciences. The book will also serve the needs of engineers, technicians, administrators, programmers, teachers, and others who need a self-study or reference text on microprocessors.

A major problem in teaching about microprocessors is that they cannot be understood solely from a software or a hardware point of view. Programmers will find that microprocessors have architectures, instruction sets, and software much like other computers with which they may be familiar. Engineers will find that microprocessors have the same physical properties, input and output signals, and operating characteristics as other integrated circuits with which they may be familiar. However, both programmers and engineers will discover that developing systems based on microprocessors requires understanding of both hardware and software. I have taken the approach in this book that the use of microprocessors does involve a shift of the design burden from hardware to software and I have, therefore, emphasized software. At the same time, I have discussed the hardware aspects of microprocessors at some length with particular emphasis on the design of memory sections, the use of standard and specialized integrated circuits, and the interfacing of simple peripherals. I have not discussed digital design since I believe that several textbooks adequately cover that subject at various levels. Thus I have written a software-oriented book while not ignoring the associated hardware problems.

Rather than surveying the entire spectrum of microprocessors or inventing an example for study, I have chosen to focus on the two most widely used devices, the Intel 8080 and the Motorola 6800. These processors are similar in performance to most of the standard devices on the market. They are also sufficiently different from each other, both in programming and interfacing techniques, to be representative of the entire range of devices. I believe that adequate surveys of microprocessors are available and that a textbook should provide a detailed treatment of one or two devices. I have based my choice on the choice of the marketplace; I see no evidence that these two processors (or any others) are superior to their competitors. This book does occasionally mention some of the special features of the various competing processors.

The basic organization of the book is as follows:

Chapter 1 introduces the subject of microprocessors. It compares microprocessors to minicomputers and large computers as well as to other large-scale integrated circuitry. It then describes semiconductor technologies and memories, discusses the advantages and disadvantages of microprocessors as compared to the competing design techniques, presents the areas in which microprocessors have been applied, and gives some specific examples of microprocessor-based products.

Chapter 2 considers the architecture of microprocessors. The various sections of a computer—central processing unit (CPU), memory, and input/output—are briefly discussed. The rest of the chapter concentrates on the CPU, describing the registers, arithmetic unit, and instruction-decoding mechanism. The final section presents the architectures of the Intel 8080 and Motorola 6800.

Chapter 3 describes instruction sets. The first sections contain a general description of instruction formats, addressing methods, and types of instructions. The last section describes the instruction sets of the Intel 8080 and Motorola 6800.

Chapter 4 deals with assemblers. The first sections discuss the advantages and disadvantages of various language levels and the general features of assemblers. The last section is a specific description of the standard Intel 8080 and Motorola 6800 assemblers.

Chapter 5 discusses assembly language programming for the Intel 8080 and Motorola 6800 processors. The chapter begins with simple programs and proceeds through loops, string and character manipulation, code conversions, arithmetic, lists and tables, and subroutines.

Chapter 6 considers the entire software development process. It describes problem definition, program design, coding, debugging, testing, documentation, and maintenance and redesign. The last section briefly discusses development systems.

Chapter 7 deals with the memory section. It describes the basic interaction between the microprocessor and memory. It goes on to consider the interfacing of simple memory sections and the design of busing structures required for more complex sections. The chapter then describes the design of memory sections for the Intel 8080 and Motorola 6800 and the operation of their instruction cycles.

Chapter 8 discusses input/output. It begins with a description of input and output procedures. It then considers simple input/output sections and more complex input/output sections which require a busing structure. The chapter then discusses some circuits that are widely used in I/O sections and some simple I/O devices. The final part of the chapter describes the specific hardware and software required to interface simple I/O devices to the Intel 8080 and Motorola 6800 microprocessors.

Chapter 9 presents interrupts. It describes the uses, advantages, and disadvantages of interrupts. It then discusses interrupt procedures, the features of interrupt systems, and the handling of specific sources of interrupts. The chapter next describes the programming and interfacing of interrupt-based systems using the Intel 8080 and Motorola 6800. The chapter concludes with a brief consideration of direct memory access.

The Appendices present background material, tables of codes, and instruction sets. Appendix 1 deals with the binary number system, Appendix 2 with logical functions, Appendix 3 with numerical and character codes, Appendix 4 with semiconductor technologies, and Appendix 5 with semiconductor memories. Appendices 6 and 7 contain the instruction sets of the Intel 8080 and Motorola 6800 microprocessors. The Appendices are followed by an extensive Glossary.

Obviously, I have omitted many subjects. I have described the purpose of microprogramming without describing the procedures for microprogramming either at the designer or user level. The microprogramming of microprocessors, in itself, probably deserves an entire book. The use of high-level languages has been explained, but no specific examples have been presented. Such techniques as multiprocessing, pipelining, parallel processing, and virtual memory have also been omitted. Microprocessor peripherals and the wide variety of associated digital and analog integrated circuitry that is currently available have been described sparingly. Direct memory access has received only a brief treatment. Some of those topics may be dealt with at a later date.

I have attempted throughout this textbook to illustrate various topics by presenting examples of the actual use of microprocessors. I have tried to develop these examples in a logical manner so that the reader can apply them directly to laboratory or engineering problems. In the hardware area, I have used standard symbols, design techniques, circuit elements, and documentation. In the software area, I have used standard flowcharting symbols, and have structured and documented all programs in accordance with the methods recommended by modern theorists. I have tried not only to present useful examples but also to show the rules of structure and documentation which I believe to be vital to the efficient development of microprocessor-based systems.

A key difficulty in writing a book about a new technology is the rapid obsolescence of information. Obviously the time required to publish and distribute this textbook will make some of its information obsolete. I have not tried to predict the future course of microprocessor technology, but I have tried to focus on processors that are widely available, have been used in significant applications, have considerable hardware and software support, and will be important factors in the marketplace for years to come. I have also attempted to present continuing trends, current problems, and promising new approaches. However, I realize that readers will have to obtain up-to-date information from the manufacturers' manuals and technical notes, articles in trade and scholarly journals, and special conferences and short courses. I have described the sources of such information and have presented basic approaches to microprocessors that will enable the user to take maximum advantage of these sources.

The field of microprocessors is clearly in a state of rapid expansion. More courses, articles, and conference sessions on this subject appear all the time. We are just beginning to see the results of this new technology in actual products. The capacity for intelligent and flexible control of everyday systems is now available at a reasonable price—the use of this control is a challenge that is open to all the readers of this book.

Acknowledgments

My special thanks go to Mr. William Tester of Grossmont College, who was responsible for introducing microprocessors into the Grossmont College curriculum and for providing much of the support which made this book possible. I would also like to thank Mr. Colin Walsh of Grossmont College for his continuing assistance and Mrs. Teddy Ferguson of Grossmont College for her typing and proofreading help. Others who have assisted me include Mr. David Bulman and Mrs. Kati Bulman of Pragmatics, Mr. Karl Amatneek of KVA Associates, Mr. Ken Reider and Mr. Tony Earle of Earle Associates, Mr. Jeffrey Haight of Data/Ware Development, Professors Fredric Harris and Nicholas Panos of San Diego State University, Mr. James Gordon and Mr. Franklin Antonio of Linkabit, Mr. Terry Benson of Intel, Dr. James Tiernan of Linkabit, Mr. Romeo Favreau of Sorrento Valley Group, and Dr. Donald Rauch of Sysdyne. Mr. Stanley Rogers of the Society for Computer Simulation deserves recognition for prodding me constantly to improve my writing style. My wife, Donna, has been patient and understanding. I, of course, bear full responsibility for the contents and organization of this book but all of those whom I have mentioned and others besides should share in any credit.

LANCE A. LEVENTHAL

Solana Beach, California

1 Introduction to Microprocessors

1.1 COMPUTING AND MICROPROCESSORS

The brief history of computers is marked by rapid advances in technology and in the number and variety of applications. The first computers, built in the late 1940s and early 1950s, were used to solve complex scientific problems. Today computers that are far more powerful than the early machines are used in such mundane applications as electronic games, cash registers, scales, calculators, and household appliances. An individual can purchase a computer like the one shown in Fig. 1.1 for a few hundred dollars and use it in a variety of home projects.

Figure 1.1 A home computer (courtesy of MITS, Inc.).

Figure 1.2 A typical microprocessor (courtesy of Motorola Semiconductor Products, Inc.).

The latest development in computer technology is the *microprocessor*, a device that has all the functions of the central processing unit (CPU) of a computer on one or a few tiny pieces of silicon. Figure 1.2 shows a typical microprocessor. Such a device can fetch instructions from a memory, decode and execute them, perform arithmetic and logical operations, accept data from input devices, and send results to output devices. A microprocessor, together with a memory and input/output channels for communication with the outside world, forms a full-fledged computer or *microcomputer*. Simple microcomputers cost as little as $10. Complete *microcomputer systems*, with a chassis, front panel, and power supply in addition to the microcomputer, cost less than a thousand dollars and have as much processing power as giant computers of the 1950s that cost hundreds of times that amount. The rapidly decreasing cost of computers contrasts sharply with the rapidly increasing cost of most other items.

The microprocessor is a continuation of the trend toward smaller computers that began in the middle 1960s. In the early years of computer development the emphasis was on larger and more powerful machines. Computers were so expensive that only large institutions could own them and only specially trained personnel could operate them. New technologies, such as transistors and integrated circuits, provided greater speed but did not reduce costs. Computers remained remote and mysterious objects.

Minicomputers started the present trend. The first minicomputers were primitive by computer standards and still cost tens of thousands of dollars. Nevertheless, laboratories, factories, and smaller institutions that could not afford large computers could now purchase a small computer like the Digital Equipment PDP-8, Data General Nova, Scientific Data Systems 92, or IBM 1130. Cheaper electronic circuits led to cheaper minicomputers; by 1970 a small minicomputer for use in a laboratory, office, factory, warehouse, or classroom cost a few thousand dollars.

Yet developments in integrated circuits went far beyond reducing the cost of minicomputers. Soon the construction of a single integrated circuit that could perform the functions of a computer became possible. Such complex circuits (called *large-scale integration* or *LSI*) can be manufactured by the thousands at costs not much greater than those of simple circuits. The cheap computer, long a favorite dream of science fiction writers, thus became a reality. Manufacturers have already produced more microprocessors than all other computers combined. By 1977, complete home computers including a keyboard, video display, and cassette recorder were available for under a thousand dollars.

Besides comparing microcomputers to other computers, the rest of this chapter describes the origin and history of microprocessors, the characteristics of the semiconductor technologies from which microprocessors are produced, the features that microprocessors share with other integrated circuits, the semiconductor memories with which microprocessors are used, and, finally, some applications of microprocessors.

1.2 LARGE AND SMALL COMPUTERS

Cheap computers have made many new computer applications possible, a trend started by the minicomputer and extended by the microprocessor. Figure 1.3 shows the costs of microcomputers, minicomputers, and large computers, along with typical quantities that a user might purchase at a time.

Figure 1.3 Computer costs and typical quantities.

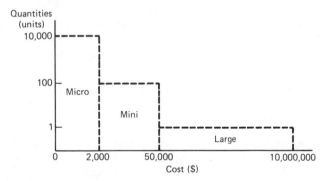

Large general-purpose computers like the IBM 370, Univac 1100, or Burroughs 6700 serve two major functions:

1. Solving complex scientific and engineering problems, such as spacecraft guidance, weather prediction, or electronic and structural design.
2. Performing large-scale data processing, such as the handling of records for banks, insurance companies, stores, utilities, and government agencies.

These tasks involve extremely large numbers of calculations or data transfers. Solving typical scientific problems requires the solution of complicated equations that could not be solved by hand. Handling business problems requires the processing of large numbers of records and the handling of large amounts of peripheral input and output.

Minicomputers and microprocessors will not replace large computers in such applications. Small computers can, of course, solve similar problems when the calculations are less complex or the amounts of data are smaller. Thus a minicomputer or microprocessor could perform laboratory calculations or handle records for a small business. Nevertheless, the greatest usage of mini and microcomputers has occurred in areas outside the typical applications of large computers.

Normal applications for mini and microcomputers have the following characteristics.

1. The computer is a system component. The overall system, which might be a piece of test equipment, a machine tool, or a banking terminal, uses the small computer much as it might a switch, power supply, or display. The computer may not even be visible from the outside.

2. The computer performs a specific task for a single system. It is not shared by different users as a large computer is. Instead the small computer is part of a particular unit, such as a medical instrument, typesetter, or factory machine.

3. The computer has a fixed program that is rarely changed. Unlike a large computer, which may solve a variety of business and engineering problems, most small computers perform a single set of tasks, such as monitoring a security system, producing graphic displays, or bending sheets of metal. Programs are often stored in a permanent medium or read-only memory.

4. The computer often performs real-time tasks in which it must obtain the answers at a particular time so as to satisfy system needs. Such applications include machine tools that must turn the cutter at the right time in order to obtain the correct pattern or missile guidance where the computer must apply thrust at the proper time in order to achieve the desired trajectory.

5. The computer performs control tasks rather than arithmetic or data processing. Its primary function might be managing a warehouse, controlling a transit system, or monitoring the condition of a patient.

Using minicomputers and microcomputers differs from using large computers. The user of a large computer system writes programs in a convenient language (such as FORTRAN, BASIC, or PL/I), submits them to the computer center staff, and receives results in printed form or on magnetic tape or other medium. The user can take advantage of a variety of peripheral devices, standard programs, and other features of a large computer center. The user need not worry about how the computer operates or how it communicates with memory and input/output devices.

Those who wish to use minicomputers or microcomputers as system components will find the situation quite different. Minicomputers and microcomputers rarely have the software and peripherals needed for convenient use. Programming small computers is tedious and time-consuming. Furthermore, the interaction of the computer with the total system is a critical problem. The designer must understand the details of how the computer works in order to use it effectively.

Small computer applications thus involve interrelated hardware and software. The designer must divide tasks between hardware and software, considering both cost and speed, and write programs to obtain data from input devices and send results to output devices. Timing considerations are critical in both hardware and software design.

The small computer that goes into the final product is generally not suitable for use in the development stage. Programs for large computers are developed on the same system on which they are used. Small computers, however, that are part of an instrument or machine tool will only have enough memory, peripherals, and software to perform their functions; anything extra would increase system cost without improving performance. As a result, such computers will not have card readers or line printers to handle input/output, compilers or debugging packages to simplify program development, or tape or disk systems to store programs or data. The computer that goes into the system can handle system functions—not system development.

Special equipment (called a *development system*) is therefore used during the development stage. This equipment may involve the same computer (*self-development system*) or other computers (*simulator* or *cross-development system*). A typical development system has peripherals for entering programs and data and recording results, a fairly large memory for holding user and system programs, software and hardware features useful in writing and debugging programs, and mass storage (disk or tape) for saving programs so that they can easily be retrieved. Such development systems include software, hardware, peripherals, and interfaces that have nothing to do with the ultimate product; they merely make designing easier. The task of developing programs, even when the programs are ultimately intended for mini or microcomputers, is better suited to large computers. A program that translates FORTRAN to machine language, for instance, can run much faster on a large computer than on a small one and can use peripherals that are part of the large system. The computer that does the translation need not be the one for which the program is intended.

The user of minicomputers or microcomputers will thus find system development quite awkward. Programs are often written in a very different environment from that in which they will ultimately run. Frequently, hardware and interfaces are developed concurrently with programs, and the user faces a difficult task of system integration. The programs must often perform complex input/output operations with real-time constraints.

1.3 COMPARISON OF TYPICAL COMPUTERS

Table 1.1 compares a large general-purpose computer, a large minicomputer, a small minicomputer, and a microcomputer. The large computer described is an IBM 370/Model 168 (see Fig. 1.4), a computer widely used for data processing. The large minicomputer described is the Digital Equipment (DEC) PDP 11/45 (see Fig. 1.5). The small minicomputer is the Computer Automation NAKED MINI (see Fig. 1.6), a popular system computer. The microcomputer is the Intel MCS-80, based on the widely used Intel 8080 microprocessor (see Fig. 1.7). Other manufacturers produce comparable machines at each level; this comparison does not, of course, imply that the computers described are superior to their competitors.

Table 1.1   Comparison of Types of Computers

	IBM 370/168	DEC PDP 11/45	Computer Automation NAKED MINI	Intel MCS-80
Cost	$4.5 million	$50,000	$2500	$250
Word length (bits)	32	16	16	8
Memory capacity (8-bit bytes)	8.4 million	256K[a]	64K	64K
Processor Add time	0.13 μs	0.9 μs	3.2 μs	2.0 μs
Maximum 1/0 data rate (bytes/second)	16 million	4 million	1,400,000	500,000
Number of general purpose registers	64	16	3	7
Peripherals (from manufacturer)	All types	Wide variety	Disk, tape, card, line printer, CRT, cassette	Paper tape reader, floppy disk, PROM programmer
Software	All types	Wide variety	Operating system, assembler, FORTRAN, BASIC	Assembler, monitor, PL/M, editor

[a]1K = 1024 bits.

Figure 1.4   IBM 370/Model 168 (photo courtesy of IBM).

Figure 1.5 Digital Equipment (DEC) PDP 11/45 (courtesy of Digital Equipment Corporation).

Figure 1.6 Computer Automation NAKED MINI (courtesy of Computer Automation, Inc.).

Figure 1.7 Photomicrograph of the Intel 8080 microprocessor (courtesy of Intel Corporation).

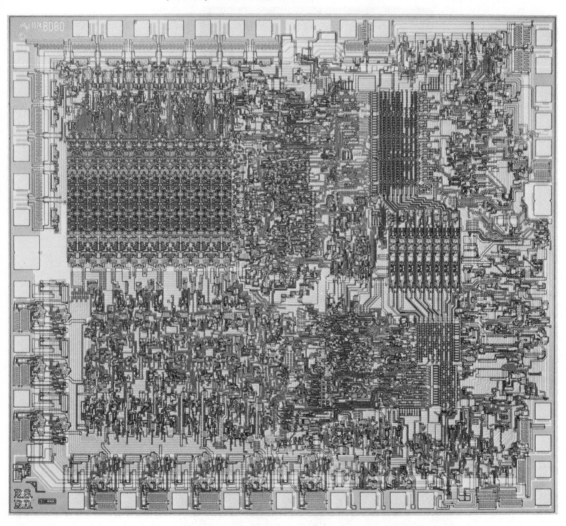

Cost

Computer	System Cost
IBM 370/168	$4.5 million
DEC PDP 11/45	$50,000
Computer Automation NAKED MINI	$2500
Intel MCS-80	$250

The large general-purpose computer is so expensive that it could only serve as a central computer facility for a large institution. Such a computer would require a specially trained staff of programmers, analysts, and operators. It would have many peripherals, such as card readers, line printers, disk and tape systems, and terminals. The computer could process vast numbers of records and handle many separate tasks.

The large minicomputer is too expensive to be part of a product but could be used by a laboratory, small business, or small industrial plant. Such minicomputers can also serve as secondary processors for large computers.

The small minicomputer is inexpensive enough to be part of a factory machine, banking terminal, or test system. However, the ultimate product would need to cost well over $10,000 to justify the cost of the computer. A product in that price range is usually not a high-volume item. An order of a hundred minicomputers by the system manufacturer would be considered substantial.

The microcomputer, on the other hand, costs one-tenth as much as the small minicomputer. It could, therefore, be part of a system costing $1000. Such applications as electronic cash registers, cathode-ray-tube (CRT) terminals, counters, and small instruments are all possible. Clearly the manufacturer of such items would use many microcomputers; an order of 10,000 devices would be considered large.

Word Length

Computer	Word Length (bits)
IBM 370/168	32
DEC PDP 11/45	16
Computer Automation NAKED MINI	16
Intel MCS-80	8

The *word length* of a computer refers to the number of binary digits (*bits*) that it can process at a time. The rate at which the computer can process data is, of course, related to how much it can process at a time and how fast it can perform operations. A computer that has twice as long a word as another computer can do twice as much work in a given amount of time even if both computers operate at the same speed.

The large computer has twice as long a word as the minicomputer and four times as long a word as the microcomputer. Typically, large computers have word lengths of 32 to 64 bits, minicomputers 12 to 32 bits, and microcomputers 4 to 16 bits. Word length is thus an important factor in measuring the power of a computer.

It is particularly important when doing arithmetic. Consider how difficult it would be to multiply two six-digit numbers if we could only handle one pair of digits at a time; the problem would be much more than six times as difficult as handling all the digits at once because of the positioning required and the many carries involved. Computers with long words can perform complicated arithmetic calculations much better than computers with short words. Such tasks as weather prediction or aircraft simulation are thus better suited to larger computers. Minicomputers and microcomputers are better at control tasks.

Note, however, that a longer word length only helps if the data is long. If the computer receives merely eight bits of information at a time, the fact that it could handle much more is no advantage. In fact, the longer word length can even be a nuisance (much like trying to read a calculator result that presents six decimal places when we only want dollars and cents). Control applications often require a computer to handle a few bits of data at a time; the computer receives such data from dials, buttons, switches, or sensors and sends it to displays, actuators, and motors. A computer with a shorter word length may be easier to use in such applications.

The computer with the shorter word length can combine data for input to a larger computer and divide the results appropriately. The large, expensive computer therefore always has full words to process. A minicomputer or microcomputer acting as a preprocessor can substantially increase the throughput of a large computer at very little additional cost. Figure 1.8 describes a system in which a 4-bit microcomputer accepts data in 4-bit segments and places them in the appropriate positions in a 32-bit register. When the microcomputer has assembled 32 bits, it signals the large computer, which reads all 32 bits with a single operation. The large computer can perform other tasks while the microcomputer is assembling the data.

Figure 1.8   A micro preprocessor.

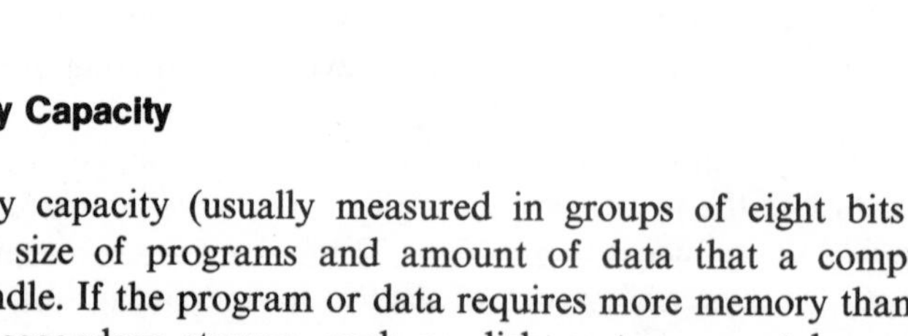

Memory Capacity

Memory capacity (usually measured in groups of eight bits or *bytes*) determines the size of programs and amount of data that a computer can conveniently handle. If the program or data requires more memory than the computer can handle, secondary storage, such as disk or tape, must be used. Secondary storage systems are expensive and much slower than the main memory. A computer with limited memory capacity will therefore take longer to execute large programs than one with a larger memory capacity; using secondary storage is like using a book of equations or tables—extra time is involved whenever the book must be used.

Computer	Memory Capacity (bytes)
IBM 370/168	8.4 million
DEC PDP 11/45	256 thousand
Computer Automation NAKED MINI	64 thousand
Intel MCS-80	64 thousand

The large computer can handle enormous programs and large amounts of data without using secondary storage. Such memory capacity is necessary to handle large files, complex calculations, and detailed reports. The large minicomputer has far less memory capacity than the large computer but still much more than the small computers. Large computers have enough memory for large operating systems and a variety of computer languages. Such programs may require hundreds of thousands of bytes of memory.

The minicomputer and microcomputer have far less memory capacity. So operating systems, compilers, and other software designed for these computers must occupy less memory or use secondary storage. Mini and microcomputers are generally used in applications involving short programs and small amounts of data. In fact, microcomputer applications requiring more than 16,000 bytes of memory are considered very large.

Addresses are more difficult to handle in a computer with a short word length. Table 1.2 shows the amount of memory that a given number of bits can address.

Table 1.2 Address Length vs. Memory Capacity

Address Length (bits)	Memory Capacity (bytes)
8	256
9	512
10	1K
11	2K
12	4K
13	8K
14	16K
15	32K
16	64K

Note that an 8-bit address can only distinguish among 256 bytes of memory; few programs could fit in such a small area. However, a microcomputer with an 8-bit data word must handle longer addresses in 8-bit segments. The instruction cycles of microprocessors with 8-bit words are complex, since the processors must fetch addresses from program memory in 8-bit segments and reassemble them inside the CPU. Addresses are even more difficult to manipulate if the microprocessor has only a 4-bit word. Consequently, minicomputers are faster than microcomputers because their longer word length allows them to address memory more efficiently.

Instruction Execution Time

Computer	Processor Add Time
IBM 370/168	0.13 μs
DEC PDP 11/45	0.9 μs
Computer Automation NAKED MINI	3.2 μs
Intel MCS-80	2.0 μs

A computer's performance depends on how rapidly it executes instructions. Although the speed of execution varies with the complexity of the instruction, the processor add time gives some measure of performance. Note that the amount of processing accomplished by the execution of an instruction depends on the word length of the computer.

The large computer is seven times as fast as the large minicomputer. The smaller computers are much slower. According to this simple comparison, the large computer has 60 times the processing power of the microcomputer, since it can handle four times as much data in one-fifteenth the time.

A true comparison must consider two other factors:

1. The longer average instruction execution time of microprocessors because of their shorter word lengths and slower addressing.
2. The more extensive instruction sets of the larger computers.

The processor add time is the time required to add the contents of two registers and does not involve additional memory accesses. Obviously the computer must get the data from the memory somewhere in the program. The data fetch requires an address that a typical microprocessor must handle in the awkward manner mentioned earlier.

The size and complexity of the computer instruction set also affect the computer's processing power. One computer may need many instruction cycles to accomplish what another can do in one cycle. For instance, subtraction is performed as follows on computers with and without subtraction instructions.

```
      FUNCTION: Z = X − Y
COMPUTER I. (HAS SUBTRACTION)
      Z = X − Y
COMPUTER II. (NO SUBTRACTION)
      W = − Y
      Z = X + W
```

Computer II uses two instruction cycles instead of one. Division and multiplication instructions, for example, are more often available on larger computers than on smaller ones. The lack of such instructions reduces the real processing power of smaller computers.

The number of instructions and the average execution time are both related to the word length of the computer. The number of distinct instructions that a computer can have is determined by the number of bits used to identify instructions as shown in Table 1.3.

Table 1.3 Number of Possible Instructions vs. Number of Instruction Bits Used

Number of Instruction Bits	Number of Possible Instructions
3	8
4	16
5	32
6	64
7	128
8	256

A computer with a long word can use seven or eight bits to distinguish instructions and still have many bits left over to determine the address of the data. A computer with a shorter word must use additional words of program memory in order to have a variety of instructions, thereby requiring additional memory accesses and longer execution times.

Maximum Input/Output Data Rate

Computer	Maximum I/O Data Rate (bytes/second)
IBM 370/168	16 million
DEC PDP 11/45	4 million
Computer Automation NAKED MINI	1.4 million
Intel MCS-80	500 thousand

Maximum I/O data rates limit the problems that the computer can handle and the types of peripherals that it can use effectively. A larger computer can transfer data at a much higher rate than a smaller one and can utilize high-speed disk systems and other devices that transfer millions of bits per second. In this category, the large computer is over 30 times as powerful as the microcomputer.

Furthermore, larger computers generally have better instructions and hardware for handling input/output. They have input/output channels and controllers that can be activated with a few instructions and can then transfer large amounts of data without further processor intervention. A small computer must frequently transfer the data one word at a time. Clearly such a computer cannot handle high-speed I/O devices and perform much other work.

The word length of the computer affects the number of separate I/O devices that can be handled easily. Each I/O device, like a memory location, must have an address for identification. A computer with a longer word can more easily distinguish among a large number of I/O devices than can one with a shorter word. Because of their lower transfer rates and shorter data words, small minicomputers and microcomputers generally use a few simple peripherals, such as control panels, numeric displays, keyboards, teletypewriters, and paper tape readers. High-speed peripherals like magnetic tapes or disks, high-speed printers, and high-speed communications lines are more often used with larger computers.

Smaller computers are used in low-speed applications. Situations involving human interaction (like electronic cash registers or video games) are ideal for microcomputers, since the response time of a person is about a tenth of a second. Controlling slowly changing quantities like temperature, pressure, or chemical concentrations is another application area for small computers. High-speed applications in which responses must occur within microseconds are best left to larger computers or special controllers.

Number of General-Purpose Registers

Registers are small memories within the central processing unit. A register has the same relationship to main memory as main memory has to disk or tape storage. If a computer has several general-purpose registers, they can hold frequently used data and intermediate results. More general-purpose registers mean fewer bottlenecks and less time spent moving data between memory and registers.

Computer	Number of General-Purpose Registers
IBM 370/168	64
DEC PDP 11/45	16
Computer Automation NAKED MINI	3
Intel MCS-80	7

The larger computers have many more general-purpose registers than the smaller ones and so can handle data more rapidly. They also have many extra registers that can be used during subroutines. The smaller computers must access the memory more often and must spend more time loading and storing the contents of registers. Subroutines must use the same registers as the main program and so must save and restore the contents of those registers.

Peripherals

Computer	Peripherals Available
IBM 370/168	All types
DEC PDP 11/45	Wide variety
Computer Automation	Disk, tape, card, line printer,
NAKED MINI	CRT, cassette
Intel MCS-80	Paper tape, floppy disk

The peripherals that are available for a given computer can have a substantial effect both on program development and on system interfacing. If we can obtain a variety of peripherals specially designed for a computer, we can develop programs faster and spend less time interfacing peripherals to the final product.

Development is much simpler with high-speed input/output and mass storage devices. If such peripherals are not immediately available, the user has two choices: (a) develop the required interfaces and (b) use slower and less convenient peripherals. The first option requires the user to develop interfaces not directly related to the final product. The second requires the user to wait for program and data entry and output. The lack of fast input devices means that a long program will take an hour to enter from a teletypewriter. The lack of mass storage results in frequent repetition of the slow entry. The lack of fast output devices makes the listing of programs or results a major task.

Many peripherals are immediately available for larger computers from computer manufacturers and independent peripheral manufacturers. The user can purchase fast peripherals for development or a particular peripheral for the final product.

Few peripherals are available with an off-the-shelf interface for small computers. The user must provide the interfaces for development and for the final product.

The cost of peripherals has not decreased as much as that of computers, since peripherals involve expensive mechanical parts. Although better peripherals are available at lower prices than in the past, their cost relative to that of the computer has increased. A card reader, typewriter, or paper tape reader and punch (together with the interface) costs as much as a small minicomputer and considerably more than a microcomputer.

Software

Computer	Software
IBM 370/168	All types
DEC PDP 11/45	Large variety
Computer Automation NAKED MINI	Operating system, assembler, FORTRAN, BASIC
Intel MCS-80	Assembler, monitor, PL/M, editor

Software presents a situation similar to peripherals except that software has steadily increased in cost. Software availability affects both the development process and the amount of new programming that is required. Systems software makes the task of developing user programs easier. Off-the-shelf software may be able to perform some or all of the ultimate system tasks.

As in the case of peripherals, far more software is available for larger than for smaller computers. Almost every computer language or other systems program can be used on an IBM 370. Not only does IBM supply a large amount of software but other sources also specialize in programs for IBM computers. Significantly less software is available for the large minicomputer, but the manufacturer and independent sources do supply several operating systems, compilers for most common languages, and other programs.

Much user software is available for larger computers; it ranges from common mathematical functions and record-handling programs to such highly specialized applications programs as accounting systems for a particular type of business or solutions for a particular class of engineering problems. The availability of compilers for common computer languages means that the vast backlog of programs written in FORTRAN, COBOL, PL/I, and APL can be used directly on large computers.

The user of smaller computers, on the other hand, will find far less systems and applications software available. A simple operating system or monitor, an assembler, and a few common compilers or interpreters are all that can be expected. Sometimes even this software requires memory and peripherals beyond those supplied with a minimum system. Applications software is generally limited to standard mathematical functions and a small user's library. The user must develop most software from scratch.

Microcomputers generally have even less software than small minicomputers. Few operating systems or compilers are available. The microcomputer user will seldom be able to use previously written programs.

Writing programs for microprocessors is complicated by the fact that microprocessors are used for different tasks than are larger computers. Most computer languages were designed for scientific problems or business data processing rather than control tasks. New software tools are needed to deal effectively with microprocessor software development.

Thus microcomputers represent a limited amount of computing power in many respects. In a continuation of the trends that started with minicomputers, microcomputers generally are cheaper, slower, have less memory and I/O capacity, use shorter words, and offer less peripheral and software support than larger computers. Small computers seldom replace larger ones; instead they perform limited tasks in situations where intelligent control would otherwise be too expensive.

1.4 HISTORY OF MICROPROCESSORS

Although they perform the same functions as larger CPUs, microprocessors are physically the same as other complex semiconductor devices, such as calculator chips, watch chips, semiconductor memories, and communications chips. Microprocessors are a product of the same technological developments that led to electronic watches and calculators. Many features of common microprocessors result from their origins in the semiconductor industry.

The first integrated circuits (or *ICs*) appeared in the early 1960s. An *integrated circuit* is a combination of circuit elements formed on a single substrate or chip (made of silicon) and produced as a unit. By the middle 1960s new processes substantially increased the amount of circuitry that could be placed on a chip. The most common was the *metal-oxide semiconductor* (MOS) process. Simple integrated circuits became known as *small-scale integration* (SSI), more complicated integrated circuits as *medium-scale integration* (MSI), and still more complicated circuits as *large-scale integration* (LSI). Figure 1.9, for instance, shows how the complexity of single-chip read/write memories has increased with time. In the ten years from 1966 to 1976 the capacity of such devices increased by a factor of 64, whereas their cost per bit decreased by a factor of a hundred.

Figure 1.9 Capacity of single-chip memories vs. time.

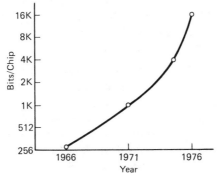

The first application of the MOS LSI technology was the memory chip. The small size and low power consumption of LSI memory chips made them ideal for small memories in communications systems, military equipment, and computers. Memory chips are easy to design and manufacture, since all the memory cells are identical and little additional circuitry is needed.

In the late 1960s calculators and terminals became important application areas for MOS LSI technology. Both calculators and terminals perform simple tasks that do not require high speed, large amounts of data, or complex operations. Conventional designs, however, did not produce satisfactory products—the standard mechanical calculator was bulky, expensive, hard to use, and could only perform simple operations; the standard terminal was slow, awkward, and had no facilities for changing or correcting data. Both applications needed some local intelligence but could not justify the cost of a minicomputer.

Calculators

Only a few years after its introduction the electronic calculator has become a standard item. Its functions (see Fig. 1.10) are simple: the calculator accepts data from a small keyboard one digit at a time, performs the required arithmetic, and shows the results on a lighted numeric display. The calculator's programs are stored in read-only memories (ROMs); the data that the user enters is stored in small read/write memories (RAMs).

What sort of electronic device does a calculator need? The following features are helpful.

1. The ability to interface easily with keyboards and lighted displays.

2. The ability to handle decimal digits as units. Since decimal digits consist of four bits (see Appendix 3), the device should be able to handle one or more 4-bit items at a time.

3. The ability to execute standard programs stored in read-only memory.

4. Extendibility so that features like percentages, square roots, and trigonometric functions can easily be added.

5. Flexibility so that the calculator can be used in custom applications like engineering, business, or programming without a complete new design.

6. Low cost, small size, and low power consumption so that the calculator can be portable and inexpensive.

Neither high speed nor large memory capacity is necessary, since human response is involved and only a few numbers need be stored.

The MOS LSI technology first resulted in special-purpose calculator chips that are cheap, small, use little power, can handle decimal digits, and can perform standard functions. They are specifically designed to accept input from a keyboard and send output to lighted numeric displays. MOS LSI technology has produced millions of calculator chips for a few dollars apiece.

Calculator chips, however, are neither flexible nor extendible. The calculator manufacturer cannot easily add new functions, custom features, or other input or output devices, such as printers or plotters. The calculator chip is ideal for simple calculators, but more complex units need a more flexible device.

The Intel 4004, the first microprocessor, was developed as a flexible calculator chip. It differs from the latter in that the user can program it to perform additional or custom functions and handle a variety of I/O devices. The Intel 4004 does, however, have the basic features of calculator chips.

1. It handles four bits (one decimal digit) at a time.

2. It has specific instructions for reading keyboards and performing decimal arithmetic.

3. It uses fixed programs stored in read-only memories and data stored in small read/write memories.

4. It can be used in simple, low-cost configurations with keyboards and displays.

However much the Intel 4004 may resemble a calculator, it is still a computer. The system manufacturer can program it to perform new functions. The advantage to the semiconductor manufacturer is that many applications can use the same device. Other industries quickly saw uses for microprocessors in their products.

Figure 1.10 The Hewlett-Packard 35 calculator (courtesy of Hewlett-Packard Co.).

Terminals

Still another leader in the use of LSI devices was the terminal industry. Terminals are used to enter data into a remote computer or to send and receive messages via telegraph or other communications lines. They range from simple teletypewriters to complex devices like the one shown in Fig. 1.11, which features a CRT display and remote operation. Data is entered from a typewriter keyboard, processed a character at a time, and usually both displayed on a CRT or printer and placed in the proper form for transmission to a computer or other terminal. Read-only memories store operating programs and the tables that produce character patterns on the CRT or printer. The data that the user enters must be saved in read/write memories until the user requests that it be transmitted or placed in backup storage.

Figure 1.11 The Beehive Brilliant Bee terminal (courtesy of Beehive International).

What sort of electronic device does a terminal need? The features below are helpful.

1. The ability to interface easily with a variety of I/O devices, including keyboards, printers, CRTs, communications lines, disks, cassettes, and other terminals.

2. The ability to handle characters as units. Since characters usually consist

of eight bits (see Appendix 3), the device should be able to handle one or more 8-bit items at a time.

3. The ability to execute standard programs stored in read-only memory and user programs stored on cassettes, cartridges, or cards.

4. Reasonably large memory capacity so that the system can run a variety of programs and store and check a full page of data before transmitting it.

5. The ability to handle blocks of data, such as an entire line or page of text. The user can then fetch a line of text from memory and edit it.

6. Rapid access to selected memory locations through pointers that contain addresses rather than data. The user may access a particular character by placing its address in a pointer.

7. Extendibility so that the manufacturer can add additional features, such as more extensive editing, different communications interfaces, error checking, other peripherals, extra memory, or graphics capability.

8. Flexibility so that the terminal can be used in custom applications, such as order entry, inventory control, remote batch processing, transaction editing, or computer control.

9. Low cost, small size, and low power consumption so that the terminal can be cheap and portable.

A small amount of computing power is very useful in terminal applications. The terminal need only be fast enough to keep pace with the human operator. However, terminals require a different type of microprocessor than do calculators. The Intel 8008 was the first microprocessor designed for terminals; its features are listed below.

1. It handles eight bits (one character) at a time.

2. It has logical and shift instructions that are useful in processing character data.

3. It can access fairly large amounts of read/write and read-only memory (16K as compared to 4K for the 4004). Programs can be placed in either type of memory.

4. It can handle complex peripherals, such as printers or CRTs.

5. It has an internal memory pointer that can be used to select and traverse a line of data.

6. It can conveniently move and process blocks of data.

Although designed for a specific terminal application, the Intel 8008 is much more like a typical computer than the Intel 4004. The instruction set, addressing methods, and registers are similar to those of common minicomputers. The Intel 8008 is much slower than a minicomputer but offers some computing power in a small package at low cost. The same characteristics that made the Intel 8008 useful in terminals have also made it useful in data acquisition systems, security monitors, test equipment, machine tools, and navigation systems. These applications require more complex programs, more program changes, and larger amounts of data than applications for which the Intel 4004 is used.

1.5 SEMICONDUCTOR TECHNOLOGIES

As complex semiconductor chips, microprocessors behave much like other devices produced from the same technologies. For instance, MOS microprocessors have speeds, operating characteristics, packages, power consumption levels, and physical characteristics similar to those of MOS memories, shift registers, and calculator chips. Microprocessors are available in many technologies; the behavior and potential applications of the devices depend on the characteristics of the technologies involved. Appendix 4 reviews these technologies in more detail.

The first question is: What characterizes a technology? Table 1.4 lists some of the features.

Table 1.4 Characteristics of a Semiconductor Technology

Speed
Density
Cost
Power consumption
Noise immunity
Ruggedness
TTL compatibility
Maturity or experience

These features determine how fast a microprocessor constructed from a particular technology will operate, how many chips a complete microcomputer will need, how much the processor will cost, how much power it will use, what kind of environments it will withstand, how easy it will be to interface with standard TTL (transistor-transistor logic) circuitry, and how easily it can be produced.

Table 1.5 compares the semiconductor technologies currently used in microprocessors, which can be briefly summarized as follows.

PMOS (P-channel metal-oxide semiconductor)—slow but cheap, considerable amount of circuitry on a single chip, not TTL-compatible, low output current levels (so that the outputs must be amplified in order to provide the signals required by other devices).

NMOS (N-channel metal-oxide semiconductor)—faster than PMOS although still slower than standard TTL, can be made TTL-compatible, low output current levels.

CMOS (complementary metal-oxide semiconductor)—moderate speed, more expensive and less dense than other MOS technologies, can be TTL-compatible, used mainly because of its low power consumption and tolerance of noisy and rugged environments.

Schottky TTL—higher speed than MOS or standard TTL but more expensive and not as dense, completely compatible with standard TTL.

ECL (emitter-coupled logic)—very high speed but expensive, high in power consumption, and difficult to interface with other technologies.

I²L (integrated injection logic)—new but may eventually combine the density and low cost of NMOS and PMOS, the TTL compatibility of Schottky TTL and CMOS, the noise immunity and ruggedness of CMOS, and the speed of standard TTL.

Table 1.5 Comparison of Semiconductor Technologies[a]

Technology	(1 = Fastest) Speed	(1 = Lowest) Power Consumption	(1 = Most Complex) Density	(1 = Most Rugged) Ruggedness	(1 = Cheapest) Cost	(1 = Longest in Use) Experience	TTL Compatibility
PMOS	6	4	2	5	1	2	No
NMOS	5	3	1	4	2	3	Sometimes
CMOS	3	1	3	1	3	4	Yes
Schottky TTL	2	5	5	2	3	1	Yes
ECL	1	6	6	6	6	5	No
I²L	3	2	3	3	3	6	?

[a]This table was originally constructed by Dr. Alex Williman of Rockwell International and is used with his permission.

We often choose a microprocessor for a particular application because of the technology from which it is constructed. Table 1.6 lists some possible requirements and the technologies that best satisfy them.

Table 1.6 Application Requirements and Appropriate Microprocessor Technologies

Requirement	Most Suitable Technologies
Low cost	PMOS, NMOS
Small size	PMOS, NMOS
High speed	Schottky TTL, ECL
Low power consumption	CMOS
Rugged environments	CMOS
Compatibility: with TTL	Schottky TTL, CMOS
with CMOS	Schottky TTL, CMOS
with ECL	ECL
Wide availability	PMOS, NMOS
Standard parts in same technology	Schottky TTL, CMOS, ECL
Large memories in same technology	PMOS, NMOS, Schottky TTL
Most support	PMOS, NMOS

PMOS and NMOS provide single-chip microprocessors; such processors are the cheapest and smallest devices and have the most software and hardware support. PMOS and NMOS also have the largest single-chip memories (read-only memories as large as 64K bits, read/write memories as large as 16K bits). However, PMOS and NMOS microprocessors are relatively slow, difficult to interface to standard TTL or other technologies, and do not have an extensive family of circuits in their own technologies that could be used in the construction of complete systems. A significant problem with PMOS and NMOS microprocessors is their low output current levels and inability to drive other devices without the assistance of amplifiers. PMOS microprocessors include the Intel 4004, Intel 4040, Intel 8008, National IMP-4, National SC/MP, National IMP-16 and PACE, Rockwell PPS-4 and PPS-8, and the Toshiba TLCS-12; NMOS microprocessors include the Fairchild F-8, General Instrument CP1600, Intel 8048, Intel 8080, Intel 8085, Motorola 6800, MOS Technology 6502, Signetics 2650, Texas Instruments 9900, and Zilog Z-80.

CMOS is primarily used in applications like automobiles or military equipment where noise and environmental conditions are significant factors or in applications like satellites and portable communication systems where low power consumption is vital. Although it does not offer the chip complexity or low cost of NMOS and PMOS, CMOS is faster, can be made compatible with standard TTL, and has a large family of standard circuits. Only a few CMOS microprocessors and moderate-sized CMOS memories are available; however, recent advances in chip complexity and speed have made CMOS more attractive. CMOS microprocessors include the Fairchild Macrologic (also available in Schottky TTL), Intersil 6100, and RCA CDP1802 (COSMAC).

Schottky TTL's main use has been in multichip microprocessors because of its high power consumption and low chip complexity. These processors are used to copy existing computers and to act as high-speed controllers in communications and signal processing applications. Schottky TTL is less dense and more expensive than PMOS or NMOS and consumes more power and is less immune to noise than CMOS; the main advantages of Schottky TTL are its speed and compatibility with the enormous family of standard TTL devices. Fairly large memories are available in Schottky TTL. Among the Schottky TTL microprocessors are the Advanced Micro Devices 2900, Fairchild Macrologic, Intel 3000, and Scientific Micro Systems Interpreter.

ECL, which is even faster and consumes more power than Schottky TTL, is used in multichip microprocessors like the Motorola MECL 10800. ECL microprocessors are extremely fast but difficult to interface and require special packaging and circuit boards because of their high power dissipation. ECL microprocessors are best suited to applications that use ECL circuitry, such as computer mainframes, high-speed communications, and precision instruments. A moderate range of circuits and some small memories are available in ECL.

I^2L has been used in one multichip microprocessor, the Texas Instruments SBP0400, and others are planned. I^2L may offer the chip complexity and low cost of NMOS and PMOS, the low power consumption of CMOS, and the speed of standard TTL; I^2L is also easier to interface to TTL than is NMOS. However, I^2L is largely unproven and no standard I^2L circuit elements or memories yet exist.

1.6 CHARACTERISTICS OF INTEGRATED CIRCUIT CHIPS

Microprocessors possess many of the same characteristics as other digital integrated circuits. As with other ICs, the size and complexity of microprocessors are limited by the maximum chip sizes that current manufacturing techniques can provide. Constraints on chip and package size limit the number of connections between the device and the outside world. The operating characteristics of micro-processors are similar to those of other ICs; typical characteristics are input and output signal levels, power supply and clock requirements, and tolerance of electrical or environmental variations.

Limitations on chip size mean that most microprocessors have a simple structure and short word length. As the processor becomes larger, it becomes more difficult to design, package, and manufacture. A chip that is close to maximum size (presently a quarter of an inch in each linear dimension) may require special manufacturing facilities; even then only one device out of every hundred may work correctly. So the cost of microprocessors increases greatly as the size approaches the maximum. Such processors as the Intel 4040, Motorola 6800, Intel 8080, Fairchild F-8, and Signetics 2650 are all less than a fifth of an inch in their longest dimension. Designers keep processors small by limiting the number and width of internal registers and data paths, the number of connections, the size and complex-ity of the instruction set, and other features. Although the maximum size of chips will increase in the future, chip size will always be a significant factor.

Package size affects both the ease with which processors can be used and their cost. LSI chips are monolithic structures—no connections can be made except via the external pins provided. We cannot observe the contents of internal registers, flags, or buses directly unless corresponding output pins are available. Nor can we change internal states directly unless there are corresponding input pins. This problem does not exist in larger computers that use discrete circuitry; there we can look at internal states on an oscilloscope and change them by applying signals directly. Testing LSI chips requires complex patterns of inputs; determining the contents of internal registers requires special programs that transfer the contents to output pins.

A large number of input and output pins simplifies system development, since more input and output signals are easily available. Nevertheless, packages with a large number of pins are expensive, use a large amount of circuit board space, and require many connections. Simpler (and cheaper) microprocessors have packages with 16 to 28 pins. Figure 1.12(a) is an example. Standard microprocessors have 40-pin packages like the Motorola 6800 shown in Fig. 1.12(b).

Figure 1.12 Pin configurations of microprocessors. (a) Intel 4004 pin configuration (courtesy of Intel Corporation); (b) Motorola 6800 pin configuration (courtesy of Motorola Semiconductor Products, Inc.).

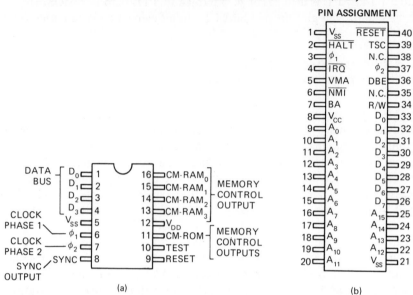

(a)

(b)

The limited number of pins means that the processor must use some pins for more than one purpose—for instance, to transfer data both to and from the memory as shown in Fig. 1.13. How does the system know which way to transfer the data? The processor may produce a control signal (READ/WRITE) that is high when the processor is reading data from the memory and low when the processor is writing data into the memory.

Figure 1.13 A bidirectional data bus.

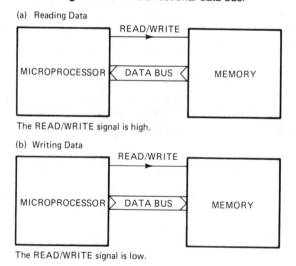

(a) Reading Data

The READ/WRITE signal is high.

(b) Writing Data

The READ/WRITE signal is low.

The processor may use the same pins to transfer data to and from input/output devices as shown in Fig. 1.14. The processor will then need another control signal (SECTION SELECT) to differentiate between memory transfers and input/output transfers. This signal could be high for memory transfers and low for I/O transfers. External gating can produce combinations of the limited number of processor signals. For example, an OR gate (see Fig. 1.15) could produce an I/O WRITE signal that is low only when the processor is transferring data to an output device.

Figure 1.14 Using a single data bus for memory and I/O.

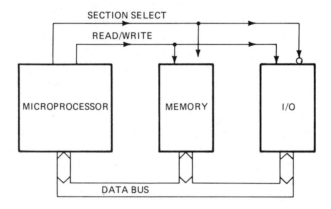

Figure 1.15 External gating of control signals.

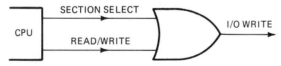

I/O WRITE is low if and only if both SECTION SELECT and READ/WRITE are low.

In addition, pin limitations mean that certain input and output pins must handle many sources or destinations. For instance, the processor may have several input devices, such as keyboards, cassettes, or paper tape readers. All these devices must send data to the processor through a single set of pins. Only one source can use the pins at a time, and sources that are not using the pins must not interfere with the one that is. A decoding system selects the particular device that will be allowed to use the pins. A special kind of bus eliminates interference; the one in common use is the *tri-state bus*. Inactive tri-state sources act like open circuits and do not affect the bus.

External gates may also combine input signals. A reset signal, for example, may come either from a remote switch or from a control panel. Figure 1.16 shows the tying of both sources to the RESET input through an OR gate. A signal on either line will reset the processor. External gates both expand the number of control signals coming from the processor and reduce the number of control signals going to the processor.

Figure 1.16 External gating of control signals.

Furthermore, the time-sharing of pins means that output data is only briefly available and that the processor may not be able to fetch input data immediately. Latches must hold the data until it can be transferred properly.

Among the important characteristics of integrated circuits are the input and output voltage levels. Input voltage levels are the levels that the circuit is guaranteed to recognize correctly; output voltage levels refer to the levels that the circuit is guaranteed to produce. The levels depend on temperature and circuit loading.

In order for two integrated circuits (such as a microprocessor and a memory) to work together, each must correctly recognize the signals produced by the other. So in the actual circuit configuration the output voltages produced by the sender must be within the limits that the receiver is guaranteed to recognize properly. The designer must allow a noise margin. If these requirements are not met, errors will occur and the system will behave erratically. Buffers or level translators will ensure that signals are received correctly. Such devices, however, add to system cost and complexity and delay the passage of signals. Level translators may be necessary in systems that contain both TTL and MOS devices, since MOS devices require higher voltage levels than TTL devices.

IC chips (particularly MOS devices) may have complex power supply and timing requirements. The most convenient situation is one in which the power supplies and clock signals of the overall system will also handle the microprocessor and memory chips. Such is usually the case for Schottky TTL and CMOS microprocessors and memories. However, the more common NMOS and PMOS devices require several power supplies at nonstandard levels (i.e., not the typical 5 V) and complex clock circuits.

Moreover, IC chips are fragile. Maximum voltage and current levels are always specified. Regulated power supplies or on-board regulation must limit voltage and current spikes. MOS chips must be handled carefully, since static charges can destroy them.

Testing of IC chips is difficult. This is particularly true of microprocessors. The number of possible combinations of inputs and outputs is far too large for each one to be checked. Expensive test systems can provide test patterns and monitor the inputs and outputs. Yet no test can absolutely ensure the proper field performance of microprocessors and other integrated circuits. Field observation indicates that such devices are highly reliable because they involve few external connections, but little test data is available.

1.7 SEMICONDUCTOR MEMORIES

Most microcomputers use semiconductor memory chips. These memory chips provide storage for programs, tables, character patterns, and data. The development of microprocessors has been closely associated with the development of memory chips that provide large amounts of storage in cheap and convenient forms. Appendix 5 describes semiconductor memories more extensively.

Three types of semiconductor memory chips are commonly used with microprocessors: read-only memories (ROMs), programmable read-only memories (PROMs), and read/write memories (generally referred to as random access memories[1] or RAMs). Almost every microprocessor-based system uses all three types either in the development or the production stage. All three types are available in most semiconductor technologies, but NMOS memories are presently the cheapest and most widely used.

ROM is the simplest and cheapest type of memory. The manufacturing process determines its contents according to a pattern (or mask) which the manufacturer must create. The manufacturer charges a fixed price (a *mask charge*, typically several hundred dollars) for each pattern. Thus ROMs are expensive to change or produce in small quantities. ROMs are used for fixed tables and for the final versions of programs in high-volume applications (involving a thousand or more memories). Standard ROMs may be purchased without a mask charge for use in producing characters on printers and CRT displays and for common code conversions. ROMs are *nonvolatile*—that is, their contents do not change when power is lost.

PROMs are memories that cannot be changed during normal operation but may be programmed under special conditions. The manufacturer produces the PROM with all the cells in the same state. The user may change cells for a particular application, usually by applying large voltage pulses for a specified amount of time. A special piece of equipment, called a *PROM programmer*, produces the required pulses.

Some PROMs can only be programmed once. Often the memory cells in these PROMs consist of links that can be broken but cannot be reconstructed. No corrections in these PROMs are possible unless the error left a cell in its original state.

Many MOS PROMs can be programmed more than once. One variety is the erasable PROM or EPROM. An EPROM can be erased by removing it from the circuit board and placing it under an ultraviolet light source for about 10 minutes. We can then program the PROM again. Note that we must erase the entire PROM even if we only want to change one bit. Another variety of reprogrammable PROM is the electrically alterable ROM or EAROM. We can change a single location in an EAROM without removing the memory from the circuit board.

---

[1] *Random access* means that all locations can be accessed in the same amount of time. Most standard memories, including ROMs and PROMs, are random access; a shift register is an example of a memory that is not. The term RAM, however, commonly refers to a random access read/write memory.

Like ROMs, PROMs are permanent storage. They are nonvolatile and cannot be changed by the program. Although somewhat more expensive than ROMs, they can be purchased in small quantities without a mask charge.

RAMs, or read/write memories, are the most complex and most expensive memories but the easiest to change. Semiconductor RAMs are *volatile*—that is, they lose their contents when power is removed. Thus a program in RAM must be reloaded each time power is applied to the system. Microcomputers may use RAM as program memory in the early stages of program development or if frequent program changes are necessary. Otherwise RAM serves only as data memory.

1.8 APPLICATIONS OF MICROPROCESSORS

Many products using microprocessors are available today. Besides describing the general areas in which microprocessors have been applied, this section also gives a specific example from each area.

Test and Instrumentation

Microprocessors have been used in counters, test equipment, calculating oscilloscopes, digital voltmeters, automatic capacitance bridges, x-ray analyzers, blood analyzers, distance meters, frequency synthesizers, data acquisition systems, and spectrum analyzers. An example is the Fluke 6010A synthesized signal generator (see Fig. 1.17), which uses a microprocessor (Intel 4004) to program the test frequencies and control their sequence, to interface with external test systems, to

Figure 1.17 The Fluke 6010A signal generator (courtesy of John Fluke Mfg. Co., Inc.).

select ranges, and to control displays. The microprocessor provides programmability, handles the interfacing with external equipment, and offers simple input procedures and flexible displays. The microprocessor is not fast enough to generate signals; instead it acts as a controller, handling coded inputs, acknowledging control signals, automatically justifying numbers, controlling display brightness, and saving input values for easy recall.

For simple instruments and test sets, the microprocessor can provide programmability, handle interfacing problems, simplify data entry, display data and warning or instructional messages in convenient forms, and automatically select parameters. The microprocessor can also provide self-test and self-calibration, internal consistency checks on data, communications with computers or computer-controlled instruments, and automatic averaging of readings. In general, it replaces standard circuitry in simple applications. The microprocessor is more reliable and makes instruments more flexible and easier to use. On the other hand, microprocessors are usually slower, more expensive, and involve more development costs than ordinary circuitry.

When large instrument systems and test equipment are involved, the microprocessor can completely or partially replace a minicomputer. The microprocessor is cheaper, physically smaller, easier to protect from severe environmental conditions, more reliable, and uses less power than a minicomputer. On the other hand, the microprocessor is slower, can handle fewer input/output devices, and has less standard software, peripherals, and interfaces than the minicomputer.

Communications

Microprocessors have been used in terminals, minicomputer networks, message switching units, repeaters, store-and-forward systems, coding and encryption devices, portable communications systems, and modems. A typical example is the Action Communications Systems' Telecontroller (see Fig. 1.18), a switching unit used in networks of private terminals. The Telecontroller uses microprocessors (the National IMP 16) as front-end processors for a minicomputer; the microprocessors convert the messages to the minicomputer's internal code, identify control sequences, check for errors, and edit the message text and header. The result of the preprocessing by the microprocessors is an order-of-magnitude increase in the throughput of the minicomputer.

In the communications area microprocessors can handle routine tasks for larger computers, perform simple conversions or calculations, detect signals and adjust analog settings, interface lines operating with different speeds or protocols, and perform editing functions. In addition, they can, as in the test and instrumentation area, provide programmability, control displays and operator messages, handle keyboards or other input devices, and allow easy customizing and interfacing of equipment. Microprocessors can increase reliability and reduce communications costs.

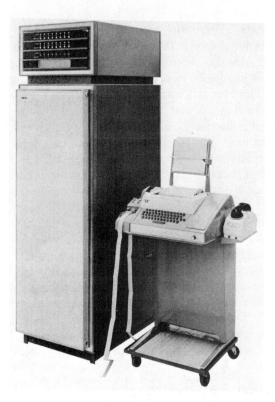

The most serious limitation of microprocessors in the communications area is speed. MOS microprocessors cannot handle data rates above 50 kilobits per second. Schottky TTL and ECL processors should permit many new applications in the communications area.

Computers

Microprocessors are used in hobby and business computers, in minicomputer CPUs and input/output controllers, and in many computer peripherals, including intelligent CRT terminals, magnetic card readers, line and character printers, typewriters, data recorders, plotters, paper tape readers and punches, optical character readers, cassette and cartridge memories, and floppy disks. A typical example is the Pertec Model 7100 CRT terminal (Fig. 1.19), which uses a microprocessor (Intel 8008) to perform text editing, error correction, and preparation of data for transmission. Functions that require high data rates (such as clearing the screen) are implemented in hardware but are triggered by the microprocessor. The microprocessor allows both additional editing facilities and the rapid customizing of the terminal in order to handle varied keyboard layouts, character sets, and communications protocols.

Microprocessors offer the same advantages in the computer peripheral area as in the test and instrumentation area. Even more significantly, microprocessors allow the distribution of system computing power. Local intelligence for terminals and other peripherals means that many tasks can be handled remotely rather than by the main computer. Not only does remote processing reduce the cost of communications and increase the throughput of the main computer but it also simplifies software and allows some work to be done even if the communications links or main computer fail. A computer consisting entirely of microprocessors would theoretically be able to assign resources to particular tasks and continue operating even if several elements failed. Such distributed systems are presently in the development phase; internal communications is a major problem.

Figure 1.19 Pertec Model 7100 CRT display terminal (courtesy of Pertec Business Systems).

Industrial

Microprocessors have been used in data-monitoring systems, smart cameras for quality control, automatic weighing and batching systems, assembly-machine control, torque certification systems, machine tool controllers, metal stretching and bending presses, lumber sorters, materials handlers, phototypesetters and composition machines, digital gas flow meters, optical page readers, graphics and drafting systems, industrial terminals, and automatic testers. A typical example is the ALMA 720 Automatic Tester (see Fig. 1.20) for watch circuits and modules that uses a Motorola 6800 microprocessor to generate test programs that check continuity, breakdown voltage, and leakage currents. The microprocessor also controls the pin electronics, handles displays, and converts units. A comparable piece of equipment using ordinary circuitry or a minicomputer would be far more expensive.

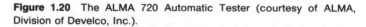

Figure 1.20   The ALMA 720 Automatic Tester (courtesy of ALMA, Division of Develco, Inc.).

The major advantages of microprocessors in industry are their low cost, high reliability, and tolerance of harsh environmental conditions. They can, therefore, be used in applications where minicomputers would be too expensive or unreliable. In most industrial applications the limited speed and computational power of the microprocessor are not major drawbacks. In process control, however, the relatively long characteristic data lengths (16 bits) and the complexity of the control algorithms require either a minicomputer or a very powerful microprocessor. Microprocessors can also be used in distributed systems where they perform local tasks and prepare data for a central computer; local intelligence allows a high degree of fault tolerance in noisy factory environments. A major shortcoming of microprocessors in industrial applications is their limited input/output capabilities. Because of short word lengths and pin limitations, they cannot handle the enormous numbers of inputs and outputs required by such industrial applications as assembly-line machines.

Business Equipment

Microprocessors have been used in small business computers, point-of-sale terminals, time-and-attendance terminals, data collection terminals, programmable calculators, check processors, teller terminals, document storage and retrieval systems, word-processing stations, and packaging equipment. A typical example is the TRW 2001 Retail Terminal (see Fig. 1.21), which uses a microprocessor (the Motorola 6800) to transmit data to the central computer for inventory and accounting purposes, to handle displays, to request credit checks, to compute totals, taxes, and discounts, and to provide instructions for the operator. The terminal can speed the checkout process by reading prices directly from tickets and performing all the calculations automatically. It also immediately enters the transaction into the accounting and inventory system and significantly reduces the number of errors made in data entry and arithmetic. Clearly a minicomputer would be far too expensive for such an application, and standard circuitry could not provide the important interactive features.

Figure 1.21   TRW 2001 Retail Terminal (courtesy of TRW Communications Systems and Services).

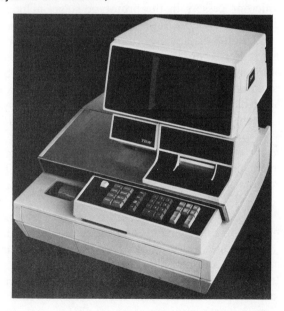

The major advantage of microprocessors in business equipment is their ability to provide interactive features at low cost. The microprocessor can easily perform most of the tasks required by clerks, salespeople, tellers, and secretaries; it can do simple calculations, record transactions, and access information quickly and accurately. Moreover, the microprocessor can provide instructions, warnings, and error messages for the operator. Thus microprocessor-based equipment can reduce errors, save training costs, and simplify changes in financial procedures, tax rates, or store policies.

Another advantage of microprocessor-based business equipment lies in its ability to communicate directly with central computer facilities. The results are faster customer service, better control over operations, and easier collection and preparation of computer input. The microprocessor can format, edit, and check the data before transmitting it to the computer. Microprocessors also allow business equipment to be customized to meet user requirements and changed to handle new situations. The drawbacks of microprocessors in business equipment are the amount of programming required of the equipment manufacturer and the relatively limited amount of software support that is presently available.

Transportation

Microprocessors have already been used extensively in traffic-light controllers and in mobile communications systems and terminals. They have also been placed in test equipment for electronic ignition and fuel-injection systems. Automotive applications of microprocessors in the prototype stage include spark-timing controllers, antiskid braking systems, on-board diagnostic systems, interior temperature controllers, and digital display and control systems. A typical example of these prototype systems is Ford's programmable spark-timing controller (Fig. 1.22 is a block diagram of the system), which uses a 12-bit custom CMOS microprocessor to calculate the desired angle of spark firing, load the angle into a custom controller, and position the exhaust gas recirculation valve or EGR system. The microprocessor-based system is expected to reduce exhaust emissions and fuel consumption significantly.

In the transportation area microprocessors can provide intelligent control at low cost, convenient operator displays, and custom features. The small size, low power consumption, reliability, and ruggedness of microprocessors are also important factors.

The major problems in applying microprocessors in transportation have been the extremely unfavorable environments and the lack of adequate development and test equipment. Automobiles, for example, require devices that can withstand large variations in temperature and humidity, unregulated power supplies, large current and voltage transients, mechanical shock and vibration, chemical and gaseous contamination, and electromagnetic and radio-frequency interference. Ships and airplanes present even worse environmental conditions, including exposure to salt spray, high vibration levels, variations in outside pressure, and nuclear radiation. The microprocessor and other supporting circuitry must be constructed from a suitable semiconductor technology (usually CMOS) and packaged to meet the environmental requirements. The transducers, sensors, actuators, and converters

Figure 1.22 Block diagram of spark-timing controller (reprinted with permission from R. H. Temple and S. S. Devlin, "The Use of Microprocessors as Automobile On-Board Controllers," *Computer*, July 1974, pp. 99–102).

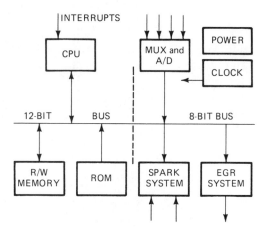

(Note: EGR SYSTEM means *exhaust gas recirculation system*.)

presently available are either too expensive, too inaccurate, or unable to withstand the harsh environments. Furthermore, microprocessor-based systems require new repair and test equipment. Although the microprocessor could help to reduce fuel consumption and exhaust emissions in vehicles and could provide improved visual displays and warning and diagnostic systems, the technical and economic problems involved in applying microprocessors in the transportation field are far from solved.

Aerospace/Military

Microprocessors have been used in navigation systems, mobile communications systems, training systems, satellite communications systems, and drone controllers. A typical example is the Litton Data Systems' Tactical Input/Output Unit (see Fig. 1.23), which uses a microprocessor (Intel 8008) to handle displays, monitor the front panel and keyboard functions, and perform self-tests. In military applications the increased reliability, flexibility, and self-diagnostic ability of microprocessor-based equipment are particularly important. Small size, low power consumption, ruggedness, and the ability to provide extensive operator displays are also significant. As in the transportation area, military applications require devices that can withstand harsh environments. The lack of standardization in microprocessors is also a problem for military applications.

Figure 1.23 Litton Data Systems' Tactical Input/Output Unit (courtesy of Litton Data Systems).

Consumer/Commercial

Microprocessor uses in the consumer area include games, slide rule calculators, home computers, liquor dispensers, appliances, and stereo and gambling equipment. A typical example is the animated bowling game, Bally Alley (see Fig. 1.24), developed by Bally Manufacturing Company, which uses a microprocessor (Intel 4004) to monitor ball placement and pin patterns, compute scores and odds, and give out free games and credits. The microprocessor provides the animation that makes the game realistic and interesting; traditional designs (ordinary pinball machines) cannot provide such varied and sophisticated animation while a minicomputer would be far too expensive. Applications of microprocessors in the consumer and commercial field are just beginning; the difficulties are the environmental conditions and the requirement for cheap, compatible actuators, sensors, analog-to-digital converters, signal conditioners, and transducers.

The number and variety of microprocessor applications demonstrate the advantages offered by this new technology. As with all new technologies, however, there are many problems and limitations. Yet the potential of cheap computers is obvious. Electronic systems can be more flexible, more reliable, less expensive, more accurate, and easier to use.

Figure 1.24 The Bally Alley Animated Bowling Game (courtesy of Bally Manufacturing Corporation).

2 Microprocessor Architecture

This chapter describes the internal structure or *architecture* of micro-processors. Our first topic is the overall structure of computers. Then the structure of the control section or central processing unit (CPU) is considered; the emphasis here is on the number and types of registers, the arithmetic unit, and the instruction-handling mechanism. The final sections discuss the special features of microprocessor architecture, including those of the Intel 8080 and Motorola 6800 devices.

2.1 GENERAL COMPUTER ARCHITECTURE

Computers have three sections: a control section that executes instructions and processes data, a memory section that stores data and instructions, and an input/output section that handles communications between the computer and the outside world. Signals travel from one section to another along paths called *buses*. Figure 2.1 shows a typical computer. After briefly describing the functions of all

Figure 2.1 Block diagram of a typical computer.

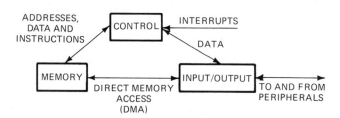

the sections and buses, we focus on the control section, or CPU. The memory and input/output sections are discussed in more detail in Chapters 7 and 8.

Memory Section

The memory section of a computer contains storage units, which usually consist of magnetic cores or semiconductor cells (Appendix 5 describes both). The storage units are binary—that is, they have two stable states that represent the values zero and one. The memory is organized into *bytes*, which are the shortest groupings of bits that the computer can handle at a time, and *words*, which have the same bit length as the computer's data registers, data buses, and arithmetic unit. A byte generally consists of 8 bits, whereas a word may be 4 to 64 bits in length. The memory is arranged sequentially into words, each of which has a unique address. The address of a word in memory should not be confused with its contents. Memory location 0, for instance, could contain any value. When referring to the contents of a memory location, we will place its address in parentheses. Thus X is an address and (X) the contents of that address. Figure 2.2 shows the arrangement of a typical memory.

Figure 2.2   A typical memory (1 word = 2 bytes).

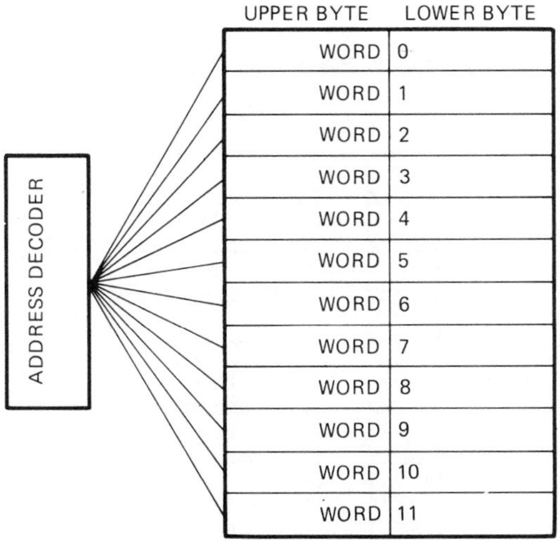

The relationship between words and bytes depends on the word length of the computer.

The address decoder takes an address sent from the control unit and selects the proper memory location. Figure 2.3 shows a simple one-line decoder. If the input line is zero, output line A is zero and output line B is one; if the input line is one, output line A is one and output line B is zero. Thus a single address line can select between two memory locations—a zero selects memory location B and a one selects memory location A.

Figure 2.3 A simple decoder.

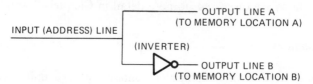

Finding the correct memory location and obtaining its contents take a certain amount of time; this time is the *access time* of the memory. The access time affects the speed of the computer, since the computer must obtain its instructions and most of its data from the memory. Computer memories are usually *random access* so that all memory locations have the same access time. The computer must wait whenever it uses the memory; typical memory access times range from 100 ns to several microseconds.

Memory sections are often subdivided into units called *pages*. The entire memory section may involve millions of words, whereas a page contains between 256 and 4K words. The computer may access a memory location by first accessing a particular page and then accessing a location on that page. Figure 2.4 shows this process. The advantage of paging is that the computer can reach several locations on the same page with just the address on the page. This process is like describing street addresses by first specifying a street and then listing the house numbers.

Figure 2.4 Accessing a paged memory.

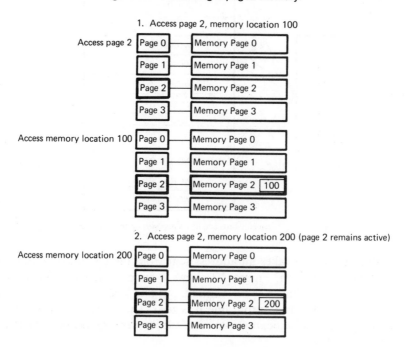

The control section transfers data to or from the memory as follows.

1. The control section sends an address to the memory.

2. The control section sends a signal (READ/WRITE) to the memory to indicate the direction of the transfer.

3. The control section waits until the transfer has been completed. This delay precedes the actual data transfer in the input case and follows it in the output case.

Several buses (see Fig. 2.5) connect the control and memory sections. The address bus carries the address of the memory location that the control section wants to use. The READ/WRITE signal determines the direction of the transfer. The data buses carry data between the sections. Some of these buses may be physically the same; for instance, a single bus may carry data in different directions or carry data and addresses at different times. A bus used for more than one purpose is said to be *time shared* or *multiplexed*. Extra control signals determine what is on the bus at a given time.

Figure 2.5 Connections between control and memory sections.

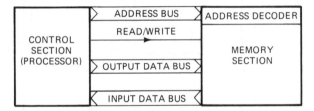

An important feature of computer memories is that they may contain either data or instructions, both of which are represented as binary numbers. A machine that uses the same format and memory for data and instructions is called a *von Neumann machine* after the mathematician who first proposed such machines. How does the control section know whether it has an instruction or a piece of data? The answer is that the control section only knows what it expects to find at a particular time. If the programmer makes an error, the control section may interpret data as instructions and vice versa.

Input/Output Section

The input/output section of a computer handles the transfer of data between the computer and external devices or peripherals. The transfer involves status and control signals as well as data. The input/output section must reconcile timing differences between the computer and the peripherals, format the data properly, handle status and control signals, and supply the required current and voltage levels. Irregular transfers may be handled with interrupts, control signals that receive the immediate attention of the control section and cause the suspension of its normal activity.

The actual transfer of data between the computer and the peripherals is rapid, but ensuring that the transfer is completed properly may take much longer. A typical input operation proceeds as follows (see Fig. 2.6).

1. The peripheral signals the control section that new data is available. The input/output section must format the signal properly and hold it until the control section accepts it.

2. The peripheral sends the data to the control section. The input/output section must hold the data until the control section is ready to read it.

3. The control section reads the data. The input/output section must have a decoding mechanism that selects a particular part of the section (or *port*). Reading the data should deactivate the signal that indicated data was available; it may also result in an acknowledgement to the peripheral so that the peripheral will know that it can send more data.

Figure 2.6 An input operation.

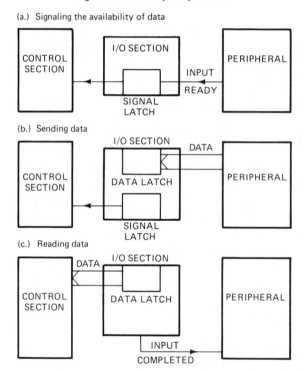

Output operations are much like input operations. The peripheral indicates to the control section that it is ready to accept data. The control section then sends the data along with a signal (a strobe) that indicates to the peripheral that the data is available. The input/output section formats the data and control signals properly and holds the data long enough for the peripheral to use it. Output data must be held much longer than input data, since mechanical devices, lighted displays, and human observers respond much more slowly than computers.

The input/output section must perform many simple interfacing tasks. It must place signals in the proper form for both the control section and the peripherals. The control section will require signals at particular voltage levels. The peripherals may use many different types of signals, including continuous (analog) signals, current levels, and different voltage levels. Amplifiers will be necessary for signals that must travel long distances or drive large loads.

The input/output section may also perform some functions that the control section could perform. These functions include conversion of data between *serial* (one bit at a time) and *parallel* (more than one bit at a time) form, the insertion or deletion of special patterns that mark the beginning or end of a data transfer, and the calculation and checking of error-detecting codes, such as parity.[1] The input/output section can perform such functions in hardware faster than the control section can perform them in software. The input/output section of a computer may be programmable or may even contain a processor so that it can handle some of the processing tasks.

Figure 2.7 shows the connections between the control and input/output sections. The address bus carries the address of the input or output port that the control section wants to use. The input/output signal determines the direction of the transfer. The data buses carry data between the sections. The control bus carries the signals indicating that data is ready and that the transfer is complete. As with buses between the control and memory sections, some of the buses may be physically the same and time shared for different purposes.

Figure 2.7 Connections between control and input/output sections.

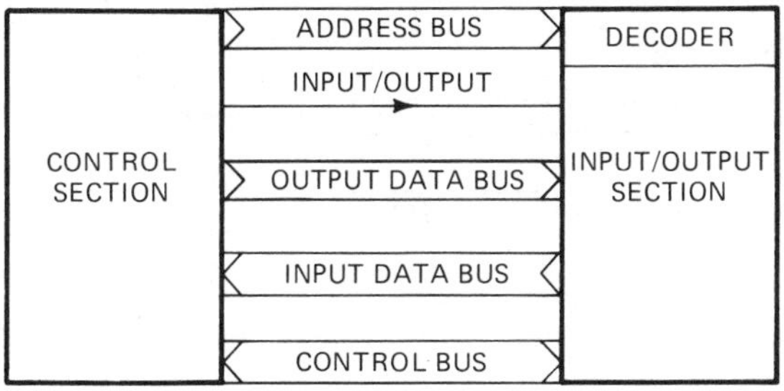

Furthermore, buses may connect the control section to both the memory and input/output sections. A single control line can distinguish between the sections. In fact, some computers (e.g., the Motorola 6800) combine the memory and input/output sections completely; they treat an input or output device just like a

---

[1]Parity is an extra bit in each word that indicates if the number of one bits in the word is even (*even parity*) or odd (*odd parity*). Parity is appended to words that are to be sent on noisy communications lines. If the receiver checks the parity and finds it to be wrong, it knows that it has not received the correct data and can ask the transmitter to repeat the message.

memory location. The memory section must then perform the additional functions required by peripherals.

Modern computers have a direct link between the memory and the input/output section that allows the transfer of data to or from peripherals without intervention by the control section. This method of transferring data is *direct memory access* (abbreviated *DMA*). The advantage of DMA is that the transfer speed is limited only by the memory access time (usually less than 1 μs). Data transfers through the control section require several instruction cycles and take 10 to 20 times as long. Direct memory access is used with high-speed peripherals, such as magnetic disks, high-speed communications lines, or CRT displays.

The connections required for direct memory access are shown in Fig. 2.8. The DMA controller, which is part of the I/O section, handles data transfers just like the CPU. A control signal (DMA REQUEST) ensures that the control section will not attempt to use the memory at the same time as the DMA controller. The buses shown may be physically the same as those that connect the control section to the input/output and memory sections.

Figure 2.8 DMA (direct memory access) connections.

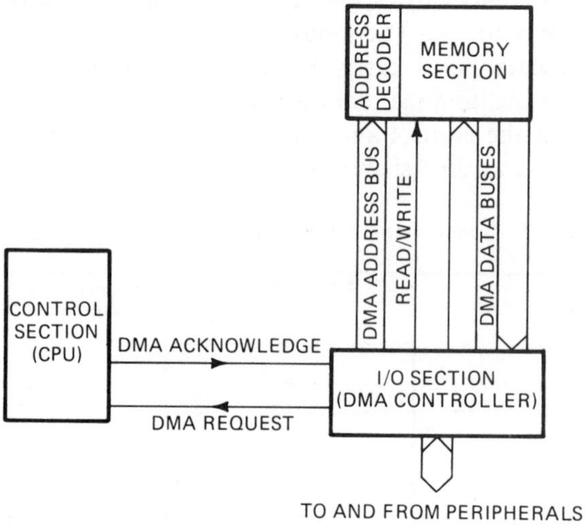

Control Section (CPU)

The control section (CPU or processor) processes the data. It fetches the instructions from memory, decodes them, and executes them. It generates timing and control signals, transfers data to or from the memory and input/output sections, performs arithmetic and logical functions, and recognizes external signals. Figure 2.9 shows a typical control section. The timing and control functions of the control section are discussed in Chapters 7 and 8.

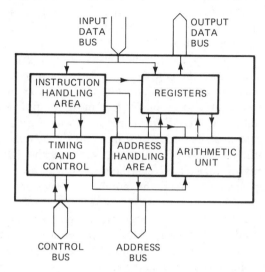

Figure 2.9 A typical computer control section.

During each instruction cycle the control section performs many tasks.

1. It places the address of the instruction on the memory address bus.

2. It takes the instruction from the input data bus and decodes it.

3. It fetches the addresses and data required by the instruction. The addresses and data may be in memory or in registers.

4. It performs the operation specified by the instruction code. The operation may be an arithmetic or logical function, a data transfer, or a management function.

5. It looks for control signals, such as interrupts, and provides appropriate responses.

6. It provides status, control, and timing signals that the memory and input/output sections can use.

The control section, or CPU, is thus the center of computer operations; it both processes data and directs the entire computer.

2.2 REGISTERS

The keys to the architecture of most CPUs are the registers. *Registers* are small memories that are part of the control section. Like the memory storage units, registers consist of binary cells and have addresses that distinguish them. The number of registers is very small, however. Data may be saved in a register until a bus or other unit is ready to receive it or until the program requires it. Registers under program control are advantageous, since the CPU can obtain data from them without a memory access. Registers that are not under program control allow the control section to save data for later use.

Registers are connected to each other, to other parts of the control section, and to external buses by means of internal buses. The registers and internal buses usually have the same word length as the rest of the computer system; however, registers and internal buses with half or double the system word length are also common. Signals generated by the instruction-handling area may place the contents of a register on a bus or the contents of a bus in a register.

The cost of registers and interconnections limits the number found in a computer. Registers were once so expensive that most computers had less than ten; the IBM 1130 and the DEC PDP-8 are computers with very few registers. Later, with the rapid decrease in semiconductor prices and the advent of LSI technology, register costs plummeted. Newer computers, such as the IBM 360 and DEC PDP-11, have dozens of registers. Nevertheless, as will be explained in a later section, limited chip sizes still keep the number of registers in microprocessors fairly small.

If the CPU has a large number of registers, programs will not require as many transfers of data to and from memory. This factor reduces the number of accesses and the length of the instructions. A large number of registers means extra internal decoding and addressing circuitry, but the trend in newer computers is toward a fairly large number, such as 50.

Figure 2.10 shows a typical set of registers. Registers may have many different purposes; some computers even allow the programmer to assign registers to particular functions. Most computers, however, permanently assign some or all their registers. Among the common types are

- Program counters
- Instruction registers
- Memory address registers
- Accumulators
- General-purpose registers
- Index registers
- Condition code registers
- Stack pointers

The program counter (PC) contains the address of the memory location that contains the next instruction. The instruction cycle begins with the CPU placing the contents of the program counter on the address bus; the CPU thereby fetches the first word of the instruction from memory. The CPU also increments the contents of the program counter so that the next instruction cycle will fetch the next sequential instruction from memory. If the instruction occupies more than one word of memory, the CPU increments the program counter each time it is used. Thus the CPU executes instructions sequentially unless an instruction (such as JUMP or BRANCH) changes the program counter.

Figure 2.10 A typical set of registers.

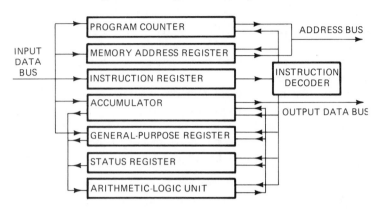

An instruction register (IR) holds the instruction until it can be decoded. The bit length of the instruction register is the bit length of the basic instruction for the computer. Some computers have two instruction registers, and so they can fetch and save one instruction while executing the previous one (this process is called *pipelining*). The programmer seldom can access the instruction register.

Memory address registers (MAR) hold the addresses of data in memory. The addresses may be part of the instructions or may be provided separately by the program. Figure 2.11 shows the use of a memory address register under program control. The LOAD ACCUMULATOR FROM MEMORY instruction loads the

Figure 2.11 Using a memory address register to increment the contents of a memory location.

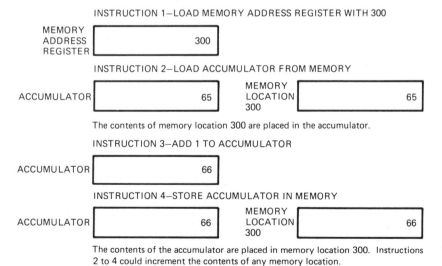

accumulator with the contents of memory location 300. The contents of the accumulator are incremented (ADD 1 TO ACCUMULATOR) and stored in memory location 300 (STORE ACCUMULATOR IN MEMORY). Thus the computer can use memory location 300 several times without specifying its address in each instruction and can use the next memory location (301) simply by adding 1 to the memory address register.

Many computers have several memory address registers. Figure 2.12 is a flowchart for a program that uses memory address registers to move ten words of data from one place in memory to another. The LOAD DATA and STORE DATA instructions in Fig. 2.12 do not need memory addresses; a single bit in the instruction could determine whether the CPU uses memory address register 1 or 2.

Figure 2.12   Using two memory address registers to move data.

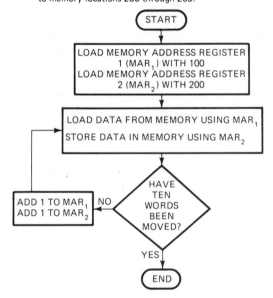

Purpose: Move ten words of data from memory locations 100 through 109
to memory locations 200 through 209.

Accumulators are temporary storage registers used during calculations. In most computers, as in calculators, the accumulator always holds one of the operands in arithmetic operations. The computer may also use accumulators in logical operations, shifts, and other instructions. So accumulators are generally the most frequently used registers in the computer. Many widely used computers (like the DEC PDP-8) have a single accumulator; programs for such computers spend much time moving data to and from the accumulator. Most newer computers have several accumulators; consequently, programs need not move data around so much. For example, Fig. 2.13 shows the instruction sequences that evaluate the expression

$A \times B + C \times D$

in a computer having one accumulator and a computer having two accumulators. With only one accumulator, the program must save the first result and then recall it; with two accumulators, the program can perform the calculations separately. However, each instruction in the two-accumulator machine must contain a code to identify which accumulator the CPU should use.

Figure 2.13 Instruction sequences with one and two accumulators.

One Accumulator	Two Accumulators
LOAD ACCUMULATOR WITH A	LOAD ACCUMULATOR 1 WITH A
MULTIPLY BY B	MULTIPLY BY B
STORE RESULT IN TEMPORARY STORAGE	LOAD ACCUMULATOR 2 WITH C
LOAD ACCUMULATOR WITH C	MULTIPLY BY D
MULTIPLY BY D	ADD ACCUMULATORS
ADD CONTENTS OF TEMPORARY STORAGE	

General-purpose registers have a variety of functions. Such registers may serve as temporary storage for data or addresses. The programmer may be able to assign them as accumulators or even as program counters.

Index registers are used for addressing. The contents of the index register are added to the memory address which an instruction would otherwise use. The sum is then the actual address of the data or the *effective address*. Thus if the contents of the index register are changed, the same instruction can be used to handle data from different addresses. We can transfer data from one place to another by using index registers as well as memory address registers; Fig. 2.14 shows the method.

In this case, the LOAD and STORE instructions must have memory addresses; however, this program uses a single index register instead of two memory address registers. Some computers, like the DEC PDP-8 and PDP-11, have *autoindexing* whereby the index register is automatically either incremented (*autoincrement*) or decremented (*autodecrement*) every time it is used. This feature is very convenient in program loops like those shown in Figs. 2.12 and 2.14. Each instruction in a computer with index registers must contain codes to indicate whether indexing is being used. If the computer has more than one index register, the instructions must also designate which one is to be used.

Condition code or status registers hold 1-bit indicators (flags) that represent the state of conditions inside the CPU or, occasionally, external serial inputs or outputs. The flags are the basis for computer decision-making. Different computers have different numbers and types of flags. Most older computers have only one or

Figure 2.14 Using an index register to move data.

Purpose: Move ten words of data from memory locations 100 throu
to memory locations 200 through 209.

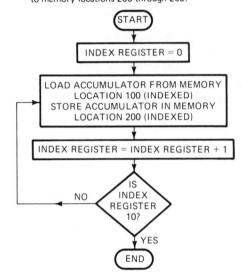

two flags because of the hardware cost involved; newer computers have several flags. Among the more common flags are the following.

CARRY—1 if the last operation generated a carry from the most significant bit. The CARRY flag can retain a single bit of information and can handle the carry from one word to the next in multiple-precison arithmetic.

ZERO—1 if the result of the last operation was zero, often used in loop control and in searching for a particular data value.

OVERFLOW—1 if the last operation produced a two's complement overflow (see Appendix 1, Section 2, for the distinction between carry and overflow); the OVERFLOW bit determines if the result of an arithmetic operation has exceeded the capacity of a word.

SIGN—1 if the most significant bit of the result of the last operation was 1 (sometimes called NEGATIVE, since 1 indicates a negative two's complement number); the SIGN bit is useful in arithmetic and in examining single bits within a word.

PARITY—1 if the number of one bits in the result of the last operation was even (even parity) or odd (odd parity). PARITY is useful in character manipulation and communicatons.

HALF-CARRY—1 if the last operation generated a carry from the lower half-word, used in 8-bit CPUs to do BCD arithmetic (see Section 5.3 and Appendix 3, Section 1).

INTERRUPT ENABLE—1 if an interrupt is allowed, 0 if not. The CPU may automatically disable interrupts during startup or service routines. The programmer may disable interrupts during critical timing loops or multi-word operations. A computer may have several interrupt enable flags if it has several interrupt inputs or levels (see Chapter 9).

A CPU may have flags that can be changed or observed externally as serial input or output lines.

A stack pointer is a register that contains the address of the top of a stack. Section 2.6 describes stacks in more detail.

2.3 ARITHMETIC UNITS

The arithmetic part of a control section can vary from a simple adder to a complex unit that can perform many arithmetic and logical functions. If the arithmetic unit cannot perform a function directly, several instructions will be necessary in order to produce the desired result.

All modern computers have binary adders. These devices accept two binary inputs and produce the binary sum and a carry from the most significant bit of the addition. Since most computers operate in two's complement (see Section A1.2), subtraction can be performed by taking the two's complement of one input before sending it to the adder. Multiplication and division may be performed by repeated additions and subtractions, respectively. Extra circuitry can form other status outputs, such as a zero indicator.

Single-chip *arithmetic-logic units* (ALUs) are widely available; these devices consist of a binary adder and other logical circuitry. Figure 2.15 shows a typical ALU; it has two data inputs, function inputs, a carry input for performing multiple-precision arithmetic, data outputs, and status outputs that set the various flags described in the previous section. The function inputs determine which function the ALU performs; typical choices are

- Addition
- Subtraction
- Logical AND
- Logical (INCLUSIVE) OR
- Logical EXCLUSIVE OR
- Logical NOT (complement)
- Increment (add 1)
- Decrement (subtract 1)
- Left shift (add input to itself)
- Clear (result is zero)

Figure 2.15 An arithmetic-logic unit.

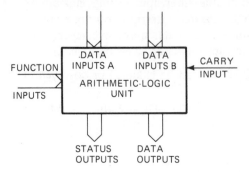

The function inputs also determine whether a bus is used at all. For instance, the value on the A bus can be incremented by blocking the B bus (so that the value entering the ALU is zero), setting the carry input to 1, and adding. Thus

OUTPUT = A + B + CARRY
= A + 0 + 1
= A + 1

Other possibilities include complementing an input or the output to produce such functions as $\overline{A} + B$ or $\overline{A} \cdot B$. An ALU can thus perform any of a variety of functions during a single cycle under the control of the function inputs.

Special circuitry can also perform other arithmetic functions, such as multiplication and division, sines and cosines, or logarithms and exponentials. The special circuitry can provide high speed, but arithmetic units capable of performing extra functions directly are much more expensive than standard units.

2.4 INSTRUCTION HANDLING AREAS

The CPU must translate the instruction it obtains from memory into the control signals that produce the desired actions. The CPU must find addresses for memory locations and registers that the instruction uses, provide function inputs for the ALU, and control the buses so that the instruction is executed properly. For instance, if the instruction is "ADD REGISTER 1 TO REGISTER 2 AND PLACE THE RESULT IN REGISTER 3," the CPU will proceed as follows, if the computer is organized as shown in Fig. 2.16(a).

1. The contents of register 1 are placed in temporary register 1 [Fig. 2.16(b)]. This step is necessary because a single bus connects the registers and the arithmetic-logic unit. So the CPU must save the contents of register 1 in a temporary register that is directly connected to the ALU.

2. The contents of register 2 are placed in temporary register 2 [Fig. 2.16(c)].

3. The addition is performed and the result is placed in register 3 [Fig. 2.16(d)].

Figure 2.16 Execution of the instruction "ADD REGISTER 1 TO REGISTER 2 AND PLACE THE RESULT IN REGISTER 3."

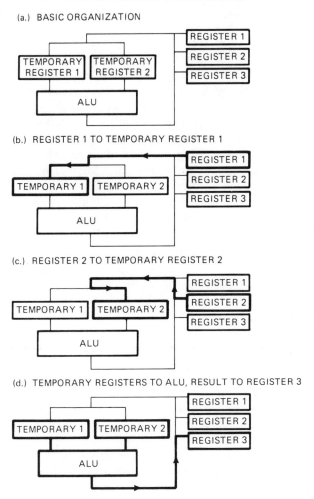

(a.) BASIC ORGANIZATION

(b.) REGISTER 1 TO TEMPORARY REGISTER 1

(c.) REGISTER 2 TO TEMPORARY REGISTER 2

(d.) TEMPORARY REGISTERS TO ALU, RESULT TO REGISTER 3

The CPU must perform the steps in the proper order and must complete a step before starting the next one. Only one piece of data can be on a bus at a given time.

The CPU must also obtain the instruction from memory, place it in the instruction register, and prepare to fetch the next instruction. The CPU will therefore perform an instruction cycle as follows.

1. The CPU places the program counter on the memory address bus in order to fetch an instruction.

2. The CPU increments the program counter so as to be ready to fetch the next instruction.

3. The CPU takes the instruction from the memory data input bus and places it in the instruction register.

4. The CPU decodes and executes the instruction.

The first three steps in the cycle are the same for every instruction.

Ordinary logic circuits may produce the required sequence of operations; a CPU built in this manner is said to be *hard wired*. However, the instruction cycle is itself a series of sequential instructions. So a control section within the control section could execute a series of instructions that would, in turn, execute the computer instructions. Writing sequences of control instructions that decode and execute computer instructions is called *microprogramming*.

Microprogramming is confusing to most students. How can a computer execute instructions by executing other instructions? Microprogramming seems like translating French to English by first translating French to German and then translating German to English. Does the process actually accomplish anything or does it simply make the problem more complex? The answer is that microprogramming replaces hardware with software and provides flexibility at the cost of speed. Note how a computer could execute an instruction as a sequence of microinstructions.

Microinstruction 1:
    PROGRAM COUNTER TO
      ADDRESS BUS
Microinstruction 2:
    INCREMENT PROGRAM COUNTER
Microinstruction 3:
    DATA INPUT BUS TO
      INSTRUCTION REGISTER

The CPU now must use the instruction to find the sequence of microinstructions required to execute it. (See Appendix 5, Section 2, for an illustration of how to do so.) For instance, the computer could execute the instruction of Figure 2.16 as follows.

Microinstruction 4:
    REGISTER 1 TO TEMPORARY REGISTER 1
Microinstruction 5:
    REGISTER 2 TO TEMPORARY REGISTER 2
Microinstruction 6:
    ADD
Microinstruction 7:
    ALU RESULT TO REGISTER 3
Microinstruction 8:
    RETURN TO MICROINSTRUCTION 1

The microinstructions are much simpler than the actual computer instructions. Consequently, the computer designer can check microinstructions more easily than regular instructions to see that they work properly. If an instruction is erroneous, the designer can correct it by changing microinstructions rather than by changing complex connections or chip designs.

Furthermore, the same microinstructions may be part of many different instructions. A SUBTRACT instruction will only require a change in microinstruction 6, for example. We can implement entire new instruction sets by changing microprograms; we may not have to change the hardware at all in order to get an improved or custom computer. In fact, a computer that executes instructions through microprograms could be made to handle the instruction set of another computer; the process is called *emulation*. Programs that ran on the original computer would run on the new computer without any changes. Emulation allows the user to get improved hardware without having to discard a substantial investment in working programs.

Of course, microprogramming has disadvantages. The process is slower than hard-wired decoding, since it requires extra fetch cycles and operates sequentially rather than in parallel. Microprograms are difficult to write and check and little support is available. A computer that has been microprogrammed will not be able to run programs not specifically written for it, and the programs that are written for it will not work on any other computer. A computer that has been microprogrammed to emulate another computer will never be an exact copy of the emulated machine; the differences can produce errors that are difficult to trace.

Note that there is no necessary relationship between microprogramming and microprocessors despite the confusing similarity in names. A microprocessor, like any other computer control section, may be microprogrammed (i.e., have its instructions decoded by microprograms) or microprogrammable (i.e., the user can change the microprograms). However, it may equally well be neither. Programs written for a microprocessor are *not* microprograms unless they are specifically designed to decode instructions in a microprogrammable microprocessor.

2.5 STACKS

Most modern computers use stacks to handle data in an organized manner. Stacks are last-in, first-out memories (or LIFOs): we can only add items to the top or remove them from the top. Adding an item to a stack is a *PUSH* operation, removing an item a *POP* or *PULL*. Figure 2.17 shows the results of pushing and popping a stack.

Some computers have stacks that are physically like the plate dispensers in cafeterias—that is, all the elements actually move when the computer adds or removes elements. The stack in Fig. 2.18 is one in which all the elements move. A shift register can form this type of stack.

Figure 2.17 Stack operations.

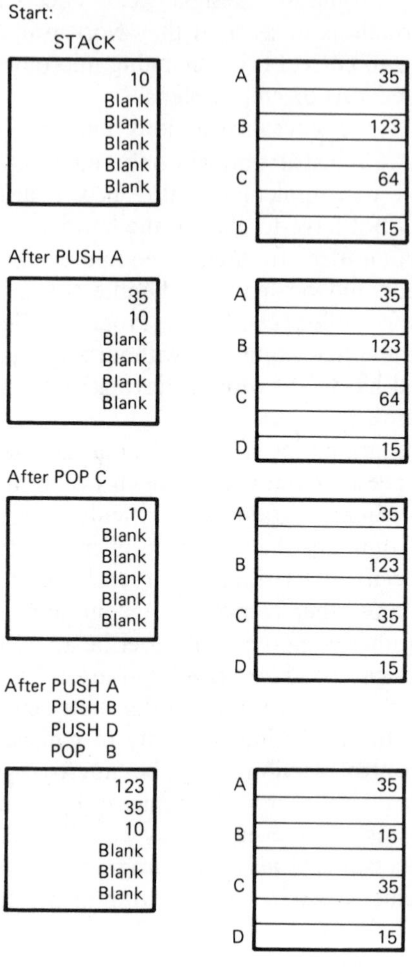

Start:

STACK

STACK		A	35
10			
Blank		B	123
Blank			
Blank			
Blank		C	64
Blank			
Blank		D	15

After PUSH A

		A	35
35			
10		B	123
Blank			
Blank			
Blank		C	64
Blank			
		D	15

After POP C

		A	35
10			
Blank		B	123
Blank			
Blank			
Blank		C	35
Blank			
		D	15

After PUSH A
    PUSH B
    PUSH D
    POP   B

		A	35
123			
35		B	15
10			
Blank		C	35
Blank			
Blank		D	15

In most computer stacks, however, the elements do not actually move. The only change that occurs is in the stack pointer, which contains the address of the top of the stack. The computer adds an element to the stack by placing the element in the memory location addressed by the stack pointer and then incrementing the stack pointer; it removes an element from the stack by decrementing the stack pointer and obtaining the element from the memory location addressed by the stack pointer. Figure 2.18 shows examples of these operations. Note that the elements in the stack do not move at all. This type of stack can be an ordinary read/write memory.

The major advantage of a stack is that we can add data to it (up to the capacity of the stack) without disturbing the data that is already there. If we store

Figure 2.18 Stack operations using a stack pointer.

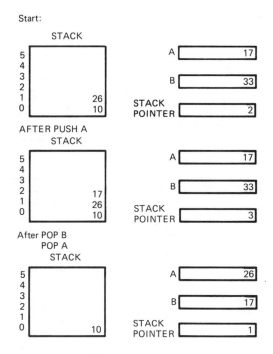

data in a memory location or register, we lose the previous contents of the storage place. So before we can use the same memory location or register again, we must save its contents somewhere else. On the other hand, we can use the stack over and over again, since its previous contents are automatically saved. Furthermore, the CPU can easily and quickly transfer data to or from the stack because the address is in the stack pointer and need not be part of the instruction. Stack instructions can be very short.

We also can use the last-in, first-out nature of the stack to advantage to store subroutine return addresses as shown in Fig. 2.19. Each JUMP TO SUBROUTINE instruction moves a return address from the program counter to the stack. Each RETURN instruction fetches a return address from the stack and places it in the program counter. Thus the program can retrace its path through the subroutines by using the stack.

The major disadvantage of stacks is the difficulty of debugging and documenting programs that use them. Since the stack does not have a fixed address, its location and contents may be difficult to remember or determine. Lists of the current contents of the stack (*stack dumps*) can serve as documentation. Errors in stack usage can be quite difficult to find; typical examples are removing items from the stack in the wrong order, placing extra items in the stack or removing extra items from it, and overflowing or underflowing the stack.

Figure 2.19 Using a stack for return addresses.

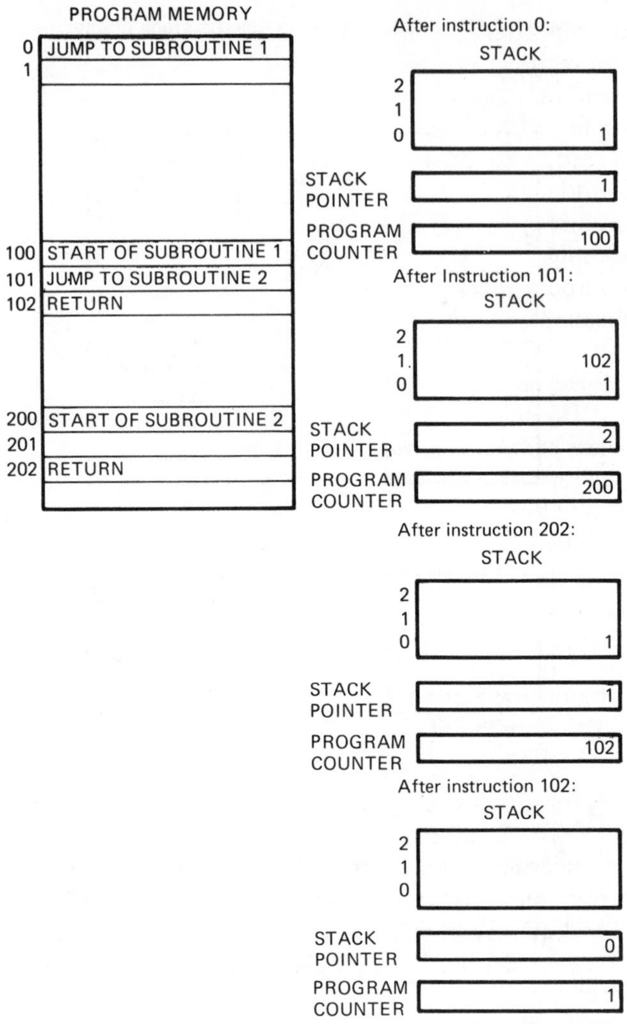

PROGRAM MEMORY

0	JUMP TO SUBROUTINE 1
1	

100	START OF SUBROUTINE 1
101	JUMP TO SUBROUTINE 2
102	RETURN

200	START OF SUBROUTINE 2
201	
202	RETURN

After instruction 0:

STACK

2	
1	
0	1

STACK POINTER: 1

PROGRAM COUNTER: 100

After Instruction 101:

STACK

2	
1	102
0	1

STACK POINTER: 2

PROGRAM COUNTER: 200

After instruction 202:

STACK

2	
1	
0	1

STACK POINTER: 1

PROGRAM COUNTER: 102

After instruction 102:

STACK

2	
1	
0	

STACK POINTER: 0

PROGRAM COUNTER: 1

2.6 SPECIFIC FEATURES OF MICROPROCESSOR ARCHITECTURE

This section is concerned with the registers, arithmetic units, and instruction-decoding mechanisms of microprocessors.

Microprocessor Registers

Microprocessor registers differ from those of larger computers for the following reasons.

1. Limited chip size. A single-chip microprocessor must have a limited number of narrow registers and buses.

2. Use of read-only program memory. Microprocessors therefore cannot save addresses or data in program memory.

3. Limited read/write memory.

4. Short word lengths. A memory address may occupy several data words.

5. Interrupt-driven operation. Registers must allow for rapid recognition and servicing of interrupts.

6. Special-purpose structures. Many microprocessors have registers designed for specific applications, such as calculators, terminals, or process control.

Obviously some of the factors mentioned require tradeoffs in the number and types of registers. The maximum chip size and the need to save registers quickly when interrupts are being serviced limit the number of registers. The short word length means that register addresses must be short in order to be handled easily. On the other hand, the use of read-only program memory and limited RAM creates a need for temporary storage in which to save data and addresses. The difficulty of addressing with short instruction words also makes a large amount of temporary storage in the microprocessor desirable. The architectural features below are typical of microprocessors.

- Most microprocessors have several general-purpose registers. The Fairchild F-8 has 64, the Intel 8080 and Signetics 2650 6, and the Intel 4040 24. A few processors, including the Motorola 6800, have no general-purpose registers at all. The Motorola 6800, however, can access certain memory locations (on page zero) very rapidly.

- Almost all microprocessors have a single accumulator. The Motorola 6800, however, has two, whereas the National PACE has four (one, though, is the only accumulator for certain instructions).

- Almost all microprocessors have a stack for saving subroutine return addresses. Some, such as the Intel 4040 and Signetics 2650, have a limited on-chip stack, usually 4 to 10 levels in depth. Others, including the Intel 8080 and Motorola 6800, keep their stacks in external read/write memory; such stacks require more read/write memory and the proper initialization of the stack pointer but allow the stack to be as long as necessary. Only a few microprocessors, such as the Scientific Micro Systems Interpreter, have no stack at all.

- Most microprocessors have special features in their registers to handle interrupts. The special feature may involve the use of a different set of registers during the interrupt service routine; the Intel 4040 and Signetics 2650 have this feature. Microprocessors with only a few registers (e.g., the Motorola 6800) can respond to interrupts quickly, since they have little to save.

The short word length of microprocessors makes the handling of addresses difficult. Registers may alleviate this problem in the following ways.

- Varied register lengths. Often some registers—particularly program counters, memory address registers, return address stacks, stack pointers, and index registers—are longer than the normal word length of the processor. Special instructions may be available to load and manipulate the contents of these long registers.
- Several memory address registers under program control. This feature allows the program to place starting addresses in these registers and then use the addresses in a series of instructions. The Zilog Z-80, Intel 4040, Intel 8080, RCA CDP1802, and Fairchild F-8 all use this method of handling addresses.
- Use of register pairs. Many microprocessors have registers that can be addressed either singly or in pairs. Programs can then use these registers either singly for decimal or character data or as pairs for addresses or longer data. The Intel 4040, Intel 8080, and RCA CDP1802 all have this feature.
- Long index registers. A few microprocessors, including the Motorola 6800, have an index register that is used like an address register. The index register is long enough to hold a complete memory address; indexed instructions provide a short offset from this address. This method differs from the common use of the index register—providing short offsets.

Microprocessor Arithmetic Facilities

Almost all microprocessors have simple arithmetic facilities. Only a few (e.g., the Data General micro-Nova and Texas Instruments 9900) have hardware multiplication and division. Some processors, such as the Intel 4004 and Texas Instruments TMS 1000NC, have no logical functions. Several processors, including the Intersil 6100 and Scientific Micro Systems Interpreter, do not even perform subtraction directly; they must complement the number to be subtracted and then add. Thus the arithmetic and logical capabilities of most microprocessors are quite limited when compared to larger computers.

Most microprocessors have an arithmetic unit with a simple bus structure. Generally one operand is derived from an accumulator and the other from a temporary register; the result is sent to the accumulator.

Many microprocessors have special read-only memories or other circuitry to perform a few common tasks. Decimal (BCD) addition is the most common such task; others include BCD subtraction, keyboard scan, and display decoding and driving.

Microprocessor Instruction Decoding

Almost all microprocessors are microprogrammed because of the difficult design process, the frequent need for changes, and the previously mentioned advantages of microprogramming. The Intel 4040 is one of the few hard-wired processors. The microprograms for most processors are stored in read-only memories on the chip itself.

The difficulties involved in programming microprocessors at any level, slow MOS speeds, and limited software aids have made microprogrammable MOS microprocessors rather unattractive. The National IMP is a series of microprogrammable MOS processors that are also available in nonmicroprogrammable forms, such as the PACE.

Most of the bipolar microprocessors, on the other hand, are microprogrammable. The only exception is the Scientific Micro Systems Interpreter. In fact, none of the other bipolar microprocessors has a standard instruction set. So far the major applications of the bipolar microprocessors have been in computer emulations where microprogrammability is a necessity. The lower density and higher speed of bipolar devices make microprogrammable processors more attractive.

2.7 EXAMPLES OF MICROPROCESSOR ARCHITECTURE

Intel 8080 Block Diagram

Figure 2.20 is a block diagram of the Intel 8080. On the right-hand side are the register array and address buffer. In the center are the data bus buffer, instruction register, and instruction-decoding facilities. On the left-hand side are the arithmetic and logical facilities, including the arithmetic-logic unit, flags, decimal adjust ROM, accumulator, and temporary register. The timing and control section, along with the input/output buses, will be discussed in Chapters 7 and 8.

Intel 8080 Registers

The Intel 8080 registers are

- Six 8-bit general-purpose registers called B, C, D, E, H, and L
- One 16-bit stack pointer
- One 16-bit program counter
- Two 8-bit temporary registers (called W and Z)

Figure 2.20 Intel 8080 block diagram (courtesy of Intel Corporation).

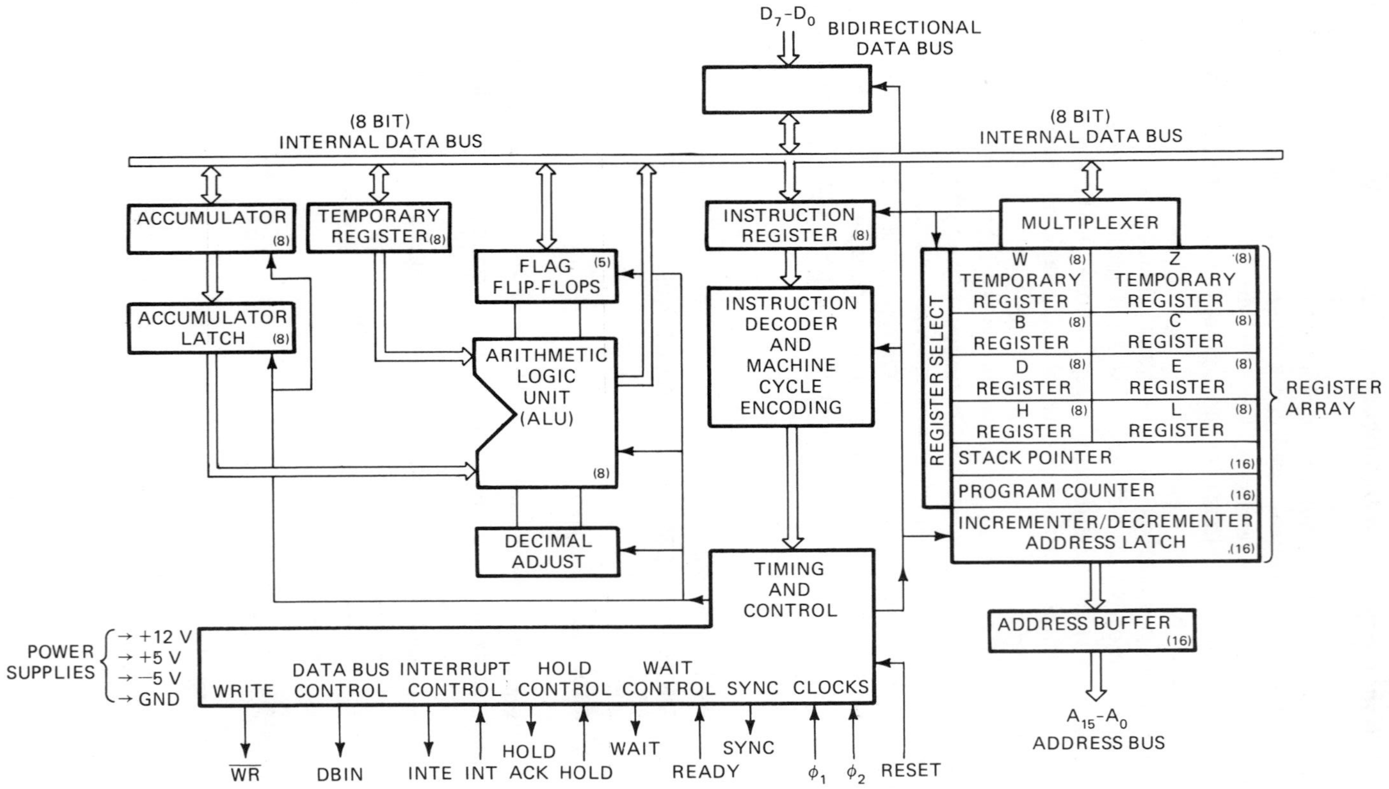

The six 8-bit general-purpose registers can also be referred to as three 16-bit registers (B and C, D and E, and H and L; the first-named register contains the eight most significant bits and the pair may be referred to by its name).

Register pair H (registers H and L) is the primary memory address register. The memory location addressed by H and L can be used just like a general-purpose register except that the CPU needs extra time to transfer data to or from it. The other register pairs may also be used as memory address registers but only to load or store the accumulator.

The registers have their own arithmetic facility. This facility allows the CPU to increment the 16-bit program counter quickly and to increment or decrement the 16-bit stack pointer and any of the 16-bit register pairs. The two 8-bit temporary registers and the incrementer/decrementer allow 16-bit addresses to be manipulated without using either the accumulator or the arithmetic-logic unit.

The stack pointer is a 16-bit register that holds the address of the last memory location (lowest address) occupied by the RAM stack. The pointer is automatically incremented after data is removed from the stack and decremented before data is added to the stack. The stack grows from higher addresses to lower addresses.

Intel 8080 Instruction Handling Area

The Intel 8080 instruction handling area contains an 8-bit instruction register and an instruction decoder. The instruction is loaded into the instruction register from the data bus via the data bus buffer.

Intel 8080 Arithmetic Facility

The Intel 8080 arithmetic facility consists of an 8-bit arithmetic-logic unit, a decimal adjust ROM, five flag flip-flops, an accumulator (or register A), and a temporary register. The arithmetic-logic unit includes facilities for addition, subtraction, four common logical functions (AND, OR, EXCLUSIVE OR, and NOT), and shifting. One operand for arithmetic and logical functions is always derived from the accumulator and the other from the temporary register. The temporary register may be loaded from any of the general-purpose registers or from the memory location addressed by registers H and L; it is loaded via the 8-bit internal bus as part of the instruction execution. The decimal adjust ROM implements the required correction for BCD addition (see Appendix 3, Section 1).

The five flags available in the Intel 8080 are

- CARRY
- ZERO
- SIGN (most significant bit)
- (Even) PARITY
- AUXILIARY (or half) CARRY

There is no two's complement overflow flag.

Motorola 6800 Block Diagram

Figure 2.21 is a block diagram of the Motorola 6800 microprocessor. The registers and arithmetic unit are on the right-hand side. The instruction facilities are on the left-hand side. The address buffer is at the top and the data buffer at the bottom.

Figure 2.21 Motorola 6800 block diagram (courtesy of Motorola Semiconductor Products Inc.).

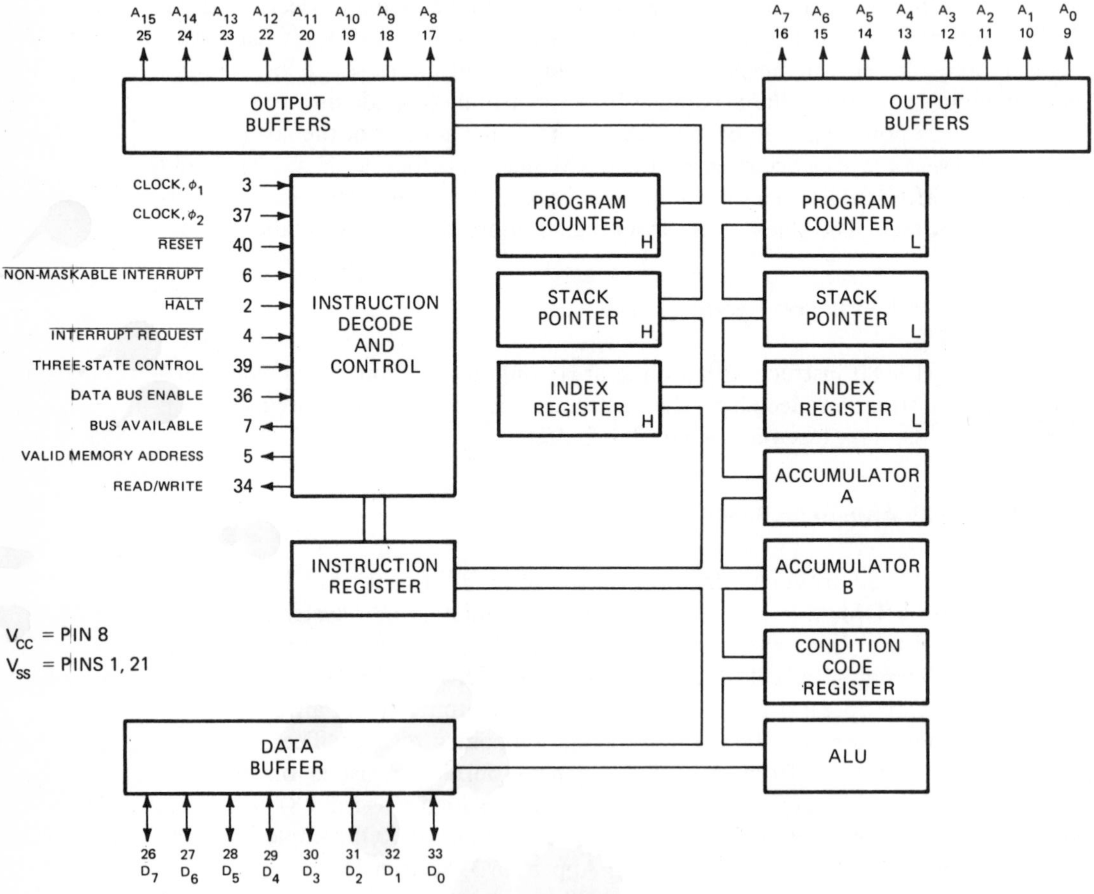

Motorola 6800 Registers

The Motorola 6800 registers are

- Two 8-bit accumulators
- One 16-bit index register

- One 16-bit program counter
- One 16-bit stack pointer
- One 8-bit condition code register
- Two 8-bit temporary registers

The 16-bit index register is used like an address register. An 8-bit offset can be added to its contents to form an effective address.

The stack pointer holds the address of the next empty location in the RAM stack; unlike the Intel 8080, the Motorola 6800 decrements the stack pointer after placing data in the stack and increments the stack pointer before removing data from the stack. The stack still grows from higher addresses to lower addresses.

Motorola 6800 Instruction Handling Area

The Motorola 6800 instruction handling area contains an 8-bit instruction register and an instruction decoder. The instruction is loaded into the instruction register from the data bus via the data buffer. A read-only memory decodes the instructions.

Motorola 6800 Arithmetic Facility

The Motorola 6800 arithmetic facility consists of an 8-bit arithmetic-logic unit and six flags. External data is placed directly into the ALU rather than into a temporary register. The ALU performs both arithmetic and logical functions. The contents of either accumulator can be used as one of the operands; the result is returned to the source accumulator.

The six flags available in the Motorola 6800 are

- CARRY
- ZERO
- NEGATIVE (sign or most significant bit)
- OVERFLOW (two's complement)
- HALF-CARRY
- INTERRUPT (DISABLE; i.e., interrupts are disabled if the bit is one)

2.8 SUMMARY

Computers have three major sections:

- The control section (CPU), which directs the activities and processes the data.
- The memory section, which stores data and instructions.
- The input/output section, which handles communications with the outside world.

The control section contains registers, an arithmetic unit, an instruction-decoding mechanism, and timing and control circuitry. Registers can serve many purposes; they can hold data, instructions, or complete or partial addresses in program or data memory. Arithmetic units may vary greatly in complexity, ranging from simple adders to complex arithmetic-logic units. The instruction-decoding mechanism may consist of ordinary circuitry or may itself be a programmed system. This second level of programming is called microprogramming. Stacks give order to data and addresses but may be difficult for the programmer to use.

A microprocessor performs the same functions as any computer control section. Microprocessors differ from other control sections because of the limitations imposed by maximum chip and package size, the use of read-only program memory and small amounts of read/write memory, and the requirements of common applications. Most microprocessors therefore have moderate numbers of registers and simple arithmetic units; they often use on-chip or RAM stacks to store subroutine return addresses. Most standard microprocessors are microprogrammed in order to simplify the design procedure.

PROBLEMS

1. How many address lines would the following sizes of memories require? Assume that we can access each byte.
    (a) 8K bytes
    (b) 64K bytes
    (c) 12K bytes
    (d) 100K bytes
    Does the number of address lines needed change if you only want to access separate words? Is the change dependent on the length of the computer word?

2. Describe how you could access the following sequences of memory locations in a computer with 1000-word pages. How should you organize the memory accesses in such a computer to obtain maximum speed?
    (a) 2150, 7270, 3480, 3490
    (b) 1100, 6000, 1200, 6300, 1300
    (c) 1100, 1200, 1300, 6000, 6300

3. Describe the errors that could occur during an input or output operation in these situations.
    (a) No signal is generated by an input device to indicate that data is available.
    (b) Two input devices have the same address.
    (c) The signal indicating that an output device is ready to receive data is not deactivated by the output operation.
    (d) The output data is not latched by the input/output section.
    (e) The output section provides a 5-V signal to a gas discharge device that requires 150 V to light the display.

4. What is the effect on the program counter of each of the following one-word instructions?

(a) ADD 1 TO ACCUMULATOR

(b) JUMP TO 300

(c) STORE DATA IN MEMORY

What happens to the program counter if the instruction occupies two or three words of program memory?

5. Use the method of Fig. 2.11 to increment the contents of memory location 500. Use the instructions ADD ACCUMULATOR TO MEMORY and INCREMENT MEMORY ADDRESS REGISTER to add the contents of memory locations 500 and 501 and place the result in memory location 502.

6. How must the program of Figure 2.12 be modified in order to do the following?

(a) Move ten words from memory locations 200 through 209 to memory locations 100 through 109.

(b) Place the ten words of data in reverse order in memory locations 200 to 209—that is, (109) in 200, and so on.

(c) Move every other word—that is, move the contents of 100 to 200, 102 to 202, 104 to 204, and so forth—so that ten words are moved in total.

7. Describe how the expression below would be evaluated on a computer having one accumulator and on a computer having two accumulators.

$$A \times (B + C \times (D - E))$$

8. How would the program of Fig. 2.14 need to be modified in order to perform the tasks described in Problem 6?

9. If the last operation performed on a computer with an 8-bit word was an addition in which the operands were 2 and 3, respectively, what would the values of the following flags be?

(a) CARRY

(b) ZERO

(c) OVERFLOW

(d) SIGN

(e) EVEN PARITY

(f) HALF-CARRY

What if the operands were −1 (two's complement) and +1?

10. How would it be possible to implement a decrement operation (i.e., subtract 1) in an ALU that could have any of its inputs blocked or complemented? How about a CLEAR operation? Assume that addition, subtraction, and the logical functions AND, OR, and EXCLUSIVE OR are available. Assume also that subtraction always subtracts the carry input—that is, the output from a subtraction is $A - B - CARRY$ INPUT.

11. Which flag bit would you use for the following purposes?

(a) To check if a counter has been decremented to zero.

(b) To check if a binary addition resulted in an answer that could be represented in a single computer word.

(c) To determine if the result of a subtraction is positive.

(d) To determine if two numbers are both positive or both negative.

(e) To check if a number is even or odd.

12. How should the sequence of Fig. 2.16 be changed in order to execute the following instructions?
    (a) SUBTRACT REGISTER 1 FROM REGISTER 2 AND PLACE THE RESULT IN REGISTER 3
    (b) LOGICALLY AND REGISTER 1 WITH REGISTER 3 AND PLACE THE RESULT IN REGISTER 1
    (c) DOUBLE REGISTER 2
    (d) CLEAR REGISTER 1

13. Describe the microinstructions required to execute the instructions of Problem 12.

14. Describe how the stack and registers of Fig. 2.17 would be affected by the sequences of instructions below if the initial conditions were the same as in Fig. 2.17.
    (a) POP B
    (b) PUSH A
        PUSH B
        POP A
        POP B
    (c) PUSH D
        POP C
        PUSH B
        POP A

How would these sequences affect the stack of Fig. 2.18? Assume that the initial conditions are as shown in Fig. 2.18 with the addition that C contains 40 and D 90.

15. How would the changes below affect the stack of Fig. 2.19? Trace the contents of the stack as the program is executed.
    (a) Memory location 0 contains JUMP 100 instead of JUMP TO SUBROUTINE 1.
    (b) Memory location 202 contains JUMP 0 instead of RETURN.
    (c) Memory location 201 contains JUMP TO SUBROUTINE 1.
    (d) Memory location 201 contains JUMP TO SUBROUTINE 3 where SUBROUTINE 3 starts in memory location 300 and ends with a RETURN instruction in memory location 370.

16. How many bits long should the stack pointer be in these cases?
    (a) The stack is four elements deep.
    (b) The stack is in the first 256 words of memory.
    (c) The stack can be anywhere in a 16K memory.

17. Describe a microinstruction sequence that would cause the computer to jump to the address contained in a register. Assume that the computer is organized as shown in Fig. 2.16; register 1 is the program counter and register 2 contains the address to be used. Describe how a monitor program could use this sequence to specify where the computer is to start executing the user program—i.e., the command GO 2000 places 2000 in the program counter.

18. An alternative to using the stack for subroutines would be to place the return address in a register. Show how the instruction JUMP TO SUBROUTINE 1 in Fig. 2.19 would be executed if register D were used to save the return address. How could the program return to the original sequence? (*Hint*: Note Problem 17.) What would happen if

SUBROUTINE 1 tried to call another subroutine? Discuss some methods for solving this problem, such as storing the return address in memory.

19. A memory address register could be used with a linked list. The address of the first element in the list would be placed in the memory address register and each subsequent element would contain the address of the succeeding element. Describe how an element could be removed from the list or added to it. What if each element in the list contained a value in the first word and the address of the next element in the second word? How could entries be removed from or added to such a list?

20. Describe how two's complement overflow from an addition could be detected on a computer that has CARRY and SIGN flags but no OVERFLOW flag. Describe when overflow can occur—that is, what must the signs of the operands be?

REFERENCES

ALLISON, D. R., "A Design Philosophy for Microcomputer Architectures," *Computer*, Vol. 10, No. 2, February 1977, pp. 35–41.

BURROUGHS CORPORATION, *Digital Computer Principles*, McGraw-Hill, New York, 1969.

CHU, Y., *Computer Organization and Microprogramming*, Prentice-Hall, Englewood Cliffs, N.J., 1972.

CUSHMAN, R. H., "The Intel 8080: First of the Second-Generation Microprocessors," *EDN*, Vol. 19, No. 9, May 5, 1974, pp. 30–36.

ECKHOUSE, R. H., JR., *Minicomputer Systems*, Prentice-Hall, Englewood Cliffs, N.J., 1975.

FINKEL, J., *Computer / Aided Experimentation*, Wiley-Interscience, New York, 1975.

GEAR, C. W., *Computer Organization and Programming*, McGraw-Hill, New York, 1974.

HUSSON, S. S., *Microprogramming: Principles and Practices*, Prentice-Hall, Englewood Cliffs, N.J., 1970.

"Intel 8080 Microcomputer Systems User's Manual," Intel Corporation, Santa Clara, Ca., July 1975.

KORN, G. A., *Minicomputers for Engineers and Scientists*, McGraw-Hill, New York, 1973.

MAZUR, T., "Microprocessor Basics. Part 4: The Motorola 6800," *Electronic Design*, Vol. 24, No. 15, July 19, 1976, pp. 66–77.

MCKENZIE, K. and A. J. NICHOLS, "Build a Compact Microcomputer," *Electronic Design*, Vol. 24, No. 10, May 10, 1976, pp. 84–92.

PEUTO, B. L. and L. J. SHUSTEK, "Current Issues in the Architecture of Microprocessors," *Computer*, Vol. 10, No. 2, February 1977, pp. 20–25.

TORRERO, E. A., "Focus on Microprocessors," *Electronic Design*, Vol. 22, No. 18, September 1, 1974, pp. 52–69.

3 Microprocessor Instruction Sets

The next four chapters deal with microprocessor software: Chapter 3 with instruction sets, Chapter 4 with assemblers, Chapter 5 with assembly language programming, and Chapter 6 with software development. Chapters 3 and 4 contain background information about instruction formats, addressing methods, types of instructions, language levels, and the features of assemblers. Chapter 5 describes the actual writing of short assembly language programs for the Intel 8080 and Motorola 6800 processors. Chapter 6 shows how to formulate system tasks as programs and how to debug, test, and document the programs. We will thus start with background information, describe the writing of short programs, and conclude by discussing the integration of program writing into a complete software development process.

This chapter describes microprocessor instruction sets. The first topics are instruction formats and addressing methods. Then the various categories of instructions and their uses are considered. The chapter concludes with a discussion of the specific features of microprocessor instruction sets and a detailed examination of the Intel 8080 and Motorola 6800 instruction sets.

3.1 COMPUTER INSTRUCTION FORMATS

Basically, the computer must receive data from the outside world, process the data, and send the results back to the outside world. The computer itself simply performs certain specified actions in response to certain binary inputs. The inputs that cause the computer to perform specified actions are called *instructions*. The series of instructions that causes the computer to perform a complete task is a *program*, and the collection of instructions that the computer recognizes is its *instruction set.* If the proper instruction is available, a program may consist of a single instruction. More often, a program will contain many instructions.

The computer receives instructions and data in the same form. Both are binary numbers that the computer stores in its memory and brings into the CPU on the data bus. Thus the computer will handle instructions as words with the same length as the data. The only difference is that the computer sends instructions to the instruction register and the instruction-decoding mechanism, whereas it sends data to data registers or the arithmetic-logic unit. (See Chapter 7 for more detail.)

Each instruction must contain a considerable amount of information. It must determine

1. The operation. The part of the instruction that specifies the operation is the *operation code field* or *opcode*.
2. The source of the data. The *address field* contains this information. An instruction like ADD or MULTIPLY requires two operands; an instruction like SHIFT or COMPLEMENT requires only one.
3. The destination of the result.
4. The source of the next instruction.

Obviously an instruction that contained all this information explicitly (see Fig. 3.1 for a possible format) would be very long. For example, if the operation code field were 4 bits long (allowing 2^4 or 16 different instructions) and each of the addresses were 12 bits long (allowing 2^{12} or 4K bytes of memory), the total instruction would be 40 bits long. Clearly such an instruction would be difficult to handle in a microcomputer with an 8- or 16-bit word. Many programs, moreover, require more than 4K bytes of memory and more than 16 different instructions. So some of the information that the computer needs must be implicit—that is, independent of the particular instruction.

Figure 3.1 A complete instruction format.

Operation Code	Address of Operand 1	Address of Operand 2	Address of Result	Address of Next Instruction

Reducing Instruction Length

There are many ways to reduce the length of computer instructions. Among the most common are

1. Having a program counter hold the address of the instruction. The CPU increments the program counter after each use and therefore fetches the next instruction from the next higher address in program memory.
2. Making the source and destination addresses implicit rather than explicit. These implicit addresses may be registers or memory locations addressed through registers.

3. Making the destination address the same as one of the sources; that is, the result replaces one of the operands.

4. Limiting addresses to be registers or the contents of registers rather than complete memory addresses.

Each of these options reduces the length of the instructions at the cost of some flexibility. Extra instructions are necessary if the programmer wants to change the implicit information, prevent the implementation of automatic features, and load or store the contents of implicit addresses. The option is worthwhile if the number of additional instructions required is small—that is, the implicit information would actually remain the same most of the time and would be repetitive if it were explicitly included in each instruction.

For instance, the use of a program counter presents the following tradeoff. There is no need to specify the address of the next instruction, if it is the next higher one in memory, but special instructions (e.g., JUMP, BRANCH, SKIP, or HALT) are necessary if it is not. The question is whether the programmer can arrange programs so that the computer proceeds sequentially most of the time. The answer is that such an arrangement is not only possible but also desirable, since it makes programs easier to enter and debug.

Using an implicit address (such as an accumulator or the address in a stack pointer or address register) means that the instruction need not include that address but that extra instructions are necessary to load it or save its contents. The question is whether the programmer can keep the number of extra instructions small. The answer is yes if the programmer places data in consecutive memory addresses and arranges operations in the proper order.

By making the destination the same as one source, one address can be omitted, but the old contents of the source are lost. Can the programmer arrange the program so that there is seldom a need to save intermediate results? The answer is yes. In most situations the intermediate results are unnecessary.

Similarly, limiting addresses to registers means that extra instructions are necessary to load the registers and save their contents. Here again the programmer can reduce the number of additional instructions by organizing the data and operations cleverly and by discarding intermediate results. Using a stack is particularly convenient, since the stack pointer is automatically changed with each use. However, the programmer must transfer data to and from the stack in the proper order. Note that all these methods reduce the length of instructions but place a larger burden on the programmer.

One-Address Instructions

Instructions in computers with short word lengths generally use an accumulator as a combined source and destination address. The instruction need not specify that the accumulator is to be used. A typical instruction is ADD B, which means "add the contents of address or register B to the contents of the accumulator and place the result in the accumulator." Such instructions are called *one-address instructions*; they are similar to calculator operations that use the latest entry and the contents of the accumulator and place the result back in the accumulator. Figure 3.2 shows the format of a one-address instruction; clearly such an instruction can be quite short.

Figure 3.2 One-address instruction format.

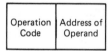

Programs consisting of one-address instructions, however, require extra instructions that place data in the accumulator originally and save the results in the memory or in general-purpose registers. These extra instructions are LOAD ACCUMULATOR and STORE ACCUMULATOR. Most programs involve many one-address instructions, since each instruction accomplishes little. Thus an evaluation of the expression

$$R = \frac{X + Y}{W + Z}$$

requires the following sequence of instructions.

Address	Instruction
START	LOAD W
START + 1	ADD Z
START + 2	STORE TEMP1
START + 3	LOAD X
START + 4	ADD Y
START + 5	DIVIDE TEMP1
START + 6	STORE R
START + 7	HALT

The instruction LOAD W places the contents of memory location W in the accumulator. The instruction STORE R places the contents of the accumulator in memory location R.

Although eliminating addresses shortens instructions, it makes programming more difficult. The programmer must keep track of the contents of the accumulator and must document programs carefully in order to avoid common errors, such as not placing a starting value in the accumulator or not saving its contents after a series of operations. Programs consisting of one-address instructions are difficult to understand, since each instruction accomplishes only part of a task and the purpose of a sequence of instructions is often unclear.

Using one-address instructions may make the accumulator into a bottleneck. More time may be spent loading and storing the contents of the accumulator than performing useful work. Some computers avoid this problem while still having short instructions by using more than one accumulator. Here there are actually two addresses in each instruction, but one address (the combined source and destination) must be one of 2, 4, or perhaps 8 accumulators. So a few bits can determine the accumulator address. The Motorola 6800, National PACE, and Signetics 2650 are examples of microprocessors having more than one accumulator.

3.2 ADDRESSING METHODS

Many different methods may specify the memory or register addresses that an instruction uses. We choose a particular addressing method for one or more of the following reasons.

1. We want to include as short an address as possible with the instruction. Short addresses take less memory space and less time to fetch.

2. We want to have easy access to as large an amount of memory as possible. Clearly this aim contradicts the first one. However, most programs use one area of memory for a while and then another. Thus the real aim is to specify any part of memory easily and use short addresses to access particular locations in the specified part.

3. We want to be able to vary the actual values of the addresses without changing the instruction. The same sequence of instructions can then be used to process all the elements in an array, table, or string. Changing the instruction creates problems in documenting and debugging the program. Furthermore, if the program memory is read-only, the instruction cannot be changed. A flexible addressing method will allow the same program to handle arrays or tables of any length.

4. We want the addressing method to be as fast as possible. A method that executes quickly is preferable to one that requires arithmetic operations or additional memory accesses.

5. We want the addressing method to be as simple as possible. The more complex a method is, the more likely we are to make mistakes using it.

Among the most widely used addressing techniques are

- Direct
- Indirect
- Immediate
- Indexed
- Relative
- Register direct
- Register indirect
- Stack

Computers use many variations and combinations of these techniques.

Direct Addressing

Direct addressing means that the actual address is part of the instruction. The one-address instruction ADD 100 causes the CPU to add the contents of memory location 100 to the contents of the accumulator—that is, (A) = (A) + (100). Note that memory location 100 does not necessarily contain the number 100. Figure 3.3 shows an instruction sequence using direct addressing that adds the contents of memory locations 100 and 101 and places the sum in memory location 102.

Direct addressing requires no calculations, is easy to understand, and can reach any location in memory at any time. However, direct addresses may be quite long. For instance, an 8-bit processor with 64K bytes of memory will need a 16-bit direct address, which it must fetch in two 8-bit sections.

Figure 3.3 An instruction sequence using direct addressing.

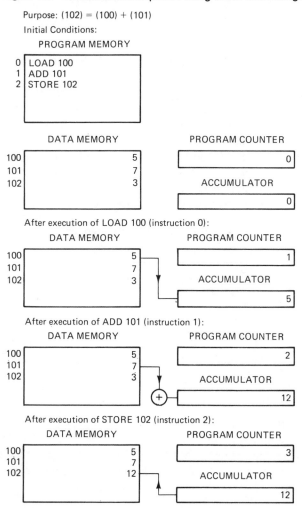

Purpose: (102) = (100) + (101)

Initial Conditions:

The direct addresses can be shortened by dividing the memory into sections or pages. We can then keep part of the address in a page register and only include the remainder with the instruction. Figure 3.4 illustrates two examples of direct addressing with a page register (the page register contains the thousands digit in the address). Of course, separate instructions must load the page register, and so the program is only shorter if it seldom requires changing pages.

Figure 3.4 Direct addressing with paging (1000-word pages).

1. INSTRUCTION   PAGE REGISTER

ADD 7		2

Result: Effective address = P007, where P is the contents of the page register.
(Accumulator) = (Accumulator) + (2007)

2. INSTRUCTION   PAGE REGISTER

STORE 36		4

Result: Effective address = P036, where P is the contents of the page register.
(4036) = (Accumulator)

By restricting the number of pages that the CPU can access at one time, the page register can be eliminated. For instance, the CPU may only be able to address memory locations directly on page zero; this method is called *page-zero addressing*. Additional addressing techniques will be required to access memory locations on the other pages. The CPU may be restricted to memory locations on the same page of memory as the instruction; this method is referred to as *current-page addressing*. These methods may be combined by including a single bit with each instruction to indicate which option is in effect. Figure 3.5 shows how the combined technique works. Such methods require no page register but only allow the CPU to easily reach locations on one or two pages of memory.

Figure 3.5 Direct addressing using the current page or page zero.

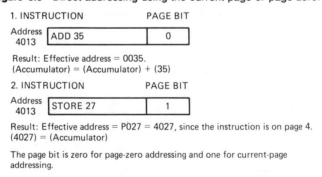

1. INSTRUCTION   PAGE BIT

Address 4013	ADD 35	0

Result: Effective address = 0035.
(Accumulator) = (Accumulator) + (35)

2. INSTRUCTION   PAGE BIT

Address 4013	STORE 27	1

Result: Effective address = P027 = 4027, since the instruction is on page 4.
(4027) = (Accumulator)

The page bit is zero for page-zero addressing and one for current-page addressing.

Direct addressing lacks the flexibility needed to process data arrays. The resulting instructions can only access a single fixed address. Note that direct addressing requires one memory access besides those needed to fetch the instruction. The CPU must place the direct address on the address bus and use it to transfer the data.

Indirect Addressing

Indirect addressing means that the address of the address rather than the address itself is part of the instruction. The one-address instruction ADD @100 (@ indicates indirect addressing) causes the CPU to add the contents of the accumulator to the contents of the memory location addressed by memory location 100—that is, $(A) = (A) + ((100))$. (Note the double parentheses to indicate "contents of contents of.") The address that is part of the instruction itself contains an address. If, for example, memory location 100 contains 227, the instruction ADD @100 is the same as the instruction ADD 227. Figure 3.6 shows an instruction sequence that uses indirect addressing to add two numbers and save the result. This

Figure 3.6 An instruction sequence using indirect addressing.

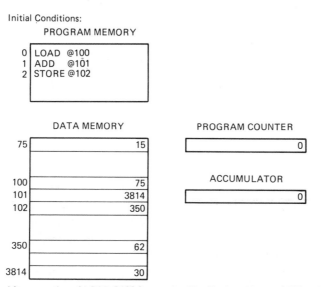

Initial Conditions:

After execution of LOAD @100 (instruction 0), effective address = (100) = 75.

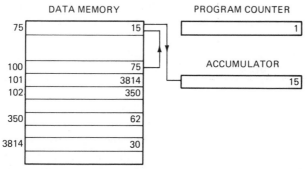

After execution of ADD @101 (instruction 1), effective address = (101) = 3814.

Figure 3.6 (cont.)

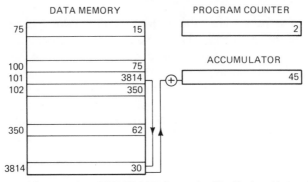

After execution of STORE @102 (instruction 2), effective address = (002) = 350.

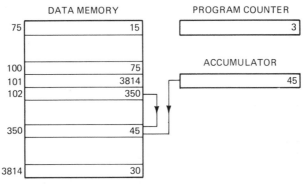

Note that the program may be in ROM, whereas the data addresses are in RAM.

sequence is more confusing and slower than the instruction sequence of Fig. 3.3. However, it can access any part of memory; the program simply changes the contents of the RAM location that holds the actual data address.

Indirect addressing is slower than direct addressing. The CPU must perform an extra memory access besides those required by direct addressing, since it must first fetch the instruction containing the indirect address from memory, then use the indirect address to fetch the effective address, and, finally, use the effective address to transfer the data. Furthermore, most programmers find indirect addressing, with its repeated distinctions between data and addresses, both confusing and error prone.

Although seemingly awkward and complex, indirect addressing is much more flexible than direct addressing. For instance, a program can save a result in memory for later use with the instruction

STORE @RESULT

Before storing the next result, we add 1 to the contents of RAM location RESULT. The same instruction will then store the next result in the next memory location. Obviously direct addressing would require a separate instruction each time. Indirect addressing is particularly convenient for subroutines, since it allows the same subroutine to process data in many different areas of memory. Figure 3.7 shows two implementations of a subroutine that finds the largest element in an array. If we use direct addressing as in Fig. 3.7(a), we must move the entire data array to the correct memory locations. If we use indirect addressing as in Fig. 3.7(b), we need only place the base address of the data array in the indirect memory location (100).

Figure 3.7 Using indirect addressing in subroutines.

Purpose: Subroutine MAX finds the largest element in an array.

(a) Using direct addressing

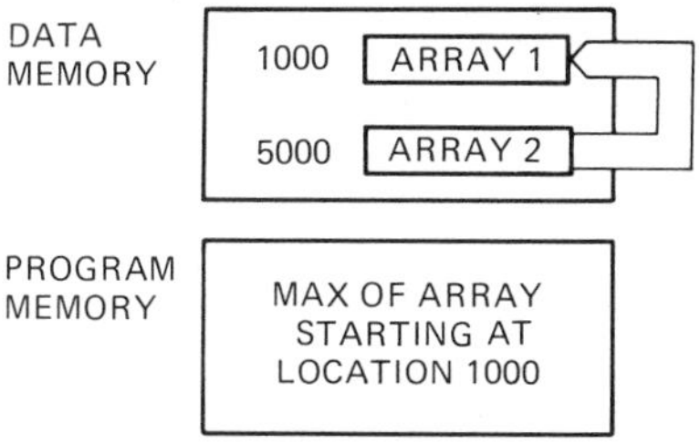

DATA MEMORY

1000 ARRAY 1

5000 ARRAY 2

PROGRAM MEMORY

MAX OF ARRAY STARTING AT LOCATION 1000

If we want to find the maximum of array 2 using subroutine MAX, we must move the entire array.

(b) Using indirect addressing

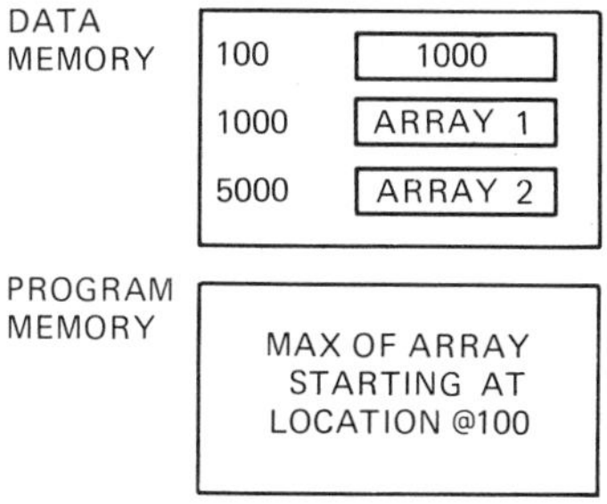

DATA MEMORY

100 1000

1000 ARRAY 1

5000 ARRAY 2

PROGRAM MEMORY

MAX OF ARRAY STARTING AT LOCATION @100

If we want to find the maximum of array 2 using subroutine MAX, we place 5000 in memory location 100.

Immediate Addressing

Immediate addressing means that the actual data is part of the instruction. The one-address instruction ADD #100 (# indicates immediate addressing) causes the CPU to add the number 100 to the old contents of the accumulator. We use immediate addressing to initialize counters and indirect addresses and to obtain constants needed in calculations. For instance, we could use the subroutine of Fig. 3.7(b) to sort the array starting in memory location 5000 with the instruction sequence

```
LOAD    #5000
STORE   100
CALL    MAX
```

We could also convert a measurement in feet to one in inches by using immediate addressing—that is,

```
LOAD      FEET
MULTIPLY  #12
STORE     INCHES
```

Instructions that use immediate addressing execute quickly because the CPU fetches the data with the instruction. Immediate addressing is also easy for the programmer to use. However, it is the least flexible of all the addressing methods, since both the address and the data are fixed. Thus immediate addressing is convenient but does not solve any major problems.

Indexed Addressing

Indexed addressing means that the CPU adds the contents of an index register to the address supplied with the instruction in order to find the effective address. The one-address instruction LOAD 100,X (,X indicates indexing) causes the CPU first to calculate the effective address by adding 100 to the contents of the index register and then to load the accumulator with the contents of the effective address. If the index register contains 35, the instruction LOAD 100,X has the same effect as the instruction LOAD 135. We use indexed addressing mainly to handle arrays and tables. Figure 3.8 shows how to calculate the average of a list of numbers by using indexed addressing. Figure 3.9 demonstrates how to access a table of squares by using indexed addressing.

Figure 3.8   Using indexed addressing to calculate an average.

```
STEP 1:
LOAD #0
LOAD INDEX REGISTER #0

STEP 2:
ADD NUMBER,X

STEP 3:
INCREMENT INDEX REGISTER BY 1

STEP 4:
If we haven't added in all the numbers, return to step 2.

STEP 5:
DIVIDE #N (N = number of elements)
STORE AVG
```

Note: # means immediate addressing.

Figure 3.9 Using indexed addressing to access a table.

Purpose: The number to be squared is in the index register. The table of squares is in memory location 100 through 109.

Initial conditions:

MEMORY

0	LOAD 100,X
100	0
101	1
102	4
103	9
104	16
105	25
106	36
107	49
108	64
109	81

PROGRAM COUNTER

0

ACCUMULATOR

0

INDEX REGISTER

3

After execution of LOAD 100,X (effective address = 100 + contents of index register = 103):

PROGRAM COUNTER

1

ACCUMULATOR

9

INDEX REGISTER

3

The accumulator now contains the square of the number in the index register.

Indexed addressing is slower than direct addressing because the CPU must perform an addition in order to obtain the effective address. Yet indexed addressing is much more flexible than direct addressing, since the same instruction can handle all the elements in an array or table. Most programmers find indexed addressing easy to use, since standard notation refers to arrays with indexes—that is, X_i is the ith element of the X array. To process the X array by using indexed addressing, we place the starting (or base) address of X in the instruction and the index i in the index register.

Relative Addressing

In relative addressing the CPU adds the contents of the program counter to the address supplied with the instruction in order to find the effective address. The one-address instruction LOAD *+100 (* or $ indicates the current value of the program counter) causes the CPU to calculate the effective address by adding 100 to the contents of the program counter and then to load the accumulator with the contents of the effective address. If the instruction LOAD *+100 were located at memory address 2000, it would have the same effect as the instruction LOAD 2100. As the name indicates, relative addressing describes addresses relative to the current instruction rather than absolutely.

Relative addressing allows us to move programs to different places in memory. In Fig. 3.10, for instance, we can move the ADD instruction and the data each by 200 locations and still preserve their relative positions. Such a program is said to be *relocatable*. Relocatable programs are useful, since they can occupy any available area of memory; they will not interfere with data or other programs.

Figure 3.10 Using relative addressing to achieve relocatability.

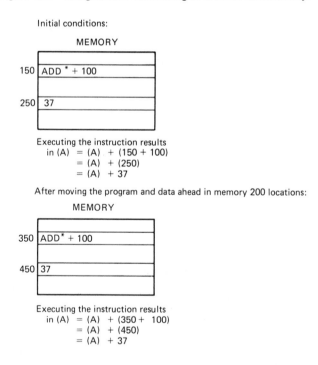

Moreover, relative addressing can result in shorter addresses when the effective address is close to the current program location. We often use relative addresses with jump instructions, since most jumps are rather short.

Register Direct Addressing

Here the procedure is the same as direct addressing except that the address is that of a register instead of a memory location. A typical one-address instruction using register direct addressing is ADD R1, which adds the contents of general-purpose register 1 to the contents of the accumulator. Some computers must use register direct addressing when performing arithmetic and logical operations.

Clearly the advantages and disadvantages are similar to those of ordinary direct addressing. Register direct addressing is even faster than direct addressing, since the CPU need not fetch data from memory. Also, instructions can be shorter because there are fewer registers than memory locations. Register direct addressing is thus the fastest addressing method available in most computers.

Its obvious disadvantage is that we must load the general-purpose register originally, keep track of its contents, and store the contents back in memory in order to save them. So the process takes extra time if the program only uses the contents of the register once. If, for instance, we want to add the contents of memory location 35 to the contents of the accumulator, the single instruction

    ADD   35

will be faster than the sequence

    LOAD   R1, 35
    ADD   R1

(The instruction LOAD R1, 35 places the contents of memory location 35 in register 1.) However, if we want to add the contents of memory location 35 to a hundred different numbers, we need only load register 1 once. The instruction ADD R1 will execute much faster than the instruction ADD 35, since the CPU need not fetch the contents of memory location 35 each time. Register direct addressing, therefore, is advantageous when the program uses the same data many times. Of course, we must allocate the limited number of registers carefully.

Register Indirect Addressing

This type is the same as indirect addressing except that the address is that of a register instead of a memory location. A typical one-address instruction using register indirect addressing is ADD@R1, which adds the contents of the memory address in register 1 to the contents of the accumulator. If register 1 contains 1200, the instruction ADD@R1 is the same as the instruction ADD 1200.

The same advantages and disadvantages apply as in ordinary indirect addressing. Register indirect addressing is faster than ordinary indirect addressing, since the CPU need not fetch the effective address from memory. Moreover, the register address is shorter than a memory address. However, we must load the register originally, and so register indirect addressing is only advantageous when the program uses the same or neighboring addresses many times. For example, the following instructions move a word of data from one area of memory to another and update the address registers.

```
LOAD  @R1
STORE  @R2
INCREMENT  R1
INCREMENT  R2
```

We must load registers 1 and 2 initially with the starting addresses of the source and destination areas. Register indirect addressing can replace ordinary indirect addressing. Figure 3.11 contains an example. The first subroutine call finds the largest element in the array starting in memory location 1000, whereas the second call finds the largest element in the array starting in memory location 6000.

Figure 3.11   Using register indirect addressing in subroutines.

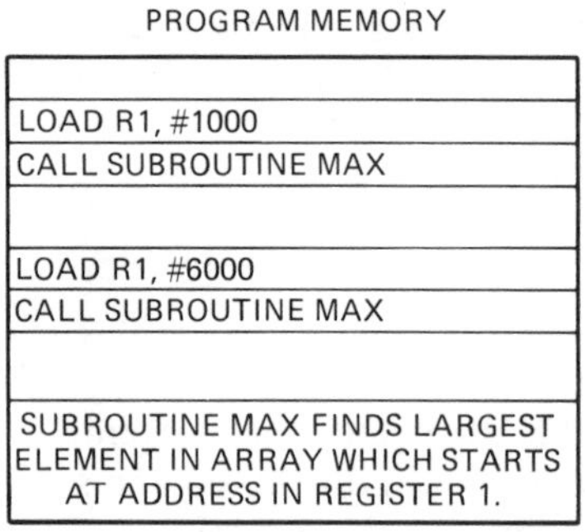

PROGRAM MEMORY

```
┌──────────────────────────────────┐
│                                  │
├──────────────────────────────────┤
│ LOAD R1, #1000                   │
├──────────────────────────────────┤
│ CALL SUBROUTINE MAX              │
├──────────────────────────────────┤
│                                  │
├──────────────────────────────────┤
│ LOAD R1, #6000                   │
├──────────────────────────────────┤
│ CALL SUBROUTINE MAX              │
├──────────────────────────────────┤
│                                  │
├──────────────────────────────────┤
│ SUBROUTINE MAX FINDS LARGEST     │
│ ELEMENT IN ARRAY WHICH STARTS    │
│ AT ADDRESS IN REGISTER 1.        │
└──────────────────────────────────┘
```

Stack Addressing

Stack addressing means that the contents of the stack pointer is the data address. Instructions that use stack addressing are obviously the shortest of all, since no explicit addresses are necessary. The method can be used much like indirect or indexed addressing but has the advantage that the address is updated as part of the execution of the instruction. Furthermore, stack addressing does not require the CPU to perform an addition in order to obtain the effective address. Since adding new data to the stack does not destroy the old data (it merely covers it up), this method can produce *reentrant* programs (which can be executed while the same program has been interrupted or temporarily suspended) or *recursive* programs (which can use themselves as subroutines).

Combinations of Addressing Methods

Each addressing method has its own special uses and advantages. Few programs use only one method. Obviously many of the methods actually depend on other methods in order to get started. We may use indexed, stack, register direct, or register indirect addressing in the parts of the program that the computer executes repeatedly; however, we will need direct, indirect, or immediate addressing in order to load counters, general-purpose registers, address registers, and stack pointers and to store the results.

If a computer has several addressing methods, each instruction must specify which one is being used (see Fig. 3.12). Clearly the more addressing methods, the more bits needed in the addressing method field. Some computers only allow certain addressing methods with certain instructions—for instance, relative addressing only with jump instructions.

Figure 3.12 Single-address instruction format with choice of addressing methods.

Operation Code Field	Addressing Method Field	Address Field

We have stressed the importance of whether an addressing method is easy for the programmer to use. The computer can handle any method properly, but most programmers find that they make more errors with certain methods. Direct, immediate, and indexed addressing are generally the easiest to use. Indirect and stack addressing are confusing to most programmers. These methods can be both convenient and powerful, but the programmer (particularly the beginner) should approach them with caution. The human factors area of software engineering is a subject that needs much more attention.

3.3 TYPES OF INSTRUCTIONS

Here we consider the operation codes that determine what the computer can do in a single instruction cycle. The section divides the instructions into several categories and then describes the size of computer instruction sets and the tradeoffs involved in determining a set.

Instruction Categories

Instructions can be categorized in various ways. Cushman[1] has suggested the following division into four major categories.

- Data manipulation instructions
- Data transfer instructions
- Program manipulation instructions
- Status management instructions

---

[1]R. H. Cushman, "Microprocessor Instruction Sets: The Vocabulary of Programming," *EDN*, Vol. 20, No. 6, March 20, 1975, pp. 35–41.

Data manipulation instructions actually transform the data in some way. Such instructions generally use the computer's arithmetic-logic unit. Among the common subcategories are

- Arithmetic instructions
- Logical instructions
- Shift instructions
- Comparison instructions
- Special-purpose instructions

Data transfer instructions move data from one place in the computer to another without actually changing the data. Among the common subcategories are

- Memory transfer instructions
- Input/output instructions
- Internal transfer instructions
- Stack instructions

Program manipulation instructions transfer program control from one place in memory to another. They change the program counter so that instructions are executed out of their normal sequential order. Among the common subcategories are

- Unconditional jump instructions
- Conditional jump instructions
- Subroutining instructions
- Halts and no operations

Status management instructions change the status conditions of the computer without affecting the data or the order in which instructions are executed. These instructions thus perform management functions rather than data processing functions. They form a minor part of most programs.

Data Manipulation Instructions: Arithmetic Operations

Table 3.1 lists common arithmetic instructions with a description of the effect of the instructions in the one-address case. A is the contents of the accumulator and M is the contents of the effective address.

Table 3.1 Arithmetic Operations

ADD	$A = A + M$
ADD WITH CARRY	$A = A + M + CARRY$
SUBTRACT	$A = A - M$
SUBTRACT WITH CARRY	$A = A - M - CARRY$
INCREMENT	$M = M + 1$
DECREMENT	$M = M - 1$
MULTIPLY	$A = A \times M$
DIVIDE	$A = A \div M$

The most common arithmetic operation is binary addition. Multiple-precision addition requires several operations and the inclusion of carries in the operations on the more significant words. The instruction ADD WITH CARRY can handle this situation. So in order to add the numbers 4327 and 5096 on a computer that can only add two digits at a time, we use the ADD instruction with the two least significant digits—that is,

$$
\begin{array}{r}
27 \\
+ \ 96 \\
\hline
23
\end{array}
$$

①
CARRY   RESULT

We then use ADD WITH CARRY with the two most significant digits—that is,

$$
\begin{array}{r}
43 \\
50 \\
+ \ \text{CARRY} \\
\hline
\end{array}
$$

$$
\begin{array}{r}
43 \\
50 \\
+ \ 1 \\
\hline
94
\end{array}
$$

RESULT

So the total result is 9423.

Another common arithmetic operation is two's complement binary subtraction. As with addition, a special instruction (SUBTRACT WITH CARRY) is necessary for multiple-precision subtraction.

Most computers also have INCREMENT and DECREMENT instructions. We use these instructions to add one to or subtract one from counters, indexes, and indirect addresses. The INCREMENT and DECREMENT instructions are shorter and faster than the ADD and SUBTRACT instructions. Furthermore, INCREMENT and DECREMENT do not affect the CARRY flag, and so they can be used in loops that perform multiple-precision arithmetic. The sequence

```
ADD WITH CARRY @R1
INCREMENT R1
DECREMENT R2
```

could add one to an indirect address in register 1 and subtract one from a counter in register 2 without affecting the carry from the addition. We can then use the carry in the next repetition of the instruction sequence.

Some computers have MULTIPLY and DIVIDE instructions. Such instructions require double-word operations, since the product of two single-word numbers is two words long and, conversely, the dividend must be two words long if the divisor, quotient, and remainder are all to be of the usual word length. If a computer lacks MULTIPLY and DIVIDE instructions, we can implement these operations with repeated addition and subtraction steps much as we would perform them by hand.

Data Manipulation Instructions: Logical Operations

Table 3.2 describes some common logical instructions (see Appendix 2 for a discussion of logical functions).

Table 3.2   Logical Operations

AND	$A = A \cdot M$
OR	$A = A + M$
EXCLUSIVE OR	$A = A \oplus M$
COMPLEMENT	$M = \overline{M}$

The most common logical instruction is AND. We use logical AND to examine parts of a word. This operation is called a *masking* process and the number with which the data is ANDed a *mask*, since its function is to mask off those bits that we do not plan to use. For example, if an 8-bit word contains two BCD digits, we can separate out the least significant digit by logically ANDing the word with the binary mask 00001111. Thus if the word was 10010110 originally,

$$\begin{array}{c} 10010110 \\ \underline{00001111} \\ 00000110 \end{array}$$

is the result. We could separate out the most significant digit by logically ANDing the original word with the binary mask 11110000. The logical AND instruction can also clear bits. For instance, to clear bit 5 of a word, we logically AND the word with a mask that has a zero in bit 5 and ones elsewhere. Bit 5 of the result is zero, whereas the other bits remain the same as they were.

A less common logical instruction is OR (sometimes called INCLUSIVE OR). The logical OR instruction can set bits. To illustrate, in order to set bit 5 of a word, we logically OR the word with a bit pattern that has a one in bit 5 and zeros elsewhere. Bit 5 of the result is one; the other bits remain the same as they were.

Other logical operations are less common. EXCLUSIVE OR is used to form checksums and COMPLEMENT is used to invert logic levels.

Data Manipulation Instructions: Shift Operations

Table 3.3 contains a list and description of the common shift operations. We use shifts to convert data between serial and parallel forms, to perform scaling and normalization, to combine data for storage or to separate it for processing, to isolate single bits or parts of words, to perform multiplication and division, and to match bit patterns.

Table 3.3 Shift Instructions

LOGICAL SHIFT	M is shifted one bit, empty bit is cleared.
ARITHMETIC SHIFT	M is shifted one bit, sign bit is retained, empty bit (if there is one) is cleared.
ROTATE	M is shifted circularly one bit, with most and least significant bits connected.
ROTATE WITH CARRY	M is shifted circularly one bit with most and least significant bits connected through the CARRY.

The LOGICAL SHIFT instruction shifts the data and clears the empty positions. Figure 3.13 shows how a logical shift of one position affects an 8-bit data word if the bit shifted from the end of the data word is placed in the CARRY.

Figure 3.13 The LOGICAL SHIFT instruction.

Original data:

CARRY   DATA

C		b_7	b_6	b_5	b_4	b_3	b_2	b_1	b_0

After LOGICAL SHIFT LEFT:

CARRY   DATA

b_7		b_6	b_5	b_4	b_3	b_2	b_1	b_0	0

After LOGICAL SHIFT RIGHT:

b_0		0	b_7	b_6	b_5	b_4	b_3	b_2	b_1

EXAMPLE

Original data:

CARRY   DATA

1		0	1	1	0	1	1	0	1

After LOGICAL SHIFT LEFT:

CARRY   DATA

0		1	1	0	1	1	0	1	0

After LOGICAL SHIFT RIGHT:

CARRY   DATA

1		0	0	1	1	0	1	1	0

For instance, to use the most significant BCD digit in an 8-bit word, we can place it in the least significant bit positions by logically shifting the word right four times. Thus if the word originally contained 10010110, the final result will be 00001001; we have moved the most significant digit to the least significant positions and cleared the four most significant bits.

The ARITHMETIC SHIFT instruction clears an empty position at the right (if the shift is left) but preserves the sign bit at the left. Figure 3.14 demonstrates arithmetic shifts with 8-bit data. An arithmetic shift right copies the sign bit into the next bit position. The procedure is called *sign extension* and is used to normalize or scale two's complement numbers. An arithmetic shift left multiplies a two's complement number by two whereas an arithmetic shift right divides the number by two.

Figure 3.14 The ARITHMETIC SHIFT instruction.

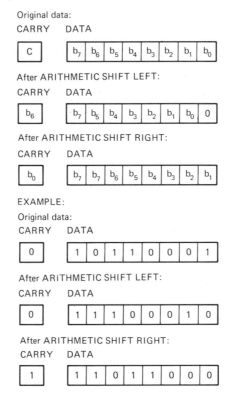

The ROTATE instruction (see Fig. 3.15) treats the data as a circular register with the most significant bit directly connected to the least significant bit. This instruction (sometimes called CIRCULAR SHIFT) preserves all the bits in the original data; the only changes are the positions of the bits and, as a rule, the contents of the CARRY.

The ROTATE WITH CARRY (or CIRCULAR SHIFT WITH CARRY) instruction is the same as the ROTATE instruction except that the CARRY bit is included in the circular register. Consequently, all the bits in the original data are retained, including the CARRY. This instruction is useful in implementing multiplication and division on computers which lack explicit instructions for those operations.

Figure 3.15 The ROTATE instruction.

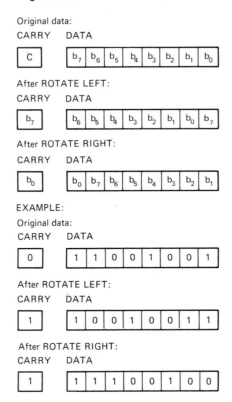

Data Manipulation Instructions: Comparison Operations

Comparison operations allow us to compare or test data without changing it. Such operations set the condition flags for later use (often in conditional jumps) but do not actually store a result anywhere. Table 3.4 describes some popular comparison instructions and their effects in the one-address case. Comparison instructions allow the program to continue the comparison process without reloading the accumulator; typical applications include looking for the first nonblank character in a string or interpreting a command character.

Table 3.4 Comparison Operations

COMPARE	Compute A − M
BIT TEST	Compute A · M
TEST	Compute M − 0
SCAN	Look for a pattern in a string

The COMPARE instruction performs a subtraction but does not return the result to the accumulator. To look for an EBCDIC blank character (hex 40) in a string, we use the instruction sequence

```
LOAD    #40
COMPARE BASE,X
```

We can increment the index register and perform the COMPARE instruction again in order to check the next character.

The BIT TEST instruction performs a logical AND without saving the result. We can thus examine particular bits or bit patterns without having to save a copy of the data before each operation. The TEST instruction sets the flags according to the contents of a particular address without performing any computation. So we can set the flags without moving data or changing any registers. The SCAN instruction (for text editing) searches a string of characters, looking for a particular pattern. A register indicates the location of the pattern, if the search is successful.

Data Manipulation Instructions:
Special-Purpose Operations

Numerous computers have specialized instructions, such as decimal arithmetic or keyboard scans for calculator applications, floating point conversions for mathematical applications, parity generation and checking for communications, and sort or merge instructions for business data processing. The availability of specialized instructions may be a significant factor in choosing a computer for a specific application. A computer without the specialized instructions will require an entire series of instructions to perform the same tasks.

Data Transfer Instructions:
Memory Transfer Operations

Memory transfer operations transfer data between registers and memory locations. The contents of the source do not change. The most common memory transfer instructions are LOAD and STORE. Special instructions (CLEAR or SET) are often available to place the value zero in a flag, register, or memory location or to place the value one in a flag.

Data Transfer Instructions:
Input/Output Operations

Input/output operations are the same as memory transfer operations except that the source or destination is an input or output port rather than a memory location. In fact, some computers treat input/output ports as memory locations and have no specific input/output instructions.

The simplest input instruction is READ or INPUT, which transfers one word of data from an input port to a register. The instruction WRITE or OUTPUT transfers one word of data from a register to an output port. Transferring more than one word at a time requires a sequence of instructions to save the input data or fetch the output data. For example, the following program can send several words to a peripheral via the accumulator.

```
LOAD BUFFER,X
WRITE DEVICE
INCREMENT INDEX REGISTER
```

Each time the CPU executes this sequence it sends a word of data to the peripheral and prepares to fetch the next word from the buffer in memory. We must count the total number of words sent or use a marker in order to indicate the end of the buffer. Some computers have BLOCK TRANSFER instructions that automatically handle all these tasks. The required parameters may be placed in registers or may be included in the instruction.

Data Transfer Instructions:
Internal Transfer Operations

Internal transfer operations move data from one register to another. We use such operations most frequently to load the accumulator or index register from a general-purpose register and to save the contents of the accumulator in a general-purpose register.

Data Transfer Instructions: Stack Operations

Stack operations transfer data between the stack and the registers (see Section 2.5). PUSH places the contents of a register in the stack; POP or PULL places the top entry from the stack in a register. Both instructions change the stack pointer.

Program Manipulation Instructions:
Unconditional Jump Operations

Unconditional jump operations (JUMP or BRANCH) vary the normal sequential execution of instructions. The instruction JUMP 150 places 150 in the program counter; the CPU will fetch the next instruction from that location. These operations only affect the program counter. The SKIP instruction bypasses the next sequential instruction.

Some computers treat the program counter like any other register. Memory transfer, internal transfer, or stack operations may then change the program counter. If, for example, register 4 is the program counter, the instruction LOAD REGISTER 4 acts as an unconditional jump. Computers that handle the program counter in this way can be very flexible. However, the programmer may find the order in which instructions are executed difficult to determine, since transfers of control are not clearly distinguished from other instructions.

Program Manipulation Instructions: Conditional Jump Operations

Conditional jump operations are an important part of most programs. Such operations allow the computer to repeat a sequence of instructions, look for particular characters, recognize errors, and check the status of peripherals. Conditional jump operations are the key to making decisions with a computer, since they allow the choice of a sequence of instructions on the basis of information derived from input data and processing operations. Conditional jump instructions turn the computer into an intelligent controller.

The most common conditional jump operation is the JUMP ON CONDITION instruction. This instruction causes a jump only if the condition is met. If the condition is not met, the computer executes the next instruction in sequence. The condition included in the instruction can take many forms. It may be the value of a status flag, such as the CARRY, ZERO, SIGN, or OVERFLOW bit. Table 3.5 contains several examples of JUMP ON CONDITION instructions involving the status flags. The condition may be an external serial input that can be directly sensed—for instance, JUMP ON TEST ZERO. Some computers allow combinations of conditions (such as JUMP ON CARRY AND OVERFLOW ZERO).

Table 3.5   Typical Conditional Jump Instruction

Address	Instruction	Result
100	JUMP ON CARRY 150	(PC) = 150 IF CARRY = 1
		(PC) = 101 IF CARRY = 0
135	JUMP ON NOT ZERO 139	(PC) = 139 IF ZERO FLAG = 0
		(PC) = 136 IF ZERO FLAG = 1
160	JUMP ON NEGATIVE 120	(PC) = 120 IF SIGN FLAG = 1
		(PC) = 161 IF SIGN FLAG = 0
145	JUMP ON OVERFLOW ZERO 147	(PC) = 147 IF OVERFLOW = 0
		(PC) = 146 IF OVERFLOW = 1

Sometimes the conditional jump instructions are named as if they always followed a COMPARE instruction. The instruction JUMP ON EQUAL then causes a jump if the two numbers compared were equal. Such conditional jump instructions as JUMP ON NOT EQUAL, JUMP ON GREATER THAN, JUMP ON LESS THAN, and so on, all result in jumps if the number in the accumulator has the specified relationship with the value to which it has just been compared.

Some computers only allow conditional SKIP instructions; that is, the CPU cannot jump conditionally but can skip the next instruction conditionally. We can then implement the conditional jump operation in two instructions. The sequence

```
SKIP ON NOT CONDITION
JUMP    LOCATE
```

has the same effect as the single instruction

```
JUMP ON CONDITION        LOCATE
```

The conditional SKIP instruction causes the computer to skip the unconditional jump instruction if the condition is not met. This technique is awkward but has the advantage that only the unconditional jump instruction requires a memory address.

We can provide missing conditional jump instructions in a similar manner. If, for example, the computer has a JUMP ON ZERO instruction but no JUMP ON NOT ZERO instruction, the sequence

```
JUMP ON  ZERO     * + 2
JUMP     ADDR
```

is the equivalent of the single instruction

```
JUMP ON NOT ZERO     ADDR
```

When controlling the execution of a program loop, we often wish to perform a certain number of iterations. A typical sequence that adds ten numbers is

Address	Instruction
0	LOAD INDEX REGISTER #10
1	CLEAR ACCUMULATOR
2	ADD 100,X
3	DECREMENT INDEX REGISTER
4	JUMP ON NOT ZERO 2

Each time through the loop (addresses 2–4), the instruction ADD 100,X adds another number (from locations 101–110) into the sum in the accumulator. The index register serves as an index for the array of numbers and as a counter for the number of iterations. Note that counting down in the index register allows the value of the ZERO flag to serve as an exit condition.

Program Manipulation Instructions: Subroutining Operations

Subroutining operations differ from ordinary jumps in that the computer must return to the original program. For example, a payroll program will frequently need subroutines that fetch data files, sort data, calculate wages and taxes, and print results. Obviously many of these subroutines can also be used by other programs and may be used at many different places in the payroll program itself. The computer must execute the correct subroutine and then resume the main program at the place where it left off.

The basic subroutining operations are the CALL and RETURN instructions. The CALL instruction transfers control just like a JUMP instruction; the difference is that CALL saves the old value of the program counter so that the main program can be resumed properly. The RETURN instruction causes the computer to jump back to the original program—that is, to restore the value of the program counter that the CALL instruction saved.

On some computers the CALL instruction saves the old program counter in the memory address to which the program jumps. This type of CALL instruction is called JUMP AND MARK PLACE or JUMP AND SAVE. Figure 3.16 shows the execution of a JUMP AND MARK PLACE instruction. The computer places the old value of the program counter in memory location 700 and starts executing the subroutine in memory location 701. No special RETURN instruction is necessary to get back to the main program. The indirect jump (JUMP @700) at the end of the subroutine causes program control to be transferred to the address that is in memory location 700. Since memory location 700 contains the address immediately following the JUMP AND MARK PLACE instruction, the computer returns to the main program.

Figure 3.16   Execution of a JUMP AND MARK PLACE instruction.

Initial conditions

PROGRAM MEMORY	PROGRAM COUNTER

200	JUMP AND MARK PLACE 700
700	
701	START OF SUBROUTINE
730	JUMP @700

PROGRAM COUNTER

200

After execution of memory location 200:

PROGRAM MEMORY	PROGRAM COUNTER

200	
700	201
701	START OF SUBROUTINE
730	JUMP @700

PROGRAM COUNTER

701

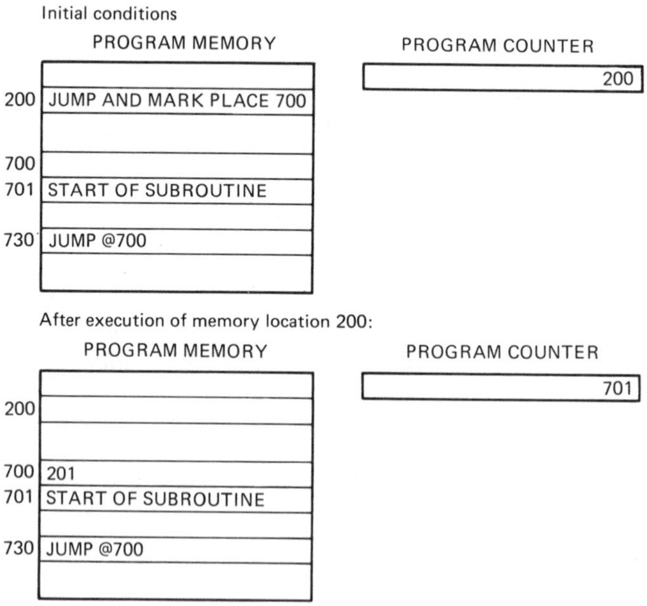

Extension of this method to several levels of subroutines is easy. A subroutine may call other subroutines in this way. However, the subroutine cannot call itself, for it would then destroy the return address that was stored in the first location. Nor is the method reentrant; we cannot share a subroutine entered by this method between two simultaneous programs or between a background program and a high-priority program that interrupts the background program. The problem is that the later program will use the first memory location for its own return address and will destroy the return address of the earlier program.

Another type of CALL instruction is the JUMP AND LINK instruction, which places the old program counter in a link register. Figure 3.17 shows an example of a JUMP AND LINK instruction. When the CPU executes the instruction in memory location 200, it places 700 in the program counter and the old program counter (201) in the link register. The RETURN instruction at the end of the subroutine (memory location 730) puts the contents of the link register back into the program counter, thereby returning control to the main program. This method of subroutining is faster than the JUMP AND MARK PLACE method, since the CPU need not store the old program counter in memory or perform the time-consuming indirect jump at the end of the subroutine. However, we obviously cannot write reentrant subroutines this way, nor can one subroutine call another unless it saves the contents of the link register somewhere or uses another link register. Registers that are used for linking will not be available for other purposes.

Figure 3.17   Execution of a JUMP AND LINK instruction.

Initial conditions:

PROGRAM MEMORY	PROGRAM COUNTER
200 JUMP AND LINK 700	200
	LINK REGISTER
700 START OF SUBROUTINE	
730 RETURN	

After execution of memory location 200

PROGRAM MEMORY	PROGRAM COUNTER
200 JUMP AND LINK 700	700
	LINK REGISTER
700 START OF SUBROUTINE	201
730 RETURN	

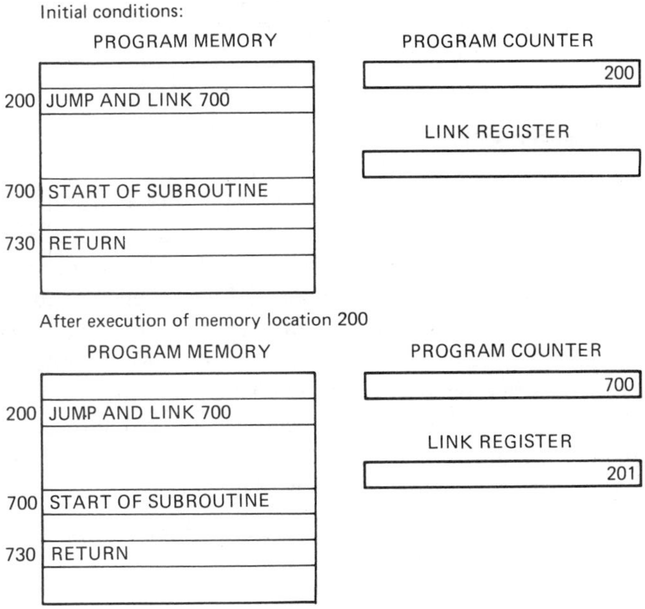

Still another type of CALL instruction saves the return address in a stack (see Fig. 2.19). The RETURN instruction then is simply an unconditional jump instruction that uses stack addressing. The CALL saves the return address in the stack; the RETURN restores it to the program counter at the end of the subroutine. This method takes extra time because it uses the stack, but it is flexible and allows many levels of subroutines (up to the capacity of the stack) and recursive or reentrant routines.

The majority of computers have a special subroutining instruction that can be used to reach subroutines located at a few specific addresses. This instruction is called TRAP or SOFTWARE INTERRUPT. TRAP instructions are short and execute quickly since their addresses are usually fixed either by the computer manufacturer or by the operating system. Some trap routines may even be in a special read-only memory; the computer may automatically execute one of these routines in the event of internal errors or failures.

Program Manipulation Instructions: Halts and No Operations

The HALT instruction causes the computer to enter a suspended state until an external signal is received. The NO OPERATION instruction does nothing except use an instruction cycle and increment the program counter. Surprisingly, such an instruction is very useful. NO OPERATION instructions can provide short delays, replace erroneous instructions, allow space for corrections, and replace subroutines that may not have been written or may not be included in a test run.

Status Management Instructions

The most common status management operations are the enabling and disabling of the interrupt system. The instructions are ENABLE (or CLEAR) INTERRUPT and DISABLE (or SET) INTERRUPT. Most computers automatically disable the interrupt system during RESET or when an interrupt has been accepted. We will want to enable the interrupts after completing the proper initialization and disable the interrupts during timing loops or other programs that could not be properly resumed. Some computers keep the interrupt enabling bits in a status register. In this case, changing the register will enable or disable all or part of the interrupt system. Other management operations include selection of a page of memory, designation of registers for particular tasks (such as program counters or memory address registers), and enabling or disabling of alarms, sense switches, or other external controls.

Combined Instructions

Some computers have instructions that perform several operations in a single cycle. One instruction may be able to not only perform an arithmetic or logical operation but also determine the carry input, shift the result, and skip the next instruction under certain conditions. Such instructions can increase throughput and reduce program memory requirements. However, combined instructions are difficult for programmers to use and document. The emergence of microprogramming has made combined instructions easier to implement, but the selection of useful combinations is difficult.

Instructions and Status Flags

The effects of instructions on status flags vary greatly from computer to computer. ADD and SUBTRACT instructions always affect the flags. Frequently, they are the only instructions that affect the CARRY flag. The INCREMENT and DECREMENT instructions usually do not affect the CARRY flag, and so they can control loops that perform multiple-precision arithmetic. Logical operations, such as OR, AND, and EXCLUSIVE OR, always affect the SIGN and ZERO flags. Shift operations may or may not affect any flags besides the CARRY. Comparison instructions have no function other than their effect on status flags. Special-purpose operations and such instructions as MULTIPLY, DIVIDE, and COMPLEMENT affect the flags differently in different computers.

An important variation in how instructions affect status flags is whether the status flags are affected by data transfer, program manipulation, and status management instructions. In many computers only the data manipulation instructions affect the status flags. Special instructions will then be necessary to set the status flags according to the contents of registers or memory locations. In other computers other types of instructions affect the status flags. We must then save the flags or check conditions immediately in order to avoid losing needed status information. The effect of instructions on status flags is peculiar to each computer, and no method seems clearly superior.

Instruction Sets

Obviously no computer has every possible instruction. Most computers have between 20 and 200 separate instructions, some of which may differ only in the addressing method used. The number of truly distinct instructions is often hard to determine, since a computer may have combined instructions or an unusual architecture. A large instruction set results in shorter programs and higher speed. However, a large instruction set also requires longer instructions and more decoding circuitry and is more difficult to learn and use effectively. Programmers rarely use many of the instructions in a large set; in fact, few programmers can effectively use instruction sets with more than 100 instructions. On the other hand, small instruction sets often require awkward implementations of common operations. Instruction sets with between 40 and 80 distinct instructions seem to be optimal; special microprogrammed instruction sets for particular applications may be preferable to one enormous set.

Most computers place some restrictions on their instruction sets. Such restrictions frequently involve addressing methods. Although a computer may have a large number of methods, certain instructions may only permit a few. Some typical restrictions are

1. Only allowing arithmetic and logical operations between registers.

To add the contents of memory location 50 to the accumulator, we must use the sequence

```
LOAD   R2, 50
ADD    R2
```

instead of the single instruction ADD 50. This restriction results in programs requiring more data transfer instructions.

2. Only allowing an accumulator to be used in such single-operand instructions as shifts, complements, increments, decrements, and special-purpose operations.

We must then move data to the accumulator and store it back in its original location after the operation. This restriction also results in more data transfer instructions.

3. Only allowing memory transfers or input/output operations through an accumulator.

Here again we will need several instructions to provide the missing operations. To move the contents of register 2 to memory location 50 will require the sequence

```
MOVE    ACC, R2
STORE·  50
```

Note that we may also have to save the previous contents of the accumulator.

4. Only allowing conditional jumps with short relative addresses.

Longer conditional jumps will require sequences of instructions. For example, the instruction sequence

```
JUMP ON NOT CONDITION * + 2
JUMP ADDR
```

has the same effect as the disallowed instruction

```
JUMP ON CONDITION ADDR
```

These and similar restrictions all simplify instruction decoding; however, they also result in longer programs that are more difficult to write and understand.

3.4 MICROPROCESSOR INSTRUCTION SETS

Instruction Formats

Microprocessor instruction sets, like microprocessor architectures, are restricted by the limited word size, read-only program memory, and limited number of buses and registers that are characteristic of microcomputers. In general, microprocessor instruction sets are significantly less powerful than the instruction sets of the newer minicomputers.

Addressing Methods

The limited word length of most microprocessors not only restricts the number of addressing methods available but also limits the usefulness of some of the methods. Since most microprocessors have only 4- or 8-bit words, the use of several instruction bits as an addressing method field is clearly undesirable. Most processors, therefore, use a limited number of methods. Table 3.6 lists the addressing methods available with some popular microprocessors. The sets of methods differ greatly.

Table 3.6 Addressing Methods of Popular Microprocessors

Addressing Method	Intel 4040	Intel 8080	Motorola 6800	Signetics 2650	Fairchild F-8
Direct	Yes	Yes	Yes	Yes	No
Page 0	No	No	Yes	No	No
Current page	Yes	No	No	No	No
Indirect	No	No	No	No	No
Indexed	No	No	Yes	Yes	No
Relative	No	No	Yes	Yes	Yes
Immediate	Yes	Yes	Yes	Yes	Yes
Register direct	Yes	Yes	Yes	Yes	Yes
Register indirect	Yes	Yes	No	No	Yes
Stack	No	Yes	Yes	No	
Comments:	Must latch register before using register indirect addressing		Has 16-bit index register	Has both autoincrement and autodecrement on four index registers	

The short word length of microprocessors makes direct addressing undesirable; consequently, most microprocessors use it sparingly. A 16-bit direct address would require two full words in an 8-bit microprocessor, thereby involving two accesses of program memory besides the one needed to fetch the original operation code. Page 0 is sometimes reserved as read/write memory so that short addresses can be used for most data.

Microprocessors seldom use true indirect addressing because of the large number of memory accesses required. Not only would one or two words be needed for the address that is part of the instruction, but the contents of two words must generally be fetched from memory to serve as the indirect address.

Indexed addressing has the same drawbacks as direct addressing, for it also requires one or two extra words of program memory. Furthermore, indexing requires an address-length addition which is time-consuming on processors that use 12- or 16-bit addresses but only have 4- or 8-bit arithmetic units.

Relative addressing is widely used in microprocessors to limit the length of addresses, particularly in jump instructions. The short word length of microprocessors means, however, that only a short offset can fit into a single-word address. Relative addressing also requires the same time-consuming addition needed by indexing.

Register direct and register indirect addressing are particularly attractive in microprocessors because they allow short instructions but do not require any address-length additions. Generally the number of registers is small so that the instructions can be one word long.

Register indirect addressing is the main memory addressing technique in such processors as the Intel 4040, Intel 8008, Intel 8080, RCA CDP1802, and Fairchild F-8. Register indirect addressing requires the programmer to organize data carefully. If data is in widely separated parts of memory, numerous instructions will be needed simply to load and store the contents of the address registers; the programmer must design both programs and data structures so as to minimize this overhead.

Stack addressing, although it would seem ideally suited to microprocessors, is not yet in wide use. Most microprocessors use stack addressing only for storing subroutine return addresses, executing RETURN instructions, and saving register contents during subroutines and interrupts. Many microprocessors have only a limited stack for return addresses; such a stack can be part of the processor chip, but it obviously cannot be used extensively. Processors like the Intel 8080 and Motorola 6800 have off-chip stacks but generally reserve them for use during interrupts and subroutines.

3.5 EXAMPLES OF MICROPROCESSOR INSTRUCTION SETS

This section describes the instruction sets of the Intel 8080 and Motorola 6800. We will use the assembly language symbolism for both instruction sets and will explain special features as we proceed.

Instruction Formats

Both the Intel 8080 and Motorola 6800 use one-address instructions almost exclusively. The Motorola 6800 has two accumulators; a single bit in most instructions indicates which accumulator is being used. The Intel 8080 uses two-address MOVE instructions to perform some transfers.

Addressing Methods

As shown in Table 3.6, the Intel 8080 and Motorola 6800 employ different addressing methods. In the Intel 8080 we find mainly register direct and register indirect addressing. Three bits in many instructions indicate one of the seven registers or the register indirect method (address in registers H and L[2]). Table 3.7 contains the Intel 8080 register addresses. The processor has single-word instructions that operate on registers or on memory through the 16-bit address in registers H and L. The Intel 8080 uses immediate addressing for initializing counters and address registers, direct addressing for accessing scattered data or indirect addresses, and stack addressing for saving and restoring register contents during subroutines or interrupt service routines.

Table 3.7   Intel 8080 Register Addresses

Code	Register
000	B
001	C
010	D
011	E
100	H
101	L
110[a]	Register indirect using the address in H and L
111	A

[a]Intel refers to code 110 as register M.

The Motorola 6800 primarily has direct and indexed addressing. Page-zero direct addresses are used for frequently accessed data. The processor has few single-word instructions but many double-word instructions with an 8-bit page-zero, indexed, or relative address (relative addressing is only used for jumps). The Motorola 6800 uses immediate addressing for loading constants and initializing the index register and stack pointer. Stack addressing is employed for temporary storage as well as for subroutines and interrupt service routines.

---

[2]The names are significant—H for "high address" and L for "low address."

Data Manipulation Instructions:
Arithmetic Operations

Table 3.8 describes the arithmetic instructions available on the Intel 8080 and Motorola 6800. Both have ADD, ADD WITH CARRY, SUBTRACT, SUBTRACT WITH CARRY (or BORROW), INCREMENT, and DECREMENT instructions. The Intel 8080 uses register direct, register indirect (through H and L), or immediate addressing with the ADD and SUBTRACT instructions. INCREMENT or DECREMENT can be applied to any register or to the memory location addressed by H and L. Typical examples are

1. ADD B

$$(A) = (A) + (B)$$

2. INR M

$$((H \text{ and } L)) = ((H \text{ and } L)) + 1$$

The INCREMENT and DECREMENT instructions do not affect the CARRY bit.

Table 3.8 Intel 8080 and Motorola 6800 Arithmetic Instructions

Instruction	Intel 8080 Opcode	Motorola 6800 Opcode
ADD	ADD or ADI[a]	ADD[b] or ABA
ADD WITH CARRY	ADC or ACI	ADC
ADD DOUBLE WORDS	DAD	
DECREMENT	DCR	DEC
DOUBLE DECREMENT	DCX	DES or DEX
INCREMENT	INR	INC
DOUBLE INCREMENT	INX	INS or INX
SUBTRACT	SUB or SUI	SUB or SBA
SUBTRACT WITH CARRY	SBB or SBI	SBC

[a] Intel uses separate operation codes (ending in the letter I) for immediate addressing.

[b] Motorola uses A or B at the end of many operation codes to designate which accumulator is used.

The Motorola 6800 uses page-zero direct, indexed, immediate, or direct[3] addressing with the ADD and SUBTRACT instructions. INCREMENT or DECREMENT can act either on the accumulators or on a memory location given by indexed or direct addressing. The INCREMENT and DECREMENT instructions do not affect the CARRY bit. Typical examples of arithmetic instructions on the

---

[3]Motorola refers to page-zero addressing as *direct* addressing and the usual direct as *extended*.

Motorola 6800 are

1. ADDA   50

$$(A) = (A) + (50)$$

2. DEC 1000

$$(1000) = (1000) - 1$$

The Motorola 6800 also has special one-word instructions for adding and subtracting the contents of the accumulators [ABA gives $(A) = (A) + (B)$ and SBA gives $(A) = (A) - (B)$].

Both the Intel 8080 and Motorola 6800 have double-length INCREMENT and DECREMENT instructions so that they can increment or decrement 16-bit addresses in one instruction cycle. The Intel 8080 instructions use the register pair addresses in Table 3.9 (the first register in a pair contains the eight most significant bits). The Motorola 6800 double-length instructions can act on either the index register or the stack pointer.

The Intel 8080 also has a double-word ADD instruction (DAD) that uses registers H and L as a 16-bit accumulator and the register pair addresses of Table 3.9 to obtain the other operand. This instruction can be used to perform indexing (place the base address in one register pair and the index in another) or a 16-bit left shift of registers H and L (DAD H).

Table 3.9 Intel 8080 Register Pair Addresses

Code	Register Pair
00	B and C
01	D and E
10	H and L
11[a]	Stack pointer

[a]Code 11 is the accumulator and flags for PUSH and POP instructions.

The Intel 8080 has some arithmetic operations with special meanings. Among them are

1. SUB A

$$(A) = (A) - (A) = 0;$$

so this instruction clears the accumulator.

2. ADD A

$$(A) = (A) + (A);$$

so this instruction shifts the accumulator left one bit logically.

Data Manipulation Instructions:
Logical Operations

The logical operations available on the Intel 8080 and Motorola 6800 are summarized in Table 3.10. The OR, AND, and EXCLUSIVE OR instructions work just like the ADD and SUBTRACT instructions on both processors. On the Motorola 6800 these instructions do not affect the CARRY bit; on the Intel 8080 they clear the CARRY bit. The COMPLEMENT instructions (both ONES and TWOS COMPLEMENT) on the Motorola 6800 can be used to complement either accumulator or a memory location (no short page-zero addresses are allowed). The COMPLEMENT instructions on the Intel 8080 can only complement the accumulator or CARRY. The COMPLEMENT instructions affect all the flags on the Motorola 6800; COMPLEMENT ACCUMULATOR does not affect any flags on the Intel 8080.

Table 3.10   Intel 8080 and Motorola 6800 Logical Instructions

Instruction	Intel 8080 Opcode	Motorola 6800 Opcode
AND	ANA or ANI	AND
COMPLEMENT (one's)	CMA or CMC[a]	COM
COMPLEMENT (two's)		NEG
EXCLUSIVE OR	XRA or XRI	EOR
OR	ORA or ORI	ORA

[a]CMA is COMPLEMENT ACCUMULATOR; CMC IS COMPLEMENT CARRY.

Some logical operations on the Intel 8080 have special meanings.

1. XRA A

$$(A) = (A) \oplus (A) = 0;$$

so this instruction clears the accumulator.

2. ORA A or ANA A

$$(A) = (A) \cdot (A) \text{ or } (A) + (A);$$

so these instructions set all the flags according to the value in the accumulator.

Typical logical operations on the Intel 8080 are

1. ANI   11110000B (B means binary in Intel 8080 assembly language)

$$(A) = (A) \cdot 11110000;$$

so this instruction masks off the four least significant bits of the accumulator.

2. ORA   M

$$(A) = (A) + ((H \text{ and } L));$$

so this instruction ORs the accumulator with the memory location addressed by registers H and L.

Typical logical operations on the Motorola 6800 are

1. ANDA #%00001111 (# means immediate and % means binary in Motorola 6800 assembly language).

$$(A) = (A) \cdot 00001111;$$

so this instruction masks off the four most significant bits of the accumulator.

2. COM 2, X

$$((\text{INDEX REGISTER}) + 2) = \overline{((\text{INDEX REGISTER}) + 2)}$$

This instruction complements the contents of the effective address.

Data Manipulation Instructions: Shift Operations

Table 3.11 describes the shift instructions available on the Intel 8080 and Motorola 6800. The Intel 8080 can only shift the accumulator; the Motorola 6800 can shift either accumulator or a memory location. Intel 8080 shift instructions do not affect any flags except the CARRY; Motorola 6800 shift instructions affect all the flags.

Table 3.11 Intel 8080 and Motorola 6800 Shift Instructions

Operation	Intel 8080 Opcode	Motorola 6800 Opcode
ARITHMETIC SHIFT RIGHT		ASR
LOGICAL SHIFT LEFT	(ADD A)	ASL
LOGICAL SHIFT RIGHT		LSR
ROTATE LEFT	RLC	
ROTATE RIGHT	RRC	
ROTATE WITH CARRY LEFT	RAL	ROL
ROTATE WITH CARRY RIGHT	RAR	ROR
OTHERS	(DAD H)	

Data Manipulation Instructions:
Comparison Operations

The comparison instructions available on the Intel 8080 and Motorola 6800 are shown in Table 3.12. The Intel 8080 COMPARE instruction performs a subtraction but does not place the result in the accumulator. The instruction affects the flags without actually changing any register contents. The Motorola 6800 has a similar COMPARE instruction (including a special form for comparing the accumulators) and also has TEST and BIT TEST instructions. TEST subtracts zero from the given address; the address can be an accumulator or a memory location. Thus TEST sets the flags according to the value of the accumulator or memory location without changing the value. BIT TEST logically ANDs the accumulator with the specified address without changing any register contents. BIT TEST thus allows the programmer to check the value of a particular bit by ANDing the word with an appropriate mask.

Table 3.12   Intel 8080 and Motorola 6800 Comparison Instructions

Operation	Intel 8080 Opcode	Motorola 6800 Opcode
BIT TEST		BIT
COMPARE	CMP or CPI	CMP or CBA
DOUBLE		CPX
TEST		TST

The Motorola 6800 also has a double-length COMPARE instruction that compares the index register to another 16-bit quantity. This instruction performs a 16-bit subtraction without changing the contents of any registers.

Typical comparison operations on the Intel 8080 are

    1. CMP   B
Sets flags as if (A) − (B) had been performed.
    2. CPI   10
Sets flags as if (A) − 10 had been performed.

Typical comparison operations on the Motorola 6800 are

    1. CMPA   #30
Sets flags as if (A) − 30 had been performed.
    2. TST   2000
Sets flags as if (2000) − 0 had been performed.

Data Manipulation Instructions:
Special-Purpose Operations

The only special-purpose operation on the Intel 8080 or Motorola 6800 is the so-called decimal correction operation, DAA or DECIMAL ADJUST AC-

CUMULATOR. This instruction changes binary addition into BCD addition (see Appendix 3, Section 1, for an explanation). The instruction sequence

        ADD
        DECIMAL ADJUST
            ACCUMULATOR

is the same as a decimal addition instruction. DECIMAL ADJUST uses both the CARRY and HALF-CARRY or AUXILIARY CARRY (from bit 3) to provide the correct result. DAA is the only instruction on either the Motorola 6800 or Intel 8080 that uses the HALF-CARRY (or AUXILIARY CARRY).

Data Transfer Instructions: Memory Transfer Operations

Both the Motorola 6800 and the Intel 8080 have single- and double-word LOAD and STORE instructions for moving data between registers and the memory. Table 3.13 summarizes these instructions.

Table 3.13   Intel 8080 and Motorola 6800 Memory Transfer Instructions

Operation	Intel 8080 Opcode	Motorola 6800 Opcode

LOAD	LDA (DIRECT)
	MOV r, M
	    (REGISTER INDIRECT
	    VIA H AND L)
	MVI r, VAL
	    (IMMEDIATE)
	LDAX
	    (REGISTER INDIRECT
	    VIA B AND C or D AND E)
		LDA

LOAD DOUBLE-WORD	LXI
	    (IMMEDIATE)
	LHLD
	    (DIRECT)
		LDS, LDX

STORE	STA
	    (DIRECT)
	MOV M, r
	    (REGISTER INDIRECT
	    VIA H AND L)
	STAX
	    (REGISTER INDIRECT
	    VIA B AND C or D AND E)
		STA

STORE DOUBLE-WORD	SHLD	STS, STX

The Motorola 6800 memory transfer operations are straightforward. LOAD and STORE move 8-bit quantities between memory and one of the two accumulators. The double-word LOAD and STORE instructions move 16-bit quantities between the memory and the index register or stack pointer. Any of these instructions can use any of the addressing methods present on the Motorola 6800. Thus we can LOAD and STORE register contents using immediate, page-zero, indexed, or direct addressing.

The Intel 8080's memory transfer instructions are more complicated. Here 8-bit data can be moved by using register indirect addressing through any register pair (operation codes MOV REG, M; MOV M, REG; LDAX; and STAX), immediate addressing (MVI), or direct addressing (STA, LDA). The programmer normally uses the register indirect method with registers H and L to process arrays or tables, LDAX and STAX to process two arrays at a time (as in moving data or merging arrays), MVI to load counters and other fixed data, and STA and LDA to reach scattered data.

It is also possible to move 16-bit data on the Intel 8080 in several different ways. We use immediate addressing (LXI) to initialize address registers with fixed quantities and direct addressing (LHLD, SHLD) to provide true indirect addressing and to initialize address registers with variable values.

Typical Motorola 6800 memory transfer instructions include

1. LDAA   #35

$$(A) = 35$$

2. STX   1515

$$(1515) = (IXH)$$
$$(1516) = (IXL)$$

where IXH and IXL are the most significant and least significant eight bits of the index register, respectively.

Typical Intel 8080 memory transfer instructions are

1. MOV   C, M

$$(C) = ((H \text{ and } L))$$

The CPU loads register C indirectly, using the address in registers H and L.

2. LXI   H, 160

$$(H \text{ and } L) = 160$$

The value 160 is placed in registers H and L.

Both processors perform double-word memory transfers one word at a time. The advantage of a double-word transfer over two single-word transfers is that the CPU need only fetch a single instruction from memory in order to perform the double-word transfer. The real savings is in overhead.

One important difference between Intel 8080 and Motorola 6800 memory transfer instructions is that the former do not affect the flags, whereas the latter do. A transfer instruction can place zero in an Intel 8080 register without setting the ZERO flag; any number that is placed in a Motorola 6800 register affects the flags.

The Motorola 6800 also has CLEAR instructions for either accumulator, an indexed or directly addressed memory location, and the CARRY and OVER-FLOW bits. It has SET instructions for the CARRY and OVERFLOW bits. The Intel 8080 has only an explicit SET instruction for the CARRY bit. Memory locations and registers must be cleared by means of logical, arithmetic, or transfer instructions as mentioned previously.

Data Transfer Instructions: Input/Output Operations

The Intel 8080 has simple input and output instructions. IN transfers a byte from the addressed input device to the accumulator. OUT transfers a byte from the accumulator to the addressed output device. Both IN and OUT use 8-bit device addresses rather than full 16-bit memory addresses. The Zilog Z-80, an advanced version of the Intel 8080, has input/output instructions that transfer an entire block of data.

The Motorola 6800 has no input/output instructions at all. It treats input/output devices as memory locations so that any instruction that transfers data to or from memory can perform input or output. The most common such instructions are LOAD and STORE; they act as I/O instructions when their addresses are actually I/O devices.

Other instructions may have less obvious effects, however. For example, we can send zero to an output device by clearing the associated memory address. We can examine input data by using the COMPARE or TEST instructions with the input device as the address.

Data Transfer Instructions: Stack Operations

Both the Motorola 6800 and the Intel 8080 have a 16-bit stack pointer and a stack that resides in external RAM. The Intel 8080's stack pointer contains the address of the last element placed in the stack; the Motorola 6800's stack pointer contains the address of the next empty location.

The Intel 8080 uses double-word stack operations. PUSH places a pair of registers in the stack and POP removes a pair of registers from the stack. The stack grows downward from the top of memory; that is, a PUSH causes the CPU to decrement the stack pointer by two. This arrangement seems awkward but allows us to use the lower RAM locations for data and allocate the rest to the stack. The Intel 8080 can PUSH or POP any of the register pairs. Register pair 3 here is a special 16-bit register called the *processor status word* (PSW); its eight most significant bits are the contents of the accumulator and its eight least significant bits are the flags organized as shown in Fig. 3.18. When the Intel 8080 places a register pair in the stack, it starts with the eight most significant bits. The POP instructions, of course, reverse the order.

Figure 3.18   Intel 8080 processor status word.

7	6	5	4	3	2	1	0
S	Z	0	AC Auxiliary	0	P Even	1	C
Sign Bit	Zero Bit	Fixed	Carry Bit	Fixed	Parity Bit	Fixed	Carry Bit

The Motorola 6800 uses single-word stack operations. PSH places the contents of an accumulator in the stack; and PUL places the top element of the stack in an accumulator. The PSH and PUL instructions can provide extra temporary storage (since the Motorola 6800 has so few registers) and can save register contents during subroutines.

Some typical stack instructions are

1. Intel 8080
   (a) PUSH D
   Initial conditions:

$$(STACK\ POINTER) = 173$$

$$(D) = 55$$

$$(E) = 37$$

Final conditions:

$$(STACK\ POINTER) = 171$$

$$(172) = 55$$

$$(171) = 37$$

   (b) POP H
   Initial conditions:

$$(STACK\ POINTER) = 200$$

$$(200) = 31$$

$$(201) = 0$$

Final conditions:

$$(STACK\ POINTER) = 202$$

$$(H) = 0$$

$$(L) = 31$$

2. Motorola 6800
   (a) **PSHA**
   Initial conditions:

$$(\text{STACK POINTER}) = 250$$

$$(A) = 64$$

Final conditions:

$$(\text{STACK POINTER}) = 249$$

$$(250) = 64$$

   (b) **PULB**
   Initial conditions:

$$(\text{STACK POINTER}) = 180$$

$$(181) = 72$$

Final conditions:

$$(\text{STACK POINTER}) = 181$$

$$(B) = 72$$

Data Transfer Instructions:
Internal Transfer Operations

Because the Motorola 6800 has few registers, it also has few internal transfer operations. The most common are TBA, which moves data from B to A, and TAB, which moves data from A to B.

The Intel 8080 uses internal transfer operations more frequently, since it has more registers. The instruction MOV can move data from any register to any other register. However, the most frequent use is to move data to and from the accumulator. The instruction XCHG exchanges register pair D and E with register pair H and L in one cycle.

Some typical Intel 8080 internal transfer instructions are

1. MOV B, A

$$(B) = (A)$$

A is unchanged.

2. MOV A, D

$$(A) = (D)$$

D is unchanged.

Program Manipulation Instructions:
Unconditional Jump Operations

The Intel 8080 has two unconditional jump instructions. JMP uses a 16-bit direct address; PCHL places the contents of register pair H and L in the program counter and so provides an indirect jump.

The Motorola 6800 also has two unconditional jump instructions. JMP can use either direct or indexed addressing. We can provide an indirect jump by using indexed addressing with a zero offset; the instruction JMP 0, X (or simply JMP X) causes the CPU to jump to the address contained in the index register. BRA (BRANCH ALWAYS) uses relative addressing. An 8-bit (one word) relative address allows a jump of 128 locations in either direction (actually, 129 forward and 126 backward, since the count starts at the end of the two-word BRANCH instruction). So we use JMP for long jumps or indirect jumps and BRA for short jumps.

Program Manipulation Instructions:
Conditional Jump Operations

Table 3.14 summarizes the conditional jump instructions available on the Intel 8080 and Motorola 6800. The Intel 8080 allows jumps conditional on any of the flags being either zero or one. All conditional jumps require a 16-bit direct address.

Table 3.14 Intel 8080 and Motorola 6800 Conditional Jump Operations

Instruction	Intel 8080 Opcode	Motorola 6800 Opcode
JUMP IF CARRY = 0	JNC	BCC
CARRY = 1	JC	BCS
JUMP IF OVERFLOW = 0		BVC
OVERFLOW = 1		BVS
JUMP IF PARITY = 0	JPO	
PARITY = 1	JPE	
JUMP IF SIGN = 0	JP	BPL
SIGN = 1	JM	BMI
JUMP IF ZERO = 0	JNZ	BNE
ZERO = 1	JZ	BEQ
JUMP IF < 0		BLT
$\leq$ 0		BLS, BLE
> 0		BHI, BGT
$\geq$ 0		BGE

The most common conditional jumps are JZ (JUMP ON ZERO) and JNZ (JUMP ON NOT ZERO); JZ causes a jump if the ZERO flag is one (i.e., the previous result was zero), whereas JNZ causes a jump if the ZERO flag is zero (i.e., the previous result was not zero). We use JZ or JNZ in most program loops; a typical sequence is

```
DCR   C
JNZ   LOOP
```

which causes the CPU to execute a program (address LOOP is at the beginning) until the contents of register C are reduced to zero. Figure 3.19 shows a typical sequence in which the required number of iterations (COUNT) is placed in register C, the main program is executed, register C is decremented, and JNZ is used to determine whether the main program will be repeated.

We can also use JZ or JNZ to look for a particular value. The sequence

```
CPI   100
JZ    F100
```

causes a jump to address F100 if the accumulator contains 100.

Figure 3.19 A typical loop.

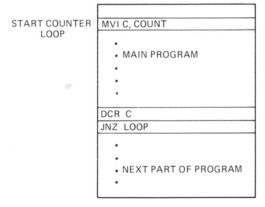

The next most common conditional jump instructions are JC (JUMP ON CARRY) and JNC (JUMP ON NOT CARRY). We often use these instructions with the COMPARE instruction (CMP or CPI). COMPARE sets the CARRY flag if the 8-bit unsigned number in the accumulator is less than the number with which we are comparing it. Thus CARRY = 1 means that a borrow would be necessary actually to perform the subtraction. The instruction sequence

```
CPI   10
JC    LSTEN
```

causes a jump to address LSTEN if the accumulator contains an unsigned number

less than 10 (CARRY = 0, if the accumulator contains 10). Similarly, the instruction sequence

```
CPI  64
JNC  LARGE
```

causes a jump to address LARGE if the accumulator contains an unsigned number
between 64 and 255.

We also use JC and JNC to check the value of a bit shifted into the CARRY.
Note that the Intel 8080 shift instructions do not affect any of the other flags. So in
order to determine if the number in the accumulator is even (least significant bit
zero), we use the sequence

```
RAR
JNC  EVEN
```

RAR shifts the least significant bit of the accumulator to the CARRY, and JNC
causes a jump to the address EVEN if the CARRY is zero.

The Motorola 6800 only uses relative addressing with conditional jumps.
Therefore, as with the unconditional BRANCH (BRA), conditional jumps are
limited to 129 locations forward or 126 backward. Longer conditional jumps can be
obtained by using the inverted sequence

```
BRANCH ON NOT CONDITION OVER
    JMP ADDR
OVER
```

The Motorola 6800 has conditional BRANCH instructions like those available on the Intel 8080 plus additional combinations. The names of most branch
instructions presume that they follow a COMPARE instruction. BEQ (BRANCH
ON EQUAL) forces a jump if the ZERO bit is one (i.e., the numbers being
compared were equal). BNE (BRANCH ON NOT EQUAL) forces a jump if the
ZERO bit is zero. As with the Intel 8080, these instructions can control loops and
check for values. A typical loop control sequence (counter in memory location 40)
is

```
DEC  40
BNE  LOOP
```

A typical search sequence is

```
CMPA  #100
BEQ   F100
```

As with the Intel 8080, we can use the CARRY bit with the COMPARE
instruction. Not only does the 6800 have BCS (BRANCH IF CARRY SET) and
BCC (BRANCH IF CARRY CLEAR) but it also has another complementary pair
—BHI (BRANCH IF HIGHER) and BLS (BRANCH IF LOWER OR SAME).
BHI and BLS simply place the equality case on the other side; that is, BLS causes a

jump if the contents of the accumulator are less than or equal to the other number and BHI causes a jump if the contents of the accumulator are greater than the other number. So after the instruction

    CMPA #64

we have the following possibilities.

1. BCS DONE

$$(PC) = DONE \text{ if } (A) < 64$$

2. BLS DONE

$$(PC) = DONE \text{ if } (A) \leqslant 64$$

3. BCC DONE

$$(PC) = DONE \text{ if } (A) \geqslant 64$$

4. BHI DONE

$$(PC) = DONE \text{ if } (A) > 64$$

Since the Motorola 6800 has an OVERFLOW bit, two's complement arithmetic is much simpler than on the Intel 8080. BVC (BRANCH IF OVERFLOW CLEAR) and BVS (BRANCH IF OVERFLOW SET) can determine if two's complement overflow has occurred. BGE (BRANCH IF GREATER THAN OR EQUAL TO ZERO), BLT (BRANCH IF LESS THAN ZERO), BGT (BRANCH IF GREATER THAN ZERO), and BLE (BRANCH IF LESS THAN OR EQUAL TO ZERO) also take into account the possibility of overflow. The various conditions can be defined in terms of logical functions of the flags (Table 3.15); you may wish to try some examples to show that these functions do, in fact, produce the desired results after a COMPARE instruction.

Table 3.15 Motorola 6800 Conditional Jump Combinations

Meaning	Branch Test
JUMP IF < 0, SIGNED (BLT)	$N \oplus V = 1$
JUMP IF $\leqslant 0$, SIGNED (BLE)	$Z + (N \oplus V) = 1$
JUMP IF $\leqslant 0$, UNSIGNED (BLS)	$C + Z = 1$
JUMP IF $\geqslant 0$, SIGNED (BGE)	$N \oplus V = 0$
JUMP IF > 0, SIGNED (BGT)	$Z + (N \oplus V) = 0$
JUMP IF > 0, UNSIGNED (BHI)	$C + Z = 0$

Program Manipulation Instructions:
Subroutining Operations

Both the Intel 8080 and Motorola 6800 use the RAM stack for subroutines. The CALL instruction on the Intel 8080 and the JSR and BSR (JUMP and BRANCH TO SUBROUTINE) instructions on the Motorola 6800 both cause the current program counter to be placed in the stack before the starting address of the subroutine is placed in the program counter. The RETURN instruction on the Intel 8080 and the RTS (RETURN FROM SUBROUTINE) instruction on the Motorola 6800 both reverse the calling process and restore the old program counter from the stack.

The Intel 8080 has conditional CALL and RETURN instructions. Although similiar to the conditional jump instructions, they are rarely used. The Intel 8080 also has a special one-word CALL instruction for reaching interrupt or trap routines. This instruction (RST or RESTART) is explained in Chapter 9.

The Motorola 6800 also has some special interrupt instructions. They are SOFTWARE INTERRUPT (SWI), which causes a jump to the address contained in memory locations FFF8 and FFF9 and saves all register contents in the stack, and RETURN FROM INTERRUPT (RTI), which restores all register contents from the stack. Chapter 9 explains the Motorola 6800 interrupt system and instructions.

Program Manipulation Instructions:
Halts and No Operations

Both the Intel 8080 and Motorola 6800 have a NO OPERATION instruction that simply increments the program counter. The Intel 8080 has a HALT instruction (HLT) that can only be cleared by an interrupt or reset signal. The Motorola 6800 has a WAIT FOR INTERRUPT (WAI) instruction that stores all the registers in the stack and waits for an interrupt. Both microprocessors also have several unused operation codes; the effects of these codes on the CPU are undefined—they are not necessarily the same as the NO OPERATION instruction.

Status Management Instructions

The only status management instructions available on the Intel 8080 or Motorola 6800 are those that enable and disable the interrupt system. On the Intel 8080 the instructions are EI (ENABLE INTERRUPTS) and DI (DISABLE INTERRUPTS). The Motorola 6800 has an interrupt mask bit I; the instruction CLI (CLEAR INTERRUPT) clears the mask bit and enables the interrupt, and SEI (SET INTERRUPT) sets the mask bit and disables the interrupt. Both processors automatically disable the interrupt system during reset and after accepting an interrupt. The Intel 8080 interrupt system must be explicity reenabled by the interrupt service routine; the Motorola 6800 interrupt system will automatically be reenabled by the RTI instruction, since this instruction restores the old value of the interrupt mask bit from the stack.

3.6 SUMMARY

An instruction is one of the binary inputs to which the CPU reacts with a specified series of actions. Each instruction must specify an operation, the sources of the data, the destination of the result, and the address of the next instruction. In most small computers much of this information is implicit—that is, independent of the particular instruction. This use of implicit information results in shorter instructions but means that more instructions are necessary in order to perform common tasks. The standard format is the one-address instruction in which the computer obtains one operand from an accumulator, places the result back in the accumulator, and sequences through a program by incrementing the program counter after each use.

Many different methods can be used to specify the address of the data. Direct addressing is simple and can handle single data items. Indirect and indexed addressing are more complex but allow the program to modify the actual or effective address so as to handle arrays and tables. Immediate addressing is useful for constants, whereas relative addressing allows the transfer of entire programs from one place in memory to another. Stack addressing depends on the last-in, first-out order of the stack; it is short and fast but difficult to use. Register addressing methods allow the programmer to place data or addresses in registers and use them repeatedly without additional memory accesses.

The instruction set itself can be divided into several basic categories: (a) data manipulation instructions that actually change the data, (b) data movement instructions that move the data from one place to another, (c) program manipulation instructions that alter the normal sequence of operations, and (d) status management instructions that affect only the machine status. Typical data manipulation instructions perform arithmetic, logical, shift, comparison, or special-purpose operations. Typical data movement instructions include memory transfers, register transfers, input/output operations, and stack transfers. Typical program manipulation instructions are unconditional and conditional jumps, subroutining operations, halts, and no operations. Typical status management instructions enable and disable the interrupts and determine other modes of operation.

A microprocessor instruction set usually contains between 40 and 80 separate instructions. The short data words and read-only program memory of most microcomputers favor short or implicit addressing methods. Register methods and stack addressing are more efficient than direct or indirect methods, which require complete addresses, or indexing, which requires an address-length addition.

The Intel 8080 and Motorola 6800 processors use different addressing techniques but have similar instruction sets. The 8080 uses an address register (registers

H and L) to refer to memory quickly; it has special instructions for loading, storing, incrementing, and decrementing that register. The 6800 uses page-zero addressing and a 16-bit index register to refer to memory; it has special instructions for loading, storing, incrementing, and decrementing the index register. Both processors use a RAM stack to store subroutine return addresses.

PROBLEMS

1. Write a sequence of instructions that evaluates the expression $S = X + W \times (Y + Z)$ on a computer using one-address instructions.

2. Write the instruction sequences required to perform the following calculations with one-address instructions.
   (a) SUM = SUM + TERM
   (b) PROD = (X + Y) × (X − Y)
   (c) REM = 1 − ANGLE
   (d) RAT = X/(1 − X)

3. How could you change the program of Fig. 3.3 so that it adds the contents of memory locations 1000 and 1001 and places the result in memory location 1002? What would you do if the program were in ROM? How about the program in Fig. 3.6? Would a ROM-based program make any difference there?

4. Assume that a computer has 64 different instructions. How many bits will be required in each one-address instruction (including operation code and direct address)?
   (a) If the address can refer to 1K different locations? 4K? 64K?
   (b) If the address must be one of eight general-purpose registers?

5. Write the sequence of instructions required to evaluate the expression

   $$Y = S + T \times (S + T)$$

   on a one-address machine where LOAD and STORE instructions may use any of 1K locations as a direct address but addition and multiplication can only be performed using the accumulator and one of four general-purpose registers (R1, R2, R3, R4).

6. Write the sequence of instructions required to evaluate the expression

   $$Y = \frac{S + R}{S - R}$$

   with one-address instructions.

7. Describe the effects of the following instructions. Assume that the one-address instructions always use a single accumulator A.
   (a) ADD 525
   (b) DIVIDE #10
   (c) JUMP @100
   (d) SUBTRACT #5
   (e) LOAD #30
   (f) LOAD @1000

8. Describe the effect of the following sequence of instructions starting in memory location 0 on the registers and data memory. The program counter is originally 0; memory location 100 contains 20 and 101 contains 5. Each instruction occupies one word of program memory. The computer has a single accumulator that originally contains 0.

        LOAD 100
        SUBTRACT 101
        MULTIPLY 101
        STORE 102

9. Describe the effect of the one-address instruction

        STORE 60

   (a) using page-zero addressing.
   (b) using current page addressing if the instruction is located at address 2030.
   (c) using 256 word pages and paged addressing if the page register contains 6.
   (d) using 1K word pages and paged addressing if the page register contains 3.

10. Describe the effect of the sequence of instructions below if the accumulator originally contains 10. Could you think of an application for the sequence?

        ADD   BASE
        STORE   ADDR
        JUMP   @ADDR

11. Describe the effect of this sequence of instructions if (VAL) = 5.

        LOAD   TABLE
        ADD   VAL
        STORE   DEST
        LOAD   @DEST

   What would be a possible application for the sequence?

12. Describe the one-address logical instructions that would have the following effects. Use the logical AND and INCLUSIVE OR functions; describe both the operation and operand needed. Do not change any bits other than those specified.
   (a) Set the least significant bit of the accumulator.
   (b) Clear the four most significant bits of the accumulator.
   (c) Set bits 2 and 3 of the accumulator.
   (d) Clear bits 3, 4, 5, and 6 of the accumulator.

13. Describe the effects of the following instructions, using indexed addressing if index register 1 contains 60.
   (a) ADD BASE, 1
   (b) INCREMENT INDEX REGISTER 1
   (c) LOAD 65, 1
   (d) STORE 237, 1

14. Show how an index register could be used to find the maximum of four numbers. Assume that the numbers are stored in memory locations BASE through BASE + 3 and that the maximum will be stored in memory location MAX.

15. What is the effect of the following instructions if $ means relative to the program counter?
(a) JUMP $ + 23
(b) ADD $ − 10
(c) STORE $ + 36
(d) LOAD $ + 66

16. (a) Use the instructions ADD and ADD WITH CARRY on a one-address machine to produce a triple-word addition. Assume that the first sequence of three words (most significant word first) is in memory locations FIRST, FIRST+1, and FIRST+2. The second sequence is in memory locations SECOND, SECOND+1, and SECOND+2; the answer replaces the first sequence.
(b) Use the instructions SUBTRACT and SUBTRACT WITH CARRY similarly to produce a triple-word subtraction.
(c) Use the instructions INCREMENT and JUMP ON ZERO to produce a double-word increment of memory locations COUNT and COUNT + 1. Assume that the most significant word is in COUNT. INCREMENT affects the ZERO flag but not the CARRY.

17. Memory location ADDR contains an 8-bit word that represents the position of four switches; that is, bits 0 and 1 describe whether switch #1 is in position 0, 1, 2, or 3; bits 2 and 3 do the same for switch #2; bits 4 and 5 describe switch #3; bits 6 and 7 describe switch #4. Write a program using one-address instructions that will place the switch settings in the two least significant bits of memory locations SW1, SW2, SW3, and SW4, respectively.
(a) Assume that we can only shift the accumulator. Describe the advantage of having a general-purpose register besides the accumulator for performing this task.
(b) Assume that we can shift a memory location. Use the instructions LOGICAL SHIFT and ROTATE WITH CARRY. What if the computer does not have a LOGICAL SHIFT instruction? How would you program this task on the Intel 8080 or Motorola 6800?

18. Memory location START contains an 8-bit ASCII character. Write a program using one-address instructions that will transfer control to memory location EDIT if START contains an E (45 hex), to SEND if START contains an S (53 hex), and to CNTRL if START contains anything else.
(a) Use the instructions COMPARE and JUMP ON ZERO.
(b) Use the instructions SUBTRACT and JUMP ON ZERO (assume that the computer does not have a COMPARE instruction).
(c) Use the instructions SUBTRACT and SKIP ON ZERO or SKIP ON NOT ZERO (assume that the computer has no conditional jump instructions).
(d) Assume that the computer does not allow immediate addressing with arithmetic instructions. Use the instructions COMPARE and JUMP ON ZERO but assume that we must use one of four general-purpose registers (R1, R2, R3, R4) with the COMPARE instruction. You may use LOAD IMMEDIATE to load the registers. How would you program this task on the Intel 8080 or Motorola 6800?

19. Subroutine SUB requires the temporary use of all eight general-purpose registers. Write programs to save all the registers at the beginning of SUB and restore them all at the end of SUB.

   (a) Assume that the computer has no stack and so we must save the registers in an area of memory. What happens if SUB calls itself or if the execution of SUB is interrupted by a program that calls SUB? Discuss how a pointer could be used to solve this problem.

   (b) Assume that the computer has a stack but can only transfer data to or from it via the accumulator. That is, PUSH places the contents of the accumulator in the stack, and PULL places the contents of the top location of the stack in the accumulator. What happens if SUB calls itself or is interrupted by a program that calls SUB? What happens if SUB is interrupted while we are saving the register contents?

   How would you save and restore register contents on the Intel 8080 or Motorola 6800?

   (c) What if the computer can transfer data to or from the stack via any register? PUSH R3 places the contents of register 3 in the stack and PULL R3 reverses the process.

20. Memory locations NEXT and NEXT + 1 (the words are eight bits long) contain the address of the next program that the CPU must execute. Write an instruction or sequence of instructions to start the CPU at the proper address.

   (a) if the computer has jump instructions with indirect addressing.

   (b) if the computer only has jump instructions with indexed addressing but the index register can hold a complete address.

   (c) if the computer only has jump instructions with register indirect addressing through register 1.

   How would you program this task on the Intel 8080 or Motorola 6800?

REFERENCES

Bond, J., "Designer's Guide to: Software for the Hardware Designer—Part I," *EDN*, Vol. 19, No. 11, June 5, 1974, pp. 40–44.

Bond, J., "Designer's Guide to Software for the Hardware Designer—Part II," *EDN*, Vol. 19, No. 15, August 5, 1974, pp. 51–56.

Cushman, R. H., "The Intel 8080," *EDN*, Vol. 19, No. 9, May 5, 1974, pp. 30–36.

Cushman, R. H., "Microprocessor Instruction Sets," *EDN*, Vol. 20, No. 6, March 20, 1975, pp. 35–41.

Cushman, R. H., "A Very Complete Chip Set Joins the Great Microprocessor Race," *EDN*, Vol. 19, No. 22, November 20, 1974, pp. 87–94.

Eckhouse, R. H., Jr., *Minicomputer Systems*, Prentice-Hall, Englewood Cliffs, N.J., 1975.

Gear, C. W., *Computer Organization and Programming*, 2nd ed., McGraw-Hill, New York, 1974.

"Intel 8080 Microcomputer Systems Manual," Intel Corporation, Santa Clara, Ca., 1975, p. 125.

KORN, G. A., *Minicomputers for Engineers and Scientists*, McGraw-Hill, New York, 1973.

LEVENTHAL, L. A., "Put Microprocessor Software to Work," *Electronic Design*, Vol. 24, No. 16, August 2, 1976, pp. 58–64.

"M6800 Microprocessor Applications Manual," Motorola, Inc., Phoenix, Ariz., 1975.

PEATMAN, J. B., *Microcomputer-Based Design*, McGraw-Hill, New York, 1977.

WEITZMAN, C., *Minicomputer Systems*, Prentice-Hall, Englewood Cliffs, N.J., 1974.

4 Microprocessor Assemblers

The features of the assembler programs that are normally used to develop software for microprocessor-based systems are the subject here. In the first section we consider the various language levels at which programs can be written and describe the advantages and disadvantages of each. Subsequent sections cover the general characteristics of assemblers and the specific properties of microprocessor assemblers. The standard Intel 8080 and Motorola 6800 assemblers are described in the final section.

4.1 COMPARISON OF LANGUAGE LEVELS

Machine Language Programming

The instructions that a computer executes are binary numbers that the CPU fetches from memory just like any other data and decodes to produce the required actions. For instance, the Intel 8080 instruction that adds the contents of general-purpose register B to the contents of the accumulator is the 8-bit binary number

$$10000000$$

This instruction looks exactly the same as the two's complement number -128, or the eight least significant bits of address 128. The computer decides whether the number is an instruction, part of an address, or simply a piece of data according to what it expects at a particular point in the instruction cycle. Thus the computer may interpret the same number from the same memory location in three entirely different ways.

The fact that data, addresses, and instructions all look the same in a computer memory is only one of the many difficulties associated with writing programs in a form that a computer can directly execute. Writing programs in this form is called *machine language programming*. For example, Fig. 4.1 shows the Intel 8080 machine language program that moves the contents of ten consecutive memory locations, starting with location 40 (hex), to ten new memory locations, starting with location 60 (hex). It is clear that understanding, correcting, or using this program would be difficult. The programmer would need a table of binary instruction codes and a pad of paper to keep track of the contents of memory locations, registers, and flags. The programmer must also be proficient in binary arithmetic and possess a detailed understanding of the Intel 8080. Working with binary numbers is difficult enough, but determining that memory location 6 contains an instruction, memory location 7 data, and memory location 14 part of an address is almost impossible. Consequently, few programmers work directly in machine language.

Figure 4.1 A machine language program.

Address	Contents
0	00100001
1	01000000
2	00000000
3	00010001
4	01100000
5	00000000
6	00000110
7	00001010
8	01111110
9	00010010
10	00100011
11	00010011
12	00000101
13	11000010
14	00001000
15	00000000
16	01110110

A simple alternative to machine language is to assign names to instructions, registers, data, and memory locations and use the names in the program instead of binary numbers. The programmer must build tables of the binary equivalents of the various names and use the tables to translate the final program into the form that the computer can execute. The computer manufacturer usually assigns names to the instructions and registers in order to simplify the description of the computer. Since the manufacturers supply tables of instruction codes like those shown in Appendixes 6 and 7 for the Intel 8080 and Motorola 6800, we will use the manufacturers' names in the interests of standardization; we used these names in discussing the instruction sets of the Intel 8080 and Motorola 6800 in Chapter 3. The names are mnemonics; that is, they suggest the actual operations performed by instructions or the functions of registers. Typical examples are

ADD—Add
SUB—Subtract
LD—Load
JMP—Jump
A—Accumulator
X—Index register

The programmer must, of course, assign names to data and addresses used in a particular program and construct tables with the binary equivalents of these names. We can now write the program of Fig. 4.1 as shown in Fig. 4.2. We have used the rules of the Intel 8080 assembler (see Section 4.4).[1] Table 4.1 translates the program-specific names into binary numbers. This method of writing programs is called *assembly language programming*, and the process of converting the programs to binary numbers is a *hand assembly*.

Figure 4.2 An assembly language program.

```
        LXI    H,BLK1    ; MEMORY POINTER 1 = START OF BLOCK 1
        LXI    D,BLK2    ; MEMORY POINTER 2 = START OF BLOCK 2
        MVI    B,COUNT   ; COUNT = LENGTH OF BLOCKS
TRANS:  MOV    A,M       ; GET ELEMENT OF BLOCK 1
        STAX   D         ; MOVE ELEMENT TO BLOCK 2
        INX    H
        INX    D
        DCR    B
        JNZ    LOOP
        HLT
```

Table 4.1 Symbol Table for Program of Figure 4.2

Names	Meaning (binary)
BLK1	01000000
BLK2	01100000
COUNT	00001010
TRANS	00001000

Since different Intel 8080 instructions occupy different numbers of words, we must determine the actual address corresponding to the name TRANS either by counting the number of words required by the instructions before that position or

---

[1]Briefly,

: is used after a label.
; is used before a comment.
, is used to separate operands.

Numbers are decimal unless specifically followed by

H—hexadecimal
B—binary

by translating the program to the binary form and finding the appropriate address in the machine language program.

Obviously the program in Fig. 4.2 is much easier to read and understand than the one in Fig. 4.1. We have distinguished data, addresses, and instructions. The manufacturer's mnemonic instruction codes suggest the actual computer operations. We have chosen names for data and addresses that similarly suggest their actual significance in the program. We can check the program before loading it into the computer and feel reasonably confident of its correctness.

Yet the programming process is still far from convenient. We must translate each operation code into a binary number; we must remember whether the instruction requires additional words for data or addresses and, if it does, the format of those additional words. We must create a table like Table 4.1, assign meanings to the various names or determine their values from the binary program, and convert data and addresses to binary. Clearly many of the tasks are repetitive, tiresome, and subject to minor but potentially disastrous errors. Additional problems exist if we want to use character or numerical codes, relative addresses, or subroutines that have been written by someone else. Assembly language programming with hand assembly is easier than machine language programming but certainly not the best way to write anything besides short programs.

Hand assembly also makes debugging difficult. In addition to the problem of dealing with such mistakes as incorrect operation codes or erroneous binary conversions, hand assembly forces the programmer to keep track of all the effects of each change. For instance, if in the program of Fig. 4.2 we had accidentally omitted the instruction MVI B,COUNT that sets the counter initially to ten, the program would not work properly. However, simply inserting the instruction would not make the program work; since the new instruction uses two additional words of memory, we must also correct all program addresses below the insertion. For example, the address TRANS would have to be changed from 6 to 8. So any change that involves the insertion or deletion of instructions or the use of different areas of data memory would force a repetition of the hand assembly. The inconvenience and high probability of error in the writing and debugging of hand assembled programs are obvious.

Machine Assembly and Assembler Programs

The operations involved in hand assembly are not difficult; such tasks as converting mnemonic codes and decimal numbers to their binary equivalents, counting words to calculate addresses, and placing data and addresses correctly in the instructions are time-consuming and repetitive. They are, in fact, ideal tasks for a computer that never makes careless mistakes, gets tired, or loses its place. We can thus use the computer to help solve the problems created by programming.

A simple example of using the computer in this way is the octal or hexadecimal monitor. Obviously machine language programs would be easier to write if we could enter octal or hexadecimal digits rather than binary digits. Only one-third or one-quarter as many entries would be necessary and the number of errors would be much smaller. The assembled programs would be shorter and easier to check. But how do we get the computer to accept octal or hexadecimal entries? The answer is that we program the computer to read octal or hexadecimal digits and convert them to binary. The task is simple; we can program it ourselves (in machine language) or use a program supplied by the computer manufacturer. Once we have written the conversion program, we can use it to simplify the writing of other programs. In fact, most computer manufacturers supply a simple octal or hexadecimal monitor (often in a read-only memory) to eliminate the need for binary entry.

The computer can do much more than merely convert octal or hexadecimal numbers to binary. The computer can perform all the tasks that the programmer must perform in hand assembly; the required program is called an *assembler*. The assembler translates the mnemonic codes to binary instruction codes, constructs the tables of names and their meanings, and replaces all the references to those names with the appropriate binary numbers. Clearly the computer can assemble programs faster and more accurately than the programmer can. The computer will never accidentally pick the wrong instruction code, transpose numbers, or convert addresses or data into binary incorrectly. Nor will the computer ever forget how many additional words of address or data an instruction requires or in what form it expects that address or data. The assembler can also, as will be shown later, provide other helpful features. The assembler is a program that accepts a program (*source code* in assembly language) as input data and produces a program (*object code* in machine language) as output data.

Of course, such advantages have a price. We must purchase or write the assembler or use it for a fee on a time-sharing service. The assembler also introduces demands of its own; it will possess methods and formats that we must learn. Still, assembly language programming with an assembler is more convenient and more productive than either machine language programming or hand assembly.

However, the entire process of writing programs in terms of the instruction set of a particular computer is inefficient. In the first place, we can only use the resulting programs on that computer. We cannot easily translate the programs into the assembly language of another computer, since the architectures, instruction sets, and addressing methods of computers vary so widely. Furthermore, we cannot easily use existing programs that were written for other computers. We may find that we are tied to a particular computer because a change would require rewriting and retesting programs.

The basic problem is that assembly language is more closely related to the structure of the computer than to the performance of engineering tasks. The assembly language programmer spends more time manipulating registers and devising instruction sequences than solving actual problems. The programmer must have very detailed knowledge of the instruction set, architecture, and addressing methods of the computer. Note the knowledge of the Intel 8080 that is necessary to write a simple program like that shown in Fig. 4.2. So assembly language programming requires a great deal of extra effort that contributes nothing directly to the solution of design problems.

The computer's instruction set reflects the limitations of the underlying technology. The manufacturer creates an instruction set that the hardware can easily and cheaply decode and execute. Thus the user rarely finds a single instruction that will perform a meaningful task. Even such simple tasks as adding numbers, making comparisons, or looking for characters require sequences of instructions. Assembly language programming is therefore time-consuming; the large number of instructions increases the probability of errors and makes programs difficult to document. The productivity of assembly language programmers is low, and the final programs bear little resemblance to engineering descriptions of the system.

Procedure-Oriented Languages

The programmer can avoid this dependence on the architecture and instruction set of a particular computer by using a *procedure-oriented language*. A procedure-oriented, or *high-level*, language is designed so that common tasks can be easily and naturally placed in a form that is comprehensible to a translator program called a *compiler*. Like an assembler, a compiler accepts programs (written in the procedure-oriented language) as input data and produces programs (in machine or assembly language) as output data. The procedure-oriented language, however, is independent of any one computer. The same program will run on any computer that has a compiler for the language. The compiler is machine-dependent but the language is not. Furthermore, we can describe the problem to the computer in a convenient form. The program will suggest what we are actually trying to do rather than consist of instruction sequences with no obvious meaning. We can formulate problems more efficiently in a high-level language and need not have a precise understanding of the architecture of the computer.

Many procedure-oriented languages exist; some are general-purpose, whereas others are specifically designed for such tasks as business data processing, circuit design, or text analysis. By far the most common procedure-oriented language is FORTRAN, originally invented in the early 1950s and named as an abbreviation of Formula Translation Language. Other procedure-oriented languages, such as PL/I, APL, BASIC, ALGOL, and PASCAL, are also used to solve engineering problems. FORTRAN compilers, however, are available for almost every computer; standard forms of the FORTRAN language are widely accepted and thousands of programs have been written in FORTRAN. Thus the FORTRAN programmer can transfer programs from one computer to another easily and can use the vast backlog of FORTRAN programs.

If we can express a task in algebraic notation, we can easily translate it into a few FORTRAN statements. The program of Figs. 4.1 and 4.2, which took 16 lines in machine language and 10 lines in assembly language, requires just 2 lines in

Figure 4.3 A FORTRAN program.

```
        DO  100    I = 1, 10
100     BLK1(I)  = BLK2 (I)
```

FORTRAN (see Fig. 4.3). This program is obviously shorter, simpler, and easier to read and understand than the assembly language or machine language versions. The FORTRAN statements resemble the description of the problem that we would write down as part of the normal design procedure. We will need much less documentation to make a FORTRAN program comprehensible than an assembly or machine language program. The FORTRAN programmer need not be concerned about the addressing methods, registers, or other features of a computer since the FORTRAN program does not depend on them.

Nevertheless, FORTRAN has some major disadvantages. The FORTRAN compiler is much more complicated and expensive than an assembler; in general, FORTRAN requires more than a minimum computer system in order to run properly. FORTRAN itself is a complex language with many rules that the programmer must follow.

The FORTRAN compiler also produces object code that is slower and uses more memory than that produced by an assembly or machine language programmer. A compiler translates FORTRAN statements accurately but unimaginatively; it will not discover shortcuts that may be obvious to an experienced programmer. However, the longer execution time and larger memories required by FORTRAN programs are serious drawbacks in many microprocessor applications. FORTRAN makes programming easier by handling much of the detail required in assembly language, but it also keeps programmers from using their knowledge of particular computers and applications to make programs more efficient.

FORTRAN itself was originally designed for tasks that are outside the realm of microprocessors. As the name suggests, FORTRAN was designed to solve scientific problems that could be described by mathematical formulas. We seldom use microprocessors to solve such problems. FORTRAN is not well suited to the real-time control applications in which microprocessors are often used. The formatting, bit manipulations, and interfacing requirements of control applications are awkward to implement in FORTRAN. Languages like ALGOL and PL/I are better suited than FORTRAN to these applications, but such languages are not as widely used and so have limited transferability and small program libraries. The near future will determine whether FORTRAN will be modified to meet the needs of microprocessor users or whether other languages (perhaps specifically designed for control) will replace it.

The computer user has several options in writing programs. Machine language programming or hand assembly requires the least support and gives the programmer the closest control over the computer. On the other hand, such methods are time-consuming and error prone. The assembler relieves the programmer of the repetitive tasks of hand assembly but leaves the programmer dependent on a particular computer. A procedure-oriented language like FORTRAN makes programming simpler, more productive, and less machine-dependent but generally results in slower programs that require more memory. At the present time the disadvantages of procedure-oriented languages outweigh their advantages as far as microprocessors are concerned; most microprocessor programming is currently being done in assembly language, and so we will concentrate on this method. In the future, however, the greater efficiency of procedure-oriented languages will undoubtedly lead to their wider use.

4.2 FEATURES OF ASSEMBLERS

The basic purpose of an assembler is to translate assembly language mnemonics into binary machine language codes. Some assemblers do very little beyond this; the programmer must still do a great deal of hand assembly in order to write programs in a convenient form. However, most assemblers now offer a variety of features, including labeling, symbolic addressing, format conversions, storage allocation, data generation, and assembly-time arithmetic. The boundary between assemblers and compilers has, in fact, become blurred as more features have been added to assemblers.

Field Structure

Assembler statements consist of several divisions or *fields*. Figure 4.4 shows a typical organization.

Figure 4.4 An assembler statement.

Label	Assembler Operation Code	Address	Comment

EXAMPLE:

LAST: JUMP START   ; RETURN TO BEGINNING OF PROGRAM

Some assemblers use a *fixed format* with certain columns on a punched card or other input form reserved for specific fields. Fixed formats have the advantage that no special symbols are needed to separate fields. Most microprocessor assemblers use *free formats* in which fields may occur anywhere on a line; the fields are then separated by specific characters, called *delimiters*. Common delimiters include the space character, colon, semicolon, comma, reverse slash, question mark, and other characters that are available on standard keyboards but would not otherwise find much use in computer programs.

Labels

The label field allows us to assign a name to the address of an instruction or piece of data. We can then use the name as an address or as data in other instructions. Most assemblers permit labels that consist of letters, numbers, and a few other characters. We will discuss the choice of labels as part of the consideration of programming techniques in Chapter 6. Labels are usually restricted in length to five or six characters; frequently, the first character must be a letter so that the assembler can easily distinguish labels from numbers. A particular label, of course, can only be used once in a program. Using operation codes and other assembler directives as labels is inadvisable and often not allowed. The label field may be empty; in fact, we only use the label field when we have a specific reason for doing so.

Assembler Operation Codes

The operation code field usually contains the mnemonic instruction code; it is the only field that can never be empty. The assembler simply compares the code to the elements of a list in memory until it finds a match. The corresponding entries in other tables contain the binary equivalent of the code and the address of a subroutine that will search for the required addresses or data. The tables may be stored in read-only memory.

Pseudo-operations

The operation code field may also contain directives to the assembler. These directives are called *pseudo-operations*, since they appear in the operation code field but are not translated into binary instruction codes. Pseudo-operations may assign programs and data to areas of memory, define symbols, allocate space for variables, generate fixed tables and data, mark the end of the program, and determine the form of the program listing. The pseudo-operations also appear in the fixed assembler mnemonic table; they have no binary equivalents but do have corresponding assembler subroutines that produce the prescribed actions.

Common pseudo-operations include (see Table 4.2)

```
ORIGIN
EQUATE or DEFINE
RESERVE
DATA
END
LIST
PAGE
SPACE
NAME or TITLE
```

The specific names that assemblers use for these pseudo-operations vary greatly.

The pseudo-operation ORIGIN (almost always abbreviated ORG) allows us to start programs or data at particular memory locations. Startup routines, interrupt service routines, and trap routines usually must start at specified memory

Table 4.2 Common Pseudo-Operations

Operation	Abbreviations	Effect
DATA	DATA, DB, DW, DDB, FW, FCC, FCB	Enters constant values into memory
DEFINE	EQU, SET, DEF	Defines a name
END	END	Marks end of assembly language program
LIST	LIST	Provides listing of assembly language program
NAME	NAME	Assigns a name to the program
ORIGIN	ORG	Defines starting point in memory of next part of program
PAGE	PAGE	Skips to next page of listing
RESERVE	RES, DS, RMB	Reserves memory space for variable data
SPACE	SPACE	Skips a line in listing

addresses. The main program, subroutines, and data must not interfere with each other or with the computer's fixed addresses. Thus a program often has several origins; Fig. 4.5 shows a typical example.

Figure 4.5 Use of the ORG pseudo-operation.

PROGRAM

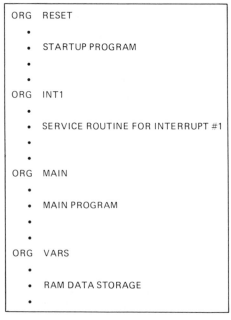

```
ORG   RESET
   •
   •    STARTUP PROGRAM
   •

ORG   INT1
   •
   •    SERVICE ROUTINE FOR INTERRUPT #1
   •
   •

ORG   MAIN
   •
   •    MAIN PROGRAM
   •
   •

ORG   VARS
   •
   •    RAM DATA STORAGE
   •
```

The pseudo-operation EQUATE (often abbreviated EQU) or DEFINE defines names for later use in the program. We place the name in the label field and the definition in the address field. Typical examples are

```
COUNT    EQU  10
THRSH    EQU  200
KBD      EQU  2
```

We frequently place all the definitions at the start of the program so that we can find them easily and use them as part of the documentation; we may divide the definitions into such groups as input/output units, variable names, fixed memory addresses, and parameters.

The pseudo-operation RESERVE (often abbreviated RES, DS for DEFINE STORAGE, or RM for RESERVE MEMORY) sets aside RAM storage for variables and may assign a name to the first address in the storage area. The pseudo-operation

```
TEMP    RESERVE    1
```

sets aside one word of memory and assigns the name TEMP to its address; we may then use TEMP later in the program. Similarly, the pseudo-operation

```
SYMTB    RESERVE    100
```

sets aside 100 RAM locations and assigns the name SYMTB to the address of the first one. Note that the program can change the data in these addresses. Some assemblers allow the programmer to place initial values in the RAM locations; we will not use this feature, since it is based on the assumption that the program (together with the initial values) will be loaded into the memory each time it is run. Most microprocessor programs are stored permanently in read-only memory; therefore they must execute properly when power is turned on and the contents of the volatile RAM are uncertain.

The pseudo-operation DATA (often called DB for DEFINE BYTE, DW for DEFINE WORD, or FCB for FORM CONSTANT BYTE) allows tables or constants to be placed in program memory. We usually can assign a name to the address of the first location in the assigned area. The pseudo-operation

```
TFAC    DATA    32
```

places the number 32 in the next word of program memory and assigns that address the name TFAC. We can place a table in program memory by using a pseudo-operation like

```
SQTAB    DATA    0, 1, 4, 9, 16, 25, 36, 49
```

which forms an eight-element table of squares and assigns the name SQTAB to the address of the first element.

Note that DATA places permanent values in program memory, whereas RESERVE establishes variable storage in data memory. So we place values in the address field of a DATA statement and the number of assigned locations in the address field of a RESERVE statement.

The pseudo-operation END simply marks the end of the assembly language program. Some assemblers allow a label in the address field of an END to indicate where the program should start executing if it is assembled without any errors. The pseudo-operation

        END   FIRST

ends the assembly language program and causes the computer to begin execution of the program at the statement labeled FIRST if the program is assembled without errors.

Pseudo-operations like LIST, PAGE, SPACE, and TITLE only affect the form of the listing that the assembler produces.

Symbol Table

The assembler places all the names used in an assembly language program in a symbol table similar to the fixed mnemonic table. Methods for constructing symbol tables are outside the scope of our discussion but are explained in several of the references at the end of this chapter. The assembler must, of course, use RAM for the symbol table.

Addresses

Most assemblers allow the programmer to describe data or addresses in many different forms. Special symbols may indicate the addressing method—for instance,

@	INDIRECT
#	IMMEDIATE
,I or ,X	INDEXED
* , \$, or ◇	RELATIVE

Sometimes the addressing method is indicated by a modified version of the mnemonic instruction code, such as

ADDI	ADD IMMEDIATE
ADDX	ADD INDEXED
ADDA	ADD TO ACCUMULATOR A.

Most assemblers allow addresses and data in the following forms.

1. Decimal numbers:

ADD 136—Add the contents of memory location 136 to the contents of the
accumulator.
MULTIPLY #5—Multiply the contents of the accumulator by 5.

Most assemblers assume all numbers to be decimal unless the programmer indicates otherwise.

2. Other number systems—octal, hexadecimal, or binary: Entries in these
number systems may be marked by a code letter at the end of the entry (e.g., B for
binary, O or Q for octal, H for hexadecimal). The assembler, of course, will convert
all numbers to binary. Hexadecimal numbers may require an initial digit (e.g., 0A
rather than A) so that the assembler can distinguish them from names.

SUBTRACT #0B3H—Subtract the hexadecimal number B3 from the contents of the accumulator.
JUMP 53Q—Jump to memory location 53 octal (43 decimal).
AND #00001111B—Logically AND the contents of the accumulator with
the binary number 00001111.

We prefer to enter data and addresses in the number systems in which their
meaning is the clearest. Thus we enter numerical constants in decimal, BCD
numbers in hexadecimal (since each BCD digit is also a hexadecimal digit), and
masks in binary (since their purposes are then more obvious although hexadecimal
may be more convenient for longer masks).

3. Symbolic names: Symbolic names can be used just like the values that they
represent. The names may represent addresses or data; we must use immediate
addressing if the name is intended as data. Usually register names are built into the
assembler—for instance,

A—accumulator
X—index register

Sometimes the registers must have an R in their names, such as R3 or R15.

EXAMPLES:

ADD INT

means to add the contents of the memory location whose address is given by the name
INT to the contents of the accumulator.

ONE   EQU   1
      SUBTRACT ONE

means to subtract the contents of memory location 1 (not necessarily the number 1) from the contents of the accumulator.

```
ONE   EQU   1
      SUBTRACT #ONE
```

means to subtract the number 1 (# means immediate) from the contents of the accumulator.

```
JUMP   TRAP
```

means to jump to the memory location whose address is given by the name TRAP.

4. The current program counter: Most assemblers refer to the current value of the program counter as $ or *. We can use this form even if the computer does not have relative addressing; the assembler will calculate the actual address.

EXAMPLE:

```
JUMP   $ + 8
```

means to jump eight locations forward.

5. Arithmetic combinations: Many assemblers allow arithmetic combinations of names, symbols, and numbers in the address field. The example ($ + 8) above is typical of the simple combinations that are most common. The way in which these combinations are evaluated differs greatly from assembler to assembler; the programmer must use them cautiously.

EXAMPLES:

```
MULTIPLY   ADDR + 2
```

means to multiply the contents of the accumulator by the contents of the address two beyond ADDR.

```
JUMP   COUNT − 1
```

means to jump to the address one before COUNT.

The assembler may also allow such functions as multiplication, integer division, and even exponentiation. Some assemblers use the FORTRAN precedence rules whereby multiplications and divisions are performed before additions and subtractions (operations with the same precedence are performed in order from left to right). Other assemblers treat all operations the same and simply perform them in order from left to right. Note that the assembler evaluates the expressions; the computer may not be able to evaluate them directly. Very complex expressions make programs unclear and hard to test and debug.

6. *Character codes*: Data can often be specified in character codes, usually either ASCII or EDCDIC (see Appendix 3 for a description of these codes). The character data is frequently enclosed in single or double quotation marks, although some assemblers use a beginning or ending symbol, such as C, A, or E.

EXAMPLES:

    COMPARE #'E'

means to compare the contents of the accumulator with the internal representation of the character E.

    LOAD #','

means to load the accumulator with the internal representation of the character , (comma).

7. *Other combinations*: Some assemblers allow the use of logical operations (AND, OR, NOT, EXCLUSIVE OR), shifts, and other functions in calculating addresses or data. Obviously complex expressions are rarely used in practice.

Note that we can use any of the address field options in DATA pseudo-operations—for instance,

    ERRM DATA   'ERROR'
    PROD DATA   C * D

We must be particularly careful if the data is too long or too short for the address field; different assemblers will truncate the data or fill the remaining bits in different ways.

Conditional Assembly

Some assemblers allow code to be either included or ignored, depending on conditions existing at assembly time. Some even allow conditional or unconditional jumps, loops, or subroutine calls to be performed as part of the assembly; we will not discuss such features here, but they are explained in some of the references. The conditional assembly facility can be controlled by the pseudo-operations IF and ENDIF. Typical examples of conditional assembly are

EXAMPLE: Choice of Addressing Modes

```
IF      X1    < 256
        ADD   X1
ENDIF
IF      X1    ⩾ 256
        LOAD   #X1
        STORE  TEMP1
        ADD    @TEMP1
ENDIF
```

We could use this construction if the computer involved could only directly address memory locations on page zero (assuming a 256-word page). If X1 is not on page zero, the assembler will use indirect addressing through a location (TEMP1) on page zero containing the address X1. The value of X1 (specified by a DEFINE pseudo-operation or a label declaration) at assembly time would determine which of the two instruction sequences would actually be included in the program.

EXAMPLE: Choice of Number of Operands

```
ADD    X1
IF    X2 ≠ 0
    ADD  X2
ENDIF
IF    X3 ≠ 0
    ADD  X3
ENDIF
```

We could exclude the additional operands by setting their addresses to zero at the start of the program. The same assembly language program could be used regardless of whether the additional operands are present. Conditional assembly is also a convenient way to include statements intended solely for debugging purposes.

Macros

If instruction sequences are used frequently or for purposes that are not obvious, the assignment of names to the sequences may be convenient. The feature in an assembler that permits this assignment is called a *macro* facility; the sequence of instructions is a *macro*. We must define the macro before using it; the pseudo-operations MACRO and ENDM or MEND mark the beginning and end of the definition. The assembler automatically replaces each reference to the macro with the sequence of instructions from the definition.

A simple macro may consist of a single instruction. Thus on a computer that has no explicit LOGICAL SHIFT LEFT instruction the required operation can be provided by adding the contents of the accumulator to itself with the instruction ADD A. We can give this instruction its own mnemonic code by defining a macro.

```
SLL    MACRO
       ADD    A
       ENDM
```

The name SLL placed in the label field of the MACRO pseudo-operation is the name of the macro. Once the macro has been defined, SLL may be used just like any of the actual instruction codes; the assembler will replace each occurrence of SLL with the binary code for the instruction ADD A.

A macro may have parameters. For example, the macro for a logical NAND (NOT AND) operation may be defined by the sequence

```
NAND   MACRO        ADDR
       AND          ADDR
       COMPLEMENT ACCUMULATOR
       ENDM
```

NAND is the name of the macro; ADDR, placed in the address field, is a parameter. NAND requires an address each time it is used; the assembler will place that address in the instruction sequence that defines the macro. For instance, the assembler will replace NAND 100 with the sequence

```
AND        100
COMPLEMENT ACCUMULATOR
```

Macros may, of course, be much more complex than these two examples. A macro may have several parameters and may contain many instructions.

EXAMPLE: Sum of an Array

```
SUM    MACRO      TOTAL, ELEM, NUM
       LOAD #0
       LOAD INDEX REGISTER NUM
LOOP   ADD ELEM, X
       DECREMENT INDEX REGISTER
       JUMP ON NOT ZERO LOOP
       STORE TOTAL
       ENDM
```

The SUM macro has three parameters: TOTAL is the address in which the sum will be stored; ELEM is the starting address of the array, and NUNUM is the address that contains the length of the array. The programmer may use the macro by placing a statement like

SUM   TOT1, A1, N1

in the assembly language program. The assembler will replace the statement by the specified sequence of instructions with the parameters replaced by their assigned values.

Macros and subroutines differ even though their forms and functions are similar. The assembler replaces each reference to a macro with the specified instruction sequence. A macro does not require CALL and RETURN instructions. A subroutine, on the other hand, is a single sequence of instructions that may be called from various places in the main program or other subroutines. A subroutine only appears once in memory; we use a CALL instruction to reach the subroutine and a RETURN instruction to get back to the main program.

Subroutines

Many assemblers have special features that simplify the use of subroutines. The assembler may allow separate assembly of subroutines. It will then mark all references to subroutines in the main program and provide this information to a special loader program (called a *linking loader*) that fills in the actual addresses. If the assembler lacks this feature, we must assemble the subroutines together with the main program. Some assemblers will automatically handle references to common subroutines supplied by the computer manufacturer (called *library* subroutines); they may include trigonometric functions, input/output routines, or other widely used programs.

Advantages and Disadvantages of Subroutines and Macros

Macros and subroutines both have the following advantages.

1. They allow the programmer to write a sequence of instructions once and use it many times.
2. They make programs easier to read and understand.
3. They allow changes to be made to a single sequence of instructions rather than to every occurrence of that sequence.
4. They allow the use of library programs, other standard instruction sequences, or instruction sequences that have been previously debugged and tested.

Macros have an advantage over subroutines in that they do not require calls or jumps, since the assembler places the instructions from the macro definition in the normal sequence. Thus macros execute faster than subroutines. In addition, a program that interrupts another program can use a macro while the same macro has been interrupted without causing any problems, since the two uses of the macro involve physically distinct instruction sequences. On the other hand, macros require more memory than subroutines because each reference to the macro causes the assembling of separate code, whereas a subroutine is assembled only once. We use macros for relatively short instruction sequences in which memory usage is not a major factor; we prefer subroutines for longer sequences, perhaps involving ten instructions or more. The programmer should be cautious in using either macros or subroutines because a single use may result in the execution of many instructions and the expenditure of much time.

Local or Global Variables

One problem occurring with macros or subroutines concerns whether names defined in the main program can be used in the macro or subroutine and vice versa. In general, names cannot be so used unless they are arguments of the macro or subroutine. A variable that is only defined in a particular subprogram is called a *local* variable; one that is defined throughout the program is referred to as *global*. Generally names and labels in macros and subroutines are local; consequently, we cannot use them outside the particular macro or subroutine. For instance, in the macro SUM described earlier, the label LOOP is local to the macro; no statement outside the macro may reference that label, nor would a second use of the macro mean that the label was doubly defined. Here again we try to avoid confusion; a variable that is needed both inside and outside a subroutine or macro should be placed in the list of arguments.

Comments

Almost all assemblers provide a commenting facility for documentation purposes. Usually the assembler requires some special symbol or a space to initiate comment fields. The comment field may be empty, but comments improve the readability of programs and are an important part of documentation. They do not affect the object code produced by the assembler.

Relocatability

Some assemblers provide a machine language program that is *relocatable*—that is, it can be placed anywhere in memory by a loader. The assembler provides the information that the loader uses to adjust all the relocatable addresses. We must be careful not to use absolute addresses except when they are actually needed to refer to fixed data locations, interrupt entry points, and so on. The loader will add the relocation constant to all the addresses that are not absolute.

Arithmetic combinations of relocatable addresses should be avoided, since such combinations can be either erroneous (like sums that would contain the relocation constant twice) or absolute (like differences). Relocatable subroutines are convenient because we can then use the same subroutines with different main programs and let the loader place the subroutines appropriately in the available memory.

One-pass and Two-pass Assemblers

Because they must read through a program twice in order to produce the correct object code, most assemblers are *two-pass assemblers*. The assembler uses the first pass to create the symbol table and collect all the definitions; during the second pass it translates the program with the aid of the definitions collected in the first pass. Generally symbols may be defined anywhere in the program, since the assembler reads through the entire program in any case; the programmer, however, will find the collection of definitions at the start of the program to be convenient for reference purposes. Most two-pass assemblers temporarily store the program being assembled on tape or disk so that no physical second pass is required; if no backup storage is available, the two-pass assembler must physically read the program twice from paper tape or cards. An assembler may even require a third pass if it must produce a paper tape or cassette output. Figure 4.6 illustrates the workings of a two-pass assembler.

Figure 4.6 The two-pass assembler.

Pass 1. Creation of symbol table

	PROGRAM			SYMBOL TABLE	
123		LOAD	X1 + 7	X1	60
124		JUMP	THRU	THRU	
125	GR:	ADD	#1	GR	125
126		DIVIDE	#10	ST	127
127	ST:	STORE	TEMP	TEMP	62

The label THRU appears later in the program.

Pass 2. Use of symbol table

	PROGRAM			NONSYMBOLIC PROGRAM	
123		LOAD	X1 + 7	LOAD	67
124		JUMP	THRU	JUMP	327
125	GR:	ADD	#1	ADD	#1
126		DIVIDE	#10	DIVIDE	#10
127	ST:	STORE	TEMP	STORE	62

The alternative to a two-pass assembler is a *one-pass assembler*, which is faster since it must read through a program only once. One-pass assemblers, however, have problems with forward references; often the loader must handle such references. In general, one-pass assemblers cannot offer as many features as two-pass assemblers. They either burden the programmer by having stricter rules for constructing addresses, using names, and allocating storage or require a more complex loader that does some of the assembly work while loading the program into memory.

Assembler Input and Output

In general, assemblers accept input from any medium. Obviously the speed of the assembly process depends on the speed of the input medium (particularly if the assembler must read the program twice).

The assembler usually provides all or most of the following output.

- A listing of the assembly language program, together with the object code that was generated.
- A list of assembly errors.
- A symbol table with the meanings of all the names used in the program.
- A cross-reference table with a list of names and all the instructions that use them.
- A list of external references (i.e., references to subroutines or variables that are defined outside the program).
- A list of subroutines or macros and their lengths.

The assembler also, if required, produces a punched paper tape or card version of the machine language program. Some assemblers automatically place a simple bootstrap loader at the start of the object code so that it will be self-loading.

Some place the program in memory and start executing it at a specified starting location. Such assemblers are called *load-and-go assemblers*. Others place the machine code on disk or tape (or in memory) and await further instructions.

Errors

Assemblers provide a variety of error messages which are described in the assembler manual. Among the more common errors are the ones in Table 4.3. The assembler usually identifies an error with a code letter or number and lists the errors and the line numbers where they occurred at the end of the program; sometimes the assembler also marks the lines where an error occurred in the output listing.

Table 4.3 Typical Assembler Errors

Error	Meaning
DEFINED SYMBOL NOT USED	A symbol has been defined but not used. Most assemblers will note this situation and inform the programmer but will still assemble the program.
ERRONEOUS LABEL	A statement is labeled that cannot have a label. Usually an ORG, END, IF, ENDIF, PAGE, NAME, LIST, or other pseudo-operation.
ILLEGAL CHARACTER	A character has been used improperly, such as something other than zero or one in a binary number or similar errors in other formats.
ILLEGAL FORMAT	An incorrect format has been used, such as an invalid delimiter, too few operands, or the wrong type of operands.
ILLEGAL LABEL	A label has been used that is not permitted by the rules of the assembler; illegal characters, too many characters, or an invalid starting character are common errors.
ILLEGAL NUMERIC	A number contains an illegal digit or character. Often caused by a misspelling or typing error.
ILLEGAL OPERAND or INVALID REGISTER	An operand or register has been specified improperly; for instance, the register does not exist or the register or operand cannot be used with the instruction.
ILLEGAL VALUE	A number has been used that is too large for the number of bits assigned to it
INVALID ASSEMBLER OPERATION	An assembler operation has been used improperly, such as an ENDM without a MACRO (or vice versa) or an ENDIF without an IF.
INVALID EXPRESSION	An expression has been formed in an illegal manner. Common problems include two operations in a row, invalid operations (typing errors or incorrect symbols), unmatched parentheses, omitted arguments, arguments of the wrong type or length, and omitted or unmatched quotation marks.
LIMIT EXCEEDED or SYMBOL TABLE OVERFLOW	The physical limits of the assembler in terms of number of symbols, number of external references, value of the program counter, number of macros, or other quantities have been exceeded.
MACRO DEPTH EXCEEDED	A macro has been defined within a macro or a macro has called itself.
MISSING LABEL	A statement that requires a label does not have one. Usually a DEFINE or MACRO pseudo-operation that does not make sense without a label.
MISSING OPERAND FIELD	An operand field has been omitted. No address is provided for an instruction that requires one.

Table 4.3 (cont.)

Error	Meaning
MULTIPLE DEFINITION	A label or symbol has been defined more than once. Often means that the same symbol or label has been accidentally used for two different purposes. This error may also be caused by symbols that have identical starting sequences, since most assemblers only use the first five or six characters in a name.
UNDEFINED OPERATION CODE	An operation code has been used that is neither in the instruction set nor defined as a macro. This error usually means that the operation code was misspelled, misplaced, or omitted.
UNDEFINED SYMBOL	A symbol has been used but not defined. The definition may have been omitted, the symbol may have been misspelled when used or defined, or the symbol may be local to a macro.

Cross-Assembly and Self-Assembly

An assembler or compiler need not run on the computer for which it produces object code. An assembler that does is called a *self-assembler* or *resident assembler*; one that runs on another computer is a *cross-assembler*. Similar distinctions apply to *self-compilers* and *cross-compilers*.

Initially cross-assembly seems somewhat mysterious. However, it is useful with microcomputers, since they usually lack the speed, memory, peripherals, and software required for convenient assembly. Program development is, as noted, a task best suited to large computer systems having high-speed input and output devices, mass storage, operating systems, editors, compilers, and other useful software and hardware.

Cross-assembly and cross-compilation do introduce additional problems. The assembler cannot simply place the resulting machine language program in memory and execute it. Instead the program is placed on paper tape or some other medium; we then take the tape and enter it into the computer which will run the program. Thus we need a loader and monitor for the microcomputer as well as a cross-assembler or cross-compiler for the larger computer. We must weigh the cost and inconvenience of cross-assemblers against their greater speed and more extensive features. Ultimately, of course, we must debug and test the program on the microcomputer; however, software development is often easier if we use a larger computer to do as much as possible and postpone the actual testing on the microcomputer.

Size of Assemblers

The size of the assembler depends on the features provided and the size of the symbol tables allowed. A simple assembler may require 2K 8-bit words of memory, whereas a more advanced assembler may require 8K or 16K 16-bit words of memory. There are tradeoffs between the amount of memory required by the assembler, the cost of the assembler, the convenience of additional assembler features, the size of programs that can be assembled, and the speed with which programs can be assembled. We must consider all such factors in evaluating an assembler. A simple assembler may be desirable if a system lacks a large memory and fast peripherals.

4.3 FEATURES OF MICROPROCESSOR ASSEMBLERS

Most microprocessor assemblers are relatively simple. They lack the advanced features that can be found in assemblers written for more powerful computers, such as the IBM 370 or DEC PDP-11. Some of the features of assemblers for larger computers are unnecessary, since microprocessors are rarely used for large-scale data processing applications.

Cross-assemblers vs. Self-assemblers

Almost all microprocessor assemblers are available both as cross-assemblers and as self-assemblers. The reasons are the relatively slow speed of microprocessors and their orientation toward control applications rather than the extensive text analysis and symbol manipulation required by an assembler. Also, the assembler requires more memory and peripherals than are usually available on a microcomputer.

Certain self-assemblers will only run on a special development system based on the microprocessor. Sometimes the self-assembler is provided in a read-only memory so that it need not be entered into the development system each time it is used. However, the self-assembler will still be slow because the development system depends on the basic speed of the microprocessor. The self-assembler will require two or three physical passes of the program unless mass storage is available.

Both the cross-assembler and the self-assembler involve an additional computer for program development. The cross-assembler uses a completely different computer. We must transfer the object code output to the microcomputer. The self-assembler requires a development system with sufficient memory, software, and peripherals. We can run the object code on the development system immediately for checkout, but eventually we must test the programs on a prototype. Program development methods for microprocessor-based systems are discussed more extensively in Chapter 6.

Almost all microprocessor cross-assemblers are written in FORTRAN because such assemblers are easy to write and can run on any computer that has FORTRAN. However, a cross-assembler written in FORTRAN uses a large amount of memory and executes slowly. A few cross-assemblers have been written in assembly language for specific computers (usually an IBM 370) to provide faster assembly in a more compact form.

Special Features

Several assembler features are particularly useful with microprocessors because of their short word length, read-only program memory, and use in interrupt-based systems. Among these features are

1. Ability to handle multiple-word instructions. Microprocessors have many multiple-word instructions. The assembler will not only choose the proper length and keep track of the program counter but will also divide multiple-word operands and addresses properly.

2. Provisions for multiple origins. Most microprocessor programs require multiple origins in order to position reset and interrupt service routines properly and to avoid memory areas reserved for data storage or input/output devices.

3. Separate allocation of fixed data and variable storage. Most microprocessor programs need this separation, since fixed data is stored in ROM, whereas variables are stored in RAM. The DATA pseudo-operation places constants in ROM; the RESERVE pseudo-operation sets aside RAM for variables.

Assembler Input/Output

Microprocessor cross-assemblers can accept input in any form that the host computer system allows; most use cards or paper tape. Self-assemblers almost always use paper tape or cassette input. Both cross-assemblers and self-assemblers usually produce the machine language program as a cassette or paper tape. We can load the tape into the microcomputer read/write memory for testing and debugging or use it to program a read-only memory.

Use and Acquisition of Microprocessor Assemblers

Microprocessor assemblers are available from the microprocessor manufacturer. The self-assembler is generally included with the microcomputer development system; the cross-assembler may be purchased either on a magnetic tape or as a card deck. Both self-assemblers and cross-assemblers for common microprocessors are available from manufacturers of microcomputers or development systems, software specialty houses, and other sources. Cross-assemblers for popular minicomputers, such as the DEC PDP-8 and PDP-11, Data General Nova, and Hewlett-Packard 2100, are often available.

The cross-assembler may thus be used on most computers. Cross-assemblers are also available through time-sharing services. The user of these services can, for a fee, take advantage of their mass storage and extensive software.

4.4 EXAMPLES OF ASSEMBLERS: THE INTEL 8080 AND MOTOROLA 6800

Intel 8080 and Motorola 6800 assemblers are available for development systems, time-sharing networks, and many large computers. Here we will discuss the standard cross-assemblers that are made available by Intel and Motorola. Other sources provide equivalent assemblers.

Field Structure

Each assembler uses the format shown in Fig. 4.4 in which each line has a label field, assembler operation code field, address field, and comment field. The label and comment fields are optional, although pseudo-operations like EQUATE (EQU) and MACRO must have labels since their function is to define the label. Both assemblers are free-form except that the Motorola assembler requires that labels start in column 1. The delimiters are

Intel 8080

1. A colon after a label except with the pseudo-operations EQU and MACRO; in these cases, the label is followed by a space.
2. A space after the entry in the operation code field.
3. Commas between operands in the address field.
4. A semicolon before a comment. The semicolon can also indicate an entire line of comments.

Motorola 6800

1. A space after a label.
2. A space after the accumulator designation in the operation code field. The designation is often added to the end of the operation code—for instance, ADDB, add to accumulator B.
3. A comma between the 8-bit offset and X for indexing—for instance, ADDB 5,X.
4. A space before a comment. An asterisk indicates an entire line of comments.

Typical Intel 8080 assembly language instructions are

```
EXTR:   ADI     30      ;   ADD OFFSET
        MVI     C,5
        RAR
```

Typical Motorola 6800 assembly language instructions are

```
EXTR    ADDA    #30     ADD OFFSET
        LDAB    #5
        RORA
```

Labels

Both assemblers allow a wide choice of labels. The Intel 8080 assembler permits five characters; the first character must be a letter, @, or ? and the label may not be one of the names reserved for registers, instruction codes, or pseudo-operations. The Motorola 6800 assembler allows six characters; the first one must be a letter and the label may not be A, B, or X, which are reserved for the accumulators and index register. Both assemblers forbid duplicate labels.

If the label is longer than the maximum allowed, the assembler will ignore the extra characters. In general, we try to avoid labels that will be truncated, could be illegal on other assemblers, are the same as instruction or pseudo-operation codes, or closely resemble other labels (such as INTI and INT1).[2] The easiest way to avoid mistakes is not to use confusing or ambiguous names. Examples of names that will be legal on almost any assembler are

```
LAST
SUM
DROP4
CHECK
ADD15
```

The assembler will discover erroneous or duplicated labels immediately; such errors are easy to correct if the programmer has chosen names sensibly.

Pseudo-operations

Table 4.4 contains a list of the pseudo-operations present in the Intel 8080 and Motorola 6800 assemblers. The only special features are the pseudo-operations that allow 8- or 16-bit data or addresses to be placed in program memory (DEFINE BYTE and DEFINE WORD on the Intel 8080, FORM CONSTANT BYTE and FORM DOUBLE CONSTANT BYTE on the Motorola 6800). The

---

[2] Note the obvious confusion between the letter O and number zero, letter I and number 1, and letter Z and number 2.

Motorola 6800 also has a pseudo-operation FORM CONSTANT CHARACTERS (FCC) that is specifically designed for entering ASCII characters into program memory.

Table 4.4   Intel 8080 and Motorola 6800 Pseudo-operations

Pseudo-operation Type	Intel 8080 Pseudo-operation	Motorola 6800 Pseudo-operation
DATA	DB—DEFINE BYTE (8-bit data)	FCB—FORM CONSTANT BYTE (8-bit data)
	DW—DEFINE WORD (16-bit data)	FDB—FORM DOUBLE CONSTANT BYTE (16-bit data)
		FCC—FORM CONSTANT CHARACTERS (ASCII data)
DEFINE	EQU SET (can be changed)	EQU
END	END	END
LIST		Many options
ORIGIN	ORG	ORG
PAGE		PAGE
RESERVE	DS—DEFINE STORAGE	RMB—RESERVE MEMORY BYTES
SPACE		SPACE

Typical pseudo-operations on the Intel 8080 are

```
        ORG   1000
FACT    EQU   35        (No colon after label.)
ZRO:    DB    0
EMESS:  DB    'ERROR'   (Quotation marks around ASCII characters.)
BUFR:   DS    100
```

The equivalent pseudo-operations on the Motorola 6800 are:

```
        ORG   1000
FACT    EQU   35        (Label must begin in column 1.)
ZRO     FCB   0
EMESS   FCC   /ERROR/   (Any identical delimiters can enclose
                         the ASCII characters.)
BUFR    RMB   100
```

Address Field

The address field in the Intel 8080 assembler may be empty if the instruction does not need any data or addresses like STC (set carry) or HLT (halt). Information in the address field can be specified in several ways.

1. Numerical data. May be hexadecimal, decimal, octal, or binary.
2. Using the current value of the program counter ($).
3. Character data (ASCII).
4. Names.
5. Arithmetic or logical expressions.

The assembler assumes that numbers are decimal unless otherwise specified. Hexadecimal, octal, and binary data must be followed by the appropriate letter (H for hexadecimal, O or Q for octal, B for binary). Hexadecimal numbers must begin with a decimal digit (0–9) to avoid confusion with names.

Typical examples of the use of numerical data are

1.

```
STRT:  MVI  C,16    ;  LOAD REGISTER C WITH 16
```

The assembler assumes 16 to be decimal, since it is unmarked.

2.

```
M1  EQU    0FFH
```

The name M1 (minus one) is defined as a hexadecimal number (note the leading zero to avoid confusion with the name FFH).

3.

```
INIT:  LXI  B,30DEH     ;  LOAD B AND C WITH 30DE
```

16-bit addresses or data are conveniently specified in hexadecimal notation.

4.

```
;  MASKS FOR REMOVING 4-BIT DIGITS
   MASKS:  DB      11110000B, 00001111B
```

Masks used to separate bit fields from words may be most clearly specified in binary notation.

We can use the address of the current instruction in the address field; it is designated by $ and the instruction

```
JMP  $ + 6
```

translates into a jump to the address located six words beyond the first word of the JMP instruction. We advise against this usage with the Intel 8080 because it has many instructions that require more than one word of program memory; the programmer can easily calculate the offset incorrectly and the actual value of the specified address may be difficult for a reader to determine. Since the Intel 8080 has no relative addressing, the method offers no time or memory savings; the programmer should use a label instead.

We can specify data to the Intel 8080 assembler as ASCII characters (7-bit characters with the most significant bit always zero).

Typical uses of ASCII characters are

1.

```
CPI    'E';  CHECK IF CHARACTER IS E
```

This instruction compares the contents of the accumulator to the ASCII character E (45 hex).

2.

```
;  ERROR MESSAGE IF DATA TOO LARGE
ERRM:  DB    'DATA TOO LARGE'
```

This message is stored as ASCII characters, starting at the word labeled ERRM.

We can use any name in the operand field. The programmer must be careful to distinguish between data and addresses. The following examples are typical.

1.

```
MASK   EQU    00001111B
       ANI    MASK  ;  REMOVE LEAST SIGNIFICANT 4 BITS
```

The name MASK is data.

2.

```
ALPH   EQU    5300H
       LDA    ALPH    ;  ALPH TO ACCUMULATOR
```

This instruction loads the accumulator with the contents of address ALPH (5300 hexadecimal).

3.

```
PNCH   EQU    5
       OUT    PNCH
```

This instruction uses the value of PNCH as an output device address.

The use of meaningful names for all input and output devices makes the program not only much clearer but also easier to change; a new device number requires the changing of a single definition instead of each of the many references.

The Intel 8080 assembler also allows arithmetic and logical functions in the address field with all types of data. All functions treat their arguments as 16-bit quantities and generate 16-bit results. The functions allowed are

+:	arithmetic sum
−:	arithmetic difference or negative
*:	arithmetic product
/:	arithmetic integer quotient
MOD:	integer remainder from division
NOT:	logical complement
AND:	bit-by-bit logical AND
OR:	bit-by-bit logical OR
XOR:	bit-by-bit logical EXCLUSIVE OR
SHL:	logical shift left
SHR:	logical shift right

Parentheses can establish the order of evaluation or make the meaning of an expression clearer. The most deeply parenthesized expressions are evaluated first. The normal order of evaluation is as follows (operators with the same precedence are evaluated left to right):

1. *, /, MOD, SHL, SHR
2. +, −
3. NOT
4. AND
5. OR, XOR

Thus the assembler performs multiplications and divisions before additions and subtractions and arithmetic functions before logical functions. Parentheses should be used to make the programmer's intent clearer; complex constructions should be avoided, since they are hard to understand and can lead to errors.

The programmer must ensure that expressions, when evaluated, result in a number within the range required by a particular instruction. Table 4.5 describes the requirements of the various instructions.

The Motorola 6800 assembler allows similar but simpler options in the address field. We can specify information in several ways.

1. Numerical data. May be binary, decimal, octal, or hexadecimal.
2. Using the current value of the program counter (*).
3. Character data (ASCII).
4. Names.
5. Arithmetic expressions.

Numerical constants are specified by

hexadecimal—$ before number
binary—% before number
octal—@ before number

Table 4.5 Operand Requirements of Intel 8080 Instructions

Instruction Code	Operand 1	Operand 2
ACI, ADI, ANI, CPI, ORI, SBI, SUI, XRI	8-bit data	
ADC, ADD, ANA, CMP, DCR, INR, ORA, SBB, SUB, XRA	Register	
CALL, CC, CM, CNC, CNZ, CP, CPE, CPO, CZ, JC, JM, JMP, JNC, JNZ, JP, JPE, JPO, JZ, LDA, LHLD, SHLD, STA	16-bit direct address	
CMA, CMC, DAA, DI, EI, HLT, NOP, PCHL, RAL, RAR, RC, RET, RLC, RM, RNC, RNZ, RP, RPE, RPO, RRC, RZ, SPHL, XCHG, XTHL	None	
DAD, DCX, INX, POP, PUSH	Register pair	
IN, OUT	8-bit device address	
LDAX, STAX	Register pair (B or D only)	
LXI	Register pair	16-bit data
MOV	Register	Register
MVI	Register	8-bit data
RST	3-bit address $(00 b_2 b_1 b_0 000)$	

The assembler assumes that numbers without special markings are decimal. Other special symbols are ' (an apostrophe) for 7-bit ASCII characters (most significant bit zero) and # for immediate addressing.

   The Motorola 6800 assembler will only handle arithmetic expressions involving the operators +, −, * (multiplication), and /. The assembler evaluates expressions from left to right; it uses neither precedence rules nor parentheses. The assembler truncates all fractional results. The Motorola 6800 assembler thus only allows simple arithmetic expressions; as noted, we seldom use more complicated expressions in any case.

Any expressions that are allowed in either assembler are evaluated during assembly and not during the execution of the program. For instance, the assemblers can perform multiplication and division even though neither the Motorola 6800 nor the Intel 8080 has specific instructions for these purposes.

Conditional Assembly

The Intel 8080 assembler allows conditional assembly using the pseudo-operations IF and ENDIF; the Motorola 6800 assembler does not. The IF pseudo-operation requires an expression constructed according to the rules just discussed. If the value of this expression at assembly time is not zero, the assembler will include the statements between the IF and ENDIF pseudo-operations in the program. If the value of the expression is zero, the statements are not included. Typical examples are

EXAMPLE 1: ONES OR TWOS COMPLEMENT

```
CMA
IF     TWOS
INR    A         ;ADD 1 FOR TWOS COMPLEMENT
ENDIF
```

If TWOS = 0, the assembler will only place the instruction CMA in the program, thus producing the one's complement. If TWOS ≠ 0, the assembler will include the additional instruction INR A, resulting in the calculation of the two's complement. The same assembly language program can provide either one's or two's complement arithmetic; the definition of TWOS prior to assembly selects the option.

EXAMPLE 2: 8- OR 16-BIT ADDITION

```
IF     L8   ; 8-BIT ADDITION
LDA    OP1
MOV    B, A
LDA    OP2
ADD    B
STA    RES
ENDIF
IF     L16  ; 16-BIT ADDITION
LHLD   OP1
XCHG
LHLD   OP2
DAD    D
SHLD   RES
ENDIF
```

This sequence allows us to select either 8- or 16-bit addition, depending on the definitions in the assembly language program. If L8 $\neq$ 0 and L16 = 0, the assembler includes the instructions that perform 8-bit addition; if L8 = 0 and L16 $\neq$ 0, the assembler includes the instructions that perform 16-bit addition.

We recommend that the programmer use conditional assembly sparingly. Its use makes programs difficult to read and debug. Separate programs for different cases is a better alternative than heavy reliance on conditional assembly. Conditional assembly may be a convenient way to include debugging features in early versions of programs.

Macros

The Intel 8080 assembler has macro capabilities while the Motorola 6800 assembler does not. We can use macros to clarify the meaning of instructions, to extend the instruction set, or to allow frequently used instruction sequences to be specified by a single statement. We must define each macro and give it a unique name. Macros may not include the definitions of other macros, nor may they refer to themselves; macros may, however, refer to other macros. The Intel 8080 assembler uses the pseudo-operations MACRO and ENDM for defining macros. Examples of macros are

EXAMPLE 1: Clear Accumulator and CARRY

```
CLR   MACRO
      SUB A
      ENDM
```

The instruction SUB A is a simple way to clear the accumulator and CARRY; the macro CLR makes the purpose of the instruction more obvious.

EXAMPLE 2: The NOR Function (complement of logical OR)

```
NOR   MACRO   REG
      ORA     REG
      CMA
      ENDM
```

The NOR macro requires an operand REG. Once we have defined this macro, we can use NOR just like the logical functions that are part of the Intel 8080 instruction set. For instance, NOR C forms the logical NOR of the accumulator and register C.

EXAMPLE 3: Indirect Addressing (LOAD ACCUMULATOR INDIRECT)

```
LIND    MACRO    ADDR
        LHLD     ADDR
        MOV      A, M
        ENDM
```

We can thus use a macro to implement indirect addressing on the Intel 8080.

The programmer should observe the rules below when using macros.

1. Each macro must have a unique name.
2. The macro definition must start with a MACRO pseudo-operation and end with an ENDM pseudo-operation.
3. Names defined within a macro are local to the macro and are not defined in the main program.
4. Macros may not contain the definitions of other macros.

Assembler Output

Both the Intel 8080 and Motorola 6800 assemblers produce paper tape output. The Intel 8080 assembler uses the so-called BNPF format. The symbols in this format have the following meaning.

B—beginning of 8-bit word
N—binary zero
P—binary one
F—ending of 8-bit word

This format is used to program Intel ROMs and PROMs.

Use of Assemblers

The Intel 8080 assembler is included with the Intellec 8/Mod 80 and the MDS development systems from Intel. Self-assemblers are also available with other Intel 8080 development systems from other manufacturers. FORTRAN versions of the cross-assembler are available from Intel and other sources for use on most computers that have FORTRAN. The cross-assembler is also available from the major time-sharing services.

The Motorola 6800 assembler is included with the Motorola Exorciser development system. In addition, it is available on other development systems, on time-sharing networks, and in suitable form for most computers that have a FORTRAN compiler.

4.5 SUMMARY

Programs can be written at various levels. Machine and assembly language do not require much software or hardware support and can produce very efficient programs. These languages, however, are machine-dependent and difficult and time-consuming for the programmer to use. High-level or procedure-oriented languages are not machine-dependent and are significantly easier to use but require a large amount of software and hardware support and usually produce inefficient programs. Most microprocessor-based systems are currently programmed in assembly language.

The basic function of the assembler is to translate mnemonic instruction codes into their binary equivalents. In addition, most assemblers provide other features, such as labeling, comments, assembly-time arithmetic, conditional assembly, and macros. Microprocessor designers generally use most of these features only in their simplest forms. Standard microprocessor assemblers are rather simple and do not provide many advanced features. They still require either another computer (cross-assembler) or a special development system (self-assembler).

PROBLEMS

1. Using Appendixes 6 and 7 for Intel 8080 and Motorola 6800 instruction codes, interpret the following binary numbers as Intel 8080 instructions, Motorola 6800 instructions, 8-bit unsigned numbers, and 8-bit two's complement numbers.
   (a) 11001001
   (b) 10000110
   (c) 01111110

2. Use Appendixes 6 and 7 to translate the Intel 8080 or Motorola 6800 instruction codes below into binary numbers.

Intel 8080	Motorola 6800
(a) RET	RTS
(b) ANA C	ANDA $40
(c) ADI 10	ADDA #10
(d) IN 5	STAA 50

3. A section of a program sets a variable RPLUS to the value of R plus 1. Write an Intel 8080 or Motorola 6800 assembly language program to perform this task. What entries would we need in the symbol table to translate this program to machine language? Assume that R is stored in memory location 50 (hex) and RPLUS in 60 (hex). Translate the program to machine language. Write a FORTRAN statement to perform the task.

4. A section of a program sets a variable MAXXY to the larger of the variables X and Y (assume that both are 8-bit unsigned numbers). Write an Intel 8080 or Motorola 6800 assembly language program to perform this task. What entries would we need in the symbol table to perform a hand assembly? Assume that X is stored in memory location

30 (hex), Y in 31 (hex), and MAXXY in 32 (hex). Translate the program to machine language. Write a FORTRAN program to perform the task.

5. Which of these labels would you use in a program? Discuss the reasons for your decision.
   (a) ADD ALL TOGETHER
   (b) ADD
   (c) LO0O0
   (d) EQU
   (e) O101
   (f) MUL8

6. What errors are present in the following assembly language statements (assuming a free-form assembler that requires a colon after a label)?
   (a) ADD
   (b) EQU   36
   (c) MOVE R1
   (d) LABL: 300

7. Describe the effects of the pseudo-operations shown.
   (a) ORIGIN 1300
   (b) LIMIT EQU 200
   (c) HBD2 EQU HBDTW
   (d) DTAB: RESERVE 100

8. A program uses memory location 0 as an entry point (it contains a jump to the start of the program), memory location 50 as an interrupt entry (it contains a jump to a service routine in memory location 3000), and memory locations 100 to 2000 for the main program. Show how you would organize this program using the ORG pseudo-operation. How would you add a trap routine in memory location 3500 that uses memory location 40 as an entry point? Does the order in which sections of the program appear in the assembly language version matter?

9. What pseudo-operations would you use to perform these tasks?
   (a) Place the message OUT OF ORDER in program memory.
   (b) Assign 20 memory locations for a page heading to be entered by the system user.
   (c) Start a program in memory location 6000.
   (d) Assign the name TOTAL to memory location 2000.
   (e) Place a table of sines in program memory.

10. Discuss whether you would use a subroutine or a macro for the tasks below.
    (a) An instruction sequence that performs a double-word two's complement (i.e., forms the two's complement of two successive words in memory).
    (b) An instruction sequence that finds the largest and smallest elements in an array.
    (c) An instruction sequence that performs a logical EXCLUSIVE NOR operation (EXCLUSIVE NOR is the complement of EXCLUSIVE OR).
    (d) An instruction sequence that calculates a logarithm from a series approximation.

11. What form would you use to enter the following quantities in the address field of an assembly language statement? Justify your answers.
    (a) The address 2A00 (hex)

(b) BCD 99

(c) The ASCII characters GO

(d) An 8-bit mask with a one in bit 5 and zeros elsewhere

(e) The number 10

(f) ASCII carriage return character (0D hex)

12. Explain the meaning of the following error messages in the lines to which they are attached.

(a) EQU 300 MISSING LABEL

(b) ADD   MISSING OPERAND FIELD

(c) RAND EQQ 500 UNDEFINED OPERATION CODE

(d) LOAD S + + 2 INVALID EXPRESSION

13. Which of the labels shown are valid in both the Intel 8080 and Motorola 6800 assemblers?

(a) 1100

(b) QQQ

(c) A

(d) RAN3

14. Write the pseudo-operations required to perform the following tasks in Intel 8080 and Motorola 6800 assembly language.

(a) Set the starting location of a program to 500.

(b) Assign the name TOP to memory location 3000.

(c) Place the table of values 1, 1, 2, 3, 5, 8, 13 in memory and assign the name FIB to the address of the first element.

(d) Establish a printer buffer consisting of 132 bytes of memory and assign the name PRBUF to the first location.

15. Explain the meaning of the following Intel 8080 pseudo-operations. What would the Motorola 6800 equivalents be?

(a) TPWRS: DB   1, 10, 100

(b) MAX   EQU   500

(c) JTAB: DW   ADDR, SUBR, MULR, DIVR

(d)   ORG   START

16. Explain how the Intel 8080 and Motorola 6800 assemblers determine which addressing method is being used. Describe where the addressing method field is located in Motorola 6800 instructions, such as ADD and SUBTRACT. How does the Motorola 6800 assembler use the accumulator code (A or B) at the end of an ADD or SUBTRACT instruction? (HINT: Compare the binary forms of the Motorola 6800 instructions for ADD DIRECT TO ACCUMULATOR A, ADD IMMEDIATE TO ACCUMULATOR A, etc.)

17. Write Intel 8080 macros to perform the following operations.

(a) LOGICAL SHIFT RIGHT ACCUMULATOR

(b) TWOS COMPLEMENT REGISTERS H AND L (16-BIT TWOS COMPLEMENT)

(c) SUBTRACT IN REVERSE; that is, SREV B subtracts the contents of the accumulator from the contents of register B. The result is placed in the accumulator.

(d) LOAD ACCUMULATOR INDEXED WITH B, that is load A from the address obtained by adding register pair B and register pair H.

18. A FORTRAN three-way IF statement IF (Y) 100, 200, 300 causes the program to transfer control to statement number 100 if $Y < 0$, to 200 if $Y = 0$, and to 300 if $Y > 0$. Assume that the statement numbers correspond to memory locations (i.e., statement number 100 is in memory location 100, etc.) and that Y is an 8-bit two's complement number stored in memory location 1250. Write an Intel 8080 or Motorola 6800 program that performs the same tasks as the FORTRAN IF statement.

19. Describe how a two-pass assembler handles forward references. Outline the steps involved. How could a one-pass assembler handle forward references? Would your solution work if the references involved assembly-time arithmetic—for instance, LAST-1, where LAST is a forward reference?

20. The Intel 8080 and Motorola 6800 both have instructions that range from one to three 8-bit words in length. Describe how this variation in instruction length affects the programmer doing hand assembly, using an assembler, or using a compiler. Discuss how the assembler could divide multiple-word operands into 8-bit sections.

REFERENCES

BARRON, D. W., *Assemblers and Loaders*, American Elsevier Inc., New York, 1972.

BLAKESLEE, T. R., *Digital Design with Standard MSI and LSI*, Wiley, New York, 1975.

BOND, J., "Designer's Guide to Software for the Hardware Designer, Part II," *EDN*, Vol. 20, No. 15, August 5, 1974, pp. 51–56.

CAMPBELL-KELLY, M., *An Introduction to Macros*, American Elsevier Inc., New York, 1973.

GEAR, C. W., *Computer Organization and Programming, 2nd ed.,* McGraw-Hill, New York, 1974.

GIBBONS, J., "When to Use Higher-Level Languages in Microcomputer-Based Systems," *Electronics*, Vol. 48, No. 16, August 7, 1975, pp. 107–111.

Intel 8080 Assembly Language Programming Manual, Intel Corporation, Santa Clara, Ca, 1974.

KNUTH, D. E., *The Art of Computer Programming: Fundamental Algorithms, Vol. 1*, Addison-Wesley, Reading, Ma., 1967.

KNUTH, D. E., *The Art of Computer Programming: Seminumerical Algorithms, Vol. 2*, Addison-Wesley, Reading, Ma., 1969.

Motorola 6800 Programming Manual, Motorola Semiconductor Products Inc., Phoenix, Az., 1974.

WEITZMAN, C., *Minicomputer Systems*, Prentice-Hall, Englewood Cliffs, N.J., 1974.

WYLAND, D. C., "Employ μP Software Tools Properly," *Electronic Design*, Vol. 23, No. 26, December 20, 1975, pp. 50–55.

5 Assembly Language Programming

This chapter concentrates on assembly language programming for the Intel 8080 and Motorola 6800. The general techniques, however, apply to other microprocessors with some differences caused by variations in addressing methods and instructions sets. The first section presents simple assembly language programs. Subsequent sections describe program loops and data arrays, arithmetic, character manipulation, and subroutines. The chapter includes detailed examples with assembly and machine language listings, flowcharts, and program traces.

All examples adhere to the following guidelines.

1. Intel 8080 or Motorola 6800 assembler notation as described in Chapter 4.

2. Hexadecimal notation for all instructions and addresses. Appendix 1 explains the hexadecimal number system; Appendixes 6 and 7 contain hexadecimal listings of the instruction sets of the Intel 8080 and Motorola 6800, respectively.

3. Various number systems for data according to which is the clearest. All nondecimal numbers are identified according to the rules of the assemblers. For the Intel 8080, H is hexadecimal and B binary; for the Motorola 6800, $ is hexadecimal and % binary.

4. A flowchart of each program that has conditional branches. The flowcharts use the standard symbols—that is,

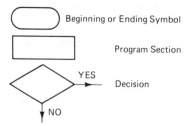

Beginning or Ending Symbol

Program Section

Decision

5. Traces of program execution. A trace follows the program through each instruction and shows the changes in registers and memory locations.

6. Comments as part of each assembly language program listing. The comments are more extensive than would generally be provided as documentation but use the normal style. Chapter 6 discusses commenting and other forms of documentation.

The Intel 8080 assembler requires a semicolon before each comment; the Motorola 6800 assembler requires a space before each comment that is on the same line as an instruction and an asterisk at the start of an entire line of comments.

7. Stress on program clarity over speed and efficient use of memory; the programs are reasonably efficient but do not use methods designed to minimize execution time and memory usage at any cost. Chapter 6 considers the tradeoffs involved here.

8. Emphasis on common microprocessor tasks and widely used instructions.

9. Consideration only of the most widely used flags—CARRY, SIGN, AND ZERO on the Intel 8080; CARRY, NEGATIVE, and ZERO on the Motorola 6800. The other flags—PARITY and AUXILIARY CARRY on the Intel 8080, OVERFLOW and HALF-CARRY on the Motorola 6800—are discussed only when actually used in a program.

10. Standard memory assignments so that all short programs start in memory location 0 and use memory locations starting with 40 (hexadecimal) for data. These programs will therefore execute on almost any microcomputer if the reader establishes consistent corresponding addresses.

11. A halt or trap instruction at the end of all programs, HLT (HALT) for the Intel 8080 and SWI (SOFTWARE INTERRUPT) for the Motorola 6800.

12. Use of standard clock rates for timing purposes—1 MHz for the Motorola 6800, 2 MHz for the Intel 8080. Instruction execution times may therefore be given in microseconds.

5.1 SIMPLE PROGRAMS

EXAMPLE 1: 8-Bit Addition

Perhaps the simplest program we can imagine is one that adds two numbers. For instance, assume that we want to add the contents of memory locations 40 and 41 (hexadecimal) and place the result in memory location 42 (hexadecimal). For the present, simply ignore the carry.

On most computers the addition requires several steps.

Step 1. LOAD ACCUMULATOR FROM MEMORY LOCATION 40 (HEX)
Step 2. ADD CONTENTS OF MEMORY LOCATION 41 (HEX)
Step 3. STORE ACCUMULATOR IN MEMORY LOCATION 42 (HEX)

So this simple task involves at least three instructions.

MOTOROLA 6800—Example 1

The Motorola 6800 addition program follows these steps closely.

M6800 EXAMPLE 1
ADDITION OF TWO NUMBERS

```
LDAA   $40    GET OPERAND 1
ADDA   $41    ADD OPERAND 2
STAA   $42    STORE RESULT
SWI
```

A step-by-step examination of this program shows

1. LDAA $40

This instruction loads accumulator A with the contents of memory location 40. Since memory location 40 is on page zero (i.e., the address is less than 100 hex), we can use the direct form of the instruction (96 hex), which requires two words of program memory and three clock cycles (or 3 μs with the Motorola 6800 standard 1 MHz clock).

2. ADDA $41

This instruction adds the contents of memory location 41 to the contents of accumulator A. The direct form of the instruction (9B hex) requires two words of program memory and 3 μs.

3. STAA $42

This instruction stores the contents of accumulator A in memory location 42. The direct form (97 hex) requires two words of program memory and 3 μs.

4. SWI

This instruction ends all the Motorola 6800 examples.

We can assemble the program by hand (see Fig. 5.1), using the Motorola 6800 instruction code tables in Appendix 7. Figure 5.2 traces the execution of the program, assuming as initial conditions that the number 5 is in memory location 40, 3 in memory location 41, and 0 in the program counter. Note particularly the effects of each instruction on the program counter and flags. Each of the first three instructions requires two words of program memory, one for the instruction and one for the 8-bit address on page zero.

Figure 5.1 Assembled Motorola 6800 addition program.

Memory Address (hexadecimal)	Instruction (mnemonic)	Memory Contents (hexadecimal)
00	LDAA $40	96
01		40
02	ADAA $41	9B
03		41
04	STAA $42	97
05		42
06	SWI	3F

Figure 5.2 Trace of Motorola 6800 addition program.

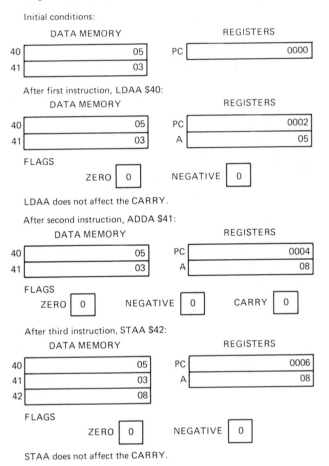

Initial conditions:

DATA MEMORY   REGISTERS

40 | 05   PC | 0000
41 | 03

After first instruction, LDAA $40:

DATA MEMORY   REGISTERS

40 | 05   PC | 0002
41 | 03   A | 05

FLAGS
ZERO | 0   NEGATIVE | 0

LDAA does not affect the CARRY.

After second instruction, ADDA $41:

DATA MEMORY   REGISTERS

40 | 05   PC | 0004
41 | 03   A | 08

FLAGS
ZERO | 0   NEGATIVE | 0   CARRY | 0

After third instruction, STAA $42:

DATA MEMORY   REGISTERS

40 | 05   PC | 0006
41 | 03   A | 08
42 | 08

FLAGS
ZERO | 0   NEGATIVE | 0

STAA does not affect the CARRY.

INTEL 8080—Example 1

The Intel 8080 addition program is more complicated because the Intel 8080 cannot perform an addition with direct addressing. An extra instruction thus must move one operand to a general-purpose register. The addition instruction can then use register direct addressing. The next example will show the use of register indirect addressing to overcome this deficiency. The steps in the present case are

```
INTEL 8080 EXAMPLE 1
ADDITION OF TWO NUMBERS

LDA     40H        ;GET OPERAND 1
MOV     B,A
```

```
LDA     41H     ;GET OPERAND 2
ADD     B       ;ADD OPERANDS
STA     42H     ;STORE RESULT
HLT
```

The program takes five instructions on the Intel 8080 compared to three on the Motorola 6800. In fact, the Intel 8080 is better at handling large amounts of data than single items. The reason is that register direct and register indirect addressing are only efficient when the program uses the register contents many times.

Let us examine the Intel 8080 program step by step (ignoring repetitive instructions).

1. LDA   40H

This instruction loads the accumulator with the contents of memory location 40. Since the Intel 8080 does not have page-zero addressing, the instruction needs a complete 16-bit address. LDA requires three words of program memory and 13 clock cycles (or 6.5 μs with the Intel 8080 standard 2 MHz clock).

2. MOV   B,A

This instruction loads register B with the contents of the accumulator. MOV B,A requires one word of program memory and 2.5 μs.

3. ADD B

This instruction adds the contents of register B to the contents of the accumulator. The instruction requires one word of program memory and 2 μs.

4. STA 42H

This instruction stores the contents of the accumulator in memory location 42. The instruction requires three words of program memory and 6.5 μs.

5. HLT

This instruction marks the end of all the Intel 8080 examples.

We can assemble the program by hand (see Fig. 5.3), using the Intel 8080 instruction code tables in Appendix 6. A trace of the program execution is in Fig. 5.4. The trace assumes the same starting conditions as before—(40) = 5, (41) = 3, (PC) = 0. Note only the ADD instruction affects the flags on the Intel 8080; note also that the program counter increases in varied steps because of the varied word lengths of the instructions.

LDA and STA both need a 16-bit direct address. The Intel 8080 stores 16-bit addresses with the eight least significant bits in the first word (lower address) and the eight most significant bits in the second word (higher address); this method is contrary to the practice on the Motorola 6800 and almost all other computers.

EXAMPLE 2: Separating out a Hexadecimal Digit

A common problem with any computer is handling data that is not the same length as the computer word. The computer always processes a word or a byte at a time. But what if the data is shorter? One, two, or four bits can represent the state of a switch, display, keyboard, relay, or motor. On the other hand, what if the data is much longer than a single word? Many bits may be needed to represent a number with

Figure 5.3 Assembled Intel 8080 addition program.

Memory Address (hexadecimal)	Instruction (mnemonic)		Memory Contents (hexadecimal)
00	LDA	40H	3A
01			40
02			00
03	MOV	B,A	47
04	LDA	41H	3A
05			41
06			00
07	ADD	B	80
08	STA	42H	32
09			42
0A			00
0B	HLT		76

Figure 5.4 Trace of Intel 8080 addition program.

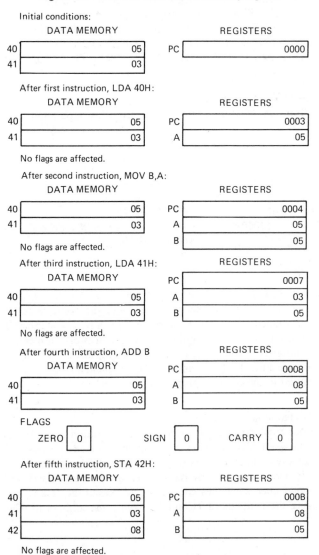

several decimal places, a control message, or an entire set of switches or displays. Let us deal with the smaller problem first and consider the larger problem in the next section.

In order to process short data fields, the program must clear the unused bits in the computer word so that they do not affect the operations. The logical AND instruction can perform the clearing. For instance, assume that we only want the four least significant bits (least significant hexadecimal digit) of a data word. The program will take the contents of memory location 40 (hex), separate out the four least significant bits, and store them in memory location 41 (hex). The separation proceeds as follows.

Step 1.   LOAD ACCUMULATOR FROM MEMORY LOCATION 40 (HEX)
Step 2.   LOGICALLY AND ACCUMULATOR WITH 00001111 (BINARY)
           The result will have the same four least significant bits as the original data (since 0 AND 1 = 0 and 1 AND 1 = 1), but its four most significant bits will all be zero (since 0 AND 0 = 0 and 1 AND 0 = 0).
Step 3.   STORE ACCUMULATOR IN MEMORY LOCATION 41 (HEX)

MOTOROLA 6800—Example 2

The Motorola 6800 program to perform this separation consists of three instructions:

```
M6800 EXAMPLE 2
SEPARATING OUT A HEXADECIMAL DIGIT

LDAA    $40             GET OPERAND
ANDA    #%00001111      MASK OFF FOUR MOST SIGNIFICANT BITS
STAA    $41             STORE RESULT
SWI
```

The only new instruction in this program is ANDA #%00001111, which logically ANDs the binary number 00001111 with the contents of accumulator A. Note the # for immediate addressing and the % for a binary number. The immediate form of the instruction (84 hex) requires two words of program memory and 2 μs.

The assembled version of the program is shown in Fig. 5.5 and the trace in Fig. 5.6. The trace assumes 87 (hex) as the data in memory location 40. Clearly this program is similar to the addition program of Example 1.

INTEL 8080—Example 2

The Intel 8080 program to perform the separation uses the register indirect feature that the assembler identifies with register code M. The programmer can use register M like any other register; however, the Intel 8080 obtains the actual data from the memory location addressed by registers H and L. Registers H and L serve as a *memory* or *data pointer*, since they contain the address of the data rather than the data itself. Changing the contents of H and L changes the address to which the pointer

Memory Address (hexadecimal)	Instruction (mnemonic)	Memory Contents (hexadecimal)
00	LDAA $40	96
01		40
02	ANDA #%00001111	84
03		0F
04	STAA $41	97
05		41
06	SWI	3F

Figure 5.6 Trace of Motorola 6800 hexadecimal digit separation program.

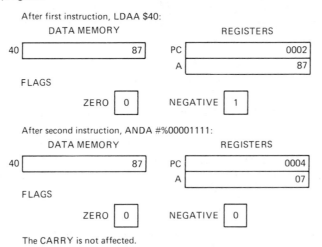

After first instruction, LDAA $40:

After second instruction, ANDA #%00001111:

The CARRY is not affected.

refers. For instance, the instruction INX H causes the pointer to refer to the next higher memory address. Of course, an instruction (often LXI) must load H and L before the program can use register indirect addressing. The digit separation program is

INTEL 8080 EXAMPLE 2
SEPARATING OUT A HEXADECIMAL DIGIT

```
LXI    H,40H
MOV    A,M              ;GET DATA
ANI    00001111B        ;MASK OFF FOUR MOST SIGNIFICANT BITS
INX    H
MOV    M,A              ;STORE RESULT
HLT
```

Here again the program needs five instructions compared to three on the Motorola 6800. Register indirect addressing is not advantageous unless the program is processing an entire array of data.

Let us examine the program step by step.

1. LXI   H,40H

This instruction loads the register pair (in this case, H and L) with the contents of the next two locations in program memory. The word immediately following the operation code goes into register L and the next word into register H. The instruction requires three words of program memory and 5 μs. Note that this instruction places a 16-bit address (0040) in H and L.

2. MOV A,M

This instruction loads the accumulator with the contents of the memory location addressed by registers H and L. The instruction requires one word of program memory and 3.5 μs.

3. ANI   00001111B

This instruction logically ANDs the binary number 00001111 with the contents of the accumulator. The instruction requires two words of program memory and 3.5 μs.

4. INX H

This instruction adds one to the 16-bit address in registers H and L. The instruction requires one word of program memory and 2.5 μs.

5. MOV M,A

The opposite of MOV A,M.

The assembled version of this program appears in Fig. 5.7; the trace of the program execution is in Fig. 5.8. We have used the same starting conditions as for the Motorola 6800—(40) = 87, (PC) = 0. Note particularly how the instructions that use register indirect addressing (MOV A,M and MOV M,A) work. These instructions are preferable to LDA and STA whenever data is stored in successive memory locations because they require less time and memory. Note also that only the ANI instruction affects the flags; INX does not. This program is much shorter than the one in Fig. 5.3., which did not use register indirect addressing.

Figure 5.7   Assembled Intel 8080 hexadecimal digit separation program.

Memory Address (hexadecimal)	Instruction (mnemonic)		Memory Contents (hexadecimal)
00	LXI	H,40H	21
01			40
02			00
03	MOV	A,M	7E
04	ANI	00001111B	E6
05			0F
06	INX	H	23
07	MOV	M,A	77
08	HLT		76

Figure 5.8 Trace of Intel 8080 hexadecimal digit separation program.

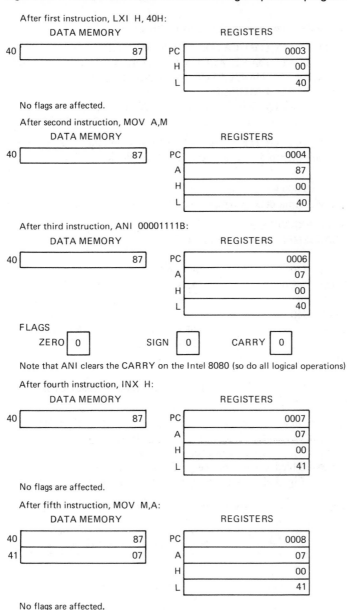

After first instruction, LXI H, 40H:

DATA MEMORY   REGISTERS

40 [87]   PC [0003]
                               H [00]
                               L [40]

No flags are affected.

After second instruction, MOV A,M

DATA MEMORY   REGISTERS

40 [87]   PC [0004]
                               A [87]
                               H [00]
                               L [40]

After third instruction, ANI 00001111B:

DATA MEMORY   REGISTERS

40 [87]   PC [0006]
                               A [07]
                               H [00]
                               L [40]

FLAGS
    ZERO [0]   SIGN [0]   CARRY [0]

Note that ANI clears the CARRY on the Intel 8080 (so do all logical operations)

After fourth instruction, INX H:

DATA MEMORY   REGISTERS

40 [87]   PC [0007]
                               A [07]
                               H [00]
                               L [41]

No flags are affected.

After fifth instruction, MOV M,A:

DATA MEMORY   REGISTERS

40 [87]   PC [0008]
41 [07]   A [07]
                               H [00]
                               L [41]

No flags are affected.

EXAMPLE 3: Disassembly of a Word

Example 2 can be extended to remove both hexadecimal digits from the original word and place them in separate memory locations. The new program places the four least significant bits in memory location 41 as before and the four most significant bits in memory location 42. The program moves the four most significant bits to the four least significant bit positions in memory location 42 so that they can be processed later

175

as ordinary data. The steps in the disassembly are

Step 1. LOAD ACCUMULATOR FROM MEMORY LOCATION 40 (HEX)
Step 2. LOGICALLY AND ACCUMULATOR WITH 00001111 (BINARY)
Step 3. STORE ACCUMULATOR IN MEMORY LOCATION 41 (HEX)
Step 4. LOAD ACCUMULATOR FROM MEMORY LOCATION 40 (HEX)
Step 5. LOGICALLY SHIFT ACCUMULATOR RIGHT FOUR BITS
Step 6. STORE ACCUMULATOR IN MEMORY LOCATION 42 (HEX)

LOGICAL SHIFT RIGHT clears the four most significant bits of the accumulator as well as shifting their old values to the four least significant bits.

MOTOROLA 6800—Example 3

The Motorola 6800 program to perform the disassembly is

```
M6800 EXAMPLE 3
DISASSEMBLY OF A WORD


LDAA   $40              GET DATA
ANDA   #%00001111       MASK OFF MOST SIGNIFICANT DIGIT
STAA   $41              STORE LEAST SIGNIFICANT DIGIT
LDAA   $40
LSRA                    SHIFT MOST SIGNIFICANT DIGIT
LSRA                       RIGHT 4 TIMES
LSRA
LSRA
STAA   $42              SAVE MOST SIGNIFICANT DIGIT
SWI
```

The only new instruction in this program is LSRA, which shifts the contents of accumulator A right one bit logically—that is, clearing the most significant bit. LSRA requires one word of program memory and 2 μs.

The assembled version of the program appears in Fig. 5.9 and a trace of one logical shift in Fig. 5.10. Try to trace the rest of the execution by hand.

Figure 5.9 Assembled Motorola 6800 word disassembly program.

Memory Address (hexadecimal)	Instruction (mnemonic)	Memory Contents (hexadecimal)
00	LDAA $40	96
01		40
02	ANDA #%00001111	84
03		0F
04	STAA $41	97
05		41
06	LDAA $40	96
07		40
08	LSRA	44
09	LSRA	44
0A	LSRA	44
0B	LSRA	44
0C	STAA $42	97
0D		42
0E	SWI	3F

Figure 5.10 Trace of Motorola 6800 word disassembly program.

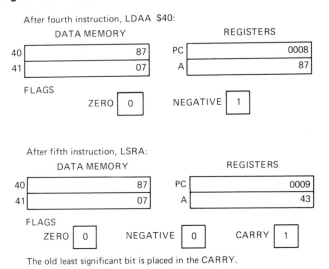

After fourth instruction, LDAA $40:

DATA MEMORY   REGISTERS

40 | 87   PC | 0008
41 | 07   A | 87

FLAGS

ZERO | 0   NEGATIVE | 1

After fifth instruction, LSRA:

DATA MEMORY   REGISTERS

40 | 87   PC | 0009
41 | 07   A | 43

FLAGS

ZERO | 0   NEGATIVE | 0   CARRY | 1

The old least significant bit is placed in the CARRY.

INTEL 8080—Example 3

The Intel 8080 disassembly program is somewhat longer than the Motorola 6800 program, since the Intel 8080 has no LOGICAL SHIFT RIGHT instruction. The Intel 8080 can, however, produce the required operation (a 4-bit LOGICAL SHIFT RIGHT) by four ROTATE RIGHT instructions followed by a logical AND that masks off the most significant digit. The program saves a copy of the data in general-purpose register B. So we can reload the accumulator from the register instead of from memory. The program is

INTEL 8080 EXAMPLE 3
DISASSEMBLY OF A WORD

```
LXI    H,40H
MOV    A,M         ;GET DATA
MOV    B,A         ;SAVE COPY OF DATA
ANI    00001111B   ;MASK OFF MOST SIGNIFICANT DIGIT
INX    H
MOV    M,A         ;STORE LEAST SIGNIFICANT DIGIT
MOV    A,B
RRC                ;SHIFT MOST SIGNIFICANT DIGIT
RRC                ;   RIGHT 4 TIMES
RRC
RRC
ANI    00001111B   ;MASK OFF LEAST SIGNIFICANT DIGIT
INX    H
MOV    M,A         ;STORE MOST SIGNIFICANT DIGIT
HLT
```

The only new instruction in the program is RRC, which shifts the accumulator right circularly one bit. It requires one word of program memory and 2 μs. Note that MOV A,B places the contents of register B in the accumulator, whereas MOV B,A is the opposite transfer. Register-to-register transfers require one word of program memory and 2.5 μs.

The assembled version of this program is shown in Fig. 5.11 and a trace of the execution of the first shift in Fig. 5.12. The starting conditions of the trace are somewhat different than the final conditions of Fig. 5.8 because of the MOV B,A instruction, which saves a copy of the data. Note the rather large number of single-word instructions; also note that the shift instructions on the Intel 8080 only affect the CARRY flag.

Figure 5.11   Assembled Intel 8080 word disassembly program.

Memory Address (hexadecimal)	Instruction (mnemonic)		Memory Contents (hexadecimal)
00	LXI	H,40H	21
01			40
02			00
03	MOV	A,M	7E
04	MOV	B,A	47
05	ANI	00001111B	E6
06			0F
07	INX	H	23
08	MOV	M,A	77
09	MOV	A,B	78
0A	RRC		0F
0B	RRC		0F
0C	RRC		0F
0D	RRC		0F
0E	ANI	00001111B	E6
0F			0F
10	INX	H	23
11	MOV	M,A	77
12	HLT		76

Figure 5.12   Trace of Intel 8080 word disassembly program.

After seventh instruction, MOV A,B:

DATA MEMORY   REGISTERS

40	87	PC	000A
41	07	A	87
		B	87
		H	00
		L	41

After eighth instruction, RRC:

DATA MEMORY   REGISTERS

40	87	PC	000B
41	07	A	C3
		B	87
		H	00
		L	41

FLAG

CARRY | 1 |

These simple examples emphasize the following features of assembly language programming.

1. Almost all the actual processing of data takes place in accumulators. The program starts by loading the accumulator with data from memory and ends by storing the result in the accumulator back into memory.

2. The programmer tries to have the CPU perform as few memory accesses as possible. You can reduce the number of memory accesses by using page-zero or register indirect addressing (thus allowing shorter instructions) and by saving data in general-purpose registers.

3. You must carefully watch the effects of instructions on flag bits. These effects vary greatly from instruction to instruction and from processor to processor.

4. The logical AND instruction can clear parts of a word so as to process data that is shorter than the word length of the computer.

5. Shift instructions can move data to other bit positions for simple processing or efficient storage.

5.2 LOOPS AND ARRAYS

Of course, real computer applications do not involve a single piece of data and a single operation. Instead they involve either many data items (i.e., an *array* or *block* of data) or single items that occupy several computer words. The program must perform the same operations on each word or item. Program loops repeat a set of instructions, counters keep track of the number of repetitions, and pointers or indexes describe the particular data items used during a repetition.

EXAMPLE 4: Sum of Data

The problem is to add a whole series of numbers. These numbers might represent the number of inputs of a particular type that a system must monitor, the number of items sold in a transaction, the number of points scored in a game, or the number of messages received during an interval. Assume that the total length of the series is in memory location 41 and that the series itself starts in memory location 42. Assume also that the sum is less than 256 so that it will fit in an 8-bit word in memory location 40.

A typical situation

$$(41) = 03$$

$$(42) = 35$$

$$(43) = 72$$

$$(44) = 1D$$

The series contains three numbers, since the contents of memory location 41 is 3. The sum is (42) + (43) + (44) = 35 + 72 + 1D = C4 (the numbers are all hexadecimal). So the result is

$$(40) = C4$$

The steps involved in adding the numbers are

Step 1.

```
COUNT = (41)
SUM   = 0
POINTER = 42
```

Step 2.

```
SUM = SUM + (POINTER)
```

Step 3.

```
COUNT = COUNT − 1
POINTER = POINTER + 1
```

Step 4.

```
IF COUNT = 0 GO TO STEP 2
```

Step 5.

```
(41) = SUM
```

The flowchart (Fig. 5.13) shows that the program has four distinct sections.

1. An initialization section that sets variables, counters, and data pointers to their starting values. Pointers contain the addresses of the data.
2. A processing section that performs the actual task.
3. A loop control section that updates counters and pointers for the next iteration and checks to see if the loop has been performed the proper number of times.
4. A concluding section that stores the result.

Section 2 actually does the addition. The other sections are, however, essential to ensure that Section 2 handles the task correctly. Figure 5.14 is a general flowchart of the sections. Sections 1 and 4 are performed only once; so most of the computer time is spent in Sections 2 and 3. The program will run appreciably faster only if the programmer can make Sections 2 and 3 execute faster; Sections 1 and 4 have little effect on program execution time.

Figure 5.13 Flowchart of sum of data program.

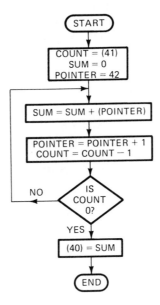

Figure 5.14 Flowchart of a typical program loop.

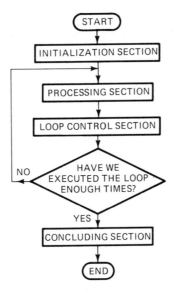

MOTOROLA 6800—Example 4

The Motorola 6800 program to add a series of numbers uses both accumulators and the index register. Accumulator A contains the sum, accumulator B the counter, and the index register the data pointer—that is, the address of the element that is being added to the sum.

```
M6800 EXAMPLE 4
SUM OF DATA

        CLRA                SUM = 0
        LDAB  $41           COUNT = LENGTH OF ARRAY
        LDX   $42           POINT TO START OF ARRAY
SUMD    ADDA  X             SUM = SUM + ELEMENT FROM ARRAY
        INX
        DECB
        BNE   SUMD
        STAA  $40           STORE SUM
        SWI
```

The new instructions in this program are

CLRA

This instruction clears accumulator A. It requires one word of program memory and 2 μs.

LDX   #$42

This instruction loads the 16-bit index register from the next two words of program memory. The eight most significant bits are in the first word and the eight least significant bits in the second word (the standard practice but opposite to the method used by Intel). The instruction requires three words of program memory and 3 μs.

ADDA   X (or 0,X)

This instruction adds the contents of the memory location addressed by the index register to the contents of the accumulator. The zero offset may be omitted from the assembly language program; the effective address is zero plus the contents of the index register. The instruction requires two words of program memory and 5 μs; the CPU needs extra time to perform the 16-bit addition of offset and index register even though the offset is zero.

INX

This instruction adds 1 to the contents of the 16-bit index (or X) register. It requires one word of program memory and 5 μs. INX increments the data pointer so that it contains the next higher address.

DECB

This instruction subtracts one from the contents of accumulator B. It requires one word of program memory and 2 μs. Accumulator B contains the number of iterations remaining.

BNE SUMD

This instruction causes a branch to the program memory location labeled SUMD if the ZERO flag is zero. The instruction uses relative addressing; the 8-bit offset is a two's complement number that represents the distance from the memory location immediately following the BRANCH instruction to the target location. BNE requires two words of program memory and 4 μs; as with indexing, the CPU uses the extra time to perform the 16-bit addition of offset and program counter. Note that if the ZERO flag is one, the CPU executes the next sequential instruction. The effect of BNE is

(PC) = SUMD if ZERO = 0
(PC) = (PC) + 2 if ZERO = 1

The assembled version of this program appears in Fig. 5.15. The new features are

1. The two words of program memory used to load the index register (00 and 42 in memory locations 4 and 5).
2. The indexed instruction code and the zero offset used with the ADDA X instruction in memory locations 6 and 7.
3. The relative offset used with the BNE instruction in memory locations A and B. We can calculate the offset by subtracting the address of the word of program memory immediately following the BRANCH instruction from the target address—that is,

$$\begin{array}{r} 06 = 06 \\ -0C +F4 \\ \hline \overline{FA} \end{array}$$

Figure 5.15 Assembled Motorola 6800 sum of data program.

Memory Address (hexadecimal)	Instruction (mnemonic)		Memory Contents (hexadecimal)
00		CLRA	4F
01		LDAB $41	D6
02			41
03		LDX #$42	CE
04			00
05			42
06	SUMD	ADDA X	AB
07			00
08		INX	08
09		DECB	5A
0A		BNE SUMD	26
0B			FA
0C		STAA $40	97
0D			40
0E		SWI	3F

Hexadecimal subtraction involves first calculating the two's complement of the number to be subtracted and then adding.

Figure 5.16 contains a partial trace of one iteration of the program, using the sample data from the typical situation. Note the effects of the indexed and relative addressing.

Figure 5.16　Trace of Motorola 6800 sum of data program.

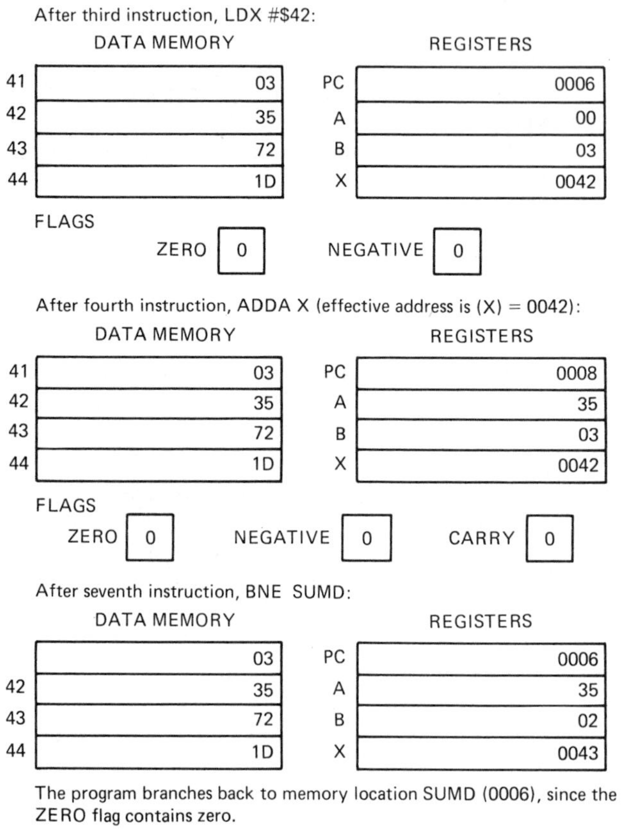

After third instruction, LDX #$42:

DATA MEMORY		REGISTERS	
41	03	PC	0006
42	35	A	00
43	72	B	03
44	1D	X	0042

FLAGS

ZERO 0　　　NEGATIVE 0

After fourth instruction, ADDA X (effective address is (X) = 0042):

DATA MEMORY		REGISTERS	
41	03	PC	0008
42	35	A	35
43	72	B	03
44	1D	X	0042

FLAGS

ZERO 0　　NEGATIVE 0　　CARRY 0

After seventh instruction, BNE SUMD:

DATA MEMORY		REGISTERS	
	03	PC	0006
42	35	A	35
43	72	B	02
44	1D	X	0043

The program branches back to memory location SUMD (0006), since the ZERO flag contains zero.

INTEL 8080—Example 4

The Intel 8080 program to add a series of numbers uses a general-purpose register as a counter and registers H and L as the data pointer.

```
INTEL 8080 EXAMPLE 4
SUM OF DATA

SUB    A        ;SUM = 0
LXI    H,41H    ;COUNT = LENGTH OF ARRAY
```

```
        MOV    B,M
SUMD:   INX    H
        ADD    M        ;SUM = SUM + DATA
        DCR    B
        JNZ    SUMD
        STA    40H      ;STORE  SUM
        HLT
```

The new instructions in this program are

SUB   A

This instruction clears the accumulator by subtracting it from itself. It requires one word of program memory and 2 μs.

ADD   M

This instruction adds the contents of the memory location addressed by registers H and L to the contents of the accumulator. It requires one word of program memory and 3.5 μs.

DCR   B

This instruction subtracts one from the contents of register B. It requires one word of program memory and 2.5 μs.

JNZ   SUMD

This instruction causes a jump to memory location SUMD if the ZERO flag is zero. It uses a 16-bit direct address with the eight least significant bits in the word immediately following the instruction and the eight most significant bits in the next word. JNZ requires three words of program memory and 5 μs.

Figure 5.17 shows an assembled version of this program; a partial trace of one iteration is in Fig. 5.18. Note particularly the use of register indirect addressing in the instructions MOV B,M and ADD M.

The Intel 8080 and Motorola 6800 programs are very similar. They require the same amount of memory, since this task uses register indirect addressing more effectively than the simple tasks. In fact, the Intel 8080 program is somewhat faster (see the time budget in Fig. 5.19) because it need not perform the 16-bit additions required by the relative and indexed addressing on the Motorola 6800.

Figure 5.17 Assembled Intel 8080 sum of data program.

Memory Address (hexadecimal)		Instruction (mnemonic)		Memory Contents (hexadecimal)
00		SUB	A	97
01		LXI	H,41H	21
02				41
03				00
04		MOV	B,M	46
05	SUMD:	INX	H	23
06		ADD	M	86
07		DCR	B	05
08		JNZ	SUMD	C2
09				05
0A				00
0B		STA	40H	32
0C				40
0D				00
0E		HLT		76

Figure 5.18 Trace of Intel 8080 sum of data program.

After third instruction, MOV B,M:

DATA MEMORY		REGISTERS	
41	03	PC	0005
42	35	A	00
43	72	B	03
44	1D	H	00
		L	41

Effective address = (H and L) = 0041
After fifth instruction, ADD M:

DATA MEMORY		REGISTERS	
41	03	PC	0007
42	35	A	35
43	72	B	03
44	1D	H	00
		L	42

Effective address = (H and L) = 0042

FLAGS
ZERO [0] SIGN [0] CARRY [0]

After seventh instruction, JNZ SUMD:

DATA MEMORY		REGISTERS	
41	03	PC	0005
42	35	A	35
43	72	B	02
44	1D	H	00
		L	42

The program branches back to memory location SUMD (0005), since the ZERO flag contains zero.

Figure 5.19 A comparative time budget.

Part 1. Initialization

Intel 8080 Instruction	Execution Time (μs)	Motorola 6800 Instruction	Execution Time (μs)
SUB A	2	CLRA	2
LXI H,41H	5	LDAB $41	3
MOV B,M	2½	LDX #$42	3
Total	9½		8

Part 2. Program loop

Intel 8080 Instruction	Execution Time (μs)	Motorola 6800 Instruction	Execution Time (μs)
INX H	2½	ADDA X	5
ADD M	3½	INX	4
DCR B	2½	DECB	2
JNZ SUMD	5	BNE SUMD	4
Total	13½		15

Part 3. Concluding section

Intel 8080 Instruction	Execution Time (μs)	Motorola 6800 Instruction	Execution Time (μs)
STA 40H	6½	STAA $40	3
Total	6½		3

EXAMPLE 5: Data Transfer

The task here is to move an array of data from one place in memory to another. We may be initializing an array, moving data to or from an area of memory used for input or output, or selecting a line for display on a CRT. Assume that the length of the data array is in memory location 40, the data originally starts in memory location 41, and the destination area for the data starts in memory location 51.

A typical situation

$$(40) = 02$$

$$(41) = 7E$$

$$(42) = 55$$

The array contains two elements in memory locations 41 and 42. The result is

$$(51) = 7E$$

$$(52) = 55$$

The contents of memory location 41 have been moved to location 51 and the contents of 42 to 52.

Figure 5.20 contains a flowchart of the required program. This program has no concluding section but does have initialization, processing, and loop control sections. Two data pointers are necessary; one contains the address of the source of the data and the other the address of the destination. However, the two addresses are always a constant distance apart so that a single index can describe both.

Figure 5.20 Flowchart of data transfer program.

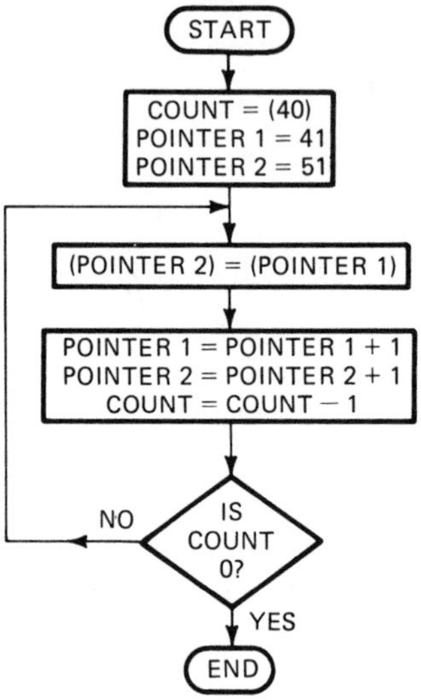

MOTOROLA 6800—Example 5

In the Motorola 6800 program the constant distance between the source and destination addresses is the offset in an indexed instruction. We can thus access both arrays with a single index register. However, the arrays must be less than 256 memory locations apart, since the offset is only eight bits long. The program is

```
MOTOROLA 6800 EXAMPLE 5
DATA TRANSFER

        LDX    #$41          POINT TO START OF ARRAY
        LDAB   $40           COUNT = LENGTH OF ARRAYS
TRANS   LDAA   X             GET DATA FROM SOURCE
        STAA   $10,X         MOVE DATA TO DESTINATION
        INX
        DECB
        BNE    TRANS
        SWI
```

The only new feature in this program is the use of indexed addressing with an offset. The effective address for the instruction STAA $10,X is 10 (hex) plus the contents of the index register. Note that 10 appears in the word immediately following the STAA instruction in the assembled program in Fig. 5.21. A trace of one iteration of the transfer instructions is in Fig. 5.22; the data is the sample case.

Figure 5.21 Assembled Motorola 6800 data transfer program.

Memory Address (hexadecimal)		Instruction (mnemonic)	Memory Contents (hexadecimal)
00		LDX #$41	CE
01			00
02			41
03		LDAB $40	D6
04			40
05	TRANS	LDAA X	A6
06			00
07		STAA $10,X	A7
08			10
09		INX	08
0A		DECB	5A
0B		BNE TRANS	26
0C			F8
0D		SWI	3F

The relative offset for BNE TRANS is

$$\begin{array}{r} 05 \\ -\ 0D \end{array} = \begin{array}{r} 05 \\ +\ F3 \\ \hline F8 \end{array}$$

Figure 5.22 Partial trace of Motorola 6800 data transfer program (first iteration).

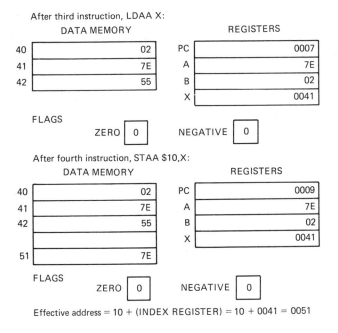

After third instruction, LDAA X:

DATA MEMORY		REGISTERS	
40	02	PC	0007
41	7E	A	7E
42	55	B	02
		X	0041

FLAGS   ZERO 0   NEGATIVE 0

After fourth instruction, STAA $10,X:

DATA MEMORY		REGISTERS	
40	02	PC	0009
41	7E	A	7E
42	55	B	02
		X	0041
51	7E		

FLAGS   ZERO 0   NEGATIVE 0

Effective address = 10 + (INDEX REGISTER) = 10 + 0041 = 0051

INTEL 8080—Example 5

The Intel 8080 program uses another register pair besides H and L as an address register. The Intel 8080 can use registers B and C (pair B) or D and E (pair D) as address registers but only to load and store the contents of the accumulator (operation codes LDAX and STAX). It cannot use these address registers to perform arithmetic or logical functions or to transfer data to or from the general-purpose registers. Such limitations are seldom significant, since the CPU must, in general, move data to the accumulator. The use of completely different instruction codes with the different address registers is confusing, however. Note that the program must update both address registers during each iteration and that the single set of registers must be shared among counters, pointers, and temporary data storage.

INTEL 8080 EXAMPLE 5
DATA TRANSFER

```
         LXI     H,40H       ;COUNT = LENGTH OF ARRAYS
         MOV     B,M
         LXI     D,50H       ;POINT TO START OF DESTINATION ARRAY
TRANS:   INX     D
         INX     H
         MOV     A,M         ;GET DATA FROM SOURCE
         STAX    D           ;MOVE DATA TO DESTINATION
         DCR     B
         JNZ     TRANS
         HLT
```

The new instruction in this program is STAX D, which stores the contents of the accumulator in the memory location addressed by registers D and E. The instruction requires one word of program memory and 3.5 μs. STAX D is the same as MOV M,A except that it uses a different address register; LDAX D is related similarly to MOV A,M.

Figure 5.23   Assembled Intel 8080 data transfer program.

Memory Address (hexadecimal)	Instruction (mnemonic)		Memory Contents (hexadecimal)
00	LXI	H,40H	21
01			40
02			00
03	MOV	B,M	46
04	LXI	D,50H	11
05			50
06			00
07	TRANS: INX	D	13
08	INX	H	23
09	MOV	A,M	7E
0A	STAX	D	12
0B	DCR	B	05
0C	JNZ	TRANS	C2
0D			07
0E			00
0F	HLT		76

Figure 5.24 Partial trace of Intel 8080 data transfer program (first iteration).

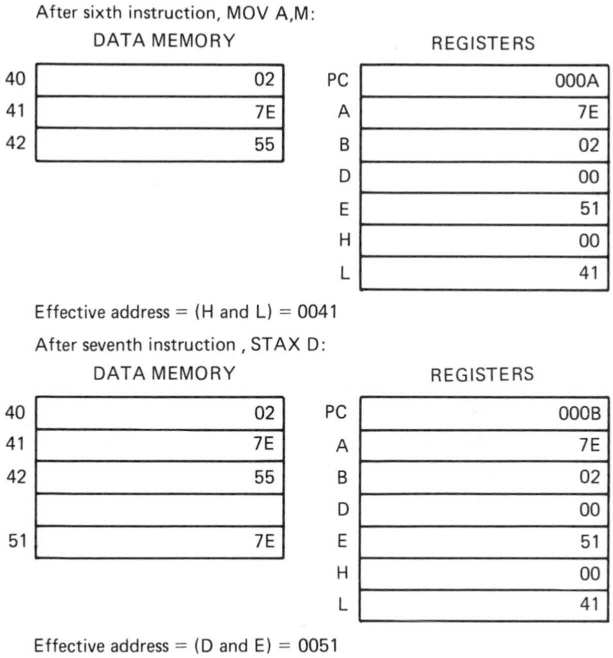

After sixth instruction, MOV A,M:

DATA MEMORY			REGISTERS	
40	02	PC		000A
41	7E	A		7E
42	55	B		02
		D		00
		E		51
		H		00
		L		41

Effective address = (H and L) = 0041

After seventh instruction , STAX D:

DATA MEMORY			REGISTERS	
40	02	PC		000B
41	7E	A		7E
42	55	B		02
		D		00
51	7E	E		51
		H		00
		L		41

Effective address = (D and E) = 0051

Figure 5.23 shows the assembled Intel 8080 program; Fig. 5.24 is a partial trace of the first iteration. The CPU must update both address registers, but it need not perform any 16-bit additions to calculate effective addresses. The data arrays in the Intel 8080 may be anywhere in memory; they need not be within 256 locations of each other as in the Motorola 6800 program.

EXAMPLE 6: Maximum Value

Obviously the processing sections of program loops are seldom as simple as those in Examples 4 and 5. Usually the sections contain a variety of operations, conditional branches, and perhaps even other program loops. The other sections of the program may be the same regardless of the complexity of the processing section.

A slightly more complex processing section is necessary in order to find the largest value in a data array. We may be sorting data, analyzing a set of test results, determining the next entry to be handled on a priority basis, or scaling input or output data for analysis or display. Assume that the length of the data array is in memory location 41 and that the array itself starts in memory location 42. The program places the maximum in memory location 40. All data entries are assumed to be 8-bit unsigned numbers.

A typical situation

$$(41) = 03$$

$$(42) = 37$$

$$(43) = F2$$

$$(44) = C6$$

The data array is three elements long and resides in memory locations 42, 43, and 44. The result is

$$(40) = F2$$

since F2 (in memory location 43) is the largest 8-bit unsigned number in the array.

Figure 5.25 shows a flowchart of the program. The processing section itself involves a conditional jump to determine if the entry being examined is larger than the old maximum. If it is, the program replaces the old maximum with the entry. The initial guess at the maximum is the first entry. The program reduces the counter by one, since the first entry need not be examined again; the program structure is the same as in the earlier examples.

Figure 5.25   Flowchart of maximum program.

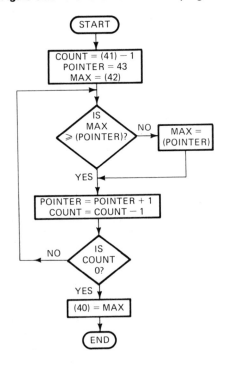

MOTOROLA 6800—Example 6

The Motorola 6800 program uses a comparison instruction (CMPA X) to determine whether the old maximum is larger than the entry currently being examined. If the comparison does not set the CARRY (indicating that no borrow would be required to perform the subtraction), the program keeps the old maximum in accumulator A. Otherwise the program replaces the old maximum with the current entry. Note the convenience of the COMPARE instruction—the old maximum is still in accumulator A for the next iteration if the current entry is not larger. The program is

```
MOTOROLA 6800 EXAMPLE 6
MAXIMUM VALUE

              LDAB   $41        COUNT = LENGTH OF ARRAY
              DECB              ADJUST COUNT TO EXCLUDE FIRST
    *                            ENTRY
              LDAA   $42        MAXIMUM IS FIRST ENTRY
              LDX    #$43
MAXM          CMPA   X          IS MAXIMUM LARGER THAN CURRENT
    *                            ENTRY?
              BCC    NOCHG      YES, KEEP MAXIMUM
              LDAA   X          NO, REPLACE WITH CURRENT ENTRY
NOCHG         INX
              DECB
              BNE    MAXM
              STAA   $40        SAVE MAXIMUM
              SWI
```

The new instructions in the program are

```
CMPA   X
```

This instruction sets the flags as if the contents of the addressed memory location had been subtracted from the contents of accumulator A. The indexed form of the instruction requires two words of program memory and 5 μs. If M is the addressed memory location, the ZERO and CARRY flags are set as follows:

$$Z = 1 \quad \text{if} \quad (A) = (M)$$

$$C = 1 \quad \text{if} \quad (M) > (A), \text{ assuming that both are unsigned.}$$

```
BCC   NOCHG
```

This instruction causes a branch to location NOCHG if the CARRY flag is zero. Like BNE, BCC uses relative addressing and requires two words of program memory and 4 μs.

Figure 5.26 contains the assembled program. This program has two conditional jumps with relative addresses. Figure 5.27 shows a trace of two iterations through the processing section of the program. Note the operation of the COMPARE instruction and the effects of the different flag values in the two iterations.

Figure 5.26 Assembled Motorola 6800 maximum program.

Memory Address (hexadecimal)		Instruction (mnemonic)		Memory Contents (hexadecimal)
00		LDAB $41		D6
01				41
02		DECB		5A
03		LDAA $42		96
04				42
05		LDX #$43		CE
06				00
07				43
08	MAXM	CMPA X		A1
09				00
0A		BCC NOCHG		24
0B				02
0C		LDAA X		A6
0D				00
0E	NOCHG	INX		08
0F		DECB		5A
10		BNE MAXM		26
11				F6
12		STAA $40		97
13				40
14		SWI		3F

The relative offset for BCC NOCHG is   The relative offset for BNE MAXM is

$$\begin{array}{r} 0E \\ -\ 0C \end{array} = \begin{array}{r} 0E \\ +\ F4 \\ \hline 02 \end{array} \qquad\qquad \begin{array}{r} 08 \\ -\ 12 \end{array} = \begin{array}{r} 08 \\ +\ EE \\ \hline F6 \end{array}$$

INTEL 8080—Example 6

The Intel 8080 program to find the maximum is similar to the Motorola 6800 program. It uses the COMPARE and JUMP ON NOT CARRY instructions to perform the required test. The program is

INTEL 8080 EXAMPLE 6
MAXIMUM VALUE

```
        LXI   H,41H
        MOV   B,M        ;COUNT = LENGTH OF ARRAY
        DCR   B          ;ADJUST COUNT TO EXCLUDE FIRST
                         ;  ENTRY
        INX   H
        MOV   A,M        ;MAXIMUM IS FIRST ENTRY
MAXM:   INX   H
        CMP   M          ;IS MAXIMUM LARGER THAN CURRENT
                         ;  ENTRY
        JNC   NOCHG      ;YES, KEEP MAXIMUM
        MOV   A,M        ;NO, REPLACE WITH CURRENT ENTRY
NOCHG:  DCR   B
        JNZ   MAXM
        STA   40H
        HLT
```

Figure 5.27 Partial trace of Motorola 6800 maximum program.

First Iteration:

After fifth instruction, CMPA X:

DATA MEMORY   REGISTERS

41	03
42	37
43	F2
44	C6

PC	000A
A	37
B	02
X	0043

FLAGS

ZERO $\boxed{0}$ NEGATIVE $\boxed{0}$ CARRY $\boxed{1}$

The flags are set as if the CPU had performed $(A) - ((X)) = (A) - (0043) = 37 - F2$

$$\begin{array}{r} 37 \\ -\ F2 \end{array} = \begin{array}{r} 37 \\ +\ 0E \\ \hline 45 \end{array}$$

Note that the CPU complements the actual carry from a subtraction so that the CARRY bit is really a borrow.

After sixth instruction, BCC NOCHG:

DATA MEMORY   REGISTERS

41	03
42	37
43	F2
44	C6

PC	000C
A	37
B	02
X	0043

No branch occurs, since CARRY = 1.

Second Iteration:

After fifth instruction, CMPA X:

DATA MEMORY   REGISTERS

41	03
42	37
43	F2
44	C6

PC	000A
A	F2
B	01
X	0044

FLAGS

ZERO $\boxed{0}$ NEGATIVE $\boxed{0}$ CARRY $\boxed{0}$

The flags are set as if the CPU had performed

$$(A) - ((X)) = (A) - (0044) = F2 - C6 = 2C$$

After sixth instruction, BCC NOCHG:

DATA MEMORY   REGISTERS

41	03
42	37
43	F2
44	C6

PC	000E
A	F2
B	01
X	0044

A branch occurs, since CARRY = 0.

The new instructions here are

CMP   M

This instruction sets the flags as if the contents of the memory location addressed by registers H and L had been subtracted from the contents of the accumulator. CMP M requires one word of program memory and 3.5 μs.

JNC   NOCHG

This instruction causes a jump to memory location NOCHG if the CARRY flag is zero. It requires three words of program memory and 5 μs.

Figure 5.28 contains the assembled version of the Intel 8080 program; Fig. 5.29 is a trace of two iterations through the processing section.

Figure 5.28   Assembled version of Intel 8080 program.

Memory Address (hexadecimal)		Instruction (mnemonic)		Memory Contents (hexadecimal)
00		LXI	H,41H	21
01				41
02				00
03		MOV	B,M	46
04		DCR	B	05
05		INX	H	23
06		MOV	A,M	7E
07	MAXM:	INX	H	23
08		CMP	M	BE
09		JNC	NOCHG	D2
0A				0D
0B				00
0C		MOV	A,M	7E
0D	NOCHG:	DCR	B	05
0E		JNZ	MAXM	C2
0F				07
10				00
11		STA	40H	32
12				40
13				00
14		HLT		76

The last three examples have emphasized certain features of assembly language programs.

1. *Simple loop structure.* Each program contains an initialization section, a processing section, and a loop control section. The computer executes the initialization section once prior to entering the loop. The loop control section determines how many times the loop is repeated; this section may be the same for a variety of processing tasks. The processing section may vary from a single statement to a complex program.

Figure 5.29 Partial trace of Intel 8080 maximum program.

First Iteration:

After seventh instruction, CMP M:

DATA MEMORY

41	03
42	37
43	F2
44	C6

REGISTERS

PC	0009
A	37
B	02
H	00
L	43

FLAGS

ZERO	0	SIGN	0	CARRY	1

The flags are set as if the CPU had performed

$$(A) - (\,(H \text{ and } L)\,) = (A) - (0043) = 37 - F2$$

The CPU complements the actual carry from the subtraction to form a borrow in the CARRY bit.

After eighth instruction, JNC NOCHG:

DATA MEMORY

41	03
42	37
43	F2
44	C6

REGISTERS

PC	000C
A	37
B	02
H	00
L	43

No jump occurs, since CARRY = 1.

Second Iteration:

After seventh instruction, CMP M:

DATA MEMORY

41	03
42	37
43	F2
44	C6

REGISTERS

PC	0009
A	F2
B	01
H	00
L	44

FLAGS

ZERO	0	SIGN	0	CARRY	0

The flags are set as if the CPU had performed

$$(A) - (\,(H \text{ and } L)\,) = (A) - (0044) = F2 - C6$$

After eighth instruction, JNC NOCHG:

DATA MEMORY

41	03
42	37
43	F2
44	C6

REGISTERS

PC	000D
A	F2
B	01
H	00
L	44

A jump occurs, since CARRY = 0.

2. *The use of pointers to access arrays.* The use of pointers reduces the number of addresses that the CPU must fetch from program memory. This reduction is particularly critical in microprocessors, since addresses are two words long. Multiple address registers and indexing add flexibility to the use of pointers. The initialization section must initialize all pointers, and the loop control section must update them during each iteration.

3. *The use of conditional branches to control loops and make decisions.* The basic loop structure initializes a counter and decrements it during each repetition of the program. The instruction JUMP ON NOT ZERO causes the computer to repeat the loop the correct number of times. The COMPARE instruction performs a subtraction and sets the flags without changing the contents of any registers. JUMP ON ZERO, JUMP ON NOT ZERO, JUMP ON CARRY, and JUMP ON NOT CARRY can select alternate instruction sequences, depending on the results of the comparison.

Using arrays and loops requires careful attention to detail. The programmer must answer these questions:

    (a) Have all variables been initialized properly before entering the loop?
    (b) Do the conditional branches have the correct addresses?
    (c) Have the conditions for the branches been chosen properly?
    (d) Are the first and last iterations being performed correctly?

We shall return to these questions as part of the discussion of program debugging in Chapter 6.

5.3 ARITHMETIC

Example 4, the sum of a series of numbers, is a simple arithmetic problem. Most arithmetic calculations require more than single-word accuracy, use decimal numbers, or involve more complex operations than addition or subtraction. In this section we discuss multiple-precision arithmetic, decimal arithmetic, and lookup tables. The programs have the loop structures developed in the previous section.

EXAMPLE 7: Multiple-Precision Arithmetic
    The task is to add two numbers that are more than one 8-bit data word in length. The numbers might be measurements from accurate analog-to-digital converters, values of trigonometric or exponential functions, poles or roots of equations, intensity levels, processing factors, or other data that needs more than eight bits of accuracy. Assume that the length (in words) of the numbers is in memory location 40 and that the numbers themselves start in memory locations 41 and 51, respectively (least significant bits first). The program places the result in the locations formerly occupied by the first number.

A typical situation

$$(40) = 03$$
$$(41) = 29$$
$$(42) = A4$$
$$(43) = 50$$

$$(51) = FB$$
$$(52) = 37$$
$$(53) = 28$$

The problem is to add the 24-bit numbers 5-A429 and 2837FB. The result is

$$(41) = 24 = 29 + FB$$
$$(42) = DC = A4 + 37 + CARRY (1)$$
$$(43) = 78 = 50 + 28 + CARRY (0)$$

The carries must be included in the addition.

Figure 5.30 shows the flowchart of the program. As in the previous examples, the program has an initialization section, a processing section, and a loop control section. The only new feature is the use of the CARRY to transfer a single bit of information from one iteration to the next.

Figure 5.30 Flowchart of multiple-precision addition program.

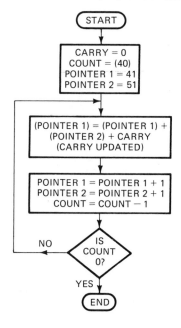

MOTOROLA 6800—Example 7

In the Motorola 6800 program, the instruction CLEAR CARRY (CLC) clears the CARRY initially and ADD WITH CARRY (ADC) performs the addition. The program is

MOTOROLA 6800 EXAMPLE 7
MULTIPLE-PRECISION ADDITION

```
            LDAB    $40       COUNT = LENGTH OF NUMBERS
            CLC               START CARRY AT ZERO
            LDX     #$41      POINT TO FIRST NUMBER
   MPADD    LDAA    X         GET 8 BITS OF FIRST NUMBER
            ADCA    $10,X     ADD 8 BITS OF SECOND NUMBER
            STAA    X         STORE SUM IN FIRST NUMBER
            INX
            DECB
            BNE     MPADD
            SWI
```

The instruction ADCA X adds the contents of the addressed memory location and the contents of the CARRY to the contents of accumulator A.

Figure 5.31 illustrates an assembled version of the program. Figure 5.32 shows the effects of two iterations of the ADD WITH CARRY instruction. The loop control instructions INX and DECB do not affect the CARRY; so its value is retained for use in the next iteration.

Figure 5.31   Assembled Motorola 6800 multiple-precision addition program.

Memory Address (hexadecimal)		Instruction (mnemonic)	Memory Contents (hexadecimal)
00		LDAB $40	D6
01			40
02		CLC	0C
03		LDX #$41	CE
04			00
05			41
06	MPADD	LDAA X	A6
07			00
08		ADCA $10,X	A9
09			10
0A		STAA X	A7
0B			00
0C		INX	08
0D		DECB	5A
0E		BNE MPADD	26
0F			F6
10		SWI	3F

The relative address for BNE MPADD is

$$
\begin{array}{cc}
06 & 06 \\
\overline{} = & \\
-\,10 & +\,\underline{F0} \\
 & F6
\end{array}
$$

Figure 5.32 Trace of ADD WITH CARRY in Motorola 6800 multiple-precision addition program.

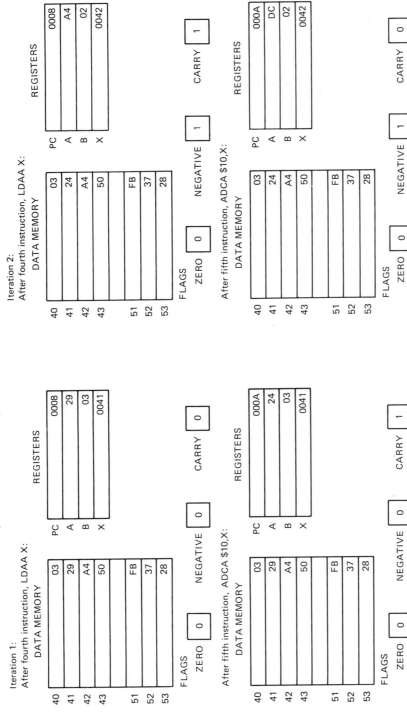

Iteration 1:
After fourth instruction, LDAA X:

DATA MEMORY

40	03
41	29
42	A4
43	50
51	FB
52	37
53	28

REGISTERS

PC	0008
A	29
B	03
X	0041

FLAGS

ZERO $\boxed{0}$ NEGATIVE $\boxed{0}$ CARRY $\boxed{0}$

After fifth instruction, ADCA $10,X:

DATA MEMORY

40	03
41	29
42	A4
43	50
51	FB
52	37
53	28

REGISTERS

PC	000A
A	24
B	03
X	0041

FLAGS

ZERO $\boxed{0}$ NEGATIVE $\boxed{0}$ CARRY $\boxed{1}$

Iteration 2:
After fourth instruction, LDAA X:

DATA MEMORY

40	03
41	24
42	A4
43	50
51	FB
52	37
53	28

REGISTERS

PC	0008
A	A4
B	02
X	0042

FLAGS

ZERO $\boxed{0}$ NEGATIVE $\boxed{1}$ CARRY $\boxed{1}$

After fifth instruction, ADCA $10,X:

DATA MEMORY

40	03
41	24
42	A4
43	50
51	FB
52	37
53	28

REGISTERS

PC	000A
A	DC
B	02
X	0042

FLAGS

ZERO $\boxed{0}$ NEGATIVE $\boxed{1}$ CARRY $\boxed{0}$

The old CARRY was zero, and so it did not affect the addition; the new CARRY, however, is one.

INTEL 8080—EXAMPLE 7

The Intel 8080 program uses SUB A to clear the CARRY (there is no CLEAR CARRY instruction) and ADD WITH CARRY (ADC) to perform the addition. The program is

INTEL 8080 EXAMPLE 7
MULTIPLE-PRECISION ADDITION

```
        SUB     A           ;START CARRY AT ZERO
        LXI     H,40H       ;COUNT = LENGTH OF NUMBERS
        MOV     B,M
        LXI     D,50H       ;POINT TO SECOND NUMBER
MPADD:  INX     D
        INX     H
        LDAX    D           ;GET 8 BITS OF SECOND NUMBER
        ADC     M           ;ADD 8 BITS OF FIRST NUMBER
        MOV     M,A         ;STORE SUM IN FIRST NUMBER
        DCR     B
        JNZ     MPADD
        HLT
```

The order of the addition on the Intel 8080 is reversed because the processor can only add indirectly using the address in registers H and L. Here again the loop control instructions INX D, INX H, and DCR B do not affect the CARRY so that it can transfer information from one iteration to the next. The instruction ADC M adds the contents of the memory location addressed by registers H and L and the contents of the CARRY to the contents of the accumulator.

Figure 5.33 shows the assembled Intel 8080 program. The ADD WITH CARRY instruction has the same effect on the Intel 8080 as on the Motorola 6800.

Figure 5.33 Assembled Intel 8080 multiple-precision addition program.

Memory Address (hexadecimal)		Instruction (mnemonic)		Memory Contents (hexadecimal)
00		SUB	A	97
01		LXI	H,40H	21
02				40
03				00
04		MOV	B,M	46
05		LXI	D,60H	11
06				60
07				00
08	MPADD:	INX	D	13
09		INX	H	23
0A		LDAX	D	1A
0B		ADC	M	8E
0C		MOV	M,A	77
0D		DCR	B	05
0E		JNZ	MPADD	C2
0F				08
10				00
11		HLT		76

EXAMPLE 8: Decimal Arithmetic

Most 8-bit microprocessors have a special instruction for adding decimal numbers. This instruction (generally called DECIMAL ADJUST) uses the CARRY and HALF-CARRY (or AUXILIARY CARRY) bits; Appendix 3 describes the method. Decimal arithmetic is essential in such common microprocessor applications as point-of-sale terminals, teller terminals, calculators, games, and navigation systems. For instance, assume the same situation as in Example 7 except that all the numbers are BCD. The length of the numbers is in memory location 40, the numbers themselves start in locations 41 and 51, respectively, and the result replaces the first number.

A typical situation

$$(40) = 03$$
$$(41) = 29$$
$$(42) = 65$$
$$(43) = 37$$

$$(51) = 88$$
$$(52) = 43$$
$$(53) = 22$$

The problem is to add two strings of six decimal digits—that is,

$$376529 + 224388$$

The result is 600917.

$$(41) = 17$$
$$(42) = 09$$
$$(43) = 60$$

The program is the same as the one flowcharted in Fig. 5.30 except that the addition is decimal rather than binary.

MOTOROLA 6800 AND INTEL 8080—Example 8

The only change required in the Motorola 6800 and Intel 8080 programs from Example 7 is a DAA (DECIMAL ADJUST ACCUMULATOR) instruction after the ADD WITH CARRY instruction. Figure 5.34 shows the effects of the DAA instruction during the first two iterations. Each decimal addition requires two instructions —an addition instruction followed by DECIMAL ADJUST. DECIMAL ADJUST only acts on accumulator A in the Motorola 6800. Other microprocessors handle the problem somewhat differently. The National PACE has a DECIMAL ADD instruction, and the MOS Technology 6502 has a decimal mode (entered with a SET DECIMAL MODE instruction) in which all arithmetic is performed in decimal.

Figure 5.34 Trace of decimal adjust instruction.

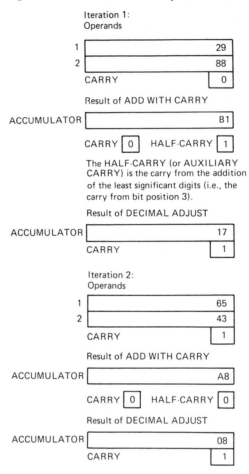

MOTOROLA 6800 EXAMPLE 8
DECIMAL ADDITION

```
        LDAB   $40        COUNT = LENGTH OF NUMBERS
        CLC               START CARRY AT ZERO
        LDX    #$41       POINT TO FIRST NUMBER
DCADD   LDAA   X          GET TWO DIGITS OF FIRST NUMBER
        ADCA   $10,X      ADD TWO DIGITS OF SECOND NUMBER
        DAA               DECIMAL CORRECTION
        STAA   X          STORE SUM IN FIRST NUMBER
        INX
        DECB
        BNE    DCADD
        SWI
```

INTEL 8080 EXAMPLE 8
DECIMAL ADDITION

```
            SUB    A          ;START CARRY AT ZERO
            LXI    H,40H
            MOV    B,M        ;COUNT = LENGTH OF NUMBERS
            LXI    D,50H      ;POINT TO SECOND NUMBER
DCADD:      INX    D
            INX    H
            LDAX   D          ;GET TWO DIGITS OF SECOND NUMBER
            ADC    M          ;ADD TWO DIGITS OF FIRST NUMBER
            DAA               ;DECIMAL CORRECTION
            MOV    M,A        ;STORE SUM IN FIRST NUMBER
            DCR    B
            JNZ    DCADD
            HLT
```

EXAMPLE 9: Table of Squares

More complicated arithmetic problems can often be solved by using lookup tables. Such tables contain all the possible results of a calculation arranged in a convenient order. The program must select the correct result for a particular problem. The tradeoff here is between time and memory; tables require less time, since no results need be calculated, but use more memory, since all possible results must be stored. As memory becomes cheaper, lookup tables are increasingly attractive. Code conversion and function lookup tables are even available in standard ROMs.

To illustrate, let us find the square of a 3-bit number. Such a task would be part of signal processing, communications, or process control applications. The lookup table consists of all the squares of 3-bit numbers organized in increasing order. We could place such a table in program memory with the assembler pseudo-operation DATA—that is,

```
SQTAB  DATA   0, 1, 4, 9, 16, 25, 36, 49
```

The index to the table is the number to be squared—in other words, the zeroth entry contains the square of zero, and so on. The program must add the 3-bit number to the base address (SQTAB) in order to find the address of the correct entry. Assume that the number between 0 and 7 is stored in memory location 40 and that the result must be placed in memory location 41.

A typical situation

$$(40) = 04$$

The task is to square the number 4. The result is

$$(41) = 10 \text{ (hex)} = 16 \text{ (decimal)}$$

The correct entry is in memory location SQTAB + 4.

Figure 5.35 is a flowchart of the program. The program must perform an addition in order to obtain the address of the table entry and then must use that address to get the actual entry.

Figure 5.35 Flowchart of table of squares program.

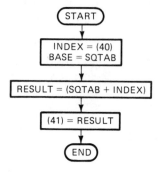

MOTOROLA 6800— Example 9

Because the Motorola 6800 has indexing, obtaining the correct table entry would seem to be simple. The obvious approach would be to place the base address of the table in the index register, the index in the offset, and then use indexed addressing to find the entry. However, this approach does not work because the offset is a fixed part of the program memory (i.e., ROM) and cannot be changed for each value that must be squared. Nor can the base address and index be interchanged, since the base address is normally 16 bits long and cannot be placed in an 8-bit offset. The solution to this problem is awkward. For a short table, we can simply place the base address in the index register and increment it by one a number of times determined by the index or entry number. Assuming that the index is in memory location 40, the program is

```
          LDX     #BASE          GET BASE ADDRESS OF TABLE
          LDAA    $40            COUNT = INDEX
LOOKT     BEQ     DONE
          INX                    INCREMENT BASE ADDRESS
  *                                COUNT TIMES
          DECA
          BRA     LOOKT
DONE      LDAB    X              GET ENTRY FROM TABLE
```

For long tables, the method is obviously slow. Instead we can move the index and the eight most significant bits of the base address to the index register via memory and use the eight least significant bits of the base address as the offset. The Motorola 6800 does not allow direct transfers between the accumulators and the index register. Assuming that BASEU and BASEL are the eight most and eight least significant bits of the base address of the table, the program is

```
          LDAA    #BASEU         GET 8 MSB'S OF BASE ADDRESS OF
  *                                TABLE
          STAA    TEMP
```

```
          LDAA       $40              GET INDEX
          STAA       TEMP + 1
          LDX        TEMP             OFFSET ADDRESS TO INDEX
  *                                     REGISTER VIA MEMORY
          LDAA       BASEL,X          GET ENTRY FROM TABLE
```

The assembler can calculate BASEU and BASEL from the expressions

```
  BASEU   EQU        BASE/256
  BUPP    EQU        BASEU * 256
  BASEL   EQU        BASE – BUPP
```

BASE/256 is simply the eight most significant bits of BASE (since dividing by 256 is equivalent to an 8-bit right shift—$256 = 2^8$). BUPP has the same eight most significant bits as BASE, but its eight least significant bits are all zero. Subtracting BUPP from BASE leaves BASEL equal to the eight least significant bits of BASE.

Using the second method, the Motorola 6800 assembly language program for accessing the table of squares is

```
  MOTOROLA 6800 EXAMPLE 9
  TABLE OF SQUARES


          LDAA       #SQTBU           GET 8 MSB'S OF BASE ADDRESS
  *                                     OF SQUARE TABLE
          STAA       TEMP
          LDAA       $40              GET INDEX
          STAA       TEMP + 1
          LDX        TEMP             OFFSET ADDRESS TO INDEX
  *                                     REGISTER VIA MEMORY
          LDAA       SQTBL,X          GET ENTRY FROM SQUARE TABLE
          STAA       $41              STORE RESULT
          SWI
  TEMP    RMB        2
  SQTAB   FCB        0, 1, 4, 9, 16, 25, 36, 49
  SQTBU   EQU        SQTAB/256
  SQUPP   EQU        SQTBU * 256
  SQTBL   EQU        SQTAB – SQUPP
```

Note that the index register contains the 8-bit index and eight bits of the base address.

The pseudo-operations are

TEMP RMB 2 reserves two words of data memory and assigns the label TEMP to the address of the first word. No values are placed in the words.

SQTAB FCB 0, 1, 4, 9, 16, 25, 36, 49 places the table of squares in memory and assigns the label SQTAB to the first address used by the table.

Figure 5.36 shows the assembled version of the program. Note the placement of the table of squares in memory. Figure 5.37 is a trace of the table access. Remember that the table entries are hexadecimal numbers.

Figure 5.36 Assembled version of Motorola 6800 table of squares program.

Memory Address (hexadecimal)	Instruction (mnemonic)			Memory Contents (hexadecimal)
00		LDAA	#SQTBU	86
01				00
02		STAA	TEMP	97
03				0F
04		LDAA	$40	97
05				40
06		STAA	TEMP + 1	97
07				10
08		LDX	TEMP	DE
09				0F
0A		LDAA	SQTBL,X	A6
0B				11
0C		STAA	$41	97
0D				41
0E		SWI		3F
0F	TEMP	RMB	2	
10				
11	SQTAB	FCB	0 (0^2)	00
12			1 (1^2)	01
13			4 (2^2)	04
14			9 (3^2)	09
15			16 (4^2)	10
16			25 (5^2)	19
17			36 (6^2)	24
18			49 (7^2)	31

Address SQTAB is 0011 so SQTBU is 00 and SQTBL is 11.

Figure 5.37 Trace of table access in Motorola 6800 table of squares program.

After fifth instruction, LDX TEMP:

After sixth instruction, LDAA SQTBL,X:

$(A) = (\ (X) + SQTBL) = (0004 + 11)$
$\quad = (0015) = 10$

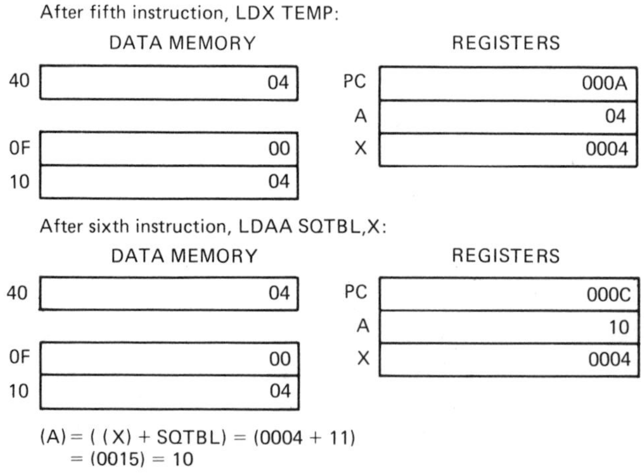

INTEL 8080—Example 9

Although the Intel 8080 does not have indexing, finding the correct table entry is relatively simple. The program uses the 16-bit addition instruction DAD to add the base address and the index. The process is somewhat awkward, since the address is 16 bits long and the index only 8 bits long. The index must be extended to 16 bits by clearing the most significant half of a register pair before DAD is executed. The program is

```
INTEL 8080 EXAMPLE 9
TABLE OF SQUARES

              LXI   D, SQTAB    ;GET BASE ADDRESS OF SQUARE TABLE
              LDA   40H         ;GET DATA
              MOV   L,A         ;DATA IS 8 LSB'S OF INDEX
              MVI   H,0         ;8 MSB'S OF INDEX ARE ZERO
              DAD   D           ;INDEX SQUARE TABLE
              MOV   A,M         ;GET SQUARE OF DATA
              STA   41H         ;STORE SQUARE OF DATA
              HLT
SQTAB:        DB    0, 1, 4, 9, 16, 25, 36, 49
```

The new instructions here are

```
    MVI   H,0
```

This instruction clears register H. It requires two words of program memory (zero is in the second word) and 3.5 μs.

```
    DAD   D
```

This instruction adds the contents of register pair D (D and E) to the contents of register pair H (H and L). The result is placed in register pair H. DAD D requires one word of program memory and 5 μs.

Figure 5.38 contains the assembled version of the Intel 8080 program, and Fig. 5.39 is a trace of the table access. The base address of the table is placed in registers D and E so that it can be used to obtain another element from the table if necessary. The procedure could be simplified if the table were always on a single 256-word page of memory—that is, if the eight most significant bits of all the addresses were the same. Then 8-bit addition could be used instead of 16-bit addition.

The last three examples have described the programming of arithmetic calculations on microprocessors. The basic loop structure can perform multiple-precision binary arithmetic and, with the special DECIMAL ADJUST instruction, multiple-precision decimal arithmetic. More complex arithmetic problems can be solved with lookup tables; most microprocessors need several instructions in order to obtain the correct result from the table.

Figure 5.38 Assembled version of Intel 8080 table of squares program.

Memory Address (hexadecimal)		Instruction (mnemonic)		Memory Contents (hexadecimal)
00		LXI	D,SQTAB	11
01				0F
02				00
03		LDA	40H	3A
04				40
05				00
06		MOV	L,A	6F
07		MVI	H,0	26
08				00
09		DAD	D	19
0A		MOV	A,M	7E
0B		STA	41H	32
0C				41
0D				00
0E		HLT		76
0F	SQTAB:	DB	0 (0^2)	00
10			1 (1^2)	00
11			4 (2^2)	04
12			9 (3^2)	09
13			16 (4^2)	10
14			25 (5^2)	19
15			36 (6^2)	24
16			49 (7^2)	31

Figure 5.39 Trace of table access in Intel 8080 table of squares program.

After fourth instruction, MVI H,0:

DATA MEMORY		REGISTERS	
40	04	PC	0009
		A	04
		D	00
		E	0F
		H	00
		L	04

After fifth instruction, DAD D:

DATA MEMORY		REGISTERS	
40	04	PC	000A
		A	04
		D	00
		E	0F
		H	00
		L	13

After sixth instruction, MOV A,M:

DATA MEMORY		REGISTERS	
40	04	PC	000B
		A	10
		D	00
		E	0F
		H	00
		L	13

(A) = ((H and L)) = (13) = 10

5.4 CHARACTER MANIPULATION

Many microprocessor applications require the manipulation of character-coded data. Not only do such common devices as keyboards, teletypewriters, printers, and CRT displays use character-coded data but so do many computers, communication lines, and instruments as well. The character code used by most microprocessors is ASCII (see Appendix 3). ASCII characters can be processed just like ordinary numbers by using the arithmetic and comparison operations. This section demonstrates how to examine a string of ASCII characters, convert data to or from the ASCII representation, and compare ASCII strings.

EXAMPLE 10: Length of an ASCII String
Determine the length of a string of ASCII characters that is stored starting in memory location 41. The end of the string is marked by an ASCII period (hex 2E). Place the result in memory location 40.

A typical situation

$$(41) = 43 \quad C$$

$$(42) = 41 \quad A$$

$$(43) = 54 \quad T$$

$$(44) = 2E$$

The ASCII period in memory location 44 marks the end of the string. The length of the string (excluding the period) is 3; so the result is

$$(40) = 03$$

Figure 5.40 is a flowchart of the program. The loop control method here differs from that in previous examples, since the number of iterations is not fixed. We assume for simplicity that all strings end with a period.

Figure 5.40 Flowchart of length of string program.

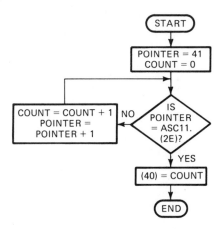

211

MOTOROLA 6800—Example 10

The Motorola 6800 program uses the COMPARE instruction to check for an ASCII period. Note that COMPARE leaves the accumulator unchanged for the next iteration. The program is

```
MOTOROLA 6800 EXAMPLE 10
LENGTH OF STRING


        CLRB              STRING LENGTH = ZERO
        LDAA    #'        GET ASCII PERIOD FOR COMPARISON
        LDX     #$41      POINT TO START OF ASCII STRING
CHPER   CMPA    X         IS CHARACTER ASCII PERIOD?
        BEQ     DONE      YES, DONE
        INCB              NO, ADD 1 TO STRING LENGTH
        INX
        BRA     CHPER
DONE    STAB    $40       SAVE STRING LENGTH
        SWI
```

The apostrophe indicates ASCII data.

Figure 5.41 contains the assembled version of the program. The ASCII data is handled just like any other data. The instruction BRA (BRANCH ALWAYS) is an unconditional jump that uses relative addressing.

Figure 5.41 Assembled version of Motorola 6800 length of string program.

Memory Address (hexadecimal)		Instruction (mnemonic)	Memory Contents (hexadecimal)
00		CLRB	5F
01		LDAA #'	86
02			2A
03		LDX #$41	CE
04			00
05			41
06	CHPER	CMPA X	A1
07			00
08		BEQ DONE	27
09			04
0A		INCB	5C
0B		INX	08
0C		BRA CHPER	20
0D			F8
0E	DONE	STAB $40	D7
0F			40
10		SWI	3F

The relative address for BEQ DONE is

$$\begin{array}{r} 0E \\ -\ 0A \\ \hline 04 \end{array}$$

The relative address for **BRA CHPER** is

$$\frac{\begin{array}{r} 06 \\ - \ 0E \end{array}}{} = \frac{\begin{array}{r} 06 \\ + \ F2 \end{array}}{F8}$$

INTEL 8080—Example 10

The Intel 8080 program is very similar to the Motorola 6800 program.

INTEL 8080 EXAMPLE 10
LENGTH OF STRING

```
        MVI    B,0        ;STRING LENGTH = ZERO
        MVI    A,'.'      ;GET ASCII PERIOD FOR COMPARISON
        LXI    H,41H      ;POINT TO START OF ASCII STRING
CHPER:  CMP    M          ;IS CHARACTER ASCII PERIOD?
        JZ     DONE       ;YES, DONE
        INR    B          ;NO, ADD 1 TO STRING LENGTH
        INX    H
        JMP    CHPER
DONE:   MOV    A,B
        STA    40H        ;SAVE STRING LENGTH
        HLT
```

Two apostrophes surround the ASCII data. Figure 5.42 contains the assembled version of the Intel 8080 program.

Figure 5.42 Assembled version of Intel 8080 length of string program.

Memory Address (hexadecimal)	Instruction (mnemonic)		Memory Contents (hexadecimal)
00	MVI	B,0	06
01			00
02	MVI	A,'.'	3E
03			2A
04	LXI	H,41H	21
05			41
06			00
07	CHPER: CMP	M	BE
08	JZ	DONE	CA
09			10
0A			00
0B	INR	B	04
0C	INX	H	23
0D	JMP	CHPER	C3
0E			07
0F			00
10	DONE: MOV	A,B	78
11	STA	40H	32
12			40
13			00
14	HLT		76

EXAMPLE 11: Converting ASCII to Decimal

Frequently, programs must convert numerical data from ASCII to decimal or binary before processing it and from decimal or binary to ASCII before printing it. The conversion is simple because the decimal digits form a numerical sequence in ASCII. All that the program must do is subtract hexadecimal 30 (ASCII zero) to convert ASCII to decimal or add the same number to convert decimal to ASCII. The program could also check to see if the ASCII character is actually a digit. Assume that the program takes an ASCII character in memory location 40 and converts it to a decimal digit in memory location 41. If the character is not a digit, the program places FF (hex) in memory location 41.

Typical situations

1. (40) = 36: 36 is the ASCII representation of decimal 6; so the result is

$$(41) = 06$$

2. (40) = 5E: 5E is not an ASCII digit; so the result is

$$(41) = FF$$

Figure 5.43 is a flowchart of the program. The procedure is to subtract ASCII zero from the original data. If the result is less than ten, the data was an ASCII digit and the result is the decimal equivalent. Otherwise the original data was not an ASCII digit and the program replaces the result with the error indicator FF (hex).

MOTOROLA 6800—Example 11

The Motorola 6800 program to convert an ASCII digit to decimal follows the flowchart closely. Figure 5.44 is the assembled version.

Figure 5.43 Flowchart of ASCII-to-decimal program.

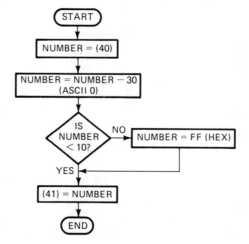

Figure 5.44 Assembled version of Motorola 6800 ASCII-to-decimal program.

Memory Address (hexadecimal)	Instruction (mnemonic)		Memory Contents (hexadecimal)
00	LDAA	$40	96
01			40
02	SUBA	#'0	80
03			30
04	CMPA	#10	81
05			0A
06	BCS	DONE	25
07			02
08	LDAA	#$FF	86
09			FF
0A	DONE STAA	$41	97
0B			41
0C	SWI		3F

MOTOROLA 6800 EXAMPLE 11
ASCII TO DECIMAL

```
      LDAA    $40      GET ASCII DATA
      SUBA    #'0      SUBTRACT ASCII ZERO
      CMPA    #10      IS RESULT LESS THAN 10?
      BCS     DONE     YES, STORE DECIMAL RESULT
      LDAA    #$FF     NO, RESULT IS FF HEX (DATA NOT DECIMAL)
DONE  STAA    $41      STORE RESULT
      SWI
```

INTEL 8080—Example 11

The Intel 8080 program to convert ASCII digits to decimal is also simple. Figure 5.45 is the assembled version.

Figure 5.45 Assembled version of Intel 8080 ASCII-to-decimal program.

Memory Address (hexadecimal)	Instruction (mnemonic)		Memory Contents (hexadecimal)
00	LDA	40H	3A
01			40
02			00
03	SUI	'0'	D6
04			30
05	CPI	10	FE
06			0A
07	JC	DONE	DA
08			0C
09			00
0A	MVI	A,0FFH	3E
0B			FF
0C	DONE: STA	41H	32
0D			41
0E			00
0F	HLT		76

INTEL 8080 EXAMPLE 11
ASCII TO DECIMAL

```
        LDA    40H       ;GET ASCII DATA
        SUI    '0'       ;SUBTRACT ASCII ZERO
        CPI    10        ;IS RESULT LESS THAN 10?
        JC     DONE      ;YES, STORE DECIMAL RESULT
        MVI    A,0FFH    ;NO, RESULT IS FF HEX (DATA NOT DECIMAL)
DONE:   STA    41H       ;STORE RESULT
        HLT
```

EXAMPLE 12: Pattern Comparison

Many applications require the recognition of strings of ASCII characters. These strings may be commands, identification codes, names, text patterns, or numbers. Recognition involves comparing the data string to a known string of characters to see if they are the same. Assume that the two ASCII strings start in memory locations 42 and 52, respectively. Memory location 41 contains the length of the strings. The program sets memory location 40 to zero if the strings are equal and to FF (hex) if they are not.

Typical situation

$$(41) = 04$$

$$(42) = 43 \quad C$$

$$(43) = 41 \quad A$$

$$(44) = 54 \quad T$$

$$(45) = 53 \quad S$$

$$(52) = 43 \quad C$$

$$(53) = 41 \quad A$$

$$(54) = 50 \quad P$$

$$(55) = 45 \quad E$$

The two strings of four characters are not the same, since the third and fourth characters do not correspond. Note that the first discrepancy concludes the search. The result is

$$(40) = FF$$

Figure 5.46 is the flowchart of the program. Clearly the program is similar to the data transfer program (Example 5) and the multiple-precision arithmetic programs (Examples 7 and 8). The loop here has two exits—one in the event of a discrepancy and one in the event that all the characters in the strings correspond. This program combines the logic of Example 10 with that of Examples 4 through 8.

Figure 5.46 Flowchart of pattern comparison program.

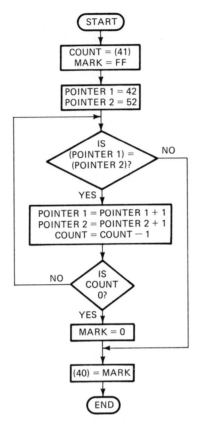

MOTOROLA 6800—Example 12

The Motorola 6800 program for pattern comparison assumes that the two strings are less than 256 locations apart so that the distance can be placed in an 8-bit offset. Figure 5.47 contains the assembled program. Note that the instruction CLR $40 requires a 16-bit address (0040) even though location 40 is on page zero. The Motorola 6800 does not use page-zero addressing with any of the single-operand instructions—CLEAR, COMPLEMENT, NEGATE, ROTATE LEFT, ROTATE RIGHT, ARITHMETIC SHIFT LEFT, ARITHMETIC SHIFT RIGHT, LOGICAL SHIFT RIGHT, and TEST. The Motorola 6800 can apply any of these instructions to the data in a memory location (unlike the Intel 8080), but the instructions must have a 16-bit direct address or an indexed offset.

MOTOROLA 6800 EXAMPLE 12
PATTERN COMPARISON

```
        LDAA    #$FF
        STAA    $40         MARK = FF HEX FOR INEQUALITY
        LDAB    $41         COUNT = LENGTH OF STRINGS
        LDX     #$42        POINT TO START OF STRINGS
```

```
PATTC   LDAA    X          GET ELEMENT OF STRING 1
        CMPA    $10,X      IS IT SAME AS ELEMENT OF STRING 2?
        BNE     DONE       NO, NO MATCH
        INX
        DECB               ALL CHARACTERS CHECKED?
        BNE     PATTC      NO, CHECK NEXT CHARACTERS
        CLR     $40        YES, MARK = 0 FOR EQUALITY
DONE    SWI
```

Figure 5.47   Assembled version of Motorola 6800 pattern comparison program.

Memory Address (hexadecimal)		Instruction (mnemonic)	Memory Contents (hexadecimal)
00		LDAA #$FF	86
01			FF
02		STAA $40	97
03			40
04		LDAB $41	D6
05			41
06		LDX #$42	CE
07			00
08			42
09	PATTC	LDAA X	A6
0A			00
0B		CMPA $10,X	A1
0C			10
0D		BNE DONE	26
0E			07
0F		INX	08
10		DECB	5A
11		BNE PATTC	26
12			F6
13		CLR $40	7F
14			00
15			40
16	DONE	SWI	3F

INTEL 8080—Example 12

The Intel 8080 program for pattern comparison allows the strings to be anywhere in memory. The assembled program is shown in Fig. 5.48.

```
INTEL 8080 EXAMPLE 12
PATTERN COMPARISON


        MVI     C,0FFH      ;MARK = FF HEX FOR INEQUALITY
        LXI     H,41H       ;COUNT = LENGTH OF STRINGS
        MOV     B,M
        LXI     D,51H       ;POINT TO START OF STRING 2
PATTC:  INX     H
```

```
            INX     D
            LDAX    D           ;GET ELEMENT OF STRING 2
            CMP     M           ;IS IT SAME AS ELEMENT OF STRING 1?
            JZ      DONE        ;NO, NO MATCH
            DCR     B           ;ALL CHARACTERS CHECKED?
            JNZ     PATTC       ;NO, CHECK NEXT CHARACTERS
            MVI     C,0         ;YES, MARK = 0 FOR EQUALITY
     DONE:  MOV     A,C
            STA     40H         ;STORE MARK
            HLT
```

Figure 5.48 Assembled version of Intel 8080 pattern comparison program.

Memory Address (hexadecimal)	Instruction (mnemonic)		Memory Contents (hexadecimal)
00		MVI C,0FFH	0E
01			FF
02		LXI H,41H	21
03			41
04			00
05		MOV B,M	46
06		LXI D,51H	11
07			51
08			00
09	PATTC:	INX H	23
0A		INX D	13
0B		LDAX D	1A
0C		CMP M	BE
0D		JZ DONE	CA
0E			16
0F			00
10		DCR B	05
11		JNZ PATTC	C2
12			09
13			00
14		MVI C,0	0E
15			00
16	DONE:	MOV A,C	79
17		STA 40H	32
18			40
19			00
1A		HLT	76

This section has described the processing of character-coded data. We have shown how to find particular characters in strings, convert data to or from character codes, and compare character strings. The simplicity of the programs shows that 8-bit microprocessors are well suited to handling data in character form. The programmer can use the ordering of the character codes to advantage, since both the number and the letters form continuous sequences.

5.5 SUBROUTINES

Any program can be made into a subroutine by labeling the first instruction or entry point and ending the program with a RETURN instruction. The main program must call the subroutine and initialize the stack pointer to ensure that return addresses are stored properly.

Nevertheless, a more general subroutine is easier to use and is not restricted to particular memory locations. In simple cases, the main program can place data and addresses in registers before calling the subroutine, and the subroutine can place its results in registers. The data and addresses required by a subroutine are called *parameters*; the process of making these items available to the subroutine is called *passing parameters*. More complex subroutines may require too many parameters for the registers available. Such subroutines can use an assigned area in memory or the stack for parameters and results.

Reentrant subroutines can be called during interrupts without affecting the resumption of the original program. Such subroutines either use the stack for parameters, results, and temporary storage or assign special areas in memory for each calling program. The use of the stack is simpler, particularly if there are several levels of subroutines or interrupts.

An ASCII-to-decimal conversion program (Example 11) would be useful as a subroutine. Clearly any program that fetches numbers from a teletypewriter would need it. We could make the example programs into subroutines by labeling the first instruction (e.g., ASDEC) and replacing the last instruction with a RETURN (RET on the Intel 8080, RTS on the Motorola 6800). The modified programs are Motorola 6800 and Intel 8080 Example 13.

EXAMPLE 13: ASCII-to-Decimal Subroutine, Simple Form

```
MOTOROLA 6800 EXAMPLE 13
ASCII-TO-DECIMAL SUBROUTINE SIMPLE FORM


ASDEC   LDAA   $40      GET ASCII DATA
        SUBA   #'0      SUBTRACT ASCII ZERO
        CMPA   #10      IS RESULT LESS THAN 10?
        BCS    DONE     YES, STORE DECIMAL RESULT
        LDAA   #$FF     NO, RESULT IS FF HEX (DATA NOT DECIMAL)
DONE    STAA   $41      STORE RESULT
        RTS
```

```
INTEL 8080 EXAMPLE 13
ASCII-TO-DECIMAL SUBROUTINE SIMPLE FORM


ASDEC:  LDA    40H      ;GET ASCII DATA
        SUI    '0'      ;SUBTRACT ASCII ZERO
        CPI    10       ;IS RESULT LESS THAN 10?
```

```
          JC      DONE    ;YES, STORE DECIMAL RESULT
          MVI     A,0FFH  ;NO, RESULT IS FF HEX (DATA NOT DECIMAL)
DONE:     STA     41H     ;STORE RESULT
          RET
```

The main program must place the data in memory location 40, call the subroutine, and interpret the result. Example 14 contains typical calling sequences. The Motorola 6800 has two CALL instructions—BSR uses relative addressing and JSR uses direct (16-bit) addressing or indexed addressing. The Intel 8080 has both conditional and unconditional CALL and RETURN instructions.

EXAMPLE 14: Calling Sequence for Simple ASCII-to-Decimal Subroutine

```
MOTOROLA 6800 EXAMPLE 14
CALLING SEQUENCE FOR SIMPLE ASCII-TO-DECIMAL SUBROUTINE

STAA    $40         STORE ASCII DATA FOR SUBROUTINE
JSR     ASDEC       CONVERT TO DECIMAL
LDAA    $41         IS RESULT A DIGIT?
CMPA    #$FF
BEQ     ERROR       NO, ERROR IN DATA


INTEL 8080 EXAMPLE 14
CALLING SEQUENCE FOR SIMPLE ASCII-TO-DECIMAL SUBROUTINE

STA     40H         STORE ASCII DATA FOR SUBROUTINE
CALL    ASDEC       CONVERT TO DECIMAL
LDA     41H         IS RESULT A DIGIT?
CPI     0FFH
JZ      ERROR       NO, ERROR IN DATA
```

Since CALL and JSR place the return address in the stack, the main program must initialize the stack pointer. On the Motorola 6800 this step can be done with the instruction LDS (LOAD STACK POINTER); on the Intel 8080 it can be done either with LXI SP (LOAD STACK POINTER IMMEDIATE) or with SPHL (TRANSFER H AND L TO STACK POINTER). Generally the stack occupies the highest addresses in a section of read/write memory. If, for example, a system has read/write memory in addresses 1000 to 13FF (hex), we will typically start the stack pointer at 1400 (Intel 8080) or 13FF (Motorola 6800).

If the subroutine uses registers for parameters and results, it need not contain the instructions that load data from memory and store results in memory. A subroutine like the ASCII-to-decimal conversion is easy to modify, since it requires a single parameter and produces a single result. Example 15 shows the modified subroutines and typical calling sequences. The documentation describes how to pass parameters to the subroutine and how to obtain results from it.

A subroutine may have widespread effects. It will almost surely change all the status flags and the contents of the accumulator. It may also change other registers and memory locations. The documentation must describe exactly what effects the subroutine has. Clearly the subroutine will be easier to use if it only affects a few registers and uses the stack for other temporary storage.

EXAMPLE 15: ASCII-to-decimal Subroutine, Modified Form

```
MOTOROLA 6800 EXAMPLE 15
ASCII-TO-DECIMAL SUBROUTINE MODIFIED FORM
*
*   SUBROUTINE ASDEC CONVERTS AN ASCII
*     CHARACTER IN ACCUMULATOR A TO A
*     DECIMAL DIGIT IN ACCUMULATOR A
*   IF THE CONTENTS OF ACCUMULATOR A ARE
*     NOT AN ASCII DIGIT, ASDEC RETURNS
*     FF (HEX) IN ACCUMULATOR A
*   REGISTERS USED:   A
*

ASDEC       SUBA      #'0       SUBTRACT ASCII ZERO
            CMPA      #10       IS RESULT LESS THAN 10?
            BCS       DONE      YES, CONVERSION DONE
            LDAA      #$FF      NO, GET ERROR MARKER
DONE        RTS

*   TYPICAL CALLING SEQUENCE
            LDAA      ASDAT     GET ASCII DATA
            JSR       ASDEC     CONVERT TO DECIMAL
            CMPA      #$FF      WAS THERE AN ERROR?
            BEQ       ERROR     YES, ERROR ROUTINE


INTEL 8080 EXAMPLE 15
ASCII-TO-DECIMAL SUBROUTINE MODIFIED FORM
;
;SUBROUTINE ASDEC CONVERTS AN ASCII
;   CHARACTER IN THE ACCUMULATOR TO
;   A DECIMAL DIGIT IN THE ACCUMULATOR
;IF THE CONTENTS OF THE ACCUMULATOR ARE
;   NOT AN ASCII DIGIT, ASDEC RETURNS
;   FF (HEX) IN ACCUMULATOR A
;REGISTERS USED:   A
ASDEC:      SUI       '0'       ;SUBTRACT ASCII ZERO
            CPI       10        ;IS RESULT LESS THAN 10?
            JC        DONE      ;YES, CONVERSION DONE
            MVI       A,0FFH    ;NO, GET ERROR MARKER
DONE:       RET

;TYPICAL CALLING SEQUENCE
            LDA       ASDAT     ;GET ASCII DATA
```

```
        CALL    ASDEC   ;CONVERT TO DECIMAL
        CPI     0FFH    ;WAS THERE AN ERROR?
        JZ      ERROR   ;YES, ERROR ROUTINE
```

The ASCII-to-decimal subroutine requires a single input, produces a single result, and uses no temporary storage. The word disassembly program (Example 3) produces two results and uses temporary storage for a copy of the data. Example 16 shows the Motorola 6800 and Intel 8080 versions of this subroutine.

The Motorola 6800 program uses the two accumulators for the final results and the stack for temporary storage. The stack instructions are

PSH places the contents of an accumulator in the memory location addressed by the stack pointer and decrements the stack pointer—that is,

$$((SP)) = (A \text{ or } B)$$
$$(SP) = (SP) - 1$$

PUL increments the stack pointer and places the contents of the memory location addressed by the stack pointer in an accumulator—that is,

$$(SP) = (SP) + 1$$
$$(A \text{ or } B) = ((SP))$$

EXAMPLE 16: Word Disassembly Subroutine

```
MOTOROLA 6800 EXAMPLE 16
WORD DISASSEMBLY SUBROUTINE

*
*   SUBROUTINE WDDIS DIVIDES A WORD
*       IN ACCUMULATOR A INTO TWO HEXADECIMAL
*       DIGITS IN ACCUMULATORS A AND B
*   THE MOST SIGNIFICANT FOUR BITS OF
*       ACCUMULATOR A ARE PLACED IN
*       THE LEAST SIGNIFICANT FOUR BIT
*       POSITIONS OF ACCUMULATOR A
*   THE LEAST SIGNIFICANT FOUR BITS OF
*       ACCUMULATOR A ARE PLACED IN
*       THE LEAST SIGNIFICANT FOUR BIT
*       POSITIONS OF ACCUMULATOR B
*   ALL OTHER BIT POSITIONS ARE ZERO
*   REGISTERS USED:   A, B
*
WDDIS   PSHA                    SAVE COPY OF DATA IN STACK
        ANDA #%00001111         MASK OFF 4 MSB'S
        TAB                     LEAST SIGNIFICANT DIGIT TO B
```

```
            PULA                    MOST SIGNIFICANT DIGIT TO A
            LSRA                    SHIFT 4 MSB'S 4 TIMES LOGICALLY
            LSRA
            LSRA
            LSRA
            RTS
```

Subroutine WDDIS will change the contents of register B. We can save those contents by storing them in the stack prior to calling WDDIS—that is,

```
    PSHB
    JSR     WDDIS
    PULB
```

The Intel 8080 program uses an extra register for the second result and the temporary storage. In this case, subroutine WDDIS changes the contents of registers B and C. If necessary, we can save that data in the stack with the single instruction PUSH B.

The Intel 8080 stack instructions save and restore register pairs. PUSH decrements the stack pointer and places the eight most significant bits of the register pair in the memory location addressed by the stack pointer and then repeats the process for the eight least significant bits—that is,

```
    (SP) = (SP) − 1
    ((SP)) = (MOST SIGNIFICANT HALF OF REGISTER PAIR)

    (SP) = (SP) − 1
    ((SP)) = (LEAST SIGNIFICANT HALF OF REGISTER PAIR)
```

POP places the contents of the memory location addressed by the stack pointer in the eight least significant bits of the register pair, increments the stack pointer, and then repeats the process for the eight most significant bits.

```
    (LEAST SIGNIFICANT HALF OF REGISTER PAIR) = ((SP))
    (SP) = (SP) + 1

    (MOST SIGNIFICANT HALF OF REGISTER PAIR) = ((SP))
    (SP) = (SP) + 1


    INTEL 8080 EXAMPLE 16
    WORD DISASSEMBLY SUBROUTINE


    ;
    ;SUBROUTINE WDDIS DIVIDES A WORD
    ;   IN THE ACCUMULATOR INTO TWO HEXADECIMAL
    ;   DIGITS IN REGISTERS B AND C
    ;THE MOST SIGNIFICANT FOUR BITS OF
    ;   THE ACCUMULATOR ARE PLACED IN
```

```
;   THE LEAST SIGNIFICANT FOUR BIT
;   POSITIONS OF REGISTER B
;THE LEAST SIGNIFICANT FOUR BITS OF THE
;   ACCUMULATOR ARE PLACED IN THE
;   LEAST SIGNIFICANT FOUR BIT POSITIONS
;   OF REGISTER C
;ALL OTHER BIT POSITIONS ARE ZERO
;REGISTERS USED: A, B, C
;
WDDIS:  MOV     B,A
        ANI     00001111B       ;MASK OFF 4 MSB'S
        MOV     C,A             ;SAVE LEAST SIGNIFICANT DIGIT
        MOV     A,B             ;RESTORE DATA
        RRC                     ;SHIFT 4 MSB'S TO LEAST
        RRC                     ;   SIGNIFICANT POSITIONS
        RRC
        RRC
        ANI     00001111B       ;MASK OFF 4 LSB'S
        MOV     B,A             ;SAVE MOST SIGNIFICANT DIGIT
        RET
```

Many subroutines require a large amount of data. For instance, try making a subroutine from the program that finds the maximum value (Example 6). If the subroutine always looks for the data in a particular area of memory, we will have to move all the data there before calling the subroutine. A better alternative is to place the starting address of the array, the length of the array, and the maximum value in registers. Example 17 shows the Motorola 6800 and Intel 8080 versions of this subroutine. The logic of the subroutine is slightly different from that of Example 6; the program now handles the first element just like the others.

The Motorola 6800 subroutine uses both accumulators and the index register. Unfortunately, there is no easy way to save the index register in the stack before entering a subroutine, and so we will have to save it in fixed memory locations. The program changes accumulator B—its value upon return to the calling program is zero.

The Intel 8080 subroutine uses registers H and L as an address register. We can easily save the old contents of H and L in the stack with the instruction PUSH H. On both processors each subroutine call requires several instructions that place the proper parameters in registers. Both subroutines are reentrant as long as the register contents are saved, since neither uses any fixed memory locations.

Some subroutines require additional parameters. For instance, the multiple-precision addition program would need

1. The starting addresses of two source arrays.
2. The length of the arrays.
3. The starting address of the destination array if this array were not one of the source arrays.

Handling a large number of parameters is quite awkward in a microprocessor with a limited number of registers. Routines that need many parameters can seldom be made reentrant without a large amount of manipulation. If the stack is used for parameters, the return address that the CALL instruction places at the top of the stack must be handled with care; it must not be destroyed or placed where it can only be retrieved with great difficulty.

EXAMPLE 17: Maximum Subroutine

```
MOTOROLA 6800 EXAMPLE 17
MAXIMUM SUBROUTINE
*
*    SUBROUTINE MXVAL FINDS THE LARGEST
*       VALUE IN AN ARRAY OF 8 BIT
*       UNSIGNED INTEGERS AND PLACES THE
*       VALUE IN ACCUMULATOR A
*    THE STARTING ADDRESS OF THE ARRAY
*       IS IN THE INDEX REGISTER AND THE
*       LENGTH OF THE ARRAY IS IN ACCUMULATOR B
*    THE ARRAY IS ASSUMED TO HAVE AT
*       LEAST ONE ELEMENT
*    REGISTERS USED:   A, B, X
*

MXVAL    LDAA   X         MAXIMUM IS CURRENT ENTRY
MAXM     DECB
         BEQ    DONE
         INX
         CMPA   X         IS MAXIMUM LARGER THAN CURRENT
*                            ENTRY?
         BCC    MAXM      YES, CHECK NEXT ENTRY
         BRA    MXVAL     NO, REPLACE MAXIMUM WITH CURRENT
*                            ENTRY
DONE     RTS
*
*    A TYPICAL CALLING SEQUENCE
         LDAB   COUNT     GET LENGTH OF ARRAY
         LDX    #BASE     GET BASE ADDRESS OF ARRAY
         JSR    MXVAL     FIND MAXIMUM
INTEL 8080 EXAMPLE 17
MAXIMUM SUBROUTINE
;
;SUBROUTINE MXVAL FINDS THE LARGEST
;    VALUE IN AN ARRAY OF 8 BIT
;    UNSIGNED NUMBERS AND PLACES THE
;    VALUE IN THE ACCUMULATOR
;THE STARTING ADDRESS OF THE ARRAY
;    IS IN REGISTERS H AND L AND THE
;    LENGTH OF THE ARRAY IS IN REGISTER B
```

```
        ;THE ARRAY IS ASSUMED TO HAVE AT
        ;   LEAST ONE ELEMENT
        ;REGISTERS USED: A, B, H, L
        MXVAL:  MOV  A,M              ;MAXIMUM IS CURRENT ENTRY
        MAXM:   DCR  B
                JZ   DONE
                INX  H
                CMP  M               ;IS MAXIMUM LARGER THAN CURRENT
                                     ;  ENTRY?
                JNC  MAXM            ;YES, CHECK NEXT ENTRY
                JMP  MXVAL           ;NO, REPLACE MAXIMUM WITH CURRENT
                                     ;  ENTRY
        DONE:   RET
        ;
        ;A TYPICAL CALLING SEQUENCE
                LDA  COUNT           ;GET LENGTH OF ARRAY
                MOV  B,A
                LXI  H,BASE          ;GET BASE ADDRESS OF ARRAY
                CALL MXVAL           ;FIND MAXIMUM
```

An area of memory may be used for parameters; a fixed area, however, results in a subroutine that is not reentrant, whereas an address register that points to an area will be awkward to load or save. The programmer may find it easier to move parameters to temporary storage before calling the subroutine and allow the subroutine to use the temporary storage area freely.

Example 18 shows an Intel 8080 subroutine that adds two multiple-precision numbers and stores the result. Five registers are used for parameters. Useful instructions for further expansion are PCHL, which loads the program counter from registers H and L, and XTHL, which exchanges the top of the stack with the contents of registers H and L, thereby providing an extra address register.

EXAMPLE 18: Multiple-Precision Addition Subroutine

```
        INTEL 8080 EXAMPLE 18
        MULTIPLE-PRECISION ADDITION SUBROUTINE
        ;
        ;SUBROUTINE MPADD ADDS TWO MULTIPLE-PRECISION
        ;   BINARY NUMBERS AND STORES THE
        ;   RESULT IN MEMORY
        ;THE STARTING ADDRESS OF ONE NUMBER
        ;   (AND THE RESULT) IS IN REGISTER PAIR H,
        ;   THE STARTING ADDRESS OF THE OTHER
        ;   NUMBER IS IN REGISTER PAIR D, AND
        ;   THE LENGTH OF THE NUMBER IS IN
        ;   REGISTER B
        ;REGISTERS USED:  A, B, D, E, H, L
        MPADD:  SUB   A              ;START CARRY AT ZERO
```

```
ADD8:    LDAX    D              ;GET 8 BITS OF FIRST NUMBER
         ADC     M              ;ADD 8 BITS OF SECOND NUMBER
         MOV     M,A            ;STORE RESULT
         INX     D
         INX     H
         DCR     B
         JNZ     ADD8
         RET
;TYPICAL CALLING SEQUENCE
         LXI     D,NUM1         ;START OF FIRST NUMBER
         LXI     H,NUM2         ;START OF SECOND NUMBER, RESULT
         LDA     COUNT          ;GET COUNT
         MOV     B,A
         CALL    MPADD          ;MULTIPLE-PRECISION ADDITION
```

A program with two pointers would be awkward on the Motorola 6800, since it only has one index register. We could use some temporary memory locations as shown in Motorola 6800 Example 18. This subroutine is not reentrant because of the use of the fixed location TEMPA; a reentrant version would be difficult to write.

```
MOTOROLA 6800 EXAMPLE 18
MULTIPLE-PRECISION ADDITION SUBROUTINE
*
*    SUBROUTINE MPADD ADDS TWO MULTIPLE PRECISION
*      BINARY NUMBERS AND STORES THE
*      RESULT IN MEMORY
*    THE STARTING ADDRESS OF ONE NUMBER
*      (AND THE RESULT) IS IN THE INDEX
*      REGISTER, THE STARTING ADDRESS OF
*      THE OTHER NUMBER IS IN MEMORY
*      LOCATIONS ANUM2 AND ANUM2 + 1
*      AND THE LENGTH OF THE NUMBERS IS
*      IN ACCUMULATOR B
*    REGISTERS USED:   A, B, X
MPADD    CLC               START CARRY AT ZERO
ADD8     LDAA   X          GET 8 BITS OF FIRST NUMBER
         STX    TEMPA      SAVE FIRST POINTER
         LDX    ANUM2      GET SECOND POINTER
         ADCA   X          ADD 8 BITS OF SECOND NUMBER
         INX
         STX    ANUM2      SAVE SECOND POINTER
         LDX    TEMPA      RESTORE FIRST POINTER
         INX
         DECB
         BNE    ADD8
         RTS
TEMPA    RES    2
*
```

```
    *  TYPICAL CALLING SEQUENCE
           LDX    #NUM2  GET START OF SECOND NUMBER
           STX    ANUM2
           LDX    #NUM1  GET START OF FIRST NUMBER
           LDAB   COUNT  GET COUNT
           JSR    MPADD  MULTIPLE-PRECISION ADDITION
```

In summary, this section has discussed the use of subroutines. Subroutines are convenient because they save memory and allow the use of programs that have already been debugged and tested. Subroutines involving only a few parameters and results are simple to write and use. The parameters and results can be placed in registers. The main program must save the old contents of these registers (if necessary) and place the correct parameters in the registers before calling the subroutine. The stack pointer must be initialized before any subroutines can be called. Programs that need an array of data can be made into subroutines by using a register to store the starting address of the array. Subroutines can also use the stack for temporary storage. More complex situations must be handled cautiously. The amount of time and memory involved increases rapidly if the amount of data exceeds the immediate capacity of the processor.

5.6 SUMMARY

This chapter has described assembly language programming for the Intel 8080 and Motorola 6800. We started with simple programs and presented program loops, array processing, arithmetic programs, character-code manipulation, and subroutines. Although we have specifically developed programs for only two microprocessors, much of the methodology is applicable to other processors as well. In general, the following conclusions can be drawn.

Simple Programs

1. Try to bring data into registers and do as much processing as possible without using slow memory accesses.
2. Use logical and SHIFT instructions to get part of a word of data into the proper form for processing.

Arrays and Loops

3. Form simple loop structures. Use counters to control the conditional jump instructions that create the loop structure.
4. Handle arrays of data by starting at the base address of the array and moving through the array continuously by incrementing an index or address register during each iteration.

Arithmetic

5. Perform simple arithmetic one word at a time by using the **CARRY** bit to transfer information between words. Many processors have special instructions for decimal arithmetic.

6. Handle more complex arithmetic problems with lookup tables. The tables store all the possible results in program memory; the arithmetic problem reduces to choosing the correct result from the table.

Character Codes

7. Process character-coded data much like any other binary data. Perform conversions with ordinary binary arithmetic or tables.

8. Use the ordering of the letters and numbers in character codes to simplify processing.

Subroutines

9. Make simple programs into subroutines by adding an entry label and a RETURN instruction. Make the subroutines more general by using registers to pass parameters and results.

10. Make subroutines reentrant by using the registers and the stack for parameters, results, and temporary storage.

PROBLEMS

1. 8-bit subtraction.

Write an Intel 8080 or Motorola 6800 program that subtracts the contents of memory location 41 from the contents of memory location 40 and places the result in memory location 42.

Example:

$$(40) = 6E$$
$$(41) = 2F$$

Result:

$$(42) = 3F$$

2. Separating out an octal digit.

Write an Intel 8080 or Motorola 6800 program that places the three least significant bits of memory location 40 in memory location 41 and clears the five most significant bits of memory location 41.

Example:

$$(40) = 3A$$

Result:

$$(41) = 02$$

3. Reassembly of a word.

Write an Intel 8080 or Motorola 6800 program that places the four least significant bits of memory location 40 in the four most significant bit positions of memory location 42 and places the four least significant bits of memory location 41 in the four least significant bit positions of memory location 42.

Example:

$$(40) = A7$$

$$(41) = 53$$

Result:

$$(42) = 73$$

4. Checksum of data.

Write an Intel 8080 or Motorola 6800 program that forms the checksum of a series of numbers. The length of the series is in memory location 41, the series begins in memory location 42, and the checksum should be placed in memory location 40. The checksum is formed by EXCLUSIVE ORing the numbers,—that is,

$$S = X_1 \oplus X_2 \oplus X_3 \oplus \cdots$$

Example:

$$(41) = 03$$

$$(42) = 68$$

$$(43) = B4$$

$$(44) = A4$$

Result:

$$(40) = 68 \oplus B4 \oplus A4 = 78$$

(The EXCLUSIVE OR function is given by $0 \oplus 0 = 0$, $0 \oplus 1 = 1$, $1 \oplus 0 = 1$, $1 \oplus 1 = 0$—that is, EITHER BUT NOT BOTH).

5. Clearing an array.

Write an Intel 8080 or Motorola 6800 program that clears all the elements in an array. The length of the array is in memory location 40 and the array itself starts in memory location 41.

Example:

$$(40) = 03$$

Result:

$$(41) = 00$$

$$(42) = 00$$

$$(43) = 00$$

6. Minimum value.
   Write an Intel 8080 or Motorola 6800 program that finds the smallest number in an array of 8-bit unsigned numbers. The length of the array is in memory location 41, the array begins in memory location 42, and the minimum value should be placed in memory location 40.

   Example:

$$(41) = 03$$
$$(42) = 37$$
$$(43) = F2$$
$$(44) = C6$$

   Result:

$$(40) = 37$$

7. Multiple-precision subtraction.
   Write an Intel 8080 or Motorola 6800 program to perform multiple-precision subtraction. The length of the numbers is in memory location 40 and the numbers themselves start in memory locations 41 and 51, respectively (least significant bits first). The result should replace the number that starts in memory location 41. The number starting in memory location 51 should be subtracted from the number starting in memory location 41.

   Example:

$$(40) = 03$$
$$(41) = 29$$
$$(42) = A4$$
$$(43) = 50$$

$$(51) = FB$$
$$(52) = 37$$
$$(53) = 28$$

   Result:

$$(41) = 2E$$
$$(42) = 6C$$
$$(43) = 28$$

   that is,

$$
\begin{array}{r}
50A429 \\
-2837FB \\
\hline
286C2E
\end{array}
$$

8. BCD subtraction.
   Assume the same conditions as in Problem 7 except that all the numbers are decimal.

Example:

$$(40) = 03$$
$$(41) = 29$$
$$(42) = 65$$
$$(43) = 37$$

$$(51) = 88$$
$$(52) = 43$$
$$(53) = 22$$

Result:

$$(41) = 41$$
$$(42) = 21$$
$$(43) = 15$$

that is,

$$
\begin{array}{r}
376529 \\
- \ 224388 \\
\hline
152141
\end{array}
$$

(*Hint*: Note that $X - Y = X + (99 - Y) + 1$, since the extra 100 only results in a carry. How do we tell if $X - Y$ is positive or negative when using this formula?)

9. Sum of squares.
Write an Intel 8080 or Motorola 6800 program that adds the contents of memory location 40 squared to the contents of memory location 41 squared and places the result in memory location 42. Use the table of squares from Example 9 and assume that memory locations 40 and 41 each contain an unsigned number less than 8.
Example:

$$(40) = 03$$
$$(41) = 06$$

Result:

$$(42) = 3^2 + 6^2 = 2D \text{ (hex)} = 45 \text{ (decimal)}$$

10. Number of nonblank characters in a string.
Write an Intel 8080 or Motorola 6800 program to find the number of nonblank characters in a string. The end of the string is marked by an ASCII period (hex 2E). An ASCII blank is hex 20. The string starts in memory location 41, and the result should be placed in memory location 40.
Example:

$$(41) = 43 \qquad \text{C}$$
$$(42) = 20 \qquad \text{space}$$

$$(43) = 20 \quad \text{space}$$
$$(44) = 41 \quad \text{A}$$
$$(45) = 54 \quad \text{T}$$
$$(46) = 2E \quad \quad .$$

Result:

$$(40) = 03.$$

Memory locations 42 and 43 are ignored, since they contain blanks.

11. Decimal to ASCII.

Write an Intel 8080 or Motorola 6800 program to convert a decimal digit in memory location 40 to an ASCII character in memory location 41. If memory location 40 does not contain a decimal digit, an ASCII question mark (3F hex) should be placed in memory location 41.

Examples:

(a)

$$(40) = 05$$

Result:

$$(41) = \text{ASCII } 5 = 35$$

(b)

$$(40) = 27$$

Result:

$$(41) = \text{ASCII } ? = 3F$$

12. Pattern ordering.

Write an Intel 8080 or Motorola 6800 program that finds the relative order of two strings. The strings start in memory locations 42 and 52, respectively, and their length is in memory location 41. If the string starting in memory location 42 is numerically larger than or equal to the string starting in memory location 52, clear memory location 40. Otherwise place FF (hex) in memory location 40.

Examples:

(a)

$$(41) = 03$$

$$(42) = 43 \quad \text{C}$$
$$(43) = 41 \quad \text{A}$$
$$(44) = 54 \quad \text{T}$$

$$(52) = 43 \quad \text{C}$$
$$(53) = 4F \quad \text{O}$$
$$(54) = 57 \quad \text{W}$$

Result:

$$(40) = FF \text{ (hex), since } 434154 < 434F57.$$

(b)

$$(41) = 03$$

$$(42) = 43 \quad C$$

$$(43) = 41 \quad A$$

$$(44) = 54 \quad T$$

$$(52) = 42 \quad B$$

$$(53) = 41 \quad A$$

$$(54) = 54 \quad T$$

Result:

$$(40) = 00 \text{ (hex), since } 434154 > 424154.$$

13. Decimal to ASCII subroutine.

Make the Intel 8080 or Motorola 6800 decimal-to-ASCII program (Problem 11) into a subroutine. First write the subroutine in the simple form in which the subroutine uses the same memory locations that the program used. Then rewrite the subroutine so that it uses registers for the data and the result. Write a calling sequence for each subroutine that obtains the original data from memory location DECEM and stores the result in memory location ASCNO.

14. Word reassembly subroutine.

Make the Intel 8080 or Motorola 6800 word reassembly program (Problem 3) into a subroutine. Write the subroutine so that it uses two registers for the original data and one register for the result. Write a calling sequence for the subroutine that obtains the original data from memory locations LSDIG and MSDIG and places the result in memory location WORD.

15. Table access subroutine.

Write an Intel 8080 or Motorola 6800 subroutine that obtains an entry from a table (Example 9). The parameters of the subroutine are the base address of the table and the index number of the required entry. Write a calling routine that obtains the base address of the table from memory locations START and START +1 and the index from memory location INDNO. The table entry should be placed in memory location TABEN.

16. Length of string subroutine.

Write an Intel 8080 or Motorola 6800 subroutine that determines the length of an ASCII string. The parameters of the subroutine are the starting address of the string and the termination character. Write a calling routine that uses address STRST as the starting address of the string, an ASCII colon (hex 3A) as the termination character, and memory location LENG as a storage place for the result. How would you change the subroutine to make the maximum length of the string another parameter? What if there were 2, 3, 4, or an entire array of termination characters (e.g., colon, semicolon, comma, period, question mark)?

17. Rewrite the multiple-precision addition subroutine for the Intel 8080 or Motorola 6800 (Examples 18 and 19) so that the result can be placed in an entirely different area of memory from either of the two sources. You need not make the program re-entrant. Write a calling routine that uses memory locations OPER1, OPER2, and RSLT as the starting locations for the two operands and the result, respectively. The length of the strings is in memory location LENG.

18. Multi-word tables.
Rewrite the table access subroutine of Problem 15 so that each table entry can be more than one word long. Use the length of each entry and the starting address of an area in memory in which the selected entry will be placed as additional parameters. Write a calling routine that uses the parameters of Problem 15, where TABEN is now the starting address of the multiword result. The length of each entry is a fixed number TBLEN.

19. Multiword maximum subroutine.
Rewrite the maximum subroutine of Example 17 so that the entries can be more than one word long. Use the same methods as in Problem 18.

20. Table search subroutine.
Write a subroutine to determine the index corresponding to a particular table entry. The parameters are the entry and the base address and length of the table. The result should be the index of the entry in the table or FF (hex) if the entry is not in the table. Write a calling program that uses address CDTAB as the base address of the table, the contents of address LTAB as its length, the contents of address ELEM as the entry, and CDELM as the storage place for the result.

REFERENCES

BLAKESLEE, T. R., *Digital Design With Standard MSI and LSI*, Wiley, New York, 1975.

CUSHMAN, R. H., "Beware of the Errors that Can Creep Intp μP Benchmark Programs," *EDN*, Vol. 20, No. 12, June 20, 1975, p. 105.

CUSHMAN, R. H., "Exposing the Black Art of Microprocessor Benchmarking," *EDN*, Vol. 20, No. 8, April 20, 1975, p. 41.

CUSHMAN, R. H., "The Intel 8080: First of the Second Generation Microprocessors," *EDN*, Vol. 19, No. 9, May 5, 1974, p. 30.

CUSHMAN, R. H., "Microprocessor Benchmarks," *EDN*, Vol. 20, No. 10, May 20, 1975, p. 43.

ECKHOUSE, R. H., Jr., *Minicomputer Systems*, Prentice-Hall, Englewood Cliffs, N.J., 1975.

Intel 8080 Assembly Language Programming Manual, Intel Corporation, Santa Clara, Ca., 1974.

Intel 8080 Microcomputer Systems User's Manual, Intel Corporation, Santa Clara, Ca., July 1975.

LEVENTHAL, L. A., "Take Advantage of 8080 and 6800 Data-Manipulation Capabilities," *Electronic Design*, Vol. 25, No. 8, April 12, 1977, pp. 90–97.

LEVENTHAL, L. A., "Cut Your Processor's Computation Time," *Electronic Design*, Vol. 25, No. 17, August 16, 1977, pp. 82–89.

LEVENTHAL, L. A., *8080A / 8085 Assembly Language Programming*, Osborne and Associates, Berkeley, Ca., 1978.

LEWANDOWSKI, R., "Preparation: The Key to Success with Microprocessors" in *Microprocessors*, McGraw-Hill, New York, 1975, p. 74.

Motorola 6800 Microprocessor Applications Manual, Motorola Semiconductor Products Inc., Phoenix, Az., 1975.

Motorola 6800 Programming Manual, Motorola Semiconductor Products Inc., Phoenix, Az., 1975.

SHIMA M., and F. FAGGIN, "In Switching to N-MOS Microprocessor Gets a Two Microsecond Cycle Time," *Electronics*, Vol. 47, No. 8, April 18, 1974, pp. 95–100.

TITUS, J., "How to Design a Microprocessor-Based Controller System," *EDN*, Vol. 19, No. 16, August 20, 1974, pp. 49–56.

WELLER, W. J., et al., *Practical Microcomputer Programming: the Intel 8080*, Northern Technology Books, Evanston, Ill., 1976.

6 Software Development for Microprocessors

In this chapter we are concerned with the various stages of software development for microprocessors and the methods that can be applied in each stage. The topics covered include problem definition, program design, coding, debugging, testing, documentation, and maintenance and redesign. The emphasis is on presenting a variety of methods and useful hints rather than stressing a single technique. Designers should be aware of the entire range of problems involved in software development and should select the methods that seem the simplest and most effective. A brief description of many modern programming methods is given; no single method has yet proved a panacea, however. Finally, some of the development systems and test equipment that are widely used in designing with microprocessors are discussed.

6.1 THE TASKS OF SOFTWARE DEVELOPMENT

Many students (and authors) commonly confuse software development with coding. *Coding* is the writing of programs in a language that is comprehensible to a computer. In fact, coding is usually a small part of software development. Although very little quantitative research has occurred, a few studies have shown that less than one-fifth of programming time is spent in coding; the rest is spent in program design testing and other stages of software development. An often-used rule is that a programmer working on a large software project will write between two and ten fully corrected lines of program per day. Since the writing of even ten lines hardly takes more than a few minutes, coding is clearly not the most time-consuming stage of software development.

Software development can be divided into several stages.

1. *Problem definition*. This stage is the formal definition of the task. It includes the specification of inputs and outputs, processing requirements, system constraints (execution time, accuracy, response time), and error-handling methods.

2. *Program design*. This stage is the design of a program to meet the requirements of the problem definition. Useful techniques include top-down design, structured programming, modular programming, and flowcharting.

3. *Coding* (the actual programming). This stage is the translation of the program design into computer instructions. These instructions are the actual program or software product. We discussed assembly language programming in Chapter 5 and alternative language levels in Chapter 4. Many manuals and guidebooks also discuss coding; therefore we consider coding only briefly in this chapter and emphasize the other stages of software development.

4. *Debugging*. This stage is the discovery and correction of programming errors (sometimes called *program verification*). Few programs run correctly the first time, and so debugging is an important and time-consuming stage of software development. Editors, debugging packages, software simulators, logic analyzers, and breakpoints are useful debugging tools. The types of errors that are most common in microprocessor programs, as well as some simple techniques to reduce their numbers, are described in this chapter.

5. *Testing*. This stage is the *validation* of the program. Testing ensures that the program correctly performs the required tasks. Important factors include the selection of test data and the development of testing methods.

6. *Documentation*. This stage is the documentation of the program so that those who must use and maintain it can understand it and so that the program can be extended for further applications. Flowcharts, comments, and memory maps are among the widely used techniques here.

7. *Maintenance*. This stage is the updating and correcting of the program to account for changing conditions or field experience. Proper testing and documentation should significantly reduce the frequency and extent of the required maintenance.

8. *Extension and redesign*. This stage is the extension of the program to solve tasks beyond those described in the initial problem definition. Obviously designers always want to take advantage of programs developed for previous tasks. Designers should not consider any task completely in isolation from those tasks that will occur subsequently.

Each stage of software development affects the other stages. Problem definition must include consideration of a test plan, documentation standards, maintenance techniques, and the possible extension to other tasks. Program design must include provisions for debugging, testing, and documentation. The programmer works on several stages at the same time—coding, debugging, testing, and documentation are often concurrent activities. Clearly a single chapter is not sufficient to deal completely with any of these stages, much less all of them. A list of references covering the various subjects in greater detail appears at the end of the chapter.

To begin, we must develop criteria for evaluating programs. These criteria will determine the aims, methods, and relative importance of the various stages of software development. The following factors should be considered in writing programs for microprocessors.

1. *Reliability*. The most important criterion for a program is whether it works reliably. Elegant structure, efficient use of time and memory, short design time, and complete documentation are all useless if the program does not work. Testing is the key stage in determining whether the program does, in fact, work. The program must be checked to see that it works correctly under test conditions that accurately reflect actual operating conditions. The selection and execution of a test plan are not simple tasks. The problem definition and program design stages must produce both a test plan and a program that can be easily and thoroughly tested.

2. *Speed*. A program that executes tasks quickly can often do more work than a slower one. Speed may determine whether the program works at all, since critical timing requirements may exist. If the speed of the overall system depends on external factors, such as operator response time, input or output data rates, or the time constants of devices like sensors, displays, switches, or converters, then program speed will be relatively unimportant. Microprocessor-based systems are more often limited by external factors than by the execution time of the programs.

3. *Hardware cost*. Each chip needed for program memory adds to system cost. Of course, a longer program only needs more chips if it fills the existing ones (each chip may contain thousands of bytes). Extra read/write memory will also add to system cost. Additional memory requires additional interconnections, board space, decoding circuitry, and provisions for adequate current and voltage supplies and power dissipation. As larger semiconductor memories have become available at much lower per bit cost, the importance of memory usage has decreased greatly. However, memory usage must still be considered, particularly in simple applications in which the cost of a single memory chip is significant.

A program may also require other circuitry besides memory. Buffers, shift registers, latches, counters, level shifters, receiver/transmitter chips, multiplexers, demultiplexers, interrupt control units, comparators, and converters are among the hardware that a program may use. In the past programmers tried to minimize memory usage and external hardware, since hardware and memory were much more expensive than software. Today the cost of memory and external hardware is greatly reduced, and so hardware requirements are less important. A conflict exists here. On the one hand, tasks that once had to be done in hardware can now be done in software because of the reduced cost of processors and memory; on the other hand, additional hardware that can substantially reduce the complexity of programming is also available at relatively low cost. A further consideration is that software costs are the same regardless of the number of units produced, whereas hardware costs are directly proportional to the number of units. Clearly the tradeoffs between hardware and software differ today from the days when programmers simply tried to take the maximum advantage of expensive hardware.

4. *Programming time and cost*. The time and cost required to develop software are important factors. Although processors, memories, and other hardware are becoming less expensive, the cost of programming time continually rises. The change in the relative costs of hardware and personnel is a major reason why so much attention centers at present on techniques like structured programming and top-down design that increase programmer productivity. Proper design, debugging, testing, and documentation reduce the overall cost of programming. Writing programs in high-level languages can greatly increase programmer productivity and make many of the stages of software development simpler. Here is an obvious tradeoff between software and hardware costs; a programmer can write and debug a program much faster in a high-level language, but the final program will require more memory than one written in assembly language. Little reliable research is available concerning which languages and design methods produce the best results. Psychological research in the programming area will become more important as the relative cost of programmer time compared to hardware continues to increase (as it apparently will in the near future).

5. *Ease of use*. A program that is easier for other programmers or the end user to work with will be more valuable than one that is relatively hard to use. Strictly defined and complicated data formats, poor error messages, and unclear outputs will make a program difficult and expensive to debug, use, and maintain. Here again the high cost of personnel relative to hardware makes this factor important. Design and documentation are particularly significant stages in determining whether a program is easy to use. A knowledge of human factors is often important when the ultimate use of the program involves human interaction. Many microprocessor-based systems are specifically designed to simplify common tasks for human operators.

6. *Error tolerance*. A program that tolerates errors is easier to maintain and use than one that does not. A program must be designed to react in some reasonable way even to errors whose specific occurrence cannot be foreseen. Error tolerance is particularly important in situations where human operators enter the data or equipment must maintain critical functions. The program should make the operator or a system element aware of erroneous inputs or malfunctions without shutting the entire system down.

7. *Extendibility*. A program that can be extended to tasks other than the one for which it is specifically designed is clearly superior in the long run to one that can only be used for a particular task. The design and documentation stages are particularly important in meeting this criterion. Modular programming is a useful tool in this area, although structured programming and top-down design can also contribute to extendibility.

Reliability and programming costs are currently the most important criteria in software development for microprocessors. The primary objective is to develop a program that works with a reasonable expenditure of time and money; improvements can be made later.

The major cost in most microprocessor projects is programming time; methods that can minimize the time required to complete a program are especially important. With the availability of larger memories, cheaper hardware, and faster processors, time, memory, and hardware constraints are not as critical in microprocessor software development as they have been in the development of software for larger computers.

Thus the major emphasis of the remainder of this chapter will be on how to write reliable programs in a reasonable amount of time and how to test and document them. Considerably less attention will be paid to the question of how to write the shortest and fastest executing programs.

6.2 PROBLEM DEFINITION

Most microprocessor-based designs involve entire systems rather than single tasks and therefore require considerable definition. The user of a microprocessor typically wishes to control an electrical or mechanical system (such as a scale, terminal, card reader, or oscilloscope), perform a variety of calculations, and generate a variety of outputs; the user seldom wishes to solve a particular type of equation, find a data record, or perform some other clearly defined task. The initial stage of software development is to define precisely the tasks that must be performed and the requirements that must be met.

A basic question concerns the form of the inputs and outputs. What devices are to be attached to the microprocessor and in what form do they send or receive data? Other input/output considerations include the maximum and average data rates, error-checking procedures, control signals with which the input/output devices indicate the availability of data or readiness to accept data, typical word lengths, formatting requirements, clocks or strobes, and protocols. We often use microprocessors in control tasks where input/output requirements are major factors in problem definition.

Another question involves processing requirements. We must decide precisely what must be done to the input data and in what order tasks must be performed. Often the order of operations is critical, since input/output signals must be sent or received in a particular sequence. The system may have time constraints, such as peripheral data rates, mechanical or electrical delay times, hold times (the length of time that the data must remain constant), settling times, recovery times, and enable and disable times. Latches and timing circuits are sometimes used to handle these constraints. Memory constraints may limit the amount of program or data memory and the size of buffers. Data frequently must be processed within a certain amount of time, and status signals must often be serviced before they change.

Still another part of problem definition is error handling. We must specify the recovery method from incorrect sequences or erroneous signals. Common errors may be handled specifically in the program; other errors may simply be handled by restarting the operating procedure. The most likely errors must be carefully described.

Moreover, problem definition may involve interactions with other programs or tables, the requirements of which must be considered.

Problem definition may thus include many factors. Input/output, time constraints, processing requirements, accuracy, memory limitations, error handling, and interfaces with other programs must all be considered. The example below demonstrates the problem definition stage in a simple case.

EXAMPLE: A Digital Scale

Purpose A microprocessor is to control a meat scale like the one shown in Fig. 6.1.

Method The operator places the meat on the weighing mechanism and enters the price per pound from the keyboard. The scale displays the weight and total cost of the meat on the seven-segment displays (like those in calculators).

Input

1. One input is from the analog-to-digital converter connected to the weighing mechanism. This input will typically be either a binary or a BCD number. The processor must start the conversion, determine when it has been completed, and fetch the data from the converter (see Section 8.5). The precise sequence of operations will depend on the particular converter being used. The processor may itself perform some of the conversion tasks. For instance, the processor may provide timing pulses or comparison levels (via a digital to analog converter). Thus the converter may consist partly of software.

2. The other input is from a simple keyboard. The keyboard consists of a matrix of switches; pressing a key closes a switch and connects a row and a column. Section 8.5 describes how to identify which key has been pressed by determining which rows and columns are connected.

Figure 6.1 A digital scale.

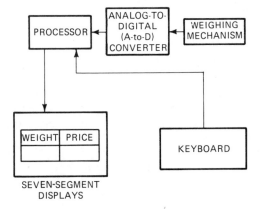

Here again the processor may perform some of the interfacing functions. The processor may debounce the keys (i.e., wait for a clean contact to be made—the key will initially bounce back and forth). The processor may also scan the keyboard, separate multiple key closures, and distinguish a single long closure from two separate closures. We will discuss these tradeoffs between hardware and software again in Chapters 8 and 9.

Output   Section A3.3 discusses the seven-segment code used by the displays. Either the program or the hardware must encode the results, send the digits to the correct displays, and ensure that the numbers are easily visible.

Processing   The program must multiply the weight by the cost per pound of the item. All numbers are decimal.

Accuracy   The weight is specified to the nearest hundredth of a pound. The program must round the total cost to the nearest penny.

Time constraints   There are no overall time requirements other than reasonable reaction time. System time constraints include the conversion time of the A/D converter, the time required for the keys to depress and bounce back, the time required to turn the displays on and off, and the pulse width and frequency needed for easy viewing of the displays. The overall speed of the system is not a high-priority factor, since the operator must prepare the input and examine and mark down the output in any case. The program must, however, observe the physical limitations of the I/O devices.

Memory constraints   Memory requirements will be small, since the program will be short and will only store a few digits. The cost of the weighing mechanism, A/D converter, and system packaging will be much higher than the cost of the processor and memory.

Error handling   A variety of erroneous inputs are possible, both human and electrical. Among them are

1. Erroneous data to or from the A/D converter.
2. Improper keyboard data. Among the possibilities are
   (a) Too many digits
   (b) Too few digits
   (c) Extra decimal points
   (d) All zeros
   (e) Two or more keys pressed at once
3. Weight or total cost too large for displays.
4. Display malfunction.
5. Processor malfunction.
6. Keyboard malfunction.

Clearly the most frequent error will be improper data from the keyboard. The program may automatically recover from some errors; it may simply ignore extra digits, extra decimal points, or multiple keys that are depressed simultaneously. The operator will discover these input errors simply by checking the displays. The program need only continue the input process in a reasonable manner—the operator will presumably correct the errors.

Some errors, however, may not be so easy to spot. For instance, a result may be too large for the displays. The program must provide a special warning, perhaps by displaying all decimal points or all zeros, to ensure that the operator is aware of this error.

Electrical or mechanical failures will clearly be less frequent than operator keyboard errors. Display failures may not be immediately obvious (0 and 8 on a seven-segment display, for example, differ only in a single segment). A solution to this problem might be a test mode in which all display segments are lit so that the operator can easily see if they are working.

Errors in the weighing mechanism or A/D converter may not be apparent. The CPU could itself check the converter by providing it with a known input. A standard weight would be needed to check the weighing mechanism. The program should provide special displays to warn the operator of these errors.

Keyboard failures, such as keys that are stuck or fail to make contact, will usually be apparent to the operator. Processor failure will also be immediately apparent. It may, however, be difficult to diagnose, and so some testing mechanism may be required.

Note the range of problems that the designer must consider in a very simple system. Obviously considerable understanding of hardware and human factors is essential in software development. Other microprocessor-based systems may need to interface with electrical or mechanical equipment without direct human interaction. Here the software must not only provide the proper interface but must also handle errors. The aim is to keep the system operating if possible and ensure that the occurrence of the error is recognized.

6.3 PROGRAM DESIGN

Once the overall problem has been defined, the next stage of software development is program design. Traditionally, program design has been linked with *flowcharting*. In fact, however, flowcharts are probably more useful in documentation than in design. Few programmers, despite the urging of numerous textbook writers, ever draw a detailed flowchart and then write a program from it. In general, programmers find that drawing a detailed flowchart from scratch is just as difficult as describing an initial working program and far less useful. Flowcharting techniques are helpful in describing program structure and in explaining programs. Other techniques, however, are more useful in actually designing programs. They include

1. *Modular programming*. A method in which long programs are divided into smaller programs or *modules* that can be designed, coded, and debugged separately with a minimum amount of interaction.

2. *Top-down design*. A method in which the overall task is first defined in terms of generalized subtasks that, in turn, are subsequently more fully defined. The process continues downward until the subtasks are defined in a form suitable for execution by the computer.

The opposite method is *bottom-up design* in which all the subtasks are first coded and then integrated into increasingly larger pieces of the overall design.

3. *Structured programming.* A method in which programs are written according to specifically defined forms; that is, only certain kinds of program logic are allowed, although the forms involved may be nested within one another to handle complex situations. Structured programming often refers to methods in which sections of a program always have a single entry and single exit.

These methods were originally developed for use in writing very long programs but can also be applied to the shorter programs commonly written for microprocessors. We will discuss flowcharting first and will then consider the other methods.

Flowcharts have the advantage over program listings in that they

(a) Show clearly the order of operations and the relationships between sections of the programs.

(b) Emphasize key decision points.

(c) Are independent of a particular computer or computer language.

(d) Have a standard set of symbols (see Fig. 6.2).

Flowcharts show the advantages of pictures over words. Despite their limitations, flowcharts remain a helpful visual aid to computer programming. In addition, they are a useful way for nonprogrammers and programmers to communicate.

Often two levels of flowcharts are desirable—one showing the general flow of the program and one providing details that are of interest mainly to programmers. Figure 6.3 shows a typical example involving a simple editor program. Too much detail makes a flowchart difficult to draw and understand; a very detailed flowchart has no advantage over the ordinary program listing.

Flowcharts can be helpful when reasonably general. However, they involve extra work and may have little connection to the structure of the data that must be

Figure 6.2   Standard flow diagram symbols.

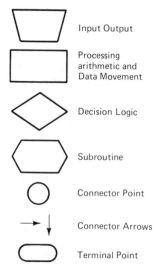

Input Output

Processing
arithmetic and
Data Movement

Decision Logic

Subroutine

Connector Point

Connector Arrows

Terminal Point

Figure 6.3 General and specific flowcharts.

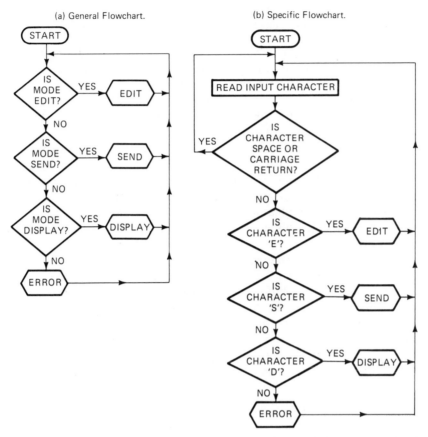

(a) General Flowchart. (b) Specific Flowchart.

processed or the hardware that must be used. Flowcharts only describe the flow of the program; they do not show the relationships of data structures or hardware elements.

Top-Down Design

Top-down design means that programs are designed by starting at the system level and successively replacing general formulations with specific programs. This method is different from the traditional bottom-up technique in which programs are written to perform specific tasks and then integrated into a complete system.

Top-down design proceeds as follows.

1. The overall supervisor program that calls the main subprograms is written and tested. The undefined subprograms are replaced by program *stubs* that either record that the subprogram has been entered or produce the result to a selected test problem. The stub should produce the same incidental effects that the ultimate program will produce.

2. Each stub is then similarly expanded. Testing and debugging can occur at each step as a stub is replaced by a working program.

3. The entire system is then tested.

Top-down design has the advantage that testing and integration occur along the way rather than at the end. Incompatibilities may be discovered early. Testing can proceed in the actual system environment rather than requiring driver programs[1] (such as to produce the numbers that will be multiplied together in the scale program) that will only be discarded later. Top-down design combines the design, coding, debugging, and testing stages of software development.

Top-down design has disadvantages, too. The overall system design may not take good advantage of the hardware; it may, in fact, require the hardware to perform tasks that it does poorly, such as requiring a 12-bit processor to manipulate 16-bit data. Top-down design is difficult when the same task occurs in several different places; the program that performs the task must interface properly in each of these places. A suitable stub may be difficult to write. Not all programs have the simple tree structures that mesh nicely with top-down design. The sharing of data by different programs can also create problems. Errors at the top level, whether in program design or coding, can have catastrophic effects on the entire project. In programming applications, top-down design has been shown to improve productivity considerably; it should not, however, be followed to such extremes that it interferes with the development of reliable programs that make efficient use of a particular processor.

Top-down design could, for instance, be used in the design of the digital scale mentioned earlier.

1. The overall flowchart is written as shown in Fig. 6.4, ignoring the possibility of errors for the time being.

The initial program would simply call the A/D input routine (a program stub), call the other routines (program stubs) if the input data was not zero, and return to reading the A/D input.

2. The program stub that reads the A/D input could then be expanded to perform the following tasks, assuming that the input from the converter consists of three BCD digits that the processor must fetch one at a time.

(a) Send a START CONVERSION signal to the A/D converter.

(b) Check the CONVERSION COMPLETED line. Wait if conversion is not finished.

(c) Fetch a digit.

(d) Check if the digit is zero.

(e) Repeat steps (c) through (d) three times.

(f) If all digits are zero, repeat the process starting with step (a).

(g) Check if converter has reached final value by waiting and then repeating steps (a) through (f).

(h) If inputs are not the same, repeat step (g) until they are the same to within the accuracy of the converter.

(i) Save final input value in memory.

---

[1] A *driver program* is a program that is written for the sole purpose of testing another program.

Figure 6.4 Flowchart for digital scale.

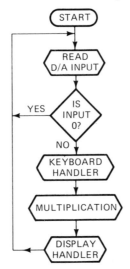

Figure 6.5 is a flowchart of the partially expanded program stub. Steps (g) through (i) are left unexpanded. The top-down procedure would continue by expanding each processing block in turn until the detail was sufficient so that all the tasks could be easily coded.

Figure 6.5 Flowchart for reading data from A/D converter.

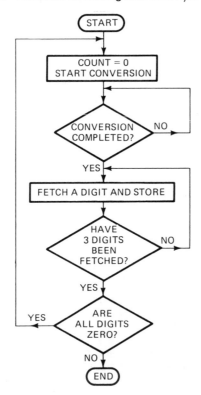

Structured Programming

In structured programming only simple logic structures are used. Bohm and Jacopini[2] showed that any program could be written by using only three structures.

1. A sequential structure in which instructions or programs are executed consecutively in the order written.

2. A conditional structure of the IF-THEN-ELSE type—that is, IF A THEN P_1 ELSE P_2, where A is a logical expression and P_1 and P_2 are programs consisting entirely of the three permitted structures. If A is true, the computer executes program P_1; if A is false, the computer executes program P_2. P_2 may be omitted if the computer is to do nothing if A is false.

EXAMPLE: (BOTH THEN AND ELSE INCLUDED)

IF X $\neq$ 0 THEN Y = 1/X ELSE Y = 0

This structure ensures that the computer will never try to divide by zero and defines Y in the case where X is zero.

EXAMPLE: (ELSE OMITTED)

IF CENTS $\geqslant$ 50 THEN DOLLARS = DOLLARS + 1

This structure rounds DOLLARS to the nearest dollar. No action is necessary if CENTS < 50.

3. A loop structure of the DO-WHILE type—that is, DO P WHILE A, where A is a logical expression and P is a program consisting entirely of the three permitted structures. The computer checks A, executes P if A is true, returns to check A again, etc. In other words, the computer executes P repeatedly as long as A is true.

EXAMPLE:

```
INDEX = 1
DO WHILE INDEX ≤ MAX
     BLK1 (INDEX) = BLK2 (INDEX)
     INDEX = INDEX + 1
     END
```

This structure moves the number of elements specified by MAX from memory locations in array 2 (BLK2) to memory locations in array 1 (BLK1).

---

[2]C. Bohm and G. Jacopini, "Flow Diagrams, Turing Machines and Languages with Only Two Formation Rules," *Communications of the ACM*, Vol. 9, No. 5, May 1966, pp. 366–371.

A *structured program* is one that is written using only this or some other complete set of structures. Figure 6.6 contains flowcharts of the conditional and loop structures.

Each structure has a single entrance and a single exit. If an error occurred during the execution of program P_1 in Fig. 6.6(a), we would know exactly how the computer reached that point. If, on the other hand, the program structure is as shown in Fig. 6.7, the error could be in any of the sequences that led to P_1. Furthermore, any correction might affect one of the other sequences. Obviously the situation would be even more complicated if the program had more than one exit as well.

Figure 6.6 Flowcharts for standard program logic structures.

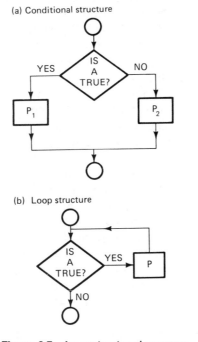

Figure 6.7 An unstructured program.

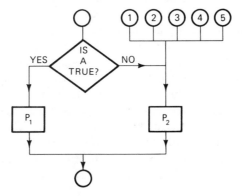

A typical example of the problem with unstructured programs is shown in the following sequence of FORTRAN statements.

```
40 COUNT = 1
   NUNIT  = XLENG / SCALE
```

Let us assume that the computer has tried to divide by zero in the calculation of NUNIT. Where is the error? We must first find all the statements that could cause a branch to statement number 40 either by examining the entire program or by using a cross-reference table. We must then determine which sequence of statements caused the error. Any corrections must not affect other sequences that also involve the altered statements. Structured programs make the debugging, testing, and maintenance stages of software development much simpler. The major difficulties in FORTRAN are the GO TO and IF statements, which can complicate program structure tremendously because the programmer may not know how the program reached a particular point. Many advocates of structured programming firmly believe in using no GO TO statements (i.e., unconditional transfers of program control). Certainly the lesson of structured programming is that a simple flow of control produces clearer, more reliable, and more easily tested programs.

So far the results of using structured programming in various environments have been encouraging. Most large programming projects presently use at least a local variation of this technique. Increases of 50 to 100% have been reported in programmer productivity, although many methods have actually been used in most cases and no carefully controlled experiments have been performed.

An important question concerns the applicability of these techniques to microprocessor programming. Structured programming has primarily been used in very large programming projects involving teams of programmers and tens of thousands of instructions; few microprocessor projects are that large. Structured programming techniques are most easily applied to programs written in high-level languages; most microprocessor programs are written in assembly or even machine language. Is structured programming actually advantageous to the microprocessor user?

The answer seems to be a qualified yes. Although microprocessor programs are seldom long by modern standards, they are difficult to debug and test because of the primitive hardware and software tools that are usually available. Techniques that make debugging and testing simpler must be carefully examined. Furthermore, few microprocessor programs are written to be used once and discarded; most are an integral part of systems and must be tested, documented, maintained, and extended just like the hardware in those systems. Structured programming can help to define system software as closely as system hardware.

The problem remains that few microprocessor designers use languages that have the actual structures of structured programming. The high-level languages based on PL/I (e.g., Intel's PL/M and Motorola's MPL) do have the needed structures and can be used to write structured programs. Popper has reported on a structured macroassembler.[3] However, most programs are presently written with simple assemblers like those described in Chapter 4. Thus structured programming must be used in the program design stage and the structured program then translated to assembly language much as an assembly language program may be hand-assembled into machine language. Since coding generally consumes only a small fraction of the total programming time, the extra step may still provide worthwhile results. Structured programs are often slower and require more memory than unstructured programs; however, as noted, execution time and memory usage are not as critical in the development of microprocessor-based systems as is the time required for program development. The use of structured programming can substantially reduce overall program development time.

A typical example of the use of structured programming is the design of a simple editor program. The program allows the user to space or backspace along the line (e.g., on a CRT or teleprinter), delete or replace characters, and end the editing phase by pressing the carriage return key. Figure 6.8 contains a structured program to perform this task (a semicolon is used to indicate comments, and indenting is used to clarify where the structures begin and end). This structured editor contains no unconditional jump (or GO TO) statements. The main loop is a DO-WHILE structure that examines characters until it finds a carriage return (the instructions in the loop will not be executed at all if the first character is a carriage return). The loop contains nested IF-THEN-ELSE statements. Indentation is used to indicate the nesting levels; otherwise the confusion as to which ELSEs do not exist and which go with which THENs is overwhelming. Some writers use an unnecessary ELSE, ENDIF, or FI (IF spelled backwards) to mark the end of the program included in a particular IF statement. Note that the same structured design can still be used even if the program must be rewritten in a different language or for a different computer. Structured programming requires considerable discipline on the part of the programmer, but the payoff seems to be substantial.

Modular Programming

Modular programming is a technique in which large programs are written, tested, and debugged in small units that are then combined into a final form. Clearly top-down design requires modular programming, but modular programming is much older and often used independently of other techniques. The modules are most often divided along functional lines; in microprocessor programming this division is particularly useful, since the modules can form a library of programs that can be used in later work. Parnas[4] has suggested a different division based on

---

[3]C. Popper, "SMAL—A Structured Macroassembly Language for a Microprocessor," *Proceedings of COMPCON* 1974, p. 147.

[4]D. L. Parnas, "On the Criteria to Be Used in Decomposing Systems into Modules," *Communications of the ACM*, Vol. 15, No. 12, December 1972, pp. 1053–1058.

Figure 6.8 A structured editor.

```
;   SET POINTER TO FIRST CHARACTER IN LINE
;      AND READ FIRST KEYBOARD INPUT
;
    CHARACTER POINTER = 1
    READ INPUT
;
;   EXAMINE CHARACTERS UNTIL CARRIAGE RETURN FOUND
;
    DO WHILE INPUT ≠ CARRIAGE RETURN
;
;   MOVE POINTER IF INPUT IS SPACE AND NOT
;      ALREADY AT END OF LINE
;
    IF INPUT = SPACE THEN
       IF CHARACTER POINTER ≠ 80 THEN
          CHARACTER POINTER = CHARACTER POINTER + 1
;
;   MOVE POINTER IF INPUT IS BACKSPACE AND
;      NOT ALREADY AT START OF LINE
;
    ELSE IF INPUT = BACKSPACE THEN
       IF CHARACTER POINTER ≠ 1 THEN
          CHARACTER POINTER = CHARACTER POINTER + 1
;
;   DELETE CHARACTER BY REPLACING WITH SPACE
;
    ELSE IF INPUT = DELETE THEN
       CHARACTER (CHARACTER POINTER) = SPACE
;
,   REPLACE WITH INPUT CHARACTER
;
    ELSE
       CHARACTER (CHARACTER POINTER) = INPUT
       IF CHARACTER POINTER ≠ 80 THEN
          CHARACTER POINTER = CHARACTER POINTER + 1
;
;   READ NEXT INPUT
;
    READ INPUT
    END
```

design decisions that are subject to change. Modular programming has obvious advantages because it limits the size of programs to be debugged and tested, provides basic programs that can be reused, and allows a division of tasks or the use of previously written programs. Its disadvantages include the additional program interfacing that is required, the extra time and memory needed to transfer control to and from modules, and the need for two separate levels of testing (i.e., module and program testing) and the writing of driver programs to test modules. Modular programming usually is hardest to apply when the structure of the data is more critical than that of the program. However, modular programming is a useful technique in developing microprocessor software regardless of other design techniques used. In the scale program described earlier the modules might be

1. A program that signals the A/D converter to begin the conversion process, waits for the conversion to be completed, and then places the results in the memory or in registers. This module would, of course, be useful in any system with the same or similar A/D converter.

2. A program that reads the keyboard and identifies the key closure. This module would be useful in any system with a similar keyboard.

3. A program that multiplies two decimal numbers. This program would be useful in any system that performs decimal arithmetic.

4. A program that displays the results. This module could be written so that the time constants of the displays could be easily varied.

The software designer can, of course, use a combination of techniques. Flowcharting, top-down design, structured programming, and modular programming are not mutually exclusive. The designer should remember that the real task is to produce a working program, not to follow the tenets of any particular design method.

6.4 CODING

Chapter 5 described assembly language coding extensively. This section presents some hints on programming style that will be useful regardless of the particular language or processor involved. Many of these hints have been inspired by the work of Kernighan and Plauger.[5]

1. Use names instead of specific memory addresses, constants, masks, I/O device numbers, or numerical factors.

The names can not only suggest the actual purpose or meaning of the particular address or data but can also make programs easier to change. For example, if output device 2 is the main system printer, the instruction

```
        OUT     2
```

will occur frequently in the program. If hardware changes require the use of another device number, the programmer will need to find each instruction and change it. If, however, the programmer has used a name, only the definition of the name need be changed. That is, if the original definition and a typical use are

```
PRNTR  EQU     2
        OUT     PRNTR
```

a change to device #3 requires the change of a single statement

```
PRNTR  EQU     3
```

---

[5]B. W. Kernighan and P. J. Plauger, *The Elements of Programming Style*, McGraw-Hill, New York, 1974.

The use of names can also reduce the confusion between addresses and data. For instance,

```
P1TOP     EQU     255
MIN1      EQU     0FFH
```

gives different names to the address 255 (P1TOP) and the number 255 (MIN1, since FF is −1 in two's complement).

2. Use meaningful names and labels. Meaningful names and labels can be helpful in documentation and maintenance as well as in debugging and integrating programs. Figure 6.9 shows the same Intel 8080 program written with and without meaningful names and labels; the extra typing pays off in clarity even without added documentation. The names should be as simple and straightforward as possible—PRNTR for the system printer, TTY for a teletypewriter, MAX for the maximum value, START for the beginning of the program. The use of meaningful names will save the programmer endless time and confusion in the various stages of software development.

3. Place definitions in groups at the start of the program. Definitions that are grouped at the start of the program can easily be located, checked, and changed when necessary. Figure 6.10 shows an example that also describes each definition with a comment. Obviously definitions that are scattered throughout the program can greatly hinder debugging and documentation.

4. Keep names and labels distinct. Distinctive names and labels reduce confusion. The use of numbers 0, 1, and 2, and letters O, I, and Z should be kept to a minimum. Certainly the programmer should not, for instance, use both MINI and MIN1 as identifiers; the chance for error is too great. Names that, for one reason or another, continually confuse the programmer should be changed; there are always enough errors in programs without inviting additional ones.

5. Avoid obscure constructions. Examples include the use of offsets from the program counter in computers that have many multiple-word instructions, the use of complex expressions that depend on the order in which operations are performed or operators that are seldom used, and complex conditional assemblies. What, precisely, does the program of Fig. 6.11 do? Even if the programmer knows the effects of an obscure construction at the moment, surely a few days or a few months time will return it to obscurity.

6. Avoid jumps when possible. Jumps make programs difficult to follow and debug. Repeating an instruction is often faster and clearer than jumping to a particular instruction. Programs with a series of jumps should be rewritten before the debugging stage.

7. Keep modules short. Divide long modules into sections. Not only will a shorter module be easier to debug and correct, but it is also more likely to be useful in subsequent programs, since its function will be a small one that is more likely to recur. One or two pages of code (50 to 75 lines) is a maximum size for a module. Modules can be implemented as macros or simply copied into the program in order

Figure 6.9 Finding a maximum.

Program 1 (without meaningful names)		Program 2 (with meaningful names)	
	LXI	H,X		LXI	H,BLOCK
Z:	MOV	A,M		NEWMX:	MOV	A,M
W:	INX	H		NEXTE:	INX	H
	DCR	B		DCR	B
	JZ	Y		JZ	DONE
	CMP	M		CMP	M
	JC	Z		JC	NEWMX
	JMP	W		JMP	NEXTE
Y:	STA	V		DONE:	STA	MAX
	HLT			HLT

Figure 6.10 Placement of definitions.

```
;  RAM LOCATIONS
   BUFR    EQU    257      ; TELETYPEWRITER INPUT BUFFER
   CLOCK   EQU    300      ; NUMBER OF CLOCK PULSES
   RFLAG   EQU    301      ; READY FLAG FOR TTY
;  TABLES
   SQR     EQU    606      ; TABLE OF SQUARES
   SSEG    EQU    520      ; SEVEN-SEGMENT CODE TABLE
;  NUMERICAL FACTORS
   MONE    EQU    -1
,  INPUT/OUTPUT DEVICES
   ADCON   EQU    4        ; INPUT UNIT FOR A/D CONVERTER
   KBD     EQU    3        ; INPUT UNIT FOR KEYBOARD
   PTAPE   EQU    2        ; INPUT UNIT FOR PAPER TAPE
   TTY     EQU    1        ; OUTPUT UNIT FOR TTY PRINTER
```

Figure 6.11 An obscure program.

```
COND    EQU    (105 SHR 2) AND 128
        IF     COND
        JNC    $ + 5
        LDA    STRT
        MVI    REG − 1, TOP OR 8
        ADD    B
        MOV    COND + 3, A
        ENDIF
```

to avoid a massive number of calls and returns (in microprocessors such calls may not only require extra time and memory but may also overflow a limited stack for storing return addresses).

8. Make modules fairly general. Obviously a module that is too specific (e.g., sorts precisely 32 elements or searches for the letter R) will find little repeated use. Greater generality can often be achieved with little or no extra code; a sort that will handle any number of elements will be no harder to write than one that handles a specific number. Generality that requires considerable extra code and ingenuity, such as writing a code conversion routine to handle both ASCII and EBCDIC characters, is not worthwhile. Simple ways to achieve generality have already been mentioned—the use of names instead of specific addresses or data, the collection of definitions at the start of the routine (perhaps including a separate heading for parameters), and the use of meaningful names that suggest the

purposes or identities of items. All these techniques can produce a program that can be used frequently and easily modified.

9. Emphasize simplicity and comprehensibility. The first objective of microprocessor programming is to write a program that works. Saving a few microseconds or a few memory locations is seldom important; the code can be optimized later. An initial program should be obvious rather than clever. Among practices to avoid are initializing variables in DATA statements, performing operations out of their obvious order, using multiple-word instructions to handle unrelated items, using leftover results to initialize variables or perform calculations, and using parameters as fixed data. Examples of practices to avoid (illustrated with Intel 8080 assembly language instructions) are

(a)

```
LXI     B, 264     ;INITIALIZE B TO 1, C TO 8
```

This statement should not be used when B and C are unrelated. Instead use

```
MVI     B, 1     ;INITIALIZE B TO 1
MVI     C, 8     ;INITIALIZE C TO 8
```

(b)

```
DCR     C
JNZ     STRT
MOV     B,C
```

This sequence should not be used to clear B. Instead use

```
DCR     C
JNZ     STRT
MVI     B,0
```

The cost in memory (one word) is small for a large increase in clarity.

This section has emphasized *defensive programming*—that is, programming in which changes can be made easily and in which misinterpretations and other errors will not occur. Obviously defensive programming takes extra time and the programmer can never anticipate all the problems that will arise. However, careful programming will pay off in fewer errors and programs that are easier to use and maintain. No programmer will always follow all the suggestions presented in this section, but a reasonable effort can make software development for microprocessors much easier.

6.5 DEBUGGING

Some of the tools used in debugging and the most common programming errors are considered here. Programming theorists often refer to program debugging and testing as verification and validation, respectively. *Verification* ensures that the program does what the programmer intends it to do. *Validation* ensures that the program produces the correct results for a set of test data. There is no clear demarcation line between these stages. The debugging of microprocessor programs is generally quite difficult because of the inability to observe register contents directly, the primitive debugging aids, the close interaction between hardware and software, the frequent dependence of programs on precise timing, and the difficulty of obtaining adequate data for real-time applications.

Among the tools that can be used to debug programs are

- Simulators
- Logic analyzers
- Breakpoints
- Trace routines
- Memory dumps
- Software interrupts

A *simulator* is a computer program that simulates the execution of programs on another computer. It does exactly what the programmer would do with pencil and paper to trace the effects of instructions; the simulator, however, is tireless, complete, and error free. Usually the simulator runs on a large computer and simulates the workings of a small computer that lacks the facilities for convenient testing. Typically, simulators, like cross-assemblers, are large FORTRAN programs that are available for purchase or through time-sharing services. These programs are useful in checking the logic of user programs, since the programmer can change data, examine the registers, and use other debugging facilities. However, simulators cannot fully model input/output or provide much help with timing problems. Sometimes the simulator is essential; the real computer may not be working, may be needed for other purposes, or may not have been built or delivered yet.

A *logic analyzer* (see Fig. 6.12) is a test instrument that is the digital bus-oriented version of the oscilloscope. The analyzer detects the states of digital signals during each clock cycle and stores them in a memory. It then displays the information on a CRT much as an oscilloscope does. As with an oscilloscope, several inputs can be monitored and displayed at once, triggering events can be defined, and thresholds can be set. Logic analyzers provide a convenient display

Figure 6.12 A logic analyzer (courtesy of Biomation, Inc.).

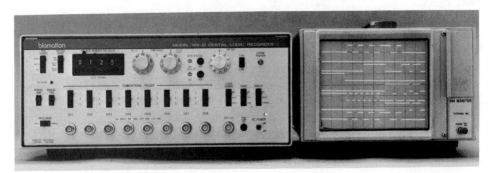

form for rapidly changing parallel digital signals. Some analyzers have such features as the ability to trigger on a particular instruction or sequence of instructions, recall previous data, and capture very short noise spikes (or *glitches*). Logic analyzers are complementary to software simulators, since their main use is in solving timing problems.

A *breakpoint* is a place in a program at which execution can be halted in order to examine the current contents of registers, memory locations, and I/O ports. Most microcomputer development systems and most simulator programs have facilities for setting breakpoints and describing the data that should be displayed or listed. Breakpoints may often be created with a TRAP instruction or a conditional jump instruction dependent on an external input that can be controlled from a panel. That is,

        JUMP ON NOT TEST $

will cause a jump to itself ($) until the TEST input is turned on. The contents of registers or memory locations can then be examined; some processors, such as the Intel 4040, will even place special status information on the buses while halted (such information might include the current contents of the accumulator, program counter, and other key registers).

A *trace* is a program that prints information concerning the status of the processor at specified intervals. Most simulator programs and some microcomputer development systems have trace facilities. Sometimes the trace will print the complete status of processor registers and flags after the execution of each instruction. Some simulator programs allow tracing of particular registers or memory locations with values being printed only when the contents change. Traces may result in massive listings that can be hard to decipher unless the programmer selects variables and formats carefully.

A *memory dump* is a listing of the current contents of a section of the memory. Most simulator programs, microcomputer development systems, and monitors can produce memory dumps. Obviously a complete memory dump will be long and difficult to interpret; such a dump will be particularly inconvenient if it must be printed on a slow teletypewriter. A memory dump is seldom an effective method for debugging, but often it is the only tool available. A complete memory dump is traditionally the program debugging technique used when other methods have failed.

The SOFTWARE INTERRUPT or TRAP instruction is frequently used for debugging purposes. The instruction usually saves the current value of the program counter and then branches to a specified memory location. That memory location can be the starting point of a debugging program that lists or displays status information—breakpoints may be inserted with TRAP instructions. For instance, when the Motorola 6800 executes a SOFTWARE INTERRUPT, it automatically saves the contents of all its registers in the memory stack; the programmer can then observe the contents directly. The Intel 8080 has a software interrupt (the RST or

RESTART instruction) but only saves the program counter in the stack. The programmer must enter the TRAP instruction into the program and provide the debugging routine if it is not part of a standard package. A monitor that can place TRAP instructions at specified addresses is useful.

Checklists and Hand Checking

Checklists are an obvious debugging tool that can be used in conjunction with flowcharts or structured design methods. The programmer should check that each variable has been initialized, each flowchart element or logic structure has been coded, all definitions are correct, and all paths are connected properly. A simple checklist can save a great deal of time.

Hand checking of long or complicated programs is usually a waste of time, since the programmer is likely to make more mistakes checking the program than coding it. However, loops and sections of programs should be hand checked to ensure that the general flow of control is correct. In the case of loops, the programmer should check by hand to see if the loop performs the first and last iterations correctly; they are usually the sources of most errors in loops (examples will be shown later). The program should also be hand checked to ensure that it handles simple cases correctly; trivial cases, such as tables with no elements and buffers that contain no data, are a source of subtle errors that are often only found in a very late stage of program or field testing. Equality cases within loops and conditional jumps are other sources of errors that should be hand checked; the problem here is usually which value of a flag to use as the jump condition and what action to take when a variable is equal to a threshold rather than above or below it. Hand checking of these troublesome cases can solve many problems at little cost.

The programmer should perform all hand checking and other debugging in a systematic manner. The programmer should never assume that the first error found is the only one in the program; the programmer should always check the entire program before executing it again in order to get the maximum value from each debugging run.

Typical Errors

Each program has its own unique errors (a modern version of Tolstoy's dictum). Nevertheless, some errors are sufficiently common to deserve mention. Some are specific to assembly language programming, but others occur in any kind of programming. They include

1. Failure to initialize variables, particularly counters and pointers. Registers, flags, and memory locations should not be assumed to contain zero at the start of the program.

2. Incrementing counters and pointers before they are used instead of afterward or not incrementing them at all. Counters and pointers must be updated regardless of which path is followed within the loop structure.

3. Failure to handle trivial cases, such as an array or table with no elements or only one element.

4. Inverting conditions, such as jumping on zero instead of on not zero. Remember that the ZERO flag is 1 if the result was zero, 0 if the result was not zero.

5. Reversing the order of operands, such as moving A to B when B to A was meant. On the Intel 8080 the instruction MOV A,B moves the contents of B to A.

6. Jumping on conditions that have been changed since they were set to the desired values. A common problem in assembly language programming is trying to use flags as jump conditions when they have been changed by intermediate instructions. The programmer must remember precisely the effects of instructions on flags.

7. Failure to handle fall-through conditions, such as an entry that is never found in a table or a condition that is never met. Such a failure can cause an endless loop.

8. Failure to save the contents of the accumulator or other register before using the register again.

9. Confusing addresses and values. Memory location 40 does not necessarily contain the number 40. Note particularly the difference between immediate addressing in which the data is part of the instruction and direct addressing in which the address of the data is part of the instruction.

10. Jumping the wrong way on equality, such as jumping if a number is nonnegative rather than positive.

11. Trying to exchange registers or memory locations without using an intermediate storage place.

```
A = B
B = A
```

sets both A and B to the previous contents of B, since the first statement destroys the previous contents of A. The sequence

```
T = A
A = B
B = T
```

will exchange the registers properly.

12. Confusing numbers and characters. ASCII zero or EBCDIC zero is not the same as the number zero. Most peripherals handle data in a particular code.

13. Confusing numbers and numerical codes. BCD 61 is not the same as binary 61.

14. Counting the length of a table or block improperly. Memory locations 40 through 48 contain nine, not eight, words of data.

15. Ignoring the direction of noncommutative operations. The assembly language command SUB C subtracts the contents of register C from the contents of the accumulator, not vice versa. Obviously the programmer must be careful with subtraction, comparison, and division.

16. Confusing two's complement and sign magnitude notation. Almost all computers use two's complement where the most significant bit is a sign but the other bits do not represent the magnitude of the number.

17. Ignoring overflow when doing signed arithmetic. Adding 64 and 64 in an 8-bit processor gives -128 (try it), whereas adding -128 and -128 gives 0.

18. Ignoring the effects of subroutines and macros. Subroutines and macros almost always change the flags and may affect registers and memory locations as well. Macros and subroutine calls may be deceptive because they seem to be single instructions.

Many other errors exist, but this list may give the programmer some idea of where to look. A typical example of debugging is the following attempt to write an Intel 8080 assembly language program to find the length of a string of ASCII characters that is known to end with a carriage return (0D hex in ASCII). Figure 6.13 contains the initial program.

Figure 6.13 Initial attempt to find length of character string.

```
MBUF     EQU  40H
CR       EQU  00001101B
         LXI  H,MBUF   ;  MEMORY POINTER = START OF STRING
         INX  H        ;
CHKCR:   INR  B        ;  CHARACTER COUNTER = CHARACTER COUNTER + 1
         CMP  M        ;  IS NEXT CHARACTER A CARRIAGE RETURN?
         JNZ  CHKCR    ;  NO, KEEP LOOKING
         HLT
```

EXAMPLE: Debugging a Program that Finds the Length of a String

A simple hand check was made with a string consisting of an ASCII carriage return character in location MBUF. The instruction INX H added one to the pointer before the data in the starting address was even examined; the carriage return character would never be recognized. Furthermore, the accumulator and register B were used within the loop but were never initialized. Correcting these errors resulted in the program of Fig. 6.14.

Figure 6.14 Second attempt to find length of character string.

```
MBUF     EQU  40H
CR       EQU  00001101B
         LXI  H,MBUF   ;  MEMORY POINTER = START OF STRING
         MVI  A,CR     ;  LOAD CARRIAGE RETURN FOR COMPARISON
CHKCR:   MVI  B,0      ;  CHARACTER COUNTER = ZERO
         CMP  M        ;  IS NEXT CHARACTER A CARRIAGE RETURN?
         JNZ  DONE     ;  YES, DONE
         INX  H        ;
         INR  B        ;  NO, INCREMENT CHARACTER COUNTER
         JMP  CHKCR    ;
DONE:    HLT
```

A hand check of this program showed that the instruction JNZ DONE should be JZ DONE in order to end the search when the character being examined is a carriage return. The result in the simple case was then a string length of zero in register B as expected.

However, trying the program on a string consisting of a space character followed by a carriage return also resulted in an answer of 0; the program was obviously incorrect. A hand check of the loop showed that the INR B instruction incremented the counter but that the program then jumped to the MVI B,0 instruction and set the counter back to zero. The label CHKCR was in the wrong place; the corrected program is shown in Fig. 6.15. This program produced the correct results on several trial strings of characters. The example shows that simple hand testing may provide as much insight into program logic as sophisticated debugging tools. Debugging real-time systems is much more difficult and requires more planning and equipment.

Figure 6.15   Final attempt to find length of character string.

```
MBUF     EQU  40H
CR       EQU  00001101B
         LXI  H,MBUF   ;  MEMORY POINTER = START OF STRING
         MVI  A,CR     ;  LOAD CARRIAGE RETURN FOR COMPARISON
         MVI  B,0      ;  CHARACTER COUNTER = ZERO
CHKCR:   CMP  M        ;  IS NEXT CHARACTER A CARRIAGE RETURN?
         JZ   DONE     ;  YES, DONE
         INX  H
         INR  B        ;  NO, INCREMENT CHARACTER COUNTER
         JMP  CHKCR
DONE:    HLT
```

6.6 TESTING

Program testing and program debugging are closely related. Testing is essentially a later stage of debugging in which the program is validated by trying it on a suitable set of test cases. Some of the test cases will certainly be the ones used in debugging—the all zeros case, the various special cases, and other obvious cases that must be checked.

Program testing is, however, more than a simple matter of exercising the program a few times. Exhaustive testing of all possible cases is the best alternative, but this process is usually impractical. A simple program that takes in 16 bits of data and produces a 16-bit result involves 4 billion possible combinations of inputs and outputs; clearly most programs are far more complicated and would have even more possible combinations. Formal validation methods exist but are only applicable to very simple programs. Thus program testing requires a choice of test cases. The situation is further complicated by the fact that many microcomputer programs depend on real-time inputs that are difficult to control or simulate; often the microprocessor must interact in a very precise manner with a large and complex system. How can the necessary data be generated and presented to the microcomputer?

Several tools are available to help with this task. Clearly debugging tools mentioned earlier will be useful, particularly logic analyzers and software simulators. Other tools include

1. *Input/output simulations* that allow a variety of devices to be simulated from a single input and a single output device. Such simulations may also provide inputs for external timing signals and other controls. Most development systems have some facilities for I/O simulation; most software simulators also provide I/O simulation but not in real time.

2. *In-circuit emulators* (see Fig. 6.16) that allow a prototype system to be directly attached to the development system or control panel and tested.

3. *ROM simulators* that allow read/write memory to be used for programs while providing the timing characteristics of the ROM that will be used in the final system.

4. Real-time operating systems or monitors that can control real-time events, provide interrupts, and allow real-time traces and breakpoints.

5. Emulations on microprogrammable computers that can execute the instruction set of a microcomputer at close to real-time speeds and that may also provide programmable input/output.

6. Special interfaces that allow a minicomputer or programmable controller to test the microprocessor program by externally controlling the input/output section.

7. Testing programs (or *exercisers*) that check each branch in a program in an automated manner. Such programs can find logical errors but cannot help with time-dependent problems.

Figure 6.16   An in-circuit emulator (courtesy of Intel Corporation).

The testing of microprocessor software is a difficult and relatively unexplored area. Most testing is presently carried out with specially built equipment suited to a particular task; few general-purpose hardware or software tools are available. Among the rules that can aid in program testing are the following.

1. Make the test plan part of the program design. Testing should be one of the factors in the problem definition, program design, and coding stages.

2. Check all trivial and special cases. Such cases may include zero inputs, no data from communications lines, special warning or alarm inputs, and other situations that are singled out for some reason. Often the simplest cases can lead to the most annoying and mysterious errors.

3. Select test data on a random basis. Doing so will eliminate any inadvertent bias caused by the programmer selecting test data. Random number tables are widely available, and most computers have random number generators.

4. Plan and document software testing just like hardware testing. Obviously testing can never prove that no errors exist; so good software design, like good hardware design, is an essential part of the testing process.

5. Use the maximum and minimum values of all variables as test data. Extreme values are often the source of special errors.

6. Use statistical methods in planning and evaluating complex tests. Methods are available for selecting data and evaluating the significance of results. Optimization techniques may suggest good choices for system parameters and efficient sets of test data.

6.7 DOCUMENTATION

Documentation is a stage of software development that is often overlooked. Yet, proper documentation is not only useful in the debugging and testing stages, it is also essential in the maintenance and redesign stages. A properly documented program can easily be used again when needed; an undocumented program usually requires so much extra work to use that the programmer might as well start over again from scratch.

Among the techniques commonly found in documentation are flowcharts, comments, memory maps, parameter and definition lists, and program library forms. Structured programming has developed some of its own documentation forms, which are described in the references.

Flowcharts are among the few visual aids available for program documentation. A general flowchart of the type shown earlier can serve as a quick pictorial description of a program. Such a flowchart is a useful part of documentation, although hardly complete in itself. A more detailed programmer's flowchart (also mentioned previously) can be invaluable to another programmer who must use or maintain the program. Usually the programmer draws this flowchart after completing the program.

Comments are a basic part of program documentation. They do not, however, substitute for proper programming style. A program with clear structure and properly chosen names can be partially self-documenting. Comments should explain the purposes of program instructions; they should not simply repeat the meaning of the instructions. Figures 6.17 and 6.18 show the same Intel 8080 assembly language program, once with commenting that adds nothing to the documentation and once with proper commenting (the program finds the maximum of an array of elements starting in location BLKST—the length of the array is in memory location LENG).

Figure 6.17 A poorly documented program.

```
              LDA   LENG        ;   LENG TO A
              MOV   B,A         ;   A TO B
              LXI   H,BLKST     ;   PUT BLKST IN H
NEWMX: MOV    A,M              ;   M TO A
NEXTE: INX    H                ;   H TO H + 1
              DCR   B           ;   B TO B − 1
              JZ    DONE        ;   GO TO DONE IF ZERO
              CMP   M           ;   COMPARE TO M
              JC    NEWMX       ;   GO TO NEWMX IF CARRY
              JMP   NEXTE       ;   GO TO NEXTE
DONE:         STA   MAX         ;   A TO MAX
              HLT
```

Figure 6.18 A properly documented program.

```
              LDA   LENG        ;   COUNT = LENGTH OF ARRAY
              MOV   B,A
              LXI   H,BLKST     ;   POINT TO START OF DATA
NEWMX: MOV    A,M              ;   ELEMENT IS NEW MAXIMUM
NEXTE: INX    H
              DCR   B
              JZ    DONE
              CMP   M           ;   IS MAXIMUM LARGER THAN CURRENT ELEMENT?
              JC    NEWMX       ;   NO, REPLACE MAXIMUM
              JMP   NEXTE       ;   YES, LOOK AT NEXT ELEMENT
DONE:         STA   MAX         ;   STORE MAXIMUM
              HLT
```

The following rules should be observed in comments.

1. Comments should explain the purposes of instructions or instruction sequences, not define operation codes.

2. Comments should be as clear as possible. Shorthand and obscure abbreviations should be avoided, although complete sentence structure is not necessary.

3. Comments should be limited to important points. Too many comments make a program difficult to follow. Standard sequences like loop controls or indexing operations need not be explained unless they are being performed in an unusual manner.

4. Comments should be placed reasonably close to the statements that they describe. The programmer should develop a standard form—repetitiveness is no evil in commenting; in fact, variations are confusing.

5. Comments should be kept up to date. Comments that refer to previous versions of a program are worse than no comments at all.

6. Comments should be brief. More complete explanations should be left to the reference documentation.

Commenting is a tool that the programmer should learn to use properly. Programmers should ask themselves what explanation they would need to understand the program and should provide it in a reasonable form. Such comments, provided in a systematic manner, can be helpful in all stages of software development.

Memory maps are lists of the memory assignments made in the program. Such maps prevent different routines from interfering with each other, simplify the passing of parameters, and help in determining the amount of memory needed and finding the locations of subroutines, tables, and temporary storage. Memory maps are particularly important in microprocessor software development because of the use of separate program and data memory (ROM and RAM), the fact that addresses are assigned as part of the hardware design, the need to conserve memory usage (particularly the more expensive RAM), and the need to know the precise locations of certain parameters that may have to be field-alterable to allow customizing.

Parameter and definition lists are part of the documentation of any computer program. Besides explaining the function of each parameter and the meaning of the various options, such lists also describe the definitions. The existence of these lists does not mean that the parameters should not also be explained in the program.

Program library forms can describe subroutines for use in subsequent programs. Among the information that the programmer should provide is the purpose of the program, the form of input and output data, the requirements (memory, time, and registers) of the program, a description of the parameters, and a sample case showing how the program works. Figure 6.19 shows a typical library program that could be either a subroutine or a macro.

Proper software documentation combines all or most of the methods mentioned. The total documentation includes

- General flowcharts
- Programmer's flowcharts
- A description of the test plan and test results
- A written description of the program
- A documented listing of each program module
- A list of parameters and definitions
- A memory map

Documentation is a time-consuming task that the programmer should perform simultaneously with the design, coding, debugging, and testing stages of software development. Good design and coding techniques make a program easier to document; good documentation, in turn, simplifies maintenance and redesign and makes subsequent programming tasks much simpler.

Figure 6.19 A library program.

```
Purpose:      The program COMPD computes a 16-bit twos complement.
Language:     Intel 8080 assembler
Initial conditions:    16-bit number in registers H and L (most significant bits in H)
Final conditions:      16-bit twos complement in registers H and L
Requirements:     Memory—8 locations
                  Time—43 clock cycles
                  Registers—A, H, L
                  No flags affected
Typical case:
    Start:
          (H) = 20 (hex)
          (L) = A4 (hex)
      End:
          (H) = DF (hex)
          (L) = 5C (hex)
Listing:
                ;
                ;    16-BIT TWOS COMPLEMENT
                ;
       COMPD: MOV   A,L    ;  ONES COMPLEMENT 8 LEAST
              CMA          ;       SIGNIFICANT BITS
              MOV   L,A
              MOV   A,H    ;  ONES COMPLEMENT 8 MOST
              CMA          ;       SIGNIFICANT BITS
              MOV   H,A
              INX   H      ;  ADD 1 FOR TWOS COMPLEMENT
              RET
```

6.8 REDESIGN

Redesign may involve adding new features or meeting new requirements; such redesign should proceed through the previously mentioned stages of software development. The process may also involve making a program meet critical time or memory requirements; this section briefly describes methods for making programs faster or shorter.

When relatively small (25% or less) increases in speed or reductions in memory usage are needed, a program can often be reorganized to meet the requirement. Program structure may have to be sacrificed. The new program must be carefully documented, since its workings will seldom be obvious. Such a reorganization may require a large amount of programmer time and should be avoided when possible.

Some rules for increasing execution speed are

1. Concentrate on loops that are executed frequently. Determine which loops they are by hand-checking or program-testing methods. Instructions that are executed only once or a few times have little impact on program execution time; changing such instructions can cause errors for no reason.

2. Try to use register operations whenever possible. Such operations will execute faster than any others but may, however, require extra initialization and manipulation. Among the register operations that may be useful are indirect jumps that are performed by transferring the contents of a register to the program counter (the Intel 8080 has such an instruction, PCHL).

3. Try to do repetitive operations outside loops. Watch for the same calculation being done every time a loop is executed; such an operation can be done outside the loop and the result stored in a register or memory location.

4. Use short forms of addressing when possible. The use of these short forms may require that data be organized cleverly.

5. Try to eliminate jump statements. They almost always take much time and memory.

6. Repeat sequences of instructions rather than use subroutines or loops.

7. Take advantage of addresses that can be manipulated as 8-bit quantities. They include addresses on page zero and even multiples of 100 (hexadecimal).

8. Use stack addressing rather than direct addressing to move data between memory and registers.

Many of the same techniques can minimize execution time and memory usage, since, for most situations, longer programs require more memory accesses and more execution time. However, subroutines represent a memory savings at the cost of the execution time required for the call and return; loops represent a similar tradeoff. When minimum execution time is required, subroutines and loops can be replaced by repeated copies of the same instructions; minimum memory usage requires the opposite replacements.

Enormous gains cannot be expected from program optimization. Unless the program is very poorly written, a speed increase or memory reduction larger than 25% is unusual. If larger increases in speed or decreases in memory usage are needed, the methods below should be considered.

1. A new algorithm. A different method may provide a large increase in speed or decrease in memory use; rearranging the present method will seldom do the job.

2. The use of microprogramming. A microprogrammable processor may be able to execute the present program at significantly higher speeds.

3. Speeding up the clock. The processor may be able to work at a higher clock rate if faster memory is available.

4. The use of external hardware. External hardware, such as multipliers, counters, UARTs, and other devices, can increase throughput by taking some of the processing burden away from the CPU.

5. Parallel processing. Two or more processors may be able to do the job at higher speed without greatly affecting system cost.

6. Distributed processing. Two or more processors may be able to do the job faster by dividing the functions.

7. Replacing program logic by large, fast ROMs. A large ROM may be able to perform the same function as part of a program. Obviously there is a tradeoff here between time and memory, as noted earlier in the discussion of lookup tables.

Relatively few microprocessors are presently being pushed to the limits of their performance; in cases where processors are so strained, the techniques just described will probably prove more helpful than attempts to obtain large increases in performance by means of program optimization.

6.9 SOFTWARE DEVELOPMENT SYSTEMS

This section deals briefly with the development systems that are used in writing software for microprocessors. Since processors themselves are difficult to use for development, a variety of systems have been devised so that programs may be developed with the aid of special-purpose software and peripherals and later transferred to the actual computer on which they will run. Among the systems used are microcomputer development systems, time-sharing services, and systems based on other computers. Some of the features of these systems have already been mentioned in earlier sections.

Microcomputer development systems consist of an actual microcomputer (or an emulation of one) with additional hardware and software suited to the development task. In general, development systems have the following characteristics.

1. Front panel status display so that the programmer can observe the contents of buses and memory locations.

2. A facility for changing the contents of memory locations.

3. A reset control that starts the processor in a known state.

4. A single step control that allows a program to be executed one step at a time for debugging purposes.

5. A run control that allows a program to be executed, beginning at a specified memory location.

6. RAM or PROM that can be used as program memory.

7. Interfaces for teletypewriters and other standard input/output devices, such as paper tape readers, keyboards, LED displays, line or character printers, cassette recorders, and floppy disk systems.

8. A bootstrap loader that enters the initial programs (such as the regular loader) into the microcomputer memory.

9. Utility programs that load user programs into the microcomputer memory from a keyboard or paper tape reader.

Even a simple development system allows the programmer to examine and change memory locations and to enter machine language programs from switches, a paper tape reader, or a teletypewriter keyboard. The user must connect the system to the teletypewriter; the development system typically includes the physical interface and the required software.

Other features provided with most development systems include

1. A self-assembler
2. A system monitor
3. A facility for setting breakpoints or initiating traces

4. Connectors for interfacing external devices to the processor buses
5. An editor that can be used to make minor changes in user programs

Figure 6.20 is a flowchart of program development with a simple development system. The process is slow because of the low speed of the standard teletypewriter (Fig. 6.21) and its paper tape mechanism. The teletypewriter prints only ten characters per second; furthermore, it is designed for moderate use and cannot be regularly employed for long listings. The paper tape reader will read ten characters per second; a teletypewriter may require half an hour to load an assembler or a long user program into the computer.

Many options can improve this situation, but each costs substantially more than the simple system based on the standard teletypewriter (the teletypewriter itself costs approximately $1000 to purchase and can be rented cheaply from many sources). Among the options are

1. A fast paper tape reader and punch (Fig. 6.22). A fast tape reader (300 characters per second) is available from many sources for about $1000. Such a tape reader will reduce the time required to load programs to a few minutes.

2. A tape cassette or cartridge system (Fig. 6.23). Such a system will be as fast as the fast paper tape reader and will provide a more convenient, although somewhat more expensive, storage medium. A cassette system will also require an interface, although a few such systems use the same interface as the standard teletypewriter. The performance of cassette systems varies widely, and some are too noisy for use with computers.

Figure 6.20   Using a simple development system.[6]

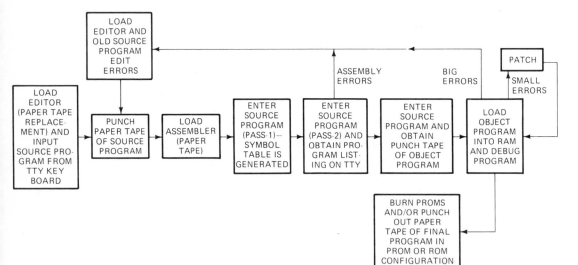

[6]This figure and Figs. 6.26 and 6.27 are reprinted with permission from G. Casilli and W. Kirn, "Microcomputer Software Development," *Digital Design*, Vol. 5, No. 7, July 1975, pp. 50–52.

Figure 6.21 A standard teletypewriter (courtesy of Teletype Corporation).

Figure 6.22 A high-speed paper tape reader (EECO Micromate).

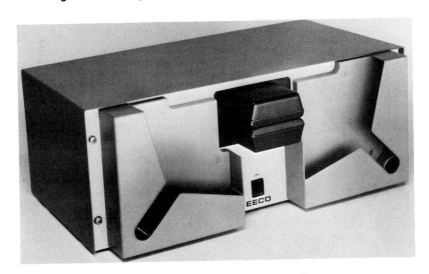

Figure 6.23 A cassette system (courtesy of Memodyne Corporation).

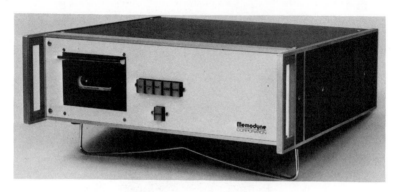

3. A floppy disk system (Fig. 6.24). Such a system can easily store and recall programs, since it has a much shorter average access time than cassettes or paper tape. A floppy disk system is, however, quite expensive and requires extensive software support.

4. A line or character printer. These printers are typically several times as fast as the standard teletypewriter and more suited to handling long listings. The user must interface the printer to the development system.

5. A CRT display. Such a display is much more convenient for debugging and editing than a printer. However, the CRT display may be more difficult to interface and does not provide hard copy.

6. An interactive editor. These programs are convenient for making small program changes but require a large amount of memory.

Figure 6.24 A floppy disk system (iCOM FD 360) (courtesy of iCOM Microperipherals, Canoga Park, Ca.).

A convenient microcomputer development system must include a fast hard-copy mechanism and a reasonable storage facility. A CRT display can also be very helpful. Obviously the more features that are added to the development system, the more useful (and more expensive) it becomes. Figure 6.25 shows a typical small development system with a keyboard for data entry and operator control, a CRT display, and dual audio cassette recorders.

Some development systems have such additional features as

1. Real-time clock
2. Analog data acquisition systems
3. A/D and D/A converter modules
4. Frequency counter modules
5. Clip-in interfaces so that prototyping boards can be attached to the system and manipulated from the control panel
6. PROM programmers that can be driven from the internal read/write memory. PROMs can then be programmed directly from the development system.
7. ROM simulator modules
8. DMA and interrupt controllers
9. Interfaces for UARTs
10. Sense switches that the program can interrogate
11. Standard bus interfaces
12. Motor controller modules

The advantages of microcomputer development systems are their relatively low cost and close relationship to the actual microcomputer. The systems are self-contained and have the same timing and interfacing properties as the microcomputer. Such systems are particularly convenient if a prototype can be attached and controlled from the panel or other system devices. The disadvantages are their

Figure 6.25 A microcomputer development system (courtesy of Futuredata Computer Corporation).

low speed, the limited software and peripherals that are usually available, and their typical limitation to a single processor. The external interfaces are useful but may complicate system development because they depend on facilities present in the development system but not in the final product. More advanced and flexible microcomputer development systems that solve many of these problems at a somewhat higher initial cost are becoming available.

Another method for developing microprocessor-based systems involves time-sharing services. Most time-sharing services have simulators and cross-assemblers for popular microprocessors. The time-sharing services also offer vast amounts of easily accessed storage, advanced interactive facilities, and high-speed peripherals.

Figure 6.26 describes the procedure for developing microprocessor software, using the time-sharing services. The advantages of time-sharing are the powerful software facilities, low initial cost, independence of a particular processor, fast mass storage, and access to high-speed peripherals. Disadvantages include the high continuing costs, inability to test programs in the real computer environment, and need to use facilities (such as a high-speed printer) that are physically located at some distance and involve extra turnaround time. Time-sharing is often a convenient way to get started on software development before other equipment becomes available.

A third method for developing microprocessor software involves the use of other computers. The simplest technique is to purchase assembler and simulator programs for use on a local large or small computer. This technique is cheaper than using time-sharing services in the long run but requires the purchase of software and its modification to meet the requirements of the local computer. Also, the method depends on the facilities of the local computer which are generally much less extensive than those of time-sharing services. Obviously, working in batch

Figure 6.26 Using a time-sharing system.

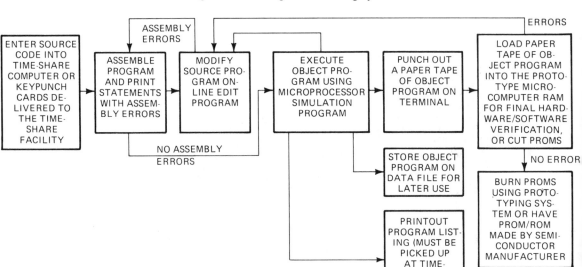

mode without an editor program and with limited storage space is considerably less convenient than using a powerful interactive system. Figure 6.27 describes the process whereby software is developed by using a batch system.

Some development systems are based on minicomputers. Large minicomputers usually have a high-speed printer, a sophisticated editor, an interactive display terminal, and a large disk system. Such a minicomputer can be used to develop programs almost as easily as time-sharing. Moreover, the minicomputer I/O bus can be interfaced so that the object code which the minicomputer generates can be transferred directly into the read/write program memory of the microcomputer. Figure 6.28 is a block diagram of such a system.

Figure 6.27 Using a local computer.

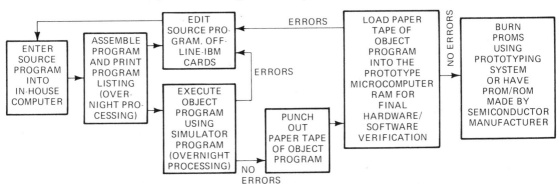

Figure 6.28 Block diagram of minicomputer-based microprocessor development system.[7]

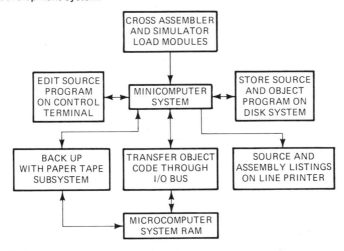

[7]Reprinted with permission from R. Martinez, "A Look at Trends in Microprocessor/Microcomputer Software Systems," *Computer Design*, Vol. 14, No. 6, June 1975, pp. 51–57. Copyright, Computer Design Publishing Corp.

Several such minicomputer/microcomputer systems exist. Some simply transfer programs to the microcomputer memory and allow all other functions to be handled from the microcomputer control system. Others allow the user to run or modify the program, monitor or produce inputs and outputs, and perform other tasks via the minicomputer and its control system. The latter systems are more convenient but require a more complex interface and more extensive software.

The minicomputer-based development systems are expensive unless the minicomputer is already available or can be shared among several projects. These systems, however, like the development systems, do allow debugging and testing of the actual hardware while also offering much of the convenience of the time-sharing services. The minicomputer-based systems can be used with a variety of processors, although a different interface is necessary for each processor. These systems appear to have great potential, particularly if direct testing and debugging facilities become available.

6.10 SUMMARY

Software development consists of many stages. Coding, the writing of instructions in a language that the computer understands, is only one of them and by no means the most important. The designer must first define the problem and design the program, then write the code, debug and test the program, document it, and later extend and redesign it. All the stages are interrelated; the designer often works on several at the same time and must consider the effects of each stage on all the others.

The definition and design stages take the task from its initial formulation to the point where an actual program can be written. Definition involves the specification of inputs and outputs, processing requirements, time and memory constraints, and error handling. Program design requires the precise formulation of program logic and timing. Flowcharting, modular programming, structured programming, and top-down design are methods for formulating programs so that they can easily be coded, debugged, and tested.

Good coding simplifies all the later stages. An emphasis on clarity and comprehensibility, simple program structure, and thorough documentation makes programs easy to debug and test. Later the designer can make programs more efficient if necessary.

Debugging, testing, and documentation should all be thorough and systematic procedures. Breakpoints, traces, dumps, and single-step modes can aid in debugging and testing. Software simulators can check program logic, whereas logic or microprocessor analyzers can help with timing or other hardware problems. Documentation requires flowcharts, well-organized and commented programs, memory maps, and other reference material.

The purpose of microprocessor software development is to provide reliable, well-documented software at reasonable cost. In most tasks doing so requires an emphasis on the design, debugging, and testing stages. Only a few high-volume products require a primary emphasis on hardware and memory costs, although the designer must always consider these factors.

PROBLEMS

1. Define the problems involved in designing a digital stopwatch with a microprocessor. The system derives inputs from a simple keyboard and counts down time on LED displays. Describe the procedures involved; input, output, processing, and accuracy requirements; time and memory constraints; and error-handling techniques. Assume that the timer displays seconds and tenths of seconds and is activated by a START key.

2. Define the problems involved in designing a digital thermometer with a microprocessor. The system derives inputs from an A/D converter attached to a temperature sensor and displays the temperature (degrees Celsius) on LED displays. Describe the procedures involved; input, output, processing, and accuracy requirements; time and memory constraints; and error-handling techniques. Assume that the thermometer displays temperatures to the nearest degree over the 0 to 50°C range. Assume that the data from the converter is a linear function of temperature. How often will the temperature have to be sampled? What changes would need to be made in the problem definition if a switch position determined whether temperature was to be displayed in degrees Celsius or degrees Fahrenheit?

3. Define the problems involved in designing a railroad crossing monitor with a microprocessor. The system derives its input from a switch that is closed by the pressure from the train. The outputs are signals that activate the warning lights, sound the alarms, and lower the crossing gates. Describe the procedures involved; input, output, processing, and accuracy requirements; time and memory constraints; and error-handling techniques. Note that you must ensure that the crossing gates remain closed until the train has completely passed the crossing. Also, the system must allow cars and people to leave the crossing before the gates are lowered. What are the time constraints if the switch is 1 mile from the crossing and the train travels at 50 miles per hour? What if trains could approach the crossing from either direction?

4. Draw a general flowchart for the following task. The processor examines an input port. If the value at the port is not zero, the processor must wait 1 ms and sample the port again. If the value remains the same, the processor must turn on a panel light. Otherwise the processor discards the first result and repeats the delay and sampling process. If the value at the port is zero (at any time), the processor turns the panel light off.

5. Draw a general flowchart for the following task. The processor reads an ASCII character from an input port. If the character is not ASCII ETX, the processor waits 5 ms and reads another character; if the character is ASCII ETX, the processor performs a message-handling routine and starts the reading process again. What changes would you need to make to the flowchart if the maximum number of characters allowed was 40? What if the message had to start with ASCII STX and characters before the STX were simply ignored?

6. Draw a general flowchart for the following task. The processor examines a simple four-key keyboard, waiting for a key to be pressed. If a key is pressed, the processor determines which key it was—key 0 causes the processor to perform an ENTER routine, key 1 a DISPLAY routine, key 2 a SEND routine, and key 3 an EXECUTE routine. The processor returns to examining the keyboard after performing the appropriate routine. What changes would you make if each key were dual purpose—that is, if the function switch were open, the keys had the meanings given above, whereas if the function switch were closed, the keys had the meanings 0—PROGRAM, 1—TEST, 2—RECEIVE, and 3—REPEAT?

7. Describe how top-down design could be used to design the digital thermometer of Problem 2.

8. Describe how top-down design could be used to design the railroad crossing monitor of Problem 3.

9. Describe how top-down design could be used to design a security system that would monitor a set of sensor-activated switches continuously and provide an alarm and a display of which switch was activated if a switch closure was found. How easily could you add more switches to your system?

10. Use structured programming to design a message editor that performs the following tasks on data that is entered in one character at a time.
(a) All characters before an ASCII STX character are ignored.
(b) The characters following the initial STX are placed in an array called MESSG.
(c) The message ends if either an ASCII ETX or 40 characters are received. The length of the message is placed in LENGM. The number of messages, NMESS, is incremented by 1.
What changes would have to be made if all space characters were to be removed from the message? What if two consecutive ASCII STX characters were required at the beginning of a valid message?

11. Use structured programming to design a display handler that processes an array of 12 ASCII characters named DSPLY. The tasks are as follows.
(a) Replace all leading zeros (before the decimal point) with blanks. Leave one zero if all the digits in the array are zero.
(b) Check all characters to ensure that they are valid. Only digits and one decimal point are allowed. Replace all erroneous characters with blanks.
(c) Round the number to two decimal places and blank any additional decimal places.

12. Use structured programming to design the security monitor of Problem 9. The number of switches is NSWCH, the array of switch positions is SWTCH, the array of indicators is DSPLY, and the array where the numbers of the switches that have been tripped is kept is IDENT. The number of switches tripped is NTRIP. The process is as follows.
(a) The program examines the switch positions in SWTCH looking for any switches that are closed (i.e., zero).
(b) If a switch is closed, the corresponding display is lit (i.e., set to one), the switch number is placed in array IDENT, and NTRIP is incremented by 1.
Assume that the computer executes the monitor once and proceeds to other routines.

13. Describe the various program modules that could be used in writing the digital thermometer program of Problems 2 and 7.

14. Describe the various program modules that could be used in writing the railroad crossing monitor program of Problems 3 and 8.

15. Discuss how the following Intel 8080 program could be improved. Input unit 2 is the teletypewriter keyboard; output unit 2 is the teletypewriter printer.

```
;LOOK FOR ASCII DIGIT
;IF NOT, PRINT AN E
        IN    2      ;INPUT FROM 2
        SUI   30H    ;SUBTRACT 30H
        CPI   10     ;COMPARE TO 10
        JNC   W      ;W IF NOT LESS
        JMP   Z      ;GO TO THRU
W:      MVI   A,45H  ;GET 45H
        OUT   2      ;OUTPUT TO 2
Z:      HLT
```

The program brings in a single ASCII character and converts it to decimal. If the character is not a digit, the program prints an E on the printer.

16. A program has been written that sorts signed numbers into ascending order. Make up a set of test data to be used in checking the program. Include the following cases.
(a) The array of numbers to be sorted contains zero or one element.
(b) The array contains elements that are equal.
(c) The array contains elements that will produce an overflow when subtracted from each other.
Indicate possible solutions for these and other potential difficulties.

17. A program has been written that checks to see if a set of numbers is greater than a set of corresponding thresholds. That is, there are N numbers $ENTRY_1$ through $ENTRY_N$ and N thresholds $THRSH_1$ through $THRSH_N$. If $ENTRY_1$ is greater than $THRSH_1$, display variable $DSPLY_1$ is set to one. Otherwise $DSPLY_1$ is set to zero. This process continues through all N cases and produces an array of indicators $DSPLY_1$ through $DSPLY_N$. Design a set of test data to be used in checking the program.
Assume that the numbers and thresholds are all unsigned. What special cases must be considered?

18. A program has been written that checks a set of switches to see if any have changed since the previous check. The previous status of the switches is in memory location SWCHS. Discuss how you would test this program. What would have to be done before entering the program the first time?

19. A program has been written that converts a decimal digit to a seven-segment code and sends the code to a display. Make up a set of test data for checking this program. What could cause the following problems?
(a) The display shows a number one less than the correct one—that is, 6 when it should show 7.

(b) The display segments are all off for the number 8 and all off except for the center bar for the number 0.

(c) The display always shows 0 regardless of the input data.

Assume that the program uses a lookup table.

20. Write an Intel 8080 or Motorola 6800 library routine that performs a 64-bit addition—that is, adds two 64-bit numbers. The result replaces one of the numbers. Document the routine properly in the library format of Fig. 6.19.

REFERENCES

ABRAHAMS, P., "Structured Programming Considered Harmful," *SIGPLAN Notices*, Vol. 10, No. 4, April 1975, pp. 13–24.

CASILLI, G., and W. KIRN, "Microcomputer Software Development," *Digital Design*, Vol. 5, No. 7, July 1975, pp. 50–52.

CHAPIN, N., *Flowcharts*, Auerbach Publishers Inc., Princeton, N.J., 1971.

DENNING, P. J., "Is Structured Programming Any Longer the Right Term?," *SIGPLAN Notices*, Vol. 9, No. 11, November 1974, pp. 4–6.

DOLLHOFF, T. "μP Software. How to Optimize Timing and Memory Usage," *Digital Design*, Vol. 6, No. 11, November 1976, pp. 56–69.

HETZEL, W., *Program Test Methods*, Prentice-Hall, Englewood Cliffs, N.J., 1973.

HUGHES, J. K., and J. I. MICHTOM, *A Structured Approach to Programming*, Prentice-Hall, Englewood, Cliffs, N.J., 1977.

KARPINSKI, R. H., "An Unstructured View of Structured Programming," *SIGPLAN Notices*, Vol. 9, No. 3, March 1974, pp. 112–119.

KNUTH, D. E., "Structured Programming with GO TO Statements," *Computing Surveys*, Vol. 6, No. 4, December 1974, pp. 261–301.

KRUMMEL, L., and G. SCHULTZ, "Advances in Microcomputer Development Systems," *Computer*, Vol. 10, No. 2, February 1977, pp. 13–19.

LEVENTHAL, L. A., "Can Structured Programming Help the Bench Programmer?" 1977 IEEE Workshop on Bench Programming of Microprocessors, Philadelphia, Pa., pp. 1–5.

McCRACKEN, D. D., "Revolution in Programming: An Overview," *Datamation*, Vol. 19, No. 12, December 1973, pp. 50–52.

McGOWAN, C. L., and J. R. KELLY, *Top-Down Structured Programming Techniques*, Petrocelli/Charter, New York, 1975.

MARTINEZ, R., "A Look at Trends in Microprocessor/Microcomputer Software Systems," *Computer Design*, Vol. 14, No. 6, June 1975, pp. 51–57.

PARNAS, D. L., "On the Criteria to be Used in Decomposing Systems into Modules," *Communications of the ACM*, Vol. 15, No. 12, December 1972, pp. 1053–1058.

PARNAS, D. L., "The Influence of Software Structure on Reliability," *SIGPLAN Notices*, Vol. 10, No. 6, June 1975, pp. 358–362.

REIFER, D. J., "Automated Aids for Reliable Software," *SIGPLAN Notices*, Vol. 10, No. 6, June 1975, pp. 131–142.

SHNEIDERMAN, B., and P. SCHEUERMANN, "Structured Data Structures," *Communications of the ACM*, Vol. 17, No. 10, October 1974, pp. 566–574.

SRINI, V. P., "Fault Diagnosis of Microprocessor Systems," *Computer*, Vol. 10, No. 1, January 1977, pp. 60–65.

YOURDON, E., *Techniques of Program Structure and Design*, Prentice-Hall, Englewood Cliffs, N.J., 1976.

7 Microcomputer Memory Sections

So far this book has considered microprocessors as isolated units that somehow fetch data and instructions from memory, store data in memory, and transfer information to and from the external world through an input/output section. The next three chapters deal with the way that the microprocessor functions as the central processing unit of a microcomputer. In this chapter the fundamental interaction between the microprocessor and the memory is described. Our first topics are the general features of this interaction, the design of simple memory sections consisting of a single read-only memory or a single read/write memory, and the design and interfacing of more complex memory sections. The final topics concern instruction cycles and the principles of memory section design for the Intel 8080 and Motorola 6800.

The memory sections discussed here are assumed to consist of semiconductor memory chips. Most microcomputers use such chips; only a few use the magnetic cores (see Section A5.1) that are common in larger computers.

The key features of semiconductor memories are

1. *Nondestructive readout*. Reading the contents of a semiconductor memory does not change those contents (unlike a magnetic core), and so there is no need to write the data back into the memory.

2. *Volatile read/write memories*. Loss of power affects the contents of semiconductor RAMs. Therefore many microcomputers use nonvolatile read-only program memory so that programs need not be loaded each time power is applied.

3. *Single-chip forms*. Semiconductor memories come as single chips with various sizes, word lengths, and organizations. Decoding and interfacing circuitry are part of the chip. Semiconductor memories behave like other digital integrated circuits of the same technology.

7.1 GENERAL FEATURES OF THE MEMORY INTERFACE

Figure 7.1 shows the interface between the microprocessor and the memory section. The connections are

1. Address bus. The CPU uses this bus to select a particular memory location as the source or destination of data.

2. Data input bus. The memory section uses this bus to send the contents of a memory location to the CPU.

3. Data output bus. The CPU uses this bus to send data to the memory.

4. Control bus. This bus transfers control and timing signals. The signals sent to the memory may include synchronization signals that make the memory accesses coincide with the processor cycle, write pulses, and address or data strobes. The signals sent to the CPU generally indicate the successful completion of the memory access.

Figure 7.1 The CPU-memory interface.

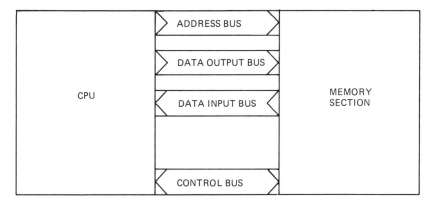

The basic interaction between the microprocessor and the memory section is the instruction fetch. The CPU must fetch an instruction from memory before it can do anything else; the instruction determines the CPU's activities during the rest of the instruction cycle. The instruction fetch proceeds as follows (see Fig. 7.2).

Step 1. The CPU places the contents of the program counter on the address bus.

Step 2. The CPU waits until data is available from the memory.

Step 3. The CPU places the data from the data input bus in the instruction register.

Figure 7.2 An instruction fetch.

STEP 1. (Program counter) placed on address bus

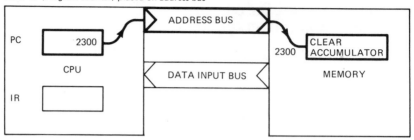

STEP 2. Wait for data to be available
        (PC) = (PC) + 1

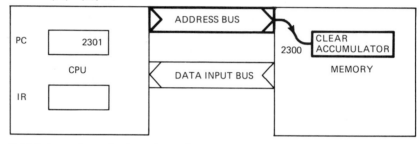

STEP 3. Instruction on data bus to instruction register

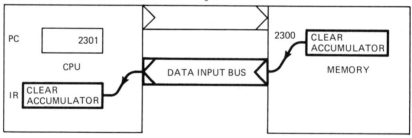

The first step determines the source of the instruction. The second step coordinates the timing of the processor and the memory so that the correct data is always transferred. The third step interprets the number received from the memory as an instruction rather than as an address or data.

Step 1 requires a timing signal that places the contents of the program counter on the address bus. The timing signal is the processor clock, which is simply a regular series of pulses produced by an oscillator. The internal characteristics of the processor determine the required frequency and pulse width of the clock.

Step 2 requires the CPU to determine when data is available from the memory. The delay depends on the access time of the memory. The contents of the address bus must, of course, remain constant throughout this interval. Clearly the delay is critical to the operation of the computer. If the CPU does not wait long enough, it may not receive the instruction correctly; such an error would be difficult to trace and could cause random results. The problem is how to determine the length of the delay. The simplest method is to design a memory section with an access time less than one clock period. Then the processor clock can determine the length of the waiting period. More complex methods will be discussed later in this chapter.

Step 3 requires a timing signal that places the contents of the data input bus in the instruction register. If the access time of the memory is less than one clock period, the timing signal can be the next cycle of the processor clock. A flip-flop can determine whether the present cycle is an address output cycle or data input cycle.

The designer must make the timing of the memory section compatible with the processor. The architecture of the CPU determines the timing signals that place the contents of the program counter on the address bus and the contents of the data input bus in the instruction register. The memory section must provide data within these constraints.

The CPU must also fetch data and addresses from memory. The differences between these fetches and an instruction fetch are the source of the address and the destination of the data. The timing of the cycles is the same as long as the access time of all parts of the memory section is the same. Other read cycles include

1. Obtaining the address part of the instruction. Here the address is the contents of the program counter, but the CPU places the data in an address register.

2. Fetching data from RAM. Here the address is the contents of an address register, and the CPU places the data in a data register.

3. Fetching immediate data. Here the address is the contents of the program counter, and the CPU places the data in a data register.

4. Fetching an indirect address. Here the address is the contents of an address register, and the CPU places the data in an address register.

To illustrate, assume that the two-word instruction ADD 150 is being executed. The first word of the instruction is the operation code for ADD; the second word is the direct address 150. This instruction requires three read cycles.

1. Instruction fetch cycle. The CPU fetches the operation code from memory and places it in the instruction register.

2. Address fetch cycle. The CPU fetches the address from memory and places it in the address register. Both the first and second cycles use and increment the program counter.

3. Data fetch cycle. The CPU uses the address register to fetch the data from memory and place it in the data register. This cycle does not use the program counter.

Figure 7.3 shows the flow of signals during the instruction execution. The timing is the same for all the cycles.

Obviously the CPU must be able to choose the source for the address bus and the destination for the input data bus. The choices are made by control signals formed by instruction decoding, internal signal generation, and the processor clock. A multiplexer or selector can determine the source for the address bus as shown in

Figure 7.3 An instruction with three read cycles (ADD 150).

1. Initial conditions:

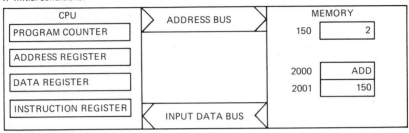

2. Instruction fetch cycle:

    (INSTRUCTION REGISTER) = (2000)
    (PROGRAM COUNTER)   = (PROGRAM COUNTER) + 1
                      = 2001

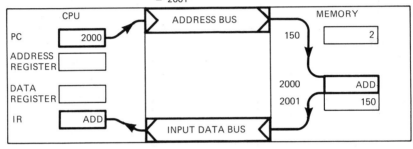

3. Address fetch cycle:

    (ADDRESS REGISTER) = (2001)
    (PROGRAM COUNTER) = (PROGRAM COUNTER) + 1
                    = 2002

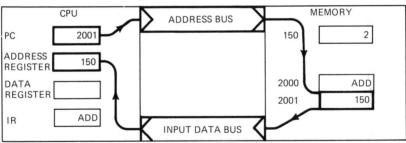

4. Data fetch cycle:

    (DATA REGISTER) = ((ADDRESS REGISTER)) = (150) = 2

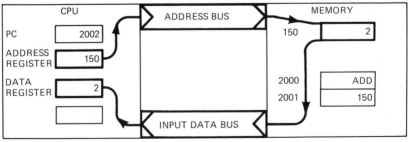

288

Figure 7.4 Selector control of address source.

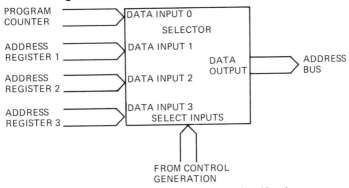

The select inputs determine which data input appears on the address bus as follows:

Select Inputs	Address Bus Contents
0	Program Counter
1	Address Register 1
2	Address Register 2
3	Address Register 3

Additional select inputs allow more sources for the address bus.

Figure 7.5 Demultiplexer control of data destination.

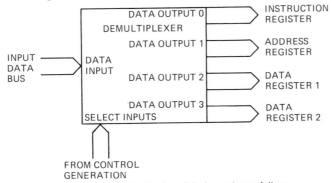

The select inputs determine the destination of the input data as follows.

Select Inputs	Destination	Function of Input Data
0	Instruction Register	Instruction
1	Address Register	Address
2	Data Register 1	Data
3	Data Register 2	Data

More select inputs allow more destinations. The demultiplexing process interprets the contents of memory as instructions, addresses, or data.

Fig. 7.4. A demultiplexer can determine the destination for the input data bus as shown in Fig. 7.5. The more sources and destinations there are, the more complex the selectors and demultiplexers and the more signals needed to control them. These internal devices also introduce delays (from input to output). Of course, selectors and demultiplexers are basic elements in computer circuits, since they produce part of the flexibility that makes the computer so useful.

In order to execute some instructions, the processor must transfer data to the memory—that is, perform a *memory write operation*. Memory write cycles are far less common than memory read cycles. Many microcomputers have no read/write memory and obviously perform no memory write operations; such systems store temporary data in registers within the microprocessor.

The memory write cycle is similar to the read cycle and proceeds as follows.

Step 1. The CPU places the contents of an address register on the address bus.

Step 2. The CPU places the contents of a data register on the data output bus.

Step 3. The CPU provides a write pulse to the memory section.

Step 4. The CPU waits for the write operation to be successfully completed.

Step 1 of the write cycle is the same as in a data fetch. Step 2 requires a clocking signal that places data on the data output bus. A selector can allow data to be obtained from several different data registers.

Step 3 requires pulse generation circuitry that provides a pulse of the proper length to the memory. In a write cycle, the order in which the memory receives signals and the precise timing relationships among those signals are very important. The order of signals in a read cycle is not important as long as the read is nondestructive. However, write operations are destructive. Thus the address must reach the memory before the write pulse begins, and the data must remain constant after the write pulse ends.

Step 4 establishes the timing for the write operation. The CPU must know when the write operation has been completed. As with the read cycle, the simplest method is to design the memory so that the write cycle can be completed in one clock period.

The write cycle is more complex than the read cycle. The read cycle only has to make the data available when the CPU needs it; what happens before and after the transfer does not matter. The write cycle must not only transfer the data correctly but must also ensure that no other transfers occur that permanently change the contents of memory locations.

Memory read and write cycles are not the only processor activities. The processor must also decode and execute instructions. Note that the CPU does not use the memory during internal decoding and execution cycles. So other devices may use the memory during these cycles without interfering with the CPU (this procedure is called *cycle stealing*).

Read and write cycles and decoding and execution cycles constitute the normal activity of the CPU. Under the control of its clock, the CPU continuously fetches, decodes, and executes instructions. This activity starts as soon as the power and the clock are turned on and ends only when one of them is turned off. An obvious question is how to start the CPU at the beginning of the program. Once this is done, the CPU will execute the program instructions until it is turned off.

The control signal that places the CPU in a known initial state is called RESET. The requirements for this signal and the precise actions that it produces vary from processor to processor. The basic effect of RESET, however, is to place a known value in the program counter. The designer must provide a program (usually in ROM) that starts at the known location and transfers control to the main program. A single jump instruction is often sufficient. The RESET signal may be applied at any time to put the processor back in the known state.

A power-up RESET signal (see Fig. 7.6) can be produced with a simple RC network attached to the power supply; a Schmitt trigger converts the slow rise of the power supply to a well-defined pulse. The flip-flop synchronizes the RESET signal with the processor clock. Many processors, such as the Zilog Z-80 and MOS Technology 6502, include this circuitry on the chip; other processors (like the Intel 8080) make it part of the system clock chip. Power-up RESET starts the processor in the known state, eliminating any transient initialization problems.

Figure 7.6 A power-up RESET circuit.

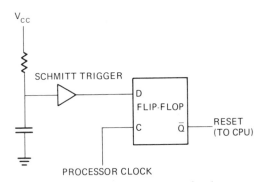

The flip-flop delays the RESET so that it occurs after the processor clock pulse. The circuit assumes that the processor RESET input is active high.

7.2 SIMPLE MEMORY SECTIONS

Simple memory sections consist of a single memory chip or a single set of chips with the same address connections. More complex memory sections require decoding circuitry that activates a particular part of the section for transfers.

A Single Read-only Memory

The simplest possible memory section consists of a single ROM. In fact, many controllers for simple applications are two-chip microcomputers consisting of a microprocessor and a ROM. Figure 7.7 shows the pin layout of a typical ROM. The address inputs determine which word will appear at the data outputs. The decoding circuitry is part of the ROM. Each address line doubles the number of

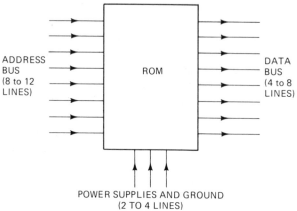

Figure 7.7 A typical ROM package.

ADDRESS
BUS
(8 to 12
LINES)

ROM

DATA
BUS
(4 to 8
LINES)

POWER SUPPLIES AND GROUND
(2 TO 4 LINES)

No explicit control signals are necessary.

addressable words, whereas the number of data lines is the length of the word. Most ROMs have 4- or 8-bit words.

ROMs have small packages, since they do not require data or control inputs. A 256 × 8 ROM needs 2 to 4 pins for power supplies and 8 pins apiece for the data and address buses. A single 18- to 24-pin package can therefore hold the entire memory for a small system.

The timing for a ROM is simple. The maximum delay from address to data is called the *maximum access time*. The manufacturer guarantees this time over a range of temperatures under certain operating conditions. This access time is the worst case that the processor must handle. The address is presumed to be stable during the accessing period.

Figure 7.8 shows the control structure of a typical microprocessor. The address outputs are the address of the location that the CPU is accessing. The data inputs are the contents of this location. The RESET input places a known value in the program counter. Microprocessor address buses are usually 8 to 16 bits wide, whereas the data buses are 4 to 8 bits wide.

In order to simplify the interface between the CPU and the ROM, we shall assume (a) a ROM with 256 8-bit words (like the common 1702 device), (b) an 8-bit processor with an 8-bit data bus and an 8-bit address bus, and (c) a RESET signal that clears the program counter. The connections can easily be changed to handle other arrangements.

Figure 7.9 shows the interface between the microprocessor and the ROM. The address outputs of the CPU are attached directly to the address inputs of the ROM. The data inputs of the CPU are attached directly to the data outputs of the ROM. The system works as follows: (a) the RESET signal starts the CPU with zero in the program counter; and (b) the CPU executes the program in the ROM, beginning at location zero. The CPU, of course, cannot write into the ROM.

Since there are only eight address lines, the total memory capacity is 256

Figure 7.8 A typical microprocessor package.

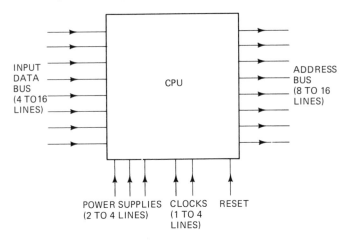

Figure 7.9 The CPU-ROM interface.

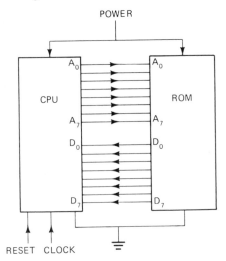

words. If the CPU did, in fact, have additional address lines, the remaining lines could simply be left unconnected in the system of Fig. 7.9. The values on the unconnected lines would not affect the decoding; so each ROM word would respond to several addresses. This redundancy may confuse the reader but does not bother the computer. The problem comes when different words respond to the same address.

The timing of the memory cycle is as follows.

1. The processor clock gates the contents of the program counter or address register on to the address bus. The maximum delay between the clock edge and the appearance of the address on the bus is t_{da} (see Fig. 7.10).

2. The processor must allow for the maximum ROM access time t_{acc}.

3. The processor clock gates the contents of the input data bus into the instruction or data register. In order for this transfer to proceed correctly, the data must be available at least a time t_{ds} before the clock pulse. t_{ds} is the *data setup time* (Fig. 7.10).

Figure 7.10 Delay and setup times for the CPU read cycle.

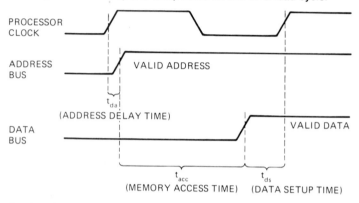

In order for the CPU and ROM to communicate properly, the maximum time needed to read data from the ROM must be less than the allowed number of processor clock cycles. This number is fixed as part of the CPU design and is usually 1 or 2 but may be as many as 10 or 20. Calling the allowed number of cycles k, the system must satisfy the equation

$$t_{da} + t_{acc} + t_{ds} < kt_p \tag{7.1}$$

where t_p is the period of the processor clock. t_{da} and t_{ds} are part of the specifications of the CPU.

EXAMPLE 1: Intel 8080-type CPU

$$t_{da} = 200 \text{ ns}$$
$$t_{ds} = 130 \text{ ns}$$
$$k = 2$$
$$t_p = 500 \text{ ns (typical)}$$

To operate this CPU at maximum speed, the access time of the ROM must be

$$t_{acc} < kt_p - t_{da} - t_{ds}$$
$$t_{acc} < 1000 - 330$$
$$t_{acc} < 670 \text{ ns}$$

EXAMPLE 2: Motorola 6800-type CPU

$$t_{da} = 300 \text{ ns}$$

$$t_{ds} = 100 \text{ ns}$$
$$k = 1$$
$$t_p = 1000 \text{ ns (typical)}$$

To operate this CPU at maximum speed, the access time of the ROM must be

$$t_{acc} < kt_p - t_{da} - t_{ds}$$
$$< 1000 - 400$$
$$< 600 \text{ ns}$$

In fact, the Intel 8080 and Motorola 6800 have even more stringent requirements (see Section 7.5), for each has two clock phases and more complex timing than we have yet discussed.

Moreover, some processors and memories cannot communicate directly because they operate at different voltage levels. In this case, the microcomputer will need buffers. The buffers may change the voltage levels, provide additional drive current, or translate between MOS and TTL levels.[1] We will discuss common buffers and drivers later in the chapter.

Equation (7.1) must be modified for the buffered system to allow for the maximum delay time of the buffers. If t_{ab} is the maximum delay time of the address buffer and t_{db} is the maximum delay time of the data buffer, the new equation for compatibility is

$$t_{da} + t_{acc} + t_{ds} + t_{ab} + t_{db} < kt_p \qquad (7.2)$$

Clearly we want the buffer delays to be as short as possible. Therefore most microcomputers use TTL buffers with delay times of 20 to 50 ns.

The need for buffers in a simple system can easily be determined from the voltage and current levels required and produced by the CPU and the ROM. Buffers are common in microcomputers because the MOS chips produce small drive currents and can seldom handle more than a single TTL load directly. Furthermore, even TTL-compatible MOS devices may require voltages closer to the nominal levels than do standard TTL devices.

The basic interface between a microprocessor and a ROM is quite simple to design. A single inequality [Equation (7.1) or (7.2)] must be satisfied to ensure proper operation.

A Single Read/Write Memory

The next step is to consider the interface between a microprocessor and a single RAM. Figure 7.11 shows a typical RAM package. We will assume that the RAM contains 256 8-bit words and is connected to an 8-bit microprocessor. The transfers now involve both input and output data as well as a write pulse.

---

[1]Nominal TTL voltage levels are 0 volts = 0, +5 volts = 1; typical MOS levels are 0 volts = 0, − 15 volts = 1.

Figure 7.11 A typical RAM package.

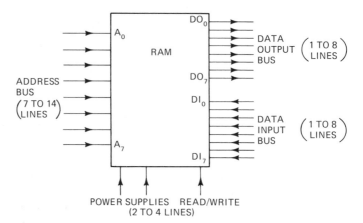

The read cycle for the RAM is the same as for the ROM. However, the system must load the program into the RAM prior to startup, since the RAM is volatile and does not retain its contents when power is lost. The processor can only start after the program is loaded.

The write cycle for the RAM is significantly more complex than the read cycle. The important RAM characteristics are

1. The minimum length of the write pulse.
2. The minimum amount of time the address must be valid before the write pulse begins.
3. The minimum amount of time the data must be valid before the write pulse ends.
4. The minimum amount of time the data must be valid after the write pulse ends.

The order of the signals is critical in the write operation. The address must be stable (t_{as} is the required setup time) before the write pulse begins and the data must be stable before (t_{ds} is the required setup time) and after (t_{dh} is the required hold time) the write pulse ends. The overlap of stable address, data, and write pulse must be a minimum length t_w. Figure 7.12 shows the write cycle timing for a RAM. There are now three inputs to consider instead of the single input required by the ROM.

The CPU timing for the write cycle is also more complex (see Fig. 7.13). The address delay time is the same as in the read cycle. However, there are also delay times for the data (t_{dd}) and the write pulse (t_{dw}). The processor must start the write pulse after the address (by t_{ew}^+) and end it before the next data and address cycle (by t_{ew}^-).

Figure 7.12 Write cycle for a RAM.

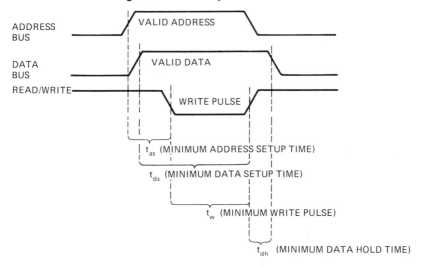

t_{as} (MINIMUM ADDRESS SETUP TIME)

t_{ds} (MINIMUM DATA SETUP TIME)

t_w (MINIMUM WRITE PULSE)

t_{dh} (MINIMUM DATA HOLD TIME)

Figure 7.13 CPU write cycle timing.

(a) DATA DELAY

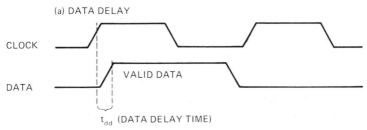

t_{dd} (DATA DELAY TIME)

t_{dd} is the maximum delay between the clock edge and the appearance of valid data on the data bus.

(b) WRITE PULSE DELAY FROM CLOCK

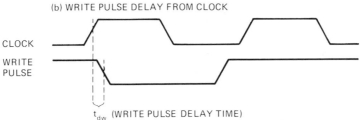

t_{dw} (WRITE PULSE DELAY TIME)

t_{dw} is the maximum delay between the clock edge and the write pulse.

(c) WRITE PULSE DELAY FROM DATA AND ADDRESS

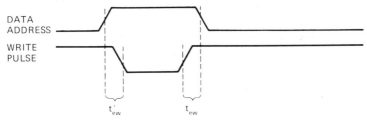

t'_{ew} t_{ew}

t'_{ew} is the minimum delay between valid address and the write pulse.
t_{ew} is the minimum delay between the end of the write pulse and a change in the data (for the next cycle).

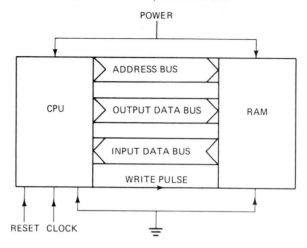

Figure 7.14 CPU/RAM interface.

The interface between the microprocessor and the RAM is shown in Fig. 7.14. The timing requirements for the write cycle consist of the following set of simultaneous equations.

1. The write pulse from the processor must exceed the minimum requirements of the memory,

$$t_{wp} > t_w \tag{7.3}$$

2. The write pulse must be delayed properly from valid address. In other words, the delay of the write pulse must be long enough to ensure that the correct address is received before the write pulse arrives.

$$t_{ew}^+ > t_{da} + t_{as} \tag{7.4}$$

3. The data must remain stable a minimum time after the write pulse ends. That is, the CPU must end the write pulse before the data changes.

$$t_{ew}^- > t_{dh} \tag{7.5}$$

4. The entire transfer must be completed within k clock periods. That is,

$$t_{da} + t_{as} + t_w + t_{ew}^- < kt_p \tag{7.6a}$$

$$t_{dd} + t_{ds} + t_{dh} < kt_p \tag{7.6b}$$

Fortunately, these inequalities are all linear, but the simultaneous solution is still not simple. The usual procedure is to allow leeway to ensure proper timing. Of course, a margin is always necessary in worst-case calculations to handle variations in power supplies, temperature, and other environmental and electrical factors.

Buffers in the system will delay data, addresses, and write pulses. The modified worst-case equations then are, assuming that the maximum buffer delay is t_b,

$$t_{wp} - t_b > t_w \tag{7.7}$$

$$t_{ew}^+ > t_{da} + t_{as} + t_b \tag{7.8}$$

298

$$t_{ew}^- > t_{dh} + t_b \tag{7.9}$$

$$t_{da} + t_{as} + t_w + t_{ew}^- + t_b < kt_p \tag{7.10a}$$

$$t_{dd} + t_{ds} + t_{dh} + t_b < kt_p \tag{7.10b}$$

The interface between the CPU and the RAM will be somewhat more complex in these common situations.

1. The RAM word is shorter than the CPU word. Two or more RAM chips must then be attached in parallel to provide a full data word. In fact, RAMs with 1-bit words are the cheapest and most widely used.

2. The CPU or the RAM uses the same buses for several different purposes. Microprocessors often have a single bidirectional data bus. Some processors only have a single bus to handle data and addresses. The RAM may also have a single set of pins for input and output data (*common I/O* as opposed to *separate I/O*).

RAMs with short words may be interfaced as follows (see Fig. 7.15).

1. The address and control connections are the same for all the memory chips.

2. Each memory chip has different connections to the data bus; these connections determine which bit or bits of the computer word the chip contains.

Figure 7.15 Connecting 1-bit memories to form an 8-bit word.

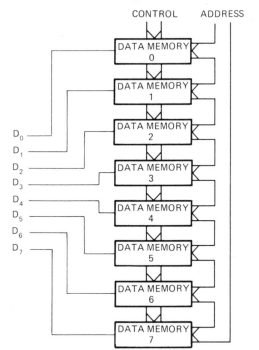

The ADDRESS and CONTROL connections are the same for all the memories.

The CPU is unaware of the physical division of the memory word. The differences for the designer are higher package count and increased loading of the address and control buses, since these lines must drive more inputs.

Memories with shorter word lengths have packaging advantages. Table 7.1 shows the number of data and address pins required by various possible arrangements of a 1-kilobit memory. Memories with short words require fewer external connections, smaller packages, and less chip area for internal connections. Most large memory sections are therefore based on RAMs with organizations like 1K by 1, 4K by 1, or 16K by 1.

Table 7.1   Pin Requirements for a 1-Kilobit Memory

Organization	Address Pins	Data Pins	Total Separate I/O	Common I/O
1K × 1	10	1	12	11
512 × 2	9	2	13	11
256 × 4	8	4	16	12
128 × 8	7	8	23	15
64 × 16	6	16	38	22

Few microprocessors have enough pins available to allow separate buses for addresses, input data, and output data. In the case of an 8-bit processor with a 16-bit address bus, the two data buses and the address bus would use 32 pins. So only 8 pins would be left in the standard 40-pin package for power supplies, clocks, and control signals. Typically, at least twice that number is necessary. Larger packages are expensive and occupy far more board space.

The common solution to this problem is to use a bidirectional data bus. Such usage does not significantly complicate processor operation, since the CPU never reads and writes during the same memory cycle. Some CPUs produce a signal (DATA BUS CONTROL) that indicates whether the data bus is in the input or output state. This signal can be used to control bidirectional buffers or drivers and receivers as shown in Fig. 7.16. A unidirectional buffer (Fig. 7.17) may be necessary to protect the outputs of a ROM from accidental write cycles.

Combined data and address buses complicate the interface between CPU and memory. The address must be externally latched so that it will remain available while the bus is being used for data. Combined buses are common in simple processors like the Intel 4040, which use very small packages, and in 16-bit processors like the National PACE, where two separate 16-bit buses could not fit easily in the standard 40-pin package.

The system must have timing signals or address and data strobes that can be used to latch the address and place data on the bus. Figure 7.18 shows an interface using address and data strobes. The operation of the computer becomes quite complicated. For example, the Intel 4040 has a single 4-bit bus that it uses for data

Figure 7.16 A bidirectional CPU/RAM interface using a RAM with separate input/output.

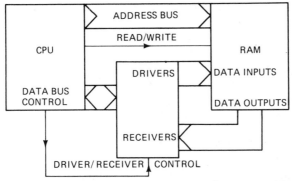

The DATA BUS CONTROL signal makes the driver/receivers into drivers during WRITE cycles and receivers during READ cycles.

Figure 7.17 A bidirectional CPU/ROM interface with a unidirectional buffer.

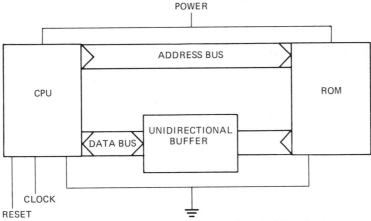

The unidirectional buffer protects the ROM data outputs from the bidirectional bus.

Figure 7.18 A CPU/ROM interface using a single bus and strobes.

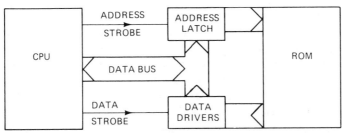

The ADDRESS STROBE places the address in the address latch. The DATA STROBE enables the data drivers and sends the instruction to the CPU. Both signals may involve external circuitry.

(4 bits), addresses (12 bits), and instructions (8 bits). The instruction cycle is divided into eight clock cycles.

Cycle 1. The CPU places the four least significant bits of the program counter on the data bus.

Cycle 2. The CPU places the four middle bits of the program counter on the data bus.

Cycle 3. The CPU places the four most significant bits of the program counter on the data bus.

Cycle 4. The ROM sends the four most significant bits of the instruction to the CPU.

Cycle 5. The ROM sends the four least significant bits of the instruction to the CPU.

Cycles 6, 7, and 8 are used for instruction decoding and execution.

In microcomputers based on the Intel 4040, special memory and interface chips produce the timing signals, latch the address, and place the data on the bus. Most processors have simpler memory cycles, since they have wider buses.

Interfacing Slow Memories

The previous discussion in this chapter has assumed that all memories have sufficiently short access times so that they can work with the processor at full speed. Yet slower memories occur often enough that most microprocessors have specific features to allow their use.

Slow memories are sometimes cheaper and more readily available than faster devices. The premium cost for faster memories, however, is becoming smaller and may disappear. Some types of memories, particularly the popular erasable MOS PROMs, were only normally available in slow forms. This situation has also changed with the introduction of faster versions of these devices. Since the use of slow memories is becoming less common, only a brief discussion of the methods for interfacing such devices is given here.

Many different techniques can slow the processor. Problems that must be considered include

1. The need to synchronize the slowdown with the processor clock. The slowdown may either involve changing the clock or using the clock to control the additional timing circuitry.

2. The need to handle memories with different speeds and cycles that do not use the memory at all. Maximum throughput occurs when the processor is only slowed during the cycles in which it is actually accessing a slow memory.

3. The minimization of delays and parts count.

4. The extension of other signals that may be needed throughout the longer cycles. Such signals may include write pulses and data strobes.

The slowdown methods include the following.

1. Slowing the processor clock. This is the simplest technique because it only requires changing the clock circuit. Most microprocessors can operate at clock rates low enough to handle slow memories. This method, however, has a dramatic effect on throughput, since it slows all the cycles.

2. Changing the clock only during the access of slow memories. This method increases throughput at the cost of more complex circuitry. The control signals that activate the slow memories must also activate the circuitry that slows the clock.

3. Adding extra clock periods to the instruction cycle when accessing slow memories. Many processors have a specific READY input for this purpose. The READY signal must be synchronized with the processor clock and may need to be held inactive for several cycles.

These methods are all transparent to the user, synchronize properly with the processor clock, and automatically cause the extension of other required control signals.

7.3 BUSING STRUCTURES

Few memory sections consist of a single memory chip or a single set of memory chips with the same address connections. More complex memory sections require a busing structure that allows the CPU to transfer data to or from different parts of memory. Two simple structures are unsuitable in practice.

1. Separate buses for each part of the memory would be wasteful, since most computers use only one part of memory at a time. Separate buses would need to be combined inside the CPU and would require a tremendous number of input and output pins.

2. Direct wiring together of outputs is impossible with standard circuit elements. Two elements trying to place opposite logic levels on a line (i.e., one element placing a zero on the line and the other a one) would produce an indeterminate result. Two elements trying to drive a line could damage inputs by exceeding their capacity. The situation in which two elements are both trying to control a bus is called *bus contention*.

Interfacing the memory section to the CPU thus requires the sharing of buses. The use of the buses can be controlled by AND and OR gates as shown in Fig. 7.19. The AND gates allow the control signals to block all except the desired input. The OR gates permit any of the inputs to control the bus. Data can be written into a particular memory by gating the write pulse with the same control signals used in the AND gates. Output cycles, of course, cannot result in bus contention.

The control signals themselves come from a series of AND gates as shown in Fig. 7.20. Only one control signal may be active during a cycle. In a read cycle two

Figure 7.19 A busing structure using simple gates.

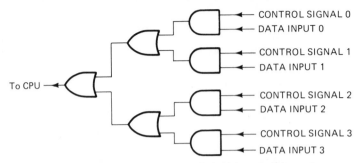

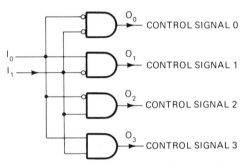

This series of two-input gates only produces a single-bit bus; parallel sets of gates with the same control signals would be necessary for parallel buses.

Figure 7.20 A circuit for generating control signals.

The four AND gates (plus some inverters) take the address inputs and produce four mutually exclusive control signals that may then be used in the busing structure.

active control signals will result in two different memories contending for the data bus. In a write cycle two active control signals will result in the same data being written into two different memories.

Before considering methods that simplify busing, let us briefly discuss criteria for a busing structure.

1. The structure should handle a large number (e.g., 50 to 200) of inputs and outputs with only a few buffers and drivers.

2. The structure should require as few parts as possible.

3. The structure should be easy to expand or modify.

4. The memory should respond properly to fixed addresses. Such addresses may include RESET and interrupt service addresses.

5. The structure should avoid bus contention and maintain proper memory timing.

Two MSI devices can simplify the busing structure.

(a) Decoders that activate particular control signals from coded inputs.

(b) Selectors that choose one of a set of possible inputs to appear at the outputs.

The decoder replaces the AND gates of Fig. 7.20. Table 7.2 is the truth table for a 2 to 4 decoder with outputs that are active-high. Decoders are available in the standard 7400 series as single-chip 2 to 4 (74139, 74155, and 74156), 3 to 8 (74138), 4 to 10 (7442), and 4 to 16 (74154 and 74159) devices. Some of these devices have outputs that are active-low (i.e., all the inactive control signals are high) or have special inputs and outputs that simplify system expansion. The most common inputs are enables that, when inactive, make all the outputs inactive so that the decoders can be cascaded as shown in Fig. 7.21. Decoders are inexpensive, widely available in a variety of sizes, and easy to use. The decoder does introduce an additional delay t_{DEC}, the maximum delay for the control signal to be generated from the input. Cascading decoders multiplies the delay time. Furthermore, there will be a brief period following a change in the inputs when two control signals are both active. Typically, the length of this period is t_{REC}, the maximum recovery time required for the previously activated signal to return to the inactive state. Other timing signals must ensure that no contention occurs during such periods.

Table 7.2 Truth Table for a 2 to 4 Decoder

Inputs		Outputs			
I_0	I_1	O_0	O_1	O_2	O_3
0	0	1	0	0	0
1	0	0	1	0	0
0	1	0	0	1	0
1	1	0	0	0	1

If the decoder also has an active-high enable E, the truth table is (X = don't care—i.e., either 0 or 1)

Inputs			Outputs			
E	I_0	I_1	O_0	O_1	O_2	O_3
0	X	X	0	0	0	0
1	0	0	1	0	0	0
1	1	0	0	1	0	0
1	0	1	0	0	1	0
1	1	1	0	0	0	1

In memory sections, decoders generate control signals from the more significant lines of the address bus that are not directly connected to the memories. All the address lines must be decoded if the designer wants to attach the maximum amount of memory. If an address line is not decoded, its value will not affect the memory selection process; addresses that differ only in the value of that line will produce the same control signals. In order to avoid bus contention, all such addresses must refer to the same memory location; this step reduces the total memory capacity of the computer and makes memory expansion difficult.

Figure 7.21 Cascading decoders to form control signals.

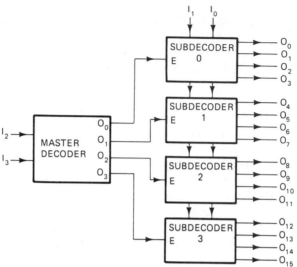

All the subdecoders have the same data inputs, but the master decoder only activates one subdecoder at a time.

The selector combines decoding and busing functions. The select inputs choose a data input to appear at the output as shown in Fig. 7.4. The select inputs may be tied directly to address lines. Table 7.3 is the truth table for a 1 of 4 selector. Selectors are available in the standard 7400 series as 1 of 2 (74157, 74158, 74257, 74258, and 74298), 1 of 4 (74153 and 74253), 1 of 8 (74151, 74152, and 74251), and 1 of 16 (74150) devices.

Selectors may have active-low outputs or special inputs and outputs that simplify system expansion. A single ENABLE input and an OR gate will allow two selectors to be combined as shown in Fig. 7.22. Here address line 2 chooses which selector will be enabled; if $A_2 = 0$, selector 0 is enabled, whereas if $A_2 = 1$, selector 1 is enabled. The output of the disabled selector will always be zero, and so it will not affect the output of the OR gate. The enable is assumed to be active-high. A

Table 7.3 Truth Table for a 1 of 4 Selector

Select Inputs		Data Inputs				Outputs
S_0	S_1	D_0	D_1	D_2	D_3	0
0	0	0	X	X	X	0
0	0	1	X	X	X	1
1	0	X	0	X	X	0
1	0	X	1	X	X	1
0	1	X	X	0	X	0
0	1	X	X	1	X	1
1	1	X	X	X	0	0
1	1	X	X	X	1	1

Figure 7.22 Combining selectors to form a busing structure.

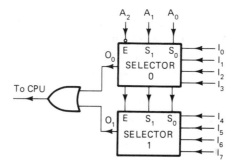

wider bus requires the combination of selectors in parallel with the same select and enable inputs. Like decoders, selectors introduce transmission delays and recovery times that may affect system timing. However, adding more selectors does not increase the transmission delay, since the data only passes through one selector.

The use of TTL decoders and selectors does introduce the following problems.

1. The additional delays may significantly slow the system. The delays can be reduced by using Schottky TTL devices, which are more expensive and consume more power but operate much faster than standard TTL devices.

2. MOS and TTL devices do not mix well on buses. MOS outputs, even when they are at TTL voltage levels, cannot drive resistive TTL loads. The MOS/TTL interface may require level translators, buffers, and drivers. MOS and TTL devices also require separate power supplies and clocks.

3. TTL devices dissipate much more power than MOS and may require heat sinks and larger power supplies. Power consumption can be reduced by using low-power Schottky TTL devices, which are more expensive than standard TTL but just as fast and consume less power.

Problems 1 and 3 create contradictory requirements for the designer. The solution is to use Schottky buffers and drivers, since their delay times are critical to system operation, and to use low-power Schottky decoders and selectors, since their delay times are not critical. Standard TTL devices may be used if device cost is the most important factor.

Open-Collector Outputs

Busing structures can be further simplified by using special outputs that can be connected together without gates. Such outputs are said to have a *wired-OR* capability. The name is a misnomer because no logical OR function is involved and only one output can be active at a time. The situation will become clearer as we discuss the open-collector and tri-state outputs that are commonly used to form buses in TTL and MOS systems.

Open-collector gates lack the final pullup resistor of an ordinary TTL gate so that their outputs are active low but not high. Open-collector gates can be wired together with a pullup resistor as shown in Fig. 7.23. The output (Table 7.4) is low if any of the wired outputs are low; it is high if and only if all the wired outputs are high.

In Fig. 7.24, open-collector gates are used to form a zero indicator. The output is high if and only if all the data lines are zero. If any data line is high, the

Table 7.4   Truth Table for Output O

| | Inputs | | | Output |
O_0	O_1	O_2	O_3	O
0	X	X	X	0
X	0	X	X	0
X	X	0	X	0
X	X	X	0	0
1	1	1	1	1

zero output of the corresponding open-collector inverter makes the total output zero. This circuit could form the ZERO status bit described in Chapter 3.

Figure 7.23   Combining open-collector gates.

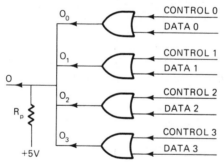

The total output is high if and only if the output of each OR gate is high. Any low gate output makes the total output low. R_p is a pullup resistor.

Figure 7.24   A zero indicator using open-collector inverter gates.

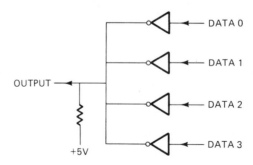

In the basic open-collector busing structure, the control signals are logically ORed with the data signals in open-collector gates (see Fig. 7.23). Table 7.5 contains the truth table for this structure. A decoder with active-low outputs can provide the required control signals.

A high control signal forces the output of the corresponding OR gate high (regardless of the data input) so that it does not affect the overall output. A low control signal makes the output of the OR gate follow the data input; therefore that data input governs the overall output.

Open-collector buses work well with ordinary TTL decoders, have a fairly simple structure, and can easily be expanded or modified. Note that open-collector buses are always active low (i.e., use *negative logic*). Thus the controlling gates are ORs rather than the ANDs of Fig. 7.19.

Table 7.5   Truth Table for Fig. 7.23[a]

| Control | | | | Data | | | | Output |
C_0	C_1	C_2	C_3	D_0	D_1	D_2	D_3	O
1	1	1	1	X	X	X	X	1
0	1	1	1	0	X	X	X	0
0	1	1	1	1	X	X	X	1
1	0	1	1	X	0	X	X	0
1	0	1	1	X	1	X	X	1
1	1	0	1	X	X	0	X	0
1	1	0	1	X	X	1	X	1
1	1	1	0	X	X	X	0	0
1	1	1	0	X	X	X	1	1

[a]The output is one if no control signals are active (i.e., are zero); the output follows the corresponding data input if a control signal is active.

Nevertheless, open-collector buses are not widely used in microcomputers for the following reasons.

1. Relatively few open-collector gates can be connected without buffering. Each high open-collector gate draws some current (typically, 0.25 mA maximum). These losses soon degrade the bus unless it is buffered. Since a standard TTL gate usually provides about 20 mA of drive current, only a few (10 to 20 maximum) open-collector gates can be wire-ORed together.

2. Gates are required to control the bus. These gates increase the parts count and use board space.

3. The pullup resistors take board space and draw current when the bus is active. This current (typically, 1 mA) further degrades the drive level of the bus.

Tri-State Outputs

In such systems as computers having many inputs, tri-state gates have superseded open-collector gates. Tri-state gates have three states: the outputs can be either high, low, or open-circuit (high impedance). In the third or open-circuit state the gate draws very little current and can be combined with other gates without affecting the overall output. Tri-state buffers with active-low enable signals can form a bus as shown in Fig. 7.25. Inactive (high) control signals force outputs into the open-circuit state (see Table 7.6) so that they do not affect the overall output.

Table 7.6   Truth Table for Tri-state Bus of Fig. 7.25

| Control | | | | Data | | | | Output |
C_0	C_1	C_2	C_3	D_0	D_1	D_2	D_3	O
1	1	1	1	X	X	X	X	?
0	1	1	1	0	X	X	X	0
0	1	1	1	1	X	X	X	1
1	0	1	1	X	0	X	X	0
1	0	1	1	X	1	X	X	1
1	1	0	1	X	X	0	X	0
1	1	0	1	X	X	1	X	1
1	1	1	0	X	X	X	0	0
1	1	1	0	X	X	X	1	1

If all the control signals are inactive, the combined output looks like an open circuit. A suitable pullup resistor (1K) will make the open circuit into a logic one.

Figure 7.25   Combining tri-state gates.

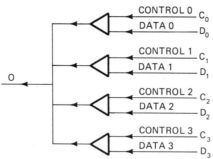

All the gates with inactive control signals are in the third or open-circuit state and do not affect the total output.

Tri-state buses are simple to expand or modify and straightforward in structure. They also have the advantages listed below.

1. Many tri-state outputs can be combined without buffering. A tri-state gate in the open-circuit state draws a maximum current of only 0.04 mA. This amount is

far less than that drawn by an inactive (high) open-collector gate; so many more tri-state outputs can be combined than open-collector outputs.

2. MSI or LSI devices can include tri-state buffers. One extra pin is needed as the "tri-state enable." If more pins are available, several enables (logically ANDed together on the chip) can be included. Proper wiring and a few inverters are often all that are needed for decoding. The MSI or LSI devices may also include the inverters.

3. No pullup resistors are necessary except to handle the case where all the outputs are open-circuit.

4. Tri-state buses can easily be controlled from several different places. For instance, tri-state buses between a processor and memory can be disabled by forcing the processor outputs into the open-circuit state. An outside controller can then use the same buses to access the memory directly.

Tri-state buses do, of course, have disadvantages.

1. Devices with ordinary outputs must be connected to the bus through tri-state buffers. This requirement increases the total parts count. However, more devices are becoming available with tri-state outputs.

2. Tri-state devices introduce new delays into the system, such as

t_{eo}—the maximum delay between enable and output
t_{dis}—the maximum delay from the time the enable is removed to the time the output enters the open-circuit state.

These delays increase the complexity of memory section design.

Tri-State Buffers and Drivers

Buffers, drivers, and receivers are often necessary in microcomputers. Popular devices include the Signetics Schottky TTL 8T97 tri-state buffer and 8T28 tri-state bus transceiver. Similar devices from other manufacturers include the National DM8097, Intel 8216, and Advanced Micro Devices AM 2915.

Figure 7.26 contains the schematic and truth table for the 8T97 buffer. Each 8T97 device has six data lines, four controlled by the DIS_4 input (active-low) and two controlled by the DIS_2 input (active-low). Buses of various widths can be created by combining sets of lines with the same control signal. The device draws a maximum current of 0.4 mA and will produce at least 40 mA of drive current. Thus the device draws far less than one standard TTL load (1.6 mA) and can drive at least 25 such loads. It introduces very little additional delay into circuits; the maximum data delay is 13 ns, the maximum output disable time is 16 ns, and the maximum enable to output delay is 25 ns.

Figure 7.27 is a schematic drawing of the 8T28 tri-state quad bus transceiver. Each 8T28 device has four data input lines (IN), four receiver output lines (R_{OUT}), and four bidirectional driver lines (D_{OUT}). The driver enable (D/E, active-high) forces the driver lines into the open-circuit state; the receiver enable (R/E, active-high) forces the receiver lines into the open-circuit state.

The 8T28 device can connect a bidirectional bus to two unidirectional buses (i.e., a CPU data bus to memory data input and output buses) simply by making the receiver enable the inverse of the driver enable. The bidirectional bus thus will not be driven both ways at the same time.

The 8T28 device draws a maximum of 0.2 mA and will produce at least 30 mA of drive current. It will also handle 300 pF of bus capacitance, an important factor since MOS devices act as capacitive loads on the line (typically, 10 pF per device). The 8T28's switching times are very short. The maximum data delay is 17 ns, the maximum output disable time is 23 ns, and the maximum enable to output delay time is 28 ns.

Figure 7.26 Logic diagram and truth table for the 8T97 tri-state buffer (courtesy of Signetics Corporation).

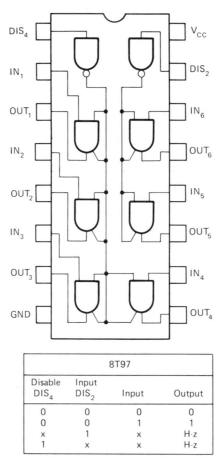

8T97			
Disable DIS$_4$	Input DIS$_2$	Input	Output
0	0	0	0
0	0	1	1
x	1	x	H-z
1	x	x	H-z

H-z is high impedance or open-circuit.

Figure 7.27 Schematic for the 8T28 bus transceiver (courtesy of Signetics Corporation).

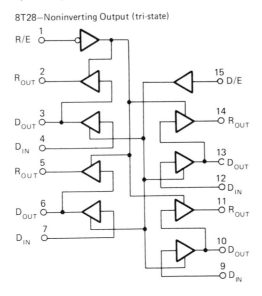

Figure 7.27 Schematic for the 8T28 bus transceiver (courtesy of Signetics Corporation).

8T28—Noninverting Output (tri-state)

7.4   DESIGN OF TRI-STATE MEMORY SECTIONS

A simple tri-state memory section is shown in Fig. 7.28. Here the outputs from the decoder are tied to the enable inputs on the memory chips. The unused address lines may disable the decoder or form a cascaded sequence of decoders. This system can easily be expanded. Large systems may, however, require many decoders as well as buffers and drivers. Only the data bus must be tri-state, since it is the only bus with more than one input in a simple system. The address bus and control signals need not be tri-state unless some external controller must also access the memory (see Chapter 9).

The decoder can be eliminated by restricting the addresses or by using memory chips with several enables. A simple way to restrict addresses is to use each available address line as an enable for a different memory. The number of memories that can be attached to the CPU by using k address lines is therefore reduced from 2^k to k. Figure 7.29 shows a memory section that uses this technique, called *linear select*. The linear select method requires no decoders but results in discontinuous memory addresses. No addresses are allowed that have more than one 1 bit in the selection lines, since each 1 bit activates a memory. Having all zeros in the selection lines is also not allowed because such addresses would activate no memories at all.

Figure 7.28 A simple tri-state memory section.

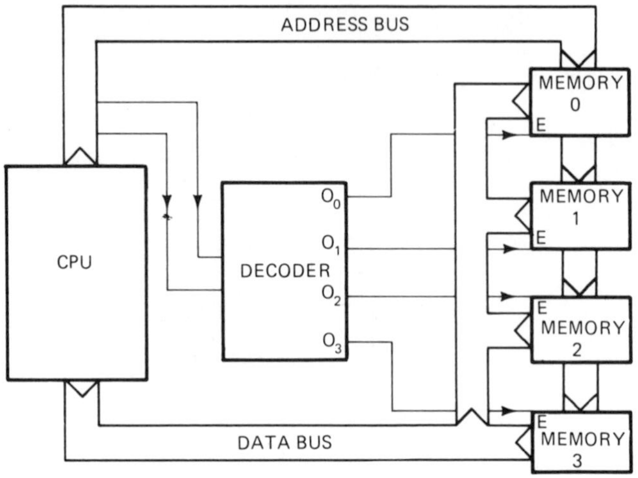

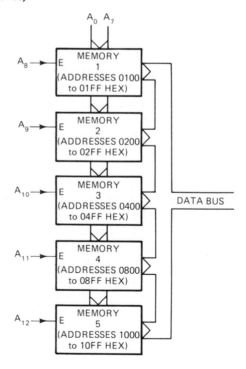

The decoder uses two of the more significant address lines to enable one of the four memories. The less significant address lines are tied directly to all the memories.

Figure 7.29 A memory section using linear select (256 word memories).

Memory chips with several enables are particularly useful if some of the enables are active-high while others are active-low. Figure 7.30 shows a memory section without decoders that uses one active-high and two active-low enables to select one of three memory chips. The memory capacity is not reduced as greatly as with linear select; moreover, the addresses need not be discontinuous. The major disadvantages of this method are that the memory sections are difficult to expand (since the address lines are not fully decoded), special memory chips with larger packages (because of the enables) are necessary, and the designer must specify the connections carefully so as to avoid conflicts.

The method is particularly useful if the CPU uses fixed memory addresses other than zero for RESET or interrupt service routines. Note that the memory section in Fig. 7.30 contains addresses at both the top and the bottom of memory. No gates or decoders are necessary. Addresses with $A_{15} = A_8 = 0$ are in memory 0, those with $A_{15} = 0$ and $A_8 = 1$ are in memory 1, and those with $A_{15} = 1$ and $A_8 = 0$ are in memory 2. Another active-high enable or an inverter would be necessary to allow addresses with $A_{15} = A_8 = 1$.

Figure 7.30 A memory section using enables (256 word memories).

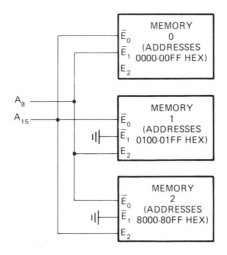

Timing Characteristics of Tri-State Memories

Tri-state memories have the same timing characteristics as other memories except for the enabling and disabling delays. The enabling does not affect the read cycle as long as the decoding system does not delay the enable too long. The maximum access time is governed by either the maximum access time from address or by the maximum access time from enable; the determining factor is which maximum time occurs later in the cycle. As long as the enable delay is no longer than the difference between the access times, it does not affect the maximum access time. The designer should not permit the maximum decoding delay to exceed that difference but need not emphasize its reduction below that figure. Low-power Schottky decoders provide adequate speed and reduce power dissipation.

The disable delay results in two control signals being simultaneously active for a while after each change of address. The old and new addresses will contend unless all outputs are disabled. Most microcomputers provide an inactive period during which addresses can change without causing bus contention. An active-phase signal can be used to enable all the memories; it is active only in the part of the cycle during which data transfers can occur.

7.5 MEMORY SECTIONS FOR SPECIFIC MICROPROCESSORS

This section describes the memory sections and read and write cycles of the Intel 8080 and Motorola 6800 microprocessors. The discussion covers the control signals, timing, addressing, and synchronization of these processors.

Intel 8080 Control Structure

Figure 7.31 shows the pin assignments for the Intel 8080 microprocessor. The signals of interest here are

1. A two-phase, nonoverlapping MOS level clock (inputs φ_1 and φ_2).
2. A 16-bit tri-state address bus, A_0–A_{15}.
3. An 8-bit tri-state, bidirectional data bus, D_0–D_7.
4. A RESET signal (pin 12). A signal lasting three clock periods on this line clears the program counter.
5. A timing signal, SYNC (pin 19), which identifies the start of each memory access cycle.
6. A write pulse, $\overline{WR}$ (pin 18), which is active (low) when the processor is sending data on the data bus.
7. A data bus directional signal, DBIN (pin 17), which designates the direction in which signals are traveling on the data bus. This is the active-phase signal used to avoid bus contention during address changes.
8. A WAIT output (pin 24) and a READY input (pin 23), which are used to add extra clock periods to the basic machine cycle in order to access slow memories.

The Intel 8080 has other status signals that are not shown in Fig. 7.31 because they do not have unique pins. The CPU places these status signals on the data bus at the start of each machine cycle; they must be externally latched if they are to be available while the data bus is being used to transfer data or instructions. Table 7.7 defines the signals and Table 7.8 relates them to the type of machine cycle being executed.

Figure 7.31 Pin configuration of the Intel 8080 microprocessor (courtesy of Intel Corporation).

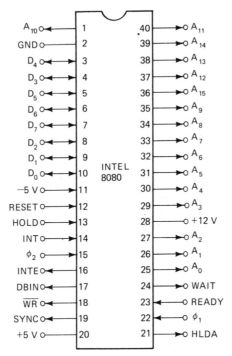

Intel 8080 Timing

The Intel 8080 clock consists of a narrow pulse φ_1 (typically, 100 ns long) followed by a wider pulse φ_2 (typically, 250 ns long). The maximum clock frequency for the standard 8080 is 2 MHz, although some versions can run twice as fast. A special clock chip, the Intel 8224 (see Fig. 7.32), is commonly used to produce MOS and TTL level clocks, synchronize the READY and RESET signals, and provide the timing signal (STATUS STROBE or STSTB) required to latch the status signals from the data bus.

The operation of the processor can be described in terms of three time intervals.

An *instruction cycle* is the time required to fetch, decode, and execute an instruction.

A *machine cycle* is the time required to transfer data to or from the memory or I/O ports.

A *state* is the interval between two successive positive-going transitions of the φ_1 clock pulse—that is, a state lasts one clock period.

Table 7.7 Definition of Intel 8080 Status Information (Courtesy of Intel Corporation)

Instructions for the 8080 require from one to five machine cycles for complete execution. The 8080 sends out eight bits of status information on the data bus at the beginning of each machine cycle (during SYNC time). The following table defines the status information.

Symbols	Data Bus Bit	STATUS INFORMATION DEFINITION Definition
INTA[a]	D_0	Acknowledge signal for INTERRUPT request. Signal should be used to gate a restart instruction onto the data bus when DBIN is active.
$\overline{WO}$	D_1	Indicates that the operation in the current machine cycle will be a WRITE memory or OUTPUT function ($\overline{WO}$ = 0). Otherwise a READ memory or INPUT operation will be executed.
STACK	D_2	Indicates that the address bus holds the pushdown stack address from the Stack Pointer.
HLTA	D_3	Acknowledge signal for HALT instruction.
OUT	D_4	Indicates that the address bus contains the address of an output device and the data bus will contain the output data when $\overline{WR}$ is active.
M_1	D_5	Provides a signal to indicate that the CPU is in the fetch cycle for the first byte of an instruction.
INP[a]	D_6	Indicates that the address bus contains the address of an input device and the input data should be placed on the data bus when DBIN is active.
MEMR[a]	D_7	Designates that the data bus will be used for memory read data.

[a]These three status bits can be used to control the flow of data onto the 8080 data bus.

Table 7.8 Intel 8080 Status Bit Definitions (courtesy of Intel Corporation).

STATUS WORD CHART

TYPE OF MACHINE CYCLE

		①	②	③	④	⑤	⑥	⑦	⑧	⑨	⑩
D_0	INTA	0	0	0	0	0	0	0	1	0	1
D_1	$\overline{WO}$	1	1	0	1	0	1	0	1	1	1
D_2	STACK	0	0	0	1	1	0	0	0	0	0
D_3	HLTA	0	0	0	0	0	0	0	0	1	1
D_4	OUT	0	0	0	0	0	0	1	0	0	0
D_5	M_1	1	0	0	0	0	0	0	1	0	1
D_6	INP	0	0	0	0	0	1	0	0	0	0
D_7	MEMR	1	1	0	1	0	0	0	0	1	0

Figure 7.32 Description of the Intel 8224 clock chip (courtesy of Intel Corporation).

PIN CONFIGURATION

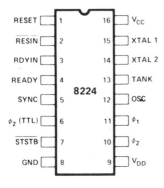

BLOCK DIAGRAM

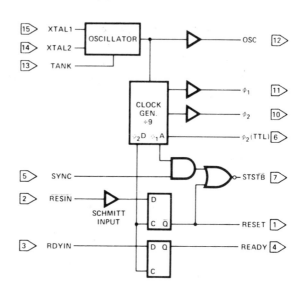

PIN NAMES

RESIN	RESET INPUT
RESET	RESET OUTPUT
RDYIN	READY INPUT
READY	READY OUTPUT
SYNC	SYNC INPUT
STSTB	STATUS STB (ACTIVE LOW)
ϕ_1	8080
ϕ_2	CLOCKS

XTAL 1	CONNECTIONS
XTAL 2	FOR CRYSTAL
TANK	USED WITH OVERTONE XTAL
OSC	OSCILLATOR OUTPUT
ϕ_2 (TTL)	ϕ_2 CLK (TTL LEVEL)
V_{CC}	+5V
V_{DD}	+12V
GND	0V

A machine cycle consists of three to five states. Three states are needed to access the memory or input/output section; the other two states, if present, are used to decode and execute the instruction.

The processor operates as follows, referring to machine cycles as M and states as T.

1. During state T_1 of cycle M_1 the CPU places the contents of the program counter on the address bus and status information (for an instruction fetch cycle) on the data bus. All these activities follow the rising edge of the ϕ_2 clock pulse. The earlier part of the cycle is used to complete the preceding cycle and to avoid overlap. The maximum address delay is 200 ns and the maximum data delay is 220 ns.

2. During state T_2 of cycle M_1 the status information is latched externally and the data bus is either used for output data or placed in the input state (DBIN = 1) to await input data. These activities all follow the rising edge of the φ_2 clock pulse except that the status is latched on the falling edge of φ_1.

3. During state T_3 of cycle M_1 either data is brought into the processor (read cycle) or the write pulse ($\overline{WR}$) is formed. In order for the data to be received properly, it must satisfy setup times during both φ_1 and φ_2. The minimum setup times are 30 ns before the falling edge of φ_1 and 130 ns before the falling edge of φ_2. The processor write pulse ends at least 130 ns before the data and address change on the rising edge of φ_2 in the next cycle.

4. States T_4 and T_5 are used to decode and execute instructions. These states are typically only present during an instruction fetch cycle. The division between instructions requiring four states and those requiring five depends on the internal decoding.

Intel 8080 Instruction Execution

Each instruction fetch and decode cycle requires four or five clock cycles. Instructions that do not need additional memory accesses or internal operations therefore execute in this length of time. Other instructions require more memory accesses, each consisting of three clock cycles, to fetch addresses or data from memory or input ports or to transfer data to memory or output ports.

EXAMPLE 1
    MOV A,M (transfer data from the memory location addressed by registers H and L to the accumulator).
    Figure 7.33 shows the execution of the MOV A,M instruction. It requires two machine cycles. During the first cycle, consisting of four states, the instruction is fetched from memory, sent to the instruction register, and decoded. During the second cycle, consisting of three states, the data is fetched from memory by using the address in registers H and L and placed in the accumulator. So the entire execution involves seven clock cycles. The first cycle is an instruction fetch ($M_1 = 1$, MEMR = 1) and the second is a memory read ($M_1 = 0$, MEMR = 1).

EXAMPLE 2
    CALL 3050H (place 3050 hexadecimal in the program counter and save the old value of the program counter in the RAM stack).
    Figure 7.34 shows the execution of the CALL 3050H instruction. This instruction requires five machine cycles and involves both read and write operations. The first three cycles fetch the instruction and address from program memory. The CPU stores the address temporarily in internal registers W and Z. The next two cycles place the program counter in the stack. The stack pointer is decremented and eight bits of the program counter are placed in the stack during each cycle (most significant bits

Figure 7.33 Execution of the MOV A,M instruction.

CYCLE 1. INSTRUCTION FETCH

(ADDRESS BUS) = (PROGRAM COUNTER)
(DATA BUS) = MOV A,M (7E hex)
(PROGRAM COUNTER) = (PROGRAM COUNTER) + 1
INSTRUCTION DECODED

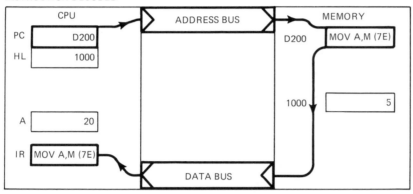

CYCLE 2. MEMORY READ

(ADDRESS BUS) = (REGISTERS H AND L)
(DATA BUS) = ((REGISTERS H AND L))
INSTRUCTION EXECUTED
(ACCUMULATOR) = ((REGISTERS H AND L))

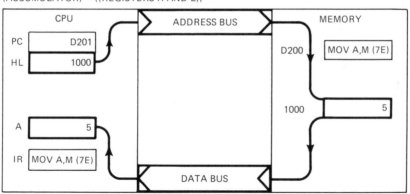

first). Finally, the CPU transfers the contents of registers W and Z to the program counter. The program counter is placed in the stack after the entire CALL instruction has been fetched so that the value saved is the address of the next instruction after the CALL. The entire instruction requires 17 clock cycles, since the instruction fetch uses five states and the two memory read cycles and two stack write cycles use three states each.

Figure 7.34 Execution of the CALL 3050H instruction.

CYCLE 1. INSTRUCTION FETCH

(ADDRESS BUS) = (PROGRAM COUNTER)
(DATA BUS) = CALL (CD hex)
(PROGRAM COUNTER) = (PROGRAM COUNTER) + 1
INSTRUCTION DECODED

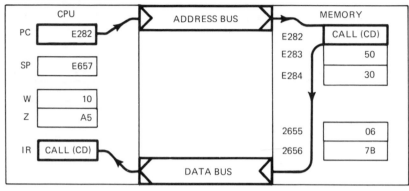

CYCLE 2. MEMORY READ

(ADDRESS BUS) = (PROGRAM COUNTER)
(DATA BUS) = ((PROGRAM COUNTER))
(PROGRAM COUNTER) = (PROGRAM COUNTER) + 1
8 LEAST SIGNIFICANT BITS OF ADDRESS MOVED TO TEMPORARY REGISTER Z

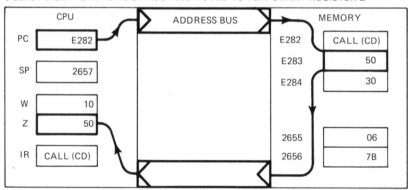

Registers W and Z are internal registers that are not accessible to the programmer.

CYCLE 3. MEMORY READ

(ADDRESS BUS) = (PROGRAM COUNTER)
(DATA BUS) = (PROGRAM COUNTER)
(PROGRAM COUNTER) = (PROGRAM COUNTER) + 1
8 MOST SIGNIFICANT BITS OF ADDRESS MOVED TO TEMPORARY REGISTER W

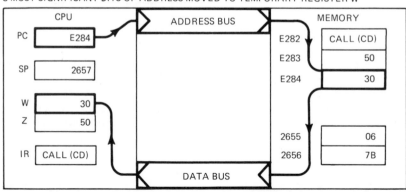

Figure 7.34 (cont.).

CYCLE 4. STACK WRITE

(STACK POINTER) = (STACK POINTER) − 1
(ADDRESS BUS) = (STACK POINTER)
(DATA BUS) = 8 MSBs OF PROGRAM COUNTER
8 MOST SIGNIFICANT BITS OF PROGRAM COUNTER PLACED IN STACK

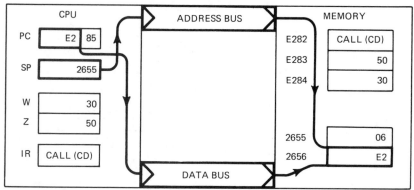

CYCLE 5. STACK WRITE

(STACK POINTER) = (STACK POINTER) − 1
(ADDRESS BUS) = (STACK POINTER)
(DATA BUS) = 8 LSBs OF PROGRAM COUNTER
8 LEAST SIGNIFICANT BITS OF PROGRAM COUNTER PLACED IN STACK
(PROGRAM COUNTER) = (W AND Z)

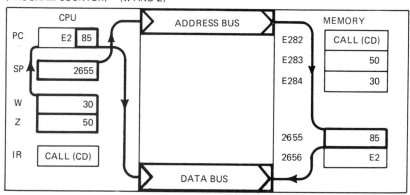

Intel 8080 Memory Design and Control

The Intel 8080 uses the signals described earlier and two derived signals to control memory transfers. The derived signals are $\overline{\text{MEMORY READ}}$ ($\overline{\text{MEMR}}$) and $\overline{\text{MEMORY WRITE}}$ ($\overline{\text{MEMW}}$). $\overline{\text{MEMORY READ}}$ is active when data is being read from memory and the data bus is in the input state (DBIN = 1). $\overline{\text{MEMORY WRITE}}$ is active when data is being written into the memory. These signals may be obtained either from gates or from the 8228 system controller and bus driver described in Fig. 7.35. The 8228 device is a combined status latch, bidirectional data bus driver, and gating array.

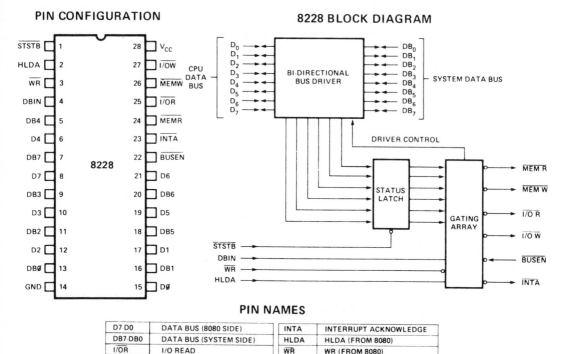

Figure 7.35 Description of the Intel 8228 system controller (courtesy of Intel Corporation).

PIN CONFIGURATION

8228 BLOCK DIAGRAM

PIN NAMES

D7-D0	DATA BUS (8080 SIDE)	INTA	INTERRUPT ACKNOWLEDGE
DB7-DB0	DATA BUS (SYSTEM SIDE)	HLDA	HLDA (FROM 8080)
I/OR	I/O READ	WR	WR (FROM 8080)
I/OW	I/O WRITE	BUSEN	BUS ENABLE INPUT
MEMR	MEMORY READ	STSTB	STATUS STROBE (FROM 8224)
MEMW	MEMORY WRITE	Vcc	+5V
DBIN	DBIN (FROM 8080)	GND	0 VOLTS

The signal $\overline{\text{MEMR}}$ can serve several purposes.

1. It can enable ROMs with tri-state outputs so that they are only active during read cycles.

2. It can enable outputs from RAMs so that outputs will only be produced during memory read cycles.

3. It can enable tri-state buffers that connect the CPU and the memory section.

4. It can eliminate bus contention during address changes. If each memory unit is enabled separately with $\overline{\text{MEMR}}$, all memories will be inactive during address changes (since $\overline{\text{MEMR}}$ includes DBIN).

$\overline{\text{MEMR}}$ may need to be combined with enabling signals from decoders in OR gates (assuming that the decoder outputs are also active-low) in order to form overall active-low enabling signals for memories or buffers.

Worst-case memory timing can easily be derived from the delay and setup times. The access time of a compatible memory, t_{acc}, is given by the minimum time that will provide the required setup times t_{ds_1} (during φ_1) and t_{ds_2} (during φ_2). That is,

$$t_{da} + t_{acc} < 2t_p - t_{ds_2} \qquad (7.11a)$$

$$t_{da} + t_{acc} < 2t_p - t_{\varphi_2} - t_{d_1} - t_{ds_1} \qquad (7.11b)$$

where

$$t_{da} \text{ (maximum address delay)} = 200 \text{ ns}$$

$$t_p \text{ (clock period)} = 500 \text{ ns (typical)}$$

$$t_{ds_2} \text{ (data setup time during } \varphi_2) = 130 \text{ ns}$$

$$t_{\varphi_2} \text{ (width of } \varphi_2) = 250 \text{ ns (typical)}$$

$$t_{d_1} \text{ (delay } \varphi_1 \text{ to } \varphi_2) = 50 \text{ ns (typical)}$$

$$t_{ds_1} \text{ (data setup time during } \varphi_1) = 30 \text{ ns}$$

So the required access time is the minimum of

$$t_{acc} < 670 \text{ ns}$$

$$t_{acc} < 470 \text{ ns}$$

The Intel 8080 thus requires a memory with a maximum access time of 470 ns in order to operate at full speed.

Memories with slower access times can be interfaced by using the READY line. If the READY line is not high at least 120 ns before the falling edge of φ_2 in state T_2, the CPU will enter a WAIT state for one clock cycle and will automatically extend all other control signals. The READY line may be synchronized to the clock by a flip-flop that is part of the 8224 clock chip.

Intel 8080 memory section design is straightforward. Since the RESET location is zero, the lowest addresses are usually ROM, so that the system can be started without loading the program each time. Decoders can generate enables for the various memories; memory sections can easily be expanded or reorganized to meet new requirements.

Motorola 6800 Control Structure

Figure 7.36 shows the pin assignments for the Motorola 6800 microprocessor. The signals of interest here are

1. A two-phase nonoverlapping TTL level clock (inputs φ_1 and φ_2).
2. A 16-bit tri-state address bus, A_0–A_{15}.
3. An 8-bit tri-state bidirectional data bus, D_0–D_7.
4. A RESET signal (pin 40). A positive edge on this line loads the program counter with the contents of the two highest addresses in memory (hexadecimal addresses FFFE and FFFF).

Figure 7.36 Pin configuration of the Motorola 6800 microprocessor (courtesy of Motorola Semiconductor Products, Inc.).

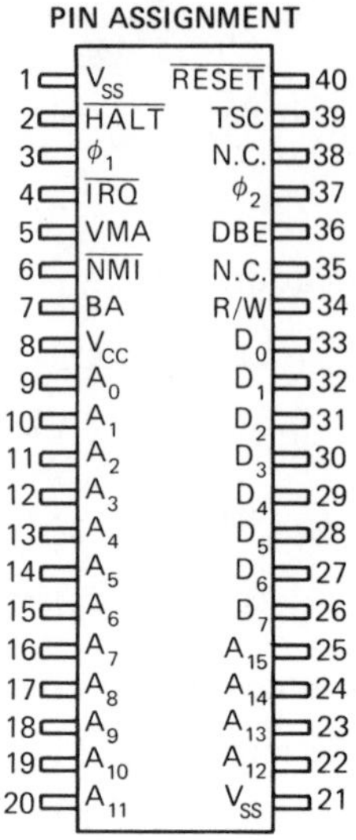

PIN ASSIGNMENT

```
 1 ⊏ V_SS    RESET ⊐ 40
 2 ⊏ HALT     TSC  ⊐ 39
 3 ⊏ φ_1      N.C. ⊐ 38
 4 ⊏ IRQ      φ_2  ⊐ 37
 5 ⊏ VMA      DBE  ⊐ 36
 6 ⊏ NMI      N.C. ⊐ 35
 7 ⊏ BA       R/W  ⊐ 34
 8 ⊏ V_CC     D_0  ⊐ 33
 9 ⊏ A_0      D_1  ⊐ 32
10 ⊏ A_1      D_2  ⊐ 31
11 ⊏ A_2      D_3  ⊐ 30
12 ⊏ A_3      D_4  ⊐ 29
13 ⊏ A_4      D_5  ⊐ 28
14 ⊏ A_5      D_6  ⊐ 27
15 ⊏ A_6      D_7  ⊐ 26
16 ⊏ A_7      A_15 ⊐ 25
17 ⊏ A_8      A_14 ⊐ 24
18 ⊏ A_9      A_13 ⊐ 23
19 ⊏ A_10     A_12 ⊐ 22
20 ⊏ A_11     V_SS ⊐ 21
```

5. A valid memory address signal, VMA (pin 5), which indicates that there is a valid address on the address bus. This signal is one during cycles that use the memory.

6. A READ/WRITE signal, R/W (pin 34), which indicates whether the processor is transferring data to or from memory (the signal is zero for writing).

7. A data bus enable input signal, DBE (pin 36), which forces the data bus into the open-circuit state if low.

The Motorola 6800 produces very few status signals directly. Other signals must be created externally. Note that the fixed RESET location is not zero but rather the address in memory locations FFFE and FFFF. Since the Motorola 6800 has page-zero direct addressing, the low addresses in a 6800 system are usually RAM; therefore the fixed ROM locations for RESET and interrupt service addresses must go elsewhere. Such placement, however, makes the design of memory sections more difficult.

Motorola 6800 Timing

The Motorola 6800 uses a two-phase, nonoverlapping clock with a maximum frequency of 1 MHz (i.e., a clock period of 1 μs). The two phases φ_1 and φ_2 are typically both about 450 ns long.

The operation of the processor is simple. Instruction execution requires between 2 and 12 clock cycles. Each cycle consists of a FETCH phase (φ_1) during which the CPU places an address on the address bus.

an EXECUTE phase (φ_2) during which the CPU transfers data to or from the memory. Normally the φ_2 clock is tied to the DATA BUS ENABLE input so that the data bus is in the open-circuit state except during φ_2.

Cycles that involve a memory access are indicated by VMA = 1; cycles that the CPU uses for internal activities are indicated by VMA = 0.

The processor operates as follows.

1. On the rising edge of φ_1, the CPU places the address, READ/WRITE, and VMA signals on the appropriate lines. The maximum delay time for all signals is 300 ns.

2. During phase φ_2 the CPU transfers data to or from the memory. The maximum data delay is 225 ns from the rising edge of φ_2, and the minimum data setup time is 100 ns from the falling edge.

Note that no write pulse is provided. Under normal conditions, the φ_2 clock pulse ends the read or write operation unless external circuitry provides a write pulse. Memories used with the Motorola 6800 must work properly under clock control; that is, the data hold time must be zero, since the READ/WRITE signal is active throughout the operation.

Motorola 6800 Instruction Execution

Each instruction or data fetch takes one clock cycle. All instructions require at least one clock cycle beyond the initial fetch. Single-word and double-word instructions that do not require further memory accesses or internal operations therefore execute in two clock cycles. Other instructions require additional clock cycles to fetch data and addresses and to perform internal operations, such as the additions required by indexed or relative addressing (both methods involve a 16-bit addition that takes two clock cycles).

EXAMPLE 1

LDAA #$40 (move immediate data—40 hexadecimal—from memory to accumulator A).

Figure 7.37 shows the execution of the LDAA #$40 instruction. Two clock cycles are required. During the first cycle the CPU fetches and decodes the instruction. During the second the CPU fetches the data and places it in accumulator A. Both cycles involve memory accesses, and so VMA is always one.

EXAMPLE 2

CMPA $20, X (compare data in the indexed memory location to the contents of accumulator A).

Figure 7.38 shows the execution of the CMPA $20, X instruction. Five clock cycles are required. The first cycle is an instruction fetch, the second cycle retrieves the offset, the third and fourth cycles are used to perform the indexing (i.e., add 20 hexadecimal to the contents of the index register), and the fifth cycle is used to fetch the data from the indexed memory location and to execute the instruction. The first, second, and fifth cycles involve memory accesses; so VMA is one. The third and fourth cycles are used for internal operations; so VMA is zero.

Figure 7.37   Execution of the LDAA #$40 instruction.

CYCLE 1. INSTRUCTION FETCH

(ADDRESS BUS) = (PROGRAM COUNTER)
(DATA BUS) = LDAA # (86 hex)
(PROGRAM COUNTER) = (PROGRAM COUNTER) + 1
INSTRUCTION DECODED

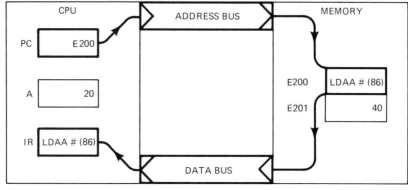

CYCLE 2. MEMORY READ

(ADDRESS BUS) = (PROGRAM COUNTER)
(DATA BUS) = ((PROGRAM COUNTER)) = 40
(PROGRAM COUNTER) = (PROGRAM COUNTER) + 1
(A) = (DATA BUS) = 40
INSTRUCTION EXECUTED

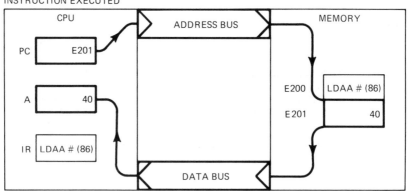

Motorola 6800 Memory Design and Control

Memory control with the Motorola 6800 is somewhat more complex than with the Intel 8080 because of the large number of cycles during which the memory is not used, the lack of a write pulse, and the use of an active clock phase. The designer may control the memory section as follows.

1. Enable all memories with φ_2 and VMA so that no bus contention occurs and external devices can use the memory during cycles when the CPU is not using

Figure 7.38 Execution of the CMPA $20, X instruction.

CYCLE 1. INSTRUCTION FETCH

(ADDRESS BUS) = (PROGRAM COUNTER)
(DATA BUS) = CMPA, X (A1 hex)
(PROGRAM COUNTER) = (PROGRAM COUNTER) + 1
INSTRUCTION DECODED

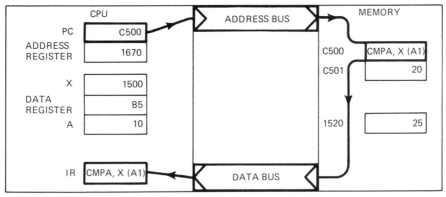

The data and address registers are temporary registers that the processor can use to hold data and addresses, respectively.

CYCLE 2. MEMORY READ

(ADDRESS BUS) = (PROGRAM COUNTER)
(DATA BUS) = ((PROGRAM COUNTER)) = 20
(PROGRAM COUNTER) = (PROGRAM COUNTER) + 1
OFFSET PLACED IN DATA REGISTER

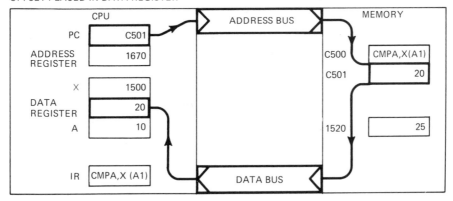

Figure 7.38 (cont.).

CYCLES 3 AND 4. EFFECTIVE ADDRESS CALCULATION

(ADDRESS BUS) = (INDEX REGISTER) IN CYCLE 3, (INDEX REGISTER)
    + OFFSET WITHOUT CARRY IN CYCLE 4
DATA BUS IS NOT USED
(ADDRESS REGISTER) = (INDEX REGISTER) + OFFSET
VMA IS LOW

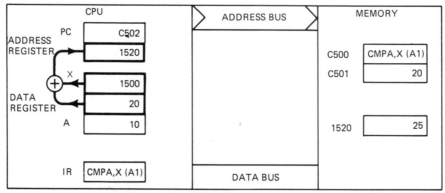

The CPU does not access memory during these cycles, and so VMA = 0.
The contents of the address bus can be examined for debugging purposes.
Note that these two cycles are used even if the offset is zero.

CYCLE 5. MEMORY READ AND INSTRUCTION EXECUTION

(ADDRESS BUS) = (ADDRESS REGISTER)
(DATA BUS) = ((ADDRESS REGISTER)) = (1520) = 25
FLAGS SET BY (A) − (DATA BUS) = 10 − 25

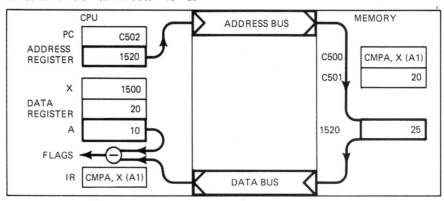

VMA = 1, since the memory is used.

it. However, remember that there is no write pulse, and so memories with no data hold time are required.

    2. Enable ROMs also with the READ/WRITE signal so that they will be inactive during write cycles.

    3. Control buffers with the φ_2 clock phase to avoid data bus contention and to allow the use of the data bus by other devices during φ_1.

The access time for a compatible memory depends on the clock characteristics, address delay time, and data setup time. The requirement is

$$t_{da} + t_{acc} < t_{\varphi_1\varphi_2} - t_{dsr} \tag{7.12}$$

where t_{da} is the address delay time, $t_{\varphi_1\varphi_2}$ the minimum total length of φ_1 and φ_2, and t_{dsr} the data setup time. The minimum is

$$t_{acc} < 965 - 300 - 100 < 565 \text{ ns}$$

Memories with slower access times can be interfaced by slowing the φ_2 clock phase. The Motorola 6800 can be slowed by any amount; the delay is not limited to an integral number of clock cycles as in the Intel 8080.

Motorola 6800 memory section design is complicated by the fact that the RESET address is at the top of memory. The ROM that contains this address must respond to memory addresses FFFE and FFFF. This ROM must therefore contain the highest available addresses and must be placed so as not to interfere with memory expansion. Furthermore, memory locations 0000 to 00FF should be RAM so that they can be used for temporary data that can be accessed with short direct (page-zero) addresses.

Large memory sections can be designed as shown previously with decoders. The following approaches are helpful in small memory sections.

1. Using memory chips with several enables. These enables can be tied to address lines, to VMA, to φ_2, and to READ/WRITE (for ROMs). The Motorola 6810 RAM, a 128×8 chip with two active-high and four active-low enables, and 6830 ROM, a $1K \times 8$ chip with four programmable enables, are convenient in small memory sections.

2. Using the most significant one or two address lines to select among ROM, RAM, and I/O. Using the two most significant address lines as shown in Fig. 7.39 permits 16K of each type of memory with addresses as described in Table 7.9.

3. Handling bus control by enabling the bus only during the φ_2 clock phase. The Motorola 6810 RAM and 6830 ROM have system-compatible access times; the 6810 RAM also has no data hold time as required for the Motorola 6800 write cycle.

Table 7.9 Memory assignments in a simple Motorola 6800 system

A_{15}	A_{14}	Meaning
0	0	RAM, including page zero
0	1	I/O
1	0	I/O
1	1	ROM, including RESET and interrupt service addresses

Figure 7.39 A simple Motorola 6800 memory section.

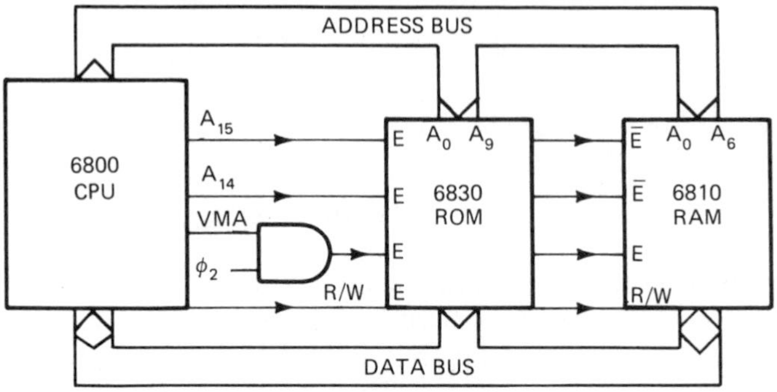

The ROM is enabled only if

$$A_{15} = 1$$
$$A_{14} = 1$$
$$VMA \cdot \phi_2 = 1$$
$$R/W = 1 \ (READ)$$

The RAM is enabled only if

$$A_{15} = 0$$
$$A_{14} = 0$$
$$VMA \cdot \phi_2 = 1$$

7.6 SUMMARY

The major activity of the microprocessor is the transfer of data and instructions to and from the memory section. The address bus contains the signals that select a particular memory location. Address signals will usually be decoded partly on the memory chips and partly in an external decoding system. The data bus contains the data or instruction. Since the memory section typically is divided into several separately addressed parts, a busing structure is necessary to ensure that only one memory will ever try to drive the data bus at a time. Tri-state outputs and buffers, mutually exclusive decoding signals, and an active-phase timing signal can provide the required structure. The timing for the memory section must ensure that input data is available to the processor at the proper time and that output data is written correctly into the memory without any erroneous destructive operations.

PROBLEMS

1. Describe the steps required to perform the following read operations. What are the contents of the data and address buses? What internal operations are necessary?
   (a) Fetch the address part of an instruction
   (b) Fetch immediate data.
   (c) Fetch data from a stack managed by a stack pointer register.

2. Describe the execution of the following two-word instructions. Show the contents of the buses during each cycle and describe the internal operations.
   (a) LOAD #100
   (b) JUMP 1000
   (c) ADD @150
   Assume that all the instructions and addresses are one word in length.

3. A processor has a stack pointer and four address registers that can be used to access data. Show how a selector could control which address is placed on the address bus (remember the program counter!). Make a table that shows the effect of each combination of select inputs.

4. A processor has eight registers to which data on a bus may be directed. Show how a demultiplexer could handle this situation. This could also be done with a decoder that activated the clock on one of the registers as shown in the figure. Describe how the processor would operate in this case. Assume that the register contents do not change unless the register is clocked.

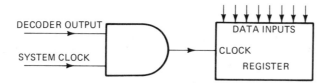

5. Explain why a processor needs a RESET input. What happens if the processor simply starts executing instructions when power comes on and how can this step be prevented?

6. Show the interface required between a CPU with a 16-bit address bus and an 8-bit data bus and a ROM with 2K 8-bit words. Assume that RESET starts the program counter at zero. What if RESET starts the program counter at 8000 (hex)? How about 1000 (hex)? How must the program be organized in these cases? What happens if some address lines are left unconnected?

7. How many clock periods are necessary between address output and data input in order for the following processor-memory systems to operate correctly?
   (a) Maximum address delay time = 250 ns
       Minimum data setup time = 200 ns
       Maximum memory access time = 650 ns
       Clock period = 250 ns
   (b) Maximum address delay time = 100 ns
       Minimum data setup time = 50 ns
       Maximum memory access time = 450 ns
       Clock period = 500 ns

8. What memory access time is necessary for maximum speed of operation if the processor has the following characteristics?
   (a) Maximum address delay time = 250 ns
       Minimum data setup time = 100 ns
       Clock period = 500 ns
       Number of clock periods (k) = 2 between address output and data input

(b) Maximum address delay time = 200 ns
Minimum data setup time = 100 ns
Clock period = 200 ns
Number of clock periods (k) = 6 between address output and data input
What effect would a data bus buffer with a maximum delay time of 50 ns have on the required access time? How about an address bus buffer with the same delay time?

9. Show the interface required between a CPU with a 16-bit address bus and an 8-bit data bus and 1K of RAM memory consisting of eight 1K by 1 chips with separate input and output. What would be necessary to start such a system?

10. Assume that a decoding system must generate enables for 20 1K memories from a 16-bit address bus. Show how this could be done using 3 to 8 decoders that have a single enabling input. What if the 3 to 8 decoders have two active-low and one active-high enabling inputs? Show all the required address connections. Describe the delays introduced by the decoding system.

11. A bus driver produces 30 mA of drive current. How many inactive (high) open-collector outputs can be placed on the bus while still maintaining 10 mA of drive current if each inactive output draws a maximum of 0.25 mA? How many inactive tri-state outputs can be placed on the bus if each draws 0.04 mA? The bus can, of course, be improved by adding another set of drivers. What are the disadvantages of doing so? Where should the drivers be placed? What problems can you foresee in expanding an unbuffered single-board computer?

12. Show the interfacing required by a tri-state memory section with the characteristics below.
(a) The CPU has an 8-bit data bus and a 16-bit address bus.
(b) The memory is organized as a 1K by 8 ROM that occupies addresses 0000 to 03FF (hex) and two 256 by 4 RAMs that occupy addresses 0400 to 04FF (hex).
(c) How should the memory section be interfaced if an open-collector bus is being used?

13. An Intel 8080 memory section is to consist of 4K of ROM and 2K of RAM. Show how such a system could be interfaced using standard tri-state memories with a single active-low chip enable. Assume that the ROMs to be used are 1K by 8, the RAMs 1K by 1 with separate input/output. What would be necessary to interface such a section to the Motorola 6800 processor? How would you need to change your design to handle twice as much memory?

14. Describe each cycle in the execution of the following Intel 8080 instructions.
(a) ADD   B
(b) LDA   1000H
(c) RET

15. Show the interfacing required for an Intel 8080 memory section consisting of 8K of ROM and 256 words of RAM. The ROMs are 1K by 8, the RAMs 256 by 4 with common I/O and an output disable. How should you change the design to attach twice as much RAM?

16. Discuss why the Intel 8080 memory read signal $\overline{\text{MEMR}}$ includes DBIN. What would happen if you used the status signal MEMR directly as an enabling signal? How could

you eliminate this problem with a buffer? How does the Motorola 6800 microprocessor handle the same problem? Describe some alternative solutions. (*Hint*: What happens in each system when the address changes?)

17. Describe each cycle in the execution of the following Motorola 6800 instructions.
(a) LDAA $2000
(b) LDX   #$0050
(c) BSR   ∗ + 8
Note: $ means hexadecimal.

18. A Motorola 6800 memory section consists of three 6830 1K ROMs and three 6810 128-word RAMs. Show how such a section could be interfaced without a decoder. Assume that the ROM enables can be chosen to be active-high or active-low as desired. How would you have to modify the section to double the RAM capacity? The ROM capacity? Each 6810 RAM has two active-high and four active-low enables; each 6810 ROM has four programmable enables; that is, you may choose them to be either active-high or active-low as part of the masking process.

19. An Intel 8080 processor must read data from a slow PROM with an access time of 1.5 μs. How many WAIT states would be needed? How long a φ_2 phase would be necessary to interface the slow memory to the Motorola 6800? What if the access time were 2.5 μs? How much would the PROM slow the execution of instructions involving various numbers of PROM and RAM accesses, assuming that the RAM has a 450 ns access time? What if all cycles (even those that did not use the PROM) were slowed?

20. Show a decoding system that can generate 64 chip enables for a 64K memory section consisting of 1K ROMs and RAMs. How would the ROM and RAM need to be organized for an Intel 8080 memory section? For a Motorola 6800 section? How long would the maximum delay through the decoders be if each decoder had a delay of 30 ns? Would this affect the computer if the address to output maximum delay were 400 ns and the chip enable to output delay were 250 ns? What if the decoder delay were 100 ns? Show the decoding system using 3 to 8 decoders with a single enable (active-low) and active-low outputs. Discuss the complications involved in using 2 to 4 decoders.

REFERENCES

BLAKESLEE, T. R., *Digital Design with Standard MSI and LSI*, Wiley, New York, 1975.

Data Manual, Signetics Co., Menlo Park, Ca., 1976.

DAVIS, S., "Selection and Application of Semiconductor Memories," *Computer Design*, Vol. 13, No. 1, January 1974, pp. 65–77.

FARNBACH, W. A., "Bring up Your μP Bit-by-Bit," *Electronic Design*, Vol. 24, No. 15, July 19, 1976, pp. 80–85.

FRANKENBERG, R. J., *Designer's Guide to Semiconductor Memories*, Cahners, Boston, Ma., 1975.

GREENE, R., and D. HOUSE, "Designing with Intel PROMs and ROMs," *Intel Application Note AP-6*, Intel Corporation, Santa Clara, Ca., 1975.

Intel 8080 Microcomputer Systems User's Manual, Intel Corporation, Santa Clara, Ca., 1975.

LEVINE, L., and W. MYERS, "Timing: a Crucial Factor in LSI-MOS Main Memory Design," *Electronics*, Vol. 48, No. 14, July 10, 1975, pp. 107–111.

LUECKE, G., et al., *Semiconductor Memory Design and Application*, McGraw-Hill, New York, 1973.

Motorola 6800 Microprocessor Applications Manual, Motorola Semiconductor Products Inc., Phoenix, Ariz., 1975.

RAPHAEL, H., "How to Expand a Microcomputer's Memory," *Electronics*, Vol. 49, No. 26, December 23, 1976, pp. 67–69.

Semiconductor Memory Data Book, Texas Instruments Inc., Dallas, Texas, 1975.

SPRINGER, J., "Designers' Guide to Semiconductor Memory Systems," *EDN*, Vol. 19, No. 16, September 5, 1974, pp. 49–56.

The TTL Data Book, Texas Instruments Inc., Dallas, Texas, 1973.

THOMAS, A. T., "Design Techniques for Microprocessor Memory Systems," *Computer Design*, Vol. 14, No. 8, August 1975, pp. 73–78.

8 Microprocessor Input/Output

This chapter deals with the input/output sections of microcomputers. We begin with the general characteristics of input and output and the interfacing of simple I/O sections consisting of a single port. Later topics include more complex I/O sections, I/O hardware, simple peripherals, and the implementation of input/output sections for the Intel 8080 and Motorola 6800 processors.

8.1 GENERAL DISCUSSION OF INPUT/OUTPUT

Input and output are similar to memory accesses. The processor can transfer data to and from peripherals in the same way that it transfers data to and from memory. In fact, memory is simply another peripheral. Why, then, are input and output such complex topics that they are often ignored in introductory courses? Why is there so little standardization of computer I/O sections?

The major problems of I/O are

1. The wide variety of types of peripherals.
2. The enormous range of speeds.
3. The variety of signal types and levels.
4. The complexity of the signal structure.

The key problem in I/O sections is variety. Memories come in a few basic types, have similar speeds, and require simple control signals. In most microcomputers the memory section consists of semiconductor chips that behave much like the CPU. Furthermore, the memory section retains its contents; the CPU need not fetch data at a precise time.

Peripherals vary tremendously. They may be mechanical, electromechanical, electronic, and so forth. They may use digital voltage signals like the processor, or they may use current signals or continuous (analog) signals. A simple I/O section may include a temperature sensor that provides data every 5 minutes, a teletypewriter that transfers 100 bits per second, and a floppy disk that transfers 250,000 bits per second. The data on input lines will, of course, change independently of the computer. Signals may be necessary to hold or transform data and control the operating modes of peripherals.

Few I/O standards exist; the most popular ones will be discussed later. Generally, however, each peripheral is a unique problem. A special interface must translate between the signals that the computer uses and those that the peripheral uses. The interface must provide the proper timing and control. With the availability of single-chip CPUs and large memories, the input/output section is the most expensive part of many microcomputers. Many complex new LSI chips perform I/O functions exclusively. For example, the Intel 8041 Universal Peripheral Interface is an entire microcomputer used as a peripheral controller in 8080-based systems.[1]

Input and output cycles themselves proceed much like memory cycles. Figure 8.1 shows the connections between the CPU and the I/O section. The various buses have the same purposes as those that serve the memory section. The control signals are often more numerous, however, in order to handle the larger variety of control functions that input/output requires.

Figure 8.1 Bus connections between CPU and I/O section.

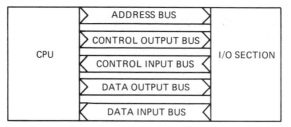

The control buses may include interrupt, DMA, timing, and strobe signals.

General Input Procedure

An input operation is similar to a memory read cycle. Three steps are necessary.

1. The CPU places an address on the address bus. This step selects a particular input unit or *port*; the physical port may be of any bit length, although ports with the word length of the CPU are the most convenient.

---

[1]D. Phillips and A. Goodman, "Slave Microcomputer Lightens Main Microprocessor Load," *Electronics*, Vol. 50, No. 14, July 7, 1977, pp. 109–112.

2. The CPU waits for data to become available.

3. The CPU reads data from the data bus and places it in a register.

The problem is how to determine when data is available. Memory cycles allow a reasonable fixed time. Since the memories are so similar to the processor, we can easily either construct a compatible memory section or add a simple delay circuit. But how can we handle the tremendous range of speeds found in peripherals? Simple delay circuits are seldom useful. Input/output requires much more complex timing.

The input cycle has the same timing as the memory read cycle. This timing is the easiest to implement since the worst-case analysis has already been derived for the memory section. Of course, establishing the timing for the cycle does not solve the overall timing problem since only a few very fast peripherals can operate just like memories. In such cases, the delay times, setup times, and hold times are the same as those described in Chapter 7.

Many methods can reconcile the timing of the CPU and the input peripherals. Typical examples are

1. Assuming that data is always available much as it is in a memory. This technique is adequate for slowly changing data from mechanical switches or sensors that measure physical quantities like temperature or pressure. The CPU need only read the data often enough to respond to changes.

2. Providing a special signal (i.e., DATA READY) to indicate that data is available. The signal may be an extra bit or strobe or a particular code that has no other meaning. This method is adequate for slow-to-moderate data rates and will handle peripherals that operate at irregular intervals or *asynchronously*. The CPU must either look for the special signal or be alerted to its appearance by an interrupt.

3. Accepting data at a rate determined by an external clock. Here the CPU simply performs input operations at a regular rate. This method will handle moderate data rates and peripherals that operate at regular intervals or *synchronously*. Transfers with higher data rates can use direct memory access. The problem here is the initial synchronization of CPU and external clock, which may require a special control line or a special synchronization message.

In the first method the CPU simply performs input operations at a reasonable rate. Often the operations need not even be periodic as long as the intervals do not exceed the maximum response time. The only problem is the transition periods. Erroneous inputs can occur when sensor levels are changing, dials are being turned, or switches are being moved to new positions. Common ways to handle transitions include

1. Changing slow or irregular transitions into pulses with one-shots (monostable multivibrators), Schmitt triggers, flip-flops, and gates.

2. Using another input (e.g., a LOAD switch) to inform the CPU that data is ready.

3. Rechecking data in software. The CPU can confirm the initial reading by taking another reading after a delay.

Method 2, providing a special DATA READY signal, is sometimes called a *handshake*. The procedure, which works as follows, is shown in Fig. 8.2.

1. The peripheral sends the data and a DATA READY signal to the I/O section.
2. The CPU determines that the DATA READY signal is active. A latch may hold the DATA READY signal until the CPU reads it.
3. The CPU reads the data.
4. The CPU sends an INPUT ACKNOWLEDGE signal to the peripheral. This signal indicates that the transfer has been completed and that the peripheral can send more data.

Figure 8.2   An input operation using handshake logic.

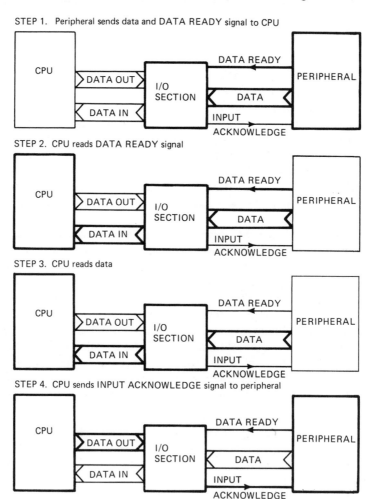

The actual transfer in step 3 is a small part of the process. An extra input operation must check the DATA READY signal, and an output operation must produce the INPUT ACKNOWLEDGE signal. The input/output section must hold the data and control signals long enough to ensure that they have been received.

Method 3, the synchronous transfer, is the fastest I/O method. Once the processor synchronizes properly with the peripheral, the transfers are regular. For example, if the peripheral is a communications line operating at 2400 bits per second, the processor must perform a serial input operation every 1/2400 of a second. The problem is how to start and stop the transfers.

A common technique is to use a special message that has no purpose other than synchronization. The end of the transfer may also be coded or specified. The problem is obviously much like that of tuning a receiver to a transmitter in a communications network. Synchronous transfer is fast but requires extra hardware and software.

General Output Procedure

An output operation is similar to a memory write cycle. Three steps are necessary.

1. The CPU places an address on the address bus.
2. The CPU places data on the data bus.
3. The CPU waits for the transfer to be successfully completed.

The output operation also requires a write pulse. As with writing into memory, the order of the steps is critical. Not only must the data be transferred correctly but no other permanent transfers can occur. Data may not be written into any other part and the output operation must be concluded properly. The timing constraints are the same as for a memory write cycle.

The problem is to determine when the transfer can begin and when it has been completed. The cycle itself uses the same timing as the memory write cycle. This timing orders the signals correctly and terminates the operation properly but cannot handle the range of speeds of peripherals. The CPU must determine whether the peripheral is ready to accept data. The output port must also hold the data long enough for the peripheral to accept it.

The same methods that handle input peripherals can also be used with output peripherals:

1. Assuming that the peripheral is always ready. This technique is adequate for slow transfers involving displays, relays, and actuators that operate at mechanical or human speeds. The CPU must not exceed the response rate of these peripherals.

2. Providing a special signal along with the data. The signal may be an extra bit or a special code. This method is adequate for low-to-moderate data rates and asynchronous peripherals.

3. Transferring data at a rate determined by an external clock. This method will handle moderate data rates and synchronous peripherals. DMA operations can provide higher data rates.

The roles of sender and receiver are the same in input and output. The receiver must determine when data is present and complete the transfer. In input, the CPU acts as receiver and must find the data. In output, the CPU acts as sender and must ensure that the peripheral finds the data.

Method 1 is adequate for many slow peripherals. The I/O section must latch the data because the CPU only briefly places it on the bus. The data must be held long enough for the peripheral to capture it. Since slow peripherals react slowly, brief changes in the output data have no effect.

Method 2, the asynchronous transfer or handshake, proceeds as follows for output.

1. The peripheral sends an OUTPUT REQUEST or PERIPHERAL READY signal to the I/O section.
2. The CPU determines that the PERIPHERAL READY signal is active. A latch may hold the signal.
3. The CPU sends an OUTPUT READY signal to the peripheral.
4. The CPU sends data to the peripheral. The next PERIPHERAL READY signal may inform the CPU that the transfer has been completed.

Here again the actual transfer of data is simply one part of the operation. Extra hardware, software, and time are necessary to ensure that the transfer proceeds properly. The I/O section must include latches and control circuitry as well as the output port itself.

Synchronous output allows the highest data rates. As in the input case, the problem is how to start and stop the transfers. A special synchronization message is a common technique.

8.2 SIMPLE INPUT/OUTPUT SECTIONS

A Single Input Port

A simple I/O section may contain a single input port. If the data changes very slowly (e.g., is derived from switches), the only connections required (see Fig. 8.3) are the data lines. No address connections are necessary, since there is only one port.

The CPU, of course, always handles words of a specified length. If the peripheral has a shorter word than the CPU, the remaining data lines can be left unconnected. A masking operation can clear the unused bits. For instance, if the peripheral provides four bits of data to an 8-bit processor, the masking operation will be

AND   #00001111B

if the four least significant data lines are used. A peripheral with longer words than the CPU will require several ports and a series of input operations.

A single input port can be used for both asynchronous and synchronous transfers. However, the CPU must determine when data is available in the asynchronous case and synchronize with the external clock in the synchronous case. A single port requires a special code for these purposes; the CPU must use its own clock for timing.

In the asynchronous case, the special code must precede each character. For example, suppose that the special code is the all ones word—that is, 11111111 binary in the 8-bit case. The transfer will then proceed as follows.

Step 1. Read the input data.
Step 2. If the input data is not the special code, return to step 1.
Step 3. Read the actual data.

The characteristics of the peripheral determine the timing of the input operations. If the peripheral transmits regularly, the program may center the reception by waiting for an extra half of a transfer period. The CPU will then sample the data at the center of the pulses rather than at the edges where the data may be changing and there is more chance for error (see Fig. 8.4).

Figure 8.3   A single input port.

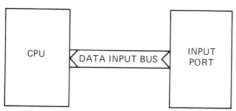

The peripheral operates slowly enough so that no timing or control signals are necessary.

Figure 8.4   Input data timing.

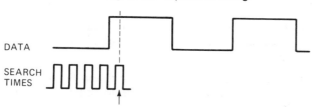

At this point, the search finds the special code. Waiting half a transfer (bit) time allows the computer to sample the data near the center of the pulses.

Figure 8.5 A simple timing loop.

1. Flowchart

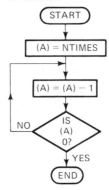

2. Time budget

Instruction	Time/Instruction	Total Time
LOAD ACCUMULATOR	t_L	t_L
DECREMENT ACCUMULATOR	t_D	NTIMES $\times t_D$
JUMP ON NOT ZERO	t_J	NTIMES $\times t_J$

The total time used is

$$\text{NTIMES} \times (t_D + t_J) + t_L$$

3. Examples

(a) Intel 8080 with 2-MHz clock

t_D = 2.5 μs (DCR A)   MVI A, NTIMES
t_J = 5 μs   (JNZ LOOP)   LOOP: DCR A
t_L = 3.5 μs (MVI A, NTIMES)   JNZ LOOP
Total time used is NTIMES $\times$ 7.5 + 3.5 μs

(b) Motorola 6800 with 1-MHz clock

t_D = 2 μs (DECA)
t_J = 4 μs (BNE LOOP)   LDAA ≠NTIMES
t_L = 2 μs (LDAA #NTIMES)   LOOP   DECA
Total time used is NTIMES $\times$ 6 + 2 μs   BNE   LOOP

EXAMPLE

Assume that the peripheral transmits data asynchronously at a maximum rate of 100 8-bit words per second and uses the all ones word to indicate the availability of data. The input procedure is

Step 1. The CPU samples the input data until it detects the all ones word.
Step 2. The CPU waits for 15 ms to find the center of the transmitted data pulse.
Step 3. The CPU reads the actual data.

In this simple case, the CPU can establish the timing from its own clock. A typical timing loop is

```
         LOAD ACCUMULATOR   #NTIMES
DELAY:   DECREMENT ACCUMULATOR
         JUMP ON NOT ZERO DELAY
```

The CPU executes the LOAD ACCUMULATOR instruction once and the DE-CREMENT ACCUMULATOR and JUMP ON NOT ZERO instructions a number of times, determined by the constant NTIMES. Figure 8.5 contains a flowchart, a time budget for the loop, and examples for the Intel 8080 and Motorola 6800 processors. The timing loop completely occupies the CPU.

The CPU can perform synchronous transfers the same way that it performs asynchronous transfers. The only difference is that the CPU continues to fetch data until the process is halted. If the peripheral in the last example were synchronous, the transfer would proceed as follows.

Step 1. The CPU reads the input data until it detects the all ones word.

Step 2. The CPU waits for 15 ms to synchronize with the input.

Step 3. The CPU reads one word of data.

Step 4. The CPU determines if the transfer is complete. If not, the CPU waits for 10 ms and returns to step 3.

The remaining question is how to end the transfer. Often the total length of the transfer is known or is included in the data. For instance, the first two characters in the data stream could be its length. Another alternative is to have a special ending character. Flowcharts for these two methods are shown in Fig. 8.6.

The single port requires little hardware. The CPU, however, must search for the data and provide timing. Furthermore, the extra starting and ending characters reduce the actual data rate.

A Single Output Port

An output port operates differently from an input port because the output data must be held for the peripheral. The connections (see Fig. 8.7) are the data lines and a write pulse (READ/WRITE signal) that latches the data. As in the input case, all CPU output operations send data to the same port, since there are no address connections.

The new feature here is the latch, which operates as follows.

1. When the clock is active, the data outputs are the same as the inputs.

2. When the clock is inactive, the outputs retain the values they had prior to the last clock transition.

Figure 8.6 Flowcharts for synchronous transfer.

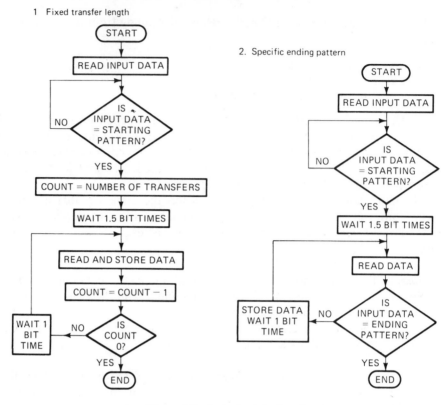

1 Fixed transfer length

2. Specific ending pattern

Figure 8.7 A single output port.

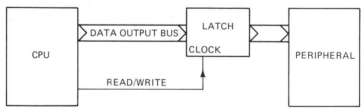

The latch is clocked by the WRITE pulse and holds the data long enough for the peripheral to capture it.

The data must be stable for minimum intervals before and after the clock transition. The latch must be activated on the proper transition of the READ/ WRITE signal.

The output port may, of course, be of any length. Data lines that are not connected to the port or to the peripheral are simply ignored; the result is to waste part of each output operation and reduce the maximum data rate. One port with the same word length as the CPU may handle several peripherals (see Fig. 8.8). The data intended for peripheral 1 is placed in the two least significant bits and so on. The same signal latches all the data.

Figure 8.8 Sharing an output port among several peripherals.

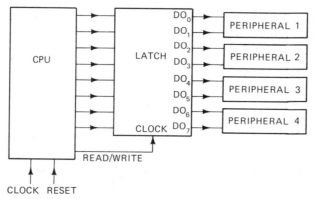

Each output operation sends two bits of data to each of the four peripherals. Bits 0 and 1 go to peripheral 1, etc. The program must prepare the output data with shift instructions.

Synchronous and asynchronous transfers require other hardware besides the output port, since the CPU must have an input that it can use to synchronize or to determine if the output device is ready. Here again simple hardware structure means a more complex signal transfer, lower data rates, and more extensive software.

In the asynchronous case, the CPU must precede each character with the special code indicating the presence of data. The transfer proceeds as follows.

Step 1. The CPU sends the special OUTPUT READY code.
Step 2. The CPU waits for one transfer period.
Step 3. The CPU sends the actual data.

The CPU controls the output operation; so there is no centering problem. The peripheral is presumed to be always ready as long as the CPU waits one transfer period between transmissions. If necessary, the CPU can send dummy characters to the peripheral to give it extra time to finish. The dummy characters are codes that the peripheral ignores; the ASCII characters SYN (synchronous idle) or NUL (null) often serve this purpose.

Synchronous output is similar to asynchronous output except that once synchronization has been achieved, transfers proceed until specifically halted. The number of transfers may be fixed or included in the data. A special ending character may complete the transfer.

Input and output differ somewhat. In the input case, the CPU must determine when the transfer begins and ends; that is, the CPU must line up its clock with the unknown peripheral clock. In the output case, the CPU determines the start and end of the transfer and must establish them so that they coincide with the peripheral's requirements. The output port must latch the data.

8.3 GENERAL INPUT/OUTPUT SECTIONS

Most input/output sections consist of more than one port. Even a single peripheral may require several ports if the length of the data exceeds the word length of the CPU or if control and status information must be transferred separately. Such I/O sections require busing structures that must be combined with those required by the memory section.

I/O Busing Structures

The input busing structure must allow the addressed input port to control the data bus without interference. The output busing structure must latch the contents of the data bus into the addressed output port. Figure 8.9 shows a tri-state input busing structure that uses control signals to enable the ports. In Fig. 8.10 an output busing structure uses control signals to clock latches. Decoders can provide mutually exclusive control signals as described in Chapter 7.

Figure 8.9 A tri-state input busing structure.

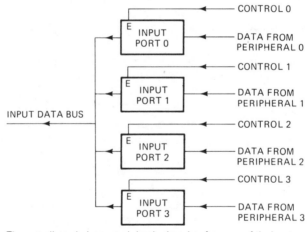

The mutually exclusive control signals place data from one of the input ports on the input data bus and force the outputs of all the other ports into the open-circuit state.

Combined Memory and Input/Output Addressing

Almost all microprocessors use the same buses for both memory and input/output transfers. The question, then, is how to distinguish the two. Three common methods exist.

1. *Isolated input/output* in which memory and I/O addresses are decoded separately.

Figure 8.10 An output busing structure.

Figure 8.10 An output busing structure.

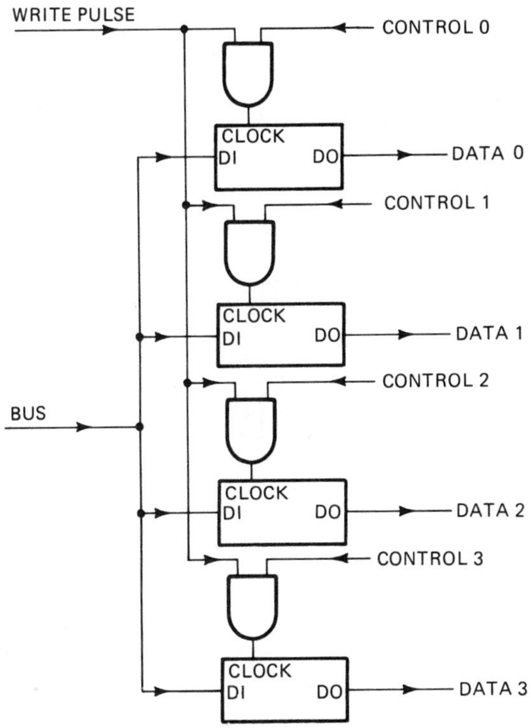

The mutually exclusive control signals determine which latch will be clocked by the write pulse and so will have its output (DO) follow its input (DI). The write pulse is assumed to be active high.

2. *Memory-mapped input/output* in which I/O ports are treated exactly the same as memory locations.

3. *Attached input/output* in which I/O ports are part of the CPU and memories and are activated by special instructions.

Figure 8.11 shows a microcomputer with an isolated I/O section. The SECTION SELECT signal distinguishes memory from I/O by enabling one or the other set of bus drivers. The signal could also activate each memory or I/O port. Separate I/O instructions are necessary; the execution of these instructions forces the SECTION SELECT signal into the I/O state. The Intel 8080, Zilog Z-80, and Signetics 2650 are examples of microprocessors that can use isolated I/O.

The advantages of isolated I/O are

1. The I/O port addresses can be short. Most systems have far fewer I/O ports than memory locations; 8-bit addresses are usually sufficient for I/O sections but inadequate for memory sections. Short I/O addresses mean simpler decoding systems and shorter instructions.

Figure 8.11 An isolated I/O section.

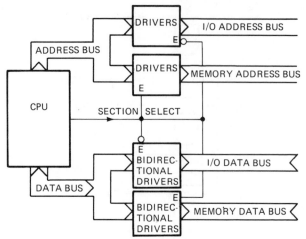

The SECTION SELECT signal indicates a memory cycle if it is high, an I/O cycle if low. The signal enables the memory buses if it is high and the I/O buses if low.

Figure 8.12 A memory-mapped I/O section.

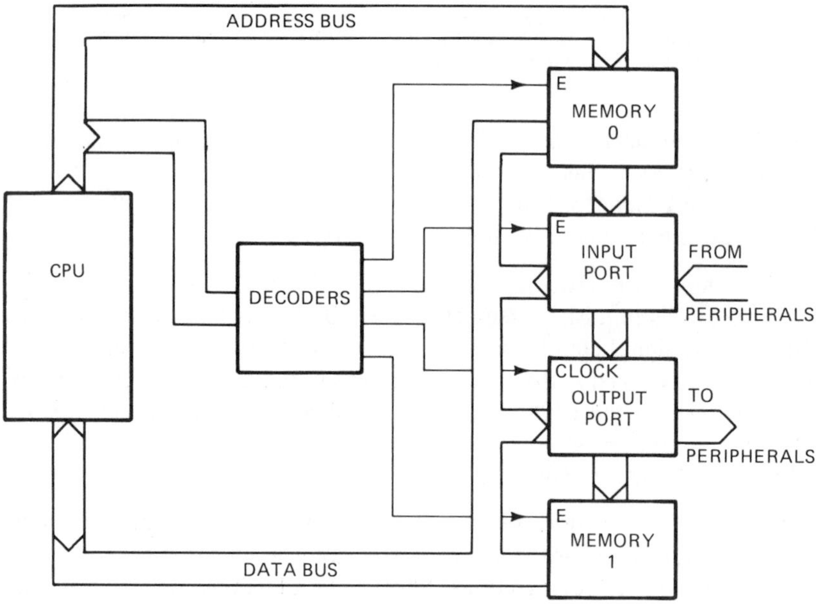

The only distinction between memory and I/O is the addresses that they occupy.

2. Extra control signals can be easily developed for I/O transfers. Memories rarely need the strobes or handshaking signals that I/O transfers often require.

3. Programs are clearer because I/O transfers are distinguished from other operations.

4. Memory and I/O design can be separated since the control structures can be independent.

Isolated I/O requires extra decoding and instructions and lacks flexibility, but it does make a natural distinction between memories and I/O ports. If the I/O ports are simple TTL devices and the peripherals are unidirectional, failure to make this distinction explicit can be confusing.

Figure 8.12 shows a microcomputer with a memory-mapped I/O section. The processor uses the same instructions for memory and I/O transfers. Processors that are specifically designed for memory-mapped I/O include the Motorola 6800, MOS Technology 6502, and National PACE. The only way to recognize an input or output port is by its address. Of course, processors with separate I/O instructions can use memory-mapped I/O merely by integrating the input/output and memory sections. The advantages of memory-mapped I/O are

1. Any instruction that operates on data in memory can operate on data at input and output ports. No separate I/O instructions are necessary, and many tasks can be greatly simplified.

2. No separate decoding or control system is necessary for input and output. This factor can save parts.

3. The system can easily incorporate LSI interfaces and special controllers. These devices often include storage elements and registers that must be programmed from the CPU. Handling such complex devices as sets of I/O ports is awkward.

Memory-mapped I/O does have drawbacks.

1. I/O transfers may be difficult to distinguish from other operations. Programs may be difficult to understand and debug if simple instructions can perform complex I/O functions.

2. I/O ports occupy some of the address space.

3. Many instructions may be difficult to understand because of the physical limitations of the I/O devices. What happens if the CPU tries to write data into a switch or read data from an output transmission line?

4. The decoding system may become complex because I/O ports occupy much less address space than memory chips. Either the decoding system must be extended or memory space must be wasted. An I/O port will seldom occupy more than a few memory addresses.

5. The method is difficult to use with standard circuitry. The control signals will not handle complex I/O. Often the interface chips must generate additional signals under program control.

In general, memory-mapped I/O is best suited to systems that use complex interface chips, whereas isolated I/O is better for systems that use small- and medium-scale integrated circuits.

Attached input/output is a useful alternative for small systems in which package count is a major factor. Here the I/O ports and control circuitry are part of the CPU or memory chips (see Fig. 8.13). The Intel 4040, Fairchild F-8, National SC/MP, Texas Instruments TMS 1000NC, and Intel 8048 allow attached I/O.

Figure 8.13 An attached I/O section.

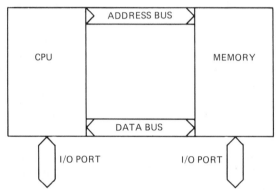

The I/O ports here are an integral part of the CPU and memory chips.

There are, of course, many limitations on these systems, including

1. The I/O requirements must be small. The CPU and memory packages can provide only a few ports and control signals.

2. The special memory chips are more expensive than standard chips. The lack of adequate control signals may make the use of standard chips very difficult.

3. System expansion is awkward and expensive.

4. Special instructions or addresses must transfer data to and from the I/O ports.

Attached input/output is useful when the cost and size of a single package are critical and expansion is unnecessary. Controllers for games, appliances, and other simple low-speed devices are typical applications for one- or two-chip microcomputers with attached input/output.

Multiport Transfers

Many peripherals require several ports. The simplest case occurs when the data word of the peripheral is longer than that of the CPU. The CPU must then transfer the data in segments. A 16-bit output operation using an 8-bit processor will proceed as follows (see Fig. 8.14).

Step 1. The CPU prepares the eight most significant bits of the data.
Step 2. The CPU sends the eight most significant bits of the data to the first port.
Step 3. The CPU prepares the eight least significant bits of the data.
Step 4. The CPU sends the eight least significant bits of the data to the second port.

Figure 8.14   A multiword output operation.

Output operation 1. Most significant bits to first port

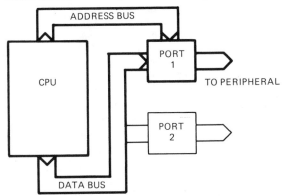

The CPU must prepare the eight most significant bits of the data first, and they are available to the peripheral first.

Output operation 2. Least significant bits to second port

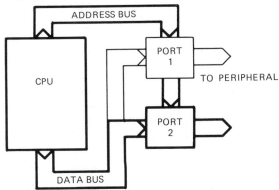

The CPU must prepare the eight least significant bits of the data and send them to port 2. After some delay, all 16 bits of the data are available to the peripheral.

In this case, the two transfers are not simultaneous. If simultaneity is necessary, a third port can control a tri-state output buffer. The program disables the buffer prior to the data transfers and enables it afterward. Then all 16 bits of the data appear simultaneously when the CPU enables the buffer.

Multiword transfers require some internal manipulation, since the CPU must transfer each word to or from its own memory or register address.

Additional ports can also handle control and status signals. Figure 8.15 shows a separate input port for a DATA READY signal and an output port for an INPUT ACKNOWLEDGE signal. No special codes are necessary, but the hardware is more complex than the single port described earlier. Either the reading of the data or the sending of INPUT ACKNOWLEDGE must clear the DATA READY signal for the next cycle. An output transfer can similarly use three ports: the data port, an input port for the PERIPHERAL READY signal, and an output port for the OUTPUT READY signal.

Figure 8.15 An I/O section with control and status ports for handshaking.

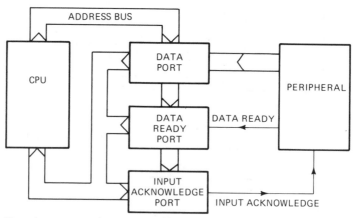

The various ports must have separate addresses.

Some microprocessors have special serial I/O lines to handle data or control signals. Specific instructions may transfer data to or from these lines or use their states as jump conditions. The Intel 8085, National PACE, General Instrument CP1600, and Texas Instruments 9900 are examples of processors with serial I/O lines.

Combining status and control ports can save hardware. Since such signals as DATA READY, INPUT ACKNOWLEDGE, PERIPHERAL READY, and OUTPUT READY are single bits, one port with the CPU's word length can handle control or status signals for several peripherals. The program must examine the proper bit position for the READY signal and change the proper bit position for the ACKNOWLEDGE signal. The control ports may be part of the data port. The data port will then latch the READY signal and provide the acknowledgement.

8.4 USEFUL INPUT/OUTPUT HARDWARE

Various hardware elements can perform some of the functions of the I/O section. Simple devices include flip-flops and one-shots. Useful MSI devices include decoders, selectors, counters, shift registers, and I/O ports. LSI I/O devices include UARTs, USRTs, and parallel interfaces.

Flip-Flops

Among the popular types are the D (delay) flip-flop, and the RS (reset-set) flip-flop. These types are widely used as counters, switches, latches, registers, and memory cells.

The D flip-flop is a clocked latch in which the output follows the input during the active clock phase and the clock transition latches the data. The RS flip-flop is an unclocked latch. The R input clears the flip-flop; the S input sets it. An RS flip-flop may hold a DATA READY or PERIPHERAL READY signal until the CPU has time to examine it. The ACKNOWLEDGE signal may then reset the flip-flop after the data transfer has been completed. A D flip-flop with the data input tied high and the signal tied to the clock input behaves like an RS device.

One-Shots

The one-shot, or *monostable multivibrator*, provides a single pulse of fixed length in response to a pulse input. This device can produce pulses of various lengths to control peripherals that the processor cannot handle directly. Such peripherals may be mechanical or electromechanical systems that operate far more slowly than the processor. They may also be signal generators or communications equipment operating at higher frequencies than the CPU. A one-shot can also convert a series of short pulses into a single long pulse.

Decoders

Decoders, which were discussed in Section 7.3, produce a single active output in response to coded inputs. The active outputs can enable or clock memories, I/O ports, registers, buffers, or other system elements. Some decoders are actually code converters. The most popular devices take BCD or ASCII inputs and convert them into the forms required by such peripherals as the widely used seven-segment display (see Section A3.3).

Selectors

The functions of selectors were described in Section 7.3. These devices can also form input ports; no decoder is necessary, since the selector can decode the address inputs. Figure 8.16 shows four 1 of 4 selectors serving as four 4-bit input ports. Each device has the same enable and select inputs but is connected to a different bit of the CPU data bus; it thus acts as one-quarter of four ports rather than as a single port. For instance, if $S_0 = S_1 = 0$, the data outputs are I_{00} from selector 1, I_{01} from selector 2, I_{02} from selector 3, and I_{03} from selector 4. A 4-bit parallel input must use one bit of each selector. The selector must have tri-state outputs to interface to a tri-state bus.

Figure 8.16 Using selectors as input ports.

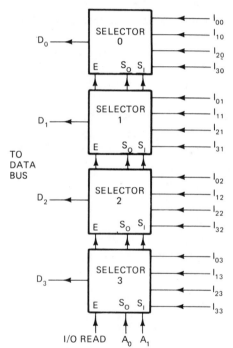

The selectors do not latch the input data.

Selector Outputs:

Address Inputs		Data Outputs			
A_1	A_0	D_3	D_2	D_1	D_0
0	0	I_{03}	I_{02}	I_{01}	I_{00}
0	1	I_{13}	I_{12}	I_{11}	I_{10}
1	0	I_{23}	I_{22}	I_{21}	I_{20}
1	1	I_{33}	I_{32}	I_{31}	I_{30}

Counters

A *counter* is a device that enters a different state with each clock pulse up to its capacity. Counters provide varied clock rates, delays, counts, and control signals for multiplexers or demultiplexers. Common counters are decimal, binary, or divide-by-12; options include counting up and down, synchronous outputs (all bits change at the same time), ability to clear or preset values, and tri-state outputs.

Figure 8.17 shows a typical application of a counter in a microcomputer. A divide-by-12 counter and a 4 to 12 decoder control a 12-digit display. The RESET signal clears the counter to start. Each write operation changes the state of the counter and directs the output to a different display. Only one output port is necessary. The processor sends the digits one at a time, and the counter and decoder automatically direct them properly. As long as each digit is latched for a reasonable amount of time and the displays are pulsed often enough, the entire 12-digit display will appear to an observer to be continuously lit. Such displays are common in calculators, instruments, monitoring systems, and terminals.

Figure 8.17 Multiplexed displays using a counter.

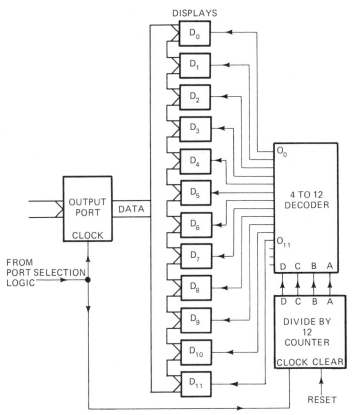

The decoder controls which display is active. The logic that selects the output port also clocks the counter.

Shift Registers

A *shift register* is a device that shifts each bit of its contents one position to the right or left with each clock pulse. Shift registers can provide expanded I/O capability, clock pulses, and delays; they can also convert data between parallel and serial forms. Common shift registers shift data to the left and have serial inputs and outputs. Options include devices with parallel inputs and outputs, synchronous outputs, serial and parallel entry, bidirectional shift ability, clear and preset, and tri-state outputs.

Figure 8.18 shows how a shift register can expand the I/O capability of a processor. Initially the CPU clears the shift registers from the control port, then sends seven bits to each shift register, and, finally, activates the displays from the control port. A 4-bit CPU can thus provide 28 bits of parallel output through one port. No multiplexing or decoding is necessary.

Figure 8.18 Expanding outputs with shift registers.

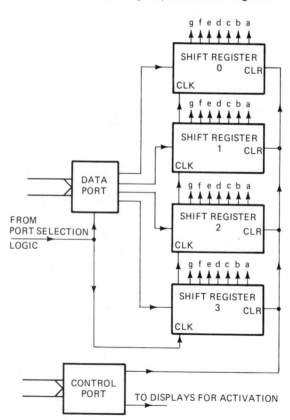

I/O Ports

MSI I/O ports combine buffers, latches, drivers, and other circuits. These ports can replace several standard devices and have some or all of the following features.

- Different input and output logic connections that the user can select.
- A clocked latch for holding data.
- A buffer with tri-state outputs.
- Bus drivers.
- An R-S latch that can hold a READY signal.
- Input and output strobes.
- Several enables for controlling port selection.
- Direct interface with bidirectional buses.
- Master enable and master clear.
- Predetermined startup state.

The Intel 8212 shown in Fig. 8.19 is a typical I/O port. It has two operating modes, one of which is chosen by the mode input (MD = 1 for output mode, 0 for input mode):

In the input mode, the peripheral latches the data into the port by sending a DATA READY signal (active-high) to the strobe input. The CPU enables the data onto the data bus with the device selection logic. In this control structure, the peripheral places the data in the port and the CPU fetches the data.

In the output mode, the CPU latches the data into the port with the device selection logic. The buffer is always enabled so that the data is immediately available to the peripheral. In this control structure, the CPU places the data in the port; no fetch is necessary, since the peripheral normally has a dedicated rather than a time-shared bus.

The Intel 8212 also has an RS flip-flop for service requests. This flip-flop is at the top of Fig. 8.19; it is active-low and is cleared by the STROBE signal from the peripheral. It is set either by the $\overline{\text{CLEAR}}$ signal or by the device selection logic. A typical sequence involving a service request proceeds as follows.

1. System reset clears the 8212 port and sets the service request flip-flop. $\overline{\text{INT}}$ output is high.

2. The STROBE (STB) signal clears the service request flip-flop and sends $\overline{\text{INT}}$ low (active).

3. The CPU selects the port by activating the device selection logic. This logic sets the service request flip-flop but holds $\overline{\text{INT}}$ low until the port is deactivated. Selection of the port brings $\overline{\text{INT}}$ low even if the strobe is not connected; in this case, $\overline{\text{INT}}$ indicates the occurrence of an I/O operation involving that port. Such a signal could multiplex displays attached to the port as shown in Fig. 8.17.

Figure 8.19 The Intel 8212 I/O port (courtesy of Intel Corp.).

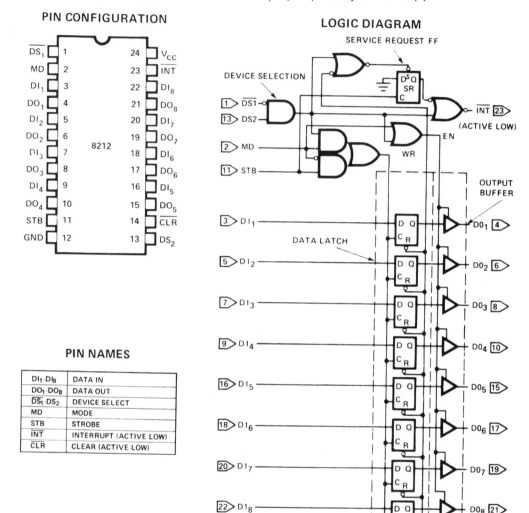

PIN NAMES

DI_1-DI_8	DATA IN
DO_1-DO_8	DATA OUT
$\overline{DS_1}$-DS_2	DEVICE SELECT
MD	MODE
STB	STROBE
$\overline{INT}$	INTERRUPT (ACTIVE LOW)
$\overline{CLR}$	CLEAR (ACTIVE LOW)

UARTs and USRTs

Serial peripherals require circuitry that generates and checks parity, adds start and stop bits to mark the beginning and ending of asynchronous transfers, and generates control signals for standard interfaces. The data rates, codes, and formats vary so that interfacing with simple logic elements is difficult.

Such tasks are sufficiently common, well defined, and slow to warrant the production of specific MOS LSI devices. Asynchronous peripherals use a *UART* or universal asynchronous receiver/transmitter. The UART performs the following tasks.

1. It converts output data from parallel to serial form and input data from serial to parallel.

2. As a transmitter it adds start and stop bits, generates parity, and clocks the data out at the required rate. As a receiver it recognizes and deletes start and stop bits, checks parity, and clocks the data in at the required rate.

3. It provides indicators that tell whether it has received data or is ready to accept data for transmission. Other indicators may signify errors in the received data.

Figure 8.20 shows the American Microsystems S1883 UART. In addition to performing the tasks mentioned above, this device has independent transmit/receive rates, tri-state outputs, and double buffering. The device can be interfaced directly to a tri-state data bus. It has a RESET signal that initially clears all the internal registers and counters, a control holding register for control options, a status word for the various indicators, and clock inputs that govern the data rates. The UART has two input ports and two output ports—one input port for received data and one for status, one output port for transmitted data and one for control.

The UART control port determines such options as

- Number of bits per character (typically, 5 to 9)
- Number of stop bits (typically, 1, $1\frac{1}{2}$, or 2)
- Parity option—that is, whether parity is included
- Type of parity—that is, odd or even

The options required for a particular application may be selected by latching data into the control port as part of the system initialization.

The UART status port holds the DATA and OUTPUT READY signals and the various error indicators. Typical status signals include

- Transmitter buffer empty—that is, the UART is ready for a new character.
- Output data available or receive buffer full—that is, the UART has received a character.
- Parity error.
- Framing error—that is, the UART has received a character without the proper number of stop bits.
- Overrun—that is, the UART has received a new character before the previous one was read.

The UART requires a clock input. The processor or a bit rate generator may supply it.

Figure 8.20 The American Microsystems S1883 UART (courtesy of American Microsystems, Inc.).

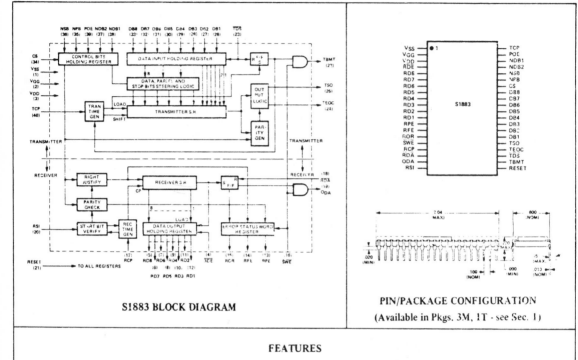

S1883 BLOCK DIAGRAM

PIN/PACKAGE CONFIGURATION

(Available in Pkgs. 3M, 1T - see Sec. 1)

FEATURES

- 12.5 K Baud Data Rate
- 5-8 Bit Word Length
- Parity Generation/Checking Odd, Even, None
- Framing and Overflow Error Detection
- 1, 1.5, or 2 Stop Bits

- Double Buffered Input/Output
- Independent Transmit/Receive Rates
- Start and Stop Bits Generated and Detected
- Interchangeable with TMS6011, COM2017, TR1602, AY-5-1013
- Tri-State Outputs

Synchronous peripherals use the *USRT* or universal synchronous receiver/transmitter. The USRT is like the UART except that data is transferred synchronously with respect to a "sync" character. The USRT receiver compares the received data to the contents of an internal register until a match is found. Then the reception is completed synchronously. The transmitter sends the "sync" character, followed by the synchronous transmission. A USRT requires a clock input and will have most of the control options and status indicators of the UART. The USRT may also have registers for a synchronization character and a fill character to be sent when no other data is available.

Unlike the simple circuits mentioned earlier, UARTs and USRTs are MOS LSI devices. They operate at lower speeds than TTL devices, provide little drive current, and require different clocks and power supplies than TTL devices. Microprocessor manufacturers often provide UARTs and USRTs that are directly compatible with a particular processor. Nevertheless, the designer should carefully integrate UARTs and USRTs into the microcomputer system and consider their timing characteristics.

Parallel Interfaces

Peripherals that handle data in parallel can be interfaced with sets of data and control ports as shown previously. Parallel interfacing, however, also presents the kind of problem that a programmable LSI device can solve. Such parallel interfaces generally provide the following features.

- Buffers and latches for input and output data
- Status and control signals for handshaking
- Other control and timing signals for peripherals
- Direct interface with the processor address, data, and control buses
- Control registers that can be programmed from the CPU to allow the devices to perform different functions

Some parallel interfaces also contain interrupt and DMA control, bidirectional lines, interval timers, and even additional program and data memory. These devices are far more complex than I/O ports or UARTs; they may contain almost as much circuitry as the CPU itself. As noted, the complexity of parallel interfaces means that they are easiest to configure and use when they can be addressed as a set of memory locations rather than as a set of input and output ports.

A popular parallel interface is the Motorola 6820 Peripheral Interface Adapter (or PIA). Figure 8.21 is a block diagram of the device. The PIA contains two ports called A and B; A is primarily intended to be an input port and B an output port. Each port contains

1. A data register. This register is latched when used for output but unlatched when used for input.

2. A data direction register that determines whether the I/O lines are inputs or outputs.

3. A control register that determines the active logic connections in the device and that also contains the DATA READY or PERIPHERAL READY bits.

4. Two control lines, CA(CB)1 and CA(CB)2, the functions of which are determined by the contents of the control register.

The PIA occupies four memory locations and can be attached directly to the Motorola 6800 buses (see Fig. 8.22). The RS (register select) lines address the internal registers and are normally connected to the two least significant bits of the address bus. The CS (chip select) lines provide addressing without decoders in small systems. In Fig. 8.22 A_{15} is tied to an active-low chip select and A_{14} to an active-high select so that the PIA addresses do not interfere with either the RAM

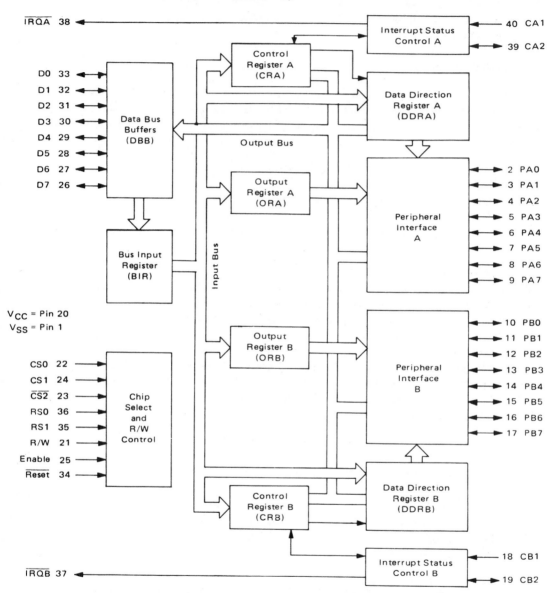

Figure 8.21 Extended block diagram and pin configuration of the Motorola 6820 Peripheral Interface Adapter (courtesy of Motorola Semiconductor Products, Inc.).

on page zero or the ROM at the highest addresses (recall the typical Motorola 6800 memory sections described in Chapter 7). One chip select is tied to VMA · A_{14} so that the PIA cannot be inadvertently changed during processor cycles that do not use the memory.

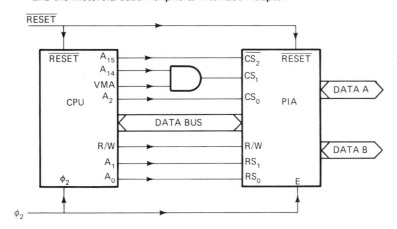

The PIA has six registers (three on each side) but only four addresses, which are assigned as shown in Table 8.1. The data and data direction registers share an address. Bit 2 of the corresponding control register selects one or the other; that bit is zero for the data direction register and one for the data register. This selection seldom causes a problem, since most systems initialize the data direction register with the appropriate values and seldom refer to it again. If a bit position in the data direction register is one, the correspondingly numbered I/O line is an output; if the bit position is zero, the I/O line is an input.

Table 8.1 Internal Addressing of the Peripheral Interface Adapter (Courtesy of Motorola Semiconductor Products, Inc.)

		Control Register Bit		
RS1	RS0	CRA-2	CRB-2	Location Selected
0	0	1	X	Peripheral Register A
0	0	0	X	Data Direction Register A
0	1	X	X	Control Register A
1	0	X	1	Peripheral Register B
1	0	X	0	Data Direction Register B
1	1	X	X	Control Register B

X = Don't Care

Figure 8.23 shows the organization of the control registers. The IRQ (interrupt request) bits are the READY bits that are set by transitions on the control lines; these bits cannot be changed by writing data into the control register. They are automatically reset by any operation that reads data from the PIA data register. These bits are also ORed together to form an interrupt output.

365

Figure 8.23 Organization of the PIA control registers (courtesy of Motorola Semiconductor Products, Inc.).

	7	6	5	4	3	2	1	0
CRA	IRQA1	IRQA2	CA2 Control			DDRA Access	CA1 Control	

	7	6	5	4	3	2	1	0
CRB	IRQB1	IRQB2	CB2 Control			DDRB Access	CB1 Control	

Control register bit 0 determines whether the interrupt output is enabled (bit 0 = 1 to enable the interrupt). Control register bit 1 determines whether bit 7 is set by high-to-low transitions (trailing edges) or low-to-high transitions (leading edges) on control line 1. Table 8.2 describes the use of bits 0 and 1. Bit 1 allows strobe signals with either polarity and triggering on either edge.

Bits 3, 4, and 5 of the control register allow the PIA to perform a variety of functions. Bit 5 determines whether control line 2 is an input or an output; if bit 5 = 0, control line 2 is an input. The A and B sides then operate identically. Control bit 6 is set by transitions on control line 2. Control bits 3 and 4 determine whether the interrupt output is active and which transitions set bit 6. Control line 2 could be an additional strobe from a single peripheral or a strobe from a multiplexed peripheral that uses the same port. Table 8.3 describes the use of CA2 and CB2 as inputs.

Table 8.2 Control of Interrupt Inputs CA1 and CB1 (Courtesy of Motorola Semiconductor Products, Inc.)

CRA-1 (CRB-1)	CRA-0 (CRB-0)	Interrupt Input CA1 (CB1)	Interrupt Flag CRA-7 (CRB-7)	MPU Interrupt Request IRQA (IRQB)
0	0	↓ Active	Set high on ↓ of CA1 (CB1)	Disabled — IRQ remains high
0	1	↓ Active	Set high on ↓ of CA1 (CB1)	Goes low when the interrupt flag bit CRA-7 (CRB-7) goes high
1	0	↑ Active	Set high on ↑ of CA1 (CB1)	Disabled — IRQ remains high
1	1	↑ Active	Set high on ↑ of CA1 (CB1)	Goes low when the interrupt flag bit CRÁ-7 (CRB-7) goes high

Notes: 1. ↑ indicates positive transition (low to high)

2. ↓ indicates negative transition (high to low)

3. The Interrupt flag bit CRA-7 is cleared by an MPU Read of the A Data Register. and CRB-7 is cleared by an MPU Read of the B Data Register.

4. If CRA-0 (CRB-0) is low when an interrupt occurs (Interrupt disabled) and is later brought high, IRQA (IRQB) occurs on the positive transition of CRA-0 (CRB-0).

Table 8.3 Control of CA2 and CB2 as Interrupt Inputs. CRA5 (CRB5) is Low. (Courtesy of Motorola Semiconductor Products Inc.)

CRA-5 (CRB-5)	CRA-4 (CRB-4)	CRA-3 (CRB-3)	Interrupt Input CA2 (CB2)	Interrupt Flag CRA-6 (CRB-6)	MPU Interrupt Request IRQA (IRQB)
0	0	0	↓ Active	Set high on ↓ of CA2 (CB2)	Disabled — IRQ remains high
0	0	1	↓ Active	Set high on ↓ of CA2 (CB2)	Goes low when the interrupt flag bit CRA-6 (CRB-6) goes high
0	1	0	↑ Active	Set high on ↑ of CA2 (CB2)	Disabled — IRQ remains high
0	1	1	↑ Active	Set high on ↑ of CA2 (CB2)	Goes low when the interrupt flag bit CRA-6 (CRB-6) goes high

Notes:
1. ↑ indicates positive transition (low to high)
2. ↓ indicates negative transition (high to low)
3. The Interrupt flag bit CRA-6 is cleared by an MPU Read of the A Data Register and CRB-6 is cleared by an MPU Read of the B Data Register.
4. If CRA-3 (CRB-3) is low when an interrupt occurs (Interrupt disabled) and is later brought high, IRQA (IRQB) occurs on the positive transition of CRA-3 (CRB-3).

If bit 5 = 1, control line 2 is an output. Here the A and B sides differ. CA2 is a read strobe, whereas CB2 is a write strobe. Table 8.4 describes the use of CB2. If bit 4 = 0, CB2 goes low on the positive transition of the first ENABLE pulse following a cycle in which the CPU writes data into data register B. Control bit 3 determines the ending condition for the strobe. If bit 3 is 1, the strobe lasts only until the next ENABLE pulse; if bit 3 is 0, the strobe lasts until an active transition on CB1 ends it. The options are a brief strobe that can latch data into the peripheral or a longer handshake acknowledgement that lasts until the peripheral begins the next transfer. The ENABLE line is tied directly to the system clock in most applications.

If bit 4 = 1, CB2 is simply a latched output (a level) with the value of bit 3. It can be used to select a status option or turn a device on or off. A separate serial control port is unnecessary.

Table 8.5 describes the use of CA2 as a read strobe which goes low after the CPU reads data from data régister A. The latched control bit option is the same as for CB2. The program can create a read strobe from side B or a write strobe from side A by following a B side read operation with a dummy write or an A side write with a dummy read. The dummy operations must not change any register contents. Reading data from the B side or writing data into the A side does not automatically produce a strobe.

Table 8.4 Control of CB2 as an Output. CRB5 is High. (Courtesy of Motorola Semiconductor Products Inc.)

| CRB-5 | CRB-4 | CRB-3 | CB2 | |
			Cleared	Set
1	0	0	Low on the positive transition of the first E pulse following an MPU Write "B" Data Register operation.	High when the interrupt flag bit CRB-7 is set by an active transition of the CB1 signal.
1	0	1	Low on the positive transition of the first E pulse following an MPU Write "B" Data Register operation.	High on the positive transition of the next "E" pulse.
1	1	0	Low when CRB-3 goes low as a result of an MPU Write in Control Register "B".	Always low as long as CRB-3 is low. Will go high on an MPU Write in Control Register "B" that changes CRB-3 to "one".
1	1	1	Always high as long as CRB-3 is high. Will be cleared when an MPU Write Control Register "B" results in clearing CRB-3 to "zero".	High when CRB-3 goes high as a result of an MPU write into control register "B".

Table 8.5 Control of CA2 as an Output. CRA5 is High. (Courtesy of Motorola Semiconductor Products Inc.)

| CRA-5 | CRA-4 | CRA-3 | CA2 | |
			Cleared	Set
1	0	0	Low on negative transition of E after an MPU Read "A" Data operation.	High on an active transition of the CA1 signal.
1	0	1	Low immediately after an MPU Read "A" Data operation.	High on the negative edge of the next "E" pulse.
1	1	0	Low when CRA-3 goes low as a result of an MPU Write in Control Register "A".	Always low as long as CRA-3 is low.
1	1	1	Always high as long as CRA-3 is high.	High when CRA-3 goes high as a result of a Write in Control Register "A".

The RESET input clears all the PIA registers. All the data and control lines are initially inputs, all interrupts are disabled, and the data direction register is selected. The program must configure the PIA from this starting point (see examples in Section 8.6).

The data lines from the two sides differ. The B side has a tri-state buffer that provides some drive capability and allows output lines to be read properly. The A side has no buffer and the output lines cannot be read properly unless they are very lightly loaded or externally buffered.

The PIA offers considerable flexibility in a single package. It can provide handshaking, interrupt control, and other functions that would normally require several ports and other circuitry.

8.5 INPUT/OUTPUT DEVICES

This section describes simple I/O devices and their interfaces with microprocessors. The devices to be considered are switches, keyboards, displays, A/D and D/A converters, and teletypewriters. More elaborate devices require more complex interfaces but use many of the same principles. Also discussed are the popular EIA RS-232 and IEEE-488 interfaces.

Simple Switches

One of the simplest input peripherals imaginable is a pushbutton that, when pressed, produces a short circuit or zero bit. The pushbutton is connected as shown in Fig. 8.24; the pullup resistor makes the output high when the pushbutton is not depressed. The button is a single-pole (single-common), single-throw (single-contact) or SPST switch.

Figure 8.24 Interfacing a pushbutton to a microprocessor.

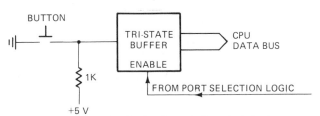

The decoding system will enable the tri-state buffer only during input operations that address the port.

A pushbutton is easy to connect to a microcomputer. The only interface necessary is an addressable tri-state buffer (see Fig. 8.24). No latch is needed, since the mechanical button changes position very slowly by computer standards.

Determining the button position is also easy. The CPU reads the buffer—that is, enables the data onto the data bus and into the processor. The data is then ANDed with a mask that has a one in the button position and zeros elsewhere. If the result is zero, the button has been depressed. If the button is connected to the least or most significant bit of the data bus, a shift operation will move the data to the CARRY and no logical AND will be necessary. The SIGN bit may also be used if available.

The only problem with a pushbutton is that a mechanical switch does not provide a clean closure. Instead the switch bounces; that is, it opens and closes randomly until a clean contact is made. The length of the bounce depends on the particular switch but is generally less than 2 ms. The bounce can be handled in two ways (the process is called *debouncing*).

1. In software by having the CPU delay after finding a closure until the bounce has stopped. The delay can be obtained by using the program in Fig. 8.5 or by having the CPU perform other tasks for the required amount of time.

2. In hardware with a one-shot. The pulse length of the one-shot must be longer than the debounce time so that the output is a single pulse.

Determining if the pushbutton has changed position is simple if an EXCLUSIVE OR instruction is available. All that must be done is

Step 1. Save record of old position.
Step 2. Read new position and EXCLUSIVE OR with old position.
Step 3. If the result is not zero, the position has changed.

An EXCLUSIVE OR instruction can also find button closures if several buttons share an input port. An EXCLUSIVE OR with an all ones word will produce a zero result if no buttons have been pressed.

The common single-pole, double-throw (SPDT) switch is a little more complicated. The switch has a common lead, a normal open (NO) lead, and a normal closed (NC) lead (see Fig. 8.25). The SPDT switch can be interfaced to the processor with a tri-state buffer. Mechanical SPDT switches can be debounced with a one-shot, with two NAND gates as shown in Fig. 8.25, or in software.

The cross-coupled NAND gates work as follows. When the switch is closed, NC is grounded, and so NAND gate 1 gives a high output (since one input is low). NO is high; so NAND gate 2 produces a low output (both inputs are high). As soon as the switch is opened, NO is grounded, gate 2 goes high, and gate 1 goes low. Intermediate (bounce) states in which NC and NO are both high do not affect the output.

The program must look for a change in position. The EXCLUSIVE OR instruction is again useful. EXCLUSIVE ORing old and new switch positions for a group of switches results in a one bit for each switch that has changed position.

Figure 8.25 Debouncing an SPDT switch with cross-coupled NAND gates.

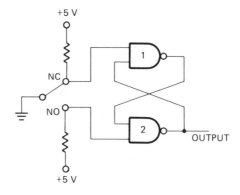

Multiposition Switches

Rotary, thumbwheel, or selector switches have many possible positions. When the switch is in a position, the lead from that position is grounded through the COMMON line. Such switches are a standard part of electronic equipment.

If the switch is not encoded, each lead must be tied to the data bus through a tri-state buffer. A program may determine the switch position by shifting the data word right until a zero bit appears in the CARRY; the number of shifts required is the switch position. Figure 8.26 is a flowchart of the method. If no zero bit is found, the switch is between positions and must be checked later. Note that a ten-position switch will require two data ports and some double-word operations on an 8-bit processor.

Clearly this interface is wasteful, since ten bits describe only ten possible positions. A BCD or hexadecimal encoded switch not only requires merely four input lines but the input also identifies the switch position without any further processing. Interfacing an encoded multiposition switch to a processor requires only an addressable tri-state buffer.

Figure 8.26   Flowchart for determining selector switch position.

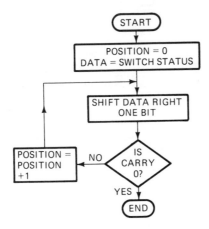

Keyboards

A keyboard is a collection of switches. Each switch may be connected independently to an input port. The interfacing and programming will then be the same as for any other collection of switches. The software must perform the tasks below.

1. Determine if any keys have been pressed. If the keys are SPST switches, this means checking for any zero bits in the inputs. A comparison with the all ones word can be used to do the checking.

2. If a key has been pressed, determine which one. This step requires a series of shifts as in Fig. 8.26.

3. Decide on an action based on the key that was pressed. This task depends on the function of the keyboard. Keys may represent data entries, mode selection, control operations, instructions, scale factors, and so on. One method is to use a table (called a *jump table*) containing the addresses of the routines that handle the various key functions. The key position determines which address is selected from the table. Figure 8.27 is a flowchart of the jump table method.

Figure 8.27   Flowchart for using a jump table.[2]

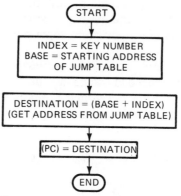

The jump table is organized as follows, starting in location JTAB.

Address	Contents
JTAB	SERVICE ADDRESS FOR KEY 0
JTAB + 1	SERVICE ADDRESS FOR KEY 1
.	.
.	.
.	.
JTAB + n	SERVICE ADDRESS FOR KEY n

In the case of an 8-bit microprocessor with 16-bit addresses, each jump table entry will occupy two words.

The problem with unencoded, independently connected keyboards is that they require a large number of input lines and many multiword operations. For example, a typewriterlike keyboard with 64 keys would need 64 input lines and a series of 8 byte operations. Looking for a single key closure would be time-consuming. The independent collection of switches is normally limited to small keyboards with 16 or fewer keys.

Encoding can reduce the input requirements. Small keyboards may use TTL encoders. Larger keyboards generally employ MOS encoders because high speed is unnecessary. The MOS encoders contain a read-only memory; common formats (such as teletypewriter) are available off the shelf, whereas custom formats require a special mask or a PROM. MOS encoders do more than simply react to key closures and code the output. Most also handle *rollover* (i.e., separate multiple key

---

[2]For some examples of actual programs, see L. A. Leventhal, "Cut Your Processor's Computation Time," *Electronic Design*, Vol. 25, No. 17, August 16, 1977, pp. 82–89.

closures and interpret them consecutively), debounce the keys, select modes (e.g., upper or lowercase), and generate a strobe that can act as a DATA READY signal and latch the data into the input port.

The encoded keyboard both recognizes and identifies the closure. The program must still decide on an action. The jump table method can be used if there are a large number of separate functions. Many programs use the same keyboard in different modes; the keyboard may provide both data and commands. Here data entries must be stored, whereas command entries must be interpreted.

Some or all of the encoding can be done in software. The I/O requirements are smaller if the keyboard is organized into a matrix with rows and columns as in Fig. 8.28. A keyboard scan determines which key has been pressed by grounding either the column or row lines from an output port. The procedure is as follows.

Step 1. Determine if any keys have been pressed.

Ground all the column lines by latching zero bits into the output port. If any of the row lines are grounded, a column-to-row connection exists and a key has been pressed. NANDing the row lines together can produce an active-high strobe.

Step 2. Determine which key has been pressed.

Once the program finds a closure, it can identify the key by grounding one column at a time. The row inputs will be all ones if the key is not in that column and will contain a zero in the bit corresponding to a particular row if the key is in that column. Table 8.6 shows the various row and column groundings that identify the keys in Fig. 8.28.

Figure 8.28 Interfacing a matrix keyboard to a microprocessor.

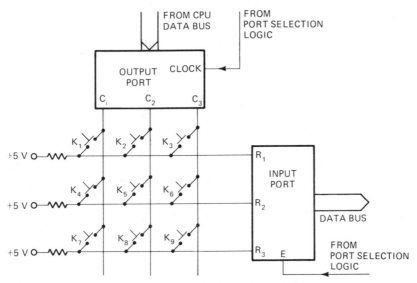

The output port for the column lines must contain a latch, whereas the input port need only be a tri-state buffer.

Table 8.6 Keyboard Identification by Column Strobes

Key	Column Grounded (Input to Keyboard)	Row Grounded (Output from Keyboard)
K1	C1	R1
K2	C2	R1
K3	C3	R1
K4	C1	R2
K5	C2	R2
K6	C3	R2
K7	C1	R3
K8	C2	R3
K9	C3	R3

The flowchart in Fig. 8.29 describes the keyboard scan. The scan requires additional time, but if the keyboard has m rows and n columns, the matrix requires only m input lines and n output lines rather than the $m \times n$ lines needed with independently connected keys. Some of the problems are

1. The average number of column scans increases linearly with the number of columns.

2. Scanning and checking become slow and cumbersome if the number of rows or columns exceeds the length of the processor data word.

3. Special procedures are necessary to handle the case where the closure ends before the scan reaches it.

Many simple systems (such as hand calculators) continuously scan their keyboards, waiting for a key to be pressed.

A different procedure uses a device like the Peripheral Interface Adapter in which the I/O lines can be programmed to be either inputs or outputs; the steps are (a) ground all the columns and save the row inputs and (b) ground all the rows and save the column inputs. The combined row and column inputs identify the key closure as shown in Table 8.7. Figure 8.30 is a flowchart of this method. No column scans or row searches are necessary, but the CPU must identify the key by searching the table of possible inputs.

Other problems still exist in interfacing a keyboard. The software or hardware must debounce mechanical key switches and deal with multiple key closures. Furthermore, the processor must distinguish one key closure from the next. A strobe can identify new data if the strobe is cleared when the processor reads the data. The clearing is automatic with an 8212 I/O port or a Peripheral Interface Adapter. If no strobe exists, the processor can simply wait for the key closure to end. The procedure is exactly the same as the first step of Fig. 8.29 except that the jump condition is inverted. In this situation, the user must wait between key closures; otherwise the system will not respond.

Figure 8.29 Flowchart for keyboard scan.

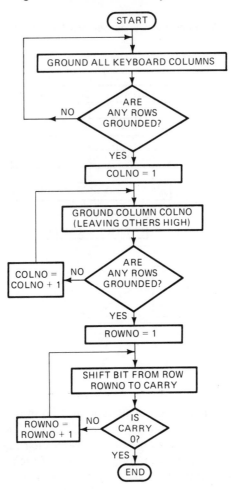

Table 8.7 Key Identification by Switching Inputs and Outputs

| Key | Column Outputs | | | Row Outputs | | | Hexadecimal |
| | C3 | C2 | C1 | R3 | R2 | R1 | Code |
	(Rows Grounded)			(Columns Grounded)			$(00C_3C_2C_1R_3R_2R_1)$
K1	1	1	0	1	1	0	36
K2	1	0	1	1	1	0	2E
K3	0	1	1	1	1	0	1E
K4	1	1	0	1	0	1	35
K5	1	0	1	1	0	1	2D
K6	0	1	1	1	0	1	1D
K7	1	1	0	0	1	1	33
K8	1	0	1	0	1	1	2B
K9	0	1	1	0	1	1	1B

Figure 8.30 Flowchart for key identification by switching inputs and outputs.

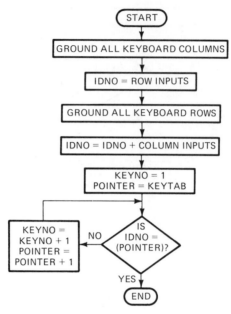

Simple Displays

A single light is a simple output peripheral. The most popular such lights at present are the so-called light-emitting diodes or LEDs. These devices emit light when biased in the forward direction—that is, when their anodes are positive with respect to their cathodes. LEDs are popular because of their small size, low current and voltage requirements, long life, low power dissipation, and low cost. LEDs are also easy to multiplex; that is, one port can handle many displays. The disadvantages of LEDs include their low brightness, temperature dependence, and limited number of colors. Other displays, such as liquid crystal, gas-discharge, incandescent, and fluorescent, are also useful and popular, but we will not discuss them here.

Figure 8.31 shows an LED circuit. The resistor limits the current through the LED to about 10 mA. Of course, the computer can apply a signal to either end of the LED. If the anode is tied to +5 V, the LED lights when the computer applies a logic zero to the cathode; if the cathode is tied to ground, the LED lights when the computer applies a logic one to the anode.

LEDs operate best from pulsed currents, since the displays produce far more light at higher current levels and the rise time for the light is short. Typical systems pulse the LEDs for a few milliseconds at 10 or 15 V; the usual pulse rate is 100 to 500 times per second. Most I/O ports cannot drive LEDs directly; either peripheral drivers or transistors are necessary.

Figure 8.31 Interface between a microprocessor and an LED.

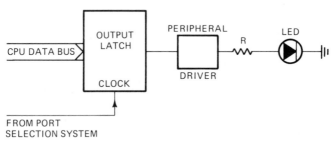

FROM PORT
SELECTION SYSTEM

The LED could also be driven from the cathode either by complementing the output logic levels or by using an inverting peripheral driver.

The length and period of the pulses (and hence the brightness of the LED) can be controlled by either hardware or software. Software control involves delay routines. Hardware control requires a timer to generate the pulses.

If the pulses are infrequent, the display will not appear to be continuously lit. Instead the light will flash if the repetition rate is 10 to 50 times per second. A flashing display can indicate malfunctions, erroneous inputs, overflow, low battery levels, or other special conditions.

The software needed to control the display is simple. The polarity of the display determines which logic level turns on the light. The program can determine the output bits as follows.

1. A bit can be set by logically ORing it with a pattern having a one bit in the appropriate position.

For instance, bit 5 in an 8-bit word can be set by a logical OR with binary 00100000.

2. A bit can be cleared by logically ANDing it with a pattern having a zero bit in the appropriate position.

For instance, bit 3 in an 8-bit word can be cleared by a logical AND with binary 11110111.

3. A bit can be complemented by logically EXCLUSIVE ORing it with a pattern having a one bit in the appropriate position.

For instance, bit 2 in an 8-bit word can be complemented by a logical EXCLUSIVE OR with binary 00000100.

To illustrate, using the interface in Fig. 8.31 (an output of one lights the display), a logical OR will turn the light on, a logical AND will turn the light off, and a logical EXCLUSIVE OR will reverse the previous condition.

Multiple Displays

Multiple displays can represent digits, alphanumeric characters, or other symbols. Figure 8.32 shows common types used in such applications as instruments, terminals, calculators, and test equipment. The seven-segment display (see

Figure 8.32 Types of displays (courtesy of Hewlett-Packard).

| 7-Segment | | Abbreviated Dot Matrix | | 14-Segment |
| Abbreviated Dot Matrix | | 5 X 7 Dot Matrix | | 9-Segment |

Section A3.3) is particularly popular, since it has the smallest number of independently controlled elements that can still produce reasonable representations of all the decimal digits and some letters and other characters as well.

The displays can be connected in one of two ways. The first method (a *common-cathode display*) ties all the cathodes together to ground; a logic one signal at an anode turns a display on. The second method (a *common-anode display*) ties all the anodes together to the power supply; a logic zero signal at a cathode turns a display on.

The basic problem is how to convert data into the proper format. Either hardware or software can perform the conversion. The usual hardware methods are special decoders, PROM-based tables, and standard ROMs, such as ASCII character generators. The hardware methods require more circuitry but less software. The CPU can perform the decoding in software with a table lookup. An 8-bit processor can easily handle seven-segment conversion but must handle 9-or 14-segment conversion in two words.[3] The hardware or software must determine the pulse width and frequency as with single displays. If the displays do not require very long pulses, they can be multiplexed from a single output port with a counter and decoder as shown in Fig. 8.17.

Digital-To-Analog Converters

Digital-to-analog converters (DACs) convert digital output data into continuous or analog signals. Analog outputs are necessary for motors, solenoids, relays, bar graphs, and other peripherals. Popular types of converters include weighted-resistor and resistor-ladder networks.[4] Most converters have fixed references, but *multiplying DACs* allow variable analog reference voltages and produce an output that is the product of the digital input times the analog reference voltage.

---

[3]L. A. Leventhal, "Cut Your Processor's Computation Time," *Electronic Design*, Vol. 25, No. 17, August 16, 1977. pp. 82–89.

[4]E. R. Hnatek, *A User's Handbook of D / A and A / D Converters*, Wiley, New York, 1976.

D/A converters specifically designed for microcomputers are available. In general, these devices have addressable input buffers that allow them to be loaded in 8-bit bytes. An example is the 10-bit Analog Devices AD7522 D/A Converter shown in Fig. 8.33.

Figure 8.33 Analog Devices AD7522 D/A Converter (courtesy of Analog Devices, Inc.).

FUNCTIONAL DIAGRAM

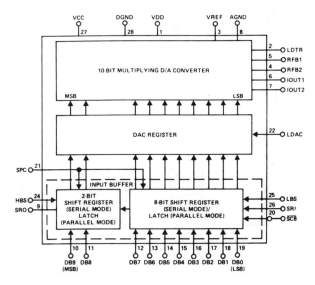

PIN CONFIGURATION

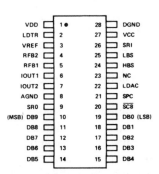

A microprocessor can load the converter in a single operation or in two bytes. The single operation requires that the same control signal enable both buffers. Loading two bytes separately requires that the two buffers have different enabling signals—that is, the high and low bytes are separate output ports. The LDAC (LOAD DAC) signal transfers data from the buffers to the DAC register; LDAC is level-activated and must be active (high) for at least 0.5 μs.

Figure 8.34 shows a typical interface between an 8-bit processor and the converter. The transfer proceeds as follows.

Step 1. CPU sends eight least significant data bits to port 0 (the least significant byte of the DAC register).

Step 2. CPU sends two most significant data bits to port 1 (the most significant byte of the DAC register).

Step 3. CPU sends a one to port 2, making LDAC high.

Step 4. CPU sends a zero to port 2, completing the pulse on LDAC.

Figure 8.34   Interfacing the D/A converter to an 8-bit processor.

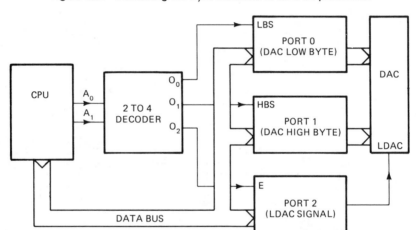

The DAC uses three output ports in this configuration. Port 0 is the low byte, port 1 the high byte, and port 2 the LOAD DAC control signal. LBS is low byte strobe; HBS is high byte strobe.

Analog-To-Digital Converters

Analog-to-digital converters convert analog input data into digital form. A processor can then derive signals from sensors, transducers, or other analog sources. Such inputs are an essential part of monitoring systems, process control, scales, machine controllers, and many other applications. Several different types of A/D converters exist, including *counter-comparator, dual-ramp, and successive approximation*. The successive approximation converter uses an analog comparator and a digital-to-analog converter to establish a value for each bit successively by comparing the input and the D/A output. This method is fast and simple but is subject to errors caused by noise in the analog input.

A/D converters specifically designed for use with microprocessors are available. These devices have tri-state outputs and separate controls for each byte to allow them to be easily interfaced to an 8-bit processor. Figure 8.35 shows a 10-bit monolithic CMOS converter, the Analog Devices AD7570, which uses a successive approximation method to perform a 10-bit conversion in a maximum of 120 ns.

Figure 8.35 The Analog Devices AD7570 10-Bit Monolithic A/D Converter (courtesy of Analog Devices, Inc.).

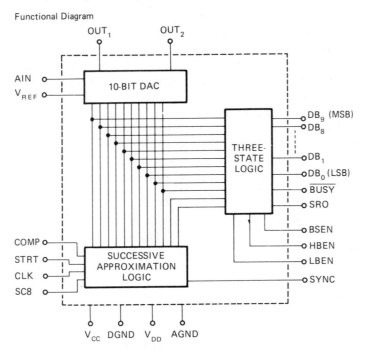

Functional Diagram

Pin Configuration

TOP VIEW

An external analog comparator (311) is necessary.

A microprocessor can fetch data from the converter in one or two input operations. There are separate tri-state enables for the high byte (two most significant bits), the low byte (eight least significant bits), and the BUSY signal. Figure 8.36 shows the interface between an 8-bit microprocessor and the converter. The processor fetches the data as follows.

1. The processor sends a one bit to output port 0, bringing the CONVERT START (STRT) line high. This step clears all the data latches except the most significant bit, which is set to one.

2. The processor sends a zero bit to output port 0, bringing the CONVERT START line low. This step starts the conversion process. CONVERT START must be high for at least 500 ns.

3. The processor reads the BUSY signal from input port 2. If this signal is zero, the conversion is still in progress.

4. Once the conversion is complete (BUSY = 1), the processor reads the eight least significant data bits from input port 0.

5. The processor reads the two most significant data bits from input port 1.

The question remains of how to interpret the digital input. The program can use (a) the equation that describes the relationship between the analog input and the quantity being measured or (b) a calibration table. The latter method is useful if the range of values is not too large; it does not require the solution of any equations but uses extra memory for the table.

Figure 8.36   Interfacing the A/D converter to an 8-bit processor.

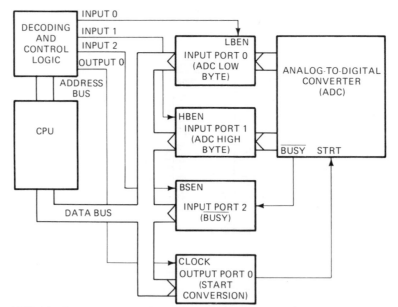

LBEN is low byte enable, HBEN high byte enable, and BSEN busy enable.

Teletypewriters

Despite improvements in computer peripherals, the most common peripheral in small systems is still the teletypewriter. The standard teletypewriter consists of

1. An ASCII keyboard that produces characters asynchronously at a maximum rate of 10 per second.
2. An ASCII printer that accepts chracters asynchronously at a maximum rate of 10 per second.
3. A 10-character-per-second (cps) paper tape reader.
4. A 10 cps paper tape punch.
5. A 20-mA current-loop interface; a current of 20 mA in a loop represents a logic one and a current of 0 mA a logic zero.

Each character consists of 11 bits (see Fig. 8.37): a start bit (logic zero), seven data bits, a parity bit (may be even, odd, or unused), and two stop bits (logic one). The line is generally in the one or *mark* state. Since the device can transfer ten 11-bit characters per second, each bit lasts 1/110 of a second or 9.1 ms.

Figure 8.37 Standard teletypewriter data format.

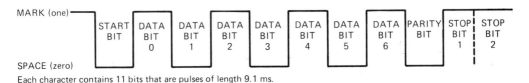

Each character contains 11 bits that are pulses of length 9.1 ms.

The teletypewriter interface must provide the following functions.

1. Conversion between current-loop signals and TTL voltage signals. The signals must be electrically isolated from each other through a transformer, relay, or optocoupler (see Fig. 8.38 for an example using an optocoupler).
2. Serial I/O for the teletypewriter.
3. Tape reader control.
4. A return or *echo* path so that keyboard entries are printed.
5. Start bit detection (receive) and addition (transmit).
6. Timing signals to allow proper spacing between bits.
7. Parity checking and generation.
8. Stop bit detection and addition.

A UART will handle most of these functions. The signal conversion, tape reader control, and return path will require additional hardware.

The interface in Fig. 8.38 (from the Motorola MEK 6800D1 Evaluation Board) provides both teletypewriter and RS-232 signals as well as a signal for

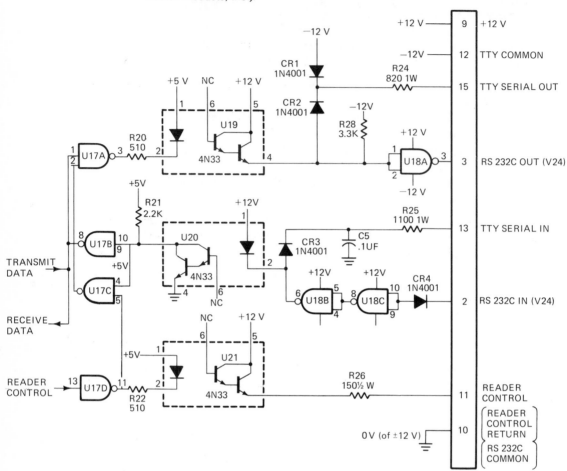

Figure 8.38 A teletypewriter interface (courtesy of Motorola Semiconductor Products, Inc.).

controlling the paper tape reader. The following active devices are present:

- An MC1489 Quad RS-232 Line Receiver (U17)
- An MC1488 Quad RS-232 Line Driver (U18)
- 3 Motorola 4N33 optocouplers (U19, U20, and U21)
- 4 Motorola 1N4001 diodes

Part of the interface can be software. A processor can perform some or all the tasks of the UART. Figure 8.39 is a flowchart of the transmission procedure, and Fig. 8.40 is a flowchart of the reception procedure. A program can perform the serial-to-parallel or parallel-to-serial conversion, handle the start and stop bits, check or generate parity, and provide proper timing. A device like the Motorola Peripheral Interface Adapter can provide lines for both serial input and output as well as control signals (such as tape reader control) and data inputs that can be tied or programmed so as to describe a particular peripheral.

Figure 8.39 Flowchart of teletypewriter transmission procedure (bit 0 of output goes to peripheral).

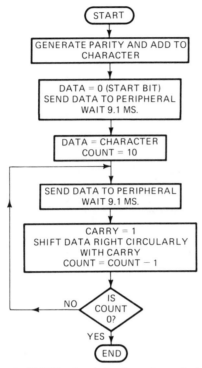

Setting the CARRY to 1 each time forms the required stop bits.

A program can handle other terminals in the same way by changing some of the parameters. For instance, the popular 30-character-per-second terminals use only one stop bit and require different timing. One method that allows the program to handle either type of terminal is to use a single input line as an indicator. This line could, for example, be tied high for a teletypewriter and low for a 30 cps terminal. The program could then establish the proper parameters according to the state of the input.

Standard Interfaces

I/O has long been complicated by the fact that each peripheral represented a unique interfacing problem. However, many peripherals now use one of the three interfaces below.

1. The teletypewriter current-loop interface.
2. The Electronic Industries Association RS-232 serial interface between data terminal equipment (DTE) and data communications equipment (DCE). The maximum data rate is 20 kilobits per second.

Figure 8.40 Flowchart of teletypewriter reception procedure (bit 7 of input is serial input from peripheral).

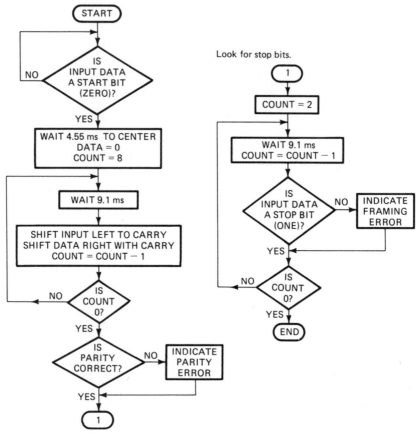

Look for start bit.

Look for stop bits.

A framing error means that the two required stop bits are not present.

3. The IEEE STD488-1975 parallel interface, the so-called IEEE Standard Digital Interface for Programmable Instrumentation. This interface is also known as the Hewlett-Packard Interface or the General Purpose Interface Bus (GPIB). The maximum data rate is 1 megabit per second.

RS-232 Interface

Table 8.8 describes the RS-232 signals, dividing them into data, control, and timing signals and marking whether they are sent to or from the data communications equipment. Few actual interfaces use all these signals.

The data lines are serial. These lines need not be physically separate. A system that has separate lines and that can receive and transmit at the same time is

Table 8.8 EIA RS-232 Serial Interface Signals (Courtesy of Electronic Industries Association)

Interchange Circuit	C.C.I.T.T. Equivalent	Description	Ground	Data from DCE	Data to DCE	Control from DCE	Control to DCE	Timing from DCE	Timing to DCE
AA	101	Protective ground	X						
AB	102	Signal ground/common return	X						
BA	103	Transmitted data			X				
BB	104	Received data		X					
CA	105	Request to send					X		
CB	106	Clear to send				X			
CC	107	Data set ready				X			
CD	108.2	Data terminal ready					X		
CE	125	Ring indicator				X			
CF	109	Received line signal detector				X			
CG	110	Signal quality detector				X			
CH	111	Data signal rate selector (DTE)					X		
CI	112	Data signal rate selector (DCE)				X			
DA	113	Transmitter signal element timing (DTE)							X
DB	114	Transmitter signal element timing (DCE)						X	
DD	115	Receiver signal element timing (DCE)						X	

called *full-duplex*. A system that can only transmit or receive at one time is *half-duplex*.

The equipment status lines indicate whether the equipment is ready to send or receive data. These signals are DATA SET READY (for the communications equipment) and DATA TERMINAL READY (for the terminal equipment). Many RS-232 interfaces omit these signals and assume that the equipment is always ready. Test modes may require these signals.

There are two transmission control signals: REQUEST TO SEND and CLEAR TO SEND. The terminal activates the REQUEST TO SEND signal when it has data to transmit. The communications equipment responds with the CLEAR TO SEND signal when it is ready to transmit the data. These signals are implemented in such devices as the Motorola 6850 Asynchronous Communications Interface Adapter, Motorola 6860 Low-Speed Modem, and the Intel 8251 Programmable Communication Interface. We will discuss the Motorola 6850 in the next section. The timing signals in the RS-232 interface locate the centers of the data bits; often these signals are not implemented.

There are three receive control signals: RING INDICATOR, RECEIVED LINE SIGNAL DETECTOR, and SIGNAL QUALITY DETECTOR. The RING INDICATOR signal means that a ringing signal is being received on the communications channel (i.e., on the telephone lines). RECEIVED LINE SIGNAL DETECTOR indicates that the communications equipment is receiving a signal (the criterion for this signal varies with the equipment). SIGNAL QUALITY DETECTOR indicates whether there is a high probability of error in the received data.

The voltage levels are somewhat different from those found in standard TTL circuits. Special line drivers and receivers are required. Popular devices include the 1488 RS-232 to TTL Voltage Level Converter and 1489 TTL to RS-232 Voltage Level Converter, and the Signetics 8T15 and 8T16 EIA Line Drivers and Receivers. These devices will convert voltage levels and provide the required drive currents and signal conditioning (see Fig. 8.38 for an example of a simple RS-232 interface). RS-232 data lines use negative logic; control lines use positive logic.

The RS-232 interface is widely used at low-to-medium data rates. Electronic devices that meet RS-232 specifications are cheap and widely available. Two serial standards that supersede RS-232 at higher data rates are RS-423 for rates up to 100 kilobits per second and RS-422 for rates up to 10 megabits per second.[5]

IEEE-488 Interface

The IEEE-488 interface was designed for use in networks of instruments. Figure 8.41 describes the signal lines; the 24-line bus consists of 8 ground lines, 8 data lines, and 8 control lines.

The network may contain up to 15 devices, which are classified into three types.

1. Talkers that can transmit data on the data lines.
2. Listeners that can receive data from the data lines.
3. Controllers that designate which devices can talk or listen.

In the control mode, the controller designates which devices talk and listen. The ATN line is set low so that all devices monitor the lines. The commands UNTALK and UNLISTEN eliminate all previous connections. The commands LISTEN ADDRESS and TALK ADDRESS then configure the bus. The addresses are assigned to the instruments in hardware by the manufacturers. Of course, only one device can talk at a time, whereas several can listen. A device can be addressed as a listener *or* talker but not both at a given time.

In the data mode, the talker provides data to the listeners. The ATN line is set high so that only previously addressed devices will participate. Listeners may

---

[5]D. Morris, "Revised Data-Interface Standards," *Electronic Design*, Vol. 25, No. 18, September 1, 1977, pp. 138–141.

use the data transfer lines to keep control of the data bus until they have had time to acquire the data. When the transmission is complete, the talker returns control of the network to the controller for reconfiguration. Devices on the bus may request attention from the controller even when they are not part of a particular configuration.

Figure 8.42 describes the constraints on the IEEE-488 Bus. Special circuits, such as the Motorola MC3400, can provide the required electrical characteristics.

Figure 8.41 IEEE-488 active signal lines (From N. Laengrich, "IEEE Std-488/1975," WESCON Technical Session 12, Paper 1, 1976. Reprinted courtesy of WESCON).

8 Data Lines.
    The data lines consist of lines DIO-1 through DIO-8. These lines are the lines over which data flows between all instruments on the bus in bit parallel, byte serial form.

3 Data Transfer Lines:
    The transfer lines consist of DAV (data valid), NRFD (not ready for data), and NDAC (not data accepted). These lines provide communication between the instrument that is talking and the instrument that is listening to synchronize the flow of information across the eight data lines.
    (a) DAV. Signifies that valid information is available on the data lines.
    (b) NDAC. Signifies instrument ready to accept information.
    (c) NRFD. Signifies information is accepted by the listener.

5 Bus Management Lines:
    The interface lines coordinate the flow of information on the bus.
    (a) IFC. Places system in a known state.
    (b) ATN. Indicates nature of information on data lines.
    (c) REN. Commands instruments to select remote operation.
    (d) SRQ. Service Request.
    (e) EOI. Indicates the end of a multiple byte transfer sequence, or, in conjunction with ATN, to execute a polling sequence.

Figure 8.42 Constraints on the IEEE-488 bus (From N. Laengrich, "IEEE Std-488/1975," 1976 WESCON Technical Session 12, Paper 1. Reprinted courtesy of WESCON).

Maximum number of devices that
may be connected to GPIB:
    15
Maximum cable length:
    2 meters times number of devices or
    20 meters (whichever is less)
Maximum data rate:
    1 megabit/s (on any line)
    Note:
    (a) Maximum 250,000 bytes/s over 20 m with load every 2 m using 48-mA open-collector drivers.
    (b) Maximum 500,000 bytes/s over 20 m with load every 2 m using 48-mA 3-State drivers
    (c) 1 Megabyte/s over maximum distance of 1 m per device using 48-mA 3-State drivers.
Maximum number of addresses available:
    31 Talk
    31 Listen

8.6 I/O DESIGN FOR SPECIFIC PROCESSORS

Intel 8080

Intel 8080 I/O sections generally use TTL devices and isolated I/O. Programmable interfaces are available, but most systems use the 8212 I/O port.

The Intel 8080 has two I/O instructions.

IN transfers eight bits of data from the addressed input port to the accumulator.

OUT transfers eight bits of data from the accumulator to the addressed output port.

Both instructions take ten clock cycles and require two words of program memory, one for the operation code and one for an 8-bit device (or port) address. The processor can therefore handle 256 input ports and 256 output ports. The CPU places the 8-bit device address on both the least significant and most significant address lines so that either set of eight lines can be decoded.

Two of the status signals produced by the Intel 8080 during the first part of each machine cycle identify I/O cycles. INP, status bit 6, indicates an input cycle; OUT, status bit 4, indicates an output cycle. These signals can be combined with the write pulse ($\overline{WR}$) and the data bus directional signal (DBIN) to form the active-low control signals $\overline{I/OW}$ and $\overline{I/OR}$, comparable to the memory control signals discussed in the previous chapter. The 8228 System Controller produces these signals directly. The following factors apply to input.

1. All input ports must have tri-state outputs or tri-state buffers. The Intel 8212 is a useful device in its input mode (MD = 0).

2. The decoding system must differentiate between I/O addresses and memory addresses. Either each input port is enabled by INP or $\overline{I/OR}$ or the input ports are isolated from the overall data bus with tri-state buffers enabled by one of these signals.

3. 8-bit device addresses must be decoded to form nonconflicting tri-state enables. Complete decoding is unnecessary unless the number of input ports is large.

4. Timing is seldom a problem, since TTL ports have much shorter delay times than MOS memories.

Figure 8.43 shows an input section with four ports. Each port is enabled by a signal from the decoder and by the $\overline{I/OR}$ signal from the 8228 System Controller. This input section can share the data bus with memories.

The factors that apply to output are discussed below.

1. All output ports must contain an addressable latch. The Intel 8212 can serve as the latch in its output mode (MD = 1). The output port need not be tri-state, since its outputs are not placed on a shared bus.

2. The system must differentiate between I/O addresses and memory addresses. Usually each output port is clocked by OUT or $\overline{I/OW}$.

3. The same decoding system can produce both input and output port addresses.

4. Timing is seldom a problem except that unlatched data will only be available briefly.

Figure 8.43 An Intel 8080 input section.

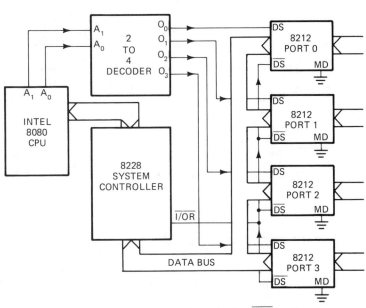

A particular port places data on the CPU data bus only when $\overline{I/OR}$ is active and the port is selected by the decoder.

Figure 8.44 shows an output section with four ports. Each port is clocked by a signal from the decoder and by the $\overline{I/OW}$ signal from the 8228 Controller. This output section can share the data bus with both memories and input ports.

Small I/O sections can use linear select as shown in Fig. 8.45. Each address line selects a port. The number of ports is limited to the number of address lines (eight), and the port numbers are powers of two as described in Table 8.9. No decoders are necessary.

The Intel 8080 can also use memory-mapped I/O. Here the I/O control signals and instructions are not used; instead some memory addresses are reserved for I/O devices. For example, address line A_{15} could differentiate between memory and I/O, allowing 32K of each with the memory occupying the lower 32K, which contains the RESET and interrupt service addresses. The resulting memory-mapped I/O section can use linear select to address 15 ports with no decoders.

Memory-mapped I/O is convenient for microcomputers that contain such devices as the 8251 Programmable Communication Interface, the 8255 Programmable Peripheral Interface, and the TMS 5501 Multifunction Input/Output Controller.

Figure 8.44 An Intel 8080 output section.

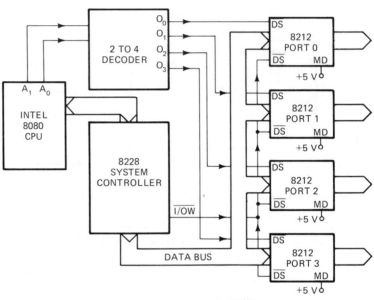

Data is only clocked into a particular output port when $\overline{I/OW}$ is active and the decoder selects that port.

Table 8.9 Port Addresses Using Linear Select (8-Bit Addresses)

Address Line Used	Port Number	
	Decimal	Hexadecimal
A_0	1	01
A_1	2	02
A_2	4	04
A_3	8	08
A_4	16	10
A_5	32	20
A_6	64	40
A_7	128	80

Figure 8.45 An Intel 8080 I/O section using linear select.

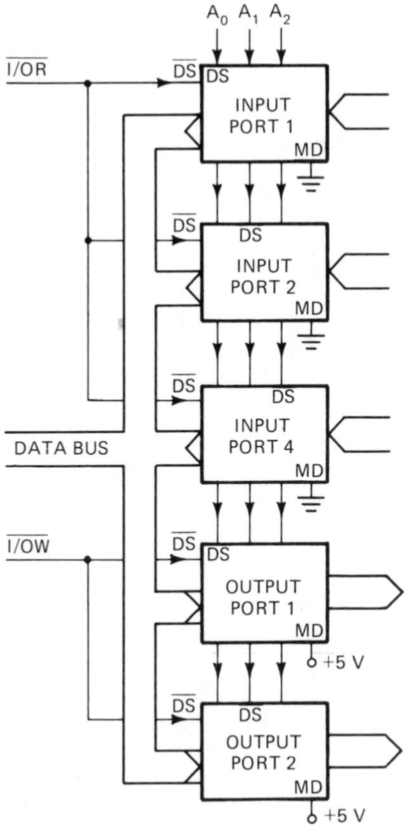

All input ports are enabled by $\overline{\text{I/OR}}$, all output ports by $\overline{\text{I/OW}}$. Address line A_0 selects port 1, A_1 port 2, A_2 port 4, etc. Port addresses with more than one address line high are not allowed.

Interfacing Simple Peripherals to the Intel 8080

EXAMPLE 1: A Two-Position Switch

The SPST or SPDT switch requires a single bit of an 8212 input port. Determining if the switch is open takes three instructions:

```
IN      PORT    ;GET SWITCH DATA
ANI     MASK    ;MASK OFF SWITCH
JZ      CLSD    ;JUMP IF SWITCH IS CLOSED
```

The parameter MASK contains a one bit in the switch position and zero bits elsewhere. If the switch is in bit positions 0, 6, or 7, the program can use the shift instructions and the SIGN or CARRY bits. For instance, a switch in bit 6 could be examined with the sequence

```
        IN      PORT        ;GET SWITCH DATA
        ADD     A           ;SWITCH TO SIGN BIT
        JP      CLSD        ;JUMP IF SWITCH IS CLOSED
```

An EXCLUSIVE OR instruction can find changes in sets of switch positions.

```
        IN      PORT        ;GET NEW SWITCH POSITIONS
        MOV     B,A
        LXI     H,OLD
        XRA     M           ;LOOK FOR CHANGES FROM OLD
                            ;  SWITCH POSITIONS
        JZ      NOCH
        MOV     M,B         ;REPLACE OLD POSITIONS IF
                            ;  CHANGES OCCURRED
```

The accumulator now has a one bit in each position where the corresponding switch changed.

EXAMPLE 2: An Unencoded Multi-Position Switch

A switch with eight positions requires one 8-bit input port. The following sequence of instructions will determine the switch position.

```
GETSW:  IN      PORT        ;GET SWITCH DATA
        CPI     0FFH        ;IS THE SWITCH IN ANY POSITION?
        JZ      GETSW       ;NO, WAIT FOR POSITION
        MVI     B,0         ;SWITCH POSITION = 0
SRPOS:  RAR                 ;IS NEXT BIT GROUNDED?
        JNC     FOUND       ;YES, POSITION FOUND
        INR     B           ;NO, POSITION = POSITION + 1
        JMP     SRPOS
FOUND:  HLT
```

The switch position (0 to 7) will be in register B at the end of the program.

EXAMPLE 3: A 3 × 3 Unencoded Keyboard

If the keyboard connections are as shown in Fig. 8.28, the program below will identify a key closure.

```
;
;   DETERMINE IF ANY KEYS PRESSED
;
CHKBD:  SUB     A
        OUT     KOUT        ;GROUND ALL COLUMNS
        IN      KIN
        ANI     00000111B   ;MASK OFF ROW BITS
```

```
                    CPI       00000111B     ;ARE ANY ROWS GROUNDED?
                    JZ        CHKBD         ;NO, KEEP LOOKING
;
;   IDENTIFY KEY COLUMN BY GROUNDING ONE COLUMN AT A TIME
;
                    MVI       B,3           ;NUMBER OF COLUMNS = 3
                    MVI       C,0           ;KEY NUMBER = 0
                    MVI       D,11111110B   ;PATTERN FOR GROUNDING FIRST
                                            ;  COLUMN
FCOL:               MOV       A,D           ;GROUND A COLUMN
                    OUT       KOUT
                    RLC                     ;FORM PATTERN FOR NEXT COLUMN
                                            ;  BY SHIFTING
                    MOV       D,A
                    IN        KIN           ;GET ROW INPUTS
                    ANI       00000111B     ;MASK OFF ROW BITS
                    CPI       00000111B     ;ARE ANY ROWS GROUNDED?
                    JNZ       FROW          ;YES, FIND KEY ROW
                    MOV       A,C           ;NO, ADJUST KEY NUMBER TO NEXT
                                            ;  COLUMN
                    ADI       3             ;KEY NUMBER = KEY NUMBER
                                            ;  +NUMBER OF ROWS
                    MOV       C,A
                    DCR       B             ;HAVE ALL COLUMNS BEEN CHECKED?
                    JNZ       FCOL          ;NO, GROUND NEXT COLUMN
                    JMP       ERROR         ;YES, ERROR, NO CLOSURE FOUND
;
;   IDENTIFY KEY ROW BY EXAMINING INPUTS
;
FROW:               INR       C             ;KEY NUMBER = KEY NUMBER + 1
                    RAR                     ;IS ROW BIT 0?
                    JC        FROW          ;NO, KEEP LOOKING
```

The key numbers may correspond to digits, characters, commands, or functions. The program must derive the meaning from the number (perhaps through a conversion table or a jump table).

EXAMPLE 4: An Encoded Keyboard with a Strobe

Figure 8.46 shows the use of two Intel 8212 ports to interface an encoded keyboard that provides an 8-bit data output and a strobe signal. The strobe latches the data into port 1 and produces an active-low status signal at port 2. Note that the CPU cannot directly determine the state of the service request flip-flop in the data port since that flip-flop is not addressable. The 8212 is designed for use in interrupt-driven systems (see Chapter 9) where $\overline{\text{INT}}$ directly affects the processor by causing an interrupt.

Figure 8.46 Interface between the Intel 8080 and an encoded keyboard.

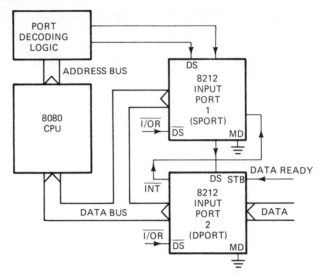

The program must determine if the status signal is active and then read the data if it is. Reading the data automatically deactivates the status signal so that the processor will not read the same data twice. The program is

```
SPORT       EQU     1               ;KEYBOARD STATUS PORT
DPORT       EQU     2               ;KEYBOARD DATA PORT
;
;   CHECK IF LATCHED STROBE IS ACTIVE-LOW
;
CHSTB:      IN      SPORT           ;GET LATCHED STATUS
            ANI     SMASK           ;IS STATUS ACTIVE (ZERO)?
            JNZ     CHSTB           ;NO, KEEP CHECKING
;
;   GET DATA
;
            IN      DPORT           ;GET DATA FROM KEYBOARD
```

The keyboard may provide data in a variety of forms. If it uses negative logic, a COMPLEMENT (CMA) instruction will be necessary. The program may also have to add or delete parity, convert codes, echo information to a printer, or interpret letters or numbers.

EXAMPLE 5: A Single Display
A single display requires one bit of an 8212 output port. The instructions needed to turn the light on or off depend on the polarity of the display. A simple sequence is

```
            MVI     A,MASK          ;GET DISPLAY DATA
```

```
            OUT       PORT          ;SEND TO DISPLAY
```

where the parameter MASK contains the appropriate bit value in the display position.
The following sequences can send the same value to a whole set of displays.

```
            SUB       A
            OUT       PORT          ;ALL DISPLAYS AT LOGIC ZERO
```

or

```
            MVI       A,0FFH
            OUT       PORT          ;ALL DISPLAYS AT LOGIC ONE
```

The control sequences are as follows for a particular display.
    (a) Display bit = one

```
            LDA       DSPLY         ;GET DISPLAY DATA
            ORI       MASK          ;SET DISPLAY BIT
            OUT       PORT          ;SEND DATA TO DISPLAY
```

MASK has a one bit in the required position.
    (b) Display bit = zero

```
            LDA       DSPLY         ;GET DISPLAY DATA
            ANI       MASK          ;CLEAR DISPLAY BIT
            OUT       PORT          ;SEND DATA TO DISPLAY
```

MASK has a zero bit in the required position.
    (c) Complement display bit

```
            LDA       DSPLY         ;GET DISPLAY DATA
            XRI       MASK          ;INVERT DISPLAY BIT
            OUT       PORT          ;SEND DATA TO DISPLAY
```

MASK has a one bit in the required position.

EXAMPLE 6: A Seven-Segment Display
    An undecoded seven-segment display may be attached to an Intel 8212 output
port as shown in Fig. 8.47. The program must convert the output data to the proper
form and send it to the port. A COMPLEMENT instruction can invert the logic
levels.
    Multiple displays may use a counter and a decoder as shown in Fig. 8.48. Here
the $\overline{\text{INT}}$ output serves as a BYTE OUT pulse that clocks the counter. A separate
output port can control the displays as shown in Fig. 8.49. The program must not only
send the data to the data port but must also send control information to the control
port. This technique can place information on any display or group of displays at any
time.

Figure 8.47 Interface between the Intel 8080 and an undecoded seven-segment display.

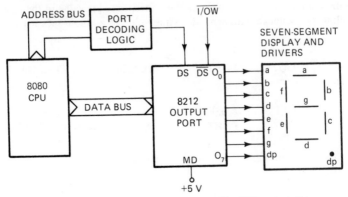

The CPU sends eight bits of data to the output port. The MSB controls the decimal point; the remaining bits control segments g, f, e, d, c, b, and a in that order. Section A3.3 describes the seven-segment display.

Figure 8.48 Interface between the Intel 8080 and multiple seven-segment displays using a counter and a decoder.

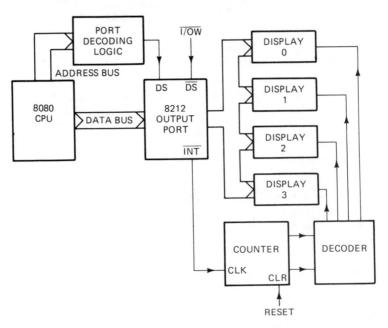

The counter and decoder control which display is active; the $\overline{\text{INT}}$ output produces a clock pulse as a result of each output transfer.

Figure 8.49 Interface between the Intel 8080 and multiple seven-segment displays using a display control port.

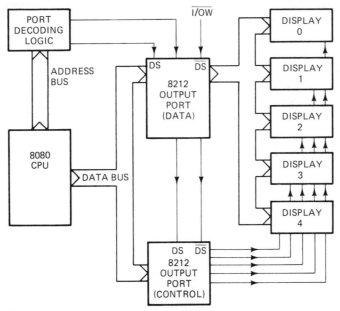

The data in the control port selects which display is active.

EXAMPLE 7: D/A Converter

A digital-to-analog converter like the Analog Devices AD7522 can be attached to an Intel 8080 system as shown in Fig. 8.50. The converter occupies three ports; one for the eight least significant data bits, one for the two most significant data bits, and one for the LOAD (LDAC) signal. The program that produces an analog output is

```
;
;  DATA TO DAC
;
            LDA       LBYTE       ;GET 8 LSB'S
            OUT       LPORT       ;SEND TO DAC
            LDA       HBYTE       ;GET 2 MSB'S
            OUT       HPORT       ;SEND TO DAC


;
;  LOAD DAC AND START CONVERSION
;
            MVI       A,LDAC1     ;PULSE LOAD DAC SIGNAL
            OUT       CPORT       ;LDAC = 1
            SUB       A
            OUT       CPORT       ;LDAC = 0
```

LDAC1 has a one bit in the appropriate position.

399

Figure 8.50 Interface between the Intel 8080 and an Analog Devices AD7522 D/A Converter.

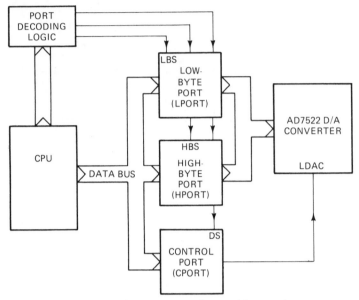

The low-byte and high-byte data ports are actually part of the converter; the control port is separate.

EXAMPLE 8: A/D Converter

An analog-to-digital converter like the Analog Devices AD7570 can be attached to an Intel 8080 system as shown in Fig. 8.51. It uses three input ports: one for the eight least significant data bits, one for the two most significant data bits, and one for the BUSY signal. It also needs one output port for a START CONVERSION signal. The three tri-state input ports are actually part of the converter. The program for acquiring data from the converter is

```
;
;   SEND START CONVERSION SIGNAL
;
            MVI       A,STCON      ;PULSE START CONVERSION SIGNAL
            OUT       CPORT        ;STRT = 1
            SUB       A
            OUT       CPORT        ;STRT = 0
;
;   WAIT FOR CONVERSION TO FINISH
;
CHBSY:      IN        BPORT        ;GET BUSY SIGNAL
            ANI       MASK         ;IS CONVERSION COMPLETE
                                   ;   (BUSY = 1)?
            JZ        CHBSY        ;NO, KEEP CHECKING
```

```
;
; GET DATA AND STORE
;
        IN      LPORT       ;GET 8 LSB'S OF DATA
        STA     LBYTE
        IN      HPORT       ;GET 2 MSB'S OF DATA
        STA     HBYTE
```

STCON must have a one bit in the correct position to pulse the start conversion (STRT) line. MASK must have a one bit in the position tied to the BUSY signal. The program would not need to check the BUSY signal if it introduced a long enough delay to ensure a successful conversion.

Figure 8.51 Interface between the Intel 8080 CPU and an Analog Devices AD7570 A/D converter.

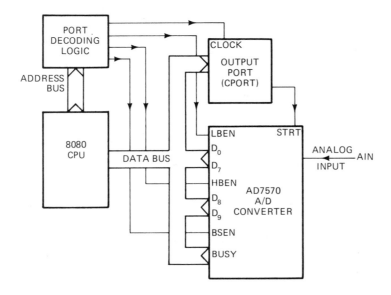

EXAMPLE 9: Teletypewriter

Intel 8080 systems can use either a hardware or a software interface to provide the conversion and formatting required by a teletypewriter. The hardware interface typically consists of a UART with tri-state outputs, an input port for examining status signals, and an output port for selecting the various UART options. The software interface requires only one input bit and one output bit but involves more programming. The low cost of UARTs and their availability in forms compatible with microprocessors have made the hardware interface very popular.

Figure 8.52 shows an interface between an Intel 8080 microprocessor and a UART with tri-state outputs. The UART contains all the input and output ports and I/O addressing inputs that can be directly attached to the port-decoding logic.

Figure 8.52 Interface between the Intel 8080 and a UART with tri-state outputs.

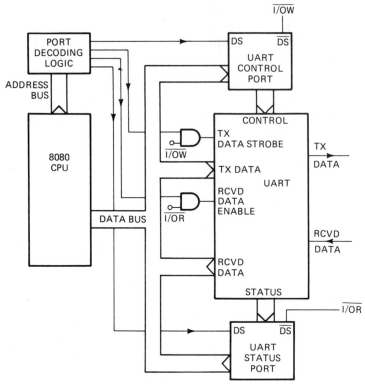

The UART includes the input and output data ports, the status input port, and the control output port.

The data transmission program requires the CPU to wait for the OUTPUT READY (TRANSMITTER BUFFER EMPTY) signal and then send the data.

```
;
;   TRANSMIT DATA TO TELETYPEWRITER VIA UART
;
;   LOOK FOR TRANSMITTER BUFFER
;       EMPTY SIGNAL
;
SRTBE:      IN      SPORT       ;GET STATUS
            ANI     TMASK       ;IS TRANSMITTER BUFFER EMPTY?
            JZ      SRTBE       ;NO, WAIT
;
;   SEND DATA TO TRANSMIT REGISTER
;
            LDA     TDATA       ;GET DATA
            OUT     TPORT       ;SEND TO TRANSMITTER REGISTER
```

The data reception program must check for errors before storing the data. A typical program is

```
;
;   RECEIVE DATA FROM TELETYPEWRITER VIA UART
;
;   LOOK FOR RECEIVER BUFFER
;      FULL SIGNAL
;
;
SRRDF:      IN          SPORT       ;GET STATUS
            ANI         RMASK       ;IS RECEIVER BUFFER FULL?
            JZ          SRRDF       ;NO,WAIT
;
;   CHECK FOR RECEIVE ERRORS
;
            IN          SPORT       ;GET STATUS
            ANI         EMASK       ;MASK OFF ERROR BITS
            JNZ         RERR        ;ERROR IF ANY BIT 1
            IN          RPORT       ;GET DATA
            STA         RDATA
```

RERR must determine the error involved and take appropriate action.

Figure 8.53 shows a direct interface between an Intel 8080 and a teletypewriter. Figure 8.39 is a flowchart of the transmission program. The start bit is a logic zero and the stop bits are one bits that are obtained by setting the CARRY to one each time through the loop. The following is a transmission program for 8-bit ASCII characters without parity, assuming that the serial output line is bit 0 and that subroutine DELAY produces a 9.1 ms delay between bit transmissions without affecting any registers.

```
;
;   SERIAL OUTPUT TO TELETYPEWRITER WITH ONE
;      START BIT, TWO STOP BITS, AND A
;      9.1 MS DELAY BETWEEN BITS
;      (OUTPUT LINE IS BIT 0)
;
            ANA         A           ;CARRY = START BIT = 0
            LDA         TDATA       ;GET CHARACTER
            RAL                     ;START BIT TO TX POSITION
            MVI         B,11        ;COUNT = 11 BITS
TRBIT:      OUT         TPORT       ;TRANSMIT A BIT
            CALL        DELAY       ;WAIT 9.1 MS BETWEEN BITS
            RAR                     ;GET NEXT BIT
            STC                     ;SET CARRY TO GENERATE STOP BITS
            DCR         B
            JNZ         TRBIT
```

Figure 8.53 Interface between the Intel 8080 and a teletypewriter.

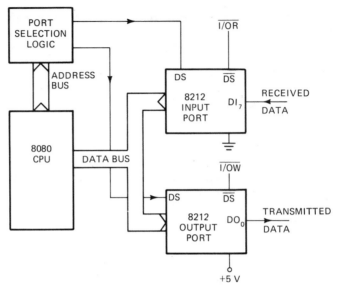

The received data is one bit of an input port; the transmitted data is one bit of an output port.

Figure 8.40 is a flowchart of the reception program. This program must look for a start bit, delay half a bit time to center the reception properly, convert the data into parallel form, and look for the stop bits. The program below assumes no parity and uses subroutine DLY2 to produce a half-bit time delay. The serial input line is bit 7.

```
;
;   SERIAL INPUT FROM TELETYPEWRITER WITH ONE
;       START BIT, TWO STOP BITS, AND A
;       9.1 MS DELAY BETWEEN BITS
;       (INPUT LINE IS BIT 7)
;
;       LOOK FOR START BIT (ZERO)
;
SRSTB:      IN      RPORT       ;GET SERIAL DATA FROM LINE 7
            ANA     A           ;IS START BIT (ZERO) PRESENT?
            JM      SRSTB       ;NO, KEEP LOOKING
;
;   CONVERT DATA TO PARALLEL FORM
;
            CALL    DLY2        ;WAIT HALF BIT TIME TO CENTER
            MVI     B,10000000B ;COUNT BIT IN MOST SIGNIFICANT BIT
                                ;   POSITION
RCVBT:      CALL    DELAY       ;WAIT 9.1 MS BETWEEN BITS
            IN      RPORT       ;GET A BIT
            RAL                 ;SAVE RECEIVED BIT IN CARRY
            MOV     A,B
```

```
            RAR                         ;MAKE RECEIVED BIT PART OF DATA
            MOV     B,A
            JNC     RCVBT               ;CONTINUE UNTIL COUNT BIT
                                        ;  TRAVERSES WORD
            STA     RDATA
;
;  CHECK FOR PROPER STOP BITS
;
            MVI     B,2                 ;NUMBER OF STOP BITS = 2
STOPS:      CALL    DELAY               ;WAIT 9.1 MS BETWEEN BITS
            IN      RPORT               ;GET A BIT
            ANA     A                   ;IS BIT A STOP BIT (ONE)?
            JP      FRERR               ;NO, FRAMING ERROR
            DCR     B
            JNZ     STOPS
```

This program only samples each bit once. If the lines are noisy, the program may sample the data several times during each period. One possibility would be to sample three times (e.g., $\frac{1}{4}$, $\frac{1}{2}$, and $\frac{3}{4}$ of the way across the bit) and use majority logic to determine the correct value. This same procedure can reduce the number of false start bits detected.

Generating and checking parity are simple on the Intel 8080 because of its (EVEN) PARITY bit. The procedures are as follows for even parity.

1. Generating parity

```
            LDA     TDATA               ;GET CHARACTER WITH BIT 7 = 0
            ANA     A                   ;IS PARITY ALREADY EVEN?
            JPE     TRANS
            ORI     10000000B           ;NO, MAKE PARITY EVEN BY SETTING
                                        ;  BIT 7
TRANS:      RAL                         START BIT TO TX POSITION
```

2. Checking parity

```
            ANA     A                   ;IS PARITY EVEN?
            JPO     PRERR               ;NO, PARITY ERROR FOUND
            STA     RDATA
```

Odd parity requires inverting the conditions used in the jump instructions.

Motorola 6800

The Motorola 6800 is designed to use LSI serial and parallel interface chips in its I/O section. It has no special I/O instructions or control signals. Although TTL devices could be used, most Motorola 6800 I/O sections are based on the 6820 Peripheral Interface Adapter.

Any 6800 instruction that references memory can perform an I/O operation. ADD, SUBTRACT, AND, OR, EXCLUSIVE OR, and other instructions can have one operand in an accumulator and the other at an input port. Some particularly useful instructions are

STORE transfers eight bits of data from an accumulator to an output port.
LOAD transfers eight bits of data from an input port to an accumulator.
CLEAR clears an output port.
TEST sets the flags according to the data at an input port.
COMPARE sets the flags as if the data at an input port had been subtracted from the contents of an accumulator.
BIT TEST sets the flags as if the data at an input port had been logically ANDed with the contents of an accumulator.

The designer must be careful in situations where input and output ports do not behave like memory locations. For example, the input data may not be latched or the output data may not be buffered. In general, writing data into an input port or reading data from an output port should be avoided unless the ports are latched and buffered. Note that such operations as TEST, SHIFT, and COMPLEMENT involve both read and write cycles and should be applied to input and output ports cautiously.

The following considerations apply to the design of I/O sections using the Peripheral Interface Adapter.

1. The decoding system must differentiate between PIA addresses and memory addresses. As noted earlier, many microcomputers use address lines A_{15} and A_{14} for this purpose. This technique is convenient, since each PIA has one active-low and two active-high chip selects. The differentiation between I/O and memory requires one active-high and one active-low chip select, leaving one active-high select available for addressing different PIAs.

2. The RS (register select) lines determine the internal PIA addresses as described in Table 8.1. If, as usual, lines RS0 and RS1 are tied to address lines A_0 and A_1 respectively, the address of data register A can be placed in the index register and all the registers in the PIA can be addressed with indexed offsets:

0,X—Data or Data Direction Register A
1,X—Control Register A
2,X—Data or Data Direction Register B
3,X—Control Register B

This procedure is convenient for configuring the PIA.

3. PIA addresses must not conflict. Complete decoding is unnecessary unless the I/O addresses are limited to a very small area of memory. Many I/O sections use linear select with a specific address bit tied to each PIA (see Fig. 8.54). Since the PIA uses bits A_0 and A_1 internally, bits A_2 through A_{13} are available to select

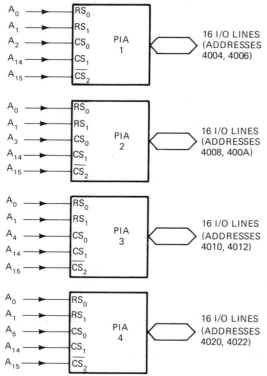

Here CS_0 is tied to a different address line for each PIA. CS_1 and $\overline{CS_2}$ differentiate between memory and I/O. RS_0 and RS_1 address the PIA registers.

24 PIAs as shown in Table 8.10. If more address bits are used for memory, fewer will be available for simple decoding of PIA addresses.

4. The maximum PIA delay times are shorter than the corresponding times for the standard 6810 RAM and 6830 ROM but may need to be considered as faster memories become available.

5. Since the PIA has no data input latch, a TTL latch will be necessary if the data is only briefly available.

6. The PIA will not directly drive output lines. An 8T97 buffer can provide higher drive currents.

7. The ENABLE on the PIA is usually tied to clock phase φ_2, since ENABLE is used to recognize interrupt transitions and to determine the length of strobes. Therefore ENABLE should be regular if these strobes are used and should be independent of the state of the processor. ENABLE should not be tied to VMA, since this connection leaves the PIA unclocked when the processor is halted.

Table 8.10   PIA Addresses in a System Using Linear Select

Address Line[a] Tied to CS	PIA Addresses (Hexadecimal) $A_{15} = 0, A_{14} = 1$	$A_{15} = 1, A_{14} = 0$
A_2	4004–4007	8004–8007
A_3	4008–400B	8008–800B
A_4	4010–4013	8010–8013
A_5	4020–4023	8020–8023
A_6	4040–4043	8040–8043
A_7	4080–4083	8080–8083
A_8	4100–4103	8100–8103
A_9	4200–4203	8200–9203
A_{10}	4400–4403	8400–8403
A_{11}	4800–4803	8800–8803
A_{12}	5000–5003	9000–9003
A_{13}	6000–6003	A000–A003

[a]A_{14} and A_{15} differentiate between memory and I/O; A_0 and A_1 address the internal PIA registers.

The various Motorola 6800 instructions operate on data in I/O ports just as they do on data in memory. The instruction cycles are exactly the same as those described in Chapter 7.

Interfacing Simple Peripherals to the Motorola 6800

EXAMPLE 1: A Two-Position Switch

The SPST or SPDT switch requires a single PIA input bit. No latch is necessary. The following program configures the PIA, using the unbuffered A side for input.

```
LDX     #PIADRA       GET BASE ADDRESS OF PIA
CLR     1,X           ACCESS DATA DIRECTION REGISTER A
LDAA    #DIRS         ESTABLISH DIRECTIONS
STAA    X
LDAA    #%00000100    ACCESS DATA REGISTER
STAA    1,X           CONFIGURE PIA CONTROL
```

The first step is to access the data direction register. Clearing control register A (bit 2 = 0) makes address zero in the PIA refer to data direction register A. The remaining steps store the appropriate bits in the data direction register (1 = output, 0 = input) and configure the control register so that all interrupts are disabled and address zero refers to the data register (control bit 2 = 1). The control lines are not used.

To determine if the switch is open takes three instructions:

```
LDAA    PIADRA      GET SWITCH DATA
ANDA    #MASK       MASK OFF SWITCH
BEQ     CLSD        JUMP IF SWITCH IS CLOSED
```

MASK contains a one bit in the switch position and zero bits elsewhere. A switch in bit 7 would require no AND instruction, since loading the accumulator would set the NEGATIVE or SIGN bit—that is,

```
LDAA    PIADRA      GET SWITCH DATA
BPL     CLSD        JUMP IF SWITCH CLOSED
```

The EXCLUSIVE OR instruction will find changes in sets of switch positions—that is,

```
LDAA    OLD         GET OLD SWITCH POSITIONS
EORA    PIADRA      LOOK FOR CHANGES IN NEW
                        POSITIONS
JZ      NOCH
LDAB    PIADRA      REPLACE OLD POSITIONS IF CHANGES
STAB    OLD
```

Accumulator A now has a one bit in each position where the corresponding switch changed.

EXAMPLE 2: An Eight-Position Switch

An eight-position selector switch will use the entire A side of a PIA. Clearing the data direction register makes all the data pins inputs—that is,

```
CLR     X           MAKE ALL LINES INPUTS
```

The program below will wait for the switch to be in a position and will determine the position (assuming that input bit 0 corresponds to switch position 0, etc.).

```
        LDAA    #$FF
CHSW    CMPA    PIADRA      IS THE SWITCH IN ANY POSITION?
        BNE     CHSW        NO, WAIT FOR POSITION
        CLRB                SWITCH POSITION = ZERO
        LDAA    PIADRA      GET SWITCH DATA
SRPOS   RORA                IS NEXT BIT GROUNDED?
        BCC     FOUND       YES, POSITION FOUND
        INCB                NO, POSITION = POSITION + 1
        BRA     SRPOS
FOUND   SWI
```

The switch position (0 to 7) will be in accumulator B at the end of the program.

EXAMPLE 3: A 3 × 3 Unencoded Keyboard

Figure 8.55 shows a simple 3 × 3 keyboard connected to the B side of a PIA. The next program identifies a key closure (see Fig. 8.30) by switching input and output lines so as to obtain a unique 6-bit code (see Table 8.7). The procedure is

1. Ground the columns and save the row inputs as the three least significant bits of the code.

2. Ground the rows and save the column inputs as the three most significant bits of the code.

3. Look up the 6-bit code in a table and find the corresponding key number.

```
*
*   KEYBOARD INPUT PROGRAM
*
*   SET UP PIA WITH COLUMN OUTPUTS AND
*       ROW INPUTS
*
              CLR     PIACRB          ACCESS DATA DIRECTION REGISTER
              LDAA    #%00111000      MAKE COLUMNS OUTPUTS, ROWS
                                         INPUTS
              STAA    PIADRB
              LDAA    #%00000100      ACCESS DATA REGISTER
              STAA    PIACRB
*
*   GROUND COLUMNS AND SAVE ROW INPUTS
*
              LDAA    #%11000111
SRKEY         STAA    PIADRB          GROUND COLUMNS
              LDAB    PIADRB          FETCH CLOSURE DATA
              ANDB    #%00000111      MASK OFF ROW INPUTS
              CMPB    #%00000111      IS A KEY CLOSED?
              BEQ     SRKEY           NO, KEEP LOOKING

*
*   SET UP PIA WITH COLUMN INPUTS AND
*       ROW OUTPUTS
*
              CLR     PIACRB          ACCESS DATA DIRECTION REGISTER
              LDAA    #%00000111      MAKE COLUMNS INPUTS, ROWS
                                         OUTPUTS
              STAA    PIADRB
              LDAA    #%00000100      ACCESS DATA REGISTER
              STAA    PIACRB
*
*   GROUND ROWS AND SAVE COLUMN INPUTS
*
              LDAA    #%11111000
              STAA    PIADRB          GROUND ROWS
              LDAA    PIADRB          FETCH CLOSURE DATA
```

Figure 8.55 Interface between the Motorola 6800 and a 3 × 3 unencoded keyboard.

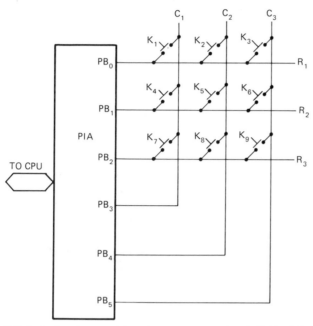

Both the keyboard rows and the columns are connected to the B side of the PIA—
the rows to the three least significant bits and the columns to the next three bits.

```
            ANDA      #%00111000   MASK OFF COLUMN INPUTS
            CMPA      #%00111000   IS A KEY CLOSED?
            BEQ       SRKEY        NO, RETURN TO SEARCHING
            ABA                    COMBINE CLOSURE DATA INTO 6-BIT
                                     CODE
*
*   USE 6 BIT CODE TO SEARCH LOOKUP TABLE
*
            LDX       #KEYTAB      GET ADDRESS OF KEY TABLE
            LDAB      #1           KEY NUMBER = 1
SRTAB       CMPA      X            IS TABLE ENTRY = 6-BIT CODE?
            BEQ       FOUND        YES, KEY FOUND
            INCB                   NO, KEY NUMBER = KEY NUMBER
                                     +1
            INX
            CPX       #KEYTAB+9    ALL OF TABLE SEARCHED?
            BNE       SRTAB        NO, KEEP LOOKING
            BRA       ERROR        YES, ERROR
FOUND       SWI
KEYTAB      FCB       $36, $2E, $1E, $35, $2D, $1D
            FCB       $33, $2B, $1B
```

In practice, remember that the B side of a PIA is buffered. The program may actually need to pull up the inputs in software by declaring all the lines as outputs and placing one bits in the appropriate positions. A scanning program like the one for the Intel 8080 could also be used.

A strobe can be obtained by logically NANDing the column lines and connecting the result to control line CB1. The program must ground the rows after identifying a closure so that the next closure will produce a strobe. Since a key closure will cause a low-to-high transition on CB1, the PIA configuration must set control register bit 1. The procedure is

```
*
*   CONFIGURE PIA FOR KEYBOARD WITH STROBE
*
            CLR     PIADRB          ACCESS DATA DIRECTION
                                        REGISTER
            LDAA    #%00000111      MAKE ROWS OUTPUTS, COLUMNS
                                        INPUTS
            STAA    PIADRB
            LDAA    #%00000110      ACCESS DATA REGISTER, SET
                                        STROBE ON RISING EDGE
            STAA    PIACRB
```

The strobe will set bit 7 of control register B. The program to examine this bit is

```
            LDAA    PIACRB          LOOK FOR STROBE
            BMI     KEYCL           IDENTIFY KEY IF STROBE 1
```

Reading data from the data register will clear the bit.

EXAMPLE 4: An Encoded Keyboard with a Strobe

Figure 8.56 shows the use of a latch and a PIA to interface an encoded keyboard that provides an 8-bit output and an active-low strobe. The strobe latches the data (the PIA has no input latch) and provides a transition on control line CA1.

Control bit 1 need not be set here, since the strobe transition is high-to-low. Using the A side of the PIA, the program is

```
            CLR     PIACRA          ACCESS DATA DIRECTION REGISTER
            CLR     PIADRA          MAKE ALL LINES INPUTS
            LDAA    #%00000100      ACCESS DATA REGISTER
            STAA    PIACRA
```

The input program is

```
*   CHECK FOR STROBE
    CHSTB:  LDAA    PIACRA          IS STROBE ACTIVE (ZERO)?
```

```
                BPL        CHSTB         NO, KEEP CHECKING
 *   GET DATA
                LDAA       PIADRA        GET DATA FROM KEYBOARD
```

A COMPLEMENT instruction will be necessary if the keyboard uses negative logic.

Figure 8.56 Interface between the Motorola 6800 and an encoded keyboard.

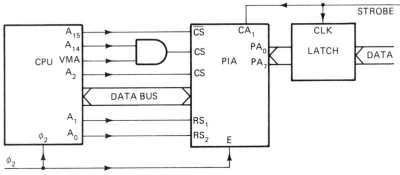

The PIA occupies addresses 4004 to 4007. An 8-bit clocked latch holds the input data from the keyboard.

EXAMPLE 5: A Single Display

A single lighted display requires one PIA output bit. Note that the PIA does contain an output latch. The exact sequences for turning the display on and off depend on the polarity of the display. An entire set of displays can be handled with the sequence

```
        LDAA      #MASK        GET DISPLAY DATA
        STAA      PIADRA       SEND TO DISPLAY
```

MASK will contain either a one bit or a zero bit in the display position, depending on polarity. The entire data register can be cleared or complemented in one operation, assuming that the output lines are buffered.

```
        CLR       PIADRA       ALL DISPLAYS AT LOGIC ZERO
        COM       PIADRA       COMPLEMENT DISPLAY DATA
```

The PIA configuration only requires that all the lines be outputs.

```
        CLR       PIACRA       ACCESS DATA DIRECTION REGISTER
        LDAA      #$FF         MAKE ALL LINES OUTPUTS
        STAA      PIADRA
        LDAA      #%00000100   ACCESS DATA REGISTER
        STAA      PIACRA       CONFIGURE PIA
```

Logical operations can change individual bits in a pattern. That is,

ORAA #MASK sets a bit if MASK has a one in the appropriate position.
ANDA #MASK clears a bit if MASK has a zero in the appropriate position.
EORA #MASK complements a bit if MASK has a one in the appropriate position.

These instructions can turn individual lights on or off or invert their states.

EXAMPLE 6: A Seven-Segment Display

An undecoded seven-segment display can be attached to a Motorola PIA as shown in Fig. 8.57. The program must convert the output data to the proper form and store it in the PIA data register. A COMPLEMENT instruction can invert the logic levels.

Figure 8.57   Interface between the Motorola 6800 and an undecoded seven-segment display.

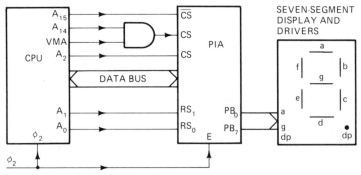

The PIA occupies addresses 4004 to 4007. The seven-segment display is attached to the B side. The most significant bit controls the decimal point, and the remaining bits control the various segments. Section A3.3 describes the seven-segment display.

Multiple displays can use a counter and a decoder as shown in Fig. 8.58. Here the CB2 control line is a BYTE OUT pulse that clocks the counter. The required values in the PIA control register are

bit 5 = 1; so CB2 is an output.
bit 4 = 0; so CB2 is a strobe.
bit 3 = 1; so CB2 is restored by the next ENABLE pulse after it is sent low; that is, the strobe is one clock period in length if ENABLE is tied to φ_2.

The program that configures the PIA is

```
CLR      PIACRB        ACCESS DATA DIRECTION
                         REGISTER
LDAA     #$FF          MAKE ALL LINES OUTPUTS
STAA     PIADRB
```

```
        LDAA    #%00101100   MAKE CB2 OUTPUT STROBE
        STAA    PIACRB
```

Bit 2 of the control register is 1 to access the data register.

Figure 8.58 Interface between the Motorola 6800 and multiple seven-segment displays using a counter and a decoder.

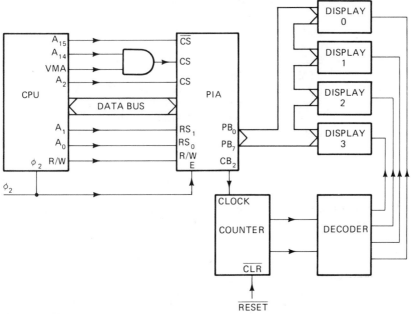

Control line CB$_2$ clocks the counter after each output operation; the counter and decoder control which display is lit.

Another method is to use the other half of the PIA to control the displays as shown in Fig. 8.59. For instance, if the B side is used for control and a logic zero activates a display, the following program will send eight words of data starting with memory location DSPLY to an eight-digit display.

```
*
*    OUTPUT TO 8 DIGIT DISPLAY
*
*
*    STEP 1:  CONFIGURE PIA
*
        LDX     #PIADRA
        CLR     1,X         ACCESS DATA DIRECTION
                            REGISTER A
        CLR     3,X         ACCESS DATA DIRECTION
                            REGISTER B
        LDAA    #$FF        MAKE ALL LINES OUTPUTS
```

```
            STAA    X
            STAA    2,X
            LDAA    #%00000100    ACCESS DATA REGISTERS
            STAA    1,X           CONFIGURE BOTH SIDES OF PIA
            STAA    3,X

*
*   STEP 2: DATA TO DISPLAYS
*
            LDX     #DSPLY        POINTER = DSPLY
            LDAB    #$7F          MOST SIGNIFICANT DISPLAY ON
            SEC                   CARRY = 1 FOR ROTATING LATER
            STAB    PIADRB
DSPLY1      LDAA    X             GET DISPLAY DATA
            STAA    PIADRA        SEND TO DISPLAYS
            JSR     DELAY         PULSE LENGTH FOR DISPLAY
            INX
            ROR     PIADRB        NEXT DISPLAY ON
            BCS     DSPLY1        CONTINUE IF ALL DATA NOT
                                     DISPLAYED
```

Figure 8.59 Interface between the Motorola 6800 and multiple seven-segment displays using a display control port.

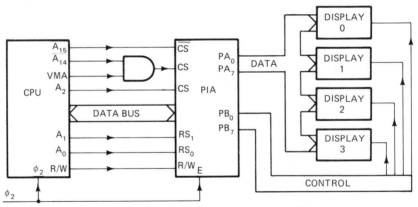

The A side of the PIA transfers data to the displays; the B side controls which display is lit.

Table 8.11 shows the register contents required to turn on the various displays. Subroutine DELAY must not affect any registers.

EXAMPLE 7: D/A Converter

A digital-to-analog converter like the AD7522 can be attached to a Motorola 6800 system as shown in Fig. 8.60. The converter uses ten output data lines and two control lines, one to strobe the data into the device (a low-to-high edge is necessary) and the other to load the DAC (a high level for at least 0.5 μs is necessary).

Table 8.11 Register Contents for Activating Multiplexed Displays

Display Number (Controlling bit)	Register Contents (Hexadecimal) Active-High	Active-Low
0	01	FE
1	02	FD
2	04	FB
3	08	F7
4	10	EF
5	20	DF
6	40	BF
7	80	7F

This interface uses many of the features of the PIA. On the A side, CA2 is a latched serial output that can produce the LDAC signal. On the B side, CB2 is a brief write strobe that places ten bits of data in the DAC buffer after the CPU has sent all ten bits to the PIA. The A control register bits are

bit 5 = 1; so CA2 is an output.
bit 4 = 1; so CA2 is a latched serial output with the value of control bit 3.
bit 3 = 0 initially to inhibit the DAC.

The B control register bits are

bit 5 = 1; so CB2 is an output.
bit 4 = 0; so CB2 is a write strobe.
bit 3 = 1; so the write strobe is one clock period in length.

Figure 8.60 Interface between the Motorola 6800 and an Analog Devices AD7522 D/A Converter.

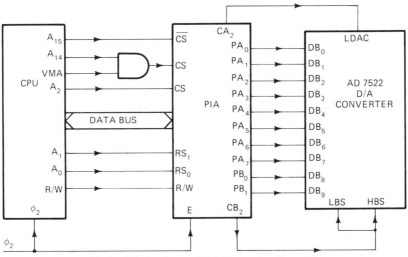

Control line CB_2 provides both the low-byte and high-byte strobes. Control line CA_2 provides the LOAD DAC signal.

The PIA configuration depends on the following factors.

1. Only the B side can produce a write strobe. Therefore the CPU uses that side for the second load operation so that the strobe will occur after all ten bits of data are available.

2. Only the latched output line can produce on active-high pulse. Therefore that configuration produces the LDAC signal. The strobes are active-low.

3. The limited number of control signals available from a PIA makes parallel loading of both bytes at once simpler than single-byte loading.

4. The byte strobes are edge-triggered and require a short pulse. The single clock period pulse controlled by the PIA ENABLE input is adequate.

Note that writing data into data register A does not produce a strobe. RESET clears all control bits and makes the control lines inputs. The hardware may have to separately inhibit the converter if RESET or changing control bits causes a problem.

The program is

```
*
*   CONFIGURE PIA FOR DIGITAL TO ANALOG CONVERTER
*
            LDAA    #%00110000   ACCESS DATA DIRECTION REGISTER A
            STAA    PIACRA
            CLR     PIACRB       ACCESS DATA DIRECTION REGISTER B
            LDAB    #$FF
            STAB    PIADRA       MAKE ALL LINES OUTPUTS
            STAB    PIADRB
            LDAA    #%00110100   CONFIGURE A SIDE WITH
            STAA    PIACRA           LDAC = 0
            LDAA    #%00101100   CONFIGURE B SIDE
            STAA    PIACRB           WITH SHORT WRITE STROBE
*
*   DATA TO DAC
*
            LDAA    LBYTE        8 LSB'S TO A SIDE
            STAA    PIADRA
            LDAA    HBYTE        2 MSB'S TO B SIDE
            STAA    PIADRB           AND STROBE DAC.
*
*   LOAD DAC WITH PULSE ON CA2 (LDAC)
*
            LDAA    #%00111100   LDAC = ONE
            STAA    PIACRA
            LDAA    #%00110100   LDAC = ZERO
            STAA    PIACRA
```

The program produces an active-high LDAC pulse that is considerably longer than the minimum required.

EXAMPLE 8: A/D Converter

An analog-to-digital converter like the Analog Devices AD7570 can be attached to a Motorola 6800 system as shown in Fig. 8.61. The converter uses ten data lines and three control lines; one input line indicates when the conversion is complete and two output lines start the conversion and enable the tri-state outputs. The BUSY ENABLE line is tied high so that BUSY can be used as a DATA READY signal (BUSY goes low when the conversion is completed). Both the START CONVERSION signal and the tri-state enables are active-high, and so the latched control options must provide them.

Figure 8.61 Interface between the Motorola 6800 and an Analog Devices AD7570 A/D Converter.

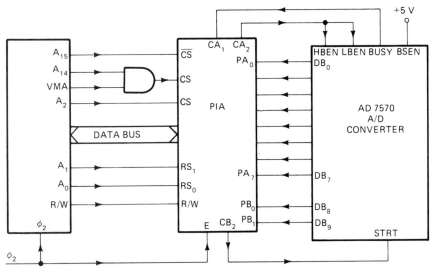

Control line CB_2 provides the START CONVERSION pulse. Control line CA_1 is the conversion completed signal. Control line CA_2 enables the tri-state data outputs of the converter.

The control register bits for the A side are

bit 5 = 1; so CA2 is an output (high- and low-byte enables).

bit 4 = 1; so CA2 is a latched serial output with the value of control bit 3 (since the enables are active-high).

bit 3 = 0 initially to disable the outputs.

bit 1 = 1; so a low-to-high transition on the BUSY line sets bit 7 to 1.

The control register for the PIA B side is as follows.

bit 5 = 1; so CB2 is an output (START CONVERSION).

bit 4 = 1; so CB2 is a latched serial output with the value of control bit 3 (since START CONVERSION is active-high).

bit 3 = 0 initially to inhibit the converter.

The program is

```
*
*   CONFIGURE PIA FOR ANALOG TO DIGITAL CONVERTER
*

            LDAA      #%00110000   ACCESS DATA DIRECTION REGISTERS
            STAA      PIACRA
            STAA      PIACRB
            CLR       PIADRA       MAKE ALL LINES INPUTS
            CLR       PIADRB
            LDAA      #%00110110   CONFIGURE PIA
            STAA      PIACRA
            STAA      PIACRB
*
*   START CONVERSION BY PULSING STRT LINE
*

            LDAA      #%00111100   STRT = 1
            STAA      PIACRB
            LDAA      #%00110100   STRT = 0
            STAA      PIACRB
*
*   WAIT FOR CONVERSION COMPLETED
*

CHBSY       LDAA      PIACRA       CHECK BUSY FLAG
            BPL       CHBSY        WAIT UNTIL FLAG = 1
*
*   ENABLE CONVERTER OUTPUTS WITH ENABLE BITS
*

            LDAA      #%00111100   ENABLE = 1 TO FETCH CONVERTER
                                       DATA
            STAA      PIACRA
*
*   GET DATA AND STORE
*

            LDAA      PIADRA       GET 8 LSB'S OF DATA
            STAA      LBYTE
            LDAA      PIADRB       GET 2 MSB'S OF DATA
            STAB      HBYTE
*
*   DISABLE CONVERTER OUTPUTS
*

            LDAA      #%00110100   DISABLE CONVERTER
            STAA      PIACRA
```

EXAMPLE 9: Teletypewriter

Motorola 6800 systems can use either a hardware or a software interface with a teletypewriter. The usual hardware interface is the Motorola 6850 Asynchronous Communications Interface Adapter (see Fig. 8.62), a UART with tri-state outputs specifically designed for use with the Motorola 6800 CPU and 6860 Low-Speed

Figure 8.62 Expanded block diagram of the Motorola MC6850 Asynchronous Communications Interface Adapter (courtesy of Motorola Semiconductor Products).

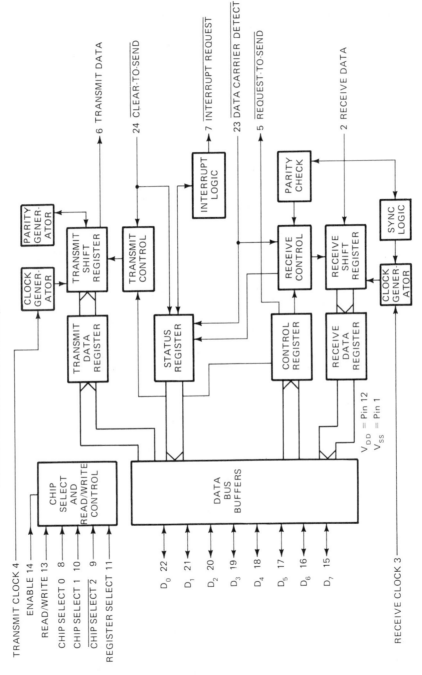

Modem. The ACIA occupies two memory locations and contains two read-only registers (receive data and status) and two write-only registers (transmit data and control). Table 8.12 defines the register contents and Table 8.13 describes the control register bits (bit 7 is the receive interrupt enable bit). Figure 8.63 shows typical connections between an ACIA and the CPU.

To illustrate, the configuration of the ACIA control register below would handle a teletypewriter that uses 7-bit characters with odd parity and two stop bits.

bit 7 = 0 to disable receive interrupt
bit 6 = 1 to make $\overline{RTS}$ high (inactive); this is the RS-232 REQUEST TO SEND signal.
bit 5 = 0 to disable transmit interrupt
bit 4 = 0 for 7-bit characters
bit 3 = 0 for two stop bits
bit 2 = 1 for odd parity
bit 1 = 0 and bit 0 = 1 for ÷ 16 clock (requires a 1760-Hz external clock)

Table 8.12 Definition of ACIA Register Contents (Courtesy of Motorola Semiconductor Products)

Data Bus Line Number	RS · $\overline{R/W}$ Transmit Data Register (write-only)	RS · R/W Receive Data Register (read-only)	Buffer Address $\overline{RS}$ · R/W Control Register (write-only)	$\overline{RS}$·R/W Status Register (read-only)
0	Data bit 0[a]	Data bit 0	Counter Divide Select 1 (CR0)	Receive Data Register Full (RDRF)
1	Data bit 1	Data bit 1	Counter Divide Select 2 (CR1)	Transmit Data Register Empty (TDRE)
2	Data bit 2	Data bit 2	Word Select 1 (CR2)	Data Carrier Detect ($\overline{DCD}$)
3	Data bit 3	Data bit 3	Word Select 2 (CR3)	Clear-to-Send ($\overline{CTS}$)
4	Data bit 4	Data bit 4	Word Select 3 (CR4)	Framing Error (FE)
5	Data bit 5	Data bit 5	Transmit Control 1 (CR5)	Receiver Overrun (OVRN)
6	Data bit 6	Data bit 6	Transmit Control 2 (CR6)	Parity Error (PE)
7	Data bit 7[c]	Data bit 7[b]	Receive Interrupt Enable (CR7)	Interrupt Request (IRQ)

[a]Leading bit = LSB = Bit 0.
[b]Data bit will be zero in 7-bit plus parity modes.
[c]Data bit is "don't care" in 7-bit plus parity modes.

CR1	CR0	Function
0	0	÷ 1
0	1	÷ 16
1	0	÷ 64
1	1	Master reset

CR4	CR3	CR2	Function
0	0	0	7 bits + even parity + 2 stop bits
0	0	1	7 bits + odd parity + 2 stop bits
0	1	0	7 bits + even parity + 1 stop bit
0	1	1	7 bits + odd parity + 1 stop bit
1	0	0	8 bits + 2 stop bits
1	0	1	8 bits + 1 stop bit
1	1	0	8 bits + even parity + 1 stop bit
1	1	1	8 bits + odd parity + 1 stop bit

CR6	CR5	Function
0	0	$\overline{\text{RTS}}$ = low, Transmitting Interrupt Disabled.
0	1	$\overline{\text{RTS}}$ = low, Transmitting Interrupt Enabled.
1	0	$\overline{\text{RTS}}$ = high, Transmitting Interrupt Disabled.
1	1	$\overline{\text{RTS}}$ = low, Transmits a Break level on the Transmit Data Output. Transmitting Interrupt Disabled.

Control register bit 7 is 1 to enable the receive interrupt, 0 to disable it.

Figure 8.63   Typical interface between the Motorola 6800 CPU and
the Motorola 6850 ACIA.

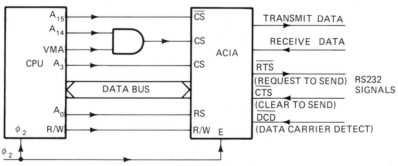

The ACIA occupies memory locations 4008 (control and status registers)
and 4009 (data registers).

423

The following program resets the ACIA, configures it, waits for the RECEIVE DATA REGISTER FULL (RDRF) signal, and reads the data.

```
*
*   RESET ACIA
*
        LDAA      #%00000011
        STAA      ACIACR        RESET ACIA
*
*   CONFIGURE ACIA
*
        LDAA      #%01000101
        STAA      ACIACR        CONFIGURE ACIA
*
*   LOOK FOR DATA READY
*
CHKDT   LDAA      ACIASR        GET ACIA STATUS
        LSRA                    MOVE RDRF TO CARRY
        BCC       CHKDT         WAIT FOR RDRF = 1
*
*   GET ACIA DATA
*
        LDAA      ACIADR        GET ACIA DATA
        STAA      RDATA
```

Note that the ACIA has no RESET input; the program must reset the device by placing ones in bits 0 and 1 of the control register. The ACIA is not like a memory location, since read and write cycles access physically distinct registers. So we cannot use the instructions that both read and write a memory location, such as TEST, INCREMENT, DECREMENT, COMPLEMENT, and SHIFT, with an ACIA.

The program below waits for the TRANSMIT DATA REGISTER EMPTY (TDRE) signal and sends the data.

```
*
*   LOOK FOR OUTPUT READY
*
        LDAA      #%00000010
CHKTR   BITA      ACIASR        LOOK AT TDRE BIT IN ACIA STATUS
        BEQ       CHKTR         WAIT FOR TDRE = 1
*
*   SEND DATA FOR TRANSMISSION
*
        LDAA      TDATA         SEND DATA
        STAA      ACIADR
```

A software interface uses one PIA input bit and one PIA output bit as shown in Fig. 8.64. A latched output control line can handle the paper tape reader and punch. The programs assume that the serial output is bit 0, the serial input is bit 7, and

Figure 8.64 Interface between the Motorola 6800 and a serial peripheral.

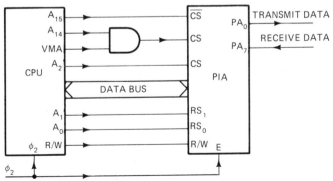

The transmission line is bit 0 of the PIA A side; the receive line is bit 7 of the PIA A side.

subroutines DELAY and DLY2 provide full and half-bit time delays, respectively, without affecting any registers or flags.

```
*
*   SERIAL OUTPUT TO TELETYPEWRITER WITH ONE
*       START BIT, TWO STOP BITS, AND A
*       9.1 MS DELAY BETWEEN BITS
*       (OUTPUT LINE IS BIT 0)
            CLC                     CARRY = START BIT = ZERO
            LDAA    TDATA           GET CHARACTER
            ROLA                    START BIT TO TX POSITION
            LDAB    #11             COUNT = 11 BITS
TRBIT       STAA    PIADRA          TRANSMIT A BIT
            JSR     DELAY           WAIT 9.1 MS BETWEEN BITS
            RORA                    GET NEXT BIT
            SEC                     SET CARRY TO GENERATE STOP BITS
            DECB
            BNE     TRBIT
*
*   SERIAL INPUT FROM TELETYPEWRITER WITH ONE
*       START BIT, TWO STOP BITS, AND A
*       9.1 MS DELAY BETWEEN BITS
*       (INPUT LINE IS BIT 7)
*
*   LOOK FOR START BIT (ZERO)
*
SRSTB       LDAA    PIADRA          IS THE SERIAL INPUT A START
                                    BIT (ZERO)?
            BMI     SRSTB           NO, KEEP LOOKING
*
*   CONVERT DATA TO PARALLEL FORM
```

```
          *
                    JSR       DLY2          WAIT HALF BIT TIME TO CENTER
                    LDAA      #%10000000    COUNT BIT IN MOST SIGNIFICANT
                                            POSITION
RCVBIT              JSR       DELAY         WAIT 9.1 MS BETWEEN BITS
                    ROL       PIADRA        DATA BIT TO CARRY
                    RORA                    DATA BIT TO DATA WORD
                    BCC       RCVBIT        CONTINUE UNTIL COUNT BIT
                                            TRAVERSES WORD

                    STAA      RDATA
          *
          *   CHECK FOR PROPER STOP BITS
          *
                    LDAA      #2            NUMBER OF STOP BITS = 2
STOPS               JSR       DELAY         WAIT 9.1 MS BETWEEN BITS
                    ROL       PIADRA        IS DATA STOP BIT (ONE)?
                    BCC       FRERR         NO, FRAMING ERROR
                    DECA
                    BNE       STOPS
```

The conversion routine can check for even parity as follows.

```
          *
          *   CONVERT DATA TO PARALLEL FORM AND
          *     CHECK FOR EVEN PARITY (INPUT LINE IS BIT 7)
          *
                    JSR       DLY2          WAIT HALF BIT TIME TO CENTER
                    LDAA      #%10000000    COUNT BIT IN MOST SIGNIFICANT
                                            POSITION
                    CLRB                    PARITY = 0
RCVBIT              JSR       DELAY         WAIT 9.1 MS BETWEEN BITS
                    EORB      PIADRA        EXCLUSIVE OR DATA BITS FOR PARITY
                    ROL       PIADRA        DATA BIT TO CARRY
                    RORA                    DATA BIT TO DATA WORD
                    BCC       RCVBIT        CONTINUE IF COUNT BIT HAS NOT
                                            TRAVERSED WORD
                    TSTB                    CHECK PARITY
                    BMI       PRERR         ERROR IF NUMBER OF 1 BITS NOT
                                            EVEN
                    STAA      RDATA
```

An odd parity check requires a BPL PRERR instruction instead of BMI PRERR.

Calculating parity requires shifting the data word and adding all the one bits in the least significant position so that no carries affect the sum (the least significant bit of a binary addition is the same as an EXCLUSIVE OR).

```
          *
          *   CALCULATE EVEN PARITY
```

```
         *
                    CLRA                   PARITY = 0
                    LDAB      TDATA        GET DATA
CALPAR              ABA                    EXCLUSIVE OR DATA BITS IN LSB
                    LSRB                   GET NEXT DATA BIT
                    BNE       CALPAR       CONTINUE UNTIL ALL BITS ZERO
         *
         *   SAVE PARITY IN MSB OF DATA
         *
                    RORA                   PARITY TO CARRY
                    BCC       DONE         IS PARITY ALREADY EVEN?
                    LDAB      TDATA        NO, SET BIT 1 OF DATA
                    ORAB      #%10000000
                    STAB      TDATA
```

Odd parity can be generated by replacing BCC with BCS.

8.7 SUMMARY

Input/output is a complex subject because of the enormous variety of peripherals that are commonly used with microcomputers. Peripherals vary widely in speeds, types of signals, and control structures. The I/O section must convert input data and status information into the form that the CPU requires and must convert output data and control information into the form that the peripherals require.

The CPU can handle simple slow peripherals like switches and displays without precise timing. The only problems are dealing with input transitions and latching the output data for a sufficient amount of time. The CPU can handle asynchronous peripherals like keyboards, multiplexed displays, teletypewriters, and converters with handshake logic. The CPU must determine the readiness of the peripheral, transfer the data, and signal the peripheral that the transfer has been completed. The CPU can handle synchronous peripherals by reconciling its clock with the peripheral clock. High-speed transfers can use direct memory access.

An I/O section with many ports requires a busing structure that must share the data and address buses with the memory section. Isolated I/O provides separate I/O control signals; these signals are particularly useful when the I/O ports are TTL circuits. Memory-mapped I/O simply reserves some addresses for input/output. This method is useful when the I/O ports are LSI devices that contain control and status registers as well as latches and buffers. Attached I/O attaches the input/output section physically to the other sections with special devices. This method can provide one- or two-chip microcomputers for limited applications but makes expansion difficult.

Standard TTL circuits and special LSI devices can simplify I/O sections. Flip-flops, one-shots, counters, selectors, and shift registers can perform useful functions. MSI I/O ports can replace many simpler elements. UARTs, USRTs, and parallel interfaces can handle a variety of control functions. Programmable devices provide increased flexibility at the cost of extra programming.

Intel 8080 I/O sections depend on specific I/O instructions and control signals. The 8212 I/O port is the basic interfacing device. Motorola 6800 I/O sections use memory-mapped I/O. The 6820 Peripheral Interface Adapter is the basic interfacing device.

PROBLEMS

1. An ASCII peripheral always transmits a B character (42 hexadecimal) to begin a message and an F character (46 hexadecimal) to end the message. All other characters are decimal numbers. Describe the procedure necessary for a microprocessor to receive a message and store it, starting at memory location BUFR. Assume that the peripheral operates at ten characters per second (in parallel). What if the transmission lines are noisy? Suggest starting and ending characters that could minimize the number of errors if all data characters are decimal numbers.

2. Describe the procedure necessary for a microprocessor to send a message starting at memory location BUFR to an ASCII peripheral that operates as in Problem 1. All messages start with the letter B and end with the letter F.

3. A line printer can print 120 8-bit characters on a line at a rate of 300 lines per minute. How often must an 8-bit processor perform a data transfer if the printer is to operate at full speed? How often would a 4-bit processor need to perform a transfer? A 16-bit processor? If the 8-bit processor had a 10 μs instruction execution time, how many instructions could it perform between data transfers? Would such a processor be able to keep up with the line printer?

4. A microcomputer contains two input and two output ports, 1K of program memory, and 1K of data memory. The microprocessor has a 16-bit address bus. What would be the advantages and disadvantages of constructing such a system using isolated, memory-mapped, or attached I/O? Describe the number of ports and the decoding system required. How could you add an extra 1K of memory to your system? How could you add two additional I/O ports? How would you modify your design if the microcomputer contained 30K of program memory and 30K of data memory?

5. Describe how an 8-bit microprocessor could handle a 32-bit input operation in which all the data is sent at once. Discuss the number of ports and the decoding system required. How would a 4-, 16-, or 32-bit CPU handle this situation?

6. Assume that a relay requires a pulse 20 ms long. How could such a pulse be produced by a CPU without any external pulse-forming hardware? How could the pulse be produced by the processor with an external one-shot? Assume that the processor takes 10 μs to execute each instruction. Discuss the advantages and disadvantages of both methods. What if the required pulse were 250 ns in length?

7. Show the hardware required to handle a ten-digit display from a single output port. Use a decade counter and a 4-line to 10-line decoder. What hardware would be necessary if ten separate output ports were used? Describe the advantages and disadvantages of each approach. What would be the advantages and disadvantages of a separate control port?

8. A high-speed communications line provides serial data at a rate of 9600 bits per second. If a microprocessor requires ten instructions to handle each bit of data, what must the processor's instruction execution time be in order to handle the line? What if an external shift register were used to convert the data to 8-bit bytes? How many instructions could an 8-bit processor then execute between input operations if its instruction execution time were 5 μs? What would be the advantages or disadvantages of a 4-, 12-, or 16-bit CPU?

9. Two ten-position selector switches together allow the operator to enter a 2-digit number. How many I/O lines are necessary if the switches are not encoded? Describe the program that would be necessary for an 8-bit processor to read the switches and display the values on two decoded seven-segment displays. Describe the required hardware and software if the switches produce BCD outputs.

10. A microprocessor must examine a switch attached to bit 5 of an input port and cause a display attached to bit 2 of an output port to be lit if the switch is closed (zero) and off if the switch is open (one). Assume that the display lights if the processor sends it a one. Show the hardware and software required by the Intel 8080 or Motorola 6800 to handle this task. Assume that the other bits of the output port are not used. What if the output port has other bits that must retain their previous values? What if the display has the opposite polarity?

11. A microprocessor must read a row of eight pushbuttons, each of which directs it to a particular subroutine as described by the following table.

Data Input Line	Subroutine
0	TEST
1	PRINT
2	FETCH
3	STORE
4	RUN
5	RECALL
6	SEND
7	LAST

Show the hardware and software required by the Intel 8080 or Motorola 6800 to perform this task. (*Hint*: Use a jump table.)

12. A microprocessor must read data from an unencoded ten-position selector switch and store the result (0 to 9) in memory location SW. Show the hardware and software required by the Intel 8080 or Motorola 6800 to perform this task.

13. A microprocessor must determine the identity of a key closure from a 4 × 4 unencoded keyboard organized like the 3 × 3 keyboard shown in Fig. 8.28. Show the hardware

and software required by the Intel 8080 or Motorola 6800 to perform this task. Would a 5 × 5 keyboard be substantially more difficult to interface? Why?

14. A microprocessor must flash a single display on and off ten times per second. The display is attached to bit 6 of an output port (the other bits are in use). Show the hardware and software required by the Intel 8080 or Motorola 6800 to perform this task. What if all eight bits were to be flashed?

15. A microprocessor must send eight words of data starting at memory location DSPLY to eight undecoded seven-segment displays. Show the hardware and software required to do this task with the Intel 8080 or Motorola 6800, assuming that a counter and decoder are used to control the displays. What if an 8-bit control port is used to control the displays (a logic zero turns a display on)?

16. A microprocessor indicates an error on eight undecoded seven-segment displays by turning on all the decimal points and leaving all the segments off. Show the hardware and software required by the Intel 8080 or Motorola 6800 to perform this task. Assume that the most significant data bit controls the decimal point. Show the program and interfacing if the displays are controlled by a counter and a decoder and if they are controlled by a separate port.

17. Modify the program of Problem 15 so that it blanks all leading zeros in the display. Assume that the display segments are active high. Will your program work properly if all the digits are zeros? How would the program and hardware need to be modified if the displays were decoded and used the four least significant data lines? Assume that the decoder is a 7447 device (a hexadecimal digit F blanks the displays).

18. A single digital-to-analog converter (AD7522) is shared among eight output devices. An output port is used to determine which device is active at a particular time (1 = active for a device). Show the hardware and software required by the Intel 8080 or Motorola 6800 to perform this task. How could data from locations LBYTE and HBYTE be sent to the output device identified by the code in location DEVNO? What if the data was always sent to the eight devices in rotation? Assume that the data is stored in an array with the least significant byte for a device followed by the most significant byte for the same device.

19. An analog-to-digital converter is used to perform both 8- and 10-bit conversions. The Analog Devices AD7570 has a short cycle 8-bits input (SC8) that causes the conversion to stop after eight bits if the input is low. In the 8-bit case, data bit 1 is high and data bit 0 is low (only data bits 2 through 9 are used). Show the hardware and software required by the Intel 8080 or Motorola 6800 to allow either 8- or 10-bit operation, depending on whether memory location NBITS contains 8 or 10.

20. A 30-character-per-second terminal is to be attached directly to a parallel input port on a microprocessor. The terminal uses 7-bit data with odd parity, one start bit, and one stop bit. Show the hardware and software required by the Intel 8080 or Motorola 6800 to interface this terminal. How could the terminal be interfaced to the Motorola 6800 with a 6850 ACIA or to the Intel 8080 with a compatible UART having tri-state outputs?

REFERENCES

ALDRIDGE, D., "Analog-to-Digital Conversion Techniques with the M6800 Microprocessor System," Motorola Application Note AN-757, Motorola Semiconductor Products Inc., Phoenix, Ariz., 1975.

Analog-Digital Conversion Handbook, Analog Devices, Inc., Norwood, Ma., 1972.

BACKLER, J., "A Display Casebook," *Digital Design*, Vol. 6, No. 2, February 1976, pp. 44–48.

BAUNACH, S. C., "An Example of an M6800-based GPIB Interface," *EDN*, Vol. 22, No. 17, September 20, 1977, pp. 125–128.

BLAKESLEE, T. R., *Digital Design with Standard MSI and LSI*, Wiley, New York, 1975.

BURSKY, D., "Focus on Data Converters," *Electronic Design*, Vol. 24, No. 19, September 13, 1976, pp. 68–79.

CONWAY, J., "What You Should Know About the 488 and 583 Interface Standards," *EDN*, Vol. 22, No. 15, August 5, 1976, pp. 49–54.

Data Manual, Signetics Corp., Mountain View, Ca., 1976.

EIA Standard RS-232-C: Interface Between Data Terminal Equipment and Data Communications Equipment Employing Serial Binary Data Interchange, Electronic Industries Association, Washington, D.C., 1969.

ETCHEVERRY, F. W., "Binary Serial Interfaces—Making the Digital Connection," *EDN*, Vol. 22, No. 8, April 20, 1976, pp. 40–43.

FULLAGAR, D., et. al., "Interfacing Data Converters and Microprocessors," *Electronics*, Vol. 49, No. 25, December 9, 1976, pp. 81–89.

Guide to Standard MOS Products, American Microsystems Inc., Santa Clara, Ca., 1975.

HILBURN, J. L., and P. N. JULICH, *Microcomputers/Microprocessors: Hardware, Software, and Applications*, Prentice-Hall, Englewood Cliffs, N.J., 1976.

HOLDERBY, W. S., "Designing a Microprocessor-Based Terminal for Factory Data Collection," *Computer Design*, Vol. 16, No. 3, March 1977, pp. 81–88.

HNATEK, E. R., *A User's Handbook of D/A and A/D Converters*, Wiley, New York, 1976.

Intel 8080 Microcomputer Systems User's Manual, Intel Corporation, Santa Clara, Ca., 1975.

KUZDRALL, J. A., "Memory, Peripherals Share Microprocessor Address Range," *Electronics*, Vol. 48, No. 24, November 27, 1975, pp. 105–107.

LAENGRICH, N., "IEEE Std-488/1975—General Purpose Means of Providing Measurement and Stimulus Instrument Communication," *WESCON 1976*, Session 12, Paper 1.

LARSEN, D. G. et. al., "INWAS: Interfacing with Asynchronous Serial Mode," *IEEE Transactions on Industrial Electronics and Control Instrumentation*, Vol. IECI-24, No. 1, February 1977, pp. 2–12.

LOGAN, J. D. and P. S. KREAGER, "Using a Microprocessor: A Real-Life Application. Part 1: Hardware," *Computer Design*, Vol 14, No. 9, September 1975, pp. 69–77.

M6800 Applications Manual, Motorola Semiconductor Products, Inc., Phoenix, Ariz., 1975.

M6800 Microcomputer System Design Data, Motorola Semiconductor Products Inc., Phoenix, Ariz., 1976.

PEATMAN, J. B, *Microcomputer-Based Design*, McGraw-Hill, New York, 1977.

PICKLES, G., "Who's Afraid of RS-232?" *Kilobaud*, Vol. 1, No. 5, May 1977, pp. 50–54.

PSHAENICH, A., "Interface Considerations for Numeric Display Systems," *Motorola Application Note AN-741*, Motorola Semiconductor Products, Inc., Phoenix, Ariz., 1975.

RONY, P. R. and D. G. LARSEN, *The Bugbook I*, E and L Instruments Inc., Derby, Conn., 1974.

RONY, P. R. and D. G. LARSEN, *The Bugbook II*, E and L Instruments Inc., Derby, Conn., 1974.

RONY, P. R. et. al., *The Bugbook III*, E and L Instruments Inc., Derby, Conn., 1975.

RUNYON, S., "Focus on Keyboards," *Electronic Design*, Vol. 20, No. 23, November 9, 1972, pp. 54–64.

The TTL Data Book, Texas Instruments Inc., Dallas, Texas, 1973.

WAKERLY, J. F. "Microprocessor Input/Output Architecture," *Computer*, Vol. 10, No. 2, February 1977, pp. 26–33.

WESTBURG, A., JR., "Displays: Today and Tomorrow," *Digital Design*, Vol. 6, No. 4, April 1976, pp. 64–72.

Microprocessor Interrupt Systems

The subject of this chapter is interrupt-driven input/output. We begin by comparing interrupt-driven I/O and regular I/O and describing the features of interrupt systems. Next, we present some simple examples of interrupts as well as a detailed description of the interrupt systems for the Intel 8080 and Motorola 6800 microprocessors. The chapter concludes with a brief discussion of direct memory access (DMA).

9.1 ADVANTAGES AND DISADVANTAGES OF INTERRUPTS

One of the most difficult problems in the design of I/O sections is timing. The CPU must determine when a peripheral has new data or is ready to accept data. Very slow peripherals like switches or lights, which do not require rapid response, are no problem. The CPU may transfer data to or from such devices at any time; the only problem is unresponsiveness if the processor waits too long.

Faster peripherals are another matter. These devices are generally neither fast enough to keep up with the computer nor slow enough so that any treatment will suffice. Keyboards, teletypewriters, printers, cassettes, modems, data acquisition systems, and many other peripherals fall in this category. As noted earlier, such devices may transfer data either asynchronously or synchronously. If the transfer is asynchronous, the CPU must be sure that the device is ready for each transfer. If synchronous, the CPU must start the process and provide the proper timing.

Waiting for signals and providing time intervals in software waste CPU time and increase the size and complexity of programs. For instance, if the CPU is waiting for the start of transmission from a device with a maximum transfer rate of ten characters per second, it will find the DATA READY flag active once every tenth of a second at most. The checking program, however, is very short:

```
CHK:   READ               DPORT
       AND                #MASK
       JUMP ON ZERO.      CHK
```

If each instruction takes 5 μs, the CPU will check the flag 6700 times in a tenth of a second. Clearly a search that is unsuccessful 99.9% of the time is inefficient.

Even several such checks will hardly occupy the CPU; for example, the CPU could check ten flags 670 times each in a tenth of a second. Furthermore, there may be additional problems. That is,

What happens if one peripheral has data ready while the CPU is servicing another?

What if the first peripheral that the program checks is almost always active?

Checking each peripheral to see if it is ready to transfer data is called *polling*. This procedure is comparable, in systems of any size or complexity, to handling a telephone switchboard by picking up each line successively to see if a caller is on it.

Synchronous peripherals require a precise time interval between transfers. The CPU can provide the delay itself (see Section 8.1) by loading a register and decrementing it a specified number of times. However, the delay completely occupies the processor. If the CPU is to perform other tasks during the interval, then either the programmer must keep track of the time used or the processor must check a timer to see if the interval is over. Both options greatly increase the complexity of the program.

The most common alternative to polling and timing programs is the use of interrupts. An *interrupt* is an input to the CPU that can directly alter the sequence of operations at the hardware level. The interrupt acts like a buzzer, causing the processor to halt its normal operations and respond to the input. Figure 9.1 shows the interrupt as a DATA READY signal; no specific instructions are necessary to examine the READY bit, since a change in its status directly affects the CPU. Figure 9.2 shows an interrupt derived from a timer. The CPU need not provide the timing itself; instead the ending of the time interval causes an interrupt.

Interrupts are obviously useful for handling input/output. It is unnecessary for the CPU to check READY flags or provide timing intervals. Other uses of interrupts include

1. Alarm inputs. Sensors, switches, or comparators may provide these inputs. Alarm conditions are uncommon, but the response time may need to be very short. Figure 9.3 shows an example of a security system.

2. Power fail warning. A power fail interrupt allows the system to save data in a low-power memory or switch to a backup power supply.

Figure 9.1 An input interrupt.

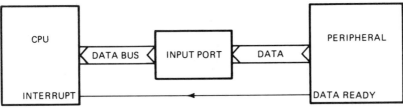

A separate DATA READY port is unnecessary. In response to the interrupt,
the CPU transfers control to the program that reads data from the input port.

Figure 9.2 A timer interrupt.

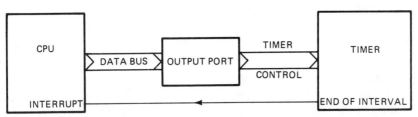

The CPU may set the timer interval and start the timer. The response to the
interrupt depends on the purpose of the timing interval.

Figure 9.3 An alarm interrupt from a security system.

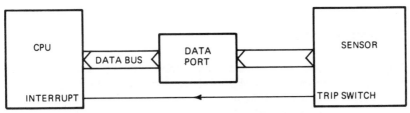

A security system is an obvious candidate for alarm interrupts. Consider the
number of wasted operations if the trip switch were only activated once every
four hours on the average but the desired response time was a fraction of a
second.

The power-fail-detection circuitry (Fig. 9.4) typically is an RC network that senses the loss of power early enough that the CPU can execute many instructions correctly before power is completely lost. Power failures are infrequent events that require immediate action. In fact, a power fail interrupt must take precedence over all other activities, since main power failure will cause a complete system shutdown.

3. Control panel or manual override. An interrupt can allow external control of a system for field maintenance, repair, testing, and debugging.

4. Debugging aids. Interrupts can allow the insertion of corrections, breakpoints, or traces.

Figure 9.4 A power fail interrupt.

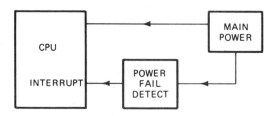

5. Hardware failure indicators.
6. Transmission error indicators.
7. Coordination for multiprocessor systems.
8. Control for direct memory access.
9. Control for operating systems.
10. Performance measurement.
11. Real-time clock. The real-time clock simply provides regularly spaced interrupts at specified intervals of time.

An important factor in determining the usefulness of interrupts is the ratio of the required response time to the time between events. If the response time is much shorter than the average time between events, the processor must check the status flag many times. For instance, if the processor must respond to an event within 1 ms while events only occur once per minute, then the processor will, on the average, search for the event unsuccessfully 120,000 times per minute. Several such bit-checking operations could seriously diminish processor throughput.

Disadvantages of Interrupts

The major disadvantage of interrupts is their random nature. Although this nature is a key to the usefulness of interrupts, it makes interrupt-driven programs difficult to debug and test. Interrupts are contrary to the modern trend toward simpler and more carefully defined programs as represented by structured programming and top-down design.

An interrupt-driven program is actually far less structured than a program with many specific transfers of control. There are, in fact, potential transfers of control everywhere in the interrupt-driven program that do not even appear in the listing. Figure 9.5 shows the structure with the possible transfers of control indicated by dashed lines. Clearly the potential for havoc is enormous.

The usual way to discover errors in interrupt-driven software is to have problems that are time dependent. Errors that occur irregularly are usually in the interrupt system, since the other parts of the program can be repeated. Obviously this approach is not scientific; the debugging and testing of any but the simplest interrupt systems are complex and uncertain. Few develoment systems can generate interrupts randomly or properly analyze test results.

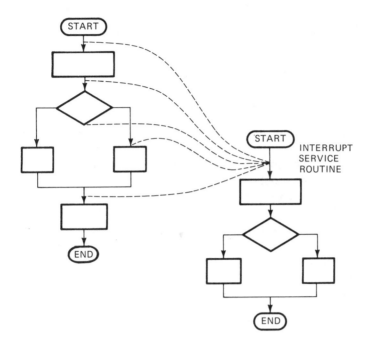

Figure 9.5 Structure of interrupt-driven programs.

Interrupt service routines are often quite difficult to write, since they must operate properly regardless of when the interrupt occurs. The routines may need to save the contents of registers, flags, and memory locations and restore them before returning. Satisfying all the possible requirements may take a large number of instructions, many of which will be wasted in the most common situations.

Interrupt systems also require extra hardware, particularly if many sources can cause interrupts. Typical hardware includes latches and flip-flops that ensure proper recognition of the interrupt signals, gates and encoders that combine interrupt signals from different sources, and data ports that identify the various sources. The amount of hardware increases as the number of sources increases, since rapid identification of the source is essential.

Interrupts are less useful when the I/O data rates are high. They still require data transfers through the CPU and the fetching and decoding of appropriate instructions. In fact, interrupts introduce additional overhead of their own. The advantages of interrupts are less important at high data rates; polling is less inefficient and timing intervals are easier to generate directly from the processor clock. The problem at data rates exceeding 10 kilobits per second is for the processor to keep up with the data transfers while still doing some useful work. Direct memory access systems, which substitute hardware for software control and provide a direct path between the memory and I/O sections, can greatly increase I/O capability at high data rates. These systems involve complex hardware; we will only briefly discuss them at the end of this chapter.

9.2 CHARACTERISTICS OF INTERRUPT SYSTEMS

Basic Features

All interrupt systems must deal with such basic problems as

1. When are the interrupt inputs examined and what signal characteristics are required?
2. How does the processor transfer control to the interrupt service routines?
3. How does the processor save the current state of the computer or *machine status* and restore it after completing the service routine?
4. How does the processor determine which source caused the interrupt?
5. How can the processor distinguish between high-priority interrupts, such as power failure or alarms, and low-priority interrupts, such as a printer that is ready for more data?
6. How can the interrupt system be disabled during programs that should not be interrupted?

Let us deal with these problems in order.

Interrupt Inputs

Although interrupt systems vary widely, most CPUs examine the interrupt inputs only at the end of instruction cycles. Resuming instruction cycles in the middle would require the saving of many intermediate results. The standard technique, therefore, is the one flowcharted in Fig. 9.6. The interrupt signal must be latched, since a complete instruction cycle may be quite long. The signal may also need to be synchronized with the processor clock to ensure recognition. A flip-flop (see Fig. 9.7) can provide the proper timing.

The number of interrupt inputs varies. Table 9.1 contains the number of inputs for some common microprocessors. A single input can, of course, have more than one source, since an OR gate can combine the signals (see Fig. 9.8). An active-low interrupt signal may be obtained without gates by combining open-collector outputs; the interrupt is high (inactive) only if all the open-collector signals are high.

Interrupt Response

The way in which a CPU responds to an interrupt can also vary considerably. The most popular techniques are

1. Executing a CALL or TRAP instruction to a specified address. The Intel 4040 uses this method.

Figure 9.6 Flowchart of instruction cycle with interrupt examination.

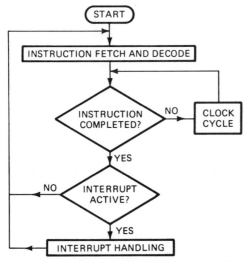

The instruction may require several clock cycles; the CPU only examines the interrupt input at the end of the last cycle.

Figure 9.7 Synchronizing an interrupt signal with the processor clock.

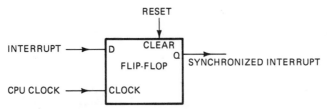

The D flip-flop ensures that the interrupt signal occurs at the proper time in the processor clock cycle.

Table 9.1 Number of Interrupt Inputs

Processor	Number of Interrupt Inputs
Intel 4040	1
Intel 8080	1
MOS Technology 6502	2
Motorola 6800	2
Rockwell PPS-8	3
RCA CDP1802	1
Signetics 2650	1
National PACE	6
Texas Instruments 9900	1
Toshiba TLCS-12	8

Figure 9.8 Combining interrupt inputs with an OR gate.

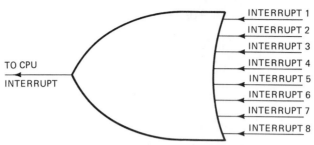

The CPU interrupt input is active (high) if any of the interrupts are high.
However, the CPU cannot distinguish the various interrupt sources internally.

2. Fetching a new value for the program counter from a specified register or memory location. The RCA CDP1802, National SC/MP, and Motorola 6800 use this method.

3. Executing a CALL instruction to an externally supplied address. The Signetics 2650 uses this method.

4. Using an output signal, INTERRUPT ACKNOWLEDGE, to gate an instruction onto the data bus as shown in Fig. 9.9. The Intel 8080 uses this method.

Figure 9.9 Using the INTERRUPT ACKNOWLEDGE signal.

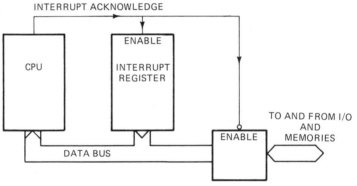

The INTERRUPT ACKNOWLEDGE signal places an instruction from the external interrupt register on the data bus and disables the normal memory access.

The basic tradeoff is between hardware and software. Methods like 1 and 2 require little external hardware but provide no way to identify a source directly. Methods like 3 and 4 are more flexible and can identify sources but require more external hardware.

The processor can transfer control to an interrupt service routine and then back to the original program in the same way that it transfers control to and from subroutines. Any of the techniques described in Chapter 3 for handling subroutines can be used. The JUMP AND MARK PLACE instruction requires a service routine in RAM. The JUMP AND LINK instruction obtains the interrupt service address from a register; this method is fast but takes a register out of normal use and cannot provide multilevel interrupts without additional instructions. The CALL instruction that places the return address in the stack is the most flexible. However, this technique requires external RAM or an on-chip stack, either of which must be shared cautiously between subroutines and interrupt service routines.

Supplying an address or instruction with external hardware can cause many timing and control problems. The external hardware must, of course, not interfere with normal memory cycles; on the other hand, the memory must not interfere with the external hardware when it takes control of the bus. Note in Fig. 9.9 that the INTERRUPT ACKNOWLEDGE signal both places the external address or instruction on the data bus and buffers the usual data from memory away from the bus. Clearly a one-word address or instruction will be much simpler to produce and control than a multiword address or instruction. TTL or MOS encoders can provide some or all the bits. However, single-word addresses or instructions limit the number of distinct inputs and may interfere with page-zero addressing. The alternative is a collection of registers and timing circuits that can place a multiword instruction on the data bus; special LSI controllers may contain the required hardware.

Saving and Restoring Status

Most CPUs automatically save some of the previous status as part of the response to the interrupt input. All CPUs save the old value of the program counter, but some save even more. The Motorola 6800, for example, saves the contents of all its registers in the stack. This method is convenient and saves time when the registers contain useful information; however, it wastes time and memory when they do not. Special instructions, such as SOFTWARE INTERRUPT, TRAP, or WAIT FOR INTERRUPT, may save register contents under program control; instructions like RETURN FROM INTERRUPT or RETURN FROM TRAP restore the status at the end of the interrupt service routine.

Most processors require several instructions to save the old status. Three methods are common.

1. *Storing the contents of registers and flags directly in the memory*. The resulting interrupt service routine cannot itself be interrupted unless a separate area of memory is available for storing the next level of register contents.

2. *Storing the register contents in a memory stack*. This method is simple because the stack pointer contains the storage address; it allows multilevel interrupts. The major inconvenience is that the stack may overflow. The return address is also in the stack, and special exits may require many stack operations.

3. *Switching between sets of registers*. A few processors, such as the Zilog Z-80 and Signetics 2650, have duplicate sets of registers. The interrupt service routine can simply use the other set. This method is faster than either of the previous two methods but means that some of the processor registers are not always available.

Switching does not allow multilevel interrupts, since only two sets of registers exist. The Texas Instruments 9900 uses a designated area of memory as registers, and so all that the interrupt must do is change the pointer that contains the starting address of the area.

Machine status must, of course, be restored before the interrupt service routine ends. The stack method requires that data be restored in the opposite order from which it was saved. The other methods have straightforward restoring techniques.

The number of registers that must be saved depends on the number used by the main program and the interrupt service routine. If the main program simply waits for the interrupt, no registers need be saved or restored. Nor does the interrupt service routine need to save registers that it does not use. In general, interrupt service routines on processors like the Motorola 6800 that have only a few registers must save and restore everything; however, this procedure can be accomplished easily and quickly. With processors like the Intel 8080 or Fairchild F-8, which have many on-chip registers, the programmer must carefully select the registers to be saved. Otherwise the response time for interrupts may become very long.

Determining Interrupt Sources

If a system has more than one potential source of interrupts, the processor must identify the actual source. Processors with several interrupt inputs can respond differently to each input—that is, transfer control to a different register or memory location. Nevertheless, recognition becomes a problem as soon as the number of sources exceeds the number of inputs.

Two common methods for identifying interrupt sources exist: polling and vectoring. *Polling* is similar to the normal examination of DATA READY or PERIPHERAL READY bits; the CPU checks each interrupt bit until it finds one that is active (see Fig. 9.10). *Vectoring* means that each interrupt source provides data (i.e., a *vector*) that the CPU can use for identification. Vectoring is faster and requires less software; polling, on the other hand, requires less hardware.

The advantage of a polling interrupt system over a normal polling system is that the CPU knows that, in the interrupt case, at least one input is active. The only hardware required is an addressable flip-flop for each interrupt bit.

Clearly a polling interrupt system is only adequate for small numbers of sources. Otherwise the time spent identifying the source becomes substantial. Clever software can reduce the average time somewhat by checking the most frequent sources first and by examining groups of sources at a time. Rotation of the order in which sources are checked can keep the average waiting time for all sources the same and can keep one source from blocking the others.

Additional improvements require more hardware. One popular method is the *daisy chain* in which an acknowledge signal propagates through the sources until it is blocked by the actual source. Figure 9.11 shows a daisy chain for an interrupt

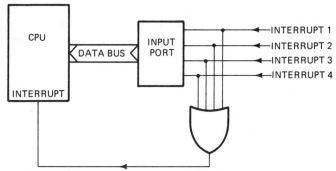

Figure 9.10 A polling interrupt system.

To determine the source of the interrupt, the interrupt service routine must examine the input port and find the active bit.

system with one input and five sources; the interrupt signals must be ORed to provide the input to the CPU. The INTERRUPT ACKNOWLEDGE signal is gated with the interrupt bit from each flip-flop before being passed on to the next one. If a particular flip-flop is set, its output prevents the INTERRUPT AC-KNOWLEDGE bit from reaching sources later in the chain. The left-hand gates produce enable signals that are active only if INTERRUPT ACKNOWLEDGE reaches them and the corresponding flip-flop is set. These enables can then produce the device identification either directly or through an encoder.

Figure 9.11 A daisy-chained interrupt system.

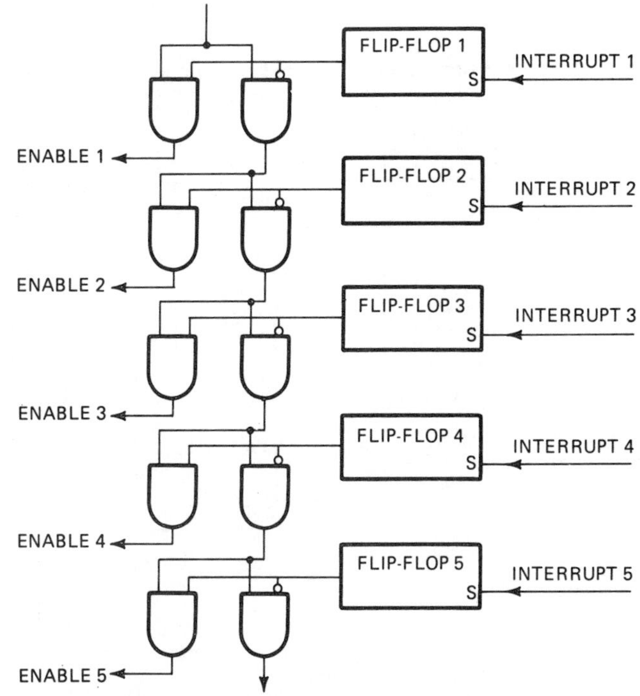

INTERRUPT ACKNOWLEDGE (FROM PROCESSOR)

FLIP-FLOP 1 INTERRUPT 1
S

ENABLE 1

FLIP-FLOP 2 INTERRUPT 2
S

ENABLE 2

FLIP-FLOP 3 INTERRUPT 3
S

ENABLE 3

FLIP-FLOP 4 INTERRUPT 4
S

ENABLE 4

FLIP-FLOP 5 INTERRUPT 5
S

ENABLE 5

The interrupt inputs set RS flip-flops. The circuitry that forms the interrupt signal for the CPU and clears the flip-flops is not shown.

The daisy chain requires no polling and only a few extra gates; additions or deletions are simple. The acknowledge and enable signals may require extra ports. The constraints on the daisy chain are that the program cannot change the priorities, and early sources in the chain will block later ones. The Fairchild F-8, which has interrupt inputs tied to each memory chip, provides a self-contained daisy chain with no external gates. Figure 9.12 shows a typical configuration with three interrupt sources. $\overline{\text{ICB}}$ (INTERRUPT CONTROL BIT) is the acknowledge bit for the daisy chain. Each ROM (3851 Program Storage Unit or PSU) has a PRI IN (PRIORITY INPUT) line and a PRI OUT (PRIORITY OUTPUT) line that form the daisy-chain connections. The active interrupt input blocks further daisy-chain connections and transfers control to an address that is masked into the ROM.

The daisy chain is a type of vectoring, since the interrupt source identifies itself. Direct vectoring systems produce the vector with encoders and control signals and place it on the data bus. Figure 9.13 shows a block diagram of a typical vectored system.

The number of different vectors depends on the complexity of the hardware. Producing a large number of vectors requires complex circuitry, such as a series of encoders or a large PROM. A large interrupt system can employ both vectoring and polling. The vectoring divides the interrupt sources into small groups; polling can then quickly identify a particular source from a group. This combined approach may be much cheaper than complete vectoring and may not require much additional time.

Figure 9.12 A Fairchild F8 daisy-chained priority interrupt system (courtesy of Fairchild Micro Systems, San Jose, Ca.).

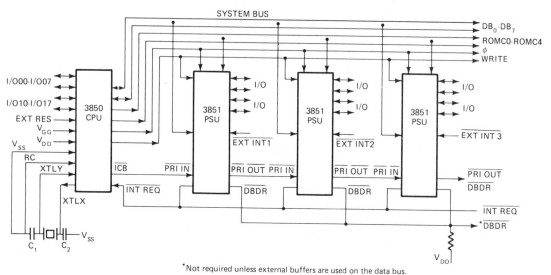

*Not required unless external buffers are used on the data bus.

There are three active-low interrupt sources ($\overline{\text{EXT INT1}}$, $\overline{\text{EXT INT2}}$, and $\overline{\text{EXT INT3}}$) that can produce an interrupt signal ($\overline{\text{INT REQ}}$) to the F8 (3850) CPU.

Figure 9.13 A vectored interrupt system.

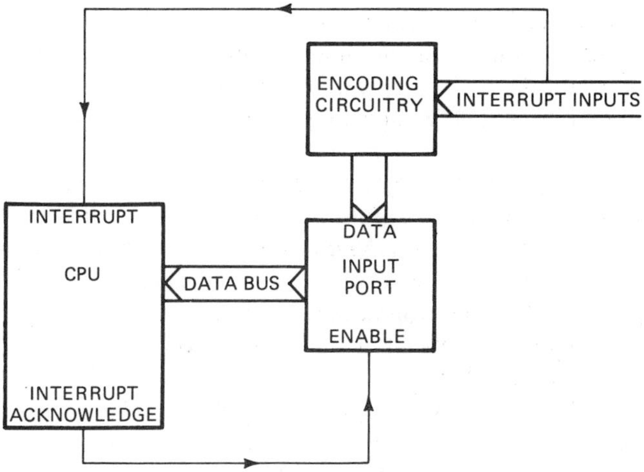

The INTERRUPT ACKNOWLEDGE signal places the vector produced by the encoding circuitry on the data bus. The encoding circuitry may consist of TTL or MOS encoders, simple gates, or a PROM.

The term vectoring refers to the common use of the identification code to produce a jump to a particular service routine. The processor may automatically force the required operation code into the instruction register or the external hardware may have to produce the operation code as well as the vector. Still another alternative is software that forms an address from the identification code and then jumps to that address. Indirect or indexed addressing can provide the jump instruction. This method is slower than the hardware techniques and often results in programs that are quite difficult to follow. The procedure on a processor with register indirect addressing is (a) LOAD REGISTER 1 with the identification code and (b) JUMP @ R1—that is, jump indirectly to the address in register 1. The procedure with indexed addressing is (a) LOAD INDEX REGISTER with the identification code and (b) JUMP 0, X—that is, jump to the address in the index register. Some processors must manipulate the identification code to form an address, since the code may be only a few bits long. A starting address for the interrupt vectors can easily be introduced into any of these procedures.

Priority

Priority methods involve several questions.

1. Which of several simultaneous interrupts will the processor service first?
2. Which interrupts will interrupt other service routines?
3. How will interrupted service routines be handled?
4. How will interrupts that are ignored because of low priority eventually be serviced?

Processors with several interrupt inputs (e.g., the National PACE) may assign a priority to each input. The highest-priority interrupt that is received at a particular time will be the one that is accepted. Other interrupts will have no effect.

Processors having only a single interrupt input can use an external priority encoder to assign priority. TTL encoders will provide a vector and block simultaneous inputs at lower levels. MOS encoders or PROMs can also provide automatic hardware priority.

The priority level may determine which interrupts will be permitted. A processor with several interrupt inputs can simply have an enable or disable associated with each input. This method is the most flexible because it allows priority levels to be individually enabled or disabled. Usually the enabling bits are saved in a register, and so the programmer can determine all the values at once. Internal hardware may set some of the bits automatically when an interrupt is accepted at a particular level.

Processors with a single interrupt input will require external hardware to enable or disable different priority levels. Figure 9.14 shows the use of an external register. Here the CPU will only respond to those interrupts whose levels have been set to one in the register. The program must initialize the register to all ones as part of the startup process; the register contents will also have to be stored in memory (since the register is write-only) so that it can be saved and restored during interrupt service routines.

Figure 9.14 An external priority enabling register.

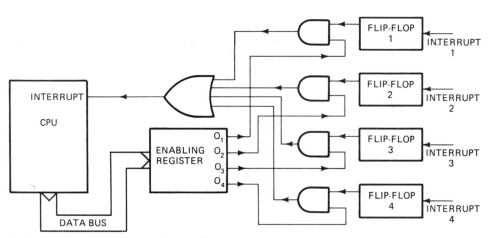

An interrupt input will only cause an interrupt if the corresponding bit of the enabling register is set. An output operation from the CPU determines the value of the enabling register, e.g.,

```
LOAD    #1111B
WRITE   EREG    ; ENABLE ALL INTERRUPTS
```

Another option is to exclude all interrupts at priority levels less than or equal to the level of the one that has just been accepted. The equal priority exclusion stops an interrupt from interrupting its own service routine. A magnitude comparator (7485) can determine if the priority of the new interrupt is greater than that of the current interrupt. The external status register must also have a priority disable bit to bypass the comparison process so that the lowest level of interrupts can be accepted (a priority of zero will only allow interrupts at levels greater than but not equal to zero). Figure 9.15 shows a priority system with a comparator.

Polling and daisy chaining automatically provide priority. Polling gives higher priority to the inputs that are examined earlier. Daisy chaining assigns priority to the earliest elements in the chain; enabling bits can easily enable or disable all interrupts beyond a particular point as shown in Fig. 9.16.

Interrupts that are ignored because of low priority may cause problems in some systems. Latches, of course, must hold the interrupt signals. However, the service times may become quite long and some interrupts may not be serviced at all. Some helpful techniques include automatically raising the priority of an interrupt each time it is passed over, disabling all or part of the priority system at certain times, or looking for lower-priority interrupts before accepting another high-priority one. Fortunately, few microprocessor interrupt systems are sufficiently complex to require any of these methods.

Figure 9.15 A priority interrupt system with a comparator.

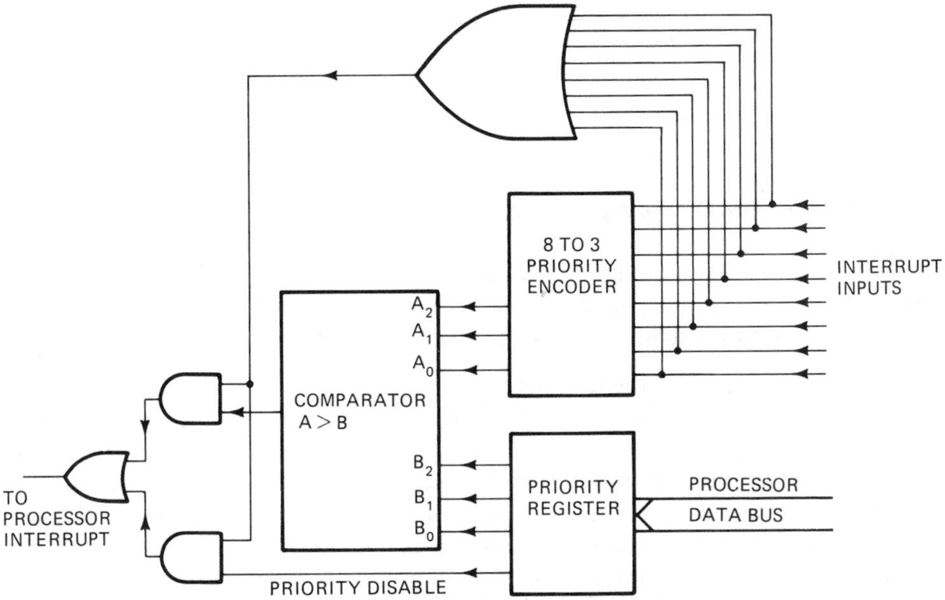

One bit of the priority register disables the comparator. If the priority disable bit is set, any input will interrupt the processor.

Figure 9.16 A daisy-chained priority interrupt system with enables.

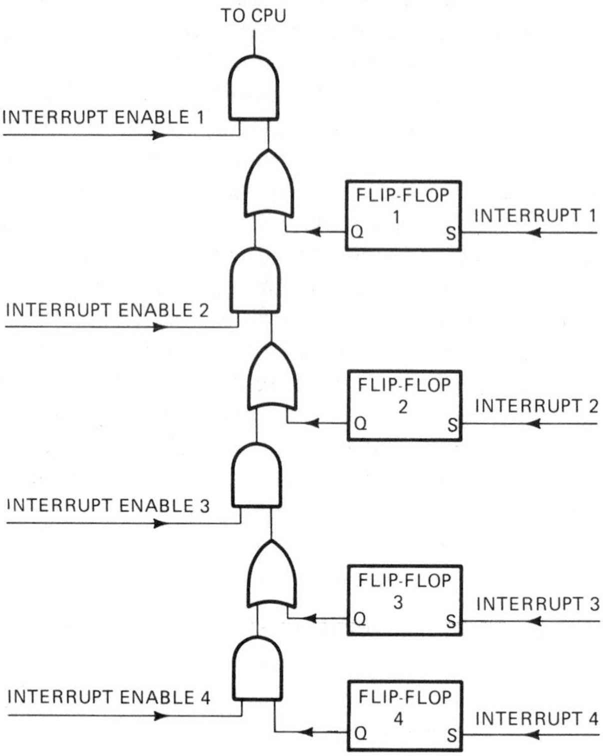

Each enable signal affects all interrupts that are farther from the CPU.

Enabling and Disabling Interrupts

We have discussed enabling and disabling (or *arming* and *disarming*) of interrupts at various times in this section. Almost all CPUs automatically disable interrupts in certain situations. These situations include

1. Reset. Disabling the interrupt system on reset allows the program to load internal and external registers and initialize variables that may be needed during interrupt service and recognition.

2. After an interrupt has been accepted. Disabling the interrupts at this time allows the identification of the interrupt source, the saving of registers, and the handling of priority to proceed without further interruption. The disabling also keeps the interrupt from interrupting its own service routine.

Note that interrupts are disabled until specifically enabled and that the interrupt system must be reenabled before the interrupt service routine ends as part of the restoration of previous status.

A few processors, including the Motorola 6800 and Intel 8085, have a *nonmaskable interrupt* that the processor cannot disable internally. Such an interrupt is useful for power failure, which obviously takes precedence over all other activities. The nonmaskable interrupt can be disabled with external hardware.

9.3 SIMPLE INTERRUPT SYSTEMS

The simplest interrupt-based systems do nothing except wait for an interrupt that indicates the presence of input data. Such data could come from a keyboard, teletypewriter, modem, or converter. Data is received so seldom that the CPU always completes the processing of one set of data before it receives the next set. The interrupt in such a simple system is more a matter of convenience than of necessity; the DATA READY signal from the peripheral is tied directly to the processor interrupt input—neither an additional port nor the software to examine that port are needed.

Figure 9.17 shows the hardware configuration. A transition on the DATA READY line sets the D flip-flop and causes an interrupt. The D flip-flop latches the signal and converts a long signal (i.e., one lasting many clock cycles) into a pulse. The CPU responds to the interrupt by performing the interrupt service routine. The logic that enables the data port during the input operation also clears the flip-flop. Another transition on the DATA READY line will be necessary to cause another interrupt. Additional hardware may be required to direct the CPU to the interrupt service routine.

The main program in such a system will consist of little more than a HALT or WAIT FOR INTERRUPT instruction. If neither is available, an instruction that causes an unconditional jump to itself will have the same effect—that is,

HERE   JUMP   HERE

The main program should start at the RESET address so that the system will operate correctly when power is turned on. Some instructions may be necessary to

Figure 9.17 A single interrupting input port.

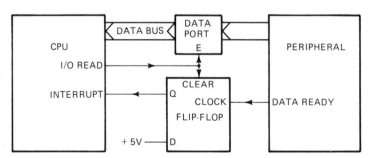

The DATA READY signal sets the flip-flop and interrupts the CPU. The enabling signal for the data port clears the interrupt flip-flop.

prepare for the transfer of control to the interrupt service routine, including initializing the stack pointer, loading a register with the interrupt service address, designating registers for various purposes, initializing a priority register, and other status management operations. The main program must also enable the interrupt system, since RESET disables it. In the system of Fig. 9.17, the service routine need not transfer control back to the main program. In fact, the interrupt service routine can end with a jump to the RESET location that will automatically restore the proper status. Of course, no registers, flags, or memory locations must be saved and no software or hardware is needed to determine the source of the interrupt, since only one source exists. RESET must also clear the external flip-flop so that the system starts in the proper state.

The entire program will be

```
ORG   RSTADD

   .
   .  CONFIGURE PROCESSOR
   .     TO FIND SERVICE
   .       ROUTINE·
   .
ENABLE INTERRUPTS
HALT

ORG   INTADD

   .
   .    PERFORM PROGRAM
   .
   .
JUMP  RSTADD
```

A separate ORIGIN (ORG) pseudo-operation starts the interrupt service routine at the proper address. Figure 9.18 shows the interrupt process through the clearing of the flip-flop.

A Single Output Interrupt

An output interrupt, signifying a device that is ready to receive data, requires a slightly different approach because the processor must prepare the data before sending it. We will examine a simple case in which a single output device provides an interrupt when it is ready to receive data. The transfers are infrequent enough so that no special procedures are necessary to ensure that data is available when the device requests it. Here again the interrupt system is convenient rather than necessary; the interrupt simply provides a direct connection between the PERIPHERAL READY signal and the CPU.

Figure 9.19 shows the hardware configuration. The only differences from the input interrupt of Fig. 9.17 are the direction of the data transfer and the identity of the processor control signal which activates the port and clears the interrupt latch.

Figure 9.18 The interrupt process in a simple case.

(a) Peripheral sends DATA READY signal (and data)

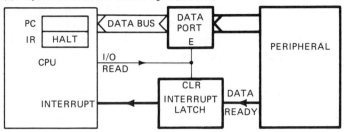

The DATA READY signal is latched and interrupts the CPU, which is executing a HALT instruction.

(b) Processor recognizes the interrupt and transfers control to service routine at memory address INTADD.

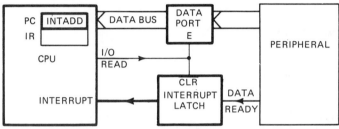

Hardware may be necessary to force address INTADD into the program counter.

(c) Processor reads data from port and clears the interrupt latch.

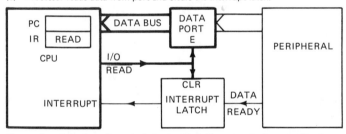

The reading of the data clears the interrupt latch. However, the interrupt is not reenabled until later so that a new pulse on the DATA READY line will be latched but not recognized.

Figure 9.19 A single interrupting output port.

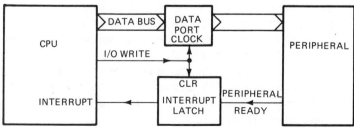

The PERIPHERAL READY signal sets the interrupt latch and interrupts the processor. The I/O WRITE signal clocks the data into the output port and clears the interrupt latch.

451

The main program for the system of Fig. 9.19 must start at the RESET address. It configures the interrupt system, prepares the output data, enables the interrupts, and waits for the PERIPHERAL READY signal. Here again there is no need to return to the main program, save the status, or determine the source of the interrupt.

The assembly language program has the following structure.

```
ORG RSTADD
 .
 .
 .   CONFIGURE PROCESSOR TO FIND
 .      INTERRUPT SERVICE ROUTINE
 .
 .
 .   PREPARE DATA FOR OUTPUT
 .
 .
ENABLE INTERRUPTS

HALT

ORG INTADD
 .
 .
 .   SEND DATA TO OUTPUT DEVICE
 .
 .
 .
 .
JUMP RSTADD
```

Figure 9.20 is a flowchart of the program. Hardware rather than software checks the interrupt bit.

An alternative would be to enable the interrupt immediately after the configuration of the interrupt system. Now the interrupt service routine must determine whether the data is ready or not. The program could employ two flags—DRDY (DATA READY), which is one if the data is ready, and PRDY (PERIPHERAL READY), which is one if the peripheral is ready. Figure 9.21 contains flowcharts of the main program and the interrupt service routine. The main program is the same as before except that ENABLE INTERRUPTS comes before the preparation of the data. The interrupt service routine checks to see if the main program has prepared the data. If the data is ready, the routine sends it and goes back to the beginning of the main program; if the data is not ready, the routine marks that the peripheral is ready by setting PRDY and returns to the main program. Note that after preparing the data, the main program must check PRDY, since the interrupt service routine may have already set it.

In this case, the interrupt service routine must save any registers that it needs to check DRDY and set PRDY, since the main program must be resumed

Figure 9.20 Flowchart of the simple output interrupt program.

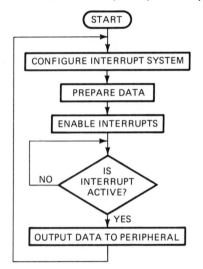

Figure 9.21 Flowchart of the extended output interrupt program.

(a) Main program

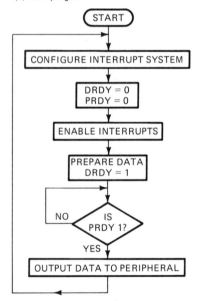

(b) Interrupt service routine

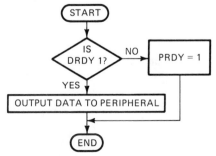

453

correctly. Note also that once an interrupt has been accepted, the interrupt system is not reenabled until after the CPU has transferred the data to the peripheral. This point is essential because the interrupt latch will remain set until the CPU clears it by writing data into the output port.

The program is organized as follows.

```
ORG RSTADD
.
.
.  CONFIGURE INTERRUPT SYSTEM
.
.
CLEAR DRDY
CLEAR PRDY
ENABLE INTERRUPTS
.
.
.  PREPARE DATA
.
.
LOAD #1
STORE DRDY
LOAD PRDY
SUBTRACT #1
JUMP ON ZERO SEND

HALT

ORG INTADD
.
.
.  SAVE REGISTERS AND FLAGS
LOAD DRDY
SUBTRACT #1
JUMP ON ZERO SEND
LOAD #1
STORE PRDY
.
.
.  RESTORE REGISTERS AND FLAGS
RETURN
ORG SEND
.
.
.  TRANSFER DATA TO PERIPHERAL
.
.
JUMP RSTADD
```

The interrupt service addresses in some computers are so close together that there is no room for complete programs. These addresses must contain jumps to the actual service routines. The ORG (origin) pseudo-instruction can place the jump instructions and the actual programs in the proper memory locations.

Although the interrupt latch is separate from the data port in Figs. 9.17 and 9.19, these two units are often a single piece of hardware. For example, both the Intel 8212 I/O port and the Motorola Peripheral Interface Adapter combine the two units as described in Chapter 8. The logic by which the RESET or port selection logic clears the latch is also part of these devices.

Combined Input/Output Interrupt Systems

We can combine the input and output interrupts into a complete interrupt-driven I/O system. Here the input interrupt starts the data preparation process; the output interrupt informs the CPU that the peripheral is ready. The CPU will then send the data as soon as the preparation is complete. Such a simple system could be a low-speed communications front-end, data acquisition system, code converter, key-to-tape or key-to-floppy disk controller, or message handler.

Figure 9.22 shows the required hardware. The input and output interrupting ports are the same as in Figs. 9.17 and 9.19. A separate input port holds the interrupt bits so that the processor can examine them and determine the source of the interrupt. Here we have assumed an interrupt system with a single input and no vectoring; we will describe the use of more complex interrupt systems later.

Figure 9.22 A combined input/output interrupt system.

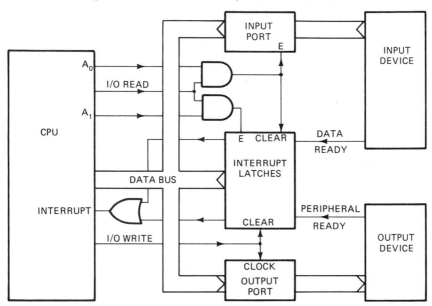

Address line A_0 selects the input data port, address line A_1 the interrupt latches.

The system operates as follows.

Step 1. Input device sends DATA READY signal and data. The DATA READY signal sets an interrupt latch and interrupts the processor (which is halted).
Step 2. In response to the interrupt the CPU starts executing the interrupt service routine at memory location INTADD.
Step 3. The CPU determines the source of the interrupt by examining the interrupt latches and transfers control to the input interrupt service routine.
Step 4. The CPU reads the input data and clears the input interrupt latch.
Step 5. The CPU prepares the output data and waits for the output interrupt.
Step 6. Output device sends PERIPHERAL READY signal. The PERIPHERAL READY signal sets an interrupt latch and interrupts the processor.
Step 7. In response to the interrupt the CPU starts executing the interrupt service routine at memory location INTADD.
Step 8. The CPU determines the source of the interrupt by examining the interrupt latches and transfers control to the output interrupt service routine.
Step 9. The CPU sends the output data (clearing the output interrupt latch) and returns to the halted state that it was in prior to step 1.

The system can simply mark the receipt of the output interrupt (as in the last example) if that interrupt occurs before the data is ready. This procedure assumes that two input operations never overlap—that is, the processor always finishes transferring one set of data before it receives more.

The program for the system of Fig. 9.22 combines the previous input and output programs. The flags DRDY and PRDY contain the status of the data and the output device. The entire program is

```
ORG RSTADD
.
.   CONFIGURE INTERRUPT SYSTEM
.
*   CLEAR DATA, PERIPHERAL FLAGS
CLEAR DRDY
CLEAR PRDY
ENABLE INTERRUPTS

HALT

ORG INTADD
.
.   SAVE REGISTERS AND FLAGS
.
```

```
*   DETERMINE INTERRUPT SOURCE
READ LATCHES
AND   IFLAG
JUMP ON NOT ZERO RCV
*   OUTPUT INTERRUPT
*   SEND DATA IF READY
LOAD DRDY
SUBTRACT #1
JUMP ON ZERO SEND
*   MARK OUTPUT DEVICE READY
LOAD #1
STORE PRDY

.   RESTORE REGISTERS AND FLAGS

.
RETURN
(IFLAG has a one bit in the input interrupt position and zeros elsewhere)
ORG   RCV
ENABLE INTERRUPTS

.
.   PREPARE DATA FOR OUTPUT
.
.
LOAD #1
STORE DRDY
LOAD PRDY
SUBTRACT #1
JUMP ON ZERO SEND

HALT

ORG SEND

.
.   TRANSFER DATA TO PERIPHERAL
.
JUMP RSTADD
```

In this situation, the programmer must carefully determine exactly when interrupts should be enabled. Some of the problem cases are

1. The output interrupt occurs first. If this is possible, the CPU must set PRDY (i.e., output device is ready) and either disable the output interrupt or send the peripheral a break character that it will ignore. The CPU must clear or disable the output interrupt without disabling the input interrupt.

2. The output interrupt occurs during data preparation. The CPU must set PRDY but not reenable the interrupts.

3. A second input interrupt occurs before the output interrupt. If this is possible, the CPU must either disable the input interrupt after accepting one or

must store the extra input data for later processing. The CPU cannot simply ignore the input interrupt without clearing it.

Interrupt service routines always have some dead time during which the interrupt system is disabled and data may be lost. If interrupts occur so frequently that this is a problem, the system should probably not be based on interrupts at all. Interrupt-driven systems work well only when the processor can handle the maximum data rates and interrupts occur many instruction cycles apart.

The program logic will be simpler if the hardware differentiates between the two interrupt sources. Either two separate interrupt inputs or a vectored system can eliminate the hardware and software required to determine which source caused the interrupt. A priority system would also be useful. The input interrupt would have lower priority and would be disabled after an input interrupt had been accepted. However, the output interrupt with higher priority would remain active. The system would not accept further input interrupts until the processor had prepared and transferred the data.

Several features of these simple interrupt-driven systems are important.

1. The program must initialize the interrupt system and other variables before enabling the interrupts.

2. The interrupt service routine can determine the source of an interrupt by examining bits from an input port. Alternatively, separate interrupt inputs or vectoring may direct the processor to a separate service routine for each source.

3. The interrupt service routine must save any registers or flags that it uses if it transfers control back to the main program.

4. The interrupt service routine must reenable the interrupts before transferring control back to the main program and may reenable them earlier if they will not interfere with the routine. Selective enabling and priority methods may block particular interrupts that could cause interference.

5. The interrupt latch must be cleared. This is often a hardware function.

6. The system design must consider the dead time during which the interrupt system is disabled. Not only must interrupt signals be latched but signals that occur too frequently may simply be lost as well. This reaction time limits the maximum rate at which the system can handle interrupts.

Reentrant programs are important in interrupt-driven systems. Not only do they allow multilevel interrupts but they also allow service routines to use subroutines that may have been in use at the time of the interrupt. Such subroutines could include code conversions, character manipulation routines, error checking and correction, and I/O handlers. Writing interrupt-driven programs is difficult enough without having to worry about the hazards of subroutines that may not be reentrant.

The single input and single output system can, of course, be extended. We could add other I/O devices, alarms, timers, control panels, power fail warnings, or breakpoint switches, all of which would provide interrupt inputs. As the number of inputs increases, additional hardware is necessary if the burden on the CPU and the programmer is not to become overwhelming. Determining the source of an interrupt, deciding which interrupts should be enabled at a particular time, and controlling the interrupt signals can all become major tasks. Vectoring can substantially reduce the amount of time, software, and hardware needed to identify the source. Most microprocessor manufacturers now provide special interrupt controllers for use in such applications as data acquisition, switching systems, process and industrial control, and monitoring and security systems. A real-time operating system will also remove much of the burden of handling interrupts from the programmer.[1]

9.4 INTERRUPT SYSTEMS FOR SPECIFIC PROCESSORS

Intel 8080

The Intel 8080 has a single interrupt input that can be disabled in software and that is automatically disabled during RESET and the acceptance of an interrupt. If an interrupt occurs while the system is enabled, the processor completes the current instruction and then executes an INTERRUPT ACKNOWLEDGE cycle. The characteristics of this cycle are

1. INTA (bit 0 of the status information) is 1.
2. MEMR (bit 7 of the status information) is 0.
3. DBIN is active to indicate an input cycle.
4. The CPU does not increment the program counter.

The CPU will thus fetch and decode an instruction but will not derive it from memory (since MEMR = 0). Software and external hardware must provide the rest of the interrupt response. Intel 8080 interrupt systems, therefore, generally require a large amount of external hardware.

The 8080 microprocessor has an instruction that is specifically intended for use in interrupt systems. This is RST (RESTART), a one-word CALL that the external hardware can place on the data bus during an INTERRUPT ACKNOWLEDGE cycle. RST places the current value of the program counter in the stack and causes a jump to address $N_2N_1N_0000$, where $N_2N_1N_0$ is a 3-bit number that is part of the instruction. RST has the binary form $11\ N_2N_1N_0\ 111$. This form is convenient because the one bits can be obtained by tying the data lines together to $+5$ V and $N_2N_1N_0$ can be obtained from an 8 to 3 encoder.

---

[1]See, for example, K. Burgett and E. F. O'Neil, "An Integral Real-Time Executive for Microcomputers," *Computer Design*, Vol. 16, No. 7, July 1977, pp. 77–82.

Table 9.2 shows the interrupt service addresses that the RST instruction can provide. Using the instruction has the following advantages.

1. The hardware need only place a single instruction word on the data bus. INTA can be used as the gating signal.

2. The hardware required to produce RST instructions is quite simple.

3. The instruction can provide eight interrupt vectors, which is enough for many systems.

4. The instruction automatically saves the return address in the stack. Note that RST requires three machine cycles, one to fetch and decode the instruction and two to store the current program counter in the stack and execute the instruction (i.e., place the new value in the program counter).

Table 9.2 Interrupt Service Addresses
Using the RST Instruction

Instruction	Service Address (hexadecimal)
RST 0	0000
RST 1	0008
RST 2	0010
RST 3	0018
RST 4	0020
RST 5	0028
RST 6	0030
RST 7	0038

Since encoders typically use negative logic, RST 7 corresponds to the lowest priority interrupt, RST 0 to the highest.

A Single Interrupt Vector

Since RST 7 is the all ones instruction (i.e., FF hex), a single interrupt vector is easy to produce. RST 7 could, in fact, be created by pullup resistors on the data bus that ensure that all lines are high when no source is driving them. Alternatively, the Intel 8228 system controller can produce the RST 7 instruction. As shown in Fig. 9.23, the $\overline{INTA}$ output of the 8228 device is tied to +12 V through a series resistor. The 8228 controller will then place the RST 7 instruction on the data bus in response to the INTA status signal. No additional hardware is necessary, but the system must poll to find the source of an interrupt. Figure 9.23 shows a typical configuration with several sources. The interrupt service routine that starts at location 38 hex (see Table 9.2) will examine the input port and jump to the correct service routine.

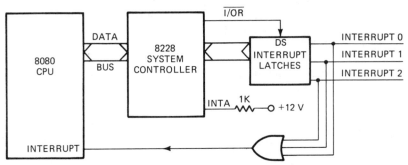

Figure 9.23 An 8080 interrupt system with a single vector.

Any of the three interrupt sources causes the processor to execute an RST 7 instruction which transfers control to the service routine starting in location 38 hex.

The program is

```
    ORG    38H
;   SAVE REGISTERS
    PUSH   PSW
    PUSH   B
    PUSH   D
    PUSH   H
;   DETERMINE INTERRUPT SOURCE
    IN     PORT     ;  GET INTERRUPT BITS
    RAR             ;  LOOK AT BIT 0
    JC     INT0
    RAR             ;  LOOK AT BIT 1
    JC     INT1
    JMP    INT2
```

The programs starting at addresses INT0, INT1, and INT2 will handle the particular interrupts. Extending this program to more sources is easy but results in more time spent examining the interrupt bits. Such systems require very little external hardware but do not take advantage of the vectoring capability of the Intel 8080. The systems are, of course, satisfactory if there are only one or two interrupt sources.

Multiple Interrupt Vectors

Creating several different vectors requires an interrupt instruction port to place one of the RST instructions on the data bus. Figure 9.24 shows the logic for such a port. INTA enables the buffers on the 8212 port and allows it to control the data bus. The circuitry forms the RST instructions by deriving input bits 2, 3, and 4 from an 8 to 3 TTL encoder (74148). The active-low encoder inputs normally come from the active-low $\overline{\text{INT}}$ outputs of 8212 I/O ports. These outputs also must produce an interrupt input to the CPU. The interrupt vectors are in inverse order as described in Table 9.3.

Figure 9.24   Generating RST instructions with a TTL encoder.

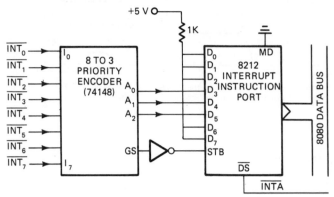

Table 9.3 contains the resulting RST instructions.

Table 9.3   Interrupt Vectors from a Priority Encoder

Highest-Priority Active Input	Instruction
0	RST 7
1	RST 6
2	RST 5
3	RST 4
4	RST 3
5	RST 2
6	RST 1
7	RST 0

A typical interrupt-driven program for a system like the one in Fig. 9.24 would have separate interrupt service routines for each peripheral. An example using the three lowest-priority inputs would be organized as follows.

```
;
;  RESET TO REACH MAIN PROGRAM
;
   ORG   0
   JMP   MAIN
;
```

```
;   SERVICE ADDRESS FOR INTERRUPT #2
;
    ORG    28H
    JMP    INT2
;
;   SERVICE ADDRESS FOR INTERRUPT #1
;
    ORG    30H
    JMP    INT1
;
;   SERVICE ADDRESS FOR INTERRUPT #0
;
    ORG    38H
    JMP    INT0
```

The service addresses themselves are too close together to allow entire programs to be placed there.

Saving Prior Status

The RST instruction automatically saves the old value of the program counter in the stack so that the interrupt service routine can restore it with a RETURN instruction. The main program must initialize the stack pointer before enabling the interrupt system. A typical sequence is

```
;
;   RESET TO REACH MAIN PROGRAM
;
    ORG    0
    JMP    MAIN
;
;   CONFIGURE INTERRUPTS AND ENABLE
;
    ORG    MAIN
    LXI    SP, LASTM    ; PLACE STACK AT END OF MEMORY
    EI                  ; ENABLE INTERRUPTS
```

The interrupt service routines must save and restore any registers, flags, and memory locations used. The simplest method is to push the prior status into the stack on entering the service routine and pop it from the stack before leaving. A typical entering sequence is

```
;   SAVE REGISTERS AND FLAGS
    PUSH   PSW
    PUSH   B
    PUSH   D
    PUSH   H
```

Restoring is performed in the opposite order—that is,

```
;   RESTORE REGISTERS AND FLAGS
    POP   H
    POP   D
    POP   B
    POP   PSW
```

Each PUSH or POP instruction transfers the contents of two registers to or from the stack. Note especially the register pair PSW (the processor status word), which consists of the accumulator (most significant bits) and the flags (least significant bits). Figure 9.25 shows how the entering sequence stores the status in the stack. The program must save the contents of the accumulator before performing any input operations for polling purposes and must restore the registers before executing a RETURN instruction.

Figure 9.25   Storing status in the Intel 8080 stack.

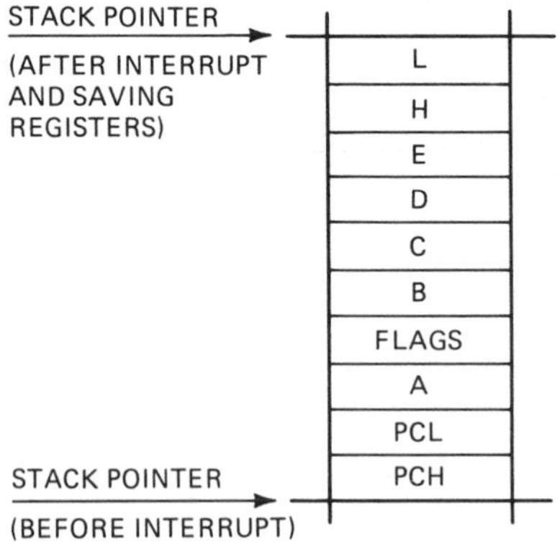

STACK POINTER	
(AFTER INTERRUPT AND SAVING REGISTERS)	L
	H
	E
	D
	C
	B
	FLAGS
	A
	PCL
STACK POINTER	PCH
(BEFORE INTERRUPT)	

PCH and PCL are the eight most and eight least significant bits of the program counter, respectively. The order of operations is RST, PUSH PSW, PUSH B, PUSH D, and PUSH H.

Priority Interrupt Systems

A priority interrupt system requires a register, an encoder, a comparator, and some gates (see Fig. 9.15). If the encoder outputs are active-low, the register must be loaded with the complement of the priority level and the interrupt signal derived from the LESS THAN output of the comparator. Remember that the comparator must have a disabling circuit in order to accept interrupts at the lowest level, since the priority circuit only permits interrupts at levels above the current priority.

This simple priority scheme works well with Intel 8080 systems because the TTL encoder can provide both the RST instruction and the comparator inputs. The Intel 8214 Priority Interrupt Control Unit (see Fig. 9.26) greatly reduces system package count by combining a priority encoder, comparator, priority register, and control circuitry. The important features of the 8214 are

1. A 4-bit current status register enabled by $\overline{ECS}$. The processor can treat the register as an output port. $\overline{SGS}$, the most significant bit of the status register, enables the priority comparator if it is low. Table 9.4 describes the status register contents that allow interrupts at various levels.

2. A request latch and priority encoder. These devices provide a 3-bit active-low output to the comparator and to external lines for use in an RST instruction.

3. A 3-bit priority comparator.

Figure 9.26 The Intel 8214 Priority Interrupt Control Unit (courtesy of Intel Corp.).

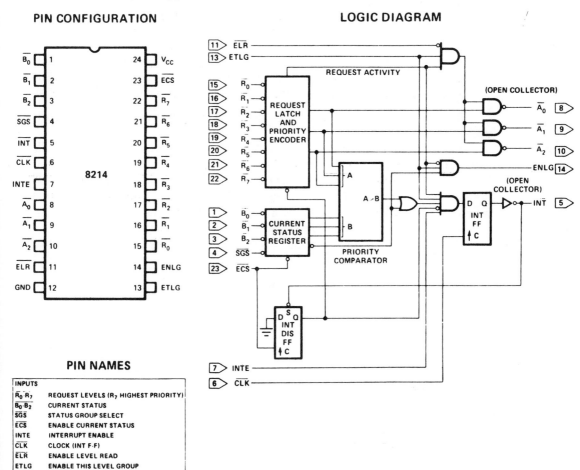

PIN CONFIGURATION

LOGIC DIAGRAM

PIN NAMES

INPUTS	
$\overline{R_0} \cdot \overline{R_7}$	REQUEST LEVELS (R_7 HIGHEST PRIORITY)
$\overline{B_0} \cdot \overline{B_2}$	CURRENT STATUS
$\overline{SGS}$	STATUS GROUP SELECT
$\overline{ECS}$	ENABLE CURRENT STATUS
INTE	INTERRUPT ENABLE
$\overline{CLK}$	CLOCK (INT F·F)
$\overline{ELR}$	ENABLE LEVEL READ
ETLG	ENABLE THIS LEVEL GROUP
OUTPUTS:	
$\overline{A_0} \cdot \overline{A_2}$	REQUEST LEVELS ⎤ OPEN
$\overline{INT}$	INTERRUPT (ACT. LOW) ⎦ COLLECTOR
ENLG	ENABLE NEXT LEVEL GROUP

Table 9.4 Intel 8214 Status Register Contents for Various Priority Levels

Minimum Request Level Accepted	Intel 8214 Status Register Contents			
	$\overline{SGS}$	$\overline{B2}$	$\overline{B1}$	$\overline{B0}$
0	1	1	1	1
1	0	1	1	1
2	0	1	1	0
3	0	1	0	1
4	0	1	0	0
5	0	0	1	1
6	0	0	1	0
7	0	0	0	1

Figure 9.27 shows the use of the 8214 Priority Interrupt Control Unit as a complete eight-level controller for an Intel 8080 priority interrupt system. The designer should note the following requirements of systems based on the Intel 8214.

1. The main program must load the priority register with all ones before enabling the interrupt system.

2. The program must save a copy of the current priority in RAM since the CPU cannot read the contents of the 8214 status register.

3. Each interrupt service routine must save the old priority in the stack, place the new priority in the 8214 status register before reenabling the interrupts, and restore the previous priority before returning to the main program.

4. All priority levels are the logical complements of the actual values.

5. The 8214 does not latch the request inputs. Usually the 8212 ports latch these inputs.

A typical interrupt-driven program using the Intel 8214 will be organized as follows.

```
;
; RESET ROUTINE
;
    ORG  0
    JMP  MAIN
;
; ENTRY POINT FOR INTERRUPT 6
;
    ORG  08H
    JMP  INT6
;
; ENTRY POINT FOR INTERRUPT 5
;
```

Figure 9.27 An eight-level Intel 8080 priority interrupt system based on the 8214 controller (courtesy of Intel Corp.).

PRIORITY REQUEST	RST	D7	D6	D5	D4	D3	D2	D1	D0
		1	1	A2	A1	A0	1	1	1
LOWEST 0	7	1	1	1	1	1	1	1	1
1	6	1	1	1	1	0	1	1	1
2	5	1	1	1	0	1	1	1	1
3	4	1	1	1	0	0	1	1	1
4	3	1	1	0	1	1	1	1	1
5	2	1	1	0	1	0	1	1	1
6	1	1	1	0	0	1	1	1	1
HIGHEST 7	*0	1	1	0	0	0	1	1	1

*RST 0 WILL VECTOR PROGRAM COUNTER TO LOCATION 0 (ZERO) AND INVOKE THE SAME ROUTINE AS "RESET" INPUT TO 8080.
THIS COULD RE-INITIALIZE THE SYSTEM BASED ON THE ROUTINE INVOKED.
(A CAUTION TO SYSTEM PROGRAMMERS.)

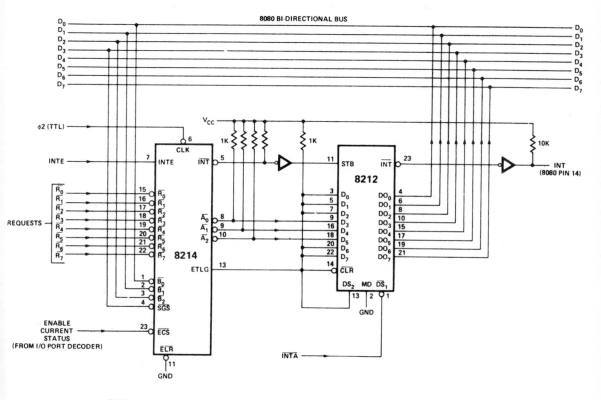

```
        ORG   10H
        JMP   INT5

;
;   ENTRY POINT FOR INTERRUPT 4
;
        ORG   18H
        JMP   INT4
;
```

```
;   ENTRY POINT FOR INTERRUPT 3
;
        ORG   20H
        JMP   INT3
;
;   ENTRY POINT FOR INTERRUPT 2
;
        ORG   28H
        JMP   INT2
;
;   ENTRY POINT FOR INTERRUPT 1
;
        ORG   30H
        JMP   INT1
;
;   ENTRY POINT FOR INTERRUPT 0
;
        ORG   38H
        JMP   INT0
;
;   MAIN PROGRAM
;
        ORG   MAIN
;
;   INITIALIZE 8214 STATUS REGISTER
;
        MVI   A, 00001111B
        OUT   SPORT           ;PRIORITY = 0
        STA   PRTY            ;SAVE COPY OF PRIORITY
        EI                    ;ENABLE INTERRUPTS
        .
        .
        .   MAIN PROGRAM
        .
;
;   INTERRUPT SERVICE ROUTINE 3
;
        ORG    INT3
        PUSH   PSW            ;SAVE REGISTERS
        PUSH   B
        PUSH   D
        PUSH   H
        LDA    PRTY
        PUSH   PSW            ;SAVE OLD PRIORITY
        MVI    A,00000100B    ;NEW PRIORITY LEVEL = 3
        OUT    SPORT          ;SAVE COPY OF NEW PRIORITY
        STA    PRTY
        EI
```

```
        .
        .
      . INTERRUPT SERVICE ROUTINE
        .
POP    PSW              ;RESTORE OLD PRIORITY
STA    PRTY
OUT    SPORT
POP    H                ;RESTORE REGISTERS
POP    D
POP    B
POP    PSW
RET
```

This example only shows the interrupt service routine at level 3 but the others are similar. Note that each service routine must store a priority value in the 8214 status register before enabling interrupts and must restore the old priority value before returning control to the interrupted program.

Extended Interrupt Systems

Interrupt systems based on the RST instruction and the 8214 controller can handle small numbers of inputs without complex hardware or software. Still, such systems have the following disadvantages in situations that involve more inputs and need more flexibility.

1. There are only eight RST instructions. Fully vectored systems with more than eight inputs require considerably more hardware and software.
2. The interrupt vectors always lie in the zeroth page of memory. Many systems need these addresses for other purposes.
3. The interrupt vector for the highest-priority input is the same as the RESET address. Extra hardware and software are necessary to differentiate between these two inputs.
4. The priority scheme is fixed. The program can only enable or disable interrupts at or below a particular level. The program cannot conveniently rotate priorities, change the levels, or update the priority of unserviced interrupts.
5. The priority method only allows groups of interrupts to be enabled or disabled. There is no provision for enabling or disabling specific levels.

The Intel 8259 Programmable Interrupt Controller can resolve many of these problems in larger systems. This device (see Fig. 9.28) permits any of a variety of priority schemes under program control; it generates a 3-byte CALL instruction with a programmable base address so that the interrupt service addresses can be placed anywhere in memory. The Intel 8228 system controller provides the three timing pulses necessary to gate the CALL instruction onto the data bus. Each 8259 device provides eight vectors, and eight such devices may be combined in the interrupt system.

Figure 9.28 The Intel 8259 Programmable Interrupt Controller (courtesy of Intel Corp.).

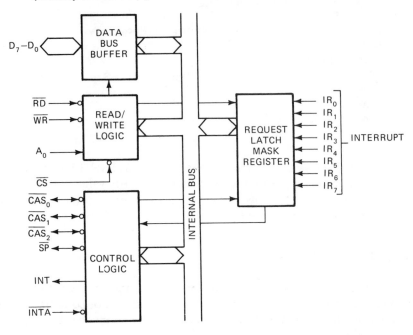

Table 9.5 describes the interrupt modes available with the Intel 8259 controller. Clearly this device provides a more flexible and more expandible system than does the Intel 8214.

Table 9.5 Programmable Interrupt Modes Using the 8259 Controller (Courtesy of Intel Corp.)

Mode	Operation
Fully nested	Interrupt request line priorities fixed at 0 as highest, 7 as lowest
Auto rotating	Equal priority. Each level, after receiving service, becomes the lowest priority level until next interrupt occurs.
Specific	System software assigns lowest-priority level. Priority of all other levels based in sequence numerically on this assignment.
Polled	System software examines priority-encoded system interrupt status via interrupt status register.

Typical 8080 Interrupts

Switch-based interrupts

Switch-based interrupts are convenient for inserting breakpoints, transferring control to an external panel, or allowing the operator to enter instructions or data. For instance, a simple breakpoint facility could print all the register contents and then resume operation.

The program is as follows (either the system monitor or the main program must initialize the stack pointer and enable interrupts).

```
        ORG     INTADD
        PUSH    PSW             ;SAVE REGISTERS IN STACK
        PUSH    B
        PUSH    D
        PUSH    H
        LXI     H,0             ;USE STACK POINTER AS
        DAD     SP              ;   DATA POINTER
        MVI     B,10            ;10 BYTES IN REGISTERS
PRREG:  MOV     A,M
        CALL    PRINT           ;PRINT CONTENTS OF A REGISTER
        INX     H
        DCR     B
        JNZ     PRREG
        POP     H               ;RESTORE REGISTERS FROM STACK
        POP     D
        POP     B
        POP     PSW
        EI                      ;ENABLE INTERRUPTS
        RET
```

This program prints the contents of all the general-purpose registers, the accumulator, the flags, and the program counter. Subroutine PRINT must perform the necessary code conversion and formatting and send the contents of the accumulator to the system printer.

Timer interrupts

Timer interrupts are convenient for generating real-time outputs and for handling peripherals. For example, a system could employ a programmable timer that uses an *RC* network to establish its basic pulse width (see Fig. 9.29). The inputs are a START pulse that begins the timing interval and 4 bits of data that determine its length.

Assume that

1. A data input FULL causes the timer to produce a pulse 9.1 ms long.

2. A data input HALF causes the timer to produce a pulse 4.55 ms long.

3. The mask START has a one bit in the position that starts the timer and zeros elsewhere; for instance, for the system in Fig. 9.29, START is 00010000.

4. Bit 7 of port TTY is a serial teletypewriter input.

Figure 9.29 Using a programmable timer (or baud rate generator).

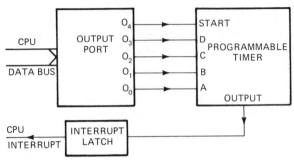

Inputs A, B, C, and D (D most significant) determine the number of stages in the timer—that is, each increase of 1 in these inputs doubles the interval length.

A teletypewriter input program based on the timer interrupt will operate as follows.

```
        ;
        ;   LOOK FOR START BIT
        ;
SRSTB:  IN      TTY         ;GET SERIAL DATA
        ANA     A           ;IS IT A START BIT (ZERO)?
        JM      SRSTB       ;NO, WAIT
        ;
        ;   CLEAR DATA, BIT COUNT
        ;
        SUB     A
        STA     TTYD        ;DATA = 0
        STA     BITCT       ;BIT COUNT = 0
        ;
        ;   SET TIME TO ONE HALF BIT TIME
        ;
        MVI     A,HALF      ;TIMER TO ONE-HALF BIT TIME
        ORI     START       ;PULSE START
        OUT     TIMER
        XRI     START
        OUT     TIMER
        ;
        ;   WAIT FOR CHARACTER
        ;
        EI
WAITC:  LDA     BITCT       ;HAVE 11 BITS BEEN RECEIVED?
        CPI     11
        JNZ     WAITC       ;NO, WAIT

        .
        .   REST OF PROGRAM
        .
```

```
        ;
        ;   TIMER INTERRUPT
        ;
            ORG     TINTP
            PUSH    PSW
            LDA     BITCT           ;BIT COUNT = BIT COUNT + 1
            INR     A
            STA     BITCT
            CPI     10              ;LOOK FOR STOP BITS IF COUNT > 9
            JNC     STOPS
            IN      TTY             ;GET SERIAL DATA
            RAL
            LDA     TTYD            ;ADD BIT TO TTY CHARACTER
            RAR
            STA     TTYD
            JMP     TDLY
        ;
        ;   LOOK FOR STOP BITS
        ;
STOPS:      IN      TTY             ;GET SERIAL DATA
            RAL
            JNC     FRERR           ;FRAMING ERROR IF STOP BIT NOT 1
            LDA     BITCT           ;LOOK FOR LAST STOP BIT
            CPI     11              :IF LAST, DO NOT SET TIMER
            JZ      LAST
        ;
        ;   SET TIMER TO 1 BIT TIME
        ;
TDLY:       MVI     A,FULL          ;TIMER TO 1 BIT TIME
            ORI     START           ;PULSE START
            OUT     TIMER
            XRI     START
            OUT     TIMER
            EI
LAST:       POP     PSW             ;RESTORE A AND FLAGS
            RET
```

The CPU can perform other tasks during the teletypewriter bit times, since it need not provide the timing. A possible modification would be to double-buffer in software—that is, to let the program handle one buffer while the input device is filling another.

Most microprocessor manufacturers provide a programmable timer specifically designed for use with their processor. The Intel 8253, for example, contains three 16-bit counters with programmable modes. The Intel SBC 80/20 Single Board Computer uses two of these devices to provide the functions described in Table 9.6. A timer is also included in the 8155 2K RAM.

Table 9.6 Programmable Timer Functions for the Intel SBC 80/20 Single Board Computer (Courtesy of Intel Corp.)

Programmable Timer Functions	
Function	Operation
Interrupt on terminal count	When terminal count is reached, an interrupt request is generated. This function is extremely useful for generation of REAL-TIME CLOCKS.
Programmable one-shot	Output goes low upon receipt of an external trigger edge or software command and returns high when terminal count is reached. This function is retriggerable.
Rate generator	Divide by N counter. The output will go low for one input clock cycle, and the period from one low-going pulse to the next is N times the input clock period.
Square-wave rate generator	Output will remain high until one half the count has been completed, and go low for the other half of the count.
Event counter	On a jumper-selectable basis, the clock input becomes an input from the external system. CPU may read the number of events occurring after the counting "window" has been enabled or an interrupt may be generated after N events occur in the system.

Timers Register Addresses (Hex notation, I/O address space)	
Control register	DF
Timer 1	DC
Timer 2	DD

Note: Timer counts loaded as two sequential output operations to same address, as given.

Input Frequencies	
Reference	1.0752 MHz $\pm$ 0.1% (0.930 μs period, nominal)
Event Rate	1.1 MHz max

Note: Maximum rate for external events in Mode 4: Event Counter.

Output Frequencies/Timing Intervals					
Mode	Function	Single Timer/Counter		Dual Timer/Counter (Two Timers Cascaded)	
		Minimum	Maximum	Minimum	Maximum
0	Real-time interrupt	1.86 μsec	60.948 msec	3.72 μsec	1.109 hrs
1	Programmable one-shot	1.86 μsec	60.948 msec	3.72 μsec	1.109 hrs
2	Rate generator	16.407 Hz	537.61 kHz	0.00025 Hz	268.81 kHz
3	Square-wave rate generator	16.407 Hz	537.61 kHz	0.00025 Hz	268.81 kHz

Keyboard interrupts

The strobe from a keyboard may serve as an interrupt input. If the keyboard causes an interrupt, the processor need not continually scan the keyboard or examine the latched strobe. For instance, the following interrupt service routine stores the input from an encoded keyboard in an array, updates the array pointer and the length of the array, and checks for an ASCII period that ends the line. Figure 9.30 is a flowchart of the program. The data pointer (KPTR and KPTR + 1) contains the address of the next empty location in the array; the array length (KLENG) contains the number of characters in the array.

Figure 9.30 Flowchart of keyboard interrupt program.

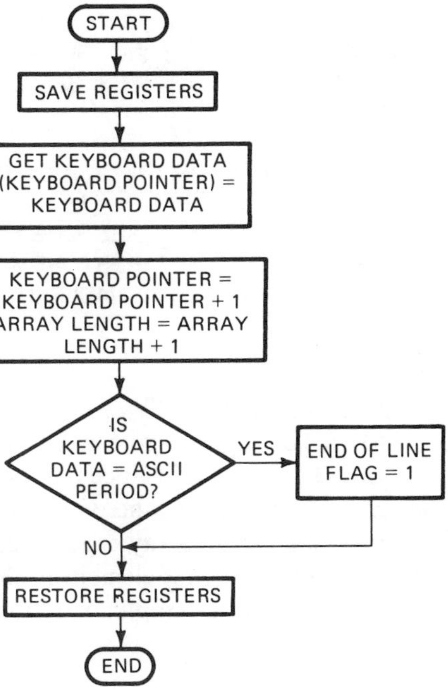

```
;
;  KEYBOARD INTERRUPT PROGRAM
;
     ORG      INTADD
;
;  SAVE REGISTERS IN STACK
;
     PUSH     PSW               ;SAVE A AND FLAGS
     PUSH     H                 ;SAVE H AND L
;
;  SAVE KEYBOARD DATA IN ARRAY
;
```

```
        LHLD    KPTR                    ;GET NEXT ADDRESS IN ARRAY
        IN      KBD                     ;GET KEYBOARD DATA
        MOV     M,A                     ;STORE DATA IN ARRAY
;
;   UPDATE ARRAY POINTER AND COUNTER
;
        INX     H
        SHLD    KPTR                    ;UPDATE ARRAY POINTER
        LXI     H,KLENG
        INR     M                       ;UPDATE ARRAY COUNTER
;
;   SET END OF LINE FLAG IF DATA IS ASCII PERIOD
;
        CPI     '.'                     ;IS CHARACTER A PERIOD?
        JNZ     ENDKY                   ;NO, GO TO END OF ROUTINE
        LXI     H,EOLF                  ;YES, SET END OF LINE FLAG
        MVI     M,1
;
;    RESTORE REGISTERS FROM STACK AND RETURN
;
ENDKY:  POP     H                       ;RESTORE H AND L
        POP     PSW                     ;RESTORE A AND FLAGS
        EI                              ;ENABLE INTERRUPTS
        RET
```

UART interrupts

The TRANSMITTER BUFFER EMPTY and RECEIVER BUFFER FULL or OUTPUT DATA AVAILABLE signals from a UART may also cause interrupts as shown in Fig. 9.31. Then the CPU need not examine these bits. The interrupt service routines can simply transfer the data and clear the interrupts.

The transmission routine can use an array exactly like the one formed by the keyboard routine. The routine sends the first element in the array if one exists and reduces the array length; if the array is empty, it sends the SYNCHRONOUS IDLE character. The program is

```
;
;   TRANSMIT INTERRUPT PROGRAM
;
        ORG     TRINT
;
;   SAVE REGISTERS IN STACK
;
        PUSH    PSW                     ;SAVE A AND FLAGS
        PUSH    H                       ;SAVE H AND L
;
;   GET SYNCHRONOUS IDLE (SYN) CHARACTER IF
;     ARRAY LENGTH IS ZERO
;
```

```
        LXI     H,LENG
        MOV     A,M             ;GET ARRAY LENGTH
        ANA     A               ;IS LENGTH 0?
        MVI     A,SYN           ;GET SYN CHARACTER
        JZ      SENDC           ;SEND SYN IF LENGTH IS ZERO
    ;
    ;   GET DATA FROM ARRAY, UPDATE POINTER AND LENGTH
    ;
        DCR     M               ;ARRAY LENGTH = ARRAY LENGTH − 1
        LHLD    DPTR            ;GET DATA POINTER
        MOV     A,M             ;GET DATA
        INX     H
        SHLD    DPTR            ;DATA POINTER = DATA POINTER + 1
    ;
    ;   SEND DATA TO UART
    ;
SENDC:  OUT     TPORT           ;DATA TO UART
    ;
    ;   RESTORE REGISTERS FROM STACK AND RETURN
    ;
        POP     H               ;RESTORE H AND L
        POP     PSW             ;RESTORE A AND FLAGS
        EI                      ;ENABLE INTERRUPTS
        RET
```

Figure 9.31 Interrupts from a UART.

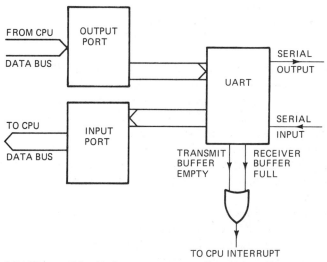

A UART compatible with the processor system will contain the I/O ports and the interrupt gating circuitry.

The interrupt service routine uses a counter and a pointer to obtain information from the main program (i.e., the data to be transmitted) and to transfer information to the main program (i.e., that one character from the array has been transmitted).

Converter interrupts

An analog-to-digital converter may interrupt the processor to indicate the completion of the conversion. The interrupt service routine can place the data in an array if necessary. The CPU need not check the conversion completed signal or execute a delay routine.

Motorola 6800

The Motorola 6800 microprocessor responds to an interrupt by fetching a new value for the program counter from a particular pair of memory locations. Table 9.7 contains the addresses used by the various inputs and instructions. The processor automatically saves all the registers in the stack (see Fig. 9.32) but has no special provisions for determining the sources of interrupt inputs.

Table 9.7 Memory Map for Motorola 6800 Interrupt Vectors (Courtesy of Motorola Semiconductor Products, Inc.)

| Vector | | Description |
MS	LS	
FFFE	FFFF	Reset
FFFC	FFFD	Nonmaskable Interrupt
FFFA	FFFB	Software Interrupt
FFF8	FFF9	Interrupt Request

The Motorola 6800 does not provide an INTERRUPT ACKNOWLEDGE signal or identify the interrupt recognition cycle other than by the address used. There are three special instructions for the interrupt system--RTI (RETURN FROM INTERRUPT), SWI (SOFTWARE INTERRUPT), and WAI (WAIT FOR INTERRUPT). RTI restores all the registers from the stack and reverses the interrupt procedure; SWI stores all the registers in the stack just like the response to an external interrupt and places the contents of memory locations FFFA and FFFB in the program counter; WAI stores all the registers in the stack and waits for an interrupt.

The Motorola 6800 actually has two active-low interrupt inputs: $\overline{IRQ}$, the regular interrupt, and $\overline{NMI}$, the nonmaskable interrupt. These inputs can provide two separate vectors. In practice, however, the nonmaskable interrupt is difficult to use because it cannot be disabled internally while the system is being configured. Our discussion here is restricted to the $\overline{IRQ}$ input.

Figure 9.32 Saving the status of the Motorola 6800 microprocessor in the stack (courtesy of Motorola Semiconductor Products, Inc.).

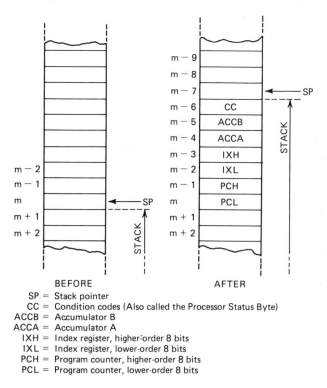

SP = Stack pointer
CC = Condition codes (Also called the Processor Status Byte)
ACCB = Accumulator B
ACCA = Accumulator A
IXH = Index register, higher-order 8 bits
IXL = Index register, lower-order 8 bits
PCH = Program counter, higher-order 8 bits
PCL = Program counter, lower-order 8 bits

The interrupt (disable) bit on the Motorola 6800 is bit 4 of the condition code register. The instruction SEI (SET INTERRUPT) disables the interrupt and CLI (CLEAR INTERRUPT) enables it. The response to an interrupt automatically saves the condition code register (and hence the INTERRUPT bit) in the stack. An RTI instruction at the end of the service routine will restore the old condition code register and reenable the interrupt unless the routine specifically changes the data in the stack.

PIA Interrupts

Most Motorola 6800 interrupt systems derive their inputs from Peripheral Interface Adapters. Each PIA has two active-low open-collector interrupt outputs, $\overline{IRQA}$ and $\overline{IRQB}$ (one for each side of the PIA). These open-collector outputs can be wire-ORed together to form the $\overline{IRQ}$ input to the processor.

The PIA contains much of the necessary interrupt circuitry. Bit 7 of the control register is the interrupt latch for signals on control line 1. The CPU can examine this bit to determine if that source caused the interrupt. Bit 6 of the control register is similarly a latch for signals on control line 2 if that line is an input. The PIA automatically resets the interrupt latches when the processor reads the corresponding data register.

Note that writing data into the data register does not clear the interrupt bits. Nor does reading or writing the control register. So the programmer must include an extra instruction that reads the data register (e.g., LOAD) in an output interrupt routine in order to clear the interrupt latch.

The contents of the PIA control register configure the interrupts for that side of the PIA. The important bits are

> bit 0 = 1 to enable the interrupt output derived from control line 1, 0 to disable the output
> bit 1 = 1 to set the interrupt latch (bit 7) from low-to-high transitions on control line 1, 0 to set the latch from high-to-low transitions.

If control line 2 is an input (control bit 5 = 0), then

> bit 3 = 1 to enable the interrupt output derived from control line 2, 0 to disable the output.
> bit 4 = 1 to set the interrupt latch (bit 6) from low-to-high transitions on control line 2, 0 to set the latch from high-to-low transitions.

The PIA control registers therefore allow individual enabling and disabling of each interrupt source. The system must enable the interrupts from each PIA separately, since RESET disables all the interrupts.

A typical interrupt configuration routine will first enable the necessary PIA interrupts and then enable the processor interrupt system. Assuming that RESET has cleared all the control registers, sample routines would be as shown below.

```
*AN INPUT PIA WITH HIGH-TO-LOW TRANSITIONS
    CLR     PIADRA          ALL LINES INPUTS
    CLR     PIADRB
    LDAA    #%00000101      ENABLE PIA INTERRUPTS
    STAA    PIACRA
    STAA    PIACRB
```

Control register bit 2 = 1 to address the data register, bit 0 = 1 to enable the interrupts.

```
*AN OUTPUT PIA WITH LOW-TO-HIGH TRANSITIONS
    LDAA    #$FF            ALL LINES OUTPUTS
    STAA    PIADRA
    STAA    PIADRB
    LDAA    #%00000111      ENABLE PIA INTERRUPTS
    STAA    PIACRA
    STAA    PIACRB
```

Control register bit $1 = 1$ to cause an interrupt from a low-to-high transition on control line 1.

```
*AN INPUT PIA WITH 2 HIGH-TO-LOW INTERRUPT INPUTS
    CLR     PIADRA          ALL LINES INPUTS
    CLR     PIADRB
    LDAA    #%00001101      ENABLE PIA INTERRUPTS
    STAA    PIACRA
    STAA    PIACRB
```

Control register bit $5 = 0$ to make control line 2 an input, bit $3 = 1$ to enable interrupts from control line 2 (a high-to-low transition on that line will cause an interrupt signal and set control register bit 6).

```
*AN OUTPUT PIA WITH 2 LOW-TO-HIGH INTERRUPT INPUTS
    LDAA    #$FF            ALL LINES OUTPUTS
    STAA    PIADRA
    STAA    PIADRB
    LDAA    #%00011111      ENABLE PIA INTERRUPTS
    STAA    PIACRA
    STAA    PIACRB
```

Control register bit $4 = 1$ to make the active transition on control line 2 low to high.

The overall routine, starting at the RESET address, will be organized as follows.

```
    ORG       RSTADD
    LDS       #LASTM        STACK TO END OF MEMORY
    .
    .
    .   CONFIGURE PIAs
    .
    .
    .
    CLI                     ENABLE INTERRUPTS
```

The original RESET address itself will contain the address RSTADD—that is,

```
    ORG       $FFFE
    FDB       RSTADD
```

The interrupt service routine need not explicitly save or restore any registers or flags. The interrupt response stores all the registers in the stack; an RTI instruction at the end of the service routine restores the original status, including the INTERRUPT bit.

Polling Interrupt Systems

The simplest Motorola 6800 interrupt systems use polling to determine the source of the interrupt. In such systems the memory locations that respond to the interrupt vector must contain the address of the start of the polling routine. Incomplete address decoding makes system expansion difficult, since the interrupt addresses (usually in ROM) must always respond to the interrupt vectors. The polling and interrupt service routines may be placed anywhere in memory.

The polling routine examines the interrupt latches in the PIA control registers —that is,

```
LDAA      PIACR
BMI       SERVE
```

The use of bit 7 as the interrupt latch is convenient because this bit is testable as the NEGATIVE bit. A logical AND instruction or a SHIFT instruction will allow the CPU to examine bit 6.

Unfortunately, examining interrupt bits is awkward because the PIA control registers generally do not have consecutive or evenly spaced addresses. So most polling programs contain separate instructions to examine each PIA. As a result, the polling programs are long, slow, and difficult to expand if the number of inputs is large. Polling, as usual, is only adequate for small systems.

Vectored Interrupt Systems

Daisy chaining (see Fig. 9.11) is one way of overcoming the deficiencies of polling in Motorola 6800 systems.[2] Since the Motorola 6800 does not produce an INTERRUPT ACKNOWLEDGE signal, the program must artificially create one for the daisy chain. The program must also fetch the output of the daisy chain and use it as a vector. Figure 9.33 shows a system that uses an extra PIA as an output port for the daisy chain and an input port for the resulting vector. INTERRUPT ACKNOWLEDGE is a latched control output from the PIA. The program uses the vector to index a jump table that contains the addresses of the service routines.

The program itself would be

```
*CONFIGURE CONTROL PIA
     LDAA        #%00110100
     STAA        CPIACR
```

This makes CA2 a latched bit with value zero.

---

[2]See, for example, J. D. Logan and P. S. Kreager, "Using a Microprocessor: a Real-Life Application. Part I—Hardware," *Computer Design*, September 1975, pp. 69–77.

```
*INTERRUPT SERVICE ROUTINE
      ORG       INTADD
      LDAA      #%00111100      INTA = 1 FOR DAISY CHAIN
      STAA      CPIACR
      LDAB      CPIADR          GET VECTOR FROM DAISY CHAIN
      LDAA      #%00110100      INTA = 0 FOR DAISY CHAIN
      STAA      CPIACR
*USE VECTOR TO INDEX JUMP TABLE
      STAB      TPTR + 1        VECTOR IS LSB'S OF OFFSET JUMP
                                   ADDRESS
      LDAB      #TBLMS          GET MSB'S OF JUMP ADDRESS
      STAB      TPTR
      LDX       TPTR
      JMP       TBLLS, X        JUMP TO ADDRESS
```

Figure 9.33 A daisy-chained interrupt system for the Motorola 6800.

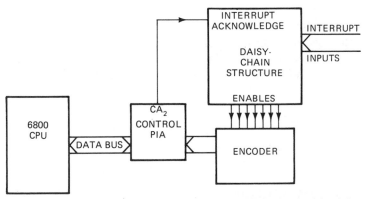

Control line CA₂ provides an INTERRUPT ACKNOWLEDGE signal to the daisy-chain
(see Fig. 9.11). The enables from the chain pass through an encoder, and
the output is available in the data register of the PIA.

TBLMS and TBLLS are the eight most and eight least significant bits of the starting address of the jump table.

Vectored interrupt systems must recognize the fixed interrupt address when it appears on the address bus, for there is no other way of identifying an interrupt response cycle. The decoding circuit that recognizes this address must then supply one of a set of interrupt service vectors to the processor. This procedure involves placing both the most significant and least significant bits of a vector on the data bus with the appropriate timing. The Motorola 6828 Priority Interrupt Controller will perform all the required tasks. The 6828 controller (a) recognizes the interrupt vector, (b) changes the eight least significant bits of this vector according to the highest-priority interrupt input that is active, and (c) inhibits any or all the interrupts according to the contents of a programmable mask register. Each 6828 device can provide eight vectors, and eight such devices can be combined.

Priority Systems

The 6828 controller has prioritizing circuitry. Such circuitry could also be added to other vectored systems. The daisy chain establishes priority according to the position of the interrupt input in the chain.

Simple polling systems may provide priorities in any of the following ways.

1. By the order in which the routine examines the interrupt flags.

2. By enabling or disabling interrupts from particular PIAs before clearing the INTERRUPT bit. This process can be time-consuming, however, since it must handle each PIA separately,

3. By using an external priority register and a comparator to disable interrupts of lower or equal priority.

Typical Interrupts

Switch-based interrupts.

Switch-based interrupts are convenient for breakpoints and control panels. If the switch is connected to line CA1 of a PIA, a breakpoint program will be as follows if the switch is normally in the open (one) position.

```
*
*   CONFIGURE PIA
*
    LDAA    #%00000101
    STAA    PIACRA          ENABLE INTERRUPT
*
*   BREAKPOINT ROUTINE
*
    ORG     INTADD
    LDAA    PIADRA          CLEAR PIA INTERRUPT BIT
    TSX                     STACK POINTER = BASE ADDRESS
                              OF AUTOMATIC REGISTER STORAGE
    LDAB    #7              7 BYTES IN REGISTERS
PRREG LDAA  X
    JSR     PRINT           PRINT CONTENTS OF A REGISTER
    INX
    DECB
    BNE     PRREG
    RTI                     RETURN TO PROGRAM
```

The Motorola 6800 interrupt system is ideally suited to this simple task, for the interrupt automatically places all the register contents in the stack and RTI automatically restores them. Subroutine PRINT must perform the necessary code conversion, formatting, and data transfers to send the contents of the accumulator to the system printer. Note the extra **LDAA PIADRA** instruction that clears the interrupt.

The breakpoint routine could enable other interrupts besides the breakpoint itself. The required program sequences would be

```
*   FIND BREAKPOINT INTERRUPT
        LDAA    PIACRA
        BMI     BRKPT
        .
        .
        .   LOOK FOR OTHER INTERRUPTS
    *   DISABLE BREAKPOINT INTERRUPT
BRKPT  ANDA    #%11111110
        STAA    PIACRA          DISABLE PIA INTERRUPT
        CLI                     ENABLE OTHER INTERRUPTS
    *   REENABLE BREAKPOINT INTERRUPT
        LDAA    PIACRA
        ORAA    #%00000001
        STAA    PIACRA          ENABLE PIA INTERRUPT
        RTI
```

The middle part of the breakpoint program will be the same as before.

Timer interrupts

A typical source of timer interrupts is the Motorola 14536 Programmable Timer, a 24-stage ripple binary counter. A 4-bit select code determines how many of the last 16 stages will be used. The device also has inputs for setting and resetting the counter, inhibiting the clock, and bypassing the first eight stages. The Motorola 6840 Programmable Timer is a similar device that is specifically designed for use with the 6800 microprocessor.

The 14536 Timer can provide various clocking functions, depending on the inputs. Figure 9.34 shows a configuration in which a PIA controls the timer. Here output bits 0 to 3 determine the number of stages to be used and output bit 4 controls the reset input. A low-to-high transition on the output line marks the ending of the time interval.

Figure 9.34   Using a PIA to control the 14536 Programmable Timer.

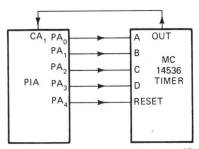

Other data and control lines could give the CPU control over other timer inputs.

The program for the interrupt will be

```
*   CONFIGURE PIA
        LDAA    #%00000110
        STAA    PIACRA
```

Bit 1 = 1 so that a low-to-high transition on CA1 will cause an interrupt.

```
*   RESET TIMER AND ENABLE INTERRUPT
        LDAA    INTRVL
        ORAA    #%00010000
        STAA    PIADRA          RESET TIMER
        ANDA    #%00001111
        STAA    PIADRA          END RESET PULSE
        LDAA    #%00000111
        STAA    PIACRA          ENABLE TIMER INTERRUPT
```

INTRVL contains a single hexadecimal digit that determines the length of the timing interval. Note that the interrupt service routine must read the timer port in order to clear the interrupt.

Keyboard interrupts

The active-low strobe from an encoded keyboard can serve as an interrupt input as shown in Fig. 9.35. The following interrupt service routine will fill an array, ignoring leading ASCII spaces (20 hex) until it receives an ASCII carriage return (0D hex). The main program waits for the line to be completed. Figure 9.36 contains the program flowcharts.

```
*   MAIN PROGRAM
*
*   INITIALIZE INPUT PIA
*
        ORG     RSTADD
        CLR     PIACRA
        CLR     PIADRA          ALL LINES INPUTS
        LDAA    #00000101
        STAA    PIACRA          ENABLE PIA INTERRUPTS
*
*   INITIALIZE LINE BUFFER AND MARKERS
*
        CLR     NONSP           NO NONBLANKS YET FOUND
        CLR     LENGTH          LINE LENGTH = 0
        CLR     EFLAG           NO END OF LINE YET
        LDX     #START          POINTER = START OF BUFFER
        STX     BPTR
*
*   ENABLE INTERRUPTS AND WAIT FOR END OF LINE
```

```
*
            CLI                         ENABLE INTERRUPTS
WAITE       LDAA     EFLAG              IS END OF LINE FLAG ZERO?
            BEQ      WAITE              YES, WAIT
*
*   CONTINUE PROGRAM
*
```

The main program configures the PIA and initializes the pointer, counter, and flags before enabling the interrupts.

Figure 9.35 An interrupt from an encoded keyboard.

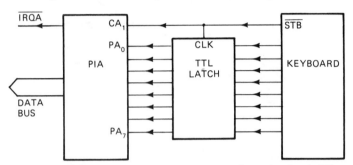

The active-low strobe from the keyboard clocks the latch (remember that the PIA has no input latch) and causes an interrupt from the PIA. Reading the input data clears the PIA interrupt bit.

Figure 9.36 Flowchart of the keyboard program.

(a) Main program

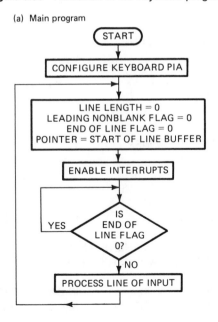

Figure 9.36 (cont.)

(b) Interrupt service routine

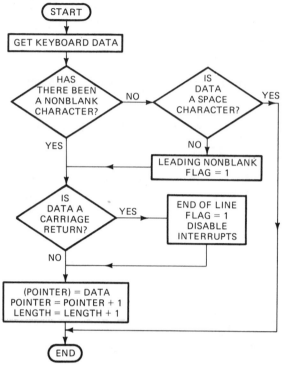

```
*
*   INTERRUPT SERVICE ROUTINE
*
            ORG     INTADD
            LDAA    PIADRA          GET KEYBOARD DATA
*
*           IGNORE LEADING SPACES
*
            LDAB    NONSP           HAS THERE BEEN A NONBLANK
                                        CHARACTER?
            BNE     NOCHK           YES, DON'T CHECK FOR BLANKS
            CMPA    #SPACE          NO, IS DATA A LEADING SPACE?
            BEQ     ENDINT          YES, IGNORE LEADING SPACE
            INC     NONSP           NO, SET NONBLANK FLAG
*
*   SET END OF LINE MARKER AND DISABLE
*       INTERRUPTS IF DATA IS CARRIAGE RETURN
*
NOCHK       CMPA    #CR             IS DATA A CARRIAGE RETURN?
            BNE     NOCR            NO, STORE IN LINE BUFFER
```

```
                INC      EFLAG          YES, SET END OF LINE FLAG
                PULB                    GET CONDITION CODES FROM STACK
                ORAB     #%00010000     DISABLE INTERRUPTS
                PSHB                    RESTORE CONDITION CODES
    *
    *   STORE DATA IN LINE BUFFER
    *
NOCR            LDX      BPTR           GET BUFFER POINTER
                STAA     X              DATA TO LINE BUFFER
                INX                     POINTER = POINTER + 1
                STX      BPTR
                INC      LENGTH         LENGTH = LENGTH + 1
ENDINT          RTI
```

The interrupt service routine sets the interrupt bit (bit 4 of the condition code register) in the stack when it finds a carriage return. Then the program can dispose of the completed line before refilling the buffer. Otherwise RTI will automatically restore the old interrupt bit and reenable the interrupts.

UART interrupts

The Motorola 6850 Asynchronous Communications Interface Adapter can provide both receiver and transmitter interrupts. The transmitter interrupt is enabled only when bit 6 of the ACIA control register is zero and bit 5 is one. The TRANSMITTER DATA REGISTER EMPTY (TDRE) bit then causes an interrupt. Writing data into the transmit data register clears the interrupt.

The receiver interrupt is enabled only when bit 7 of the ACIA control register is one. The RECEIVE DATA REGISTER FULL (RDRF) bit will then cause an interrupt. The CPU can only determine the interrupt source by examining the ACIA status register:

RDRF = bit 0
TDRE = bit 1
IRQ = bit 7

Reading the data will clear an interrupt from the RDRF bit.

In the case of a teletypewriter with 7-bit data, odd parity, and two stop bits, the program to configure the ACIA for both receiver and transmitter interrupts is

```
    *
    *   RESET ACIA
    *
                LDAA     #%00000011
                STAA     ACIACR         MASTER RESET (CLEAR ACIA)
    *
    *   CONFIGURE ACIA
    *
                LDAA     #10100100
                STAA     ACIACR         CONFIGURE ACIA
```

The master reset clears the ACIA, which has no RESET input. The control bits are

bit 7 = 1 to enable receiver interrupt.
bit 6 = 0, bit 5 = 1 to enable transmitter interrupt.
bit 4 = 0, bit 3 = 0, bit 2 = 1 to determine the data format.
bit 1 = 0, bit 0 = 0 to select the clock divide ratio as divide by 1.

The following interrupt service routine will handle both receiver and transmitter interrupts. The steps are (see Fig. 9.37)

1. Determine from the status register whether the interrupt is a receiver or transmitter interrupt (bit 0 = one for receiver, bit 1 = one for transmitter).
2. If the interrupt is a receiver interrupt, place the data in the receiver buffer. RPTR contains the address of the next empty location; RCTR is the number of words in the buffer.
3. If the interrupt is a transmitter interrupt, check if there is data in the transmitter buffer (governed by TPTR and TCTR). If there is, send a word of data to the ACIA; if not, force the ACIA to transmit a break character (FF hex).
4. Transfer control back to the main program.

```
*
*   ACIA INTERRUPT PROGRAM
*
            ORG      AINT
*
*   DETERMINE RECEIVER OR TRANSMITTER FROM REGISTER STATUS
*
            LDAA     ACIASR          GET ACIA STATUS
            RORA                     IS RECEIVE BIT 1?
            BCS      RINT            YES, RECEIVER INTERRUPT
            RORA                     IS TRANSMIT BIT 1?
            BCC      DONE            NO, DONE
*
*   TRANSMITTER INTERRUPT
*
*   DETERMINE IF TRANSMIT DATA AVAILABLE
*
            LDAA     #$FF            GET BREAK CHARACTER
            TST      TCTR            IS TRANSMIT DATA AVAILABLE?
            BEQ      TDATA           NO, TRANSMIT BREAK CHARACTER
*
*   GET DATA FROM TRANSMITTER BUFFER
*
            LDX      TPTR            GET TRANSMITTER BUFFER POINTER
            LDAA     X               GET DATA
            INX
```

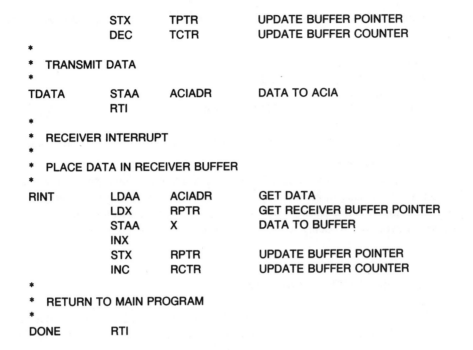

```
                STX      TPTR          UPDATE BUFFER POINTER
                DEC      TCTR          UPDATE BUFFER COUNTER
*
*   TRANSMIT DATA
*
TDATA           STAA     ACIADR        DATA TO ACIA
                RTI
*
*   RECEIVER INTERRUPT
*
*   PLACE DATA IN RECEIVER BUFFER
*
RINT            LDAA     ACIADR        GET DATA
                LDX      RPTR          GET RECEIVER BUFFER POINTER
                STAA     X             DATA TO BUFFER
                INX
                STX      RPTR          UPDATE BUFFER POINTER
                INC      RCTR          UPDATE BUFFER COUNTER
*
*   RETURN TO MAIN PROGRAM
*
DONE            RTI
```

Figure 9.37 Flowchart of ACIA interrupt routine.

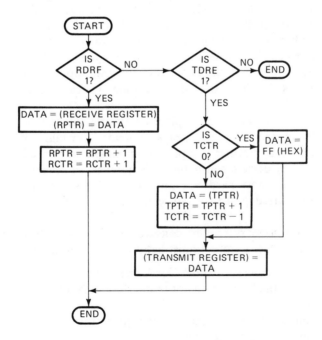

The program could also transmit a break level by setting bit 6 of the ACIA control register to 1—that is,

```
LDAA    #%11100100
STAA    ACIACR          BREAK LEVEL
LDAA    #%10100100
STAA    ACIACR          RESTORE TRANSMITTER INTERRUPT
```

Remember that we cannot examine the write-only control register of an ACIA.

Converter interrupts

The Analog Devices AD7570 Analog-to-Digital Converter described in Chapter 8 can be used in an interrupt mode merely by enabling the interrupt from the BUSY line. A low-to-high transition on this line indicates the end of the conversion process. No delay will then be necessary in the converter program.

9.5   DIRECT MEMORY ACCESS

Direct memory access is an I/O method in which special hardware performs the entire I/O operation. The CPU turns over control of the buses to the DMA controller, which then transfers data directly between the memory and the I/O section. The DMA controller will usually transfer an entire block of data; it will provide addresses and control signals to the memory, update the addresses, count the number of words in the transfer, and signal the end of the operation.

The advantage of direct memory access is speed. Transfers can proceed at a rate only limited by the access time of the memory. The CPU need not fetch and decode the instructions that would transfer the data, update the address and the counter, and check for the end of the operation. Instead the controller performs these tasks at hardware speed.

As is usual when hardware replaces software, the tradeoff is between the speed of hardware and the lower cost and greater flexibility of software. DMA controllers are normally rather complex; even simple ones need 50 to 100 chips, although special LSI devices can reduce this number. In general, the fastest DMA systems involve the most hardware and highest cost. The DMA controller is essentially a specialized processor, since it transfers data much like the regular CPU.

Most microprocessors require considerable hardware to implement DMA. Various methods are used, but all must handle such basic problems as

1. Alerting the processor to the DMA operation.
2. Controlling the buses so as not to interfere with normal processor activities or cause bus contention.
3. Determining the length and location of the transfer.
4. Marking the end of the operation.

As a rule, the processor will do little more than halt its operations and indicate that it is not using the buses. The DMA controller must do the rest.

A simple DMA method is to use cycles when the processor is not accessing the memory. The DMA controller can then use the buses without informing the processor. This technique is called *cycle stealing*. The major problems are identifying the proper cycles and avoiding overlap with processor operations. Some processors produce a signal (for example, VMA on the Motorola 6800) that indicates whether memory is being used. Recognizing internal cycles on other processors requires decoding. For example, the Intel 8080 never accesses the memory during states T_4 and T_5 but a special circuit would be necessary to identify these states. Cycle stealing does not slow processor operations but may require complex timing circuits and allow only occasional and irregular data transfers.

A more common method is to force the processor to relinquish control of the buses for a DMA operation. DMA REQUEST is the signal to the CPU; DMA ACKNOWLEDGE is the response from the CPU. DMA ACKNOWLEDGE can disable tri-state bus buffers and activate the DMA controller. Figure 9.38 shows the required control signals. Common processors like the Intel 8080, Motorola 6800, Signetics 2650, and General Instrument CP-1600 have this type of DMA capability.

Figure 9.38 Control signals for simple DMA capability.

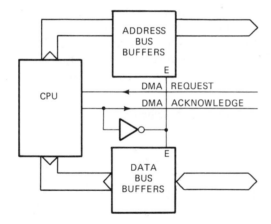

DMA recognition and timing

The DMA REQUEST signal is handled much like the interrupt signal; in other words, the processor only looks for the signal at certain times during normal operations. The signal must be synchronized with the clock. The processor may complete part or all of the current instruction. The Intel 8080 will finish the current machine cycle but will relinquish the buses as soon as it is no longer using them (it will, however, perform actions at the end of the cycle, such as decoding or executing instructions that do not involve the buses). The Motorola 6800 has two separate controls, one of which (TSC or tri-state control) waits only until the end of the clock cycle, whereas the other (HALT) waits until the end of the current instruction. The DMA REQUEST signal must be removed during the last cycle that is being used for DMA. The DMA controller must synchronize all the signals properly.

Controlling the DMA Transfer

Processors use various techniques to determine the starting address and length of a DMA operation. One simple method is for the controller to fetch these parameters from registers. For example, the RCA CDP1802 uses an internal register as the address for a DMA operation; the register contents are automatically incremented at the end of each transfer. This method simplifies the external hardware but requires the initialization and dedication of a register. Processors more commonly manage DMA transfers through the normal input/output channels. To illustrate, the processor may send a starting address, word count, and activation signal to the DMA controller; the DMA controller must contain the required ports and counters.

Like a complex interrupt system, the DMA system may have additional features. Several DMA channels may exist. These channels may have a priority scheme and may interrupt each other. They may also have enabling or disabling mechanisms either individually for each channel or through a priority system. External hardware or special controllers can provide such features. The Intel 8257 Programmable DMA Controller (see Fig. 9.39) has four DMA channels, priority logic, channel inhibit logic, counters, and other circuitry.

Programming of DMA-Based Systems

DMA-based systems are generally easier to program than interrupt-driven systems, since the transfers occur under hardware control. The memory in a DMA-based system acts like an I/O device; the processor must determine when new input data is ready or when output data can be sent. The programmer must make the same provisions for a DMA transfer as for any other I/O transfer. DMA transfers, unlike interrupts, do not affect program structure because no transfer of program control is involved. However, DMA-based systems usually require precise timing and understanding of the I/O transfer; the programming of DMA-based systems shows that well-structured programs must consider the flow of data as well as the flow of control.[3]

---

[3]B. Shneiderman and P. Scheuermann, "Structured Data Structures," *Communications of the ACM*, Vol. 17, No. 10, October 1974, pp. 566–574.

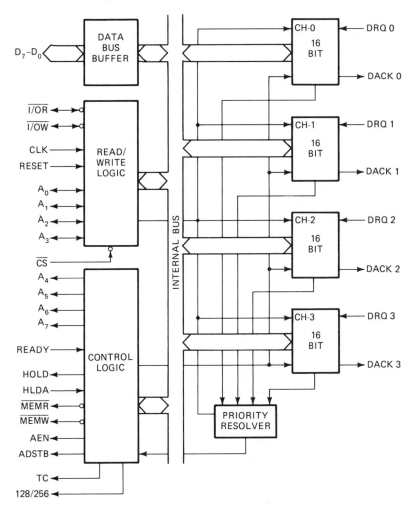

Figure 9.39 Block diagram of Intel 8257 Programmable DMA Controller (courtesy of Intel Corp.).

9.6 SUMMARY

Interrupts are inputs that cause the CPU to suspend its normal operations and respond to external events. Interrupts allow the checking of DATA READY or PERIPHERAL READY flags in hardware rather than in software. They are also useful in handling breakpoints, alarms, power failure, and timing. Their major disadvantages include the extra hardware involved and the effects on program structure. The interrupt system may determine the source of an interrupt either by examining the latched signals (polling) or by obtaining an identification code from the interrupting device (vectoring). Complex interrupt systems may involve multiple inputs or levels and priorities. Intel 8080 interrupt systems depend on external hardware that is activated by the INTERRUPT ACKNOWLEDGE signal and places a RESTART or CALL instruction on the data bus. Motorola 6800 interrupt systems use specific memory addresses that contain a vector; the interrupt service routine can differentiate among interrupt sources by polling the PIAs. Direct memory access is a faster I/O method that uses a separate controller to perform entire block transfers; it provides higher speed at the cost of greater hardware complexity.

PROBLEMS

1. A system has two interrupt-driven inputs: a teletypewriter and a card reader. Describe the differences in the hardware and software requirements for a processor with a single interrupt input and one with two interrupt inputs. What would be the advantages and disadvantages of vectoring or a priority system?

2. A microprocessor-based calculator simply waits for data to be entered from its keyboard. Would such a system require interrupts? What if the calculator could also receive data from a communications line?

3. A processor responds to an interrupt by automatically exchanging the program counter and an address register. What initialization would be necessary before interrupts could be enabled? How could such a processor provide multilevel interrupts? What are the advantages and disadvantages of this technique?

4. A processor uses an on-chip stack of limited length for all return addresses (interrupts and subroutines). How many levels of interrupts and subroutines could a program for such a processor use? How many levels are possible when interrupts are disabled, when interrupts are enabled, or when an interrupt service routine is being executed?

5. An 8-bit microprocessor automatically places a JUMP TO SUBROUTINE instruction in the instruction register in response to an interrupt. However, the external hardware must provide the jump address. Describe how this step could be performed if the processor produced an INTERRUPT ACKNOWLEDGE signal during the next memory cycle and the address only had to be 8 bits long. How could the external hardware provide 8 or 16 different vectors? What would be the additional complications if a 16-bit address were necessary? How many vectors can an 8-bit address provide if jump instructions are two words long? Three words long? Remember that the service addresses must be far enough apart to allow room for a jump to the actual service routine.

6. A daisy-chained interrupt system has four inputs. Describe the process whereby the INTERRUPT ACKNOWLEDGE signal passes through the chain and produces a code at an input port. How could an encoder reduce the number of input lines needed? Show the connection for an eight-input system that produces the interrupt level at the input port—that is, if interrupt 2 is the source, the data at the port should be 2.

7. How would you modify the daisy-chain system of Fig. 9.11 so that the contents of an output port would determine whether each level was enabled (one in the corresponding bit in the output port) or disabled (zero)? How could the interrupt service routine save

and restore the contents of the enabling port if the port were write-only? How would this system differ from the priority interrupt system of Fig. 9.16?

8. Show the hardware required for a single interrupting input port, a single interrupting output port, and one of each, using the Intel 8212 I/O port or the Motorola Peripheral Interface Adapter.

9. How would you implement a two-source interrupt system with the Intel 8080 or Motorola 6800 microprocessors? Assume that both interrupt sources are input devices that provide one character per interrupt. Describe both the hardware and software necessary. Assume that both interrupts are infrequent, both are never active at the same time, and neither is active during the time required to service the other. What would you have to add to the system to accommodate three sources? Four sources? Ten sources?

10. How would you modify the two-source system of Problem 9 so that one interrupt had priority over the other and could interrupt the other's service routine? How would you modify the system so that a lower-priority interrupt never had to wait for more than two higher-priority interrupts to be serviced? Which of the following pairs of devices would you assign as the higher priority and why? Teletypewriter and floppy disk, panel switch and CRT, card reader and 4800 bits per second communications line.

11. A system uses a one-shot as the source of a timer interrupt with a fixed length. Show the interfacing necessary to create such an interrupt with an Intel 8080 or Motorola 6800 microprocessor. Write a starting routine that configures the interrupt system and starts the timing interval and a service routine that sets memory location LATE to one in response to the interrupt. How would you change the service routine so that it did not reenable the interrupts? What if the routine were to enable all interrupts except the timer?

12. What is the minimum separation of interrupt vectors required in the Intel 8080 or Motorola 6800 systems? Describe the advantages and disadvantages of tightly packed and widely spaced vectors—for instance, which are easiest to generate, which requires the least memory, and so on?

13. A rotating priority system means that each interrupt increases in priority by one each time an interrupt is accepted. The highest-priority interrupt becomes the lowest priority. Describe the advantages and disadvantages of such a system. How could it be implemented in an Intel 8080- or Motorola 6800-based microcomputer?

14. A 16-input priority interrupt system may first use an 8 to 3 encoder to divide the 16 inputs into 8 vectored levels. It can then use polling to separate the 2 inputs at each level. Assume that the 8-level vectored system exists and show the additional hardware and software needed to distinguish between the 2 inputs at each level for a Motorola 6800 or Intel 8080 CPU. How could the 2 inputs be given separate priorities?

15. A switch-based interrupt causes an Intel 8080 or Motorola 6800 microprocessor to set a clock from thumbwheel switches as follows.
   (a) Read hours from two BCD-coded thumbwheel switches attached to an input port and place the result in memory location HRS.
   (b) Read minutes from two other BCD-coded thumbwheel switches attached to another input port and place the result in memory location MINS.

(c) Read seconds from two other BCD-coded thumbwheel switches attached to another input port and place the result in memory location SECS.

(d) Resume the interrupted program.

The clock-loading routine cannot itself be interrupted. Show the required hardware and software for the clock-loading interrupt. Would such an interrupt be advantageous if the operator typically set the clock twice a day to one second accuracy? Why?

16. A system uses four presettable 4-bit BCD counters to provide interrupts from 1 to 10,000 clock pulses in length. Show the circuitry required to do so in an Intel 8080 or Motorola 6800 system. Assume that each counter has an ENABLE input. Write a routine that starts the timer interrupt. What if a multiplexer selected one of eight possible clocks for the counter? Show how the microprocessor could control the state of the multiplexer through an output port.

17. The ERROR RESET line (active low) from a keyboard causes an interrupt that empties the keyboard buffer. That is, BCTR is set to zero, BPTR is set to BUFST, the START OF LINE flag (SOLF) is set to zero, and control is transferred to memory location START. Show the hardware and software required to implement such an interrupt on the Motorola 6800 or Intel 8080. Be sure to clear the return address and other register contents from the stack before transferring control to location START.

18. A UART receiver interrupt places the received character in a buffer (RPTR is the next empty address, RCTR is the number of characters in the buffer), and checks for the following ending conditions.

(a) Character = ASCII carriage return—that is, 0D hex.

(b) RCTR = 80

If either condition holds, the routine sets memory location EOLF to 1 and disables the interrupt system in the main program. Write the required interrupt service routine for the Intel 8080 or Motorola 6800 microprocessor.

19. A 16-bit analog-to-digital converter provides an interrupt that results in the data being loaded into memory locations ADAT and ADAT + 1, the flag in memory location DRCV being set to 1, and the interrupt system disabled. Write the required interrupt service routine for the Intel 8080 or Motorola 6800 microprocessor. Show the necessary hardware.

20. How would you modify the system of Problem 18 or Problem 19 so that the disabling only affected that particular interrupt input? What if the only interrupt allowed after the disabling was the real-time clock? Show both the hardware and software required for either the Intel 8080 or Motorola 6800.

REFERENCES

BALDRIDGE, R. L., "Interrupts Add Power, Complexity to μC-System Design," *EDN*, Vol. 22, No. 15, Aug. 5, 1977, pp. 67–73.

BURGETT, K. and E. F. O'NEIL, "An Integral Real-Time Executive for Microcomputers," *Computer Design*, Vol. 16, No. 7, July 1977, pp. 77–82.

CUSHMAN, R. H., "Let the Interrupts Do Their Work," *EDN*, Vol. 21, No. 11, June 5, 1976, pp. 92–97.

CUSHMAN, R. H., "Single-Chip Microprocessors Move into the 16-Bit Arena," *EDN*, Vol. 20, No. 4, February 20, 1975, pp. 24–30.

ECKHOUSE, R. H., Jr., *Minicomputer Systems*, Prentice-Hall, Englewood Cliffs, N.J., 1975.

F8 Microprocessor User's Manual, Fairchild Semiconductor, Menlo Park, Ca., 1975.

FALK, H., "Linking Microprocessors to the Real World," *IEEE Spectrum*, Vol. 11, No. 9, September 1974, pp. 59–67.

FISHER, E., "Speed Microprocessor Responses," *Electronic Design*, Vol. 23, No. 23, November 8, 1975, pp. 78–83.

GRANDBOIS, G.,"Log Data Under μP Control," *Electronic Design*, Vol. 24, No. 10, May 10, 1976, pp. 94–101.

Intel 8080 Microcomputer Systems User's Manual, Intel Corporation, Santa Clara, Ca., 1975.

KHANNA, V., and T. DALY, "Making the Most of Your Micro," *Digital Design*, Vol. 5, No. 7, July 1975, pp. 36–49.

LANE, A., "Microprocessor System Design," *Digital Design*, Vol. 5, No. 8, August 1975, pp. 62–70.

LEWIN, M. H., "Integrated Microprocessors," *IEEE Transactions on Circuits and Systems*, Vol. CAS-22, No. 7, July 1975, pp. 577–585.

LOGAN, J. D., and P. S. KREAGER, "Using a Microprocessor: A Real-Life Application. Part I —Hardware," *Computer Design*, Vol. 14, No. 9, September 1975, pp. 69–77.

MOORE, A., and M. EIDSON, *Printer Control: A Minor Task for a Fast Microprocessor*, Motorola Semiconductor Products, Phoenix, Ariz., 1975.

OSBORNE, A., *An Introduction to Microcomputers, Vol. I, Basic Concepts*, Adam Osborne and Associates, Berkeley, Ca., 1975.

OSBORNE, A., *An Introduction to Microcomputers. Vol. II. Some Real Products*, Adam Osborne and Associates, Berkeley, Ca., 1977.

RIPPS, D. L., "Multitasking Operating Systems Simplify μC Software Development," *EDN*, Vol. 22, No. 2, January 20, 1977, pp. 67–69.

The TTL Data Book, Texas Instruments, Inc., Dallas, Texas, 1973.

VACROUX, A. G., "Explore Microcomputer I/O Capabilities," *Electronic Design*, Vol. 23, No. 10, May 10, 1975, pp. 114–119.

WEISBECKER, J., "A Simplified Microcomputer Architecture," *Computer*, Vol. 7, No. 3, March 1974, pp. 41–47.

WEITZMAN, C., *Minicomputer Systems*, Prentice-Hall, Englewood Cliffs, N.J., 1974.

WELLER, W. J. et al., *Practical Microcomputer Programming. The Intel 8080*, Northern Technology Books, Evanston, Ill., 1976.

WYLAND, D. C., "Increase Microcomputer Efficiency," *Electronic Design*, Vol. 23, No. 23, November 8, 1975, pp. 70–75.

Appendix

1 The Binary Number System

A1.1 INTRODUCTION TO BINARY NUMBERS

Although the decimal number system is in everyday use, computers use the binary system. Using a different number base is rather discomforting for most people even though the decimal system has no justification other than the number of fingers we have. In fact, we occasionally use other number systems, such as base 12 in counting hours, inches, or dozens; base 60 in counting seconds or minutes; and base 7 in keeping track of the days of the week.

The binary number system has only two digits—zero and one. Computers use the binary system because it is easy to tell if electrical devices are on (1) or off (0). Furthermore, electrical and magnetic storage devices having two stable states are simple to construct. Of course, such devices could be combined to handle numbers with larger bases. However, circuitry is the simplest and communications most efficient if only two states are allowed.

Binary numbers are constructed just like decimal numbers except that the base is 2 instead of 10. Thus

$$378 \text{ (decimal)} = 3 \times 10^2 + 7 \times 10^1 + 8 \times 10^0$$

In the same way,

$$101 \text{ (binary)} = 1 \times 2^2 + 0 \times 2^1 + 1 \times 2^0$$
$$= 5 \text{ (decimal)}$$

Table A1.1 contains the binary representations of the first few decimal numbers.

Table A1.1 Decimal-
to-Binary Conversion

Decimal	Binary
0	0
1	1
2	10
3	11
4	100
5	101
6	110
7	111
8	1000
9	1001
10	1010
11	1011
12	1100

In the decimal system the first place is for 1s, the second for 10s, the third for 100s, the fourth for 1000s—that is, each place has a value (or weight) ten times the previous place. In the binary number system the factor is 2 instead of 10; the first place is still for 1s, but the second is for 2s, the third for 4s, the fourth for 8s, the fifth for 16s. Note that between three and four binary digits (the shorthand for binary digit is *bit*) correspond to one decimal digit.

EXAMPLES:
1. 101101 (binary)

$$= 1 \times 2^5 + 0 \times 2^4 + 1 \times 2^3 + 1 \times 2^2 + 0 \times 2^1 + 1 \times 2^0$$
$$= 45$$

2. 11011 (binary)

$$= 1 \times 2^4 + 1 \times 2^3 + 0 \times 2^2 + 1 \times 2^1 + 1 \times 2^0$$
$$= 27$$

Converting Binary to Decimal

Converting binary numbers to decimal is simple, since a bit can only be zero or one. The procedure below will perform the conversion.

1. Multiply the rightmost bit by one.
2. Going right to left, multiply each succeeding bit by twice the factor used with the previous bit.
3. Add the products according to the usual rules of decimal addition.

EXAMPLE: 1110101 (binary)

$$= 1 \times 1 + 0 \times 2 + 1 \times 4 + 0 \times 8 + 1 \times 16 + 1 \times 32 + 1 \times 64$$
$$= 117 \text{ (decimal)}$$

Binary numbers are simple but rather long and cumbersome.

Converting Decimal to Binary

Converting decimal numbers to binary is somewhat more difficult than converting binary numbers to decimal. However, a division procedure can be used. The remainder from a division by 2 is the rightmost bit of the binary representation of the decimal number. This procedure can be extended as follows.

1. Divide the decimal number by 2. Save the remainder.
2. If the quotient is zero, proceed to step 3. If the quotient is not zero, replace the number with the quotient and repeat step 1.
3. The binary representation of the decimal number is the remainders, starting with the first remainder at the right.

EXAMPLES:
1. Convert 105 (decimal) to binary.

Dividing 105 by 2 gives 52,   1 remainder
Dividing 52 by 2 gives 26,   0 remainder
Dividing 26 by 2 gives 13,   0 remainder
Dividing 13 by 2 gives 6,   1 remainder
Dividing 6 by 2 gives 3,   0 remainder
Dividing 3 by 2 gives 1,   1 remainder
Dividing 1 by 2 gives 0,   1 remainder

So 105 (decimal) = 1101001 (binary).
Check:
1101001 (binary)

$$= 1 \times 1 + 0 \times 2 + 0 \times 4 + 1 \times 8 + 0 \times 16 + 1 \times 32 + 1 \times 64$$
$$= 1 + 8 + 32 + 64$$
$$= 105 \text{ (decimal)}$$

2. Convert 531 (decimal) to binary.

Dividing 531 by 2 gives 265,   1 remainder
Dividing 265 by 2 gives 132,   1 remainder
Dividing 132 by 2 gives 66,   0 remainder
Dividing 66 by 2 gives 33,   0 remainder
Dividing 33 by 2 gives 16,   1 remainder
Dividing 16 by 2 gives 8,   0 remainder
Dividing 8 by 2 gives 4,   0 remainder
Dividing 4 by 2 gives 2,   0 remainder
Dividing 2 by 2 gives 1,   0 remainder
Dividing 1 by 2 gives 0,   1 remainder

So 531 (decimal) = 1000010011 (binary).
  Check:
  1000010011 (binary)
$$= 1 \times 1 + 1 \times 2 + 0 \times 4 + 0 \times 8 + 1 \times 16 + 0 \times 32 + 0 \times 64$$
$$+0 \times 128 + 0 \times 256 + 1 \times 512$$
$$= 1 + 2 + 16 + 512$$
$$= 531 \text{ (decimal)}$$

A check of the conversion will ensure that the answer is correct.

The binary number system becomes simple with use. The major inconvenience of the system is that 10 is not an integer power of 2. If computers had preceded people, they would have constructed people with either 8 or 16 fingers so as to overcome this problem. Science fiction writers could probably suggest numerous ways to eliminate this incompatibility.

A1.2 BINARY ARITHMETIC

Binary Addition

Binary addition is exactly like decimal addition except that the rules are much simpler. The addition rules are shown in Table A1.2.

Table A1.2 Binary Addition Table

A	B	A + B
0	0	0
0	1	1
1	0	1
1	1	10

The final entry is the binary version of $1 + 1 = 2$. Binary addition is simple but tiresome, since the numbers are long and the carries numerous.

EXAMPLES:
  1. Add 101101 and 100110

$$\begin{array}{r} 101101 \\ +100110 \\ \hline 1010011 \end{array}$$

Note that there are carries from the second, third, and fifth bit positions (counting from the right and starting with the zeroth position).

Check:

101101 (binary)

$= 1 \times 1 + 0 \times 2 + 1 \times 4 + 1 \times 8 + 0 \times 16 + 1 \times 32$

$= 45$ (decimal)

100110 (binary)

$= 0 \times 1 + 1 \times 2 + 1 \times 4 + 0 \times 8 + 0 \times 16 + 1 \times 32$

$= 38$ (decimal)

1010011 (binary)

$= 1 \times 1 + 1 \times 2 + 0 \times 4 + 0 \times 8 + 1 \times 16 + 0 \times 32 + 1 \times 64$

$= 83$ (decimal)

2. Add 11111 and 111

$$
\begin{array}{r}
11111 \\
+ \quad 111 \\
\hline
100110
\end{array}
$$

Here there are carries from all the first five bit positions.

Check:

11111 (binary)

$= 1 \times 1 + 1 \times 2 + 1 \times 4 + 1 \times 8 + 1 \times 16$

$= 31$ (decimal)

111 (binary)

$= 1 \times 1 + 1 \times 2 + 1 \times 4$

$= 7$ (decimal)

100110 (binary)

$= 0 \times 1 + 1 \times 2 + 1 \times 4 + 0 \times 8 + 0 \times 16 + 1 \times 32$

$= 38$ (decimal)

As with conversions, checking will ensure that the answer is correct.

Representing Negative Numbers

Since subtraction can produce negative results, it requires a binary representation of negative numbers. Normally, the most significant bit is used for the sign; that bit is zero if the number is positive and one if the number is negative. Of course, the numerical position of the most significant bit depends on the word length of the computer; we will assume that all numbers in this discussion are eight bits long. Reserving one bit for the sign reduces the magnitude of the largest number that can be represented by a word, since one less bit is available.

There are several common methods for representing negative numbers, including (a) sign-magnitude, (b) one's complement, and (c) two's complement.

In the sign-magnitude method, the negative number is simply the positive number with the sign bit inverted.

EXAMPLES:

$$7 \text{ (decimal)} = 00000111$$

$$-7 \text{ (decimal)} = 10000111 \quad \text{(sign-magnitude)}$$

$$21 \text{ (decimal)} = 00010101$$

$$-21 \text{ (decimal)} = 10010101 \quad \text{(sign-magnitude)}$$

The sign-magnitude representation makes it easy to obtain the magnitude and the negative of a number. The magnitude is obtained by clearing the most significant bit and the negative by inverting the most significant bit. The sign-magnitude representation is frequently used in A/D and D/A conversion and in accessing such tables as sines, cosines, or squares, which are independent of the sign of the argument (or only sign-dependent on the sign). However, the sign-magnitude representation makes arithmetic difficult because the binary sum of a number and its sign-magnitude negative is not zero.

EXAMPLE:

$$1 \text{ (decimal)} = 00000001$$

$$-1 \text{ (decimal)} = 10000001 \quad \text{(sign-magnitude)}$$

The binary sum of 1 and -1 is

$$
\begin{array}{r}
00000001 \\
+ \ 10000001 \\
\hline
10000010
\end{array}
$$

$$= -2 \quad \text{(sign-magnitude)!}$$

Sign-magnitude numbers are usually converted to another form before arithmetic operations are performed.

In the one's complement representation, the negative of a number is the logical complement (i.e., replace all the zeros in the binary representation by ones and all the ones by zeros).

EXAMPLES:

$$7 \text{ (decimal)} = 00000111$$

$$-7 \text{ (decimal)} = 11111000 \text{ (one's complement)}$$

$$21 \text{ (decimal)} = 00010101$$

$$-21 \text{ (decimal)} = 11101010 \text{ (one's complement)}$$

The one's complement representation is fairly convenient, since the negative of a number is simply its logical complement and the magnitude is either the seven least significant bits or their complement, depending on the most significant bit. The problem with one's complement is that the one's complement of zero is not zero—that is,

$$0 \text{ (decimal)} = 00000000$$

$$-0 \qquad\qquad = 11111111 \text{ (one's complement)}$$

Thus there are two zeros (0 and -0) in one's complement arithmetic. This confusion has made the one's complement representation of negative numbers obsolete.

In the two's complement representation, the negative of a number is the logical complement plus one.

EXAMPLES:
   1.

$$
\begin{array}{rcl}
7 \text{ (decimal)} & = & 00000111 \\
-7 \text{ (decimal)} & = & 11111000 \\
& + & \underline{1} \\
& = & 11111001
\end{array}
$$

   2.

$$
\begin{array}{rcl}
21 \text{ (decimal)} & = & 00010101 \\
-21 \text{ (decimal)} & = & 11101010 \\
& + & \underline{1} \\
& & 11101011
\end{array}
$$

The two's complement representation makes the calculation of negatives and magnitudes more difficult, since it requires a logical complement and an addition. However, twos complement numbers can be easily handled with binary arithmetic circuits.

EXAMPLES:
   1. Add $+2$ and -2 in two's complement binary arithmetic.

$$
\begin{array}{rcl}
+2 & = & 00000010 \\
-2 & = & 11111101 \\
& + & \underline{1} \\
& = & 11111110
\end{array}
$$

Adding gives

$$
\begin{array}{rl}
& 00000000 \\
+ & \underline{11111110} \\
& 00000000
\end{array}
$$

The final carry (at the left) is lost. We will discuss the actual handling of carries later in this section.

  2. Add −7 and +5

$$+5 = \quad 00000101$$

$$-7 = \quad 11111000$$

$$+ \quad \underline{\qquad 1}$$

$$\overline{11111001}$$

Adding gives

$$00000101$$
$$+ \quad \underline{11111001}$$
$$\overline{11111110}$$

The result is the two's complement representation of −2 from Example 1.

Binary Subtraction

Once negative numbers are represented in the two's complement form, binary subtraction becomes quite simple. Subtraction can be performed by adding the two's complement of the number to be subtracted. Carries at the left are lost.

EXAMPLES:
  1.

$$00001011$$
$$- \quad 00000110$$

The two's complement of 00000110 is

$$11111001$$
$$+ \quad \underline{\qquad 1}$$
$$\overline{11111010}$$

So the subtraction is equivalent to the following addition.

$$00001011$$
$$+ \quad \underline{11111010}$$
$$\overline{00000101}$$

  Check:

$$00001011 = 1 \times 1 + 1 \times 2 + 0 \times 4 + 1 \times 8$$
$$= 11$$
$$00000110 = 0 \times 1 + 1 \times 2 + 1 \times 4$$
$$= 6$$
$$00000101 = 1 \times 1 + 0 \times 2 + 1 \times 4$$
$$= 5$$

so $11 - 6 = 5$.
   2.

$$11000011$$
$$- \quad 10110100$$

The two's complement of 10110100 is

$$01001011$$
$$+ \qquad 1$$
$$\overline{01001100}$$

so the subtraction is equivalent to the following addition.

$$11000011$$
$$+ \quad 01001100$$
$$\overline{00001111}$$

Check:

11000011 is clearly a negative number, since its sign bit is one. Taking its two's complement gives

$$00111100$$
$$+ \qquad 1$$
$$\overline{00111101}$$

$$00111101 = 1 \times 1 + 0 \times 2 + 1 \times 4 + 1 \times 8 + 1 \times 16 + 1 \times 32$$
$$= 61 \text{ (decimal)}$$

So 11000011 (binary) $= -61$.

The two's complement of 10110100 has already been found to be 01001100.

$$01001100 = 0 \times 1 + 0 \times 2 + 1 \times 4 + 1 \times 8 + 0 \times 16 + 0 \times 32 + 1 \times 64$$
$$= 76$$

So $10110100 = -76$.

The binary result was

$$00001111 = 1 \times 1 + 1 \times 2 + 1 \times 4 + 1 \times 8$$
$$= 15$$

The decimal arithmetic check gives

$$\begin{array}{rr} 11000011 & -61 \\ - \quad 10110100 & - \quad -76 \\ \hline 00001111 & 15 \end{array}$$

The largest positive number that can be represented by one 8-bit word using the two's complement method is

$$01111111 = 1 \times 1 + 1 \times 2 + 1 \times 4 + 1 \times 8 + 1 \times 16 + 1 \times 32 + 1 \times 64$$
$$= 127$$

The most negative number is

$$10000000$$

The positive number with the same magnitude cannot be represented by eight bits, since the two's complement of the most negative number is itself—that is,

$$
\begin{array}{r}
01111111 \\
+ \qquad 1 \\
\hline
10000000
\end{array}
$$

However, the number is obviously one less than -127, which is given by

$$
\begin{array}{r}
10000000 \\
+ \qquad 1 \\
\hline
10000001
\end{array}
$$

Therefore it must equal -128. This slight asymmetry is characteristic of two's complement representations.

Carry and Overflow

Most computers have a one-bit flag or condition code that saves the carry from the most significant bit of an addition or subtraction. This flag (or CARRY) can be used to implement carries or borrows between words in multiple-precision arithmetic.

EXAMPLE:
Add

$$
\begin{array}{r}
1011000110011100 \\
+ \; 0000100111100001
\end{array}
$$

using 8-bit arithmetic.

Step 1. Add the least significant eight bits of the numbers.

$$
\begin{array}{r}
10011100 \\
+ \; 11100001 \\
\hline
01111101 \quad \text{and a carry}
\end{array}
$$

Step 2. Add the most significant eight bits of the two numbers plus the carry from step 1.

$$
\begin{array}{r}
10110001 \\
+ \quad 00001001 \\
+ \qquad\quad 1 \\
\hline
10111011
\end{array}
$$

So the answer is

$$
1011101101111101.
$$

Note that adding 16-bit numbers on an 8-bit computer requires more than simply two additions, since the second addition must include the CARRY.

Many computers also have a two's complement OVERFLOW flag. This flag is set when the result overflows into the bit position used for the sign.

EXAMPLES:
  1.

$$
\begin{array}{r}
01000000 \\
+ \quad 01000000 \\
\hline
10000000
\end{array}
$$

The answer is clearly incorrect if the numbers are signed because it is negative, whereas the two numbers being added are positive. The OVERFLOW flag is set by this operation. Note that, since 01000000 is decimal 64, the addition is

$$64 + 64 = 128$$

The result is too large for 8-bit two's complement representation.
  2.

$$
\begin{array}{r}
10100000 \\
+ \quad 11000000 \\
\hline
01100000
\end{array}
$$

This answer is also incorrect if the numbers are signed because it is positive, whereas the two numbers being added are negative. This operation would also set the OVERFLOW flag.

Thus the rules for the CARRY and OVERFLOW flags are as follows.

1. The CARRY flag is 1 if there is a carry from the most significant bit position. The CARRY flag is used in multiple-precision arithmetic.

2. The OVERFLOW flag is 1 if the two operands in an addition have the same sign but the result has the opposite sign. The OVERFLOW flag shows whether the magnitude of the result has affected the sign bit. The OVERFLOW flag is only meaningful in signed arithmetic. Overflows from the less significant words are meaningless in multiple-precision arithmetic.

A1.3 OCTAL AND HEXADECIMAL
NUMBER SYSTEMS

Since binary numbers are long and cumbersome, more convenient representations combine groups of three or four bits into octal (base 8) or hexadecimal (base 16) digits. Both representations are much shorter and more convenient than binary but awkward for a user who is accustomed to decimal numbers.

Octal Number System

Table A1.3 contains the octal representations of groups of three binary digits.

Table A1.3 Binary-to-Octal Conversion

Binary	Octal
000	0
001	1
010	2
011	3
100	4
101	5
110	6
111	7

A binary number can be converted to its octal representation by converting each 3-bit segment, starting with the three least significant bits.

EXAMPLES:

1. 00110010 is divided as follows.

$$00|110|010$$

Each 3-bit segment is then converted to an octal digit according to Table A1.3.

$$000 = 0 \text{ (octal)} \qquad \text{The leading zero is assumed.}$$
$$110 = 6 \text{ (octal)}$$
$$010 = 2 \text{ (octal)}$$

So

$$00110010 = 062 \text{ (octal)}.$$

2. 1101101011001 is divided as follows.

$$1|101|101|011|001$$

Each 3-bit segment is again converted to an octal digit according to Table A1.3.

$$001 = 1 \text{ (octal)}$$
$$101 = 5 \text{ (octal)}$$
$$101 = 5 \text{ (octal)}$$
$$011 = 3 \text{ (octal)}$$
$$001 = 1 \text{ (octal)}$$

The answer thus is

$$1101101011001 \text{ (binary)} = 15531 \text{ (octal)}$$

Converting binary numbers to octal is simple, and the octal representation is much shorter. The same table can also be used to convert octal numbers to binary.

EXAMPLES:
1. Convert 276 (octal) to binary. According to Table A1.3,

$$2 = 010 \text{ (binary)}$$
$$7 = 111 \text{ (binary)}$$
$$6 = 110 \text{ (binary)}$$

so

$$276 \text{ (octal)} = 010111110 \text{ (binary)}.$$

2. Convert 405 (octal) to binary. According to Table A1.3,

$$4 = 100 \text{ (binary)}$$
$$0 = 000 \text{ (binary)}$$
$$5 = 101 \text{ (binary)}$$

so

$$405 \text{ (octal)} = 100000101 \text{ (binary)}.$$

Octal numbers can be converted to decimal by using the rules below.

1. Multiply the rightmost octal digit by one.
2. Going right to left, multiply each succeeding digit by eight times the factor used with the previous digit.
3. Add the results, using ordinary decimal addition.

EXAMPLES:
1. Convert 237 (octal) to decimal.

$$237 = 7 \times 1 + 3 \times 8 + 2 \times 64$$
$$= 7 + 24 + 128$$
$$= 159 \text{ (decimal)}$$

2. Convert 3156 (octal) to decimal.

$$3156 = 6 \times 1 + 5 \times 8 + 1 \times 64 + 3 \times 512$$
$$= 6 + 40 + 64 + 1536$$
$$= 1646 \text{ (decimal)}$$

Decimal numbers can be converted to octal by first converting them to binary and then to octal.

Addition, subtraction, multiplication, and division of octal numbers are slightly different than the same operations with decimal numbers because the base is 8 instead of 10. (The octal operations are standard on planets where inhabitants have 8 fingers.)

Table A1.4 Octal Addition Table

+	0	1	2	3	4	5	6	7
0	0	1	2	3	4	5	6	7
1	1	2	3	4	5	6	7	10
2	2	3	4	5	6	7	10	11
3	3	4	5	6	7	10	11	12
4	4	5	6	7	10	11	12	13
5	5	6	7	10	11	12	13	14
6	6	7	10	11	12	13	14	15
7	7	10	11	12	13	14	15	16

Table A1.4 can be used in performing octal arithmetic as follows.

EXAMPLES:

1. Add 136 (octal) and 275 (octal). Adding digit by digit gives

$$6 + 5 = 13 = 3 + \text{a carry}$$

$$3 + 7 = 12 = 2 + \text{a carry}$$

$$2 + 1 \text{ (previous carry)} = 3$$

$$1 + 2 = 3$$

$$3 + 1 \text{ (previous carry)} = 4$$

so

$$
\begin{array}{r}
136 \\
+ \quad 275 \\
\hline
433
\end{array}
$$

2. Add 607 (octal) and 126 (octal). Again adding digit by digit,

$$7 + 6 = 15 = 5 + \text{a carry}$$

$$0 + 2 = 2$$

$$2 + 1 \text{ (previous carry)} = 3$$

$$6 + 1 = 7$$

So

$$
\begin{array}{r}
607 \\
+ \quad 126 \\
\hline
735
\end{array}
$$

Similar tables can be constructed for octal subtraction and multiplications.

Hexadecimal Number System

Table A1.5 contains the hexadecimal representations of groups of four binary digits.

Table A1.5 Binary-to-Hexadecimal Table

Binary	Hexadecimal
0000	0
0001	1
0010	2
0011	3
0100	4
0101	5
0110	6
0111	7
1000	8
1001	9
1010	A
1011	B
1100	C
1101	D
1110	E
1111	F

Note that letters are used for the hexadecimal digits with values 10 through 15. This usage is confusing as well as awkward because numbers constructed in this way can resemble names or words.

Converting a binary number to its hexadecimal representation requires the coding of each 4-bit segment, starting with the four least significant bits.

EXAMPLES:
1. 100110010 is divided as follows.

$$1|0011|0010$$

Each 4-bit segment is then converted to a hexadecimal digit.

$$0001 = 1 \text{ (hex)}$$

$$0011 = 3 \text{ (hex)}$$

$$0010 = 2 \text{ (hex)}$$

so

$$100110010 \text{ (binary)} = 132 \text{ (hex)}.$$

2. 10111011110 is divided as follows.

$$101|1101|1110$$

Each 4-bit segment is then converted to a hexadecimal digit.

$$0101 = 5 \text{ (hex)}$$
$$1101 = D \text{ (hex)}$$
$$1110 = E \text{ (hex)}$$

so

$$10111011110 \text{ (binary)} = 5DE \text{ (hex)}.$$

The hexadecimal representation is more difficult to obtain than the octal representation but is shorter. Converting a hexadecimal number to binary requires using Table A1.5 in reverse.

EXAMPLES:

1. Convert 3BC (hex) to binary. According to Table A1.5,

$$3 = 0011 \text{ (binary)}$$
$$B = 1011 \text{ (binary)}$$
$$C = 1100 \text{ (binary)}$$

so

$$3BC \text{ (hex)} = 001110111100 \text{ (binary)}.$$

2. Convert E09 (hex) to binary. According to Table A1.5,

$$E = 1110 \text{ (binary)}$$
$$0 = 0000 \text{ (binary)}$$
$$9 = 1001 \text{ (binary)}$$

so

$$E09 \text{ (hex)} = 111000001001 \text{ (binary)}.$$

Table A1.6 can be used to convert hexadecimal digits to decimal. The first ten entries are the same in both representations. The rules below allow the conversion of hexadecimal numbers to decimal.

1. Convert each hexadecimal digit to its decimal equivalent using Table A1.6.
2. Multiply the rightmost decimal equivalent by one.
3. Going right to left, multiply each succeeding decimal equivalent by 16 times the factor used with the previous decimal equivalent.

4. Add the results, using decimal addition.

Table A1.6   Hexadecimal-to-Decimal Table

Hex	Decimal
0	0
1	1
2	2
3	3
4	4
5	5
6	6
7	7
8	8
9	9
A	10
B	11
C	12
D	13
E	14
F	15

EXAMPLES:
1. Convert 7EC (hex) to decimal.

$$7EC = 7\ 14\ 12$$

$$= 12 \times 1 + 14 \times 16 + 7 \times 256$$

$$= 12 + 224 + 1792$$

$$= 2028 \text{ (decimal)}$$

2. Convert A03F (hex) to decimal.

$$A03F = 10\ 0\ 3\ 15$$

$$= 15 \times 1 + 3 \times 16 + 0 \times 256 + 10 \times 4096$$

$$= 15 + 48 + 40,960$$

$$= 41,023 \text{ (decimal)}$$

Decimal numbers can be converted to hexadecimal by first converting them to binary and then to hexadecimal.

Hexadecimal numbers can be added, subtracted, multiplied, and divided just like decimal numbers except that the rules are slightly different, since the base is 16 instead of 10. (These rules are standard on planets where inhabitants have 16 fingers.)

Table A1.7 Hexadecimal Addition Table

+	0	1	2	3	4	5	6	7	8	9	A	B	C	D	E	F
0	0	1	2	3	4	5	6	7	8	9	A	B	C	D	E	F
1	1	2	3	4	5	6	7	8	9	A	B	C	D	E	F	10
2	2	3	4	5	6	7	8	9	A	B	C	D	E	F	10	11
3	3	4	5	6	7	8	9	A	B	C	D	E	F	10	11	12
4	4	5	6	7	8	9	A	B	C	D	E	F	10	11	12	13
5	5	6	7	8	9	A	B	C	D	E	F	10	11	12	13	14
6	6	7	8	9	A	B	C	D	E	F	10	11	12	13	14	15
7	7	8	9	A	B	C	D	E	F	10	11	12	13	14	15	16
8	8	9	A	B	C	D	E	F	10	11	12	13	14	15	16	17
9	9	A	B	C	D	E	F	10	11	12	13	14	15	16	17	18
A	A	B	C	D	E	F	10	11	12	13	14	15	16	17	18	19
B	B	C	D	E	F	10	11	12	13	14	15	16	17	18	19	1A
C	C	D	E	F	10	11	12	13	14	15	16	17	18	19	1A	1B
D	D	E	F	10	11	12	13	14	15	16	17	18	19	1A	1B	1C
E	E	F	10	11	12	13	14	15	16	17	18	19	1A	1B	1C	1D
F	F	10	11	12	13	14	15	16	17	18	19	1A	1B	1C	1D	1E

Table A1.7 can be used to perform hexadecimal addition as follows.

EXAMPLES:

1. Add A3F (hex) and 7BA (hex). Adding digit by digit gives

$$F + A = 19 = 9 + \text{a carry}$$

$$3 + B = E$$

$$E + 1 \text{ (previous carry)} = F$$

$$A + 7 = 11 = 1 + \text{a carry}$$

so

$$
\begin{array}{r}
A3F \\
+ \ 7BA \\
\hline
11F9
\end{array}
$$

2. Add 20C (hex) and AF8 (hex). Adding digit by digit gives

$$C + 8 = 14 = 4 + \text{a carry}$$

$$0 + F = F$$

$$F + 1 \text{ (previous carry)} = 10 = 0 + \text{a carry}$$

$$2 + A = C$$

$$C + 1 \text{ (previous carry)} = D$$

so

$$
\begin{array}{r}
20C \\
+ \ AF8 \\
\hline
D04
\end{array}
$$

Similar tables can be constructed for hexadecimal subtraction and multiplication.

Comparison of Octal and Hexadecimal

The hexadecimal representation has the following advantages over the octal representation.

1. It is significantly shorter, particularly for long computer word lengths, such as 48 or 64 bits.

2. The hexadecimal representation is more convenient when the word length is divisible by 4 but not by 3. A 4-, 8-, 16-, or 32-bit word divides evenly into hexadecimal digits but not into octal digits. The octal representation thus requires the placing of zeros ahead of the most significant bit to complete the leading digit.

The octal representation has these advantages over the hexadecimal representation.

1. It is easier to derive from a binary number.

2. Octal numbers cannot be confused with names or words.

3. Converting octal numbers to decimal is simpler, since the digits need not be changed. (All octal digits are also decimal digits, whereas hexadecimal has some letters as well.)

4. Octal arithmetic is simpler and less confusing than hexadecimal arithmetic. Both the octal and the hexadecimal representations of binary numbers are frequently used in computer programming. In fact, special electronic calculators that perform conversions and arithmetic in these number systems are available.

REFERENCES

BARTEE, T. C., *Digital Computer Fundamentals*, McGraw-Hill, New York, 1974.

CHU, Y., *Introduction to Computer Organization*, Prentice-Hall, Englewood Cliffs, N.J., 1970.

ECKHOUSE, R. H., JR., *Minicomputer Systems*, Prentice-Hall, Englewood Cliffs, N.J., 1975.

KATZAN, H., *Introduction to Computer Science*, Petrocelli, New York, 1975.

Appendix

2 Introduction to Logical Functions

This appendix defines the common logical functions and presents some examples of their uses in computer programming and interfacing. It does not deal with logic design or with the implementation of logical functions by circuits.

Mathematicians developed methods (Boolean algebra) for dealing with logical functions in the early nineteenth century. However, these methods remained a mathematical curiosity until the advent of electronic circuit design. Logical functions allow complex circuits to be simply described in terms of their inputs and outputs. Logical functions are useful not only to the hardware designer in implementing circuits but also to the software designer in making decisions, performing arithmetic, recognizing characters and patterns, checking for errors, formatting outputs, and assembling and disassembling data.

A2.1 THE AND FUNCTION

The AND function is well known to everyone. Just as in normal usage, the AND of two inputs is true if and only if each input is individually true. The AND function can be described by a series circuit with two switches as shown in the figure. Obviously current will only flow in this circuit if both switch A and switch B are closed. A common mathematical way to describe a function like the AND is by means of a *truth table*, which gives the value of the function for all possible values (true or false) of the inputs. The following shorthand is used.

1 = true = switch closed
0 = false = switch open

The table below describes the AND function (the shorthand for A and B is A · B—not to be confused with multiplication, although the similarity will be noted later).

A	B	A · B
0	0	0
0	1	0
1	0	0
1	1	1

One of the common uses of logical functions is in implementing binary arithmetic. For example, the next table describes binary addition.

A	B	SUM	CARRY
0	0	0	0
0	1	1	0
1	0	1	0
1	1	0	1

The carry bit is the same as A · B. Thus an AND gate can produce the carry from binary addition.

Binary multiplication also involves the AND function.

A	B	A × B
0	0	0
0	1	0
1	0	0
1	1	1

A × B is equal to A · B, the AND function.

AND gates have three major uses in microcomputer design:

1. To form new control signals externally by combining processor or decoder signals.
2. To select a data input for a shared bus.
3. To determine whether external hardware functions will be activated.

Figure A2.1 shows AND gates used to form new control signals. The CPU has only a limited number of pins for control signals; external gates must form the others. Common combined signals are write pulses for particular sections or parts of sections, activity signals that eliminate bus contention, and pulses that identify particular input or output operations.

Figure A2.1 Forming control signals with AND gates.

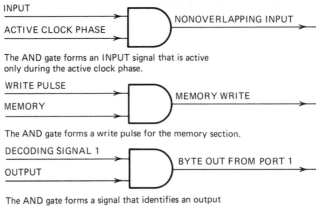

The AND gate forms an INPUT signal that is active
only during the active clock phase.

The AND gate forms a write pulse for the memory section.

The AND gate forms a signal that identifies an output
operation directed to port 1.

Figure A2.2 shows AND gates used to form a busing structure. Mutually exclusive control signals only permit one source to place data on the bus at a time. The inactive (zero) control signals force the outputs of the other AND gates to zero regardless of the values of the data inputs.

Figure A2.2 Forming a busing structure.

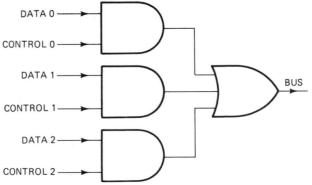

The mutually exclusive control signals (only one is high) determine which data
input appears on the bus.

Figure A2.3 shows an AND gate used to determine whether a counter will be clocked. This structure allows direct computer control of external functions. The CPU can send the control bits to an output port and thereby determine which functions will be activated.

The most frequent use of the AND function in programming is in separating part of a word for examination. This process is called *masking*, since it is accomplished by means of a mask or pattern that selects the desired part of the word.

Figure A2.3 Controlling external functions with AND gates.

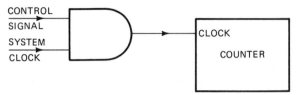

The control signal determines whether the system clock affects the counter.

EXAMPLES:

1. Determine if a binary number is even or odd.

Solution: A binary number is odd if its least significant bit is one, even if its least significant bit is zero. So the determination requires a logical AND of the number with a pattern having a one in the least significant bit and zeros elsewhere. The result will be zero if the number is even and nonzero if it is odd. For instance, using 8-bit numbers,

(a) Is 00010110 even or odd? AND it with the mask

$$00000001$$

Using the truth table for AND on a bit-by-bit basis gives

$$
\begin{array}{r}
00010110 \\
\cdot\ \ 00000001 \\
\hline
00000000
\end{array}
$$

The result is zero; so the original number was even.

(b) Is 10111101 even or odd? ANDing it with the mask on a bit-by-bit basis gives

$$
\begin{array}{r}
10111101 \\
\cdot\ \ 00000001 \\
\hline
00000001
\end{array}
$$

The result is one; so the original number was odd.

2. Determine if a two's complement binary number is positive or negative.

Solution: A two's complement binary number is positive if its most significant bit is zero, negative if its most significant bit is one. So the solution is the same as in Example 1 except that the mask has a one in the most significant bit and zeros elsewhere. In the 8-bit case, the mask is

$$10000000$$

If an 8-bit two's complement binary number is ANDed with this mask, the result will be zero if the number is positive and nonzero if the number is negative.

3. The settings of two ten-position switches (0 to 9) have been stored in an 8-bit word (each requires four bits) and must be retrieved separately.

Solution: The setting in the four least significant bits of an 8-bit word can be determined by ANDing the word with a mask having zeros in the four most significant bits and ones in the four least significant bits—that is,

$$00001111$$

For instance, if the 8-bit word is

$$01110100$$

it can be ANDed with the mask to give

$$00000100$$

(or decimal 4), which now contains only the desired setting.

The setting in the four most significant bits can be determined by ANDing the word with a mask having ones in the four most significant bits and zeros in the four least significant bits—that is,

$$11110000$$

For instance, if the 8-bit word was

$$01110100$$

it can be ANDed with the mask to give

$$01110000$$

which now contains only the desired setting. The program must, however, shift this result right four bits logically to obtain the switch setting.

The AND function can also clear individual bits or groups of bits in a word. The programmer can then clear flag bits, turn a single display on or off (depending on its polarity), or bring a single control output low. For example, to clear bit 4 of an 8-bit word, the required instruction is a logical AND with the pattern 11101111. The pattern has a zero in each position that is to be cleared and a one in each position that is to remain the same.

A2.2 THE NOT FUNCTION

The NOT function, or complement, is the simplest logical function because it has only one input. NOT inverts logic levels; the following truth table describes the function (a bar over an expression means NOT).

A	$\bar{A}$
0	1
1	0

Inverter (or NOT) gates can invert external logic levels or help produce mutually exclusive control signals. Inverted logic levels are useful in transferring data to or from peripherals that use negative logic; typical examples are common-anode displays, keyboards, and encoders. A logic zero in these cases is the active state; a logic one is inactive. Many processors and memories also require or produce active-low control signals; inverter gates are often necessary to form the correct interface.

Mutually exclusive control signals require inverters. For instance, if a single control output (SECTION SELECT) determines whether the processor is accessing memory (one) or input/output devices (zero), Fig. A2.4 shows the formation of mutually exclusive write pulses for the memory and input/output sections. Figure A2.5 shows the use of inverters to form the mutually exclusive control signals required by a busing structure. The A and B inputs determine which of the four data inputs appears on the bus as follows.

B	A	BUS OUTPUT
0	0	D_0
0	1	D_1
1	0	D_2
1	1	D_3

Figure A2.4   Forming mutually exclusive control signals.

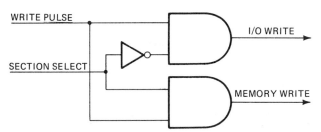

The two signals are mutually exclusive, since SECTION SELECT is either zero or one.

Figure A2.5   Forming a busing structure with inverter gates.

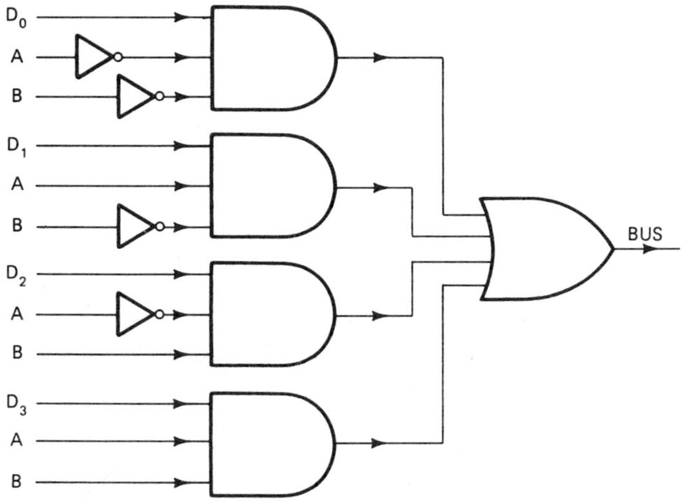

The inverter gates form four mutually exclusive control signals that ensure that only one data input will appear on the bus at a time. The diagram shows four inverters, although only two are actually necessary.

The uses of the NOT function in programming include inverting logic levels for input and output and producing the one's or two's complement for arithmetic.

EXAMPLES:
1. Find the one's complement of

01101011

Applying the NOT function to each bit gives

10010100

2. Find the one's complement of

10001000

Applying the NOT function to each bit gives

01110111

3. Find the negative (two's complement) of the number 10010011. The two's complement is the one's complement plus 1—that is,

$$\begin{array}{r} 01101100 \\ + 1 \\ \hline 01101101 \end{array}$$

A2.3   THE INCLUSIVE OR FUNCTION

The INCLUSIVE OR, or OR, function is also well known, although there is some confusion with the EXCLUSIVE OR, which is described later. The INCLU-SIVE OR of two inputs is true if either one of the inputs is true or if both are true. The OR function can be described by the following truth table (a plus sign usually means OR).

A	B	A + B
0	0	0
0	1	1
1	0	1
1	1	1

The truth table for the OR function has three ones and a zero compared to the three zeros and a one of an AND function. Clearly the two functions are in some sense complementary—the complement of an AND function is an OR and vice versa. The OR function can be described in terms of parallel switches as shown below. Current will flow in this circuit if either of the switches is closed or if both are closed.

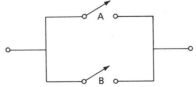

OR gates can combine input signals. Most microprocessors have only a few input pins for such control signals as interrupts, RESET, or DMA requests. OR gates allow several different sources for these signals as shown in Fig. A2.6. The OR gate also can combine signals for a bus as shown in Figs. A2.2 and A2.5.

Figure A2.6 Combining input signals in OR gates.

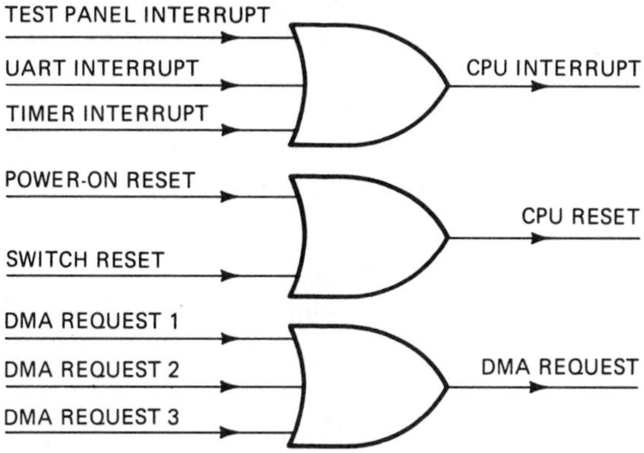

TEST PANEL INTERRUPT

UART INTERRUPT   CPU INTERRUPT

TIMER INTERRUPT

POWER-ON RESET

CPU RESET

SWITCH RESET

DMA REQUEST 1

DMA REQUEST 2   DMA REQUEST

DMA REQUEST 3

If the CPU has only a single input pin, an OR gate will allow several sources for that input. However, the processor cannot internally determine which source produced the input.

Programming uses of the logical OR include assembling words from bits or partial words, setting bits, and combining conditions. The logical OR has the opposite functions from the logical AND. A logical OR can assemble data into a word for output much as the logical AND disassembles the word after input. The logical OR can also set output or flag bits; the procedure is to perform a logical OR with a pattern that has one bits in the positions to be set and zero bits in the positions that are to remain the same.

EXAMPLES:

1. Set the sign bit of a sign-magnitude number.

Solution: The sign bit may be set by ORing the number with a pattern that has a one in the most significant bit position and zeros elsewhere—that is,

$$10000000$$

in the 8-bit case. Since the sign bit of the pattern is one, the sign bit of the result will be one regardless of the value of the sign bit of the original number; since the other bits of the pattern are all zero, the other bits of the result will be the same as in the original number. For instance,

(a) The original number is 01101001. ORing this number bit by bit with 10000000 gives

$$
\begin{array}{r}
01101001 \\
+\ \ 10000000 \\
\hline
11101001
\end{array}
$$

(b) The original number is 10111111. ORing this number bit by bit with 10000000 gives

$$
\begin{array}{r}
10111111 \\
+ \quad 10000000 \\
\hline
10111111
\end{array}
$$

Note that the + sign here means "OR" and not "add."

2. Store two 4-bit numbers in one 8-bit word. (This is the opposite of the masking problem, which was handled with an AND function.) The 4-bit numbers could each represent a decimal digit for a numeric display.

Solution: Shift one of the 4-bit numbers left logically four times and OR it with the other number. For instance, if the two numbers were

$$0100 \quad \text{and} \quad 0111$$

the second number would be shifted left four times, giving

$$01110000$$

The shifted number would then be ORed with the other number as follows.

$$
\begin{array}{r}
01110000 \\
+ \quad\quad 0100 \\
\hline
01110100
\end{array}
$$

The two 4-bit numbers now form a single 8-bit word.

A2.4 THE EXCLUSIVE OR FUNCTION

The EXCLUSIVE OR function is the same as the INCLUSIVE OR except that it is false in the case where both inputs are true. The EXCLUSIVE OR of two inputs is true if either one of the inputs is true but not both. The following truth table describes the EXCLUSIVE OR function ($\oplus$ is a common symbol for EXCLUSIVE OR).

A	B	A $\oplus$ B
0	0	0
0	1	1
1	0	1
1	1	0

A $\oplus$ B is thus zero if A and B are equal and one if they are not equal.

The EXCLUSIVE OR function can form the sum in binary addition.

A	B	SUM	CARRY
0	0	0	0
0	1	1	0
1	0	1	0
1	1	0	1

The sum is given by A ⊕ B. Another hardware application for the EXCLUSIVE OR function is a circuit that determines if two numbers are equal. For example, in Figure A2.7 the EXCLUSIVE OR gates produce zero results if the register outputs and data bits are equal. The OR gate then produces a zero result if and only if all the EXCLUSIVE OR outputs are zero. The net result is a logic one if the data bits are equal to the contents of the register and a logic zero otherwise. In Fig. A2.8, the output O follows the data D only if A and B are equal.

Figure A2.7 Forming a comparator with EXCLUSIVE OR gates.

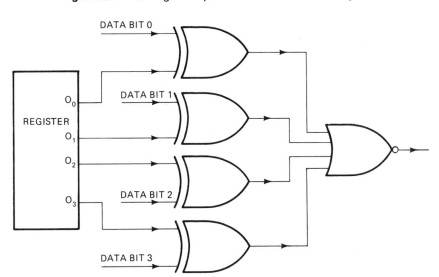

Figure A2.8 Forming a control signal with an EXCLUSIVE OR gate.

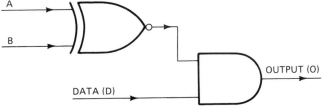

The AND gate only allows the data to affect the output if A and B are equal.

The programming uses of the EXCLUSIVE OR function are complementing bits or flags, looking for pattern matches, clearing registers, and checking and generating parity. The EXCLUSIVE OR is not used as often as OR and AND; the function may be obtained by combining the other logical functions—that is,

$$A \oplus B = \overline{A} \cdot B + A \cdot \overline{B}$$

The EXCLUSIVE OR can complement single bits much as AND clears bits and OR sets them. The required pattern has a one bit in each position that is to be complemented and a zero bit in each position that is to remain unchanged. Note that EXCLUSIVE ORing a number with the all ones pattern produces the logical complement, whereas EXCLUSIVE ORing a number with itself produces zero.

The EXCLUSIVE OR can also check for pattern matches. If two bit patterns are the same, their EXCLUSIVE OR is zero; if they are not the same, the EXCLUSIVE OR has a one bit in each position where the patterns differ. Such a function is useful in searching for message headings in cases where one or more transmission errors are permitted.

The EXCLUSIVE OR function is widely used to check and generate parity. The transmitter generates parity by EXCLUSIVE ORing all the bits and sends it along with the data. The receiver checks parity by generating it again from the data and comparing the result to the transmitted parity. If the two do not agree, the receiver knows that the data is incorrect and can request retransmission. EXCLU-SIVE ORs can also form checksums for tape or disk records.

EXAMPLES:

1. Find the negative of a sign-magnitude number.

Solution: Complement the most significant bit by EXCLUSIVE ORing the number with a pattern having a one in the most significant bit and zeros elsewhere—that is,

$$10000000$$

in the 8-bit case. For instance,

(a) The original number is 01101001. EXCLUSIVE ORing this number bit-by-bit with 10000000 gives

$$
\begin{array}{r}
01101001 \\
\oplus \quad 10000000 \\
\hline
11101001
\end{array}
$$

(b) The original number is 10111111. EXCLUSIVE ORing this number bit-by-bit with 10000000 gives

$$
\begin{array}{r}
10111111 \\
\oplus \quad 10000000 \\
\hline
00111111
\end{array}
$$

2. Check the parity of eight serial inputs. The eighth bit is odd parity—that is, zero if an odd number of the first seven bits are ones and one otherwise. (The total number of ones in the eight bits is always odd.) For instance, if the first seven bits are

$$1011010$$

the parity bit is one, since four of the bits are one. The 8-bit number with parity is

$$10110101$$

If the first seven bits are

$$0010000$$

there is one 1 and so the parity bit is zero. The 8-bit number with parity is

$$00100000$$

Solution: Check parity by clearing a register and EXCLUSIVE ORing it with each of the input bits in succession. If the result is one, the parity is correct; if the result is zero, the parity is erroneous. Note that we can calculate the original parity by EXCLUSIVE ORing the first seven bits and complementing the result.

(a) The eight inputs are

$$1, 0, 1, 1, 0, 1, 0, 1$$

Starting with zero, the successive results are

$$0 \oplus 1 = 1$$
$$1 \oplus 0 = 1$$
$$1 \oplus 1 = 0$$
$$0 \oplus 1 = 1$$
$$1 \oplus 0 = 1$$
$$1 \oplus 1 = 0$$
$$0 \oplus 0 = 0$$
$$0 \oplus 1 = 1$$

The final result is one; so the parity is correct. The result of EXCLUSIVE ORing the first seven bits is the complement of the eighth or parity bit.

(b) The eight inputs are

$$1, 1, 0, 0, 1, 1, 0, 0$$

Starting with zero, the successive results are

$$0 \oplus 1 = 1$$
$$1 \oplus 1 = 0$$
$$0 \oplus 0 = 0$$
$$0 \oplus 0 = 0$$
$$0 \oplus 1 = 1$$
$$1 \oplus 1 = 0$$
$$0 \oplus 0 = 0$$
$$0 \oplus 0 = 0$$

The final result is zero; so the parity is incorrect. The example clearly has an even number (4) of one bits.

3. Determine if two 8-bit numbers are the same.

Solution: EXCLUSIVE OR the two numbers. If they are the same, the result will be zero. If they are different, the result will have a one in each bit position where the numbers differed. For instance,

(a) The 8-bit numbers are

$$10110101 \quad \text{and} \quad 11000101$$

EXCLUSIVE ORing them gives

$$01110000$$

There is a one in each position where the corresponding bits differ.

(b) The 8-bit numbers are

$$01001010 \quad \text{and} \quad 01001010$$

EXCLUSIVE ORing them gives

$$00000000$$

so they are equal.

REFERENCES

BARTEE, T. C., *Digital Computer Fundamentals*, McGraw-Hill, New York, 1974.

ECKHOUSE, R. H., JR., *Minicomputer Systems*, Prentice-Hall, Englewood Cliffs, N.J., 1975.

HELLERMAN, H., *Digital Computer System Principles*, McGraw-Hill, New York, 1967.

PHISTER, M., *Logical Design of Digital Computers*, Wiley, New York, 1958.

Appendix

3   Numerical and Character Codes

This appendix briefly describes various codes that are commonly used with microprocessors. The first section discusses numerical codes with particular emphasis on the standard or 8, 4, 2, 1 BCD representation of decimal numbers. Brief descriptions of other BCD codes and Gray codes are also included. The second section deals with the Baudot, ASCII, and EBCDIC character codes. The third section describes the seven-segment display code.

A3.1   NUMERICAL CODES

BCD (Binary-Coded-Decimal) codes are widely used with microprocessors and calculators. These codes represent decimal numbers by coding each decimal digit separately into four bits. The representation uses extra memory but is convenient if the system input, processing, and output all involve decimal numbers.

The most common BCD code is the standard or 8, 4, 2, 1 code (so-called because of the weights given to the places in the representation—the same weights as in ordinary binary). Table A3.1 shows the coding for each decimal digit in the standard BCD representation.

Decimal numbers between 0 and 9 have the same representations in standard BCD and binary. Numbers larger than 9 have different representations; Table A3.2 shows some examples.

The standard BCD representation does not use the binary numbers 1010 (10) through 1111 (15). Therefore standard BCD requires additional memory; for instance, an 8-bit word can represent a number as large as 11111111 or decimal 255 in binary but only 10011001 or decimal 99 in BCD. However, storing decimal digits in BCD requires only a 4-bit shift and a logical OR. Storage in binary requires the

Table A3.1 Standard (8, 4, 2, 1) BCD Representation

Decimal Number	Standard BCD Representation
0	0000
1	0001
2	0010
3	0011
4	0100
5	0101
6	0110
7	0111
8	1000
9	1001

Table A3.2 Examples of Standard (8, 4, 2, 1) BCD Representations of Numbers Larger than Nine

Decimal Number	Standard BCD Representation	Binary
10	00010000	1010
11	00010001	1011
12	00010010	1100
13	00010011	1101
20	00100000	10100
37	00110111	100101
63	01100011	111111
94	10010100	1011110

multiplication of each digit by the appropriate power of ten. Multiplication is time-consuming even on computers that have a multiplication instruction; it is very awkward on those computers that must perform the operation in software. The decimal output process is equally simple if the results are in BCD and awkward if the results are in binary. Many switches, keyboards, and converters automatically produce data in BCD, and many displays directly accept such data. The following examples show the input and output procedures for decimal digits if the internal storage is BCD or binary.

EXAMPLES:

1. Enter 37 from a decimal keyboard and store it in memory. The keyboard provides the decimal digits separately.
   (a) STORAGE IN BCD

534

The procedure is to shift the previous digits left four bits logically and OR them with the new digit. This process works as follows.

Step 1. PLACE FIRST ENTRY IN STORAGE LOCATION (value is 3).
Step 2. SHIFT CONTENTS OF STORAGE LOCATION LEFT FOUR BITS (3 shifted left four bits gives 30 hexadecimal or 48 decimal).
Step 3. LOGICALLY OR STORAGE LOCATION WITH SECOND ENTRY (result is 37 hexadecimal or 55 decimal).

(b) STORAGE IN BINARY
The procedure is to multiply the previous digits by ten and add the product to the new digit. It works as follows.

Step 1. PLACE FIRST ENTRY IN STORAGE LOCATION (value is 3).
Step 2. MULTIPLY CONTENTS OF STORAGE LOCATION BY 10 (result is 30 decimal or 1E hexadecimal).
Step 3. ADD STORAGE LOCATION TO SECOND ENTRY (result is 37 decimal or 25 hexadecimal).

Binary storage of decimal digits requires a multiplication instead of a 4-bit shift.

2. Display 37 on a two-digit decimal display. The displays contain decoders.
(a) STORAGE IN BCD
The procedure is to shift the contents of the storage location right four bits and mask off the least significant digit. It works as follows.

Step 1. MASK OFF FIRST DIGIT BY LOGICALLY ANDING STORAGE LOCATION WITH A MASK (value is 7). The mask has ones in the four least significant bit positions and zeros elsewhere.
Step 2. SHIFT CONTENTS OF STORAGE LOCATION RIGHT FOUR BITS (result is 3).
Step 3. MASK OFF SECOND DIGIT (value is 3).

(b) STORAGE IN BINARY
The procedure is to divide the contents of the storage location by ten; the required digits are the quotient and the remainder. This works as follows.

Step 1. DIVIDE CONTENTS OF STORAGE LOCATION BY 10.
Step 2. REMAINDER IS LEAST SIGNIFICANT DIGIT (7), QUOTIENT IS MOST SIGNIFICANT DIGIT (3).

Displaying decimal digits stored in binary thus requires a division instead of a 4-bit shift.

Entering and displaying decimal numbers are clearly simpler when the numbers are stored in BCD rather than in binary. The added convenience is even greater in the case of microprocessors with short word lengths. The 4-, 8-, 12-, and 16-bit words that are typical of microprocessors can all handle a whole number of 4-bit BCD digits. Particularly in the case of 4-or 8-bit words where almost all decimal numbers occupy more than one word, entering and displaying decimal numbers stored in binary involves many multiword operations. On the other hand, entering and displaying decimal numbers stored in BCD requires no multiword operations, since the 4-bit BCD digits fit evenly into 4-or 8-bit words.

Thus the BCD representation is most convenient when (a) numbers are entered and displayed in decimal and (b) the computer word length is very short.

BCD does have disadvantages; numbers stored in BCD are longer and BCD arithmetic is more complex. We can easily estimate the extra work required by the greater length of BCD numbers. The number 1000 requires 10 bits in binary (since $2^{10} = 1024 \sim 1000$) and 12 bits in BCD (three decimal digits). So the BCD representation uses about 20% more memory and arithmetic operations simply because of the additional length of the numbers involved.

BCD arithmetic requires extra steps when the arithmetic unit only performs binary operations. For instance, standard BCD addition is the same as binary addition if the sum of each pair of digits is less than 9, since numbers between 0 and 9 are the same in binary and standard BCD.

EXAMPLES:
    1. Add 31 and 42, using the standard BCD representation.
    Solution: Simply perform binary addition.

$$31 \text{ (standard BCD)} = 00110001$$

$$42 \text{ (standard BCD)} = 01000010$$

Adding gives

$$
\begin{array}{r}
00110001 \\
+ \quad 01000010 \\
\hline
01110011
\end{array}
$$

which is 73 in the standard BCD representation.
    2. Add 57 and 12, using the standard BCD representation.

$$57 \text{ (standard BCD)} = 01010111$$

$$12 \text{ (standard BCD)} = 00010010$$

Adding gives

$$
\begin{array}{r}
01010111 \\
+ \quad 00010010 \\
\hline
01101001
\end{array}
$$

which is 69 in the standard BCD representation.

But if the sum of any pair of digits is greater than 9, standard BCD addition differs from binary addition.

EXAMPLES:

    1. Add 37 and 36, using the standard BCD representation.

$$37 \text{ (standard BCD)} = 00110111$$

$$36 \text{ (standard BCD)} = 00110110$$

Adding gives

$$
\begin{array}{r}
00110111 \\
+ \quad 00110110 \\
\hline
01101101
\end{array}
$$

The four least significant bits are not a valid BCD digit.

    2. Add 75 and 85, using the standard BCD representation.

$$75 \text{ (standard BCD)} = 01110101$$

$$85 \text{ (standard BCD)} = 10000101$$

Adding gives

$$
\begin{array}{r}
01110101 \\
+ \quad 10000101 \\
\hline
11111010
\end{array}
$$

In this case, neither the four least significant bits nor the four most significant bits are a valid BCD digit.

    3. Add 38 and 29, using the standard BCD representation.

$$38 \text{ (standard BCD)} = 00111000$$

$$29 \text{ (standard BCD)} = 00101001$$

Adding gives

$$
\begin{array}{r}
00111000 \\
+ \quad 00101001 \\
\hline
01100001
\end{array}
$$

In this case, both the four most and the four least significant bits are valid BCD digits, but the result is the standard BCD representation of 61, which is certainly not correct.

    The problem is the gap between the representations of 9 and 10 in standard BCD. The difference between 1 and 2, 2 and 3, or any of the other consecutive digits in the standard BCD representation is 1. However, as shown in Table A3.2, the standard BCD representation of 10 is the same as binary 16, not binary 10. Thus the difference between the standard BCD representation of 9 and the standard BCD representation of 10 is 7, not 1. This extra factor of 6 must be added whenever the sum of two BCD digits is 10 or more.

The rules for converting binary addition to standard BCD addition are

1. If the binary sum of a pair of digits is less than 10, leave it alone.
2. If the binary sum of a pair is greater than or equal to 10, add 6 to the sum.

If the problem is stated as $S = A + B$, where S_i is the ith standard BCD digit of the sum and A_i and B_i are the ith standard BCD digits of A and B, the rules are

1. If $A_i + B_i +$ carry (if one exists) is less than 10,
$$S_i = A_i + B_i + \text{carry}$$
2. If $A_i + B_i +$ carry (if one exists) is greater than or equal to 10,
$$S_i = A_i + B_i + \text{carry} + 6$$

Adding 6 may generate further carries.

EXAMPLES:
1. Add 37 and 36, using the standard BCD representation

$$37 \text{ (standard BCD)} = 00110111$$
$$36 \text{ (standard BCD)} = 00110110$$

Adding gives

$$\begin{array}{r} 00110111 \\ + \quad 00110110 \\ \hline 01101101 \end{array}$$

Since the sum of the least significant digits is greater than 9, add 6 to it.

$$\begin{array}{r} 01101101 \\ + \quad 00000110 \\ \hline 01110011 \end{array}$$

The result is the standard BCD representation of 73.
2. Add 75 and 85, using the standard BCD representation.

$$75 \text{ (standard BCD)} = 01110101$$
$$85 \text{ (standard BCD)} = 10000101$$

Adding gives

$$\begin{array}{r} 01110101 \\ + \quad 10000101 \\ \hline 11111010 \end{array}$$

Since the sum of the least significant digits and the sum of the most significant digits are both greater than 9, add 6 to each of them.

$$\begin{array}{r} 11111010 \\ + \quad 01100110 \\ \hline 01100000 + \text{a carry} \end{array}$$

The result is the standard BCD representation of 160 (the carry is the leading 1).
3. Add 38 and 29, using the standard BCD representation.

$$38 \text{ (standard BCD)} = 00111000$$
$$29 \text{ (standard BCD)} = 00101001$$

Adding gives

$$
\begin{array}{r}
00111000 \\
+ \quad 00101001 \\
\hline
01100001
\end{array}
$$

Since the sum of the least significant digits is greater than 9, add 6 to it.

$$
\begin{array}{r}
01100001 \\
+ \quad 00000110 \\
\hline
01100111
\end{array}
$$

The result is the standard BCD representation of 67. In this case, the binary sum does not indicate that the answer is incorrect; the only way to see if the answer is correct is to determine if there was a carry from the most significant bit of the least significant digit. If there was, the sum of the least significant digits was greater than 9 and the binary sum is incorrect.

The difficulty of performing arithmetic in standard BCD with binary arithmetic circuits is a serious drawback to using this representation even though it makes the entry and display of decimal numbers much easier. The addition of standard BCD numbers using a binary adder requires the following steps.

1. Add the numbers in the binary adder.
2. Check the sum of each pair of digits to see if it exceeds 9.
3. Add 6 to each digit of the sum where step 2 finds an excess.

Calculating the sum involves checking each digit and the carry from the leading bit of each digit (since the sum of the digits could exceed 15, thus carrying properly to the next digit but leaving an incorrect result behind). Programming this procedure is difficult. For instance, if the word length is eight bits, the program must examine both the regular carry and the carry from bit 3 (least significant digit). Since microprocessors are often used in applications that involve decimal arithmetic, most of them have special BCD arithmetic instructions. The usual feature is a decimal adjust instruction that corrects a binary sum to the BCD result. Four-bit processors like the Intel 4040 need only the regular CARRY to perform decimal addition. Eight-bit processors like the Intel 8080 or Motorola 6800 need the carry from the least significant digit (usually called a HALF-CARRY) to perform decimal addition. Some microprocessors (e.g., the Intel 4040) also have special instructions for standard BCD subtraction.

Other BCD Codes

Other BCD codes besides the 8, 4, 2, 1 code are sometimes used in calculators, instruments, and other applications. Since these codes simplify BCD arithmetic, they can be used with microprocessors that lack specialized BCD instructions.

One such code can be derived by examining the rules for standard BCD addition. As noted, if the standard BCD addition problem is $S = A + B$, where S_i is the ith standard BCD digit of the sum and A_i and B_i are the ith standard BCD digits of A and B, respectively, the rules are

1. If $A_i + B_i +$ the carry from the previous digit is less than 10,

$$S_i = A_i + B_i + \text{carry}$$

2. If $A_i + B_i +$ the carry from the previous digit is greater than or equal to 10,

$$S_i = A_i + B_i + \text{carry} + 6$$

Next, make the following substitutions.

$$A_i' = A_i + 3$$
$$B_i' = B_i + 3$$
$$S_i' = S_i + 3$$

The primed addition rules are

1. If $A_i' + B_i' +$ the carry from the previous digit is less than 16,

$$S_i' = A_i' + B_i' + \text{carry} - 3$$

2. If $A_i' + B_i' +$ the carry from the previous digit is greater than or equal to 16,

$$S_i' = A_i' + B_i' + \text{carry} + 3$$

The primed rules have the following advantages over the original BCD rules.

1. The correction always has the same magnitude (3); the only difference is the sign.

2. The sign of the correction depends only on whether the binary addition of the digits produces a carry. The transition point is 16 rather than 10. There is no longer a distinction between the case where the sum is an invalid character (Examples 1 and 2) and the case where the sum produces a valid carry and a valid but incorrect remainder (Example 3).

The BCD representation (see Table A3.3) that uses the primed values is the *Excess-3 BCD* code.

The Excess-3 BCD representation of a decimal digit is the digit plus 3. An additional convenience of the Excess-3 BCD representation is that complementing each bit of a decimal number gives the nine's complement of the number (i.e., each digit in the nine's complement is nine minus the digit in the original number). We can thus easily implement decimal subtraction as the addition of the nine's complement plus 1.

EXAMPLES:

1. Find the nine's complement of the Excess-3 BCD representation of 1.
Solution: The Excess-3 BCD representation of 1 is

0100

Complementing each bit gives

1011

which is the Excess-3 BCD representation of 8.

    2. Find the nine's complement of the Excess-3 BCD representation of 5.
Solution: The Excess-3 BCD representation of 5 is

1000

Complementing each bit gives

0111

which is the Excess-3 BCD representation of 4.

Table A3.3   Excess-3 BCD Representation

Decimal Number	Excess-3 BCD Representation
0	0011
1	0100
2	0101
3	0110
4	0111
5	1000
6	1001
7	1010
8	1011
9	1100

Decimal subtraction of Excess-3 BCD numbers requires the following steps:

1. Find the nine's complement of the number to be subtracted by logically complementing the number.

2. Add the other number plus one.

Note, however, that Excess-3 BCD is not as convenient as standard BCD for entering and displaying decimal digits, since the factor of 3 must be added to each input and subtracted from each output. The 7443 decoder converts Excess-3 BCD to decimal. But few other devices will handle the Excess-3 code, and so custom hardware or software conversion is usually necessary.

Still another BCD code (see Table A3.4) is the 2, 4, 2, 1 code. The 2, 4, 2, 1 BCD representation differs from the 8, 4, 2, 1 representation in that the leading bit has a weight of 2 rather than 8. As in the Excess-3 BCD representation, the one's complement of a decimal digit in the 2, 4, 2, 1 BCD representation is the same as its nine's complement. So the 2, 4, 2, 1 BCD code also makes decimal subtraction easy to implement. Like Excess-3 BCD, the 2, 4, 2, 1 representation is not as convenient as standard BCD for entry and display.

Table A3.4 2, 4, 2, 1 BCD Representation

Decimal Number	2, 4, 2, 1 BCD Representation
0	0000
1	0001
2	0010
3	0011
4	0100
5	1011
6	1100
7	1101
8	1110
9	1111

Gray Codes

Gray codes are binary codes in which only one bit changes in a transition from one number to the next larger number. Such codes are used in applications like shaft encoders where if more than one bit changed in the transition from one number to the next, completely erroneous intermediate results could occur.

EXAMPLE:
Assume that a binary encoder is changing from 7 (0111) to 8 (1000). If an external device reads the output when all the bits have changed except bit 2, it would read the data as 12 (1100). However, if the encoder uses the Gray code of Table A3.5, the device could only read the output as 7 or 8. Gray coded input must be converted to binary for computations.

Table A3.5 A Sample Gray Code

Decimal	Binary	Gray
0	0000	0000
1	0001	0001
2	0010	0011
3	0011	0010
4	0100	0110
5	0101	0111
6	0110	0101
7	0111	0100
8	1000	1100
9	1001	1101

A3.2 CHARACTER CODES

Baudot Code

The 5-bit Baudot code is commonly used in telegraph systems and in some teletypewriters. The code has both upper and lowercase forms, usually referred to as *letter* case and *figure* case. The blank, space, carriage return, and line feed characters are nonprinting and are recognized in either case. Two special characters—the letter shift and the figure shift—control whether the characters that follow are in letter case or figure case. When a letter shift is sent, all characters that follow it are in letter case until a figure shift is sent.

The letter case characters have standard printing forms, but there are three different printing conventions for the figure case: the international form or CCITT International Alphabet No. 2, the USA Commercial form, and the USA AT and T form. Table A3.6 contains all three forms.

Simple terminals with limited character sets use the Baudot code in order to speed transmission. Code conversion is necessary in order to use a Baudot terminal with a computer.

ASCII Code

The ASCII code or American Standard Code for Information Interchange is an industry (and government) standard code developed in the early 1960s. It has replaced many of the special codes that were previously used by manufacturers and is employed extensively in small computers, terminals, instruments, peripherals, and communications devices. However, manufacturers of large computers (particularly IBM) use the competing EBCDIC code, although some of their machines will accept ASCII. ASCII is the standard character code for digital communications, whereas EBCDIC is the standard character code for large computers.

Table A3.7 describes the ASCII code. The basic code is seven bits long; the eighth bit can be even or odd parity or can be permanently zero or one. The ASCII code includes lowercase letters; single-case machines must either reject lowercase letters or convert them to their uppercase equivalents.

ASCII has special control characters that are used in serial communications: they include ENQ, enquiry, used to request the status of the receiver; ACK, acknowledge, used to indicate successful reception after error checking has been completed; and NAK, or negative acknowledge, used to indicate errors in reception and often to request retransmission.

EBCDIC Code

The EBCDIC, or Extended Binary Coded Decimal Interchange Code, is used in most large computers, particularly those made by IBM and Burroughs. EBCDIC is an 8-bit code that fits evenly into 8-bit bytes and can be represented by two hexadecimal digits; EBCDIC can also provide a more extensive character set than ASCII. On the other hand, EBCDIC is longer than ASCII and does not provide for parity within an 8-bit byte. Table A3.8 contains the EBCDIC code.

Table A3.6   Baudot Codes

Code	Letter Case	CCITT Int. Alph. No. 2	USA Comm.	USA AT & T
11000	A	-	-	-
10011	B	?	?	$\frac{5}{8}$
01110	C	:	:	$\frac{1}{8}$
10010	D	who are you	$	$
10000	E	3	3	3
10110	F		!	$\frac{1}{4}$
01011	G		&	&
00101	H		#	
01100	I	8	8	8
11010	J	Bell	Bell	,
11110	K	(	(	$\frac{1}{2}$
01001	L	)	)	$\frac{3}{4}$
00111	M	.	.	.
00110	N	,	,	$\frac{7}{8}$
00011	O	9	9	9
01101	P	0	0	0
11101	Q	1	1	1
01010	R	4	4	4
10100	S	!	!	Bell
00001	T	5	5	5
11100	U	7	7	7
01111	V	=	;	$\frac{3}{8}$
11001	W	2	2	2
10111	X	/	/	/
10101	Y	6	6	6
10001	Z	+	"	"
00000	Blank			
11111	Letters shift			
11011	Figures shift			
00100	Space			
00100	Space			
00010	Carriage return			
01000	Line feed			

Table A3.7 ASCII Code (Hexadecimal with most significant bit zero)

ASCII Code	Character	ASCII Code	Character	ASCII Code	Character
00	NUL	2B	+	56	V
01	SOH	2C	,	57	W
02	STX	2D	-	58	X
03	ETX	2E	.	59	Y
04	EOT	2F	/	5A	Z
05	ENQ	30	0	5B	[
06	ACK	31	1	5C	\
07	BEL	32	2	5D	]
08	BS	33	3	5E	∧(↑)
09	HT	34	4	5F	−(←)
0A	LF	35	5	60	\
0B	VT	36	6	61	a
0C	FF	37	7	62	b
0D	CR	38	8	63	c
0E	SO	39	9	64	d
0F	SI	3A	:	65	e
10	DLE	3B	;	66	f
11	DC1 (X-ON)	3C	<	67	g
12	DC2 (TAPE)	3D	=	68	h
13	DC3 (X-OFF)	3E	>	69	i
14	DC4	3F	?	6A	j
15	NAK	40	@	6B	k
16	SYN	41	A	6C	1
17	ETB	42	B	6D	m
18	CAN	43	C	6E	n
19	EM	44	D	6F	o
1A	SUB	45	E	70	p
1B	ESC	46	F	71	q
1C	FS	47	G	72	r
1D	GS	48	H	73	s
1E	RS	49	I	74	t
1F	US	4A	J	75	u
20	SP	4B	K	76	v
21	!	4C	L	77	w
22	"	4D	M	78	x
23	#	4E	N	79	y
24	$	4F	O	7A	z
25	%	50	P	7B	{
26	&	51	Q	7C	|
27	'	52	R	7D	} (ALT MODE)
28	(	53	S	7E	−
29	)	54	T	7F	DEL (RUB OUT)
2A	*	55	U		

Table A3.8 EBCDIC Code (Hexadecimal)

EBCDIC Code	Character	EBCDIC Code	Character	EBCDIC Code	Character
00	(null)	38		71	
01		39		72	
02		3A		73	
03		3B		74	
04		3C		75	
05	(tab)	3D		76	
06		3E		77	
07	(delete)	3F		78	
08		40	(space)	79	
09		41		7A	
0A		42		7B	
0B		43		7C	
0C		44		7D	=
0D		45		7E	"
0E		46		7F	
0F		47		80	
10		48		81	a
11		49		82	b
12		4A	₤	83	c
13		4B	.	84	d
14		4C	<	85	e
15	(new line)	4D	(	86	f
16		4E	-	87	g
17		4F	|	88	h
18		50	&	89	i
19		51		8A	
1A		52		8B	
1B		53		8C	
1C		54		8D	
1D		55		8E	
1E		56		8F	
1F		57		90	
20		58		91	j
21		59		92	k
22	(field	5A	!	93	l
	separator)	5B	$	94	m
23		5C	*	95	n
24		5D	)	96	o
25	(line feed)	5E	;	97	p
26		5F	–	98	q
27		60	–	99	r
28		61	/	9A	
29		62		9B	
2A		63		9C	
2B	(tab)	64		9D	
2C		65		9E	
2D	(carr. ret.)	66		9F	
2E		67		A0	
2F		68		A1	
30		69		A2	s
31		6A	∧	A3	t

EBCDIC Code	Character	EBCDIC Code	Character	EBCDIC Code	Character
32		6B	,	A4	u
33		6C	%	A5	v
34		6D	—•—	A6	w
35		6E	>	A7	x
36		6F	?	A8	y
37	(EOT)	70		A9	z
AA		C7	G	E4	U
AB		C8	H	E5	V
AC		C9	I	E6	W
AD		CA		E7	X
AE		CB		E8	Y
AF		CC		E9	Z
B0		CD		EA	
B1		CE		EB	
B2		CF		EC	
B3		D0		ED	
B4		D1	J	EE	
B5		D2	K	EF	
B6		D3	L	F0	0
B7		D4	M	F1	1
B8		D5	N	F2	2
B9		D6	O	F3	3
BA		D7	P	F4	4
BB		D8	Q	F5	5
BC		D9	R	F6	6
BD		DA		F7	7
BE		DB		F8	8
BF		DC		F9	9
CO		DD		FA	
C1	A	DE		FB	
C2	B	DF		FC	
C3	C	E0	(blank)	FD	
C4	D	E1		FE	
C5	E	E2	S	FF	
C6	F	E3	T		

A3.3 SEVEN-SEGMENT CODE

The seven-segment display is the most widely used numeric display. Figure A3.1 shows the organization and naming of the segments. This display has the smallest number of separately controlled elements that can still provide recognizable forms of all the decimal digits. Seven-segment displays can also produce some letters; Table A3.9 contains the codes for the digits and the various upper and lowercase letters that can be formed. Some of the numbers and letters are difficult to read unless the observer is accustomed to them; the widespread use of electronic calculators and watches has, however, made the seven-segment forms relatively familiar. Many integrated circuits produce seven-segment outputs; the 7447 BCD to Seven-Segment Decoder is an example that is frequently used in display circuitry.

Table A3.9 Seven-Segment Code
(1 = segment on, 0 = segment off)[a]

Decimal Digit	Seven-Segment Code (hexadecimal)
0	3F
1	06
2	5B
3	4F
4	66
5	6D
6	7C or 7D
7	07
8	7F
9	6F or 67

Uppercase Letter	Seven-Segment Code (hexadecimal)
A	77
C	39
E	79
F	71
H	76
J	1E
L	38
O	3F
P	73
U	3E
Y	6E

Lowercase Letter	Seven-Segment Code (hexadecimal)
b	7C
c	58
d	5E
h	74
n	54
o	5C
r	50
u	1C

[a]The bytes are organized with a most significant bit of zero, followed by the bits for segments g, f, e, d, c, b, and a in that order.

Figure A3.1 Seven-segment display organization.

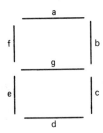

REFERENCES

BACON, M. D., and G. M. BULL, *Data Transmission*, American Elsevier, New York, 1973.

BARTEE, T. C., *Digital Computer Fundamentals*, McGraw-Hill, New York, 1974.

BUCKLEY, J. E., "Communications Code Compatibility," *Computer Design*, Vol. 13, No. 6, May 1974, pp. 11–14.

FLETCHER, J. G., "ASCII Plus One," *Datamation*, Vol. 20, No. 10, October 1974, pp. 42–47.

PRIEL, U., "7-Segment to BCD Converter: The Last Word?," *EDN*, Vol. 19, No. 16, August 20, 1974.

SCHMID, H., *Decimal Computation*, Wiley, New York, 1974.

SU, S., "Logic Design and Its Recent Development," *Computer Design*, Vol. 12, No. 10, October 1973, pp. 93–98.

Appendix

4 Semiconductor Technologies

Here we describe the semiconductor technologies used in microprocessors and memories. The emphasis is on the physical characteristics, costs, and state of development of the technologies rather than their inner workings or manufacturing processes. In addition, we describe technologies from the point of view of the microprocessor user; the references contain more complete information.

The first section summarizes the technologies. It discusses their major characteristics and their ability to satisfy various performance requirements. The next two sections contain more detailed information about the MOS and bipolar technologies, respectively.

A4.1 OVERVIEW OF SEMICONDUCTOR TECHNOLOGIES

Today microprocessors are available in many different technologies, but the most common processors are the cheap, single-chip, metal-oxide semiconductor (MOS) devices. Bipolar microprocessors are faster but generally require many chips to form a complete CPU.

Many of the characteristics of a semiconductor technology affect the properties of the resulting microprocessors. Among the significant characteristics are

1. Speed. Clearly the speed of the technology affects the instruction execution time of the microprocessors. The delay of a gate is a common measure of speed. If the delay is short, the microprocessor can decode instructions, perform arithmetic, and calculate addresses rapidly. The speed of a technology depends on its *switching time* (the time required to change from one logic state to the other).

2. Density. The density of a technology affects the complexity of the chips that can be produced. The typical size of a gate is a measure of density. Very dense technologies can produce single-chip microprocessors that are cheap to manufacture, small in size, and require few connections or additional components. Less dense technologies produce processor slices that are two or four bits wide; a CPU requires several processor slices and a large amount of additional circuitry. The density of a particular technology depends on the power dissipated by the gates and the coupling between separate structures.

3. Cost. The cost of production of a particular technology obviously affects the cost of microprocessors. Material costs, process complexity, and length of experience all affect the cost of production. A measure of cost is the typical cost of a gate.

4. Power Consumption. The power consumption of a technology is important because of the cost of energy and the additional equipment that may be necessary to produce power and dissipate heat. The operating power requirements of a technology determine the size of the needed power supplies and the amount of heat that is produced during operation. The standby power requirements determine how much power is needed to retain data during periods when the microprocessor is not operating. A measure of power consumption is the power dissipated in a gate.

5. Noise Immunity. Noise immunity affects overall system cost and the applicability of microprocessors using a technology to various systems. Noise immunity measures the range of supply voltages and currents over which a particular technology operates properly. Variations in voltages and currents may be caused by unregulated power supplies, electromagnetic and radio-frequency interference, cross-talk, nuclear radiation, initial transients, or other factors. If the variations that are typical of an application will affect the performance of a particular technology, the designer must either use another technology or protect the system with regulated power supplies, bypass networks, filters, shielding, additional grounding, or special noise immunity logic. Such protection can be expensive. A measure of noise immunity is the variations permitted in voltage levels before a logic transition occurs.

6. Ruggedness. The ruggedness of a technology determines whether a microprocessor produced from that technology can meet the environmental requirements of an application. Ruggedness refers to the ability to withstand extreme conditions or variations in such factors as temperature, pressure, humidity, shock, torque, vibration, chemical conditions (such as acidity and salt buildup), and nuclear radiation. Ruggedness is particularly important in applications like military equipment, automobiles, airplanes, ships, factories, and satellites.

7. TTL Compatibility. TTL compatibility is important because most electronic systems are built with standard TTL circuits. Thus if the technology is TTL compatible, the resulting microprocessor will be simple to interface and can use the same power supplies and clocks as the rest of the system. Otherwise level shifters, pullup resistors, additional power supplies and clocks, and other interfacing circuitry may be necessary.

8. Maturity. The maturity of a technology refers to the experience, level of support, and level of standardization that has been achieved in that technology. A mature semiconductor technology has standard specifications, high yields, off-the-shelf availability, a wide variety of standard functions, alternate sources, supporting hardware and literature, and significant field and test experience. Use of a mature technology makes system implementation simpler and avoids many of the difficulties that are always associated with state-of-the-art devices.

Obviously tradeoffs are required among these characteristics. If a technology, for example, has very fast switching time or high speed, it must have logic levels that are relatively close together, and so it cannot be as immune to noise as a lower-speed technology. High speed also normally results in high power dissipation.

Table A4.1 shows the typical characteristics of the major semiconductor technologies. Since many of these technologies (particularly CMOS, low-power Schottky TTL, ECL, and I^2L) are still in a state of active development, the figures are approximations at best. Standard TTL is included for comparison. We can characterize the technologies as follows.

PMOS (P-channel MOS). A relatively dense, cheap, but slow technology.

NMOS (N-channel MOS). A dense, cheap, medium-speed technology.

CMOS (Complementary MOS). A low-power, high-noise immunity technology. Recent developments have greatly increased the speed and density of CMOS and decreased its price.

SCHOTTKY TTL. A high-speed, high-power, fully TTL compatible technology that is not as dense as MOS.

LOW-POWER SCHOTTKY TTL. A low-power version of Schottky TTL.

ECL (emitter-coupled logic). An ultra-high-speed, high-power technology.

I^2L. A new technology that may have many of the best characteristics of the other technologies. Theoretical predictions imply that I^2L could eventually be denser and cheaper than NMOS, faster than TTL, and as low in power consumption and as high in noise immunity as CMOS.

Each characteristic tends to favor certain technologies. The user must choose a technology on the basis of which characteristics are the most important in a particular application. The technologies favored by the various characteristics are

1. Speed. ECL and Schottky TTL microprocessors are the fastest.

2. Density. PMOS and NMOS are the densest processes and produce single-chip microprocessors.

3. Cost. PMOS and NMOS microprocessors are currently the cheapest.

4. Noise Immunity. CMOS microprocessors have the highest noise immunity. I^2L has considerable potential here. CMOS, however, may be damaged by large current variations or static charges.

5. Power Consumption. CMOS microprocessors consume the least power, ECL and Schottky TTL the most. I^2L could challenge CMOS in this area.

Table A4.1 Typical Characteristics of Semiconductor Technologies

Technology	Typical Gate Size (square mils)[a]	Typical Delay/Gate (nanoseconds)	Typical Power/Gate	Typical Cost/Gate (cents)	Typical Noise Immunity (volts)
PMOS	3	100 ns	0.2 mW	0.1–2	1.0
NMOS	2	50 ns	0.2 mW	0.1–2	0.4
CMOS	12	25 ns	10 μW	10–30	4.0
TTL	13	10 ns	10 mW	5–15	0.4
Schottky TTL	5	3 ns	20 mW	25	0.3
Low-Power Schottky TTL	5	10 ns	2 mW	25	0.3
ECL	8	2 ns	30 mW	30–40	0.125
I²L	1	25 ns	50 μW	5–50	0.2

[a] One square mil = 6.45×10^{-6} square centimeters.

6. Ruggedness. CMOS microprocessors are the most rugged. I²L has potential here, too.

7. TTL compatibility. Schottky TTL microprocessors are completely TTL compatible. Some of the newer NMOS and CMOS processors are also TTL compatible.

8. Maturity. PMOS is the most common LSI technology, whereas NMOS and Schottky TTL offer the most standardization.

A4.2 MOS TECHNOLOGIES

Most microprocessors are constructed from PMOS and NMOS technologies, among the important characteristics of which are

- High density. LSI chips were first built in MOS. Memories with thousands of bits on a chip as well as other complex devices are commonplace.
- Low cost. PMOS and NMOS provide inexpensive devices. Calculator chips, microprocessors, and large memories cost only a few dollars apiece and prices continue to decrease.
- Low speed. MOS chips are significantly slower than TTL, although their speed has improved. MOS memories have access times of 100 ns to 2 μs; MOS microprocessors have instruction execution times of 1 to 20 μs.
- Low power dissipation. MOS chips dissipate much less power than TTL. MOS LSI chips rarely require special cooling equipment.
- Moderate noise immunity and ruggedness. MOS chips require special design or packaging for rugged or noisy environments. Current pulses or static charges may destroy MOS chips, so they must be protected. MOS chips will usually operate only within the commercial temperature range—0 to 70°C.

- Operation at MOS voltage levels. MOS chips often require a 15 or 17 V difference between a logic zero and a logic one. The resulting voltage levels are incompatible with standard TTL levels (0 V = 0,+5 V = 1).
- Low output currents. MOS LSI chips produce small output currents and cannot drive TTL loads or bus lines. Drivers are necessary to interface MOS microprocessors to TTL systems.
- Need for several power supplies. MOS chips usually need several different power supplies to operate properly. This requirement can greatly increase system cost and complexity.
- Wide availability. MOS chips are available from many manufacturers. Yields are high for most chips and the technology is quite common.
- Limited functions. Although there are many different MOS chips, the number of available functions is much smaller than for TTL. The lack of functions is the result of the low speed of MOS. In general, MOS devices must be interfaced with TTL circuits.
- Limited standardization. There are very few standard families in MOS. Only a few microprocessors or memories even have two sources. Manufacturers have different procedures for describing characteristics, using controls, clocks, and power supplies, and determining input and output current and voltage levels. Specific features of MOS chips and MOS processes are often proprietary, and information about them is difficult to obtain. Standards are beginning to emerge in this area.

PMOS

PMOS is the original MOS technology. It provides high density but low speed. PMOS chips are in widespread production, but most new developments are occurring in more promising technologies. PMOS remains the least expensive LSI technology for low-speed applications.

Common PMOS devices include calculators, microprocessors, UARTs, and memories. PMOS microprocessors have instruction execution times between 5 and 20 μs; typical examples are the 4-bit Intel 4040, Texas Instruments TMS 1000 NC, and Rockwell PPS-4; the 8-bit National SC/MP and Rockwell PPS-8; the 12-bit Toshiba TLCS-12; and the 16-bit National IMP-16 and PACE. PMOS memories are available in many types and sizes (see Appendix 5) and have access times of about 1 μs.

PMOS microprocessors, memories, and other LSI devices generally operate in moderate environments. Some specially packaged devices are available for hostile environments at premium prices. Very few high reliability PMOS chips exist.

Most PMOS chips operate at MOS voltage levels, although some have TTL compatible outputs. Usually pullup resistors are needed to produce TTL voltage levels. Inputs are almost always at MOS levels and require level shifters when the sources are TTL elements.

PMOS chips generally produce very small output currents, often less than 0.25 mA. This amount is not enough to drive even one standard TTL load (1.6 mA) and so drivers are almost always necessary. The Texas Instruments TMS 1000 NC microprocessor contains level shifters and drivers on the chip and delivers an output current of 10 mA at TTL voltage levels.

Most PMOS LSI chips require several power supplies. For instance, the Intel 4040 microprocessor requires -10 and $+5$ V, the National PACE -12 and $+5$ V. The Rockwell PPS-4 and PPS-8 microprocessors require only one power supply, but it is a nonstandard 17-V supply. PMOS chips also may require several clocks, which are usually produced from a more noise-immune technology, such as CMOS. Power and clocking requirements can thus complicate the use of PMOS microprocessors and memories.

Relatively few circuits have been implemented in PMOS because it is too slow. Usually the only PMOS elements in a system are the LSI chips; the other elements are TTL. A working system thus involves considerable interfacing.

There are very few standard PMOS devices. The chips generally perform highly specialized functions and have often been developed for particular applications. Few PMOS chips have a second source. Even products from the same manufacturer are often incompatible.

NMOS

NMOS is a newer technology than PMOS. In comparison to PMOS, NMOS is denser and faster but somewhat more expensive. NMOS chips are in widespread production at the present time, and significant improvements have occurred in speed, density, and TTL compatibility. NMOS is currently the state-of-the-art LSI technology for medium-speed applications.

NMOS devices include microprocessors, interface chips, and memories. NMOS microprocessors have instruction execution times in the 1 to 10 μs range; typical NMOS microprocessors are the 8-bit Intel 8080 and 8085, Motorola 6800, Fairchild F-8, Signetics 2650, MOS Technology 6502, and Zilog Z-80, and the 16-bit General Instrument CP-1600 and Texas Instruments 9900. Table A4.2 summarizes the NMOS and PMOS microprocessors. NMOS microprocessors can handle more demanding applications than PMOS microprocessors; examples are test equipment, intelligent terminals, industrial control systems, and data acquisition systems. NMOS memories are available in many types and sizes and have access time between 100 ns and 1 μs.

NMOS microprocessors, memories, and other LSI chips operate in moderate environments. Some high-reliability versions of NMOS chips are available, including versions of the most widely used microprocessors and memories. However, high-reliability NMOS devices are difficult to produce; the availability of parts is uncertain and their cost is high.

Most NMOS chips operate internally at MOS voltage levels but have TTL-

Table A4.2 Characteristics of MOS Microprocessors

Processor	Word Length	Technology	Register Add Time	Voltages Required	TTL Compatibility Comments
Fairchild F-8	8	NMOS	2 µs	+5, +12	Yes
Fairchild Macrologic	4-bit slice	CMOS	0.5 µs	+5	Yes, compatible with Schottky TTL Macrologic
General Instrument CP-1600	16	NMOS	2.4 µs	+5	Yes
Intel 4004	4	PMOS	10.8 µs	−10, +5	No
Intel 4040	4	PMOS	10.8 µs	−10, +5	No
Intel 8008	8	PMOS	12.5 µs	−9, +5	Yes
Intel 8048	8	NMOS	2.5 µs	+5	Yes
Intel 8080	8	NMOS	2 µs	−5, +5, +12	Yes
Intel 8085	8	NMOS	1.3 µs	+5	Yes
Intersil 6100	12	CMOS	5 µs	+5	Yes, faster with +10-V supply
MOS Technology 6502	8	NMOS	2 µs	+5	Yes
Motorola 6800	8	NMOS	2 µs	+5	Yes
National IMP-4	4	PMOS	12 µs	−12, +5	No
National IMP-8	8	PMOS	4.6 µs	−12, +5	No
National IMP-16	16	PMOS	4.6 µs	−12, +5	Yes
National PACE	16	PMOS	10 µs	−12, +5	Yes
National SC/MP	8	PMOS	10 µs	−12, +5	Yes
RCA CDP1802	8	CMOS	2.5 µs	+5–10	Yes
Rockwell PPS-4	4	PMOS	5 µs	+17	No
Rockwell PPS-8	8	PMOS	4 µs	+17	No
Signetics 2650	8	NMOS	4.8 µs	+5	Yes
Texas Instuments TMS 1000NC	4	PMOS	24 µs	+15	Yes
Texas Instuments TMS 9900	16	NMOS	4.7 µs	−5, +5, +12	Yes
Toshiba TLCS-12	12	PMOS	13 µs	−5, +5	No
Western Digital CP-1611	8	NMOS	300 ns	+5	Yes
Zilog Z-80	8	NMOS	1.5 µs	+5	Yes

compatible inputs and outputs. The drive currents of NMOS chips vary widely, but most NMOS chips require drivers if they are to handle several TTL loads or drive bus lines. Special chips, often produced from Schottky TTL for high speed, may act as buffers between the NMOS microprocessor and the external system.

NMOS microprocessors, memories, and other LSI chips may require several power supplies or may only need the standard 5-V supply, depending on the particular NMOS process used. The Intel 8080 microprocessor requires three power supplies (-5, $+5$, $+12$) and the Fairchild F-8 microprocessor two ($+5$ and $+12$). On the other hand, the Motorola 6800, Signetics 2650, and Zilog Z-80 microprocessors require only a single $+5$-V supply. However, many widely used memories (particularly erasable PROMs) require additional power supplies. NMOS chips may also require several clocks. The power supply and clocking requirements of NMOS chips vary greatly; chips with simple requirements are clearly the future trend.

As with PMOS, few circuits have been implemented in NMOS because of its low speed compared to standard TTL. Thus NMOS LSI chips are usually combined with TTL elements to form a complete system. The interfacing is not as difficult as with PMOS, since most NMOS LSI devices operate externally at TTL voltage levels and many use TTL-level power supplies and clocks.

More NMOS chips than PMOS chips have standard forms. One reason for this standardization is that NMOS chips are used in such general applications as microprocessors and large memories where support and second-sourcing are important rather than in specific applications like calculators where custom features and low prices are more significant. Many NMOS memories and microprocessors are available from several sources. Agreements and technology exchanges have become common.

CMOS

Although CMOS employs a combination of the p-channel and n-channel MOS transistors used in PMOS and NMOS, it has very different operating characteristics. CMOS has a balanced inverter structure based on n-and p-channel transistors connected in parallel. This structure results in low power consumption and high noise immunity. CMOS is a general-purpose logic family that replaces standard TTL in high-noise environments like automobiles and factories and in low power applications like portable equipment, watches, and satellites. At present, improved yields, speeds, and densities have made CMOS competitive with TTL in many applications.

Among the important characteristics of CMOS are

- Extremely low power dissipation. CMOS uses far less operating power than any of the competing technologies. Therefore CMOS is useful in battery-powered systems like digital watches and portable communication systems.

CMOS also requires very little standby power and so it is suitable for backup systems that retain data if the main power supply fails. The power dissipation of CMOS is, however, frequency dependent and rises significantly above 10 kHz.

- High noise immunity. CMOS is virtually immune to noise. As noted, high noise immunity has made CMOS useful in environments like factories and automobiles. Portable systems, watches, and satellites also clearly require this characteristic.
- Ruggedness. CMOS is very rugged. Its performance is insensitive to temperature, which means that it is suitable for such environments as automobiles, factories, ships, and airplanes. CMOS is also relatively insensitive to most other environmental factors. However, like other MOS devices, CMOS devices can be destroyed by large current pulses. Since CMOS is also sensitive to static charge, CMOS devices must be handled carefully.
- Variable power supplies. Unlike most other semiconductor technologies, CMOS can run from almost any power supply. This ability contributes to the high noise immunity and ruggedness of CMOS. Since CMOS devices do not require expensive regulated power supplies or on-card regulation circuits, they can be used in automobiles, satellites, watches, and other battery-powered applications. However, the characteristics of CMOS devices depend on the power supply; the devices will run faster and dissipate more power when a larger power supply is used. Many CMOS device specifications are valid only with a 5-V supply.
- Moderate density. CMOS is only about a third as dense as NMOS or PMOS because of the required separation of the p-and n-channel elements.
- Moderate speed. CMOS is faster than PMOS or NMOS but slower than TTL.
- Moderate fan-out. CMOS devices can supply more output current than PMOS or NMOS devices. CMOS outputs can drive many CMOS inputs, although they can only drive one or two TTL loads.
- Single power supply operation. CMOS devices almost always use a single power supply, which can, as noted, be a standard 5-V supply.
- Moderate availability. CMOS devices are available from several manufacturers. Yields are improving and prices declining substantially.
- Wide range of functions. Almost all TTL elements are also available in CMOS. Thus an entire system can consist of CMOS, unlike PMOS or NMOS; interfacing TTL elements is not as large a problem. However, CMOS circuits are slower and more expensive than TTL and require careful handling. Mixing CMOS and TTL is difficult because CMOS inputs are capacitive, whereas TTL inputs are resistive.
- Limited standardization. The various CMOS logic families are not as standardized as TTL. Specifications vary with the manufacturer, particularly in the case of performance at power supply levels other than 5 V. More standard CMOS will be available in the future.

CMOS microprocessors and memories are not common because of the relatively low densities that have been obtained. Commercial CMOS microprocessors include the RCA CDP1802, an 8-bit processor, the Intersil 6100, a 12-bit processor, and the Fairchild Macrologic, a 4-bit processor slice. These microprocessors have instruction execution times in the 2 to 10 μs range, although they may operate faster with a larger power supply. CMOS microprocessors have found their main uses in traditional CMOS application areas. CMOS memories are usually small (256 or 512 bits) and are used mainly in low power applications.

Future Trends in MOS

PMOS is a mature technology. New interface chips, somewhat larger memories, and some new microprocessors will undoubtedly appear, but no large-scale improvement in performance is expected. PMOS will continue to offer the cheapest LSI chips for many low-speed applications.

NMOS will offer some improvements, including larger and faster memories, faster microprocessors, and additional interface chips. NMOS will be the standard microprocessor technology in the near future.

The future position of CMOS is unclear. It may become a general-purpose logic family or may be supplanted by newer technologies like I^2L. One method of improving CMOS speeds and densities is the use of insulating substrates, such as sapphire. The SOS (silicon-on-sapphire) processes could make CMOS as fast as TTL and as dense as PMOS; however, the insulating substrates are more expensive than the usual silicon and yields have been poor. Several manufacturers are planning CMOS/SOS microprocessors.

The trends toward greater standardization of MOS parts and easier interfacing with TTL circuitry will undoubtedly continue. Additional MOS devices will be available from many sources, and they will have voltage levels, power supplies, and clocks compatible with TTL.

A4.3 BIPOLAR TECHNOLOGIES

Table A4.3 summarizes the bipolar microprocessors. Schottky TTL, ECL (emitter-coupled logic), and I^2L are the dominant bipolar technologies used for microprocessors. I^2L has not yet been fully characterized, but the major properties of the bipolar technologies are as follows.

- High speed. The bipolar technologies are much faster than MOS. ECL is the fastest, followed by Schottky TTL and I^2L.
- High power dissipation. The bipolar technologies use much more power than MOS. However, I^2L is a low-power technology.
- High frequency operation. The bipolar technologies operate at very high

frequencies. ECL can operate up to 500 MHz, Schottky TTL up to 100 MHz. I^2L operates at frequencies of 10 MHz or more.

- Medium noise immunity and ruggedness. Bipolar chips require special design and packaging for rugged or noisy environments. I^2L may eventually compete with CMOS in this area. Bipolar chips generally require regulated power supplies or regulating circuits.
- Large output currents and fan-out. Bipolar chips can handle buses or many standard loads without drivers.
- Low-to-medium density. Because of their high power dissipation, bipolar technologies are not as dense as MOS. However, the density of both Schottky TTL and ECL has increased.
- Medium to high cost. Bipolar LSI chips are significantly more expensive than MOS.

Table A4.3   Characteristics of Bipolar Microprocessors

Processors	Word Length	Technology	Instruction Cycle Time	Comments
Advanced Micro Devices Am 2901, Am 2903	4	Low-power	100 ns	
Fairchild Macrologic 9405	4	Schottky TTL	100 ns	Compatible with CMOS Macrologic
Intel 3002	2	Schottky TTL	150 ns	
Monolithic Memories 6701	4	Schottky TTL	200 ns	
Motorola 10800	4	ECL	55 ns	
Scientific Micro Systems Interpreter (Signetics 8X300)	8	Schottky TTL	300 ns	A complete working system
Signetics 3002	2	Schottky TTL	150 ns	
Texas Instruments SBP 0400	4	I^2L	1 μs	
Texas Instruments 74S481	4	Schottky TTL	100 ns.	

Schottky TTL

Schottky TTL is the most widely used bipolar technology for microprocessors. It offers high speed, moderate density, and complete compatibility with standard TTL. Most Schottky TTL microprocessors are 2- or 4-bit slices; 10 to 20 LSI devices and other circuitry may be needed to make a microcomputer. Schottky TTL microprocessors have instruction execution times in the 100 to 300 ns range. Typical examples are the Advanced Micro Devices Am 2901 (a 4-bit low-power Schottky device), the Fairchild Macrologic (a 4-bit slice), the Intel 3002 (a 2-bit slice), and the Monolithic Memories 6701 (a 4-bit slice). The Scientific Micro Systems Interpreter (Signetics 8X300) is an 8-bit Schottky TTL microprocessor on a single chip. Except for the Interpreter, all the Schottky TTL processors require microprogramming. So far their main uses have been in minicomputers, signal processing, and special military computers. Schottky TTL memories are available in many types in relatively small sizes (see Appendix 5); they have access times of 30 to 100 ns.

Schottky TTL LSI chips are often available in forms suitable for hostile environments (at premium prices, of course). Generally Schottky devices can withstand any environment in which TTL can be used; in both cases, standard devices will only operate in moderate environments. Low-power Schottky is also available in both commercial and high-reliability forms.

Since Schottky TTL is completely compatible with standard TTL (and low-power Schottky), the designer can use Schottky devices interchangeably with standard TTL devices and selectively upgrade critical parts of a system to operate at higher speeds. Schottky TTL microprocessors, memories, and other LSI chips can operate with any TTL circuitry. Schottky TTL chips present far fewer problems in system design than do LSI chips from any of the other technologies.

A major difficulty with Schottky TTL chips is their high power dissipation. Low-power Schottky does offer lower power dissipation but at reduced speeds. Schottky TTL has a very large family of devices. Almost all the TTL elements are available in both Schottky and low-power Schottky. There are fewer sources, however, for Schottky TTL and prices are significantly higher (50 to 200%). Schottky TTL memories, microprocessors, and other LSI chips have not yet been standardized, although some second sourcing does exist. Standard designs will emerge, since the rest of the TTL line is standardized.

ECL

ECL is the standard technology for such ultra high-speed applications as computer mainframes, add-on memories, and high-speed communications. Some ECL families have propagation delays under 1 ns. The high power dissipation of ECL has limited its use in LSI circuits; ECL LSI chips dissipate far more power than any other technology. Although ECL dissipates more power than Schottky TTL at low and medium frequencies (under 50 MHz), its power dissipation does not rise very much with frequency and is less than that of Schottky TTL at high frequencies (over 100 MHz).

Few ECL LSI chips are available. Motorola produces a 4-bit processor slice, the 10800, and an associated sequencer. ECL memories are available in small sizes at rather high cost. ECL microprocessors have instruction execution times in the 50 to 100 ns range; ECL memories have access times in the 10 to 50 ns range and often serve as small, fast cache memories.

ECL LSI chips operate in moderate environments. Since ECL is used mainly in high-speed systems, special packaging is often necessary even in moderate environments in order to reduce noise and dissipate power. A few ECL devices are available for hostile environments, but high-speed systems must usually be protected from large variations in environmental factors in any case.

A major problem with ECL is that it is not compatible with standard TTL. ECL operates at different voltage levels, requires different power supplies, and has very different input and output characteristics. Interfacing ECL and TTL requires level shifters, power supply reroutings, and other complex circuitry. In general, designers do not mix ECL and TTL in systems; one or the other technology is used exclusively. This is a serious disadvantage for ECL, since TTL parts are far more widely available and much cheaper than ECL parts. Those parts of a system that do not require ECL speeds must either be constructed in ECL anyway or built from TTL devices and interfaced at considerable cost.

ECL's high power dissipation is another serious disadvantage. ECL LSI chips require expensive special packages. ECL circuitry generally needs special circuit boards in order to operate properly. Adequate cooling is a major electrical and mechanical design factor in ECL circuitry.

ECL also requires special power supplies in order to operate with the best noise immunity. Two carefully regulated power supplies are necessary; typical values are -5.2 and -2 V.

ECL differs greatly from other logic families. Many ECL characteristics are particularly important in high-speed circuits. Among the characteristics are

1. ECL is better suited than Schottky TTL to drive transmission lines.
2. ECL can provide inverted outputs without external inverters.
3. ECL provides wired-OR outputs.
4. ECL circuits produce little noise and can be used in systems that require accuracy and stability.
5. ECL can drive very large loads without any deterioration in performance. ECL rarely needs drivers.
6. ECL's noise immunity is independent of temperature and supply voltage.

ECL is not as widely available as MOS or Schottky TTL, nor does it have nearly as large a variety of elements. ECL will undoubtedly find greater use in the future in high-speed, high-frequency applications. Wider use of ECL will certainly lead to more suppliers, more elements, and more standardization.

I²L

I²L is a new LSI technology that is under development by many semiconductor companies. Only a few products have appeared and problems will certainly occur, but I²L may well fulfill its initial promise. I²L is much denser than TTL and may even be as dense as PMOS and NMOS. It is not yet as fast as TTL, although laboratory devices have operated at TTL speeds. Schottky I²L, like Schottky TTL, could offer higher speeds at the cost of somewhat higher power dissipation. The power dissipation of I²L is much lower than TTL and can even be as low as CMOS; furthermore, I²L can operate at higher frequencies than CMOS, and its power dissipation is not as strongly frequency dependent. I²L is simpler to produce than TTL; in fact, of all the semiconductor technologies I²L is the simplest except for PMOS.

I^2L has only begun to appear in LSI form. Texas Instruments has introduced a 4-bit processor slice, the SBP 0400, which has an instruction execution time of 1 μs. Although somewhat slower than the Schottky TTL processors, it offers more arithmetic functions and dissipates about a tenth as much power.

I^2L is too new for much to be said about its uses, sources, product lines, or standardization. It does, however, have the following characteristics.

- It can operate from almost any power supply, including a 5-V TTL supply.
- It is not TTL compatible, since its voltage levels are very different from TTL. The problems involved in mixing I^2L and TTL devices are unknown.
- It has good drive capabilities, particularly when compared to MOS.
- It has great temperature stability and can easily be made into high-reliability circuits.
- It allows both digital and analog circuits to be placed on the same chip.

The next few years should give a clearer idea of the overall capabilities of I^2L, but so far it seems to provide a new balance with respect to cost, device complexity, and device performance that is markedly superior to any other semiconductor technology.

REFERENCES

Among the more useful books on semiconductor technologies are the following.

Components Group of Texas Instruments, *MOS/LSI Design and Application*, McGraw-Hill, New York, 1973.

Engineering Staff of American Micro-Systems, *MOS Integrated Circuits*, Wiley, New York, 1972.

Engineering Staff of Texas Instruments, *Solid-State Communications*, McGraw-Hill, New York, 1972.

IC Applications Staff of Texas Instruments, *Designing with TTL Integrated Circuits*, McGraw-Hill, New York, 1972.

LENK, J. D., *Manual for MOS Users*, McGraw-Hill, New York, 1975.

WEBER, S., *Large and Medium Scale Integration*, McGraw-Hill, New York, 1973.

Among the articles in this continually changing area are

ALTMAN, L., "Advances in Design and New Processes Yield Surprising Performance," *Electronics*, Vol. 49, No. 7, April 1, 1976, pp. 73–81.

ALTMAN, L., "Logic's Leap Ahead Creates New Design Tools," *Electronics*, Vol. 47, No. 4, February 21, 1974, pp. 81–96.

ALTMAN, L., "MOS Makers Worry about I^2L Progress," *Electronics*, Vol. 48, No. 15, July 24, 1975, pp. 70–71.

ALTMAN, L., "The New LSI," *Electronics*, Vol. 48, No. 14, July 10, 1975, pp. 81–92.

ALTMAN, L., "Special Report: C-MOS Enlarges Its Territory," *Electronics*, Vol. 48, No. 10, May 15, 1975, pp. 77–88.

BUTLER, M. K., "Prospective Capabilities in Hardware," *Proceedings of the 1976 National Computer Conference*, pp. 323–336.

EATON, S. S., "Sapphire Brings Out the Best in CMOS," *Electronics*, Vol. 48, No. 12, June 12, 1975, pp. 115–120.

GILDER, J. H., "New Bipolar Technologies to Compete with CMOS and ECL," *Electronic Design*, Vol. 24, No. 5, March 1, 1976, pp. 18–19.

HART, C. M., et al., "Bipolar LSI Takes a New Direction with Integrated Injection Logic," *Electronics*, Vol. 47, No. 20, October 3, 1974, pp. 111–118.

HORTON, R. L., et al., "I^{2}L Takes Bipolar Integration a Significant Step Forward," *Electronics*, Vol. 48, No. 3, February 6, 1975, pp. 83–90.

HUME, S., "Consider 1, 024-bit CMOS RAMS for Small Static-Memory Systems," *Electronics*, Vol. 48, No. 15, July 24, 1975, pp. 102–106.

JAEGER, R., "Designing Microprocessors with Standard-Logic Devices, Part I," *Electronics*, Vol. 48, No. 2, January 23, 1975, pp. 90–95.

JAEGER, R., "Designing Microprocessors with Standard-Logic Devices, Part II," *Electronics*, Vol. 48, No. 3, February 6, 1975, pp. 102–107.

JAEGER, R., "ECL 10,000 Interconnects Economically," *Electronic Design*, Vol. 22, No. 20, September 27, 1974, pp. 90–94.

JURISON, J., et al., "Design Considerations for Aerospace Digital Computers," *Computer Design*, Vol. 13, No. 8, August 1974, pp. 113–123.

McMOS Idea Book, Motorola Semiconductor Products, Phoenix, Ariz., 1975.

MECL—General Information, Motorola Semiconductor Products, Phoenix, Ariz., 1974.

MECL 10,000 and Schottky TTL, an Engineering Comparison Study, Motorola Semiconductor Products, Phoenix, Ariz., 1974.

MICK, J. R., and J. SPRINGER, "Single-Chip Multiplier Expands Digital Role in Signal Processing," *Electronics*, Vol. 49, No. 10, May 13, 1976, pp. 103–108.

A New Concept in Processor ICs, Motorola Semiconductor Products, Phoenix, Ariz., 1975.

ORMOND, T., "IC Logic Families: They Keep Growing in Numbers and Size," *EDN*, Vol. 19, No. 18, October 5, 1974, pp. 30–35.

STEPHENSON, K., "CMOS: Opportunities Are Limited if You Ignore the Failure Modes," *EDN*, Vol. 20, No. 11, June 5, 1975, pp. 50–54.

STEPHENSON, K., "CMOS: Opportunities Unlimited," *EDN*, Vol. 20, No. 3, February 5, 1975.

Appendix

5 Semiconductor Memories

This appendix describes the semiconductor memories that are commonly used with microprocessors. Emphasis is on physical characteristics, sizes, and costs rather than internal operation. The references offer additional information on the construction and operation of memories. As in Appendix 4 on semiconductor technologies, the point of view here is that of the microprocessor user.

The first section presents an overall view of semiconductor memories. It includes a comparison of semiconductor and core memories as well as a description of the different types of semiconductor memories and their typical features and uses. Finally, the advantages and disadvantages of memories specifically designed for use with a particular microprocessor are discussed.

Section A5.2 presents further details about random access memories (RAMs) and read-only memories (ROMs). Section A5.3 deals with programmable read-only memories (PROMs), erasable PROMs (EPROMs), and electrically alterable ROMs (EAROMs). The programming of the various devices plus their advantages and disadvantages are described. Shift registers, buffers, and future trends in memories are covered in the final section.

A5.1 OVERVIEW OF SEMICONDUCTOR MEMORIES

Semiconductor memories have found many uses in recent years. Electronic memories were formerly too expensive for anything but low-capacity, cost-insensitive applications. Larger memories in computers, terminals, and communications systems consisted of magnetic cores.

Advances in LSI techniques have greatly reduced the cost of semiconductor memories. At the same time the development of calculators, microprocessors, and other LSI chips has increased the market for such memories; almost all microcomputers use semiconductor memory rather than core because of the former's greater compatibility, smaller size, and lower power consumption. Semiconductor memories also have replaced core memories in some larger computers. Table A5.1 compares core memory and the most common semiconductor memory.

Table A5.1 Comparison Between Core and Semiconductor Memory (Typical Parameter Values)

Memory Technology	Readout Type	Storage Type	Read Cycle Time (μs)	Write Cycle Time (μs)
Core Dynamic NMOS	Destructive	Nonvolatile	1	1
Semiconductor	Nondestructive	Volatile	0.5	0.5

Access Time (μs)	Volume (cm^3/bit)	Weight (gram/bit)	Power (volt/bit)	Cost (cents/bit)	Modularity
0.4	5.7×10^{-3}	6.4×10^{-3}	3.7×10^{-4}	$3 - 5$	16K $\times$ 16 blocks
0.3	1.6×10^{-3}	2.3×10^{-3}	7×10^{-5}	1	4K $\times$ 1 chips

A key difference is that core memory has destructive readout, whereas semiconductor memory has nondestructive readout. *Destructive readout* means that the process of reading the data changes the contents of the memory. A system using core memory must restore the data after reading it. The restoration requires additional time and circuitry; most computers use the extra time to perform operations that do not involve memory.

Another key difference is that core memory is nonvolatile, whereas semiconductor memory is volatile. Volatility means that the contents of the memory are lost when power is lost. Clearly volatility is a problem both in systems that have occasional power supply transients and in those that are regularly turned on and off. A semiconductor memory would not only lose current data but would also require the reloading of fixed data and programs each time the system was turned on. Some systems overcome this problem by saving fixed data and programs in read-only memories (ROMs) or by using a backup battery (preferably with a low-power technology like CMOS). However, the first method reduces the flexibility of the system, since it makes changing data or programs difficult. The second involves additional expense, both for the battery and for the low-power technology. The volatility of semiconductor memories is particularly inconvenient when programs are being developed and many changes are being made.

Not only are semiconductor memories volatile, but the largest are dynamic as well. A *dynamic memory* stores data in capacitive memory cells; it therefore loses its contents after a certain length of time and so must be periodically *refreshed* (usually every 2 ms). *Refresh* simply means restoring the data in the cells—that is, recharging the capacitors. Refresh requires additional circuitry and complicates the use of the memory. Some microprocessors have on-chip refresh circuitry; special LSI refresh controllers are also available. *Static memories*, which do not require refresh, are often available, but these memories are more expensive and use more power.

The read cycles, write cycles, and access times of cores and MOS memories are similar. The range of cycle and access times available with core memories is much smaller than with semiconductor memories. Semiconductor memories are available at significantly higher prices with access times as low as a few nanoseconds.

Semiconductor memories are smaller, lighter, and use less power than core memories. Obviously these differences are important in applications where size, weight, and power consumption are critical, such as portable communications systems, small instruments, automobiles, airplanes, and satellites.

Semiconductor memories are somewhat cheaper than core memories. The prices are difficult to compare because core and semiconductor memories require very different circuitry to provide power, handle addressing, and perform other overhead functions. Generally core memories are cheaper in large systems, such as computers; semiconductor memories are cheaper in small systems, such as terminals, instruments, or calculators.

Cores are available in much larger blocks than are semiconductor memories. The block size of cores depends on the methods used in manufacturing and connecting them. Small memory requirements (under 1K bytes) can only be met by semiconductor memories (although at somewhat higher cost per bit than indicated in Table A5.1).

The following lists summarize the important characteristics of core and semiconductor memories.

Core

  Destructive readout
  Nonvolatile
  Limited range of cycle and access times (around 1 μs)
  Relatively large and heavy
  High power consumption
  Moderately priced
  Available only in large blocks
  Best for large memories

Semiconductor

  Nondestructive readout
  Volatile (sometimes also dynamic)

Wide range of cycle and access times (10 ns to 2 μs)
Relatively small and light
Low power consumption (depends on technology)
Low to moderately priced (depends on technology)
Available in a wide variety of sizes up to 64K bits.
Best for small- or medium-sized memories.

Types of Semiconductor Memory

Many different types of semiconductor memory (see Table A5.2) are commonly used with microprocessors. The most common are *ROMs* (read-only memories) and *RAMs* (random access memories, more properly referred to as random access read/write memories). *ROMs* that the user can change under special conditions (although not in normal operation) are called *PROMs* (programmable read-only memories); PROMs that the user can erase and reuse are called *EPROMs* (erasable PROMs) or *EAROMs* (electrically alterable ROMs). Other types of memories used with microprocessors are shift registers and buffers. Sections A5.2 and A5.3 describe which types are available in particular semiconductor technologies.

Table A5.2 Types of Semiconductor Memory

Memory Type	Variability	Technologies	Volatility	Typical Size (bits)	Use
ROM	Fixed	All	Nonvolatile	16K	Program memory, tables
PROM	Programmed once	Most	Nonvolatile	1K to 16K	Program memory, tables
EPROM	Can be reprogrammed	MOS	Nonvolatile	2K to 32K	Program memory, tables
EAROM	Can be reprogrammed	Few	Nonvolatile	1K	Program memory, tables
RAM	Variable	All	Volatile	1K to 16K	Data
Shift register	Variable	All	Volatile	8–256	Input/output
Buffer	Variable	Most	Volatile	32–256	Input/output

ROMs are the most common memories in microcomputers. They are programmed at the factory as part of the manufacturing process; the customer, of course, supplies the program. ROMs are simple, since they have only the circuitry necessary for reading the memory. Thus they are cheap in large quantities (about one-fifth the cost of read/write memory), dense (about ten times as dense as read/write memory), and easy to interface. The semiconductor manufacturers add a mask charge (usually several hundred dollars) for each new ROM pattern;

consequently, ROMs are cheap only when the customer orders large quantities of the same pattern. ROMs are mainly used with microprocessors as program storage, although they may also hold mathematical tables (e.g., sines, cosines, or squares), code conversion tables (e.g., ASCII to EBCDIC or BCD to seven-segment), logical functions, character generation patterns for cathode-ray tubes or printers, and other fixed data.

RAMs are also a common part of microcomputers. *Random access* means that all words in the memory can be accessed in the same amount of time; ROMs are also random access, but shift registers and buffers are not. RAMs are ordinary read/write memories like cores. The circuitry involved is more complex than in ROMs, since the contents must be changed as well as read; RAMs are therefore less dense and more costly than ROMs. RAMs are available in every semiconductor technology in a variety of sizes. In microprocessor-based systems, RAMs serve as data storage and as program storage in the early stages of development.

PROMs are the other type of semiconductor memory most often used with microprocessors. The PROM cannot be changed under operating conditions but the user can program it with special equipment. However, standard PROMs can only be programmed once. PROMs are more expensive than ROMs but less expensive than RAMs. They serve the same purposes as ROMs but may be purchased economically in small quantities and programmed by the user in a few minutes. PROMs are used in low-volume applications and even in high-volume applications before final debugging and field testing.

Certain PROMs can be erased and reused. They are thus read/write memories, although changing them may require high voltages or special equipment and usually takes between a few milliseconds and a few minutes. Such PROMs are non-volatile but can still be changed in a relatively short time. Erasable and electrically alterable PROMs are more expensive than regular PROMs. All PROMs involve some extra expense because they must be programmed; Section A5.3 describes the programming of PROMs and the use of erasable and electrically alterable devices.

Other types of semiconductor memory are less often used with microprocessors. Shift registers are sequential-access memories, i.e., data can only be clocked out in the order in which it was entered. Available in many sizes in all the semiconductor technologies, they can provide delays, expand the number of input or output lines, and convert data from serial to parallel or from parallel to serial form. Section A5.4 describes shift registers.

Buffers are also sometimes used with microprocessors. These devices may be organized on a first-in, first-out or a last-in, first-out basis. Such devices often hold data in interfaces until the processor can handle it. They may also serve as address or data stacks or queues; the data can be automatically retrieved in a particular order. Different types of buffers are available in various semiconductor technologies, usually in small sizes.

Comparison of System Memories
and Standard Memories

The designer can usually obtain both standard memory chips and those specially designed for use with a particular microprocessor. The advantages of the specially designed system chips are compatibility with the processor and support from the manufacturer. The advantages of the general-purpose chips are the wider range of types and sizes available, the competitive supply and pricing, and the standardization of testing and design procedures.

The compatibility between system memory chips and the microprocessor may cover such features as access time, control signals, power supplies and clocks, and data and address organization. The system memory chip may also have decoding functions or input/output structure specifically designed for use with the microprocessor. Such features are most important with the simpler processors, which often have narrow buses and few control lines. Part of the instruction execution thus actually takes place on the memory chip; the Intel 4040 is a microprocessor that uses its system memory chips in this way. The system memory chips may also include I/O ports, timers, and interrupt or DMA circuitry.

A further advantage of the system chips is the support offered by the manufacturer. Frequently, manuals and technical notes show sample systems. The manufacturer will use the same chips in development systems, evaluation kits, and single-board computers. However, the system memory chips have the disadvantages of limited variety of size and organization, few sources, limited range of access times, and higher cost than standard chips (because they are produced in smaller volumes). Furthermore, system memory chips generally are not state of the art in size, access time, or other characteristics.

Standard memory chips have complementary advantages and disadvantages. They come in various sizes, organizations, and access times and can be purchased at competitive prices from many sources. The use of standard chips permits the development of standard interfacing techniques, testing methods, and circuit boards and reduces costs because of volume discounts. Furthermore, system needs (such as a backup battery-powered state or a speed requirement) may necessitate the use of a different semiconductor technology (like CMOS or Schottky TTL).

Thus the tradeoff for the designer is between the compatibility of the system chips and the lower cost and wider variety of the standard chips. The system memory chips are fully compatible with a particular microprocessor and easy to interface. Still, they are relatively expensive and offer little variety in size, organization, access time, or technology. Standard chips must be interfaced with the microprocessor but are relatively cheap, widely available, and offer a variety of sizes, organizations, and characteristics.

A5.2 RAMS AND ROMS

RAMs

Table A5.3 summarizes the sizes and characteristics of RAMs available in the various semiconductor technologies. The costs shown are approximate, since prices change rapidly and depend on volume.

Table A5.3   Available Semiconductor RAMs

Technology	Maximum Size (bits)	Typical Size (bits)	Typical Access Time	Dynamic or Static	Typical Cost
PMOS	4K	1K	1 μs	Both	$3/1K bits
NMOS	16K	1K	300–500 ns	Both	2/1K bits
CMOS	1K	256	100–500 ns	Static	20/1K bits
Schottky TTL	1K	256	50–100 ns	Static	20/1K bits
ECL	1K	128	10–50 ns	Static	15/128 bits
I^{2}L	4K	–	100 ns	Static	–

The largest and most widely used RAMs are NMOS. 4K and 16K dynamic RAMs are standard items; such memories are available from many sources, and prices continue to drop.

Table A5.4 contains the characteristics of a typical 4K NMOS RAM, the Intel 2107B. This RAM is organized as 4096 1-bit words in order to simplify the packaging and output circuitry; other organizations are available. Access and cycle times are typically several hundred nanoseconds. Power supply and clock requirements vary somewhat, but most 4K RAMs require two or three power supplies and between one and three clocks at various voltage levels. Most 4K RAMs have TTL inputs and outputs. The refresh period of 2 ms is typical. Both 16-pin and 22-pin packages are common; the 16-pin variety requires additional multiplexing of inputs. 4K static RAMs are also available at a somewhat higher cost.

1K NMOS RAMs are also commonly available. They are used in microcomputers with small RAM requirements (1K to 2K is average for microprocessor applications, according to a recent survey). Larger NMOS RAMs are useful in applications that require large amounts of read/write memory, such as intelligent terminals, test equipment, communications systems, computers, and data acquisition and monitoring systems.

CMOS RAMs are used mainly because of their low power requirements; a CMOS memory can save critical data with power supplied by a small battery and so can serve as a backup memory or as a main memory in portable gear. 1K CMOS memories are available from several manufacturers at moderate prices with

Table A5.4 Characteristics of a Typical NMOS 4K RAM (Intel 2107B)

Characteristic	
Words × bits	4096 × 1
Access time	200 ns
Read cycle time	400 ns
Write cycle time	400 ns
Read-modify-write cycle time	520 ns
Power supplies	−5, +5, +12V
Operating power	650 mW
Standby power	10 mW
Clock requirements	one 12-V clock
Compatibility	TTL (tri-state)
Refresh period	2 ms
Package type	22-pin
Comments	Industry standard pin arrangements, several slower versions available

access times of 300 to 700 ns. CMOS RAMs consume less power, are more immune to noise, and have less stringent power supply and clock requirements than NMOS RAMs. CMOS RAMs are particularly easy to use if the rest of the system is CMOS.

Schottky TTL RAMs often serve as small cache and buffer memories in computers and communications systems. Their major advantage over MOS is their speed (access times of about 50 to 100 ns). Small sizes (256 bits) are typical, but 1K devices are available and 4K devices are planned. Schottky TTL memories are easy to interface with TTL circuitry, since the technology (see Appendix 4) is completely TTL compatible.

ECL RAMs are mainly used as small cache and buffer memories in ECL systems. They have access times as low as 10 ns and are compatible with other ECL circuitry. ECL RAMs are quite expensive, but interfacing other semiconductor technologies to ECL is also expensive.

Using RAMs with Microprocessors

RAMs are mainly used as temporary storage for current data in microcomputers. The following examples show typical organizations and sizes.

EXAMPLE 1: Calculator Memory
Calculator entries are usually stored in BCD (see Appendix 3); each decimal digit therefore requires four bits. Additional storage is necessary for an exponent and for the signs of the entry and the exponent. Assuming a 16-digit number and a

two-digit exponent, the number

$$0.1372994157387406 \times 10^{-59}$$

would be stored in a RAM as shown in Fig. A5.1. Here the signs are arbitrarily represented by zero for positive and one for negative. A single calculator entry stored in this manner requires 80 bits of RAM.

Figure A5.1 RAM storage of a calculator entry (courtesy of Intel Corporation).

Decimal digit 6	0	1	1	0
Decimal digit 0	0	0	0	0
Decimal digit 4	0	1	0	0
Decimal digit 7	0	1	1	1
Decimal digit 8	1	0	0	0
Decimal digit 3	0	0	1	1
Decimal digit 7	0	1	1	1
Decimal digit 5	0	1	0	1
Decimal digit 1	0	0	0	1
Decimal digit 4	0	1	0	0
Decimal digit 9	1	0	0	1
Decimal digit 9	1	0	0	1
Decimal digit 2	0	0	1	0
Decimal digit 7	0	1	1	1
Decimal digit 3	0	0	1	1
Decimal digit 1	0	0	0	1
Exponent Value 59	1	0	0	1
	0	1	0	1
Exponent Sign—Negative	0	0	0	1
Mantissa Sign—Positive	0	0	0	0

EXAMPLE 2: CRT Terminal Memory

Most CRT terminals display lines with 40 to 80 characters. The characters are stored internally in ASCII (see Appendix 3); the most significant bit is parity. Assuming a 40-character line and odd parity ASCII, the FORTRAN statement

```
123  7   9    11  13  15
100  X   =    Y   +   Z
```

(the number above the line indicates column location) would be stored in RAM as shown in Table A5.5.

In this case, the storage of a single 40-character line requires 320 bits of RAM. Since CRT terminals usually display 40 to 48 such lines, about 12 to 15K of RAM would be needed to hold an entire terminal display. Clearly CRT terminals require large RAMs; 8-bit organizations are convenient but not necessary.

Table A5.5 RAM Storage of Terminal Data (100 X = Y + Z)

Character Number	Character	Data (hexadecimal)
1	1	31
2	0	B0
3	0	B0
4	Blank	20
5	Blank	20
6	Blank	20
7	X	58
8	Blank	20
9	=	3D
10	Blank	20
11	Y	D9
12	Blank	20
13	+	AB
14	Blank	20
15	Z	DA
16	Blank	20
17	Blank	20
18	Blank	20
19	Blank	20
20	Blank	20
21	Blank	20
22	Blank	20
23	Blank	20
24	Blank	20
25	Blank	20
26	Blank	20
27	Blank	20
28	Blank	20
29	Blank	20
30	Blank	20
31	Blank	20
32	Blank	20
33	Blank	20
34	Blank	20
35	Blank	20
36	Blank	20
37	Blank	20
38	Blank	20
39	Blank	20
40	Blank	20

ROMs

Table A5.6 summarizes the sizes and characteristics of ROMs available in the various semiconductor technologies. Prices are, as always, approximate at best.

Table A5.6   Available Semiconductor ROMs

Technology	Maximum Size (bits)	Typical Size (bits)	Typical Access Time	Typical Cost
PMOS	64K	16K	800 ns–1.5 μs	$25/16K
NMOS	64K	16K	100 ns–1 μs	25/16K
CMOS	12K	1K	100–500 ns	50/12K
Schottky TTL	16K	1K	50–100 ns	10/1K

Most ROMs are produced from three technologies: PMOS, NMOS, and Schottky TTL. PMOS ROMs are the largest and slowest, NMOS ROMs are significantly faster, and Schottky TTL ROMs are the fastest but more expensive and generally available in smaller sizes.

ROMs are available with a wide variety of organizations and access times. Eight-bit words are most commonly used with microprocessors. Other organizations are used for tables, functions, and character generators, such as the $64 \times 5 \times 7$ devices that produce 64 different 5×7 dot matrix patterns for CRTs or printers. Access times for MOS ROMs range from a few hundred nanoseconds to 2 μs, for Schottky TTL ROMs from 50 to 100 ns.

ROMs are much easier to interface than RAMs. Almost all are static (they need no clocks), and most use only a single power supply and have TTL-compatible inputs and outputs.

ROMs have a wide variety of uses, including program storage, function tables (sine, cosine, square root, logarithm, exponentials), code conversion tables, character-generation tables, mathematical or unit conversions, linearization tables, clock generation, random logic function generators, division and multiplication tables, instruction or diagnostic decoders (for microprogrammed systems), bootstrap loaders for computers, standard computer programs (debugging packages, assemblers, and compilers), pattern generators, diagnostic or error messages, and teaching aids. Large ROMs can hold programs and permanent data and can also produce any logical function of the inputs with a single access.

Most microprocessor applications require fairly large ROMs. According to several surveys, the microprocessor program generally occupies 1K to 4K words of ROM or 4K to 32K bits. Conversion tables, arithmetic functions, and other applications can often use several thousand bits of ROM (the standard dot matrix character generator requires over 2K bits, and a converter between ASCII and EBCDIC requires 1K). Thus 32K and 64K ROMs are useful with microprocessors, particularly if many different tables must be stored.

A typical ROM used with microprocessors is the 2048×8-bit NMOS Motorola 6832, designed for use with the Motorola 6800. The ROM has the characteristics listed in Table A5.7.

This particular ROM requires three power supplies: however, it needs no clocks and has TTL-compatible outputs with tri-state bus compatibility. The CHIP

Table A5.7 Characteristics of a Typical ROM (Motorola 6832)

Characteristic	
Organization	2048 × 8
Mode of operation	Static
Access time: typical	320 ns
maximum	550 ns
Power supplies	−5, +5, +12 V
Clocks	None
Outputs	TTL, Tri-state
Select (enable) features	Programmable select

SELECT input is made either active-high or active-low during production. Motorola will accept either paper tapes produced by 6800 software or hexadecimal-coded punched cards for programming ROMs; other methods require special arrangements.

Using ROMs with Microprocessors

The use of ROMs as program storage is straightforward. The examples below demonstrate their usage as code converters, logical function generators, and micro-program storage.

EXAMPLE 1: BCD to Seven-Segment Converter (see Section A3.3)

Table A5.8 requires 80 bits of ROM organized as ten 8-bit words. The entries are the seven-segment representations of the decimal digits. In order to use the table, the CPU must add the decimal data to the starting address. The result is the address of the required seven-segment code.[1]

Table A5.8 BCD to Seven-Segment Conversion Table

Entry Number	Entry (hexadecimal)
0	3F
1	06
2	5B
3	4F
4	66
5	6D
6	7D
7	07
8	7F
9	6F

---

[1]For example programs, see L. A. Leventhal, "Cut Your Processor's Computation Time," *Electronic Design*, Vol. 25, No. 17, August 16, 1977, pp. 82–89.

A ROM table (Table A5.9) could convert ASCII characters to seven-segment codes. A zero entry indicates a character that has no seven-segment representation. Some zero entries have been omitted from Table A5.9.

Table A5.9 Partial ASCII to Seven-Segment Conversion Table

Entry Number	Character	Entry (hexadecimal)	Entry Number	Character	Entry (hexadecimal)
0	NUL	00	69	E	79
1	SOH	00	70	F	71
2	STX	00	71	G	00
3	ETX	00	72	H	76
4	EOT	00	73	I	06
5	ENQ	00	74	J	1E
⋮	⋮	⋮	75	K	00
			76	L	38
44	,	00	77	M	00
45	-	40	78	N	00
46	.	00	79	O	3F
47	/	00	80	P	73
48	0	3F	81	R	00
49	1	06	82	S	00
50	2	5B	83	T	00
51	3	4F	84	U	3E
52	4	66	98	Y	6E
53	5	6D	99	b	7C
54	6	7D	100	c	58
55	7	07	104	d	5E
56	8	7F	105	h	74
57	9	6F	110	n	54
58	:	00	111	o	5C
65	A	77	114	r	50
66	B	00	117	u	4C
67	C	39			
68	D	00			

An alternative approach would be to use the most significant bit to indicate whether the character has a seven-segment representation. This approach would differentiate between a character that has no representation and a space character. Letter entries could give the other case form if only one case has a representation (such as J or n). This table requires 128 8-bit words or 1K of ROM.

EXAMPLE 2: Parity Table (see Section A3.2)

We can calculate parity by EXCLUSIVE ORing the bits of the word, but such a process involves many operations. Table A5.10 will provide odd parity for a 5-bit code like Baudot.

In this case, each ROM entry is only a single bit, and merely 32 bits of ROM are necessary. A similar table for a 7-bit code like ASCII would require a 128 × 1 ROM and for an 8-bit code like EBCDIC a 256 × 1 ROM. An alternative would be to

Table A5.10 5-Bit Odd Parity Table

Entry Number	Entry
0	1
1	0
2	0
3	1
4	0
5	1
6	1
7	0
8	0
9	1
10	1
11	0
12	1
13	0
14	0
15	1
16	0
17	1
18	1
19	0
20	1
21	0
22	0
23	1
24	1
25	0
26	0
27	1
28	0
29	1
30	1
31	0

use a ROM organized into 8-bit words and store other short results in the same word (the retrieval process would have to mask the required bits from the 8-bit table entry). If, for example, the table contained parity in the most significant bit of each word, a shift or a logical AND with the binary number 10000000 would determine the parity value.

EXAMPLE 3: Microprogramming

Let us assume that a computer instruction word is constructed as shown in Fig. A5.2. The operation code is contained in the three most significant bits. The instruction decoder will access the microprogram for the instruction by masking off the three most significant bits and adding the result to a base address. Figure A5.3 shows the organization of the microprogram memory. Here the instruction decoding process

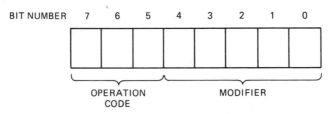

Figure A5.2   A computer instruction word.

BIT NUMBER 7   6   5   4   3   2   1   0

OPERATION
CODE

MODIFIER

Figure A5.3   Organization of microprogram memory.

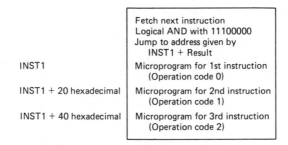

begins at address FETCH. The CPU fetches an instruction (macroinstruction) from the main memory, logically ANDs it with the appropriate mask, and uses the result to access the desired microprogram. If the instruction code is 0, the jump address (in microprogram memory) is INST1; if the instruction code is 1, the jump address is INST1 + 00100000 or INST1 + 20 hex. The microprogram will then use the five modifier bits to execute the instruction.

Advantages of ROMs and RAMs

The advantages of ROMs are

- ROMs are nonvolatile, and so they do not lose their contents when power is lost.
- ROMs are cheaper than RAMs.
- ROMs are available in larger sizes than RAMs.
- The contents of the ROM are always known and can be verified. ROMs are easy to test.
- ROMs are more reliable than RAMs because their circuitry is simpler.
- ROMs are static and do not require refresh.
- ROMs are easier to interface than RAMs.
- ROMs cannot be accidentally changed.

The advantages of RAMs are

- RAMs can be updated or corrected.
- RAMs can serve as temporary data storage.
- RAMs do not require lead time like ROMs or long programming times like PROMs.
- RAMs do not require special programming equipment like PROMs.

A5.3 PROMS

Ordinary (Unerasable) PROMs

The only difference between unerasable PROMs and ROMs is that the manufacturer determines the contents of the ROM, whereas the user can determine the contents of the PROM. PROMs are available in many technologies as noted in Table A5.11. Most MOS PROMs are erasable.

PROM prices have been steadily dropping. Like ROMs, PROMs are available with many convenient features—static operation, TTL-compatible outputs, chip enables, tri-state outputs, and operation without clocks and from a single 5-V power supply. Many PROMs are compatible with ROMs from the same manufacturer, thereby simplifying a transition from PROM to ROM.

Table A5.11 Available PROMs

Technology	Sizes (bits)	Typical Access Times	Typical Programming Time	Typical Cost
PMOS	1K–8K	1–2 μs	2 min	$20/2K
NMOS	1K–32K	300 ns–1 μs	2 min	20/8K
TTL	512–4K	50–100 ns	30 s	22/1K
Schottky TTL	512–16K	50–100 ns	30 s	6/1K
ECL	1K	10–50 ns		

PROMs are preferable to ROMs in the cases below.

1. Low-volume applications where the ROM mask charge is a factor.

2. Initial units for field testing. Many users wait for six months to a year of field testing before changing from PROMs to ROMs.

3. Custom features, such as varied character sets in terminals, operator instruction sequences, or units for display (e.g., °C or °F for temperature). A small PROM can configure the equipment to the needs of the user.

4. Local variables, such as tax formulas for point-of-sale terminals.

5. Immediate requirements where the ROM delivery time is a factor.

PROM Programming

The user programs a PROM by applying pulses to the program input on the chip. The PROM usually comes with all bits in the one state, and so the bits that are to be zero must be changed. The user can construct the programming circuitry, but the voltage and current levels may involve close tolerances and the sizes and lengths of pulses must often be precise. Furthermore, the user must verify if the PROM has been programmed correctly. Programming PROMs without special equipment is a complex, time-consuming, and error-prone process.

Special PROM programmers (see Fig. A5.4) are available from many sources. These devices may have such features as paper tape, teletypewriter, or card input, screening to reject bad PROMs, RAMs for storing data during verification, various kinds of displays, copying features, and automatic re-pulsing if the PROM bit is not correctly programmed at first. Some programmers will work only with a specific PROM; others have *personality cards* so that they can handle many different PROMs. PROM programmers cost from several hundred to several thousand dollars, depending on their features; extra personality cards cost a few hundred dollars. Thus PROM programmers are convenient but expensive. Distributors and suppliers will often program PROMs for a small charge.

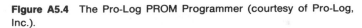

Figure A5.4   The Pro-Log PROM Programmer (courtesy of Pro-Log, Inc.).

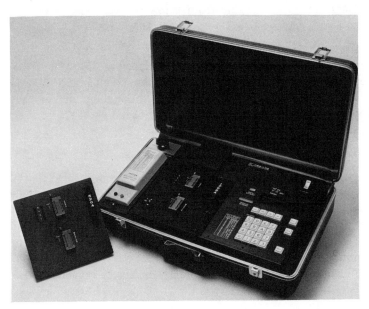

EPROMs

EPROMs or erasable PROMs are available only in the MOS technologies. The user can erase EPROMs by exposing them to high-intensity short-wave ultraviolet light. The user must remove the EPROM from the circuit board and expose it to the light for 10 to 20 minutes, being careful not to overexpose the device (or the user). Standard UV sources with wavelengths of 2537 Å may be used; the recommended dose is 6 W-s/cm². An EPROM can be reused indefinitely if it is not overexposed. Some PROM programmers will determine if an EPROM is completely erased.

EPROMs are actually read-mostly memories; the user can change their contents but not conveniently. Among the drawbacks of EPROMs are the required removal from the circuit board, the need for an ultraviolet light source, and the limitation of complete erasure (i.e., the user cannot correct a single error). However, EPROMs are cheap, reliable, and widely available.

EAROMs

Electrically alterable ROMs, or EAROMs, are like PROMs except that they can be reprogrammed electrically without removal from the circuit board. The user can change an EAROM in a matter of milliseconds rather than minutes; such an alteration time is very long by computer standards but short in comparison to EPROMs.

EAROMs are only available from a few sources. They have the following advantages.

- Nonvolatility and nondestructive readout
- Low power requirements
- Reprogramming without removal from the circuit board
- Availability in small sizes without the additional circuitry required by cores
- High resistance to damage from nuclear radiation
- Partial or complete reprogramming

The disadvantages of EAROMs are as follows.

- The technologies are new and yields are uncertain.
- Devices may change state under certain environmental conditions.
- Voltage levels for writing may change; some devices may not be reprogrammed after ten erasures.
- The technologies are not directly compatible with other semiconductor technologies.
- The devices may require nonstandard or closely regulated power supplies.

A5.4   OTHER MEMORIES AND FUTURE TRENDS

Shift Registers

Shift registers are available in almost every semiconductor technology. MOS shift registers are the largest, but small devices are available in other technologies. Table A5.12 describes typical shift registers. Like MOS memories, MOS shift registers may be dynamic or static, may require one or several power supplies and clocks, and may have TTL compatible inputs and outputs.

Shift registers may have parallel or serial inputs and outputs. Microcomputers often employ such registers to expand inputs or outputs, to perform parallel-to-serial or serial-to-parallel conversions, to produce delays, to convert voltage levels, and to synchronize communications.

Table A5.12 Typical Shift Registers

Technology	Sizes (bits)	Maximum Operating Frequency (MHz)	Cost
PMOS	up to 2K	1	$5/1K
NMOS	up to 2K	1–10	$5/single 1K dynamic
CMOS	up to 200	5	$6/200 bits
Schottky TTL	4 or 8	50–70	$2–$10
ECL	4 or 8	100	$10–$15

Using Shift Registers with Microprocessors

The following examples show the uses of shift registers with microprocessors.

EXAMPLE 1: Serial Output
An 8-bit microprocessor can produce a serial output by simply clocking the data out of an 8-bit parallel-in, serial-out shift register as shown in Fig. A5.5. The CPU sends eight bits to the shift register in one output operation. The system may then clock the data out serially either by having the CPU send clock pulses to the register or by using another clocking mechanism (perhaps even the microprocessor's clock). Thus the shift register rather than the microprocessor performs the serialization.

Figure A5.5 Serial output from a shift register.

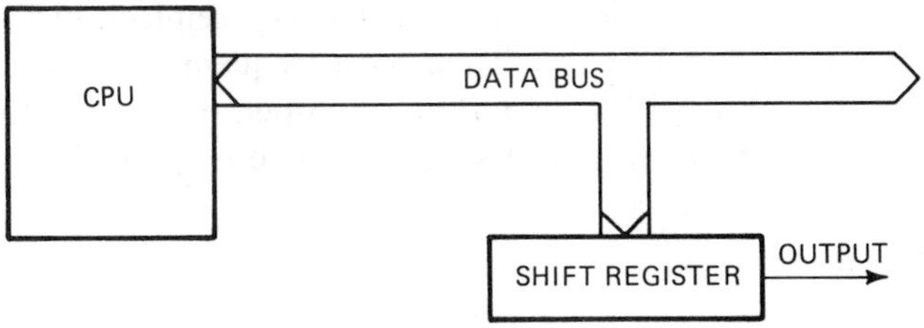

EXAMPLE 2: Synchronizing Communications
In communications systems the transmitter usually precedes its message with synchronization characters so that the receiver can detect the signal properly. For instance, the ASCII character SYN (16 hex) may precede the message. The receiver would then decode each bit, put it in a shift register, and look for a match between the pattern in the shift register and the required pattern. The end result is that the receiver

knows when the transmitter is starting its characters and can detect the message properly. Figure A5.6 shows the hardware necessary to search for a heading consisting of two SYN characters. A microprocessor could perform the comparison or just control it if the data rate is too high.

Figure A5.6   Using shift registers in synchronization.

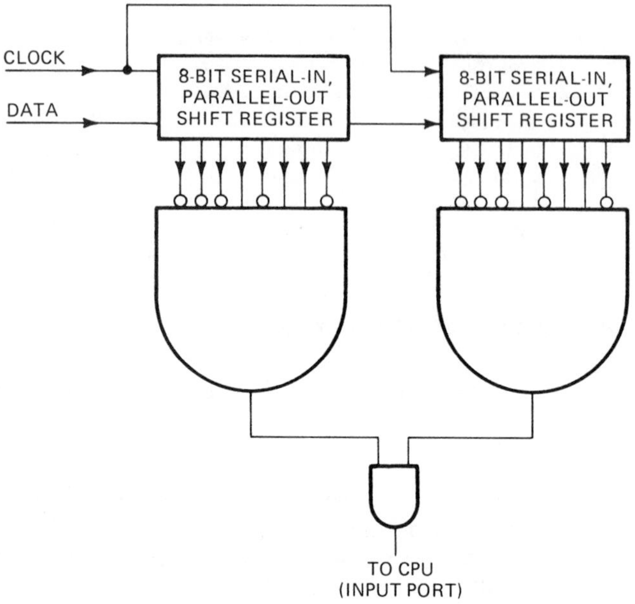

Buffers

Buffers are small memories with special organizations, such as queues (first-in, first-out or FIFO memories) or stacks (last-in, first-out or LIFO memories). Such memories are available in almost every semiconductor technology; common sizes are 16×4 and 64×9. Their most frequent use is to hold data until a processor is able to deal with it or until a line operating at a different speed is ready for it. They may also be used to stack or queue requests.

Future Trends

Future trends in memory development are clear: larger memories with shorter access times at lower prices. Maximum MOS memory sizes and speeds have not yet been achieved; the I^2L technology will make bipolar memories larger and cheaper. Clearly future memories will offer more standard features, such as operation from single power supplies and clocks, on-chip decoding mechanisms, and complete I/O compatibility with various logic families. Future memories will be easier to use and have more standard specifications, controls, power supplies, clocks, and other features.

Many more far-reaching developments are in the planning or sample stage, including

- A nonvolatile RAM. The MNOS technology used for EAROMs could provide such a device.
- CCDs and bubble memories. Charge-coupled devices and bubble memories may replace slower storage devices like disks or tapes, since they can store large amounts of data cheaply and provide high data rates and short access times.
- Subnanosecond memories. Such memories may be possible with faster versions of ECL or other new technologies.

REFERENCES

Books in the fast-changing area of semiconductor memories are soon out of date. The following books, however, are useful.

ENGINEERING STAFF OF TEXAS INSTRUMENTS, *Semiconductor Memory Design and Application*, McGraw-Hill, New York, 1973.

HNATEK, E. R., *A User's Handbook of Semiconductor Memories*, Wiley, New York, 1977.

HODGES, D. A. (Ed.), *Semiconductor Memories*, IEEE Press, New York, 1972.

Among the articles in this area are

ALTMAN, L., "Memories," *Electronics*, Vol. 50, No. 2, January 20, 1977, pp. 81–96.

ALTMAN, L., "Special Report: C-MOS Enlarges Its Territory," *Electronics*, Vol. 48, No. 10, May 15, 1975, pp. 77–88.

ALTMAN, L., "The New LSI," *Electronics*, Vol. 48, No. 14, July 10, 1975, pp. 81–92.

CAYTON, B., "Designing with Nitride-type EAROMs," *Electronics*, Vol. 50, No. 19, September 15, 1977, pp. 107–113.

COLE, B., "Next Goal: Nonvolatile Memory," *Electronics*, Vol. 49, No. 9, April 29, 1976, pp. 75–76.

CUNNINGHAM, J., and J. JAFFE, "Insight into RAM Costs Aids Memory-System Design," *Electronics*, Vol. 48, No. 25, Dec. 11, 1975, pp. 101–103.

DAVIS, S., "Selection and Application of Semiconductor Memories," *Computer Design*, Vol. 13, No. 1, January 1974, pp. 65–77.

"Designing with TTL PROMs and ROMs," *Texas Instruments Bulletin CB-162*, Dallas, Texas, 1975.

FRANSON, P., "Semiconductor Memories," *EDN*, Vol. 22, No. 12, June 20, 1977, pp. 46–57.

GREENE, B., and D. HOUSE, "Designing with Intel PROMs and ROMs," *Intel Application Note No. AP-6*, Santa Clara, Ca., 1975.

HACKMEISTER, R., "Focus on Semiconductor RAMs," *Electronic Design*, Vol. 25, No. 17, August 16, 1977, pp. 56–62.

HUME, S., "Consider 1, 024-bit CMOS RAMs for Small Static-Memory Systems," *Electronics*, Vol. 48, No. 15, July 24, 1975, pp. 102–106.

Isoplanar CMOS Data Book, Fairchild Semiconductor, Mountain View, Ca., 1975.

JURISON, J., et al., "Design Considerations for Aerospace Digital Computers," *Computer Design*, Vol. 13, No. 8, August 1974, pp. 113–123.

KOEHLER, H. F., "Advances in Memory Technology," *Computer Design*, Vol. 13, No. 6, June 1974, pp. 71–77.

KOPPEL, R. J., and I. MALTZ, "Predicting the Real Costs of Semiconductor-Memory Systems," *Electronics*, Vol. 49, No. 24, November 25, 1976, pp. 117–122.

KUO, C., et al., "16-K RAM Built with Proven Process," *Electronics*, Vol. 49, No. 10, May 13, 1976, pp. 81–86.

LEVINE, L., and W. MYERS, "Semiconductor Memory Reliability with Error Detecting and Correcting Codes," *Computer*, Vol. 9, No. 10, October 1976, pp. 43–50.

LEVINE, L., and W. MYERS, "Timing: A Crucial Factor in LSI-MOS Main-Memory Design," *Electronics*, Vol. 48, No. 14, July 10, 1975, pp. 107–111.

McDOWELL, J., "Large Bipolar ROMs and p/ROMs Revolutionize Logic and Systems Design," *Computer Design*, Vol. 13, No. 6, June 1974, pp. 100–104.

McMULLEN, J., "Programming the pROM; A Make or Buy Decision," *EDN*, Vol. 19, No. 5, March 5, 1974, pp. 59–62.

SANDER, W. B., et al., "Dynamic I²L Random-Access Memory Competes with MOS Designs," *Electronics*, Vol. 49, No. 17, August 19, 1976, pp. 99–102.

SPRINGER, J., "Applications of Dynamic Shift Registers," *Advanced Micro Devices Application Note*, Sunnyvale, Ca., July 1973.

TORRERO, E. A., "Focus on Semiconductor Memories," *Electronic Design*, Vol. 23, No. 7, April 1, 1975, pp. 98–107.

Appendix

6 The Intel 8080 Instruction Set[1]

SILICON GATE MOS M8080A

INSTRUCTION SET

The accumulator group instructions include arithmetic and logical operators with direct, indirect, and immediate addressing modes.

Move, load, and store instruction groups provide the ability to move either 8 or 16 bits of data between memory, the six working registers and the accumulator using direct, indirect, and immediate addressing modes.

The ability to branch to different portions of the program is provided with jump, jump conditional, and computed jumps. Also the ability to call to and return from subroutines is provided both conditionally and unconditionally. The RESTART (or single byte call instruction) is useful for interrupt vector operation.

Double precision operators such as stack manipulation and double add instructions extend both the arithmetic and interrupt handling capability of the M8080A. The ability to increment and decrement memory, the six general registers and the accumulator is provided as well as extended increment and decrement instructions to operate on the register pairs and stack pointer. Further capability is provided by the ability to rotate the accumulator left or right through or around the carry bit.

Input and output may be accomplished using memory addresses as I/O ports or the directly addressed I/O provided for in the M8080A instruction set.

The following special instruction group completes the M8080A instruction set: the NOP instruction, HALT to stop processor execution and the DAA instructions provide decimal arithmetic capability. STC allows the carry flag to be directly set, and the CMC instruction allows it to be complemented. CMA complements the contents of the accumulator and XCHG exchanges the contents of two 16-bit register pairs directly.

---

[1]Courtesy of Intel Corporation.

Data and Instruction Formats

Data in the M8080A is stored in the form of 8-bit binary integers. All data transfers to the system data bus will be in the same format.

D_7	D_6	D_5	D_4	D_3	D_2	D_1	D_0

DATA WORD

The program instructions may be one, two, or three bytes in length. Multiple byte instructions must be stored in successive words in program memory. The instruction formats then depend on the particular operation executed.

TYPICAL INSTRUCTIONS

One Byte Instructions

D_7	D_6	D_5	D_4	D_3	D_2	D_1	D_0

OP CODE — Register to register, memory reference, arithmetic or logical, rotate, return, push, pop, enable or disable Interrupt instructions

Two Byte Instructions

D_7	D_6	D_5	D_4	D_3	D_2	D_1	D_0

OP CODE

D_7	D_6	D_5	D_4	D_3	D_2	D_1	D_0

OPERAND — Immediate mode or I/O instructions

Three Byte Instructions

D_7	D_6	D_5	D_4	D_3	D_2	D_1	D_0

OP CODE

D_7	D_6	D_5	D_4	D_3	D_2	D_1	D_0

LOW ADDRESS OR OPERAND 1 — Jump, call or direct load and store instructions

D_7	D_6	D_5	D_4	D_3	D_2	D_1	D_0

HIGH ADDRESS OR OPERAND 2

For the M8080A a logic "1" is defined as a high level and a logic "0" is defined as a low level.

588

INSTRUCTION SET (BINARY)

Summary of Processor Instructions

Mnemonic	Description	D7	D6	D5	D4	D3	D2	D1	D0	Clock[2] Cycles
MOV r1,r2	Move register to register	0	1	D	D	D	S	S	S	5
MOV M,r	Move register to memory	0	1	1	1	0	S	S	S	7
MOV r,M	Move memory to register	0	1	D	D	D	1	1	0	7
HLT	Halt	0	1	1	1	0	1	1	0	7
MVI r	Move immediate register	0	0	D	D	D	1	1	0	7
MVI M	Move immediate memory	0	0	1	1	0	1	1	0	10
INR r	Increment register	0	0	D	D	D	1	0	0	5
DCR r	Decrement register	0	0	D	D	D	1	0	1	5
INR M	Increment memory	0	0	1	1	0	1	0	0	10
DCR M	Decrement memory	0	0	1	1	0	1	0	1	10
ADD r	Add register to A	1	0	0	0	0	S	S	S	4
ADC r	Add register to A with carry	1	0	0	0	1	S	S	S	4
SUB r	Subtract register from A	1	0	0	1	0	S	S	S	4
SBB r	Subtract register from A with borrow	1	0	0	1	1	S	S	S	4
ANA r	And register with A	1	0	1	0	0	S	S	S	4
XRA r	Exclusive Or register with A	1	0	1	0	1	S	S	S	4
ORA r	Or register with A	1	0	1	1	0	S	S	S	4
CMP r	Compare register with A	1	0	1	1	1	S	S	S	4
ADD M	Add memory to A	1	0	0	0	0	1	1	0	7
ADC M	Add memory to A with carry	1	0	0	0	1	1	1	0	7
SUB M	Subtract memory from A	1	0	0	1	0	1	1	0	7
SBB M	Subtract memory from A with borrow	1	0	0	1	1	1	1	0	7
ANA M	And memory with A	1	0	1	0	0	1	1	0	7
XRA M	Exclusive Or memory with A	1	0	1	0	1	1	1	0	7
ORA M	Or memory with A	1	0	1	1	0	1	1	0	7
CMP M	Compare memory with A	1	0	1	1	1	1	1	0	7
ADI	Add immediate to A	1	1	0	0	0	1	1	0	7
ACI	Add immediate to A with carry	1	1	0	0	1	1	1	0	7
SUI	Subtract immediate from A	1	1	0	1	0	1	1	0	7
SBI	Subtract immediate from A with borrow	1	1	0	1	1	1	1	0	7
ANI	And immediate with A	1	1	1	0	0	1	1	0	7
XRI	Exclusive Or immediate with A	1	1	1	0	1	1	1	0	7
ORI	Or immediate with A	1	1	1	1	0	1	1	0	7
CPI	Compare immediate with A	1	1	1	1	1	1	1	0	7
RLC	Rotate A left	0	0	0	0	0	1	1	1	4
RRC	Rotate A right	0	0	0	0	1	1	1	1	4
RAL	Rotate A left through carry	0	0	0	1	0	1	1	1	4
RAR	Rotate A right through carry	0	0	0	1	1	1	1	1	4
JMP	Jump unconditional	1	1	0	0	0	0	1	1	10
JC	Jump on carry	1	1	0	1	1	0	1	0	10
JNC	Jump on no carry	1	1	0	1	0	0	1	0	10
JZ	Jump on zero	1	1	0	0	1	0	1	0	10
JNZ	Jump on no zero	1	1	0	0	0	0	1	0	10
JP	Jump on positive	1	1	1	1	0	0	1	0	10
JM	Jump on minus	1	1	1	1	1	0	1	0	10
JPE	Jump on parity even	1	1	1	0	1	0	1	0	10
JPO	Jump on parity odd	1	1	1	0	0	0	1	0	10
CALL	Call unconditional	1	1	0	0	1	1	0	1	17
CC	Call on carry	1	1	0	1	1	1	0	0	11/17
CNC	Call on no carry	1	1	0	1	0	1	0	0	11/17
CZ	Call on zero	1	1	0	0	1	1	0	0	11/17
CNZ	Call on no zero	1	1	0	0	0	1	0	0	11/17
CP	Call on positive	1	1	1	1	0	1	0	0	11/17
CM	Call on minus	1	1	1	1	1	1	0	0	11/17
CPE	Call on parity even	1	1	1	0	1	1	0	0	11/17
CPO	Call on parity odd	1	1	1	0	0	1	0	0	11/17
RET	Return	1	1	0	0	1	0	0	1	10
RC	Return on carry	1	1	0	1	1	0	0	0	5/11
RNC	Return on no carry	1	1	0	1	0	0	0	0	5/11
RZ	Return on zero	1	1	0	0	1	0	0	0	5/11
RNZ	Return on no zero	1	1	0	0	0	0	0	0	5/11
RP	Return on positive	1	1	1	1	0	0	0	0	5/11
RM	Return on minus	1	1	1	1	1	0	0	0	5/11
RPE	Return on parity even	1	1	1	0	1	0	0	0	5/11
RPO	Return on parity odd	1	1	1	0	0	0	0	0	5/11
RST	Restart	1	1	A	A	A	1	1	1	11
IN	Input	1	1	0	1	1	0	1	1	10
OUT	Output	1	1	0	1	0	0	1	1	10
LXI B	Load immediate register Pair B & C	0	0	0	0	0	0	0	1	10
LXI D	Load immediate register Pair D & E	0	0	0	1	0	0	0	1	10
LXI H	Load immediate register Pair H & L	0	0	1	0	0	0	0	1	10
LXI SP	Load immediate stack pointer	0	0	1	1	0	0	0	1	10
PUSH B	Push register Pair B & C on stack	1	1	0	0	0	1	0	1	11
PUSH D	Push register Pair D & E on stack	1	1	0	1	0	1	0	1	11
PUSH H	Push register Pair H & L on stack	1	1	1	0	0	1	0	1	11
PUSH PSW	Push A and Flags on stack	1	1	1	1	0	1	0	1	11
POP B	Pop register pair B & C off stack	1	1	0	0	0	0	0	1	10
POP D	Pop register pair D & E off stack	1	1	0	1	0	0	0	1	10
POP H	Pop register pair H & L off stack	1	1	1	0	0	0	0	1	10
POP PSW	Pop A and Flags off stack	1	1	1	1	0	0	0	1	10
STA	Store A direct	0	0	1	1	0	0	1	0	13
LDA	Load A direct	0	0	1	1	1	0	1	0	13
XCHG	Exchange D & E, H & L Registers	1	1	1	0	1	0	1	1	4
XTHL	Exchange top of stack, H & L	1	1	1	0	0	0	1	1	18
SPHL	H & L to stack pointer	1	1	1	1	1	0	0	1	5
PCHL	H & L to program counter	1	1	1	0	1	0	0	1	5
DAD B	Add B & C to H & L	0	0	0	0	1	0	0	1	10
DAD D	Add D & E to H & L	0	0	0	1	1	0	0	1	10
DAD H	Add H & L to H & L	0	0	1	0	1	0	0	1	10
DAD SP	Add stack pointer to H & L	0	0	1	1	1	0	0	1	10
STAX B	Store A indirect	0	0	0	0	0	0	1	0	7
STAX D	Store A indirect	0	0	0	1	0	0	1	0	7
LDAX B	Load A indirect	0	0	0	0	1	0	1	0	7
LDAX D	Load A indirect	0	0	0	1	1	0	1	0	7
INX B	Increment B & C registers	0	0	0	0	0	0	1	1	5
INX D	Increment D & E registers	0	0	0	1	0	0	1	1	5
INX H	Increment H & L registers	0	0	1	0	0	0	1	1	5
INX SP	Increment stack pointer	0	0	1	1	0	0	1	1	5
DCX B	Decrement B & C	0	0	0	0	1	0	1	1	5
DCX D	Decrement D & E	0	0	0	1	1	0	1	1	5
DCX H	Decrement H & L	0	0	1	0	1	0	1	1	5
DCX SP	Decrement stack pointer	0	0	1	1	1	0	1	1	5
CMA	Complement A	0	0	1	0	1	1	1	1	4
STC	Set carry	0	0	1	1	0	1	1	1	4
CMC	Complement carry	0	0	1	1	1	1	1	1	4
DAA	Decimal adjust A	0	0	1	0	0	1	1	1	4
SHLD	Store H & L direct	0	0	1	0	0	0	1	0	16
LHLD	Load H & L direct	0	0	1	0	1	0	1	0	16
EI	Enable Interrupts	1	1	1	1	1	0	1	1	4
DI	Disable interrupt	1	1	1	1	0	0	1	1	4
NOP	No-operation	0	0	0	0	0	0	0	0	4

NOTES: 1. DDD or SSS – 000 B – 001 C – 010 D – 011 E – 100 H – 101 L – 110 Memory – 111 A.
2. Two possible cycle times, (5/11) indicate instruction cycles dependent on condition flags.

INTEL 8080 Hexadecimal Instruction Codes

JUMP

C3	JMP	
C2	JNZ	
CA	JZ	
D2	JNC	
DA	JC	Adr
E2	JPO	
EA	JPE	
F2	JP	
FA	JM	
E9	PCHL	

CALL

CD	CALL	
C4	CNZ	
CC	CZ	
D4	CNC	
DC	CC	Adr
E4	CPO	
EC	CPE	
F4	CP	
FC	CM	

RETURN

C9	RET
C0	RNZ
C8	RZ
D0	RNC
D8	RC
E0	RPO
E8	RPE
F0	RP
F8	RM

RESTART

C7	RST	0
CF	RST	1
D7	RST	2
DF	RST	3
E7	RST	4
EF	RST	5
F7	RST	6
FF	RST	7

MOVE IMMEDIATE

06	MVI	B,
0E	MVI	C,
16	MVI	D,
1E	MVI	E, D8
26	MVI	H,
2E	MVI	L,
36	MVI	M,
3E	MVI	A,

Acc IMMEDIATE*

C6	ADI	
CE	ACI	
D6	SUI	
DE	SBI	D8
E6	ANI	
EE	XRI	
F6	ORI	
FE	CPI	

LOAD IMMEDIATE

01	LXI	B,
11	LXI	D, D16
21	LXI	H,
31	LXI	SP,

DOUBLE ADD†

09	DAD	B
19	DAD	D
29	DAD	H
39	DAD	SP

LOAD/STORE

0A	LDAX	B
1A	LDAX	D
2A	LHLD	Adr
3A	LDA	Adr
02	STAX	B
12	STAX	D
22	SHLD	Adr
32	STA	Adr

STACK OPS

C5	PUSH	B
D5	PUSH	D
E5	PUSH	H
F5	PUSH	PSW
C1	POP	B
D1	POP	D
E1	POP	H
F1	POP	PSW*
E3	XTHL	
F9	SPHL	

SPECIALS

EB	XCHG	
27	DAA*	
37	STC†	
3F	CMC†	
2F	CMA	

INPUT/OUTPUT

D3	OUT	} D8
DB	IN	

INCREMENT**

04	INR	B
0C	INR	C
14	INR	D
1C	INR	E
24	INR	H
2C	INR	L
34	INR	M
3C	INR	A
03	INX	B
13	INX	D
23	INX	H
33	INX	SP

DECREMENT**

05	DCR	B
0D	DCR	C
15	DCR	D
1D	DCR	E
25	DCR	H
2D	DCR	L
35	DCR	M
3D	DCR	A
0B	DCX	B
1B	DCX	D
2B	DCX	H
3B	DCX	SP

MOVE

40	MOV	B,B	58	MOV	E,B			
41	MOV	B,C	59	MOV	E,C			
42	MOV	B,D	5A	MOV	E,D			
43	MOV	B,E	5B	MOV	E,E			
44	MOV	B,H	5C	MOV	E,H			
45	MOV	B,L	5D	MOV	E,L			
46	MOV	B,M	5E	MOV	E,M			
47	MOV	B,A	5F	MOV	E,A			
48	MOV	C,B	60	MOV	H,B			
49	MOV	C,C	61	MOV	H,C			
4A	MOV	C,D	62	MOV	H,D			
4B	MOV	C,E	63	MOV	H,E			
4C	MOV	C,H	64	MOV	H,H			
4D	MOV	C,L	65	MOV	H,L			
4E	MOV	C,M	66	MOV	H,M			
4F	MOV	C,A	67	MOV	H,A			
50	MOV	D,B	68	MOV	L,B			
51	MOV	D,C	69	MOV	L,C			
52	MOV	D,D	6A	MOV	L,D			
53	MOV	D,E	6B	MOV	L,E			
54	MOV	D,H	6C	MOV	L,H			
55	MOV	D,L	6D	MOV	L,L			
56	MOV	D,M	6E	MOV	L,M			
57	MOV	D,A	6F	MOV	L,A			
70	MOV	M,B	78	MOV	A,B			
71	MOV	M,C	79	MOV	A,C			
72	MOV	M,D	7A	MOV	A,D			
73	MOV	M,E	7B	MOV	A,E			
74	MOV	M,H	7C	MOV	A,H			
75	MOV	M,L	7D	MOV	A,L			
77	MOV	M,A	7E	MOV	A,M			
			7F	MOV	A,A			

ROTATE†

07	RLC
0F	RRC
17	RAL
1F	RAR

CONTROL

00	NOP
76	HLT
F3	DI
FB	EI

ACCUMULATOR*

80	ADD	B	88	ADC	B	
81	ADD	C	89	ADC	C	
82	ADD	D	8A	ADC	D	
83	ADD	E	8B	ADC	E	
84	ADD	H	8C	ADC	H	
85	ADD	L	8D	ADC	L	
86	ADD	M	8E	ADC	M	
87	ADD	A	8F	ADC	A	
90	SUB	B	98	SBB	B	
91	SUB	C	99	SBB	C	
92	SUB	D	9A	SBB	D	
93	SUB	E	9B	SBB	E	
94	SUB	H	9C	SBB	H	
95	SUB	L	9D	SBB	L	
96	SUB	M	9E	SBB	M	
97	SUB	A	9F	SBB	A	
A0	ANA	B	A8	XRA	B	
A1	ANA	C	A9	XRA	C	
A2	ANA	D	AA	XRA	D	
A3	ANA	E	AB	XRA	E	
A4	ANA	H	AC	XRA	H	
A5	ANA	L	AD	XRA	L	
A6	ANA	M	AE	XRA	M	
A7	ANA	A	AF	XRA	A	
B0	ORA	B	B8	CMP	B	
B1	ORA	C	B9	CMP	C	
B2	ORA	D	BA	CMP	D	
B3	ORA	E	BB	CMP	E	
B4	ORA	H	BC	CMP	H	
B5	ORA	L	BD	CMP	L	
B6	ORA	M	BE	CMP	M	
B7	ORA	A	BF	CMP	A	

PSEUDO INSTRUCTION

ORG	Adr
END	
EQU	D16
SET	D16
DS	D16
DB	D8 [ ]
DW	D16 [ ]
IF	D16
ENDIF	
MACRO	[ ]
ENDM	

CONSTANT DEFINITION

0BDH	} Hex
1AH	
105D	} Decimal
105	
72O	} Octal
72Q	
11011B	} Binary
00110B	
'TEST'	} ASCII
'A' 'B'	

OPERATORS

(.)
* / MOD,SHL,SHR
+, -
NOT
AND
OR,XOR

STANDARD SETS

A	SET	7
B	SET	0
C	SET	1
D	SET	2
E	SET	3
H	SET	4
L	SET	5
M	SET	6
SP	SET	6
PSW	SET	6

Adr = 16 bit address

** = all Flags except CARRY affected; (exception: INX & DCX affect no Flags)

D16 = constant, or logical/arithmetic expression that evaluates to a 16 bit data quantity.

† = only CARRY affected

D8 = constant, or logical/arithmetic expression that evaluates to an 8 bit data quantity.

* = all Flags (C, Z, S, P, AC) affected

Appendix

7 The Motorola 6800 Instruction Set[1]

this location when it fetches the immediate instruction for execution. These are two or three-byte instructions.

Direct Addressing — In direct addressing, the address of the operand is contained in the second byte of the instruction. Direct addressing allows the user to directly address the lowest 256 bytes in the machine i.e., locations zero through 255. Enhanced execution times are achieved by storing data in these locations. In most configurations, it should be a random access memory. These are two-byte instructions.

Extended Addressing — In extended addressing, the address contained in the second byte of the instruction is used as the higher eight-bits of the address of the operand. The third byte of the instruction is used as the lower eight-bits of the address for the operand. This is an absolute address in memory. These are three-byte instructions.

Indexed Addressing — In indexed addressing, the address contained in the second byte of the instruction is added to the index register's lowest eight bits in the MPU. The carry is then added to the higher order eight bits of the index register. This result is then used to address memory. The modified address is held in a temporary address register so there is no change to the index register. These are two-byte instructions.

Implied Addressing — In the implied addressing mode the instruction gives the address (i.e., stack pointer, index register, etc.). These are one-byte instructions.

Relative Addressing — In relative addressing, the address contained in the second byte of the instruction is added to the program counter's lowest eight bits plus two. The carry or borrow is then added to the high eight bits. This allows the user to address data within a range of –125 to +129 bytes of the present instruction. These are two-byte instructions.

MPU INSTRUCTION SET

The MC6800 has a set of 72 different instructions. Included are binary and decimal arithmetic, logical, shift, rotate, load, store, conditional or unconditional branch, interrupt and stack manipulation instructions (Tables 2 thru 6).

MPU ADDRESSING MODES

The MC6800 eight-bit microprocessing unit has seven address modes that can be used by a programmer, with the addressing mode a function of both the type of instruction and the coding within the instruction. A summary of the addressing modes for a particular instruction can be found in Table 7 along with the associated instruction execution time that is given in machine cycles. With a clock frequency of 1 MHz, these times would be microseconds.

Accumulator (ACCX) Addressing — In accumulator only addressing, either accumulator A or accumulator B is specified. These are one-byte instructions.

Immediate Addressing — In immediate addressing, the operand is contained in the second byte of the instruction except LDS and LDX which have the operand in the second and third bytes of the instruction. The MPU addresses

---

[1]Courtesy of Motorola Semiconductor Products, Inc.

TABLE 2 – MICROPROCESSOR INSTRUCTION SET – ALPHABETIC SEQUENCE

ABA	Add Accumulators	CLR	Clear	PUL	Pull Data
ADC	Add with Carry	CLV	Clear Overflow	ROL	Rotate Left
ADD	Add	CMP	Compare	ROR	Rotate Right
AND	Logical And	COM	Complement	RTI	Return from Interrupt
ASL	Arithmetic Shift Left	CPX	Compare Index Register	RTS	Return from Subroutine
ASR	Arithmetic Shift Right				
		DAA	Decimal Adjust	SBA	Subtract Accumulators
BCC	Branch if Carry Clear	DEC	Decrement	SBC	Subtract with Carry
BCS	Branch if Carry Set	DES	Decrement Stack Pointer	SEC	Set Carry
BEQ	Branch if Equal to Zero	DEX	Decrement Index Register	SEI	Set Interrupt Mask
BGE	Branch if Greater or Equal Zero			SEV	Set Overflow
BGT	Branch if Greater than Zero	EOR	Exclusive OR	STA	Store Accumulator
BHI	Branch if Higher			STS	Store Stack Register
BIT	Bit Test	INC	Increment	STX	Store Index Register
BLE	Branch if Less or Equal	INS	Increment Stack Pointer	SUB	Subtract
BLS	Branch if Lower or Same	INX	Increment Index Register	SWI	Software Interrupt
BLT	Branch if Less than Zero				
BMI	Branch if Minus	JMP	Jump	TAB	Transfer Accumulators
BNE	Branch if Not Equal to Zero	JSR	Jump to Subroutine	TAP	Transfer Accumulators to Condition Code Reg.
BPL	Branch if Plus	LDA	Load Accumulator	TBA	Transfer Accumulators
BRA	Branch Always	LDS	Load Stack Pointer	TPA	Transfer Condition Code Reg. to Accumulator
BSR	Branch to Subroutine	LDX	Load Index Register	TST	Test
BVC	Branch if Overflow Clear	LSR	Logical Shift Right	TSX	Transfer Stack Pointer to Index Register
BVS	Branch if Overflow Set			TXS	Transfer Index Register to Stack Pointer
		NEG	Negate		
CBA	Compare Accumulators	NOP	No Operation	WAI	Wait for Interrupt
CLC	Clear Carry	ORA	Inclusive OR Accumulator		
CLI	Clear Interrupt Mask	PSH	Push Data		

TABLE 3 – ACCUMULATOR AND MEMORY INSTRUCTIONS

OPERATIONS	MNEMONIC	IMMED OP	~	=	DIRECT OP	~	=	INDEX OP	~	=	EXTND OP	~	=	IMPLIED OP	~	=	BOOLEAN/ARITHMETIC OPERATION (All register labels refer to contents)	5 H	4 I	3 N	2 Z	1 V	0 C
Add	ADDA	8B	2	2	9B	3	2	AB	5	2	BB	4	3				A + M → A	↕	●	↕	↕	↕	↕
	ADDB	CB	2	2	DB	3	2	EB	5	2	FB	4	3				B + M → B	↕	●	↕	↕	↕	↕
Add Acmltrs	ABA													1B	2	1	A + B → A	↕	●	↕	↕	↕	↕
Add with Carry	ADCA	89	2	2	99	3	2	A9	5	2	B9	4	3				A + M + C → A	↕	●	↕	↕	↕	↕
	ADCB	C9	2	2	D9	3	2	E9	5	2	F9	4	3				B + M + C → B	↕	●	↕	↕	↕	↕
And	ANDA	84	2	2	94	3	2	A4	5	2	B4	4	3				A · M → A	●	●	↕	↕	R	●
	ANDB	C4	2	2	D4	3	2	E4	5	2	F4	4	3				B · M → B	●	●	↕	↕	R	●
Bit Test	BITA	85	2	2	95	3	2	A5	5	2	B5	4	3				A · M	●	●	↕	↕	R	●
	BITB	C5	2	2	D5	3	2	E5	5	2	F5	4	3				B · M	●	●	↕	↕	R	●
Clear	CLR							6F	7	2	7F	6	3				00 → M	●	●	R	S	R	R
	CLRA													4F	2	1	00 → A	●	●	R	S	R	R
	CLRB													5F	2	1	00 → B	●	●	R	S	R	R
Compare	CMPA	81	2	2	91	3	2	A1	5	2	B1	4	3				A − M	●	●	↕	↕	↕	↕
	CMPB	C1	2	2	D1	3	2	E1	5	2	F1	4	3				B − M	●	●	↕	↕	↕	↕
Compare Acmltrs	CBA													11	2	1	A − B	●	●	↕	↕	↕	↕
Complement, 1's	COM							63	7	2	73	6	3				M̄ → M	●	●	↕	↕	R	S
	COMA													43	2	1	Ā → A	●	●	↕	↕	R	S
	COMB													53	2	1	B̄ → B	●	●	↕	↕	R	S
Complement, 2's	NEG							60	7	2	70	6	3				00 − M → M	●	●	↕	↕	①	②
(Negate)	NEGA													40	2	1	00 − A → A	●	●	↕	↕	①	②
	NEGB													50	2	1	00 − B → B	●	●	↕	↕	①	②
Decimal Adjust, A	DAA													19	2	1	Converts Binary Add. of BCD Characters into BCD Format	●	●	↕	↕	↕	③
Decrement	DEC							6A	7	2	7A	6	3				M − 1 → M	●	●	↕	↕	④	●
	DECA													4A	2	1	A − 1 → A	●	●	↕	↕	④	●
	DECB													5A	2	1	B − 1 → B	●	●	↕	↕	④	●
Exclusive OR	EORA	88	2	2	98	3	2	A8	5	2	B8	4	3				A ⊕ M → A	●	●	↕	↕	R	●
	EORB	C8	2	2	D8	3	2	E8	5	2	F8	4	3				B ⊕ M → B	●	●	↕	↕	R	●
Increment	INC							6C	7	2	7C	6	3				M + 1 → M	●	●	↕	↕	⑤	●
	INCA													4C	2	1	A + 1 → A	●	●	↕	↕	⑤	●
	INCB													5C	2	1	B + 1 → B	●	●	↕	↕	⑤	●
Load Acmltr	LDAA	86	2	2	96	3	2	A6	5	2	B6	4	3				M → A	●	●	↕	↕	R	●
	LDAB	C6	2	2	D6	3	2	E6	5	2	F6	4	3				M → B	●	●	↕	↕	R	●
Or, Inclusive	ORAA	8A	2	2	9A	3	2	AA	5	2	BA	4	3				A + M → A	●	●	↕	↕	R	●
	ORAB	CA	2	2	DA	3	2	EA	5	2	FA	4	3				B + M → B	●	●	↕	↕	R	●
Push Data	PSHA													36	4	1	A → M_SP, SP − 1 → SP	●	●	●	●	●	●
	PSHB													37	4	1	B → M_SP, SP − 1 → SP	●	●	●	●	●	●
Pull Data	PULA													32	4	1	SP + 1 → SP, M_SP → A	●	●	●	●	●	●
	PULB													33	4	1	SP + 1 → SP, M_SP → B	●	●	●	●	●	●
Rotate Left	ROL							69	7	2	79	6	3				M	●	●	↕	↕	⑥	↕
	ROLA													49	2	1	A	●	●	↕	↕	⑥	↕
	ROLB													59	2	1	B	●	●	↕	↕	⑥	↕
Rotate Right	ROR							66	7	2	76	6	3				M	●	●	↕	↕	⑥	↕
	RORA													46	2	1	A	●	●	↕	↕	⑥	↕
	RORB													56	2	1	B	●	●	↕	↕	⑥	↕
Shift Left, Arithmetic	ASL							68	7	2	78	6	3				M	●	●	↕	↕	⑥	↕
	ASLA													48	2	1	A	●	●	↕	↕	⑥	↕
	ASLB													58	2	1	B	●	●	↕	↕	⑥	↕
Shift Right, Arithmetic	ASR							67	7	2	77	6	3				M	●	●	↕	↕	⑥	↕
	ASRA													47	2	1	A	●	●	↕	↕	⑥	↕
	ASRB													57	2	1	B	●	●	↕	↕	⑥	↕
Shift Right, Logic	LSR							64	7	2	74	6	3				M	●	●	R	↕	⑥	↕
	LSRA													44	2	1	A	●	●	R	↕	⑥	↕
	LSRB													54	2	1	B	●	●	R	↕	⑥	↕
Store Acmltr.	STAA				97	4	2	A7	6	2	B7	5	3				A → M	●	●	↕	↕	R	●
	STAB				D7	4	2	E7	6	2	F7	5	3				B → M	●	●	↕	↕	R	●
Subtract	SUBA	80	2	2	90	3	2	A0	5	2	B0	4	3				A − M → A	●	●	↕	↕	↕	↕
	SUBB	C0	2	2	D0	3	2	E0	5	2	F0	4	3				B − M → B	●	●	↕	↕	↕	↕
Subtract Acmltrs.	SBA													10	2	1	A − B → A	●	●	↕	↕	↕	↕
Subtr. with Carry	SBCA	82	2	2	92	3	2	A2	5	2	B2	4	3				A − M − C → A	●	●	↕	↕	↕	↕
	SBCB	C2	2	2	D2	3	2	E2	5	2	F2	4	3				B − M − C → B	●	●	↕	↕	↕	↕
Transfer Acmltrs	TAB													16	2	1	A → B	●	●	↕	↕	R	●
	TBA													17	2	1	B → A	●	●	↕	↕	R	●
Test, Zero or Minus	TST							6D	7	2	7D	6	3				M − 00	●	●	↕	↕	R	R
	TSTA													4D	2	1	A − 00	●	●	↕	↕	R	R
	TSTB													5D	2	1	B − 00	●	●	↕	↕	R	R
																		H	I	N	Z	V	C

LEGEND:

OP   Operation Code (Hexadecimal);
~   Number of MPU Cycles;
=   Number of Program Bytes;
+   Arithmetic Plus;
−   Arithmetic Minus;
·   Boolean AND;
M_SP Contents of memory location pointed to be Stack Pointer;

+   Boolean Inclusive OR;
⊙   Boolean Exclusive OR;
M̄   Complement of M;
→   Transfer Into;
0   Bit = Zero;
00   Byte = Zero;

CONDITION CODE SYMBOLS:

H   Half carry from bit 3;
I   Interrupt mask
N   Negative (sign bit)
Z   Zero (byte)
V   Overflow, 2's complement
C   Carry from bit 7
R   Reset Always
S   Set Always
↕   Test and set if true, cleared otherwise
●   Not Affected

Note − Accumulator addressing mode instructions are included in the column for IMPLIED addressing

593

TABLE 4 — INDEX REGISTER AND STACK MANIPULATION INSTRUCTIONS

POINTER OPERATIONS	MNEMONIC	IMMED OP	~	#	DIRECT OP	~	#	INDEX OP	~	#	EXTND OP	~	#	IMPLIED OP	~	#	BOOLEAN/ARITHMETIC OPERATION	5 H	4 I	3 N	2 Z	1 V	0 C
Compare Index Reg	CPX	8C	3	3	9C	4	2	AC	6	2	BC	5	3				$X_H - M$, $X_L - (M+1)$	•	•	⑦	↕	⑧	•
Decrement Index Reg	DEX													09	4	1	$X - 1 \rightarrow X$	•	•	•	↕	•	•
Decrement Stack Pntr	DES													34	4	1	$SP - 1 \rightarrow SP$	•	•	•	•	•	•
Increment Index Reg	INX													08	4	1	$X + 1 \rightarrow X$	•	•	•	↕	•	•
Increment Stack Pntr	INS													31	4	1	$SP + 1 \rightarrow SP$	•	•	•	•	•	•
Load Index Reg	LDX	CE	3	3	DE	4	2	EE	6	2	FE	5	3				$M \rightarrow X_H$, $(M+1) \rightarrow X_L$	•	•	⑨	↕	R	•
Load Stack Pntr	LDS	8E	3	3	9E	4	2	AE	6	2	BE	5	3				$M \rightarrow SP_H$, $(M+1) \rightarrow SP_L$	•	•	⑨	↕	R	•
Store Index Reg	STX				DF	5	2	EF	7	2	FF	6	3				$X_H \rightarrow M$, $X_L \rightarrow (M+1)$	•	•	⑨	↕	R	•
Store Stack Pntr	STS				9F	5	2	AF	7	2	BF	6	3				$SP_H \rightarrow M$, $SP_L \rightarrow (M+1)$	•	•	⑨	↕	R	•
Indx Reg → Stack Pntr	TXS													35	4	1	$X - 1 \rightarrow SP$	•	•	•	•	•	•
Stack Pntr → Indx Reg	TSX													30	4	1	$SP + 1 \rightarrow X$	•	•	•	•	•	•

COND. CODE REG.

TABLE 5 — JUMP AND BRANCH INSTRUCTIONS

COND. CODE REG.

OPERATIONS	MNEMONIC	RELATIVE OP	~	#	INDEX OP	~	#	EXTND OP	~	#	IMPLIED OP	~	#	BRANCH TEST	5 H	4 I	3 N	2 Z	1 V	0 C
Branch Always	BRA	20	4	2										None	•	•	•	•	•	•
Branch If Carry Clear	BCC	24	4	2										$C = 0$	•	•	•	•	•	•
Branch If Carry Set	BCS	25	4	2										$C = 1$	•	•	•	•	•	•
Branch If = Zero	BEQ	27	4	2										$Z = 1$	•	•	•	•	•	•
Branch If ≥ Zero	BGE	2C	4	2										$N \oplus V = 0$	•	•	•	•	•	•
Branch If > Zero	BGT	2E	4	2										$Z + (N \oplus V) = 0$	•	•	•	•	•	•
Branch If Higher	BHI	22	4	2										$C + Z = 0$	•	•	•	•	•	•
Branch If ≤ Zero	BLE	2F	4	2										$Z + (N \oplus V) = 1$	•	•	•	•	•	•
Branch If Lower Or Same	BLS	23	4	2										$C + Z = 1$	•	•	•	•	•	•
Branch If < Zero	BLT	2D	4	2										$N \oplus V = 1$	•	•	•	•	•	•
Branch If Minus	BMI	2B	4	2										$N = 1$	•	•	•	•	•	•
Branch If Not Equal Zero	BNE	26	4	2										$Z = 0$	•	•	•	•	•	•
Branch If Overflow Clear	BVC	28	4	2										$V = 0$	•	•	•	•	•	•
Branch If Overflow Set	BVS	29	4	2										$V = 1$	•	•	•	•	•	•
Branch If Plus	BPL	2A	4	2										$N = 0$	•	•	•	•	•	•
Branch To Subroutine	BSR	8D	8	2											•	•	•	•	•	•
Jump	JMP				6E	4	2	7E	3	3				See Special Operations	•	•	•	•	•	•
Jump To Subroutine	JSR				AD	8	2	BD	9	3					•	•	•	•	•	•
No Operation	NOP										01	2	1	Advances Prog. Cntr. Only	•	•	•	•	•	•
Return From Interrupt	RTI										3B	10	1		← ⑩ →					
Return From Subroutine	RTS										39	5	1	See Special Operations	•	•	•	•	•	•
Software Interrupt	SWI										3F	12	1		•	•	•	•	•	•
Wait for Interrupt *	WAI										3E	9	1		•	⑪	•	•	•	•

*WAI puts Address Bus, R/W, and Data Bus in the three-state mode while VMA is held low.

SPECIAL OPERATIONS

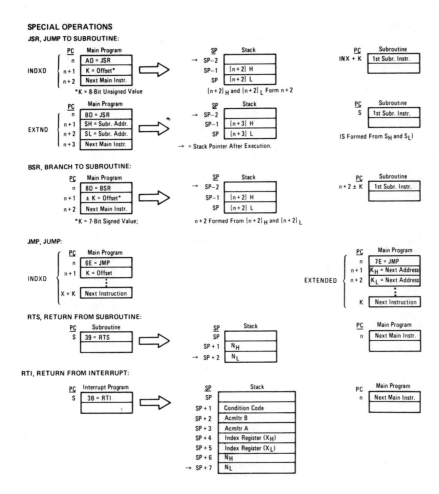

JSR, JUMP TO SUBROUTINE:

INDXD
PC	Main Program
n	AD = JSR
n + 1	K = Offset*
n + 2	Next Main Instr.

*K = 8-Bit Unsigned Value

SP	Stack
→ SP−2	
SP−1	[n + 2] H
SP	[n + 2] L

[n + 2]_H and [n + 2]_L Form n + 2

PC	Subroutine
INX + K	1st Subr. Instr.

EXTND
PC	Main Program
n	BD = JSR
n + 1	SH = Subr. Addr.
n + 2	SL = Subr. Addr.
n + 3	Next Main Instr.

SP	Stack
→ SP−2	
SP−1	[n + 3] H
SP	[n + 3] L

→ = Stack Pointer After Execution.

PC	Subroutine
S	1st Subr. Instr.

(S Formed From S_H and S_L)

BSR, BRANCH TO SUBROUTINE:

PC	Main Program
n	8D = BSR
n + 1	± K = Offset*
n + 2	Next Main Instr.

*K = 7-Bit Signed Value;

SP	Stack
→ SP−2	
SP−1	[n + 2] H
SP	[n + 2] L

n + 2 Formed From [n + 2]_H and [n + 2]_L

PC	Subroutine
n + 2 ± K	1st Subr. Instr.

JMP, JUMP:

INDXD
PC	Main Program
n	6E = JMP
n + 1	K = Offset
⋮	
X + K	Next Instruction

EXTENDED
PC	Main Program
n	7E = JMP
n + 1	K_H = Next Address
n + 2	K_L = Next Address
⋮	
K	Next Instruction

RTS, RETURN FROM SUBROUTINE:

PC	Subroutine
S	39 = RTS

SP	Stack
SP	
SP + 1	N_H
→ SP + 2	N_L

PC	Main Program
n	Next Main Instr.

RTI, RETURN FROM INTERRUPT:

PC	Interrupt Program
S	3B = RTI

SP	Stack
SP	
SP + 1	Condition Code
SP + 2	Acmltr B
SP + 3	Acmltr A
SP + 4	Index Register (X_H)
SP + 5	Index Register (X_L)
SP + 6	N_H
→ SP + 7	N_L

PC	Main Program
n	Next Main Instr.

TABLE 6 – CONDITION CODE REGISTER MANIPULATION INSTRUCTIONS

OPERATIONS	MNEMONIC	IMPLIED OP	IMPLIED ~	IMPLIED #	BOOLEAN OPERATION	5 H	4 I	3 N	2 Z	1 V	0 C
Clear Carry	CLC	0C	2	1	0 → C	●	●	●	●	●	R
Clear Interrupt Mask	CLI	0E	2	1	0 → I	●	R	●	●	●	●
Clear Overflow	CLV	0A	2	1	0 → V	●	●	●	●	R	●
Set Carry	SEC	0D	2	1	1 → C	●	●	●	●	●	S
Set Interrupt Mask	SEI	0F	2	1	1 → I	●	S	●	●	●	●
Set Overflow	SEV	0B	2	1	1 → V	●	●	●	●	S	●
Acmltr A → CCR	TAP	06	2	1	A → CCR	(12)					
CCR → Acmltr A	TPA	07	2	1	CCR → A	●	●	●	●	●	●

CONDITION CODE REGISTER NOTES: (Bit set if test is true and cleared otherwise)

1. (Bit V) Test: Result = 10000000?
2. (Bit C) Test: Result = 00000000?
3. (Bit C) Test: Decimal value of most significant BCD Character greater than nine? (Not cleared if previously set.)
4. (Bit V) Test: Operand = 10000000 prior to execution?
5. (Bit V) Test: Operand = 01111111 prior to execution?
6. (Bit V) Test: Set equal to result of N⊕C after shift has occurred.

7. (Bit N) Test: Sign bit of most significant (MS) byte = 1?
8. (Bit V) Test: 2's complement overflow from subtraction of MS bytes?
9. (Bit N) Test: Result less than zero? (Bit 15 = 1)
10. (All) Load Condition Code Register from Stack. (See Special Operations)
11. (Bit I) Set when interrupt occurs. If previously set, a Non-Maskable Interrupt is required to exit the wait state.
12. (All) Set according to the contents of Accumulator A.

TABLE 7 — INSTRUCTION ADDRESSING MODES AND ASSOCIATED EXECUTION TIMES
(Times in Machine Cycles)

	(Dual Operand)	ACCX	Immediate	Direct	Extended	Indexed	Implied	Relative
ABA	•	•	•	•	•	•	2	•
ADC	x	•	2	3	4	5	•	•
ADD	x	•	2	3	4	5	•	•
AND	x	•	2	3	4	5	•	•
ASL	•	2	•	•	6	7	•	•
ASR	•	2	•	•	6	7	•	•
BCC	•	•	•	•	•	•	•	4
BCS	•	•	•	•	•	•	•	4
BEA	•	•	•	•	•	•	•	4
BGE	•	•	•	•	•	•	•	4
BGT	•	•	•	•	•	•	•	4
BHI	•	•	•	•	•	•	•	4
BIT	x	•	2	3	4	5	•	•
BLE	•	•	•	•	•	•	•	4
BLS	•	•	•	•	•	•	•	4
BLT	•	•	•	•	•	•	•	4
BMI	•	•	•	•	•	•	•	4
BNE	•	•	•	•	•	•	•	4
BPL	•	•	•	•	•	•	•	4
BRA	•	•	•	•	•	•	•	4
BSR	•	•	•	•	•	•	•	8
BVC	•	•	•	•	•	•	•	4
BVS	•	•	•	•	•	•	•	4
CBA	•	•	•	•	•	•	2	•
CLC	•	•	•	•	•	•	2	•
CLI	•	•	•	•	•	•	2	•
CLR	•	2	•	•	6	7	•	•
CLV	•	•	•	•	•	•	2	•
CMP	x	•	2	3	4	5	•	•
COM	•	2	•	•	6	7	•	•
CPX	•	•	3	4	5	6	•	•
DAA	•	•	•	•	•	•	2	•
DEC	•	2	•	•	6	7	•	•
DES	•	•	•	•	•	•	4	•
DEX	•	•	•	•	•	•	4	•
EOR	x	•	2	3	4	5	•	•

	(Dual Operand)	ACCX	Immediate	Direct	Extended	Indexed	Implied
INC	•	2	•	•	6	7	•
INS	•	•	•	•	•	•	4
INX	•	•	•	•	•	•	4
JMP	•	•	•	•	3	4	•
JSR	•	•	•	•	9	8	•
LDA	x	•	2	3	4	5	•
LDS	•	•	3	4	5	6	•
LDX	•	•	3	4	5	6	•
LSR	•	2	•	•	6	7	•
NEG	•	2	•	•	6	7	•
NOP	•	•	•	•	•	•	2
ORA	x	•	2	3	4	5	•
PSH	•	•	•	•	•	•	4
PUL	•	•	•	•	•	•	4
ROL	•	2	•	•	6	7	•
ROR	•	2	•	•	6	7	•
RTI	•	•	•	•	•	•	10
RTS	•	•	•	•	•	•	5
SBA	•	•	•	•	•	•	2
SBC	x	•	2	3	4	5	•
SEC	•	•	•	•	•	•	2
SEI	•	•	•	•	•	•	2
SEV	•	•	•	•	•	•	2
STA	x	•	•	4	5	6	•
STS	•	•	•	5	6	7	•
STX	•	•	•	5	6	7	•
SUB	x	•	2	3	4	5	•
SWI	•	•	•	•	•	•	12
TAB	•	•	•	•	•	•	2
TAP	•	•	•	•	•	•	2
TBA	•	•	•	•	•	•	2
TPA	•	•	•	•	•	•	2
TST	•	2	•	•	6	7	•
TSX	•	•	•	•	•	•	4
TSX	•	•	•	•	•	•	4
WAI	•	•	•	•	•	•	9

NOTE: Interrupt time is 12 cycles from the end of the instruction being executed, except following a WAI instruction. Then it is 4 cycles.

596

Glossary

Access Time The delay between the time when a memory receives an address and the time when the data from that address is available at the outputs.

Accumulator A register that is the source of one operand and the destination of the result for most arithmetic and logical operations.

Active-High The active state is the one state.

Active-Low The active state is the zero state.

Address The identification code that distinguishes one memory location or input/output port from another and that can be used to select a specific one.

Addressing Methods (Modes) The methods for specifying the addresses to be used in an instruction. Common addressing methods include direct, indirect, indexed, relative, and stack.

ALGOL Algorithmic Language, a widely used high-level language designed for systems and scientific applications.

Analog Continuous signal or representation of a quantity that can take any value.

Anode Positive terminal.

Architecture Structure of a system. Computer architecture often refers specifically to the CPU.

Arithmetic-Logic Unit (ALU) A device that can perform any of a variety of arithmetic or logical functions under the control of function inputs.

Arithmetic Shift A shift operation that preserves the value of the sign bit (most significant bit).

Arm See Enable, but particularly applied to enabling interrupts.

ASCII American Standard Code for Information Interchange, a 7-bit character code widely used in computers and communications.

Assembler A computer program that converts assembly language programs into a form (machine language) that the computer can understand. The assembler translates mnemonic instruction codes into binary numbers, replaces names with their binary equivalents, and assigns locations in memory to data and instructions.

Assembly Language A programming language in which the programmer can use mnemonic instruction codes, labels, and names to refer directly to their binary equivalents. The assembler is a low-level language, since each assembly language instruction translates directly into a specific machine language instruction.

Asynchronous Operating without reference to an overall timing source, that is, operating at irregular intervals.

Attached Input/Output An addressing method for input/output ports that identifies the ports either directly (if the port is attached to the CPU) or from the address in memory to which the port is attached. The port is usually selected with special instructions that are decoded either in the CPU or in the memory section. Systems using attached I/O are frequently based on LSI devices that combine memory, input/output, and processor functions.

Autoindex An index register that is automatically incremented (*autoincrement*) or decremented (*autodecrement*) with each use.

Auxiliary Carry Bit See Half-Carry Bit.

Bank A directly addressable set of registers or memory locations. The register or other storage device that selects banks is called a *bank switch*.

Baud A communications measure for serial data transmission, bits per second but including both data bits and bits used for synchronization, error checking, and other purposes.

Baud Rate Generator A device that generates the proper timing interval between bits for serial data transmission.

Baudot Code A 5-bit character code used in telegraphy and some communications terminals.

BCD (Binary-Coded Decimal) A method for representing decimal numbers whereby each decimal digit is separately coded into a binary number.

Benchmark Program A sample program used to evaluate and compare computers.

Bidirectional Capable of transporting signals in either direction.

Binary Number system with base 2; having two distinct levels.

Bit A binary digit, possible values zero or one.

Bit Manipulation (or Bit Banging) The examination and changing of single bits or small groups of bits within a word.

Bit Slice A section of a CPU that may be combined in parallel with other such sections to form complete CPUs with various word lengths.

Bootstrap Loader (or Bootstrap)   Technique for loading first instructions of a program into memory and then using these instructions to bring in the rest of the program. The first instructions (called the *bootstrap*) may reside in a special read-only memory.

Borrow   A status bit that is one if the result of an unsigned subtraction was negative.

Bottom-Up Design   A design method in which parts (or modules) of a system are designed and tested separately before being combined.

Bounce   Moving back and forth between states before reaching a final state.

Branch Instruction   See Jump Instruction.

Breakpoint   A location specified by the user at which program execution is to end temporarily. Used as an aid in program debugging.

Bus   A group of parallel lines that connect two or more devices.

Bus Contention   A situation in which two or more devices are trying to place data on a bus at the same time.

Bus Driver   A device that amplifies outputs sufficiently so that they can be recognized by the devices on a bus.

Bus Isolation   Buffering parts of the bus away from other parts with buffers and drivers.

Bus Transceiver   A device that acts as both a bus driver and bus receiver; that is, it interfaces a bidirectional bus to two unidirectional buses.

Byte   The basic grouping of bits that the computer handles as a unit, most often eight bits in length.

Call   See Subroutine.

Carry Bit   A status bit that is one if the last operation generated a carry from the most significant bit.

Cartridge (or 3M Mag-Tape Cartridge)   A compact, enclosed package of magnetic tape that uses $\frac{1}{4}$-inch tape and records 1600 bits per inch at 30 in./s on four tracks.

Cassette   An enclosed package of magnetic tape usually housed in a plastic container. Both audio and digital versions exist; the digital ones are more reliable and more expensive. The standard unit is the Philips-type cartridge, which consists of 282 feet of 0.015-in. magnetic tape, phase encoded at 800 bits per inch.

Cathode   Negative terminal.

Central Processing Unit (CPU)   The control section of a computer. It contains the arithmetic unit, registers, instruction-decoding mechanism, and timing and control circuitry.

Checksum   A logical sum of data that is included in a record as a guard against recording or transmission errors.

Chip   A substrate containing a single integrated circuit.

Clear   Set state to zero; an input to a device that sets the state to zero.

Clock   A regular timing signal that governs transitions in a system.

CMOS Complementary metal-oxide semiconductor, a logic family that uses complementary N-channel and P-channel MOS field-effect transistors to provide high noise immunity and low power consumption.

Coding The writing of programs in a language that is comprehensible to a computer system.

Common-Anode Display A multiple display in which signals are applied to the cathodes of the individual displays and the anodes are tied together to the power supply; uses negative logic (i.e., a logic zero turns a display on).

Common-Cathode Display A multiple display in which signals are applied to the anodes of the individual displays and the cathodes are tied together to ground. Uses positive logic (i.e., a logic one turns a display on).

Common I/O Uses the same lines for input and output.

Comparator A device that produces outputs that show whether one input is greater than, equal to, or less than the other input. Both analog and digital comparators exist.

Compiler A program that converts a program in a high-level or procedure-oriented language into an assembly or machine language program.

Condition Code (or Flag) A single bit that indicates a condition within the computer, often used to choose between alternate instruction sequences.

Condition Code Register A register that contains one or more condition codes.

Control Memory A memory that holds microprograms—that is, a memory used to decode computer instructions.

Core Memory A magnetic memory that can be magnetized in one of two directions so as to represent a bit of data.

Counter A clocked device that enters a different state after each clock pulse (up to its capacity) and produces an output that reflects the total number of clock pulses it has received. Counters are also referred to as *dividers*, since they divide the input frequency by n, where n is the capacity of the counter.

Cross-Assembler An assembler that runs on a computer other than the one for which it assembles programs.

CRT Cathode-ray tube.

Current Page The page of memory on which the present instruction is located.

Current-Loop Interface (or Teletype Interface) An interface that allows connections between digital logic and a device that uses current-loop signals—that is, typically the presence of 20 mA in the loop is a logic one and the absence of that current is a logic zero.

Cycle Stealing Using a cycle during which the CPU is not accessing the memory for a DMA operation.

Cycle Time Time interval at which a set of operations is repeated regularly in the same sequence.

Cyclic Redundancy Check (CRC)   An error-detecting code generated from a polynomial that can be added to a data record or sector.

Daisy-Chain   An input or output method whereby signals pass from one device to another until accepted or blocked. Activity near the control unit for the chain will block activity farther from the control unit.

Data Acquisition System   A system that will accept several analog inputs and produce corresponding digital data. The system usually includes sample and hold circuitry, multiplexers, and converters.

Data Fetch Cycle   A computer operation cycle during which data is brought from memory to the CPU.

Data Pointer (or Pointer)   A register or memory location that holds an address rather than the data itself.

Debounce   Convert the output from a contact with bounce into a single, clean transition between states.

Debounce Time   The amount of time required to debounce a closure.

Debug   To eliminate programming errors, sometimes referred to as verifying the program.

Debugger (or Debug Program)   A program that helps in finding and correcting errors in a user program.

Decade Counter   A counter with ten different states.

Decimal Adjust   An operation that converts a binary arithmetic result to a decimal (BCD) result.

Decoder   A device that produces unencoded outputs from coded inputs.

Delay Time   The amount of time between the clocking signal and the actual appearance of output data, or the time between input and output.

Demultiplexer   A device that directs a time-shared input to one of several possible outputs, according to the state of the select inputs.

Destructive Readout (DRO)   The contents cannot be determined without changing them.

Development System   A special computer system that includes hardware and software specifically designed for developing programs and interfaces.

Diagnostic (Program)   A program that checks part of a system for proper operation.

Digital   Having discrete levels, quantized into a series of distinct levels.

Direct Addressing   An addressing method whereby the address of the operand is part of the instruction.

Directly Addressable   Can be addressed without changing the contents of any registers or bank switches.

Direct Execution A method whereby the computer directly executes statements in a high-level language rather than translating those statements into machine or assembly language.

Direct Memory Access (DMA) An input/output method whereby an external controller directly transfers data between the memory and input/output sections without processor intervention.

Disable Prohibit an activity from proceeding or a device from producing data outputs.

(Output) Disable Time The amount of time required for an active tri-state output to enter the third or open-circuit state.

Disarm See Disable, but particularly applied to disabling interrupts.

Disk Operating System (DOS) An operating system that transfers programs and data to and from a disk, which may be either flexible or fixed-head; the operating system may itself be largely resident on the disk.

Diskette See Floppy Disk.

Divider See Counter.

Dual Inline Package (DIP or Bug) A semiconductor chip package having two rows of pins perpendicular to the edges of the package, sometimes called a *bug*, since it appears to have legs.

Dynamic Memory A memory that loses its contents gradually without any external causes.

EAROM Electrically alterable ROM, a nonvolatile RAM, often with a relatively long write time.

EBCDIC Expanded Binary-Coded Decimal Interchange Code, an 8-bit character code often used in large computers.

ECL Emitter-coupled logic, a high-speed bipolar technology often used in computer mainframes.

Editor A program that manipulates text material and allows the user to make corrections, additions, deletions, and other changes.

Effective Address The actual address used by a particular instruction to fetch or store data.

Emulator A microprogrammed copy of an existing system.

Enable Allow an activity to proceed or a device to produce data outputs.

Encoder A device that produces coded outputs from unencoded inputs.

EPROM (or EROM) Erasable PROM, a PROM that can be completely erased by exposure to ultraviolet light.

Error-Correcting Code A code that can be used by the receiver to correct errors in the messages to which the code is attached; the code itself does not contain any additional message.

False Start Bit   A start bit that does not last the minimum required amount of time, usually caused by noise on the transmission line.

Fan-In   The number of inputs connected to a gate.

Fan-Out   The maximum number of outputs of the same family that can be connected to a gate without causing current overload.

Field-Programmable Logic Array (FPLA)   A programmable logic array that can be programmed by the user.

Firmware   Microprograms, usually implemented in read-only memories.

Fixed-Instruction Computer   A computer for which the manufacturer determines the instruction set. As opposed to microprogrammable computer.

Fixed Memory   See ROM.

Flag   See Condition Code.

Flatpack   A semiconductor chip package in which the pins are in the same plane as the package rather than perpendicular to it as in a DIP.

Flip-Flop   A digital electronic device with two stable states that can be made to switch from one state to the other in a reproducible manner.

Floating   Not tied to any logic level, often applied to tri-state outputs that are in the high-impedance state. TTL devices usually interpret a floating input as a logic one.

Floppy Disk (or Flexible Disk)   A flexible magnetic surface that can be used as a data storage device; the surface is divided into sectors. An IBM-compatible floppy disk is one that uses formatting and sectoring techniques originally introduced by IBM. The individual floppy disk is sometimes called a *diskette*.

Flowchart   A graphical representation of a procedure or computer program.

FORTRAN   A high-level (procedure-oriented) programming language devised for expressing scientific problems in algebraic notation. Short for Formula Translation Language.

Gate   A digital logic element where the binary value of the output depends on the values of the inputs according to some logic rule.

General-Purpose Interface Bus (GPIB or Hewlett-Packard Bus)   A standard interface for the transmission of parallel data in a network of instruments. The GPIB has 8 data lines, 8 control lines, and 8 ground lines.

General-Purpose Register   A register that can be used for temporary data storage.

Gray Code   A binary code sequence in which only one bit changes in a transition to the next higher or lower value.

Half-Carry (or Auxiliary Carry) Bit   A status bit that is one if the last operation produced a carry from bit 3 of an 8-bit word. Used on 8-bit microprocessors to make the correction between binary and decimal (BCD) arithmetic.

Hardware   Physical equipment forming a computer system.

Hex (1) Containing six distinct logic elements, as in hex buffers; (2) abbreviation for hexadecimal or base 16.

Hexadecimal Number system with base 16. The digits are the decimal numbers 0 through 9, followed by the letters A through F.

High-Impedance State See Tri-State.

High-Level Language (or Procedure-Oriented Language) A programming language in which the statements represent procedures rather than single machine instructions. FORTRAN, COBOL, and BASIC are three common high-level languages. A high-level language requires a compiler that translates each statement into a series of machine language instructions.

Hold Time The amount of time after the end of an activity signal during which some other signal must be stable to ensure the achievement of the correct final state.

IEEE Standard 488 Bus See General-Purpose Interface Bus.

Immediate Addressing An addressing method in which the operand is part of the instruction itself.

Immediate Data Data that is part of the instruction that uses it.

Implied (or Inherent) Addressing The operation code itself specifies all the required addresses.

In-Circuit Emulator A device that allows a prototype to be attached to a development system for testing and debugging purposes.

Index Register A register that can be used to modify memory addresses.

Indexed Addressing An addressing method in which the address included in the instruction is modified by the contents of an index register in order to find the actual address of the data.

Indirect Addressing An addressing method in which the address of the data, rather than the data itself, is in the memory location specified by the instruction.

Input/Output (Section) The section of the computer that handles communications with external devices.

Instruction A group of bits that defines a computer operation and is part of the instruction set.

Instruction Cycle The process of fetching, decoding, and executing an instruction.

Instruction Execution The process of performing the operations indicated by an instruction.

Instruction (Execution) Time The time required to fetch, decode, and execute an instruction.

Instruction Fetch The process of addressing memory and reading an instruction word into the CPU for decoding.

Instruction Length The number of words of memory needed to store a complete instruction.

Instruction Repertoire See Instruction Set.

Instruction Set The set of general-purpose instructions available with a given computer—that is, the set of inputs to which the CPU will produce a known response during the instruction fetch cycle.

Integrated Circuit (IC) A complete circuit on a single substrate or chip.

I²L Integrated-injection logic, a bipolar technology that uses only transistors (both vertical and lateral) to provide moderate speed, low power consumption, and high density.

Intelligent Terminal (or Smart Terminal) A terminal that has some data processing capability or local computing capability.

Interpreter A program that fetches and executes instructions written in a high-level language. An interpreter executes each instruction as soon as it reads the instruction; it does not produce an object program, as a compiler does.

Interrupt A computer input that temporarily suspends the normal sequence of operations and transfers control to a special routine.

Interrupt-Driven System A system that depends on interrupts to handle input and output or that idles until it receives an interrupt.

Interrupt Mask (Interrupt Enable) A mechanism that allows the program to specify whether interrupts will be accepted.

Interrupt Service Routine A program that performs the actions required to respond to an interrupt.

Inverter A logic device that complements the input.

Isolated Input/Output An addressing method for I/O ports that uses an addressing system distinct from that used by the memory section.

Jump Instruction An instruction that places a new value in the program counter, thus departing from the normal one-step incrementing. Jump instructions may be conditional; that is, the new value may only be placed in the program counter if certain conditions are met.

Jump Table A table that contains the addresses of routines to which the computer can transfer control.

K 2^{10} or 1024 words, a unit of memory.

Keyboard A collection of keyswitches.

Keyboard Encoder A device that produces a unique output code for each possible closure on a keyboard.

Keyboard Scan The process of examining the rows and columns of a matrix keyboard to determine which keys have been pressed.

Kilobit   1000 bits.

Label   A name attached to a particular instruction or statement in a program that identifies the location in memory of the object code or assignment produced from that instruction or statement.

Large-Scale Integration (LSI)   An integrated circuit with complexity equivalent to over 100 ordinary gates.

Latch   A temporary storage device controlled by a timing signal. The contents of the latch are fixed at their current values by a transition of the timing signal (clock) and remain fixed until the next transition.

Light-Emitting Diode (LED)   A semiconductor device that emits light when biased in the forward direction.

Linear Select   Using coded bus lines individually for selection purposes rather than decoding the lines. Linear select requires no decoders but allows only n separate devices to be connected rather than 2^n, where n is the number of lines.

Linking Loader   A loader that will enter a series of programs and subroutines into memory and provide the required interconnections.

Loader   A program that reads a user or system program from an input device into memory.

Logic Analyzer   A test instrument that detects and displays the state of parallel digital signals.

Logic Design   Design using digital logic circuits.

Logical Shift   A shift operation that places zeros in the empty bits.

Logical Sum   A bit-by-bit EXCLUSIVE-ORing of two binary numbers.

Lookahead Carry   A device that forms the carry bit from a binary addition without using the carries from each bit position.

Loop   A self-contained sequence of instructions that the processor repeats until a terminal condition is reached. A conditional jump instruction can determine if the loop should be continued or terminated.

Low-Level Language   A language in which each statement is directly translated into a single machine language instruction. See Assembly Language and Machine Language.

Low-Power Schottky TTL   A low-power variant of standard TTL.

Machine Code   See Machine Language.

Machine Cycle   The basic CPU cycle. One machine cycle is the time required to fetch data from memory or execute a single-word operation.

Machine Language   The programming language that the computer can directly understand with no translation other than numeric conversions. A machine language program can be loaded into memory and executed. The value of every bit in every instruction in the program must be specified.

Macro　A name that represents a sequence of instructions. The assembler replaces a reference to the macro with a copy of the sequence.

Macroassembler　An assembler that has facilities for macros.

Macroinstruction　An overall computer instruction fetched from the main memory in a microprogrammed computer.

Majority Logic　A combinational logic function that is true when more than half the inputs are true.

Mark　The one state on a serial data communications line.

Mask　(1) A glass photographic plate that defines the diffusion patterns in integrated circuit production. (2) A bit pattern that isolates one or more bits from a group of bits.

Maskable Interrupt　An interrupt that the system can disable.

Matrix Keyboard　A keyboard in which the keys are connected in rows and columns.

Medium-Scale Integration (MSI)　An integrated circuit with a complexity of between 10 and 100 gates.

Megabit　One million bits.

Memory (Section)　The section of a computer that serves as storage for data and instructions. Each item in the memory has a unique address that the CPU can use to fetch it.

Memory Address Register (or Storage Address Register)　A register that holds the address of the memory location being accessed.

Memory-Mapped Input/Output　An addressing method for I/O ports that uses the same addressing system as that used by the memory section.

Meta-Assembler　An assembler for which the input instruction patterns can be defined and that can, therefore, assemble programs for different computers.

Microassembler　An assembler specifically designed for writing microprograms.

Microcomputer　A computer whose CPU is a microprocessor. A microprocessor plus memory and input/output circuitry.

Microcontroller　A microprogrammed control system without arithmetic capabilities.

Microinstruction　One of the words in a control memory—that is, one of the organized sequence of control signals that form the instructions at the control level.

Microprocessor　The central processing unit of a small computer, implemented on one or a few LSI chips.

Microprocessor Analyzer　A piece of test equipment that can be used to trace and debug the operations of a microprocessor.

Microprogram　A program written at the control level and stored in a control memory.

Microprogrammable　Having a microprogrammed control function that the user can change. That is, the user can add, enter, or replace microprograms.

Microprogrammed Having the control function implemented through microprogramming.

Microprogramming The implementation of the control function of a processing system as a sequence of control signals that is organized into words and stored in a control memory.

Mnemonics Symbolic names or abbreviations for instructions, registers, memory locations, etc., which suggest their actual functions or purposes.

Modem *Mo*dulator/*dem*odulator, a device that adds or removes a carrier frequency, thereby allowing data to be transmitted on a high-frequency channel or received from such a channel.

Modular Programming A programming method whereby the entire task is divided into logically separate sections or modules.

Monitor A simple operating system that allows the user to enter or change programs and data, to run programs, and to observe the status of the various sections of the computer.

Monostable Multivibrator (or One-Shot) A device that produces a single pulse of known length in response to a pulse input.

MOS Metal-oxide semiconductor, a semiconductor process that uses field-effect transistors in which the current is controlled by the electric field around a gate.

Multiplexer (or Selector) A device that selects one of several possible inputs to be placed on a time-shared output bus according to the state of the select inputs.

Multiprocessing Utilizing two or more processors in a single system, operating out of a common memory.

Nanosecond 10^{-9} second, abbreviated ns.

Negative Logic Circuitry in which a logic zero is the active or ON state.

Nesting Constructing subroutines or interrupt service routines so that one transfers control to another and so on. The nesting level is the number of transfers required to reach a particular routine without returning.

Nibble A sequence of four bits operated on as a unit.

N-Key Rollover (NKRO) Resolving any number of simultaneous key closures into consecutive output codes.

NMOS N-channel metal-oxide semiconductor, a logic family that uses N-channel MOS field-effect transistors to provide high density and medium speed.

Noise Margin The noise voltage required to make logic circuits malfunction.

Nondestructive Readout (NDRO) The contents of the device can be determined without changing those contents.

Nonmaskable Interrupt An interrupt that the system cannot disable.

Nonvolatile Memory A memory that does not lose its contents when power is removed.

No-Op (or No Operation) An instruction that does nothing other than increment the program counter.

Object Program (or Object Code)   The program that is the output of a translator program, such as an assembler or compiler. Usually a machine language program ready for execution.

Octal   Number system with base 8. The digits are the decimal numbers 0 through 7.

Offset   A number that is to be added to another number to calculate an effective address.

One-Address Instruction   An instruction in which only one data address must be specified. The other data, if necessary, is presumed to be in the accumulator.

One's Complement   A bit-by-bit logical complement of a binary number.

One-Shot   See Monostable Multivibrator.

On-Line System   A computer system in which information reflecting current activity is introduced as soon as it occurs.

Open-Collector Output   A special output that is active-low but not high. Such outputs can be wire-ORed to form a bus employing negative logic.

Operating System   System software that controls the overall operation of a computer system and performs such tasks as memory allocation, input and output distribution, interrupt processing, and job scheduling.

Operation Code (Op Code)   The part of an instruction that specifies the operation to be performed during the next cycle.

Optoisolator   Semiconductor device consisting of an LED and a photodiode or phototransistor in close proximity. Current through the LED causes internal light emission that forces current to flow in the phototransistor. Voltage differences have no effect because the devices are electrically separated.

Overflow Bit   A status bit that is one if the last operation produced a two's complement overflow.

Overlay   The section of a program that is actually resident in memory at a particular time. A large program can be divided into overlays and run on a computer having limited memory but backup storage for the rest of the program.

Page   A subdivision of the memory section.

Page Zero   The first page of memory; the most significant address bits (or page number) are zero.

Parallel   More than one bit at a time.

Parity   A 1-bit code that makes the total number of one bits in the word, including the parity bit, odd (*odd parity*) or even (*even parity*).

Parity Bit   A status bit that is one if the last operation produced a result with even (if even parity) or odd (if odd parity) parity.

Passing Parameters   See Subroutine.

Pipelining   Overlapping cycles so that different parts of consecutive cycles are performed at the same time.

PL/I   Programming Language I, a high-level language developed by IBM that combines many of the features of earlier languages, such as ALGOL, COBOL, and FORTRAN. Many versions exist for microprocessors, such as PL/M, MPL, SM/PL, and PLµS.

PMOS   P-channel metal-oxide semiconductor, a logic family that uses P-channel MOS field-effect transistors to provide high density and low speed.

Pointer   Register or memory location that contains an address rather than data.

Polling   Determining the state of peripherals or other devices by examining each one in succession.

Pop (or Pull)   Remove an operand from a stack.

Port   The basic addressable unit of the computer input/output section.

Power-On Reset   A circuit that automatically causes a RESET signal when the power is turned on, thus starting the system in a known state.

Printed Circuit Board (PC Board)   A circuit board in which the connections are made by etching with a mask.

Priority Interrupt System   An interrupt system in which some interrupts have precedence over others—that is, will be serviced first or can interrupt the others' service routines.

Procedure-Oriented Language   See High-Level Language.

Program   A sequence of instructions properly ordered to perform a particular task.

Program Counter   A register that specifies the address of the next instruction to be fetched from program memory.

Program Library   A collection of debugged and documented programs.

Programmable Interface   An interface device that can have its active logic structure varied under program control.

Programmable Logic Array (PLA)   An array of logic elements that can be programmed to perform a specific logic function; like a ROM except that only certain addresses are decoded.

Programmable Timer   A device that can provide various timing modes and intervals under program control.

Programmed Input/Output (I/O)   Input/output performed under program control without using interrupts or direct memory access.

PROM   Programmable read-only memory, a memory that cannot be changed during normal operation but that can be programmed by the user under special conditions. The programming is generally not reversible.

PROM Programmer   A piece of equipment that is used to change the contents of a PROM.

Prototyping System (or Development System)   A hardware system used to breadboard a computer-based product. Contains the computer plus the software and hardware required for efficient development.

Pseudo-Operation (or Pseudo-Instruction)   An assembly language operation code that directs the assembler to perform some action but does not result in a machine language instruction.

Pull   See Pop.

Pullup Resistor   A resistor connected to the power supply that ensures that an otherwise open circuit will be at the voltage level of the power supply.

Pulse Generator   A device that produces a single pulse or a series of pulses of predetermined length in response to an input signal.

Push   Enter an operand into a stack.

Queue (or FIFO)   A set of registers or memory locations that are accessed in a first-in, first-out manner. That is, the first data entered into the queue will be the first data read.

RAM   Random-access (read/write) memory, a memory that can be both read and altered (written) in normal operation.

Random Access   All internal storage locations can be accessed in the same amount of time.

Real Time   In synchronization with the actual occurrence of events.

Real Time Clock   A device that interrupts a CPU at regular time intervals.

Recursive Subroutine   A subroutine that calls itself as part of its execution.

Reentrant Subroutine   A subroutine that can be executed correctly even while the same routine is being interrupted or otherwise held in abeyance.

Refresh   The process of restoring the contents of a dynamic memory before they are lost.

Register   A storage location used to hold bits or words inside the CPU.

Register Direct Addressing   An addressing method that is the same as direct addressing except that the address is a register rather than a memory location.

Register Indirect Addressing   An addressing method that is the same as indirect addressing except that the address is in a register rather than in a memory location.

Relative Addressing   An addressing method in which the address specified in the instruction is the offset from a base address. The base address may be the contents of the program counter or a base register. Relative addressing allows programs to be easily relocated in memory.

Relocatable   Can be placed in any part of memory without changes—that is, a program that can occupy any set of consecutive memory addresses.

Reset   A signal that starts a system in a known state.

Resident Software   Software that can run on the computer itself, unlike cross-assemblers or cross-compilers, which must run on another computer.

Ripple Carry   Forming the carry bit from a binary addition by using the carries from each bit position.

ROM   Read-only memory, a memory that contains a fixed pattern of data permanently defined as part of the manufacturing process.

ROM Simulator A device that allows read/write memory to act like ROM during system development; the simulator usually has special display and debugging features.

Routine A program or subprogram.

RS Flip-Flop A flip-flop that can be placed in the 1 state by a signal on the SET input or in the 0 state by a signal on the RESET input.

RS-232 A standard interface for the transmission of serial digital data.

Schmitt Trigger A circuit used to produce a single, sharp transition (i.e., a pulse) from a slowly changing input.

Schottky TTL A high-speed variant of standard TTL.

Scratch-Pad Memory Memory locations or registers that are used to store temporary or intermediate results.

Second Source A manufacturer who supplies a device or product originated by another manufacturer.

Self-Assembler An assembler that runs on the computer for which it assembles programs.

Self-Checking Number A number in which some of the digits serve to check for possible errors in the other digits and do not contain any additional information.

Self-Test A procedure whereby a system checks the correctness of its own operation.

Separate I/O Uses different lines for input and output.

Sequencer A device that controls the ordering in time of the states of a system or the order in which instructions are executed.

Serial One bit at a time.

Serial-Access A storage device (such as a magnetic tape) from which data can only be reached or retrieved by passing through all intermediate locations between the desired one and the currently available one.

Set Make state a logic one.

Setup Time The time, prior to a clock transition, during which data must be stable for proper operation.

Seven-Segment Code The code required to represent decimal digits or other characters on a seven-segment display.

Seven-Segment Display A display made up of seven separately controlled elements that can represent decimal digits or other characters.

Shift Register A clocked device that moves its contents one bit to the left or right during each clock cycle.

Sign Bit The most significant bit of a register or memory location; a status bit that is one if the most significant bit of the result of the previous operation was one.

Sign Extension The result of a right arithmetic shift that copies the sign bit into the succeeding less significant bits.

Sign-Magnitude Number A number in which the most significant bit represents the sign or polarity and the remaining bits represent the magnitude.

Signal Conditioning Making a signal compatible with the input requirements of a particular device through buffering, level translation, amplification, etc.

Signature Analysis A method whereby faults can be found in bus-oriented digital systems by examining the time histories of signals at particular nodes.

(Software) Simulator A computer program that follows the actions of a system in detail and that can be used for debugging or testing.

Sink Current The ability of a device to accept current from external loads.

Small-Scale Integration (SSI) An integrated circuit with a complexity of ten gates or less.

Snapshot Record of the entire state of a system at a particular point in time.

(Computer) Software Computer programs.

Software Interrupt See Trap.

SOS Silicon-on-sapphire, a faster MOS technology that uses an insulating sapphire substrate.

Source Program Computer program written in an assembly or high-level language.

Space The zero state on a serial data communications line.

SPDT Switch Single-pole, double-throw switch with one common line and two output lines.

SPST Switch Single-pole, single-throw switch with one common line and one output line.

Stack A sequence of registers or memory locations that are used in a last-in, first-out manner—that is, the last data entered is the first to be removed and vice versa.

Stack Addressing An addressing method whereby the data to be used is in a stack.

Stack Pointer A register or memory location that is used to address a stack.

Stand-Alone System A computer system that does not require a connection to another computer.

Standard Teletypewriter A teletypewriter that operates asynchronously at a rate of ten characters per second.

Standby (or Quiescent) Power The amount of power required to maintain the contents of a memory when it is not being accessed.

Start Bit A one-bit signal that indicates the start of data transmission by an asynchronous device.

State Counter A counter that contains the number of states that have occurred in the current operation.

Static Memory A memory that does not change its contents without external causes, opposite of dynamic memory.

Status Bit   See Condition Code.

Status Register (or Status Word)   A register whose contents reflect the current status of the computer; may be the same as condition code register.

Stop Bit   A one-bit signal that indicates the end of data transmission by an asynchronous device.

Strobe   A one-bit signal that identifies or describes another set of signals and that can be used to clock or enable a register.

Structured Programming   A programming method whereby all programs consist of structures from a limited but complete set; each structure should have a single entry and a single exit.

Subroutine   A subprogram that can be reached from more than one place in a main program. The process of passing control from the main program to a subroutine is a *Subroutine Call* and the mechanism is a *Subroutine Linkage*. The data and addresses that the main program makes available to the subroutine are *Parameters*, and the process of making them available is called *Passing Parameters*.

Subroutine Call   See Subroutine.

Synchro-To-Digital Converter   A device that converts an analog angle to a corresponding digital value.

Synchronous Operation   Operating according to an overall timing source, i.e., at regular intervals.

Synchronization   Making two signals operate according to the same clocking signal.

Syntax   The rules governing sentence or statement structure in a language.

Teleprinter   See Teletypewriter.

Teletypewriter   A device containing a keyboard and a serial printer that is often used in communications and with computers.

Terminal   An input/output device at which data enters or leaves a computer system.

Time-Shared Bus   A bus that is used for different purposes at different times.

Top-Down Design   A design method whereby the overall structure is designed first and parts of the structure are subsequently defined in greater detail.

Trap   An instruction that forces a program to jump to a specific address, often used to produce breakpoints or to indicate hardware or software errors.

Tri-State (or Three-State)   Logic outputs with three possible states—high, low, and an inactive (high-impedance or open-circuit) state that can be combined with other similar outputs in a busing structure.

Tri-State Enable (or Select)   An input that, if not active, forces the outputs of a tri-state device into the inactive or open-circuit state.

TTL (Transistor-Transistor Logic) The most widely used bipolar technology for digital integrated circuits. Popular variants include high-speed Schottky TTL and low-power Schottky (or LS) TTL.

TTL-Compatible Uses voltage levels that are within the range of TTL devices and can be used with TTL devices without level shifting, although buffering may be necessary.

2-Key Rollover (2KRO) Resolving two (but not more) simultaneous key closures into two consecutive output codes.

Two's Complement A binary number that, when added to the original number in a binary adder, produces a zero result. The two's complement is the one's complement plus one.

Two's Complement Overflow A situation in which a signed arithmetic operation produces a result that cannot be represented correctly—that is, the magnitude overflows into the sign bit.

Unbundling Pricing certain types of software and services separately from the hardware.

Universal Asynchronous Receiver/Transmitter (UART) An LSI device that acts as an interface between systems that handle data in parallel and devices that handle data in asynchronous serial form.

Universal Synchronous Receiver/Transmitter (USRT) An LSI device that acts as an interface between systems that handle data in parallel and devices that handle data in synchronous serial form.

Utility Program A program that provides basic functions, such as loading and saving programs, initiating program execution, observing and changing the contents of memory locations, or setting breakpoints and tracing.

UVPROM (or UVROM) See EPROM.

Vectored Interrupt An interrupt that provides the CPU with an identification code that the CPU can use to transfer control to the corresponding service routine.

Volatile Memory A memory that loses its contents when power is removed.

Wired-OR Connecting outputs together without gates to form a busing structure; requires special outputs of which only one is active at a time.

Word The basic grouping of bits that the computer can manipulate in a single cycle.

Word Length The number of bits in the computer word, usually the length of the computer's data bus and data and instruction registers.

Working Register See General-Purpose Register.

Zero Bit A status bit that is one if the last operation produced a zero result.

Index